MURDER

BOOK

MURDER BOOK

A Graphic Memoir of a True Crime Obsession

hilary fitzgerald campbell

Andrews McMeel
PUBLISHING®

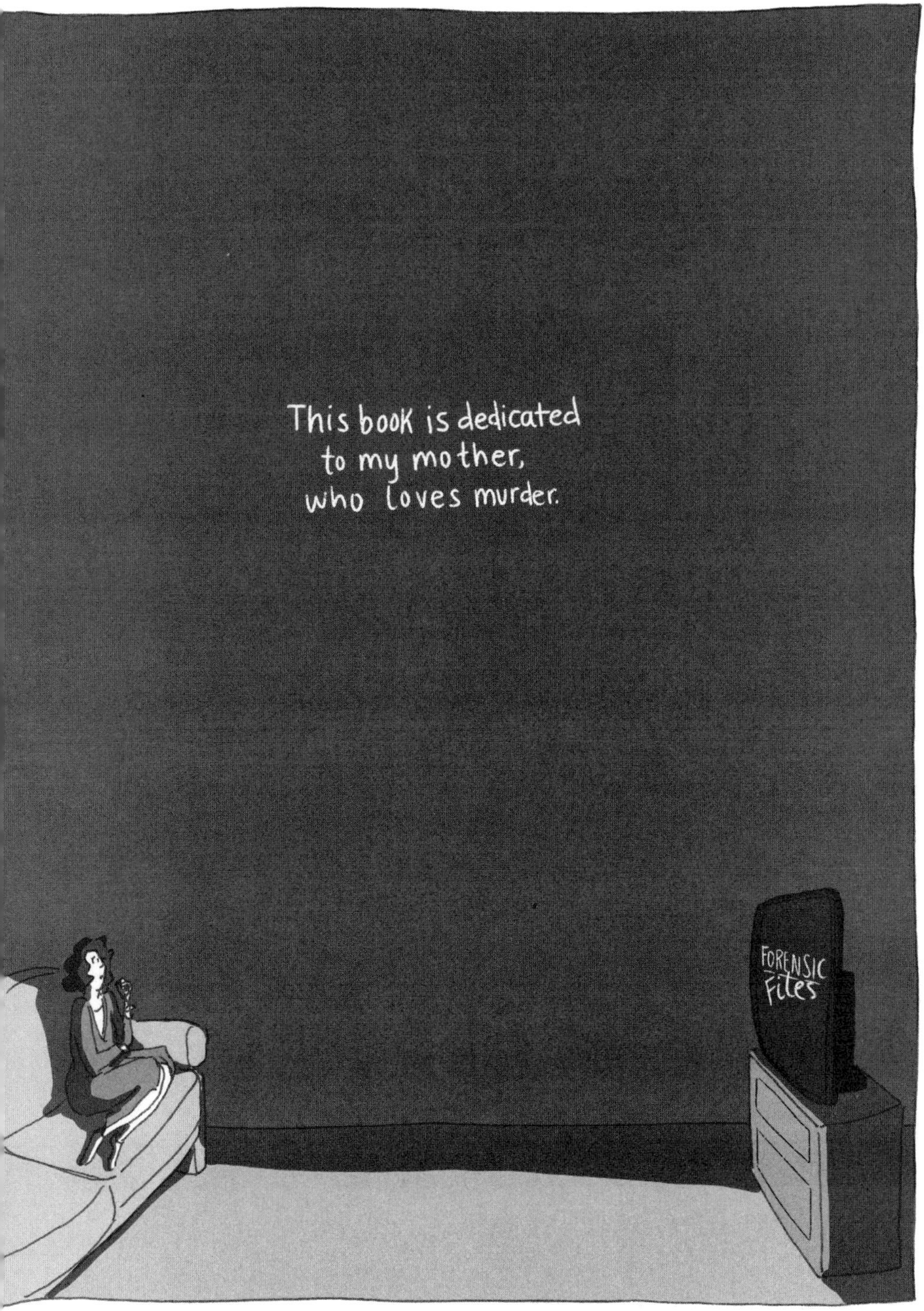
This book is dedicated
to my mother,
who loves murder.
FORENSIC
Files

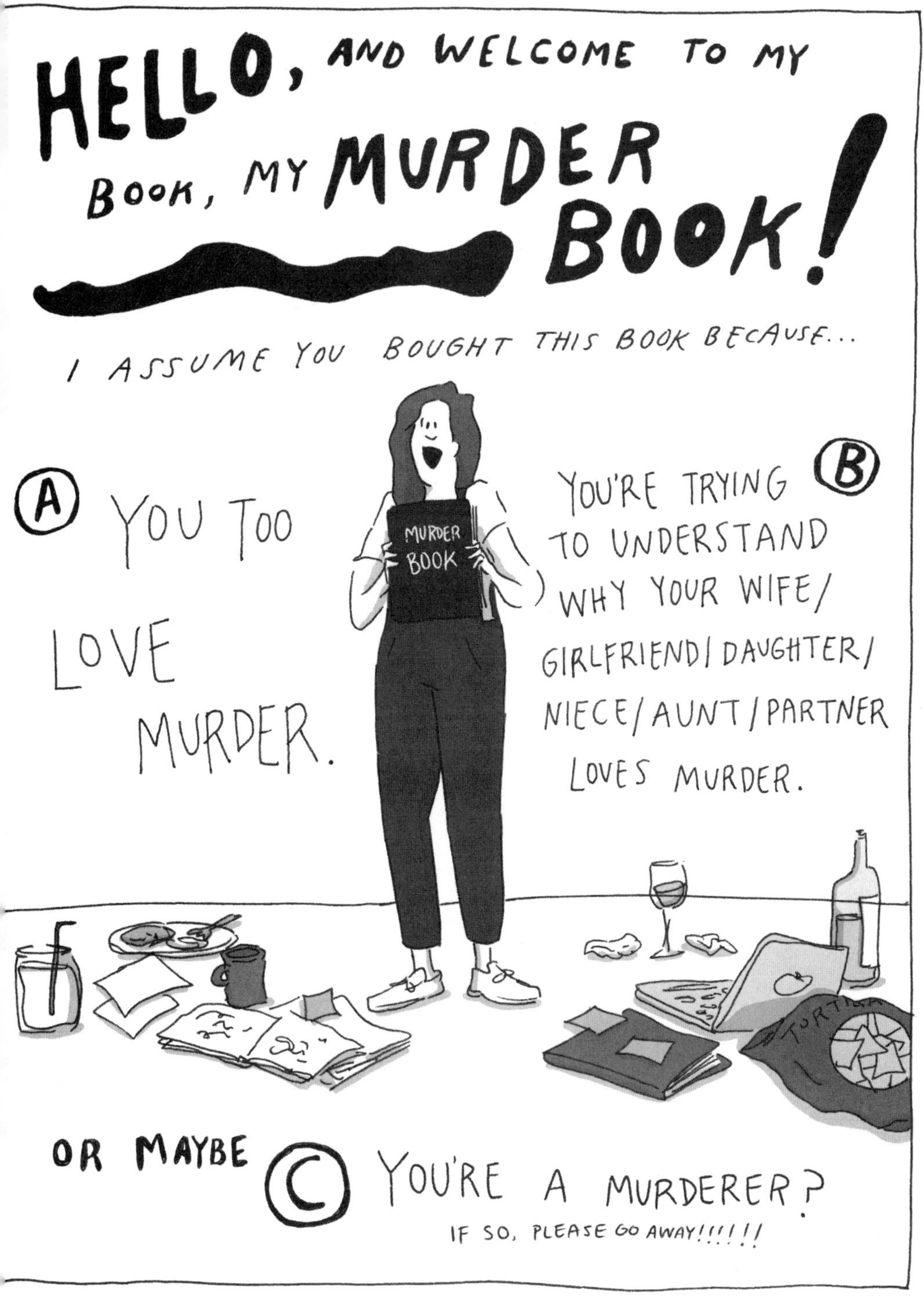
HELLO, AND WELCOME TO MY BOOK, MY MURDER BOOK!
I ASSUME YOU BOUGHT THIS BOOK BECAUSE...
A YOU TOO LOVE MURDER.
MURDER BOOK
B YOU'RE TRYING TO UNDERSTAND WHY YOUR WIFE/ GIRLFRIEND/ DAUGHTER/ NIECE/ AUNT/ PARTNER LOVES MURDER.
OR MAYBE C YOU'RE A MURDERER?
IF SO, PLEASE GO AWAY!!!!!!

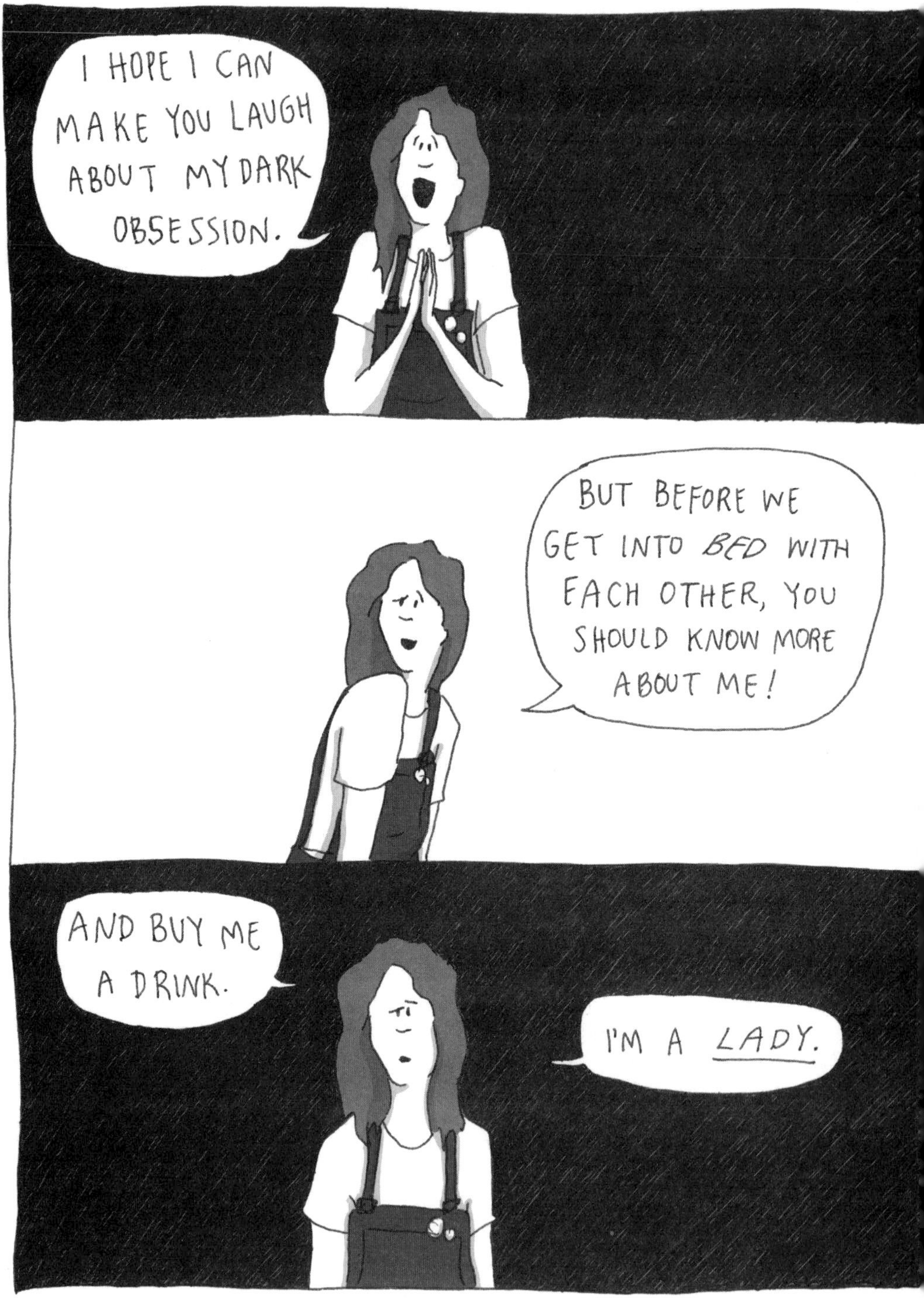
I HOPE I CAN MAKE YOU LAUGH ABOUT MY DARK OBSESSION.
BUT BEFORE WE GET INTO *BED* WITH EACH OTHER, YOU SHOULD KNOW MORE ABOUT ME!
AND BUY ME A DRINK.
I'M A LADY.

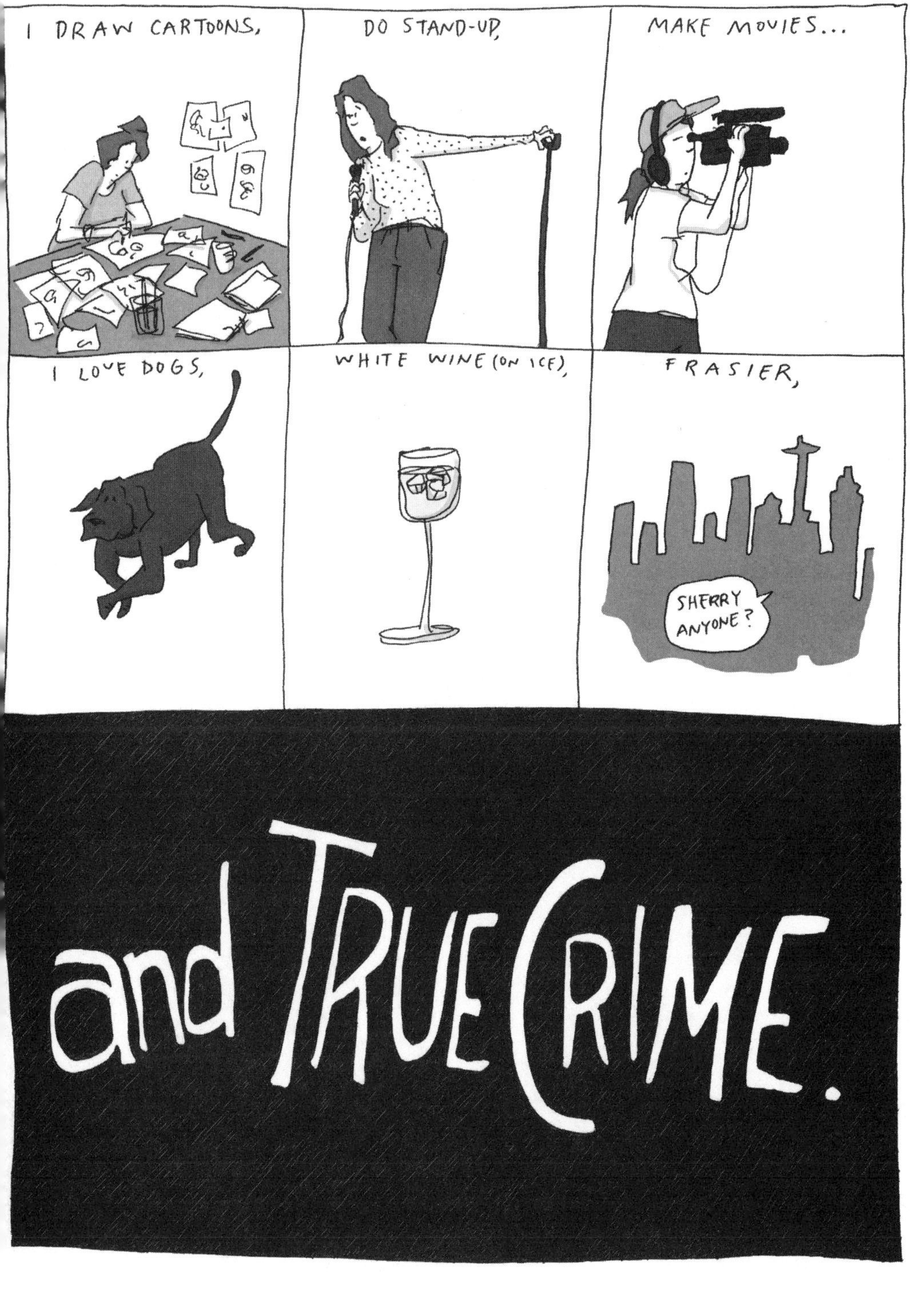
I DRAW CARTOONS,
DO STAND-UP,
MAKE MOVIES...
I LOVE DOGS,
WHITE WINE (ON ICE),
FRASIER,
SHERRY ANYONE?
and TRUE CRIME.

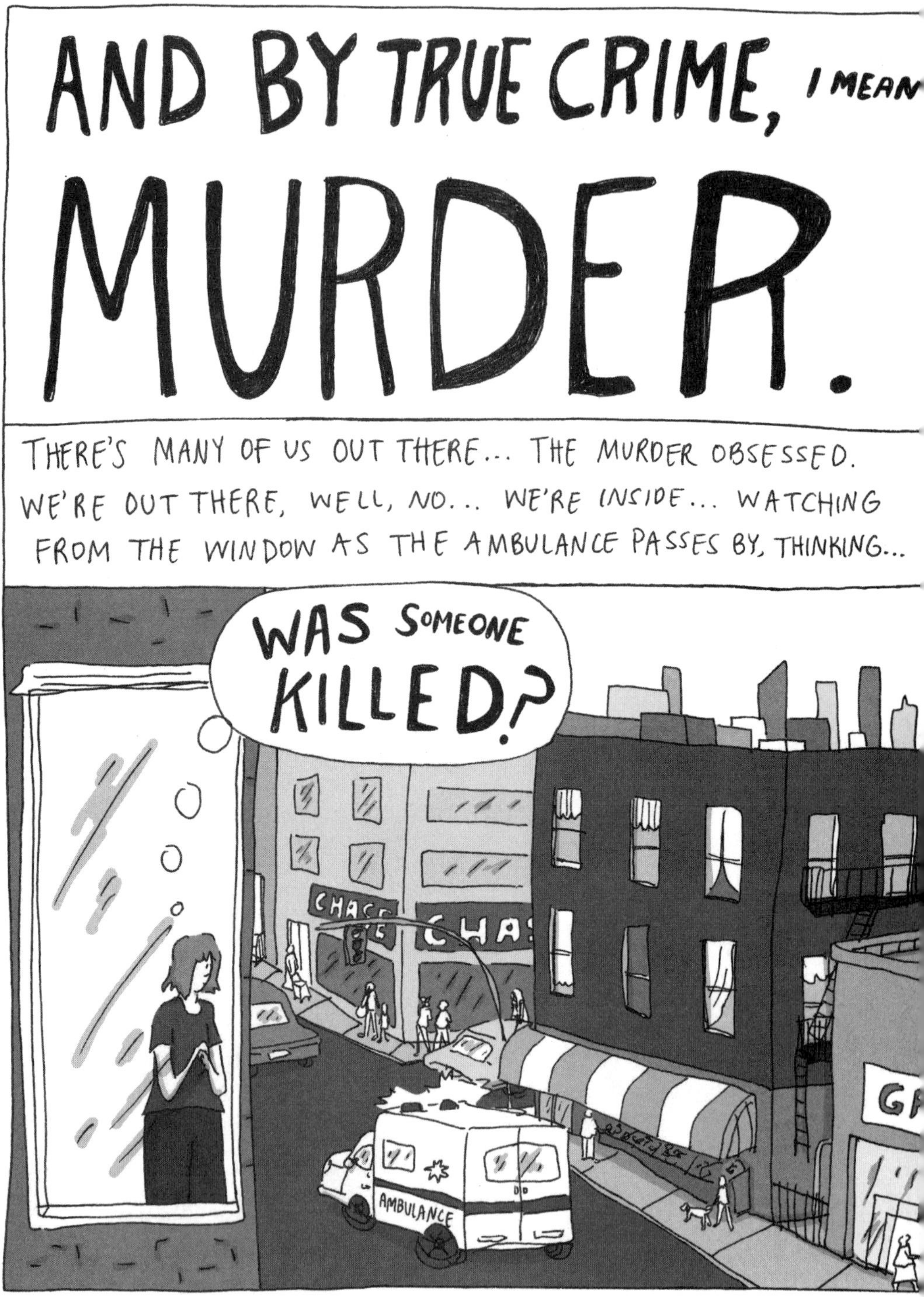
AND BY TRUE CRIME, I MEAN
MURDER.
THERE'S MANY OF US OUT THERE... THE MURDER OBSESSED. WE'RE OUT THERE, WELL, NO... WE'RE INSIDE... WATCHING FROM THE WINDOW AS THE AMBULANCE PASSES BY, THINKING...
WAS SOMEONE KILLED?
AMBULANCE

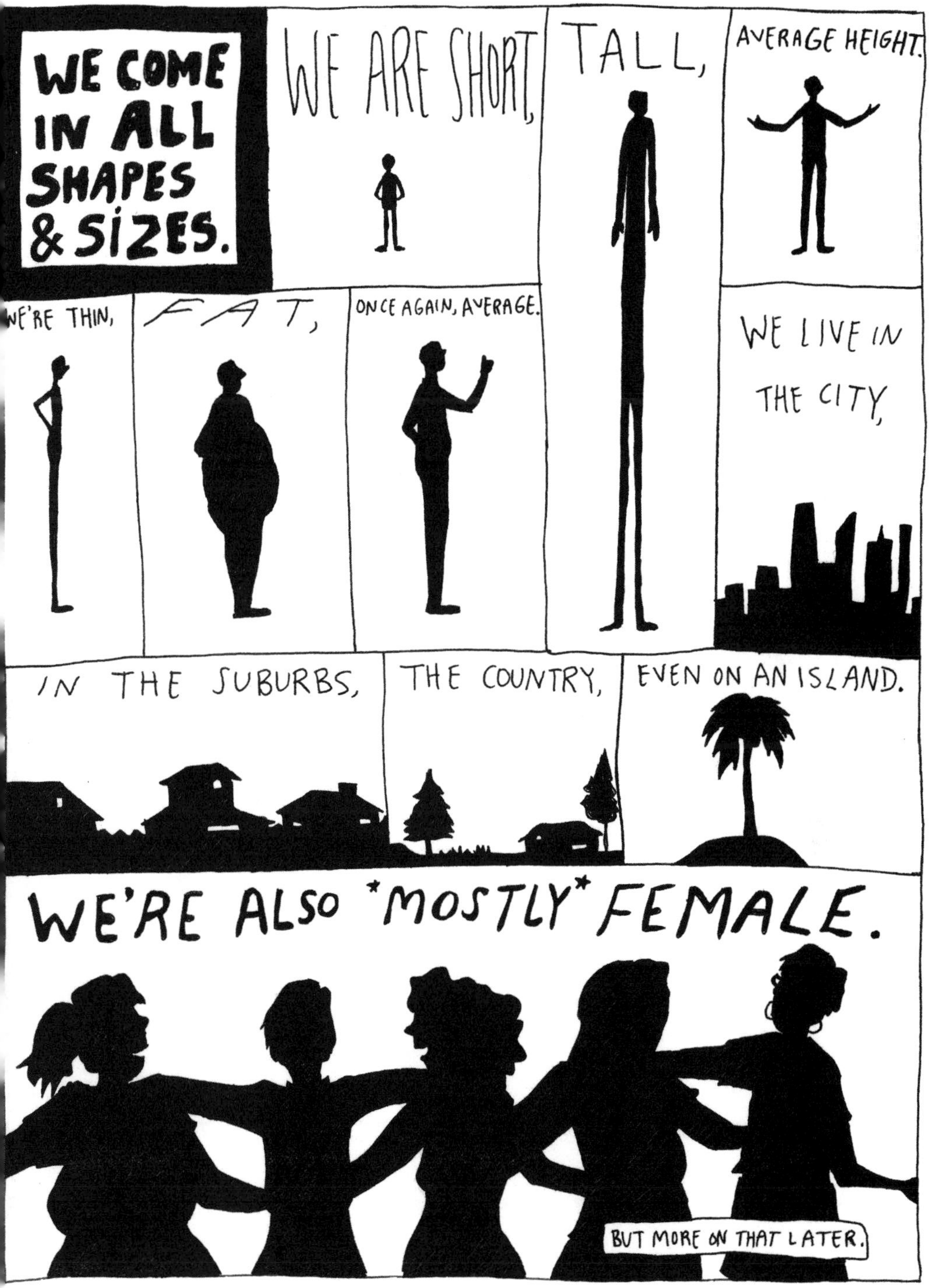
WE COME IN ALL SHAPES & SIZES.
WE ARE SHORT,
TALL,
AVERAGE HEIGHT.
WE'RE THIN,
FAT,
ONCE AGAIN, AVERAGE.
WE LIVE IN THE CITY,
IN THE SUBURBS,
THE COUNTRY,
EVEN ON AN ISLAND.
WE'RE ALSO *MOSTLY* FEMALE.
BUT MORE ON THAT LATER.

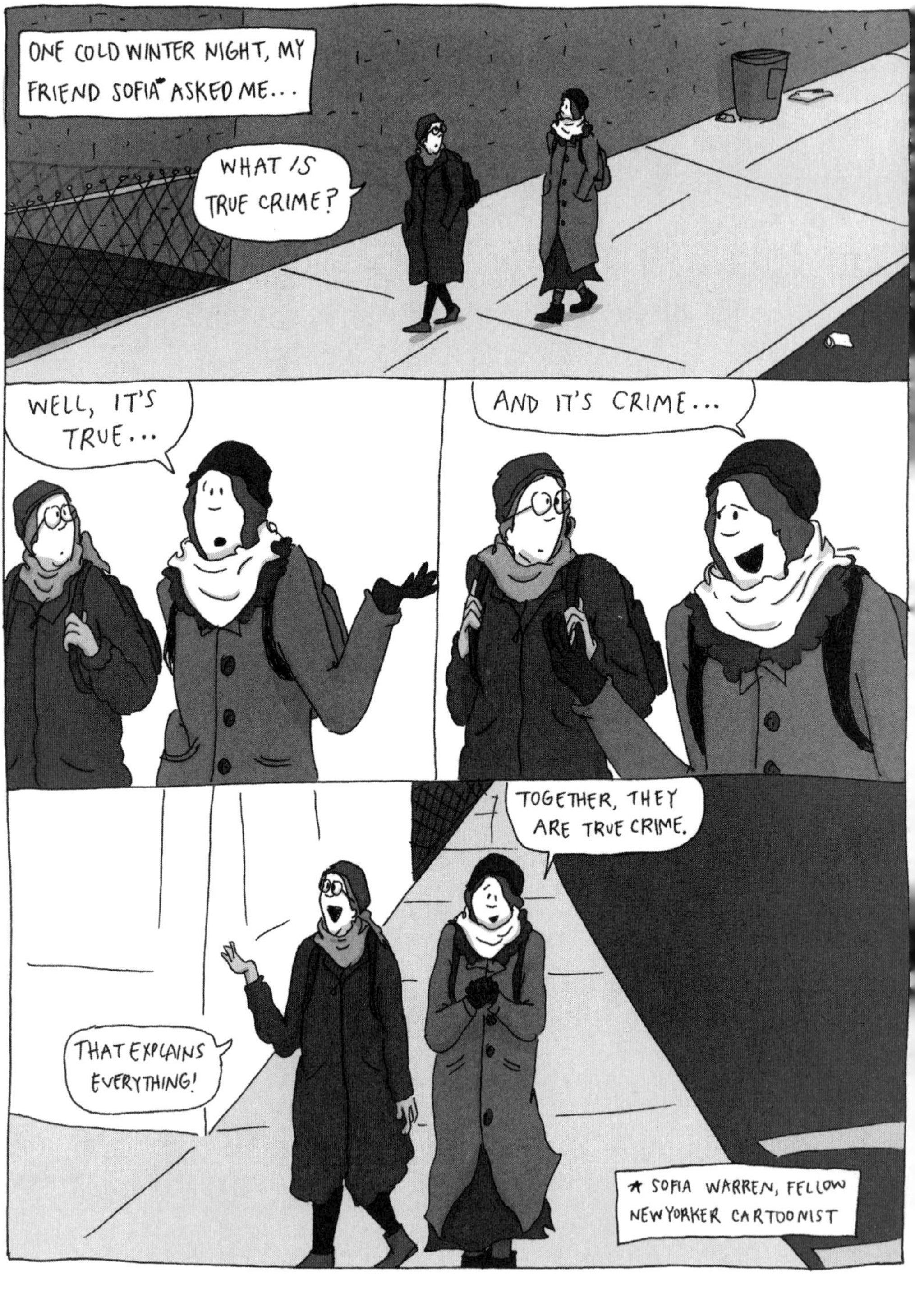
ONE COLD WINTER NIGHT, MY FRIEND SOFIA* ASKED ME...
WHAT IS TRUE CRIME?
WELL, IT'S TRUE...
AND IT'S CRIME...
TOGETHER, THEY ARE TRUE CRIME.
THAT EXPLAINS EVERYTHING!
* SOFIA WARREN, FELLOW NEW YORKER CARTOONIST

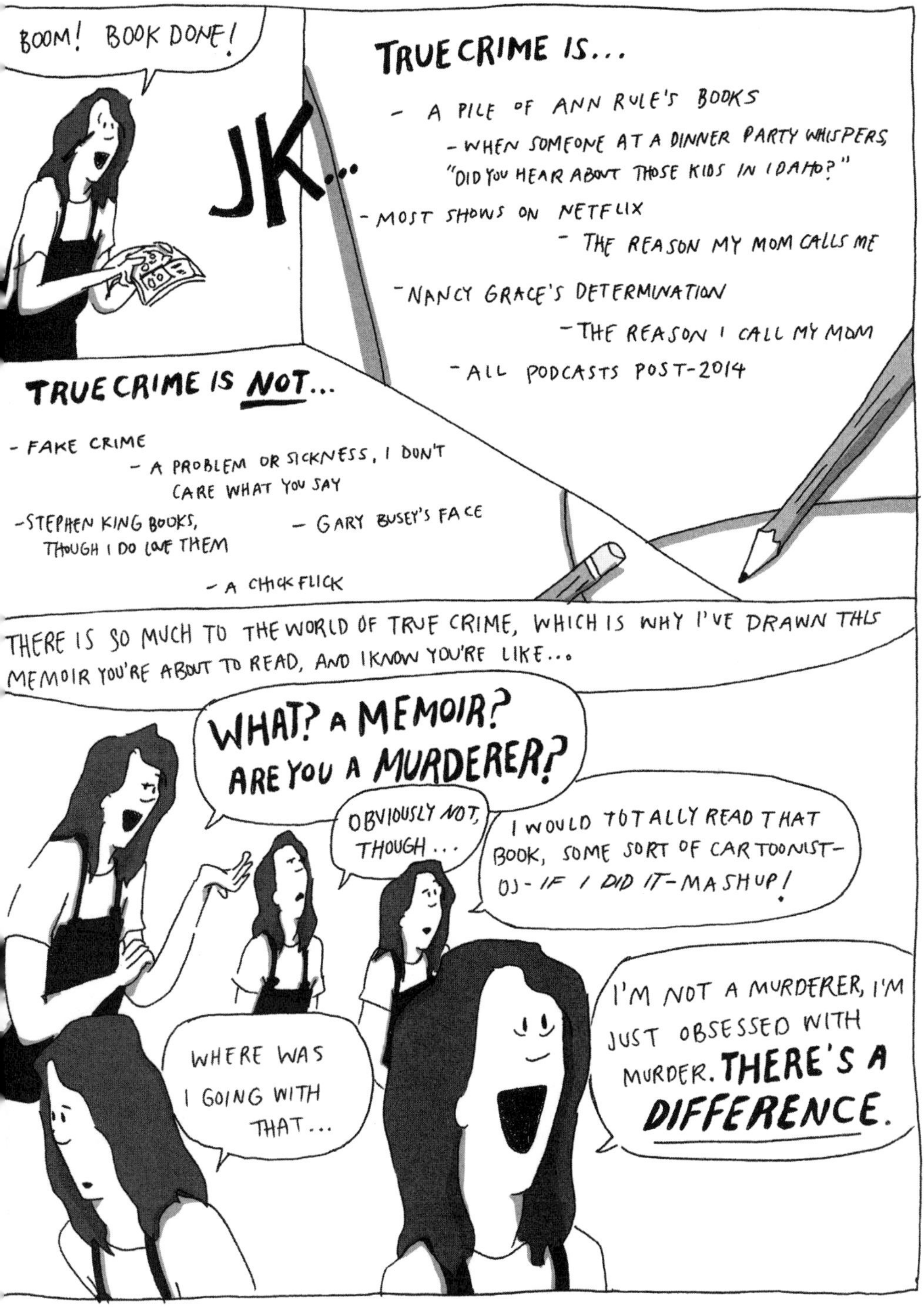
BOOM! BOOK DONE!
JK...
TRUE CRIME IS...
- A PILE OF ANN RULE'S BOOKS
- WHEN SOMEONE AT A DINNER PARTY WHISPERS, "DID YOU HEAR ABOUT THOSE KIDS IN IDAHO?"
- MOST SHOWS ON NETFLIX
- THE REASON MY MOM CALLS ME
- NANCY GRACE'S DETERMINATION
- THE REASON I CALL MY MOM
- ALL PODCASTS POST-2014
TRUE CRIME IS NOT...
- FAKE CRIME
- A PROBLEM OR SICKNESS, I DON'T CARE WHAT YOU SAY
- STEPHEN KING BOOKS, THOUGH I DO LOVE THEM
- GARY BUSEY'S FACE
- A CHICK FLICK
THERE IS SO MUCH TO THE WORLD OF TRUE CRIME, WHICH IS WHY I'VE DRAWN THIS MEMOIR YOU'RE ABOUT TO READ, AND I KNOW YOU'RE LIKE...
WHAT? A MEMOIR? ARE YOU A MURDERER?
OBVIOUSLY NOT, THOUGH...
I WOULD TOTALLY READ THAT BOOK, SOME SORT OF CARTOONIST-OJ-IF I DID IT-MASHUP!
WHERE WAS I GOING WITH THAT...
I'M NOT A MURDERER, I'M JUST OBSESSED WITH MURDER. THERE'S A DIFFERENCE.

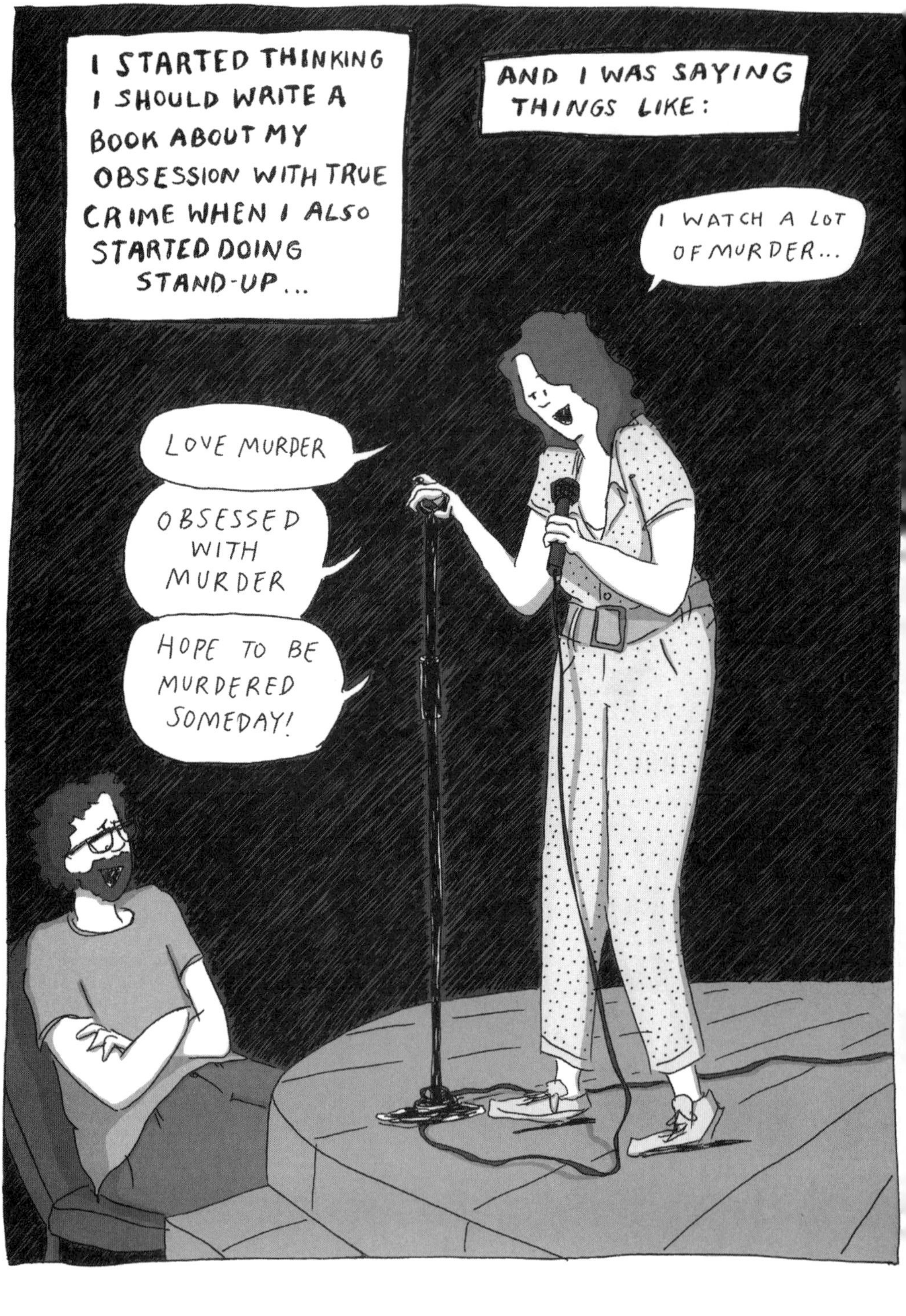
I STARTED THINKING I SHOULD WRITE A BOOK ABOUT MY OBSESSION WITH TRUE CRIME WHEN I ALSO STARTED DOING STAND-UP...
AND I WAS SAYING THINGS LIKE:
I WATCH A LOT OF MURDER...
LOVE MURDER
OBSESSED WITH MURDER
HOPE TO BE MURDERED SOMEDAY!

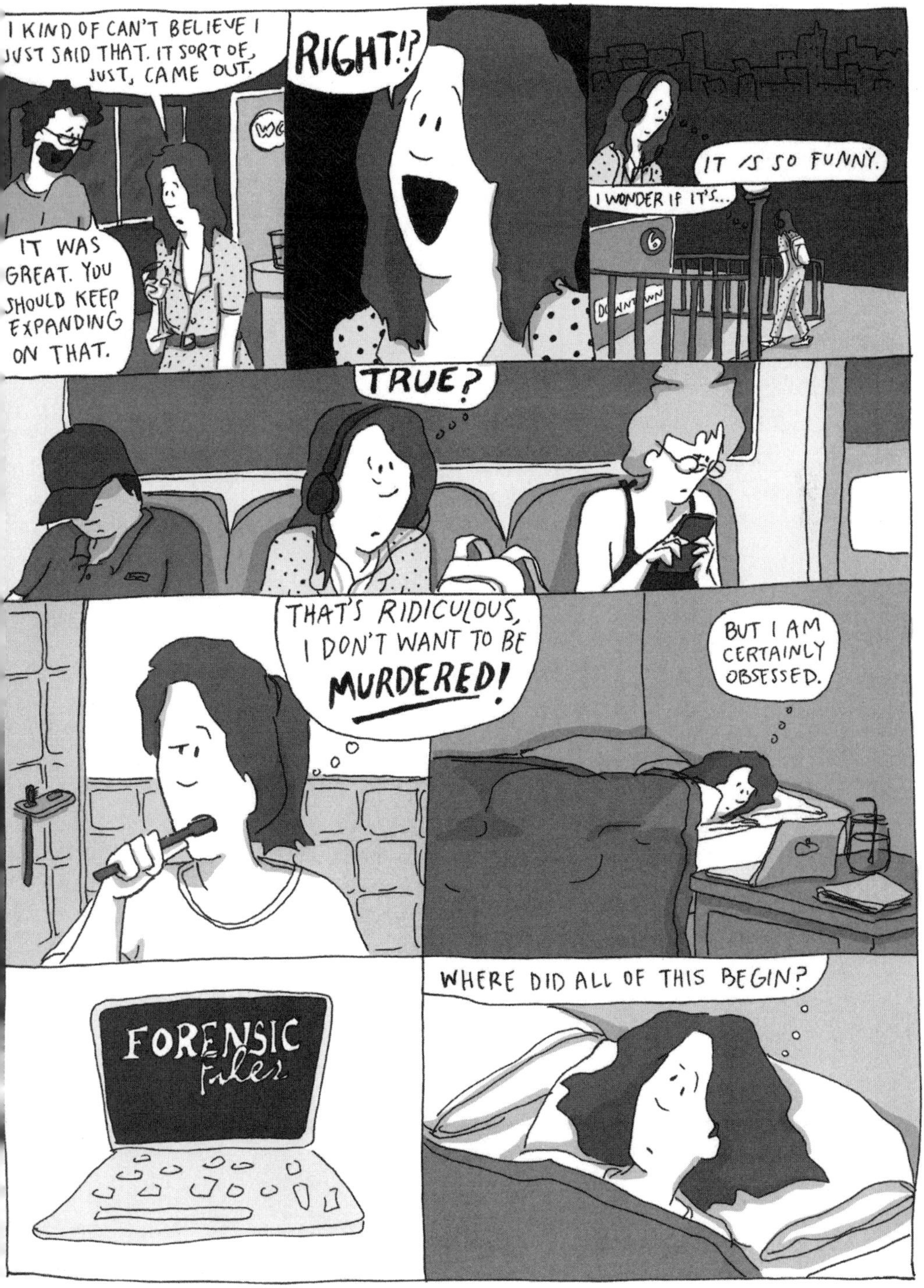
I KIND OF CAN'T BELIEVE I JUST SAID THAT. IT SORT OF, JUST, CAME OUT.
IT WAS GREAT. YOU SHOULD KEEP EXPANDING ON THAT.
RIGHT!?
I WONDER IF IT'S...
IT IS SO FUNNY.
DOWNTOWN
TRUE?
THAT'S RIDICULOUS, I DON'T WANT TO BE MURDERED!
BUT I AM CERTAINLY OBSESSED.
FORENSIC files
WHERE DID ALL OF THIS BEGIN?

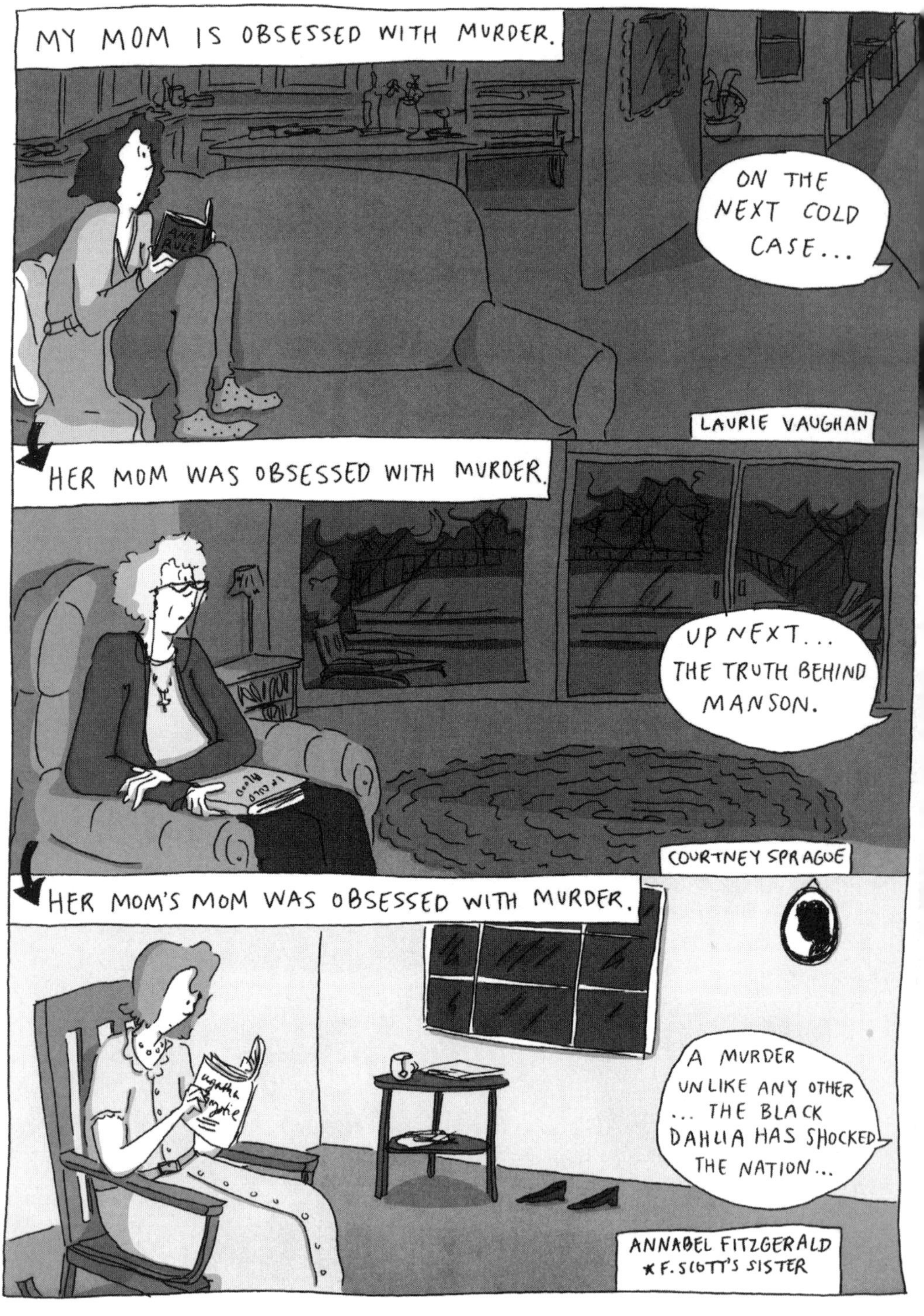
MY MOM IS OBSESSED WITH MURDER.
ON THE NEXT COLD CASE...
LAURIE VAUGHAN
HER MOM WAS OBSESSED WITH MURDER.
UP NEXT... THE TRUTH BEHIND MANSON.
COURTNEY SPRAGUE
HER MOM'S MOM WAS OBSESSED WITH MURDER.
A MURDER UNLIKE ANY OTHER ... THE BLACK DAHLIA HAS SHOCKED THE NATION...
ANNABEL FITZGERALD
*F. SCOTT'S SISTER

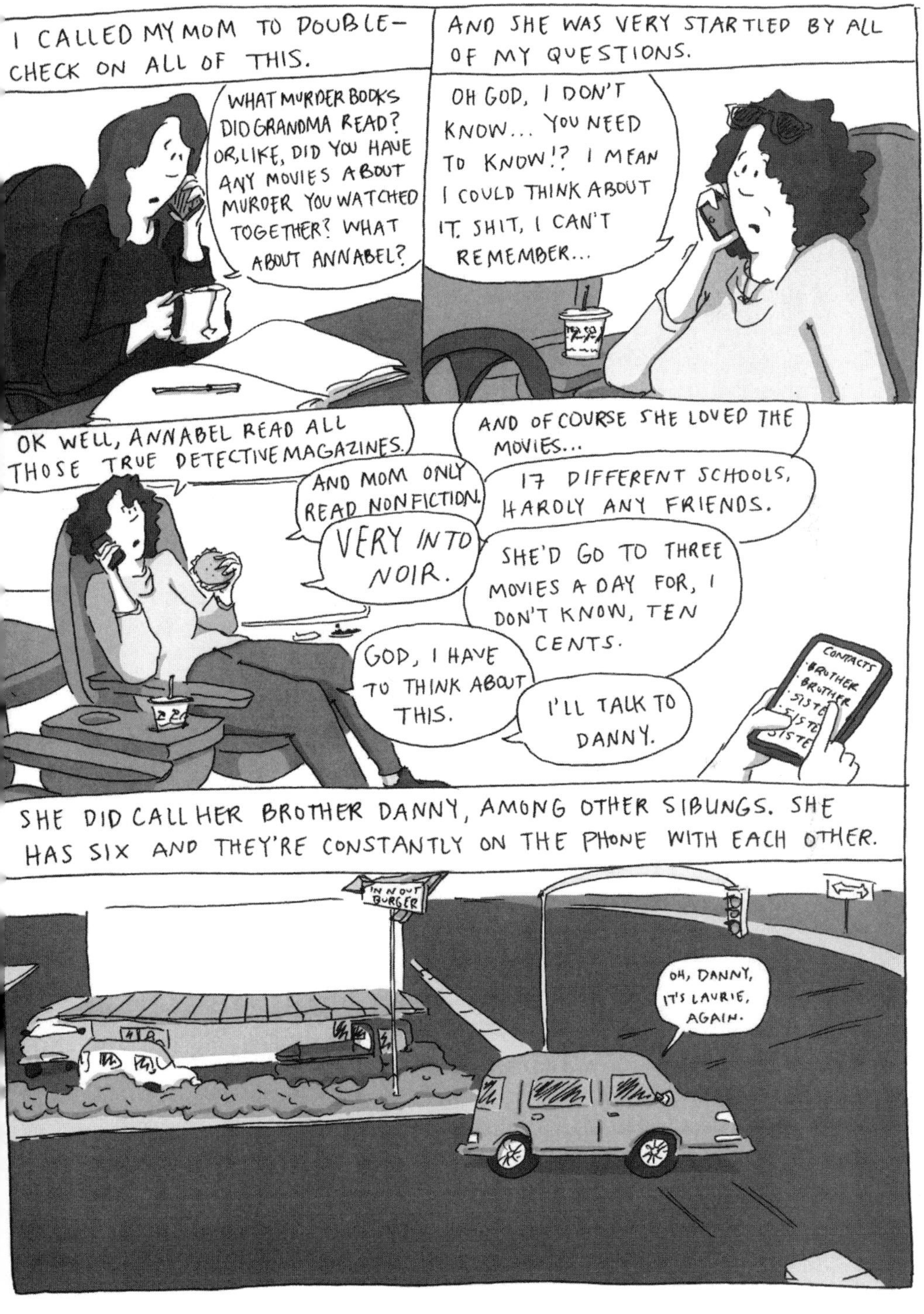
I CALLED MY MOM TO DOUBLE-CHECK ON ALL OF THIS.
WHAT MURDER BOOKS DID GRANDMA READ? OR, LIKE, DID YOU HAVE ANY MOVIES ABOUT MURDER YOU WATCHED TOGETHER? WHAT ABOUT ANNABEL?
AND SHE WAS VERY STARTLED BY ALL OF MY QUESTIONS.
OH GOD, I DON'T KNOW... YOU NEED TO KNOW!? I MEAN I COULD THINK ABOUT IT. SHIT, I CAN'T REMEMBER...
OK WELL, ANNABEL READ ALL THOSE TRUE DETECTIVE MAGAZINES.
AND MOM ONLY READ NONFICTION.
VERY INTO NOIR.
AND OF COURSE SHE LOVED THE MOVIES...
17 DIFFERENT SCHOOLS, HARDLY ANY FRIENDS.
SHE'D GO TO THREE MOVIES A DAY FOR, I DON'T KNOW, TEN CENTS.
GOD, I HAVE TO THINK ABOUT THIS.
I'LL TALK TO DANNY.
CONTACTS
BROTHER
BROTHER
SHE DID CALL HER BROTHER DANNY, AMONG OTHER SIBLINGS. SHE HAS SIX AND THEY'RE CONSTANTLY ON THE PHONE WITH EACH OTHER.
IN N OUT BURGER
OH, DANNY, IT'S LAURIE, AGAIN.

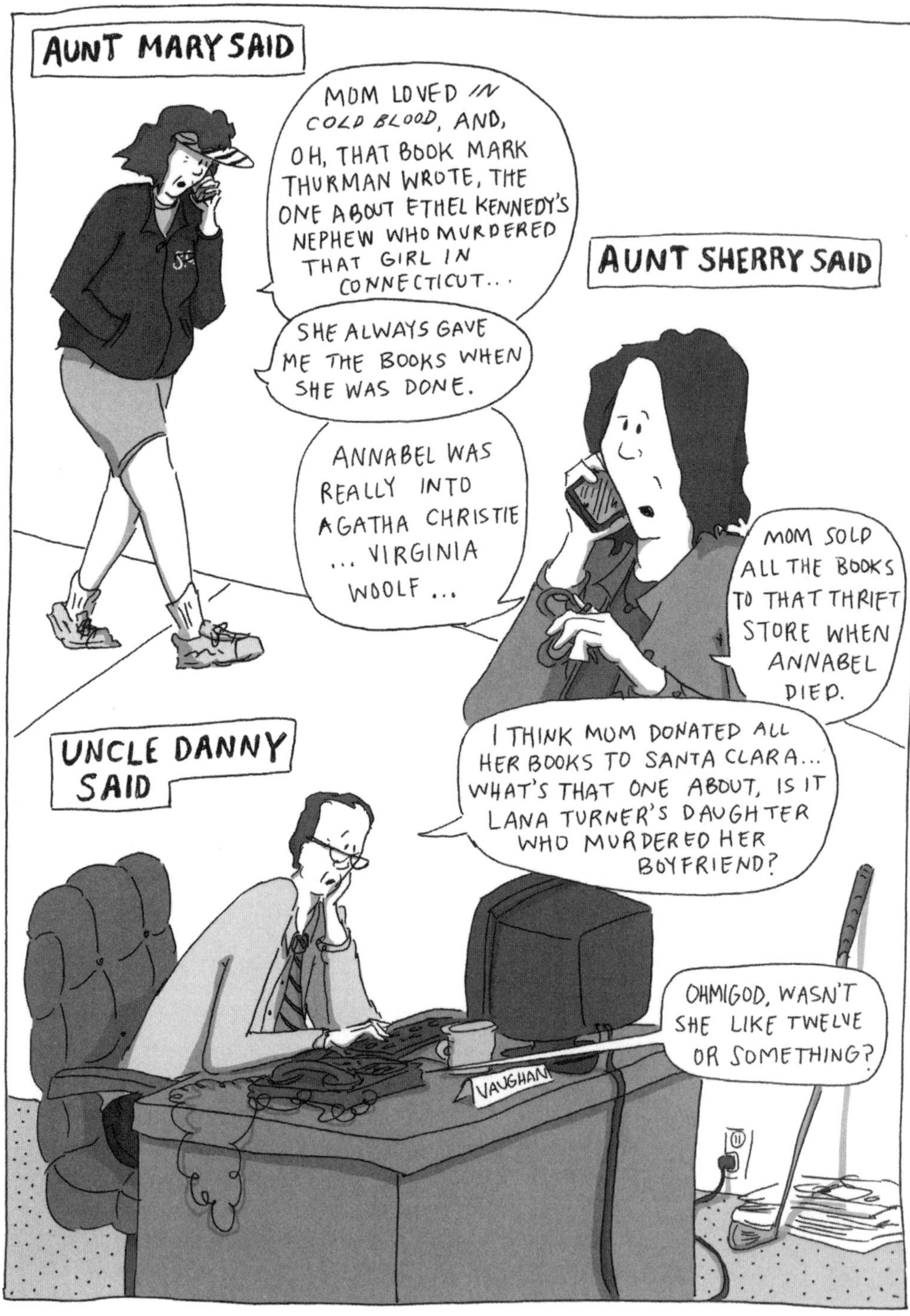

AUNT MARY SAID
MOM LOVED *IN COLD BLOOD*, AND, OH, THAT BOOK MARK THURMAN WROTE, THE ONE ABOUT ETHEL KENNEDY'S NEPHEW WHO MURDERED THAT GIRL IN CONNECTICUT...
SHE ALWAYS GAVE ME THE BOOKS WHEN SHE WAS DONE.
ANNABEL WAS REALLY INTO AGATHA CHRISTIE ... VIRGINIA WOOLF ...
AUNT SHERRY SAID
MOM SOLD ALL THE BOOKS TO THAT THRIFT STORE WHEN ANNABEL DIED.
UNCLE DANNY SAID
I THINK MOM DONATED ALL HER BOOKS TO SANTA CLARA... WHAT'S THAT ONE ABOUT, IS IT LANA TURNER'S DAUGHTER WHO MURDERED HER BOYFRIEND?
OHMIGOD, WASN'T SHE LIKE TWELVE OR SOMETHING?
VAUGHAN

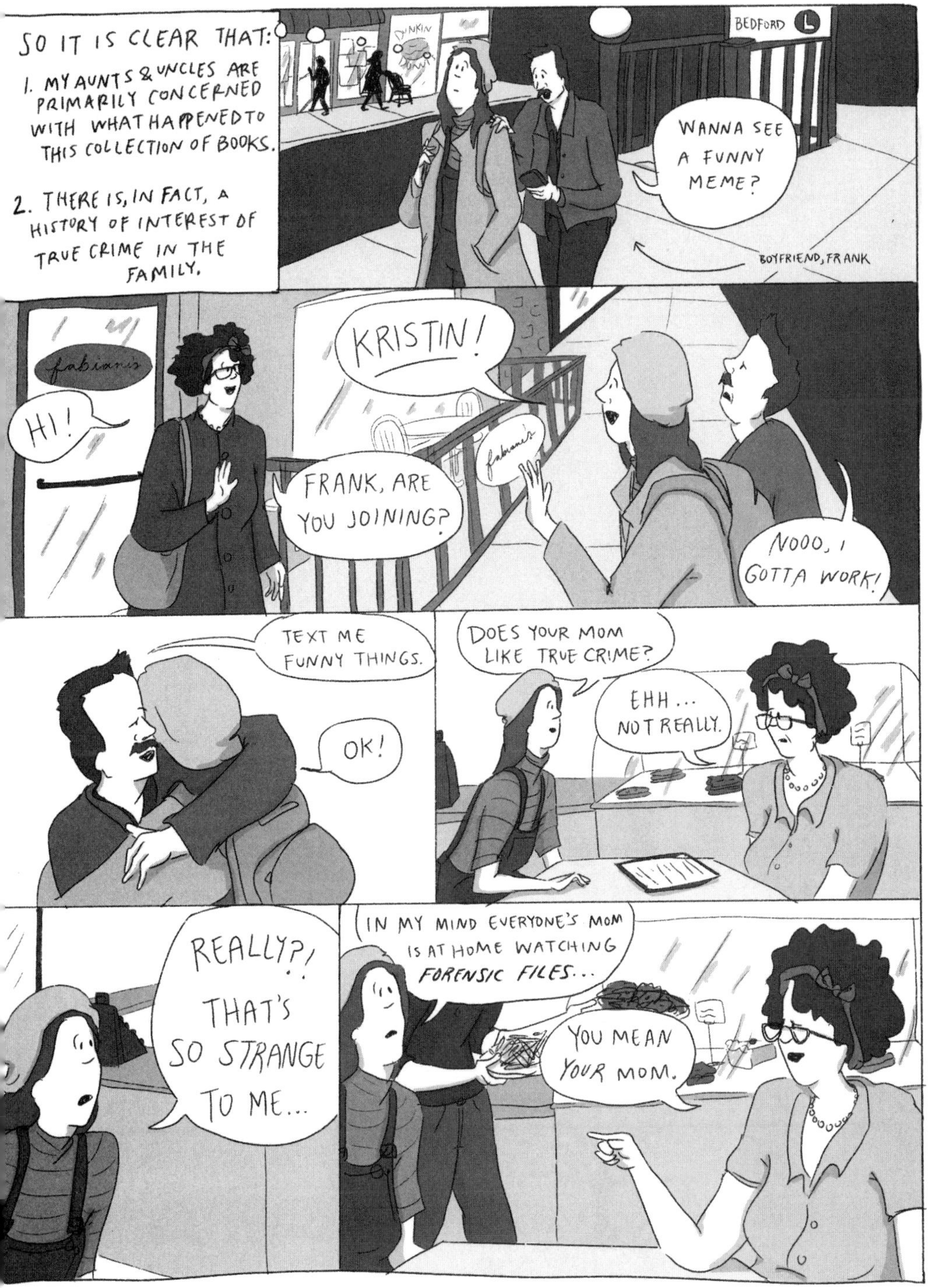

SO IT IS CLEAR THAT:
1. MY AUNTS & UNCLES ARE PRIMARILY CONCERNED WITH WHAT HAPPENED TO THIS COLLECTION OF BOOKS.
2. THERE IS, IN FACT, A HISTORY OF INTEREST OF TRUE CRIME IN THE FAMILY.
BEDFORD
WANNA SEE A FUNNY MEME?
BOYFRIEND, FRANK
KRISTIN!
HI!
FRANK, ARE YOU JOINING?
NOOO, I GOTTA WORK!
TEXT ME FUNNY THINGS.
OK!
DOES YOUR MOM LIKE TRUE CRIME?
EHH... NOT REALLY.
REALLY?! THAT'S SO STRANGE TO ME...
IN MY MIND EVERYONE'S MOM IS AT HOME WATCHING *FORENSIC FILES*...
YOU MEAN *YOUR* MOM.

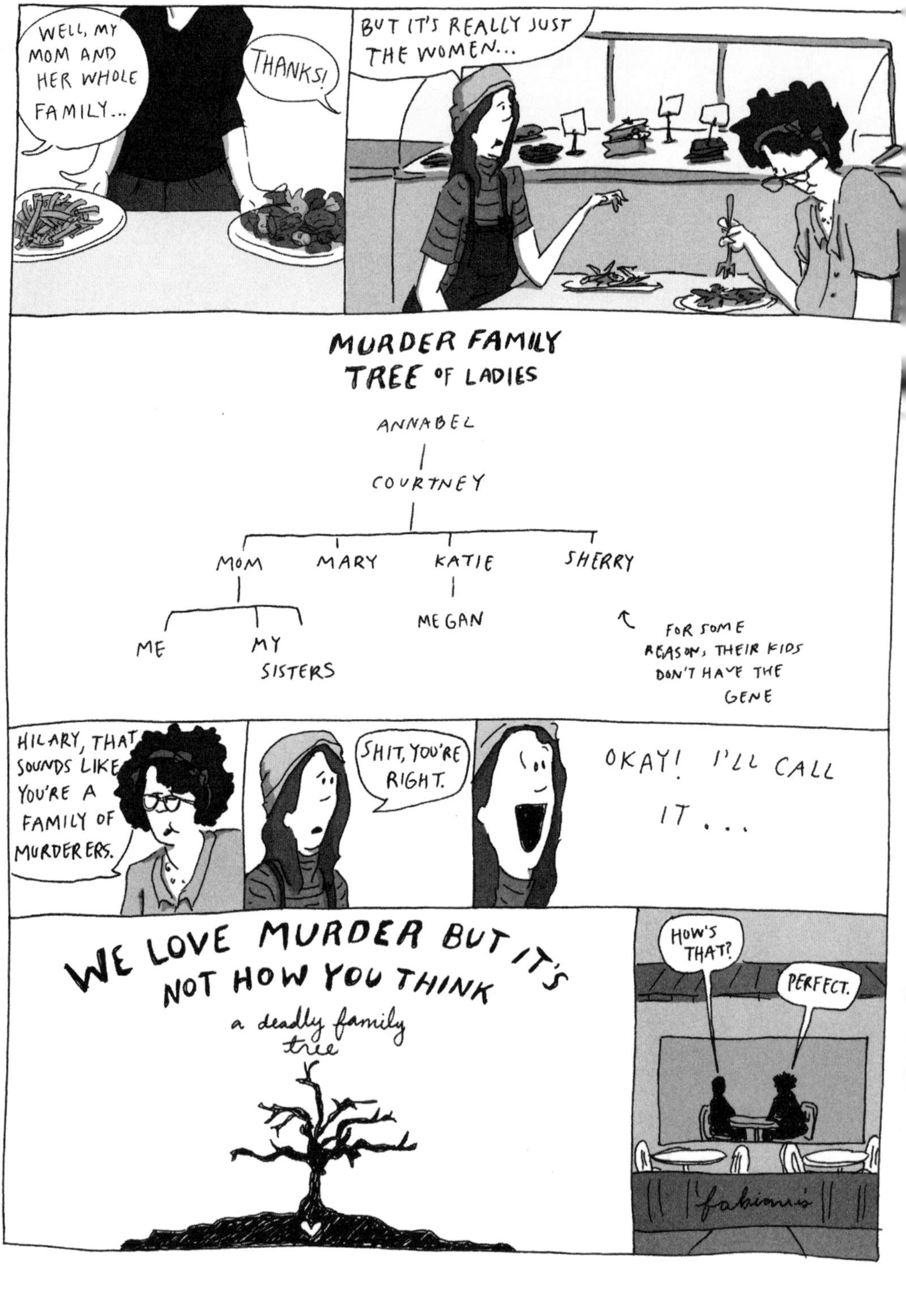
WELL, MY MOM AND HER WHOLE FAMILY...
THANKS!
BUT IT'S REALLY JUST THE WOMEN...
MURDER FAMILY TREE OF LADIES
ANNABEL
COURTNEY
MOM
MARY
KATIE
SHERRY
ME
MY SISTERS
MEGAN
FOR SOME REASON, THEIR KIDS DON'T HAVE THE GENE
HILARY, THAT SOUNDS LIKE YOU'RE A FAMILY OF MURDERERS.
SHIT, YOU'RE RIGHT.
OKAY! I'LL CALL IT...
WE LOVE MURDER BUT IT'S NOT HOW YOU THINK
a deadly family tree
HOW'S THAT?
PERFECT.
fabiani's

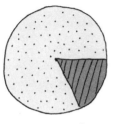

IT IS TRUE THAT, STATISTICALLY, Women ARE THE LARGEST AUDIENCE of the TRUE CRIME GENRE.
PODCASTS
BOOKS
MOVIES & TV
WOMEN
MEN
BUT I FEEL LIKE IT'S SO TRENDY TO BE A TRUE CRIME FANATIC TODAY.
EVERYONE THINKS THEY'RE SO DARK & UNIQUE BECAUSE THEY KNOW ABOUT TED BUNDY AND I'M JUST LIKE, HELLO I'VE BEEN HERE SINCE I WAS FIVE!
!!
PREACH, GIRL.
WHERE ARE YOU GOING?
I GOTTA GO DRAW.

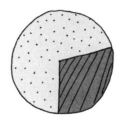

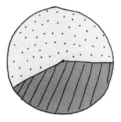

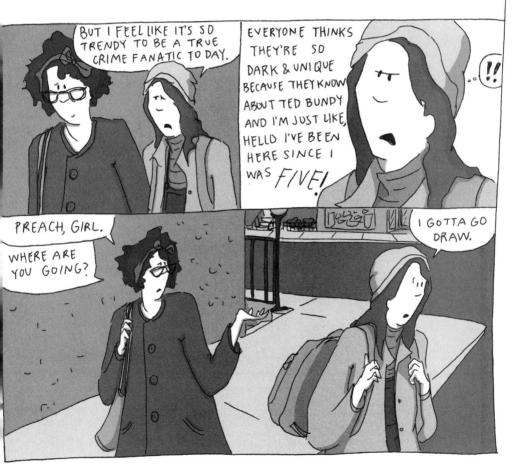

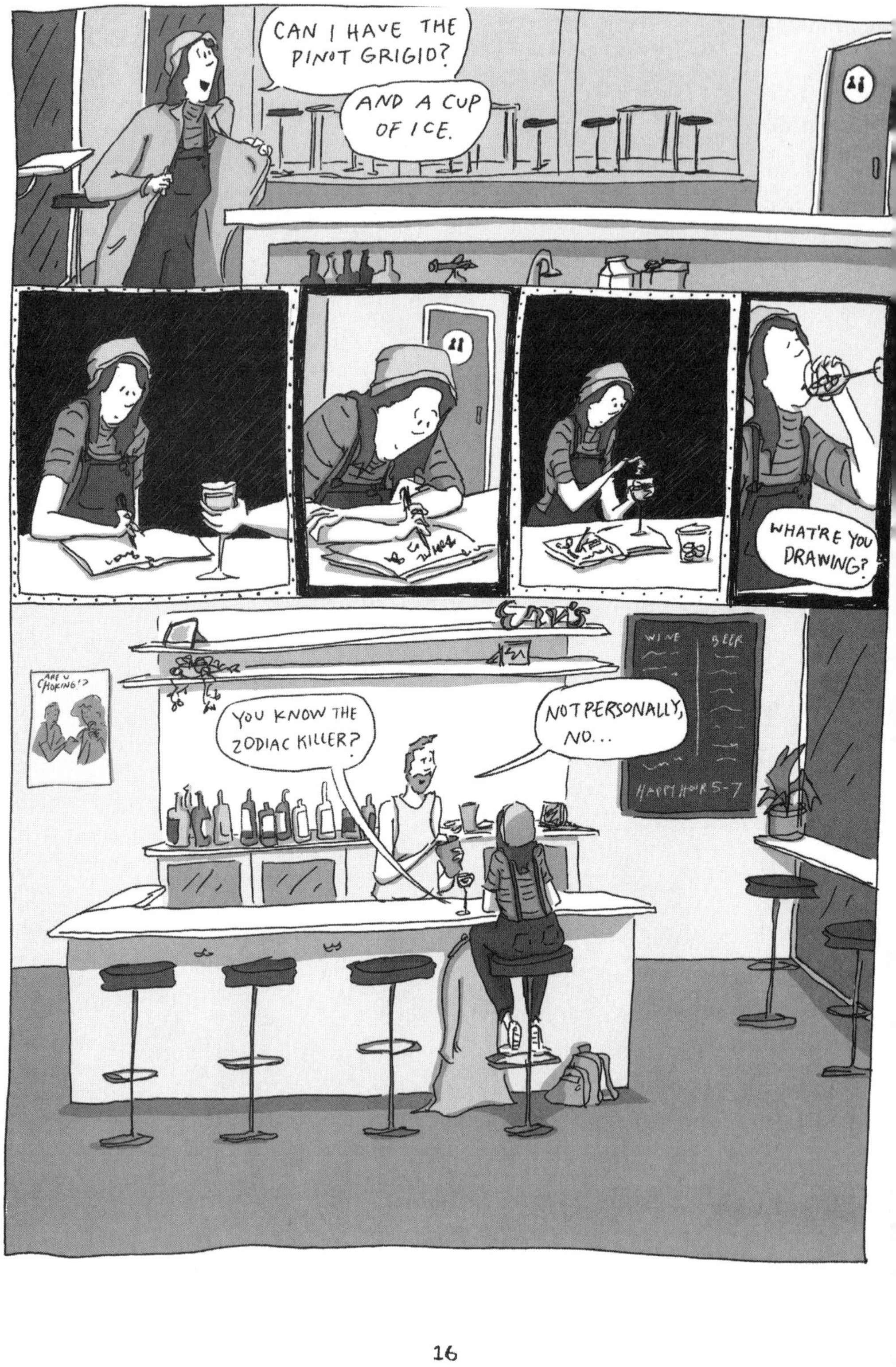
CAN I HAVE THE PINOT GRIGIO?
AND A CUP OF ICE.
WHAT'RE YOU DRAWING?
ARE U CHOKING!?
YOU KNOW THE ZODIAC KILLER?
NOT PERSONALLY, NO...
WINE
BEER
HAPPY HOUR 5-7

THIS IS THE

ZODIAC

SPEAKING

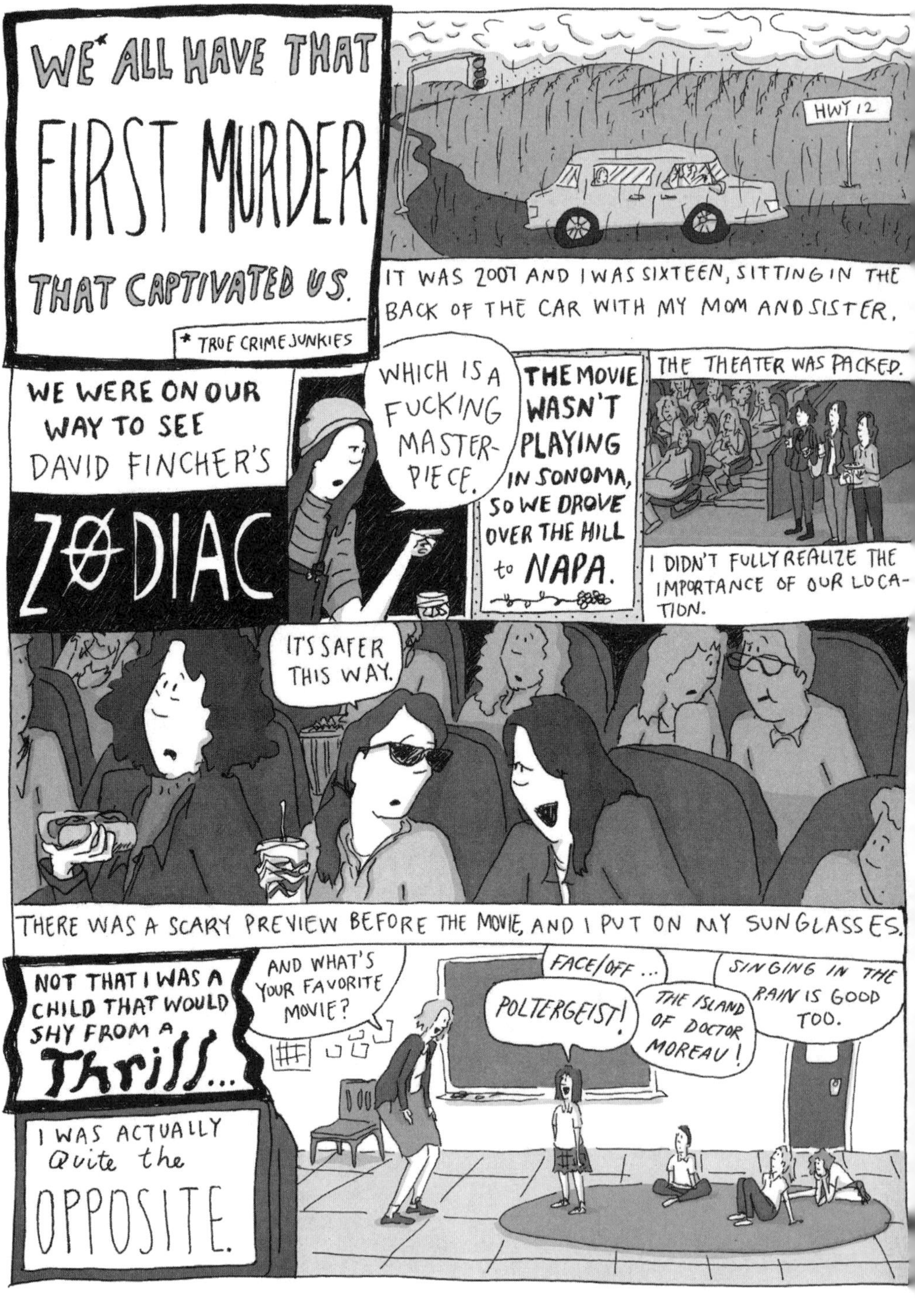
WE* ALL HAVE THAT
FIRST MURDER
THAT CAPTIVATED US.
* TRUE CRIME JUNKIES
HWY 12
IT WAS 2007 AND I WAS SIXTEEN, SITTING IN THE BACK OF THE CAR WITH MY MOM AND SISTER.
WE WERE ON OUR WAY TO SEE DAVID FINCHER'S
ZØDIAC
WHICH IS A FUCKING MASTER-PIECE.
THE MOVIE WASN'T PLAYING IN SONOMA, SO WE DROVE OVER THE HILL to NAPA.
THE THEATER WAS PACKED.
I DIDN'T FULLY REALIZE THE IMPORTANCE OF OUR LOCA-TION.
IT'S SAFER THIS WAY.
THERE WAS A SCARY PREVIEW BEFORE THE MOVIE, AND I PUT ON MY SUNGLASSES.
NOT THAT I WAS A CHILD THAT WOULD SHY FROM A Thrill...
I WAS ACTUALLY Quite the OPPOSITE.
AND WHAT'S YOUR FAVORITE MOVIE?
FACE/OFF ...
POLTERGEIST!
THE ISLAND OF DOCTOR MOREAU!
SINGING IN THE RAIN IS GOOD TOO.

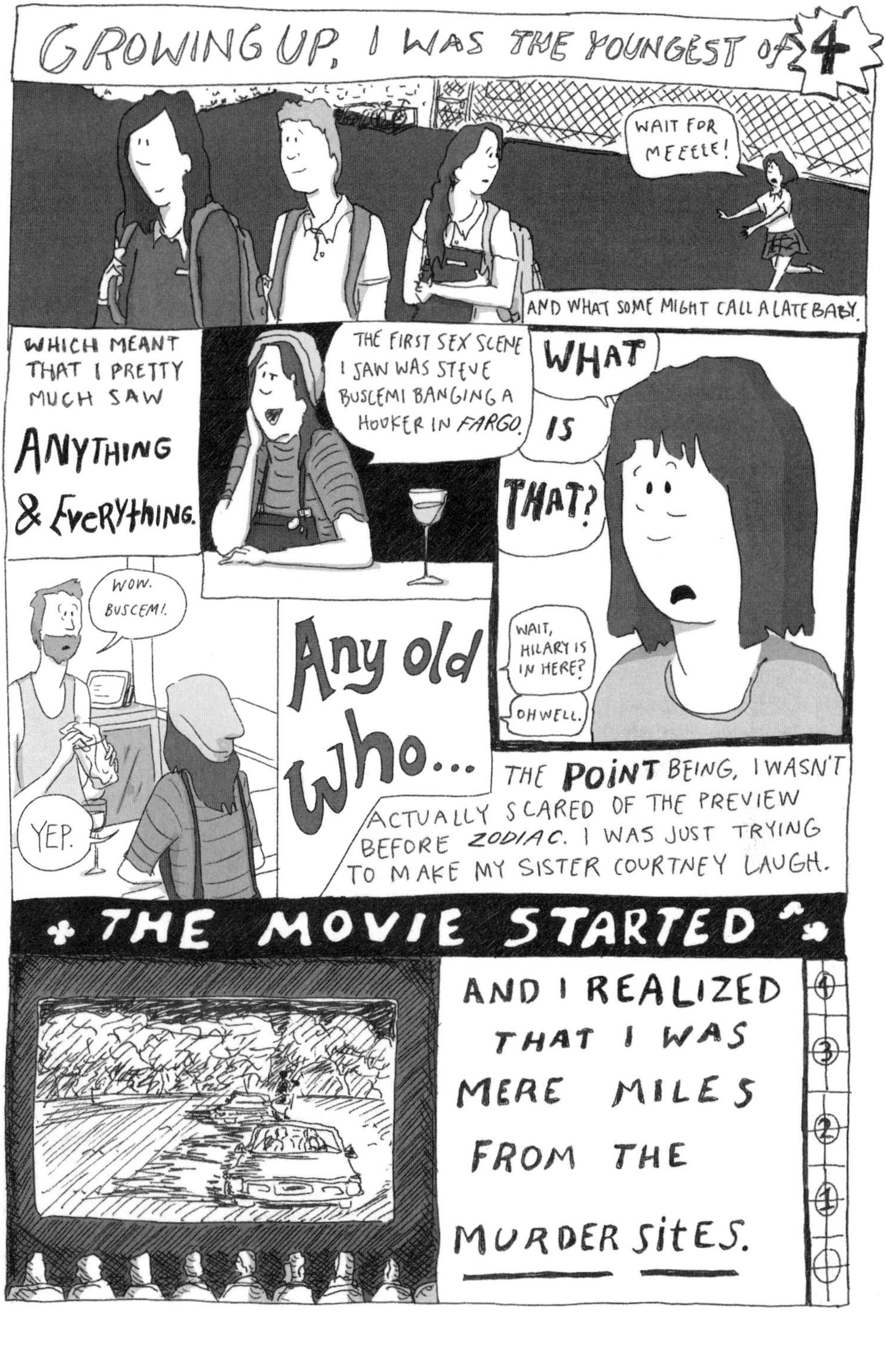
GROWING UP, I WAS THE YOUNGEST OF 4
WAIT FOR MEEEEE!
AND WHAT SOME MIGHT CALL A LATE BABY.
WHICH MEANT THAT I PRETTY MUCH SAW ANYTHING & EVERYTHING.
THE FIRST SEX SCENE I SAW WAS STEVE BUSCEMI BANGING A HOOKER IN FARGO.
WHAT IS THAT?
WAIT, HILARY IS IN HERE?
OH WELL.
WOW. BUSCEMI.
YEP.
Any old who...
THE POINT BEING, I WASN'T ACTUALLY SCARED OF THE PREVIEW BEFORE ZODIAC. I WAS JUST TRYING TO MAKE MY SISTER COURTNEY LAUGH.
THE MOVIE STARTED
AND I REALIZED THAT I WAS MERE MILES FROM THE MURDER SITES.
4
3
2
1

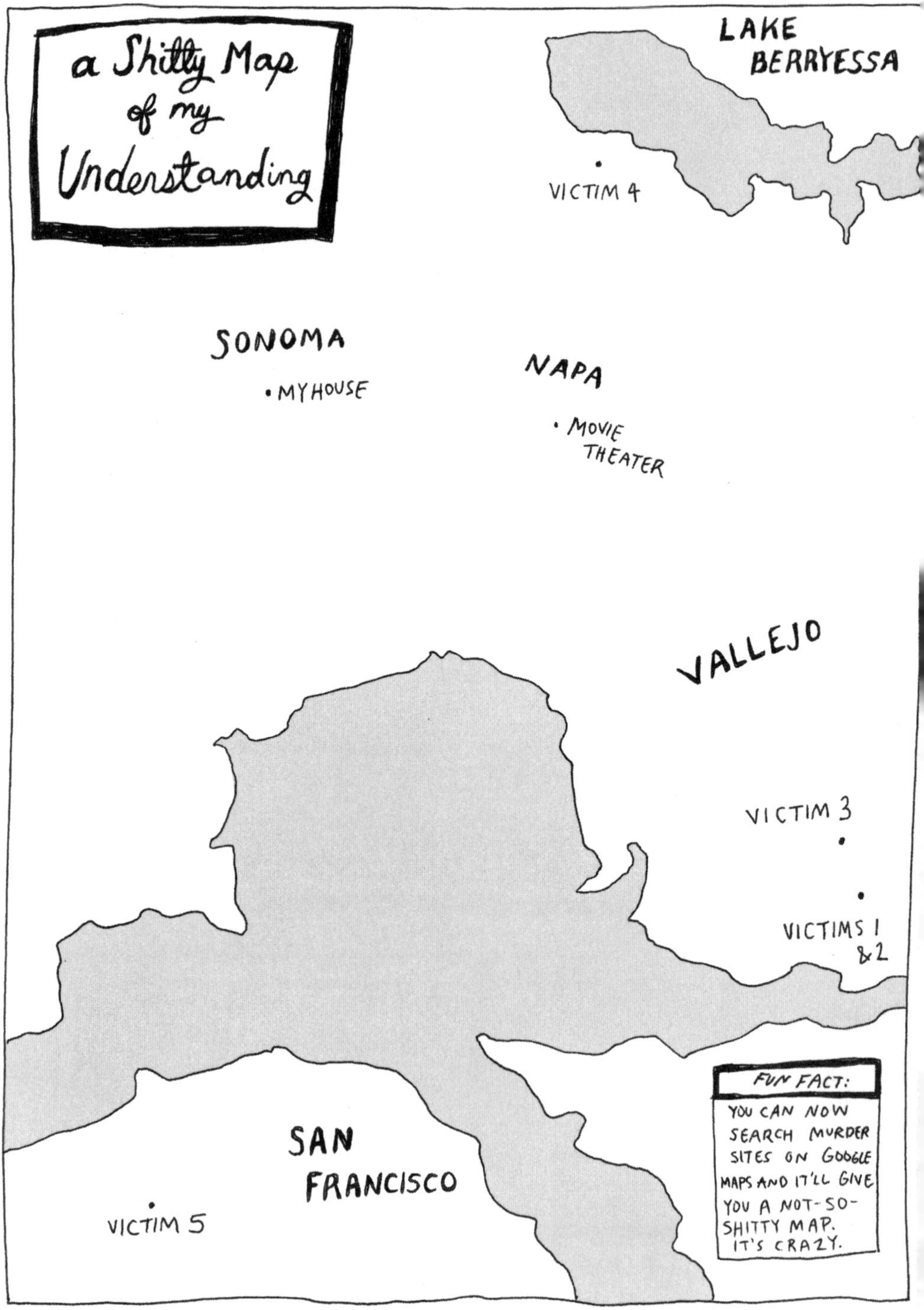
a Shitty Map of my Understanding
LAKE BERRYESSA
VICTIM 4
SONOMA
• MYHOUSE
NAPA
• MOVIE THEATER
VALLEJO
VICTIM 3
VICTIMS 1 & 2
SAN FRANCISCO
VICTIM 5
FUN FACT:
YOU CAN NOW SEARCH MURDER SITES ON GOOGLE MAPS AND IT'LL GIVE YOU A NOT-SO-SHITTY MAP. IT'S CRAZY.

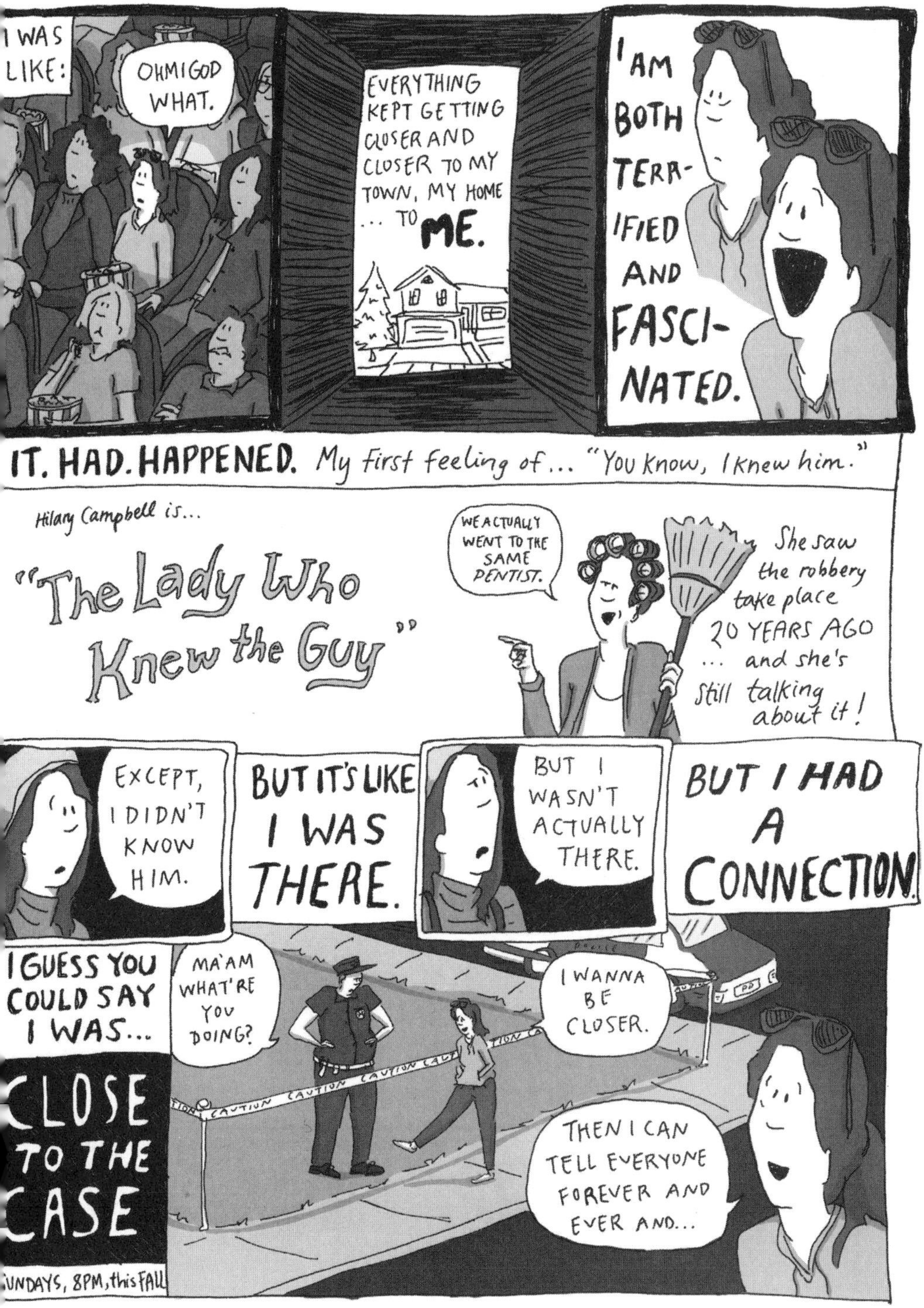
I WAS LIKE:
OHMIGOD WHAT.
EVERYTHING KEPT GETTING CLOSER AND CLOSER TO MY TOWN, MY HOME ... TO ME.
I AM BOTH TERRIFIED AND FASCINATED.
IT. HAD. HAPPENED. My first feeling of... "You know, I knew him."
Hilary Campbell is...
"The Lady Who Knew the Guy"
WE ACTUALLY WENT TO THE SAME DENTIST.
She saw the robbery take place 20 YEARS AGO ... and she's still talking about it!
EXCEPT, I DIDN'T KNOW HIM.
BUT IT'S LIKE I WAS THERE.
BUT I WASN'T ACTUALLY THERE.
BUT I HAD A CONNECTION.
I GUESS YOU COULD SAY I WAS...
CLOSE TO THE CASE
SUNDAYS, 8PM, this FALL
MA'AM WHAT'RE YOU DOING?
I WANNA BE CLOSER.
THEN I CAN TELL EVERYONE FOREVER AND EVER AND...

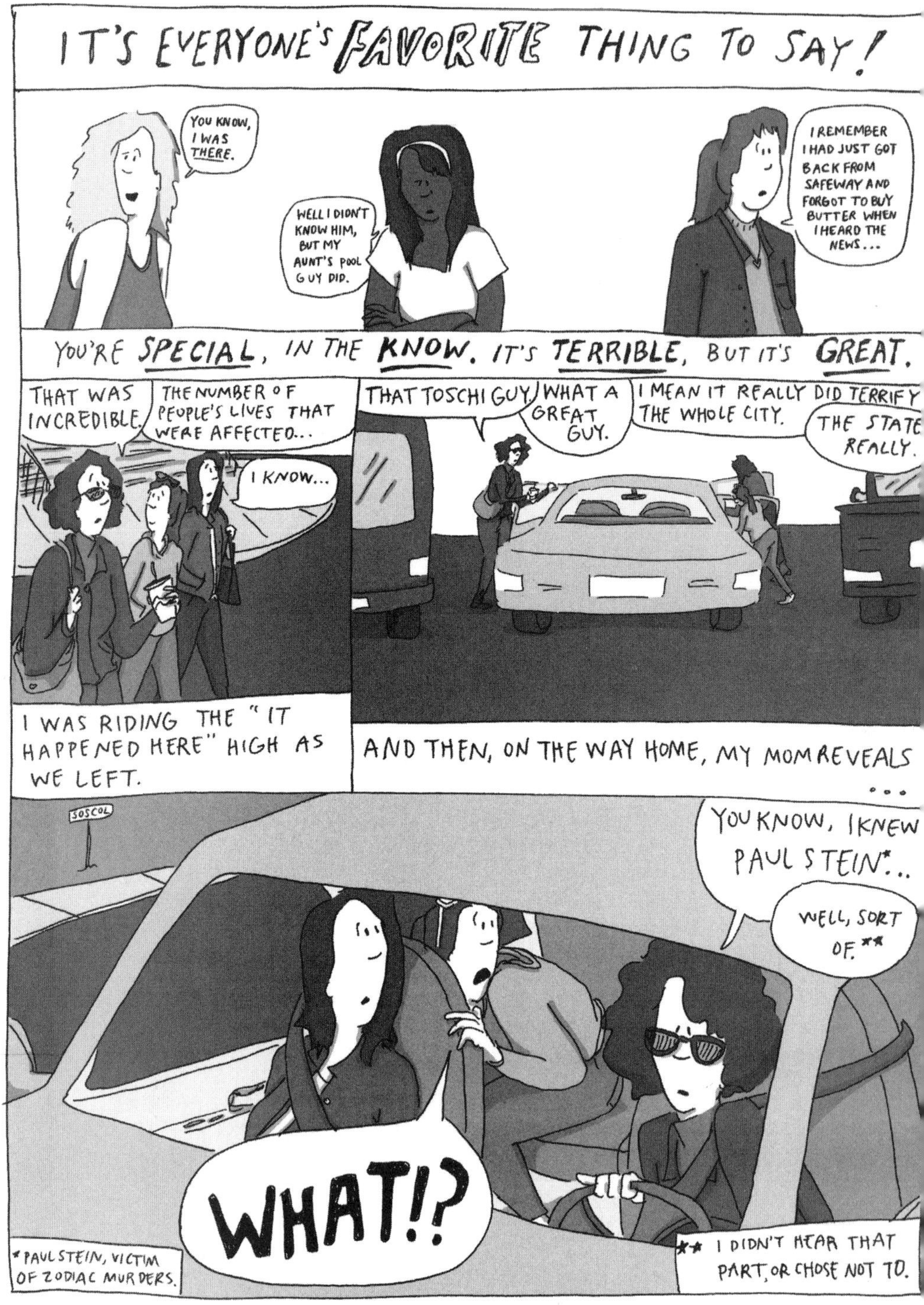
IT'S EVERYONE'S FAVORITE THING TO SAY!
YOU KNOW, I WAS THERE.
WELL I DIDN'T KNOW HIM, BUT MY AUNT'S POOL GUY DID.
I REMEMBER I HAD JUST GOT BACK FROM SAFEWAY AND FORGOT TO BUY BUTTER WHEN I HEARD THE NEWS...
YOU'RE SPECIAL, IN THE KNOW. IT'S TERRIBLE, BUT IT'S GREAT.
THAT WAS INCREDIBLE.
THE NUMBER OF PEOPLE'S LIVES THAT WERE AFFECTED...
I KNOW...
I WAS RIDING THE "IT HAPPENED HERE" HIGH AS WE LEFT.
THAT TOSCHI GUY.
WHAT A GREAT GUY.
I MEAN IT REALLY DID TERRIFY THE WHOLE CITY.
THE STATE REALLY.
AND THEN, ON THE WAY HOME, MY MOM REVEALS...
SOSCOL
YOU KNOW, I KNEW PAUL STEIN*...
WELL, SORT OF.**
WHAT!?
*PAUL STEIN, VICTIM OF ZODIAC MURDERS.
** I DIDN'T HEAR THAT PART, OR CHOSE NOT TO.

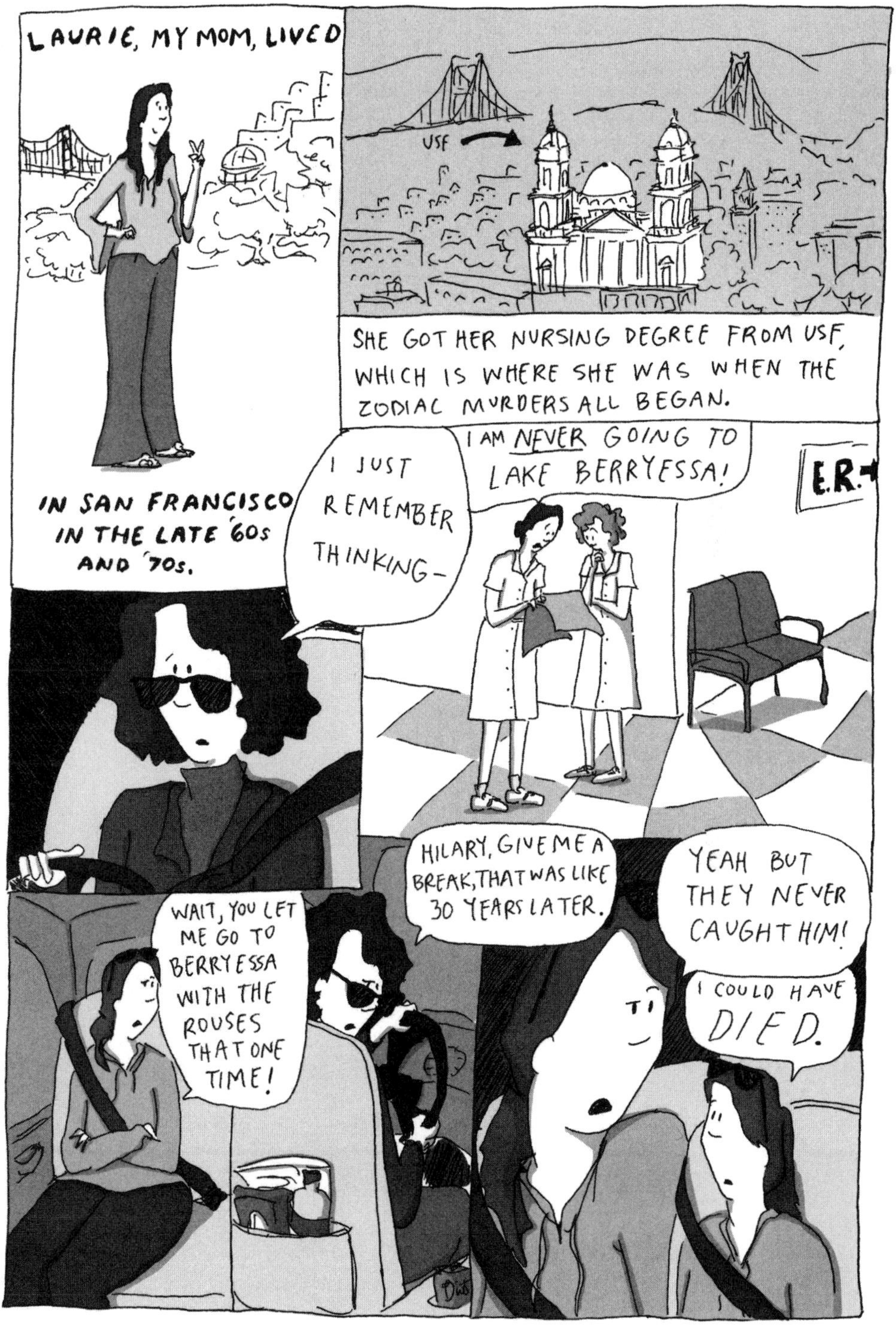
LAURIE, MY MOM, LIVED
IN SAN FRANCISCO IN THE LATE '60s AND '70s.
USF
SHE GOT HER NURSING DEGREE FROM USF, WHICH IS WHERE SHE WAS WHEN THE ZODIAC MURDERS ALL BEGAN.
I JUST REMEMBER THINKING—
I AM NEVER GOING TO LAKE BERRYESSA!
E.R.
WAIT, YOU LET ME GO TO BERRYESSA WITH THE ROUSES THAT ONE TIME!
HILARY, GIVE ME A BREAK, THAT WAS LIKE 30 YEARS LATER.
YEAH BUT THEY NEVER CAUGHT HIM!
I COULD HAVE DIED.

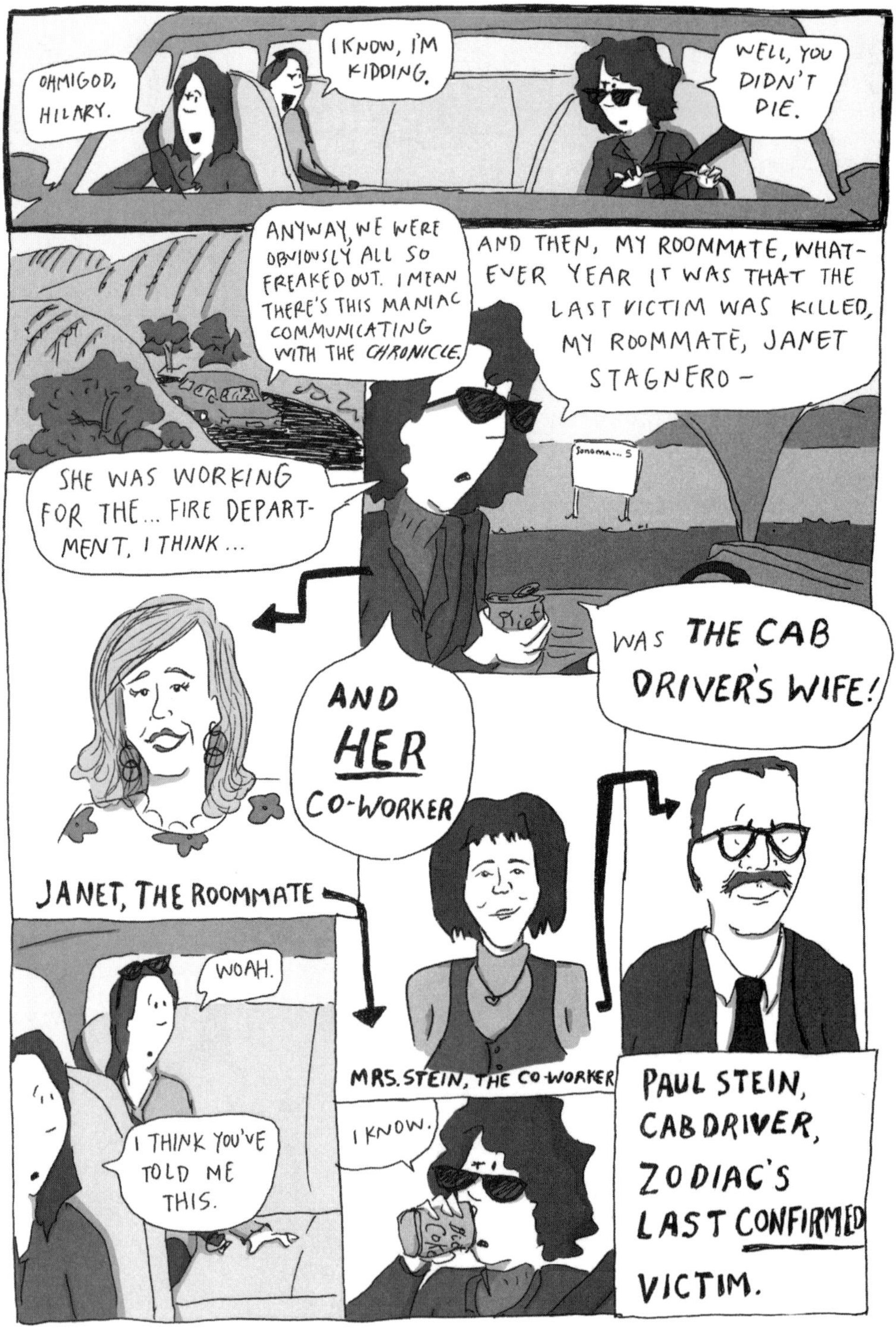
OHMIGOD, HILARY.
I KNOW, I'M KIDDING.
WELL, YOU DIDN'T DIE.
ANYWAY, WE WERE OBVIOUSLY ALL SO FREAKED OUT. I MEAN THERE'S THIS MANIAC COMMUNICATING WITH THE CHRONICLE.
AND THEN, MY ROOMMATE, WHATEVER YEAR IT WAS THAT THE LAST VICTIM WAS KILLED, MY ROOMMATE, JANET STAGNERO -
SHE WAS WORKING FOR THE... FIRE DEPARTMENT, I THINK...
AND HER CO-WORKER
WAS THE CAB DRIVER'S WIFE!
JANET, THE ROOMMATE
MRS. STEIN, THE CO-WORKER
PAUL STEIN, CAB DRIVER, ZODIAC'S LAST CONFIRMED VICTIM.
WOAH.
I THINK YOU'VE TOLD ME THIS.
I KNOW.

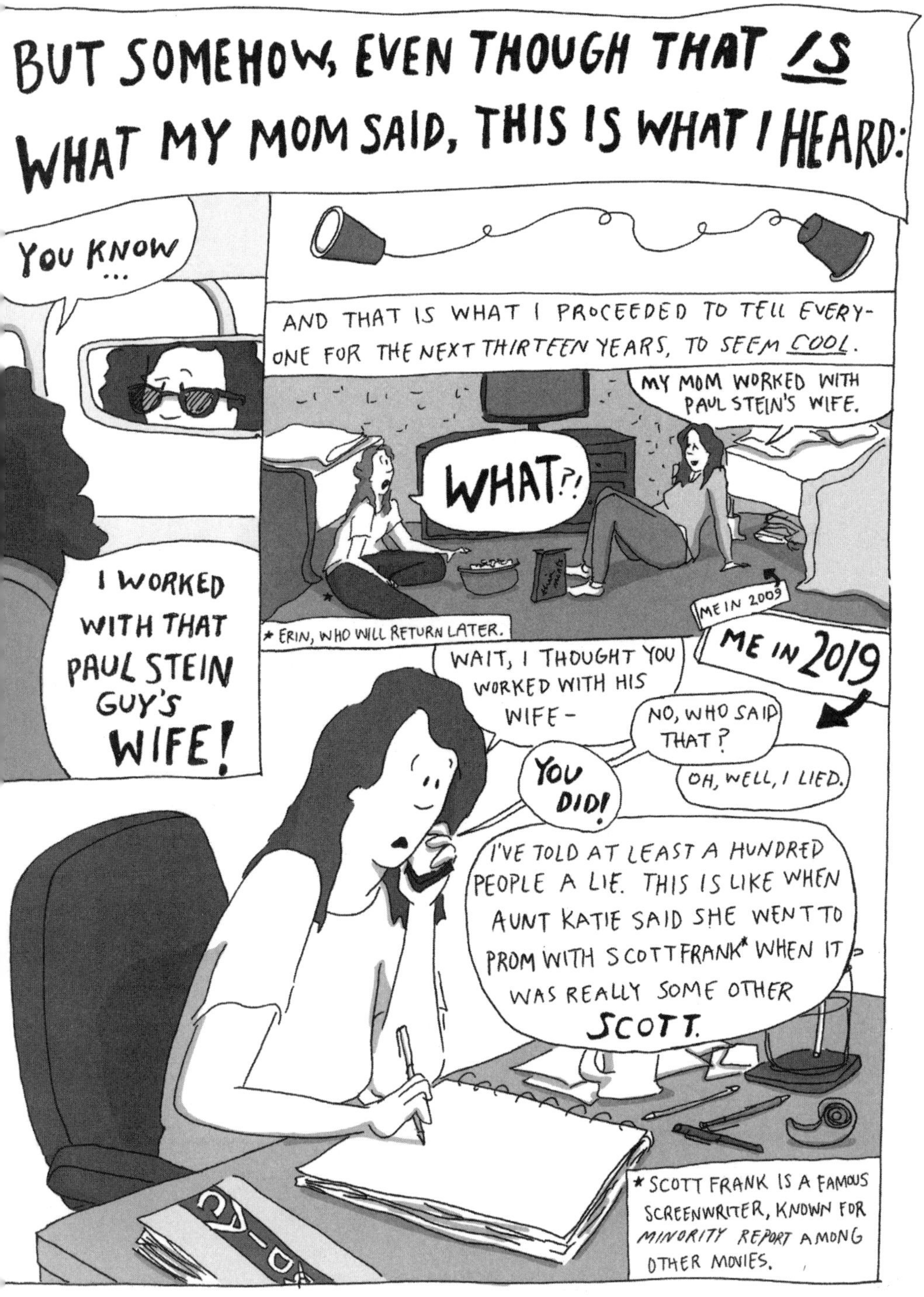
BUT SOMEHOW, EVEN THOUGH THAT IS WHAT MY MOM SAID, THIS IS WHAT I HEARD:
YOU KNOW...
I WORKED WITH THAT PAUL STEIN GUY'S WIFE!
AND THAT IS WHAT I PROCEEDED TO TELL EVERYONE FOR THE NEXT THIRTEEN YEARS, TO SEEM COOL.
MY MOM WORKED WITH PAUL STEIN'S WIFE.
WHAT?!
ME IN 2009
* ERIN, WHO WILL RETURN LATER.
ME IN 2019
WAIT, I THOUGHT YOU WORKED WITH HIS WIFE-
NO, WHO SAID THAT?
YOU DID!
OH, WELL, I LIED.
I'VE TOLD AT LEAST A HUNDRED PEOPLE A LIE. THIS IS LIKE WHEN AUNT KATIE SAID SHE WENT TO PROM WITH SCOTT FRANK* WHEN IT WAS REALLY SOME OTHER SCOTT.
* SCOTT FRANK IS A FAMOUS SCREENWRITER, KNOWN FOR MINORITY REPORT AMONG OTHER MOVIES.

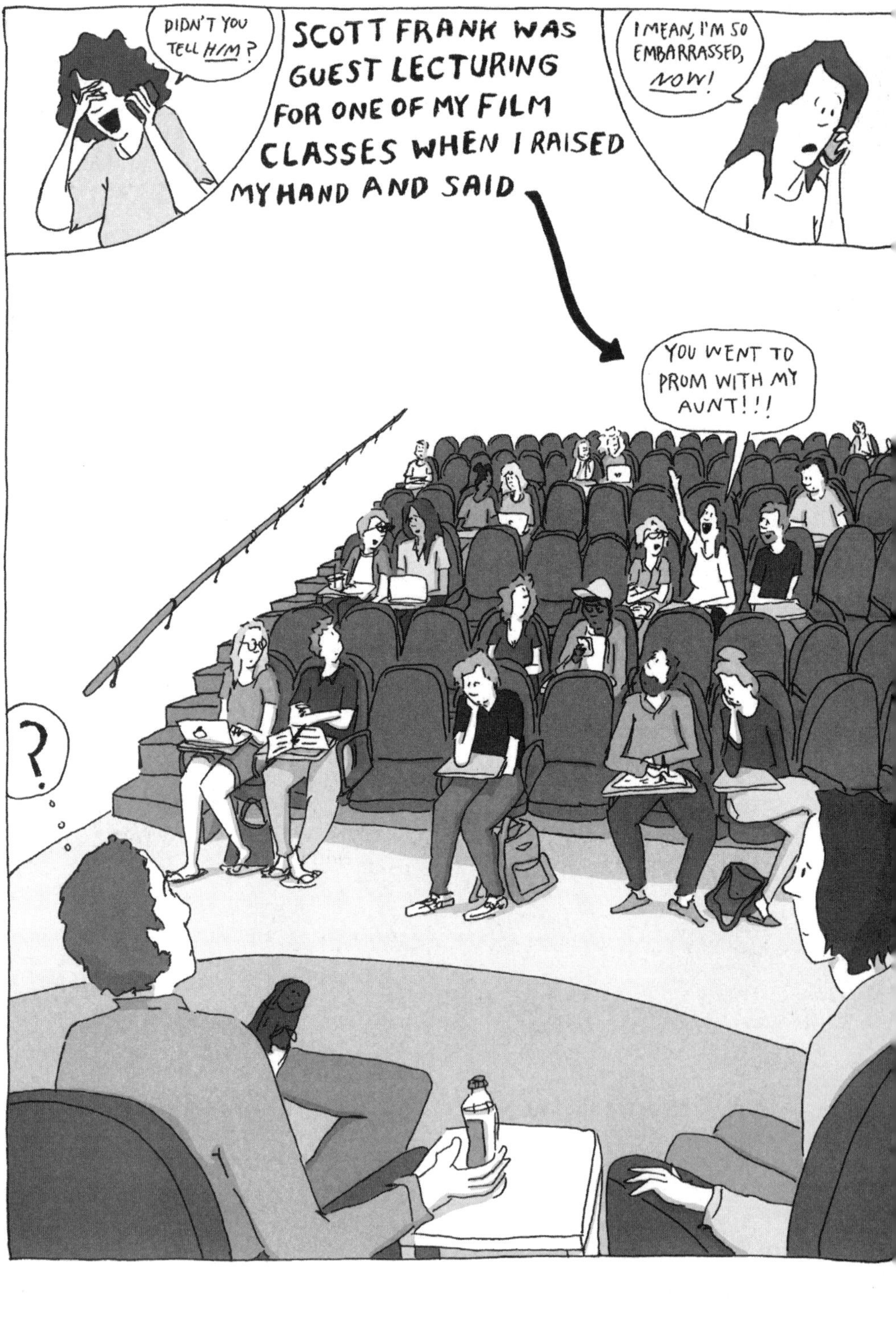
DIDN'T YOU TELL HIM?
SCOTT FRANK WAS GUEST LECTURING FOR ONE OF MY FILM CLASSES WHEN I RAISED MY HAND AND SAID
I MEAN, I'M SO EMBARRASSED, NOW!
YOU WENT TO PROM WITH MY AUNT!!!
?

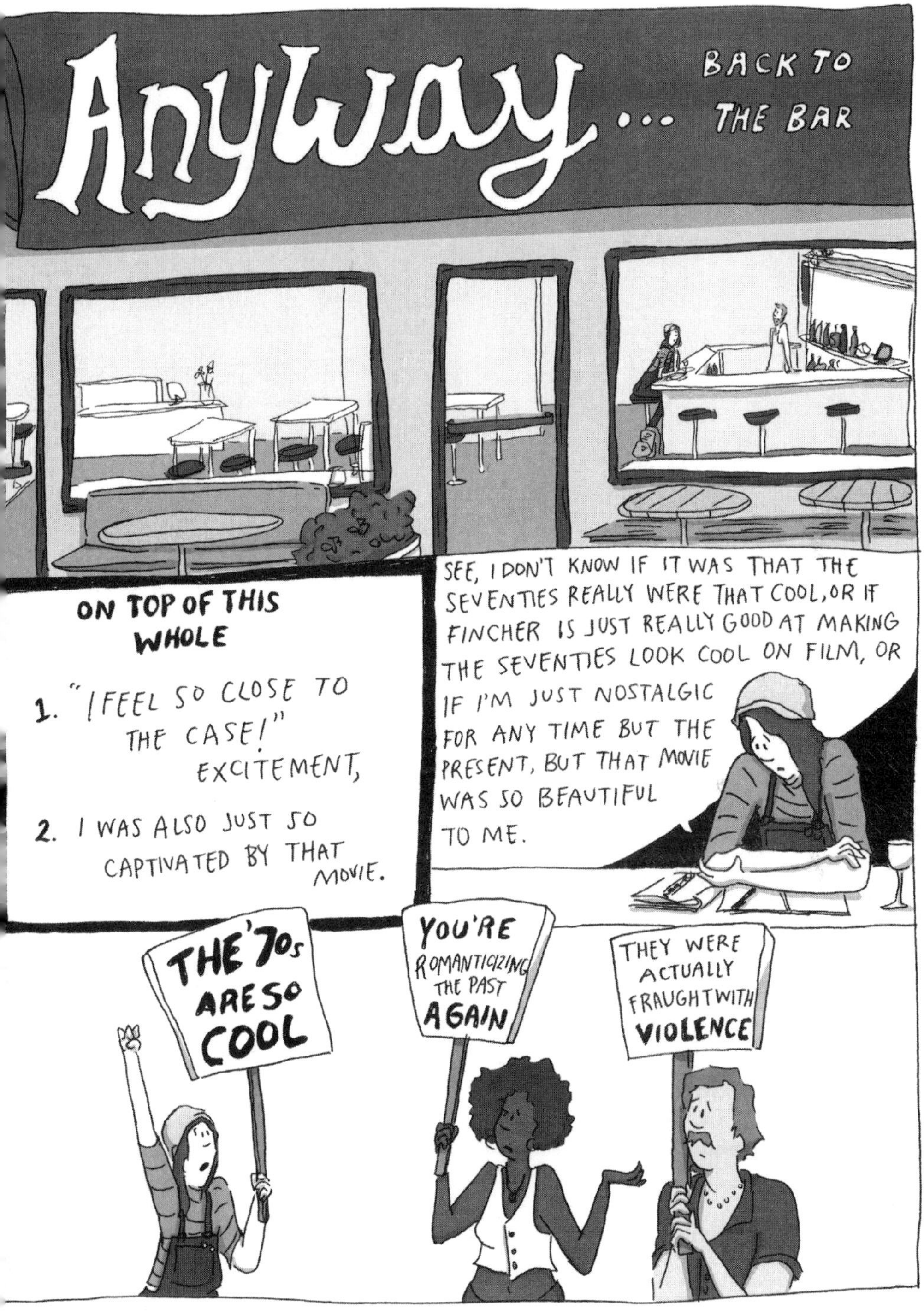

Anyway... BACK TO THE BAR
ON TOP OF THIS WHOLE
1. "I FEEL SO CLOSE TO THE CASE!" EXCITEMENT,
2. I WAS ALSO JUST SO CAPTIVATED BY THAT MOVIE.
SEE, I DON'T KNOW IF IT WAS THAT THE SEVENTIES REALLY WERE THAT COOL, OR IF FINCHER IS JUST REALLY GOOD AT MAKING THE SEVENTIES LOOK COOL ON FILM, OR IF I'M JUST NOSTALGIC FOR ANY TIME BUT THE PRESENT, BUT THAT MOVIE WAS SO BEAUTIFUL TO ME.
THE '70s ARE SO COOL
YOU'RE ROMANTICIZING THE PAST AGAIN
THEY WERE ACTUALLY FRAUGHT WITH VIOLENCE

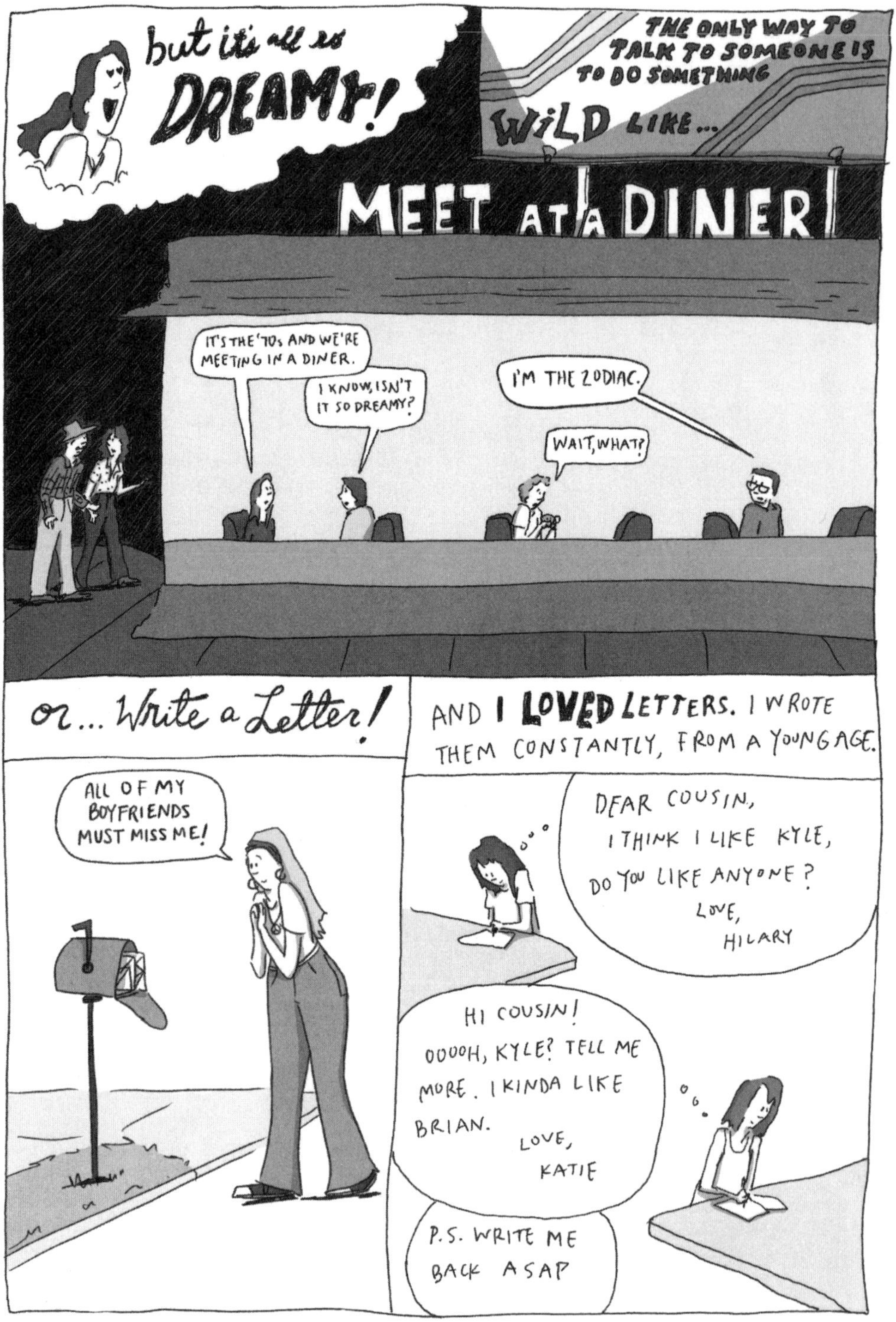
but it's all so DREAMY!
THE ONLY WAY TO TALK TO SOMEONE IS TO DO SOMETHING WILD LIKE...
MEET AT A DINER
IT'S THE '70s AND WE'RE MEETING IN A DINER.
I KNOW, ISN'T IT SO DREAMY?
I'M THE ZODIAC.
WAIT, WHAT?
or... Write a Letter!
AND I LOVED LETTERS. I WROTE THEM CONSTANTLY, FROM A YOUNG AGE.
ALL OF MY BOYFRIENDS MUST MISS ME!
DEAR COUSIN, I THINK I LIKE KYLE, DO YOU LIKE ANYONE? LOVE, HILARY
HI COUSIN! OOOOH, KYLE? TELL ME MORE. I KINDA LIKE BRIAN. LOVE, KATIE
P.S. WRITE ME BACK ASAP

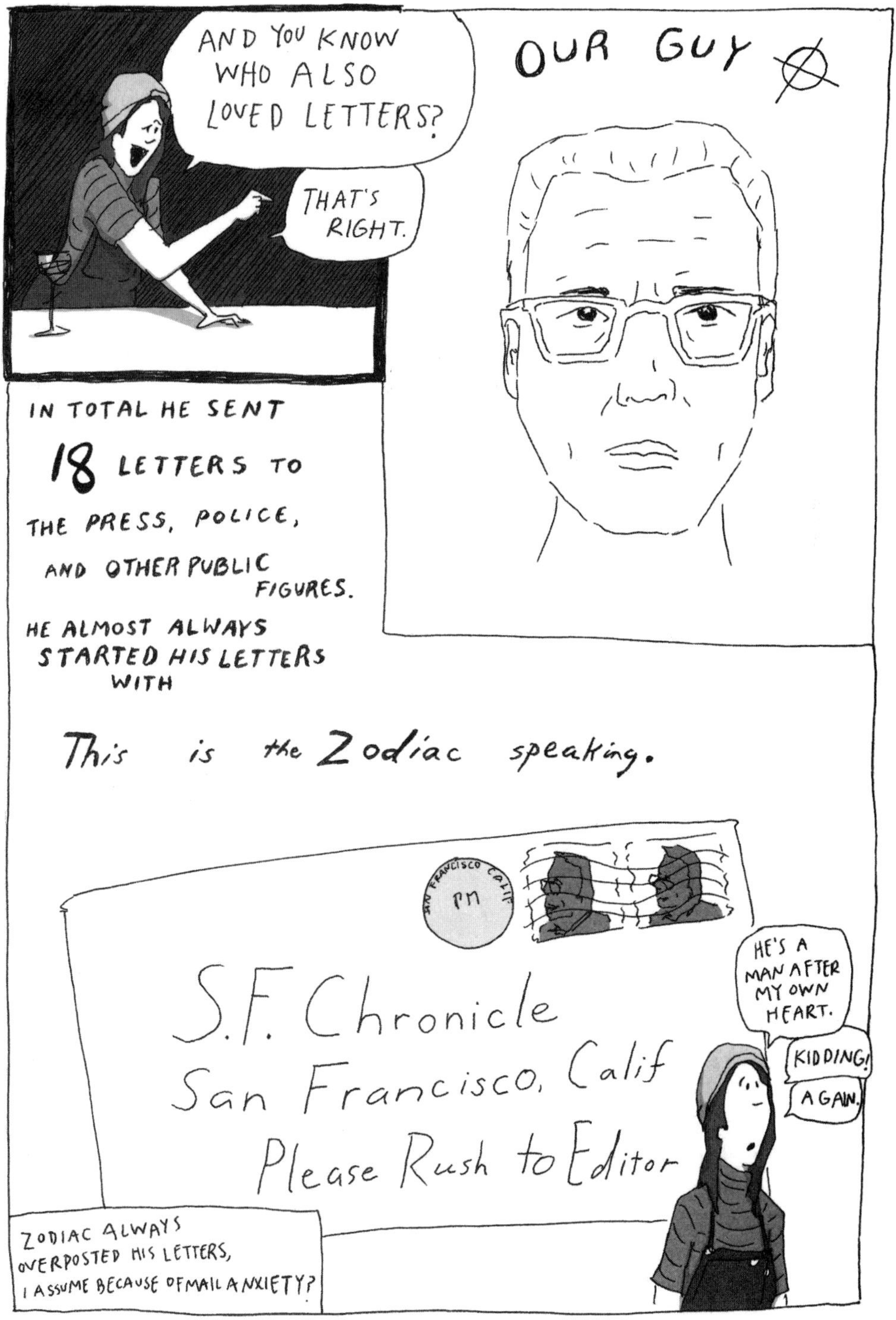

AND YOU KNOW WHO ALSO LOVED LETTERS?
THAT'S RIGHT.
OUR GUY
IN TOTAL HE SENT 18 LETTERS TO THE PRESS, POLICE, AND OTHER PUBLIC FIGURES.
HE ALMOST ALWAYS STARTED HIS LETTERS WITH
This is the Zodiac speaking.
SAN FRANCISCO CALIF
PM
S.F. Chronicle
San Francisco, Calif
Please Rush to Editor
HE'S A MAN AFTER MY OWN HEART.
KIDDING!
AGAIN.
ZODIAC ALWAYS OVERPOSTED HIS LETTERS, I ASSUME BECAUSE OF MAIL ANXIETY?

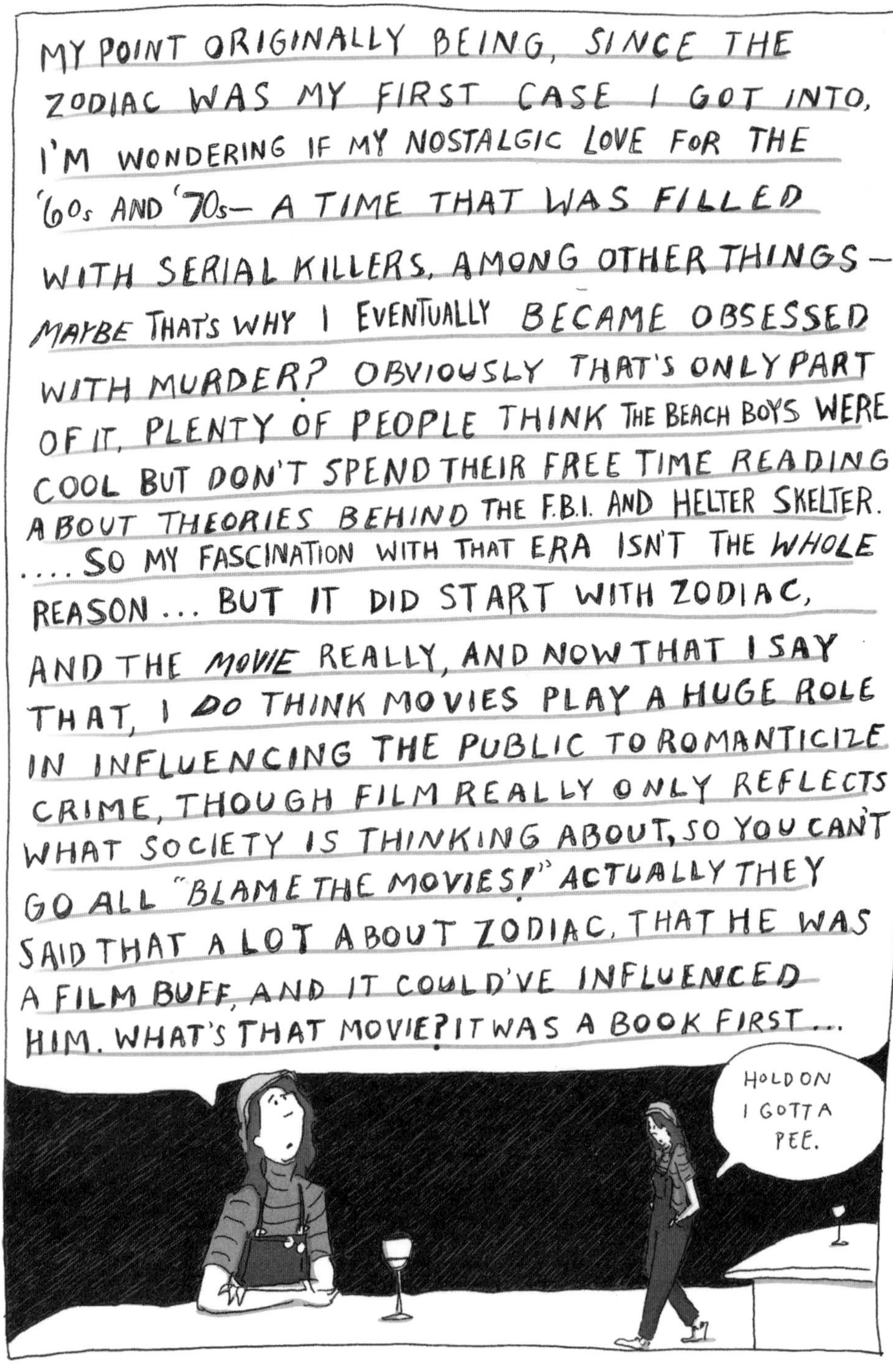
MY POINT ORIGINALLY BEING, SINCE THE ZODIAC WAS MY FIRST CASE I GOT INTO, I'M WONDERING IF MY NOSTALGIC LOVE FOR THE '60s AND '70s— A TIME THAT WAS FILLED WITH SERIAL KILLERS, AMONG OTHER THINGS— MAYBE THAT'S WHY I EVENTUALLY BECAME OBSESSED WITH MURDER? OBVIOUSLY THAT'S ONLY PART OF IT. PLENTY OF PEOPLE THINK THE BEACH BOYS WERE COOL BUT DON'T SPEND THEIR FREE TIME READING ABOUT THEORIES BEHIND THE F.B.I. AND HELTER SKELTER. ....SO MY FASCINATION WITH THAT ERA ISN'T THE WHOLE REASON... BUT IT DID START WITH ZODIAC, AND THE MOVIE REALLY, AND NOW THAT I SAY THAT, I DO THINK MOVIES PLAY A HUGE ROLE IN INFLUENCING THE PUBLIC TO ROMANTICIZE CRIME, THOUGH FILM REALLY ONLY REFLECTS WHAT SOCIETY IS THINKING ABOUT, SO YOU CAN'T GO ALL "BLAME THE MOVIES!" ACTUALLY THEY SAID THAT A LOT ABOUT ZODIAC, THAT HE WAS A FILM BUFF, AND IT COULD'VE INFLUENCED HIM. WHAT'S THAT MOVIE? IT WAS A BOOK FIRST...
HOLD ON I GOTTA PEE.

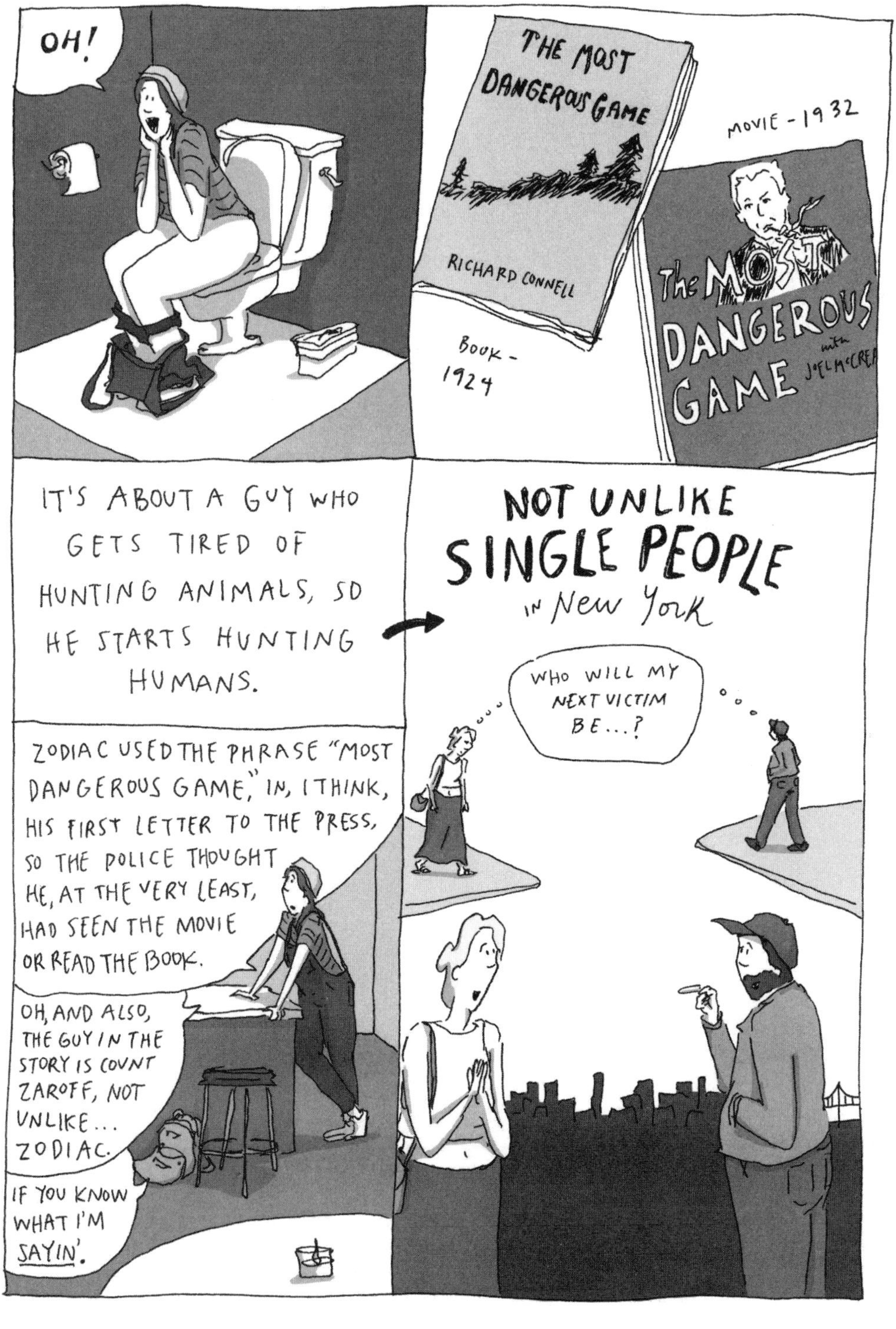
OH!
THE MOST DANGEROUS GAME
RICHARD CONNELL
BOOK - 1924
MOVIE - 1932
The MOST DANGEROUS GAME with JOEL McCREA
IT'S ABOUT A GUY WHO GETS TIRED OF HUNTING ANIMALS, SO HE STARTS HUNTING HUMANS.
NOT UNLIKE SINGLE PEOPLE IN New York
WHO WILL MY NEXT VICTIM BE...?
ZODIAC USED THE PHRASE "MOST DANGEROUS GAME," IN, I THINK, HIS FIRST LETTER TO THE PRESS, SO THE POLICE THOUGHT HE, AT THE VERY LEAST, HAD SEEN THE MOVIE OR READ THE BOOK.
OH, AND ALSO, THE GUY IN THE STORY IS COUNT ZAROFF, NOT UNLIKE... ZODIAC.
IF YOU KNOW WHAT I'M SAYIN'.

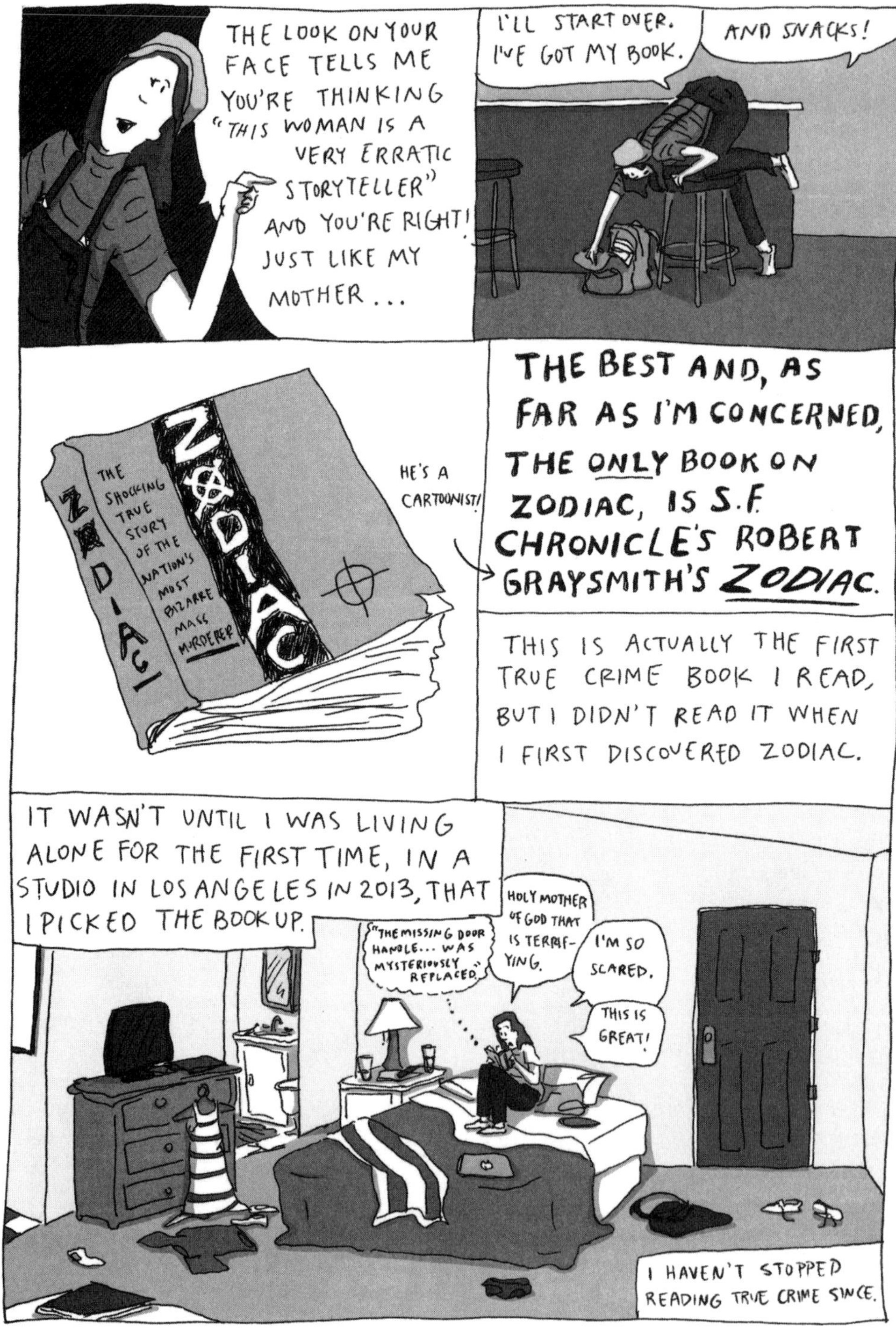
THE LOOK ON YOUR FACE TELLS ME YOU'RE THINKING "THIS WOMAN IS A VERY ERRATIC STORYTELLER" AND YOU'RE RIGHT! JUST LIKE MY MOTHER...
I'LL START OVER. I'VE GOT MY BOOK.
AND SNACKS!
ZODIAC
THE SHOCKING TRUE STORY OF THE NATION'S MOST BIZARRE MASS MURDERER
HE'S A CARTOONIST!
THE BEST AND, AS FAR AS I'M CONCERNED, THE ONLY BOOK ON ZODIAC, IS S.F. CHRONICLE'S ROBERT GRAYSMITH'S ZODIAC.
THIS IS ACTUALLY THE FIRST TRUE CRIME BOOK I READ, BUT I DIDN'T READ IT WHEN I FIRST DISCOVERED ZODIAC.
IT WASN'T UNTIL I WAS LIVING ALONE FOR THE FIRST TIME, IN A STUDIO IN LOS ANGELES IN 2013, THAT I PICKED THE BOOK UP.
"THE MISSING DOOR HANDLE... WAS MYSTERIOUSLY REPLACED."
HOLY MOTHER OF GOD THAT IS TERRIF-YING.
I'M SO SCARED.
THIS IS GREAT!
I HAVEN'T STOPPED READING TRUE CRIME SINCE.

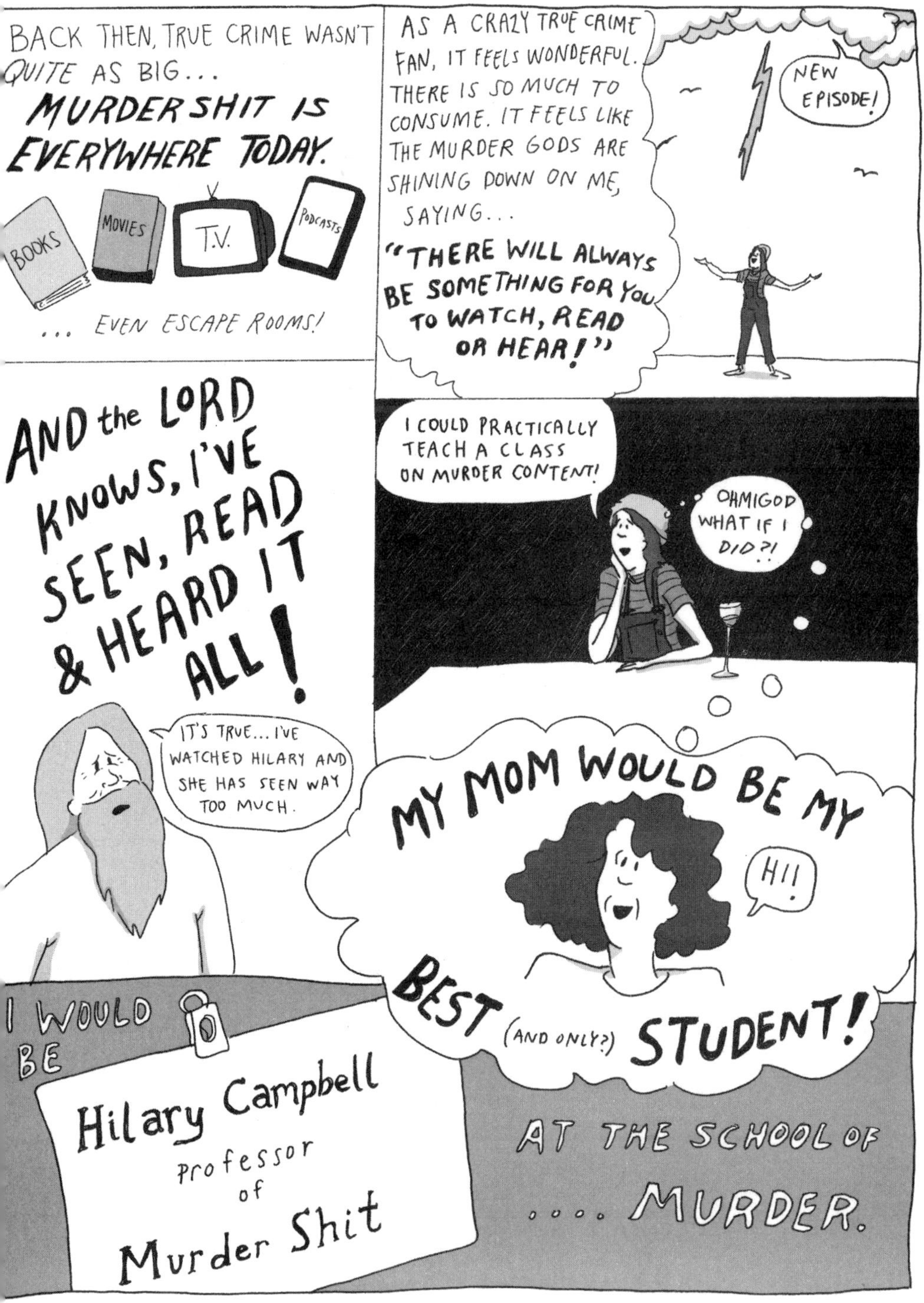
BACK THEN, TRUE CRIME WASN'T QUITE AS BIG...
MURDERSHIT IS EVERYWHERE TODAY.
BOOKS
MOVIES
T.V.
PODCASTS
... EVEN ESCAPE ROOMS!
AS A CRAZY TRUE CRIME FAN, IT FEELS WONDERFUL. THERE IS SO MUCH TO CONSUME. IT FEELS LIKE THE MURDER GODS ARE SHINING DOWN ON ME, SAYING...
"THERE WILL ALWAYS BE SOMETHING FOR YOU TO WATCH, READ OR HEAR!"
NEW EPISODE!
AND the LORD KNOWS, I'VE SEEN, READ & HEARD IT ALL!
IT'S TRUE... I'VE WATCHED HILARY AND SHE HAS SEEN WAY TOO MUCH.
I COULD PRACTICALLY TEACH A CLASS ON MURDER CONTENT!
OHMIGOD WHAT IF I DID?!
MY MOM WOULD BE MY BEST (AND ONLY?) STUDENT!
HI!
I WOULD BE
Hilary Campbell
professor of
Murder Shit
AT THE SCHOOL OF .... MURDER.

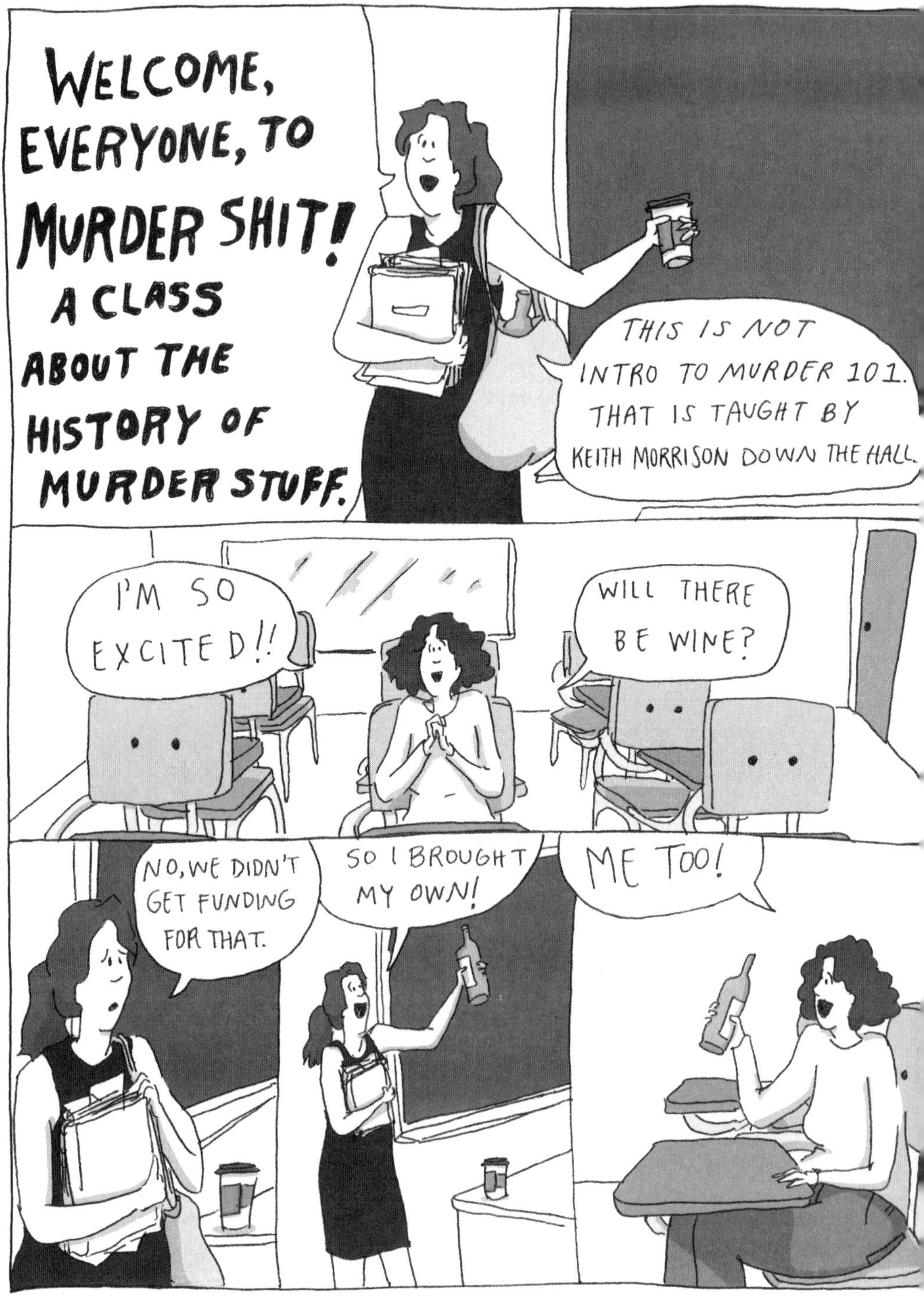
WELCOME, EVERYONE, TO MURDER SHIT! A CLASS ABOUT THE HISTORY OF MURDER STUFF.
THIS IS NOT INTRO TO MURDER 101. THAT IS TAUGHT BY KEITH MORRISON DOWN THE HALL.
I'M SO EXCITED!!
WILL THERE BE WINE?
NO, WE DIDN'T GET FUNDING FOR THAT.
SO I BROUGHT MY OWN!
ME TOO!

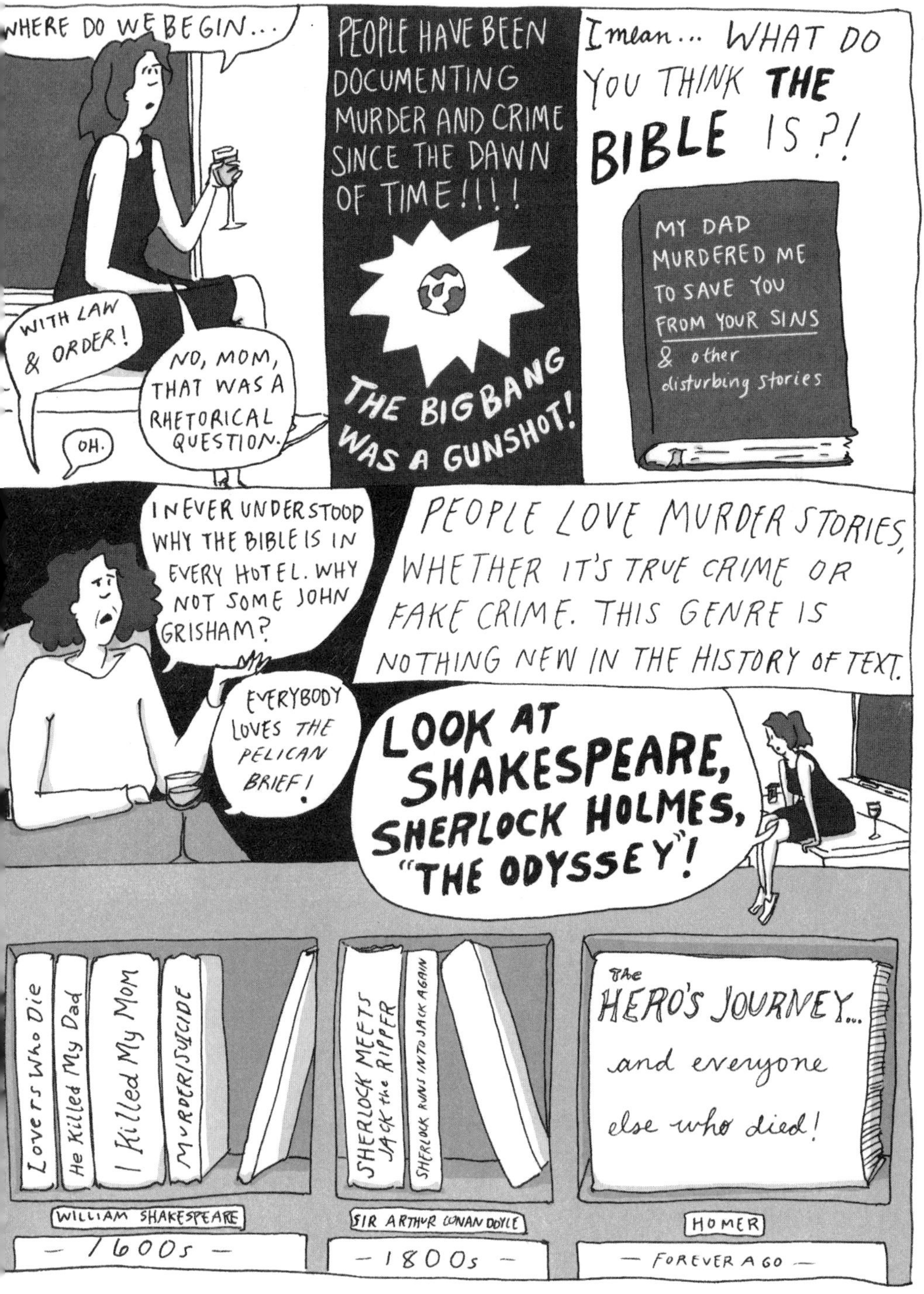
WHERE DO WE BEGIN...
WITH LAW & ORDER!
NO, MOM, THAT WAS A RHETORICAL QUESTION.
OH.
PEOPLE HAVE BEEN DOCUMENTING MURDER AND CRIME SINCE THE DAWN OF TIME!!!!
THE BIG BANG WAS A GUNSHOT!
I mean... WHAT DO YOU THINK THE BIBLE IS?!
MY DAD MURDERED ME TO SAVE YOU FROM YOUR SINS
& other disturbing stories
I NEVER UNDERSTOOD WHY THE BIBLE IS IN EVERY HOTEL. WHY NOT SOME JOHN GRISHAM?
EVERYBODY LOVES THE PELICAN BRIEF!
PEOPLE LOVE MURDER STORIES, WHETHER IT'S TRUE CRIME OR FAKE CRIME. THIS GENRE IS NOTHING NEW IN THE HISTORY OF TEXT.
LOOK AT SHAKESPEARE, SHERLOCK HOLMES, "THE ODYSSEY"!
Lovers Who Die
He Killed My Dad
I Killed My Mom
MURDER/SUICIDE
WILLIAM SHAKESPEARE
— 1600s —
SHERLOCK MEETS JACK the RIPPER
SHERLOCK RUNS INTO JACK AGAIN
SIR ARTHUR CONAN DOYLE
— 1800s —
The HERO'S JOURNEY... and everyone else who died!
HOMER
— FOREVER AGO —

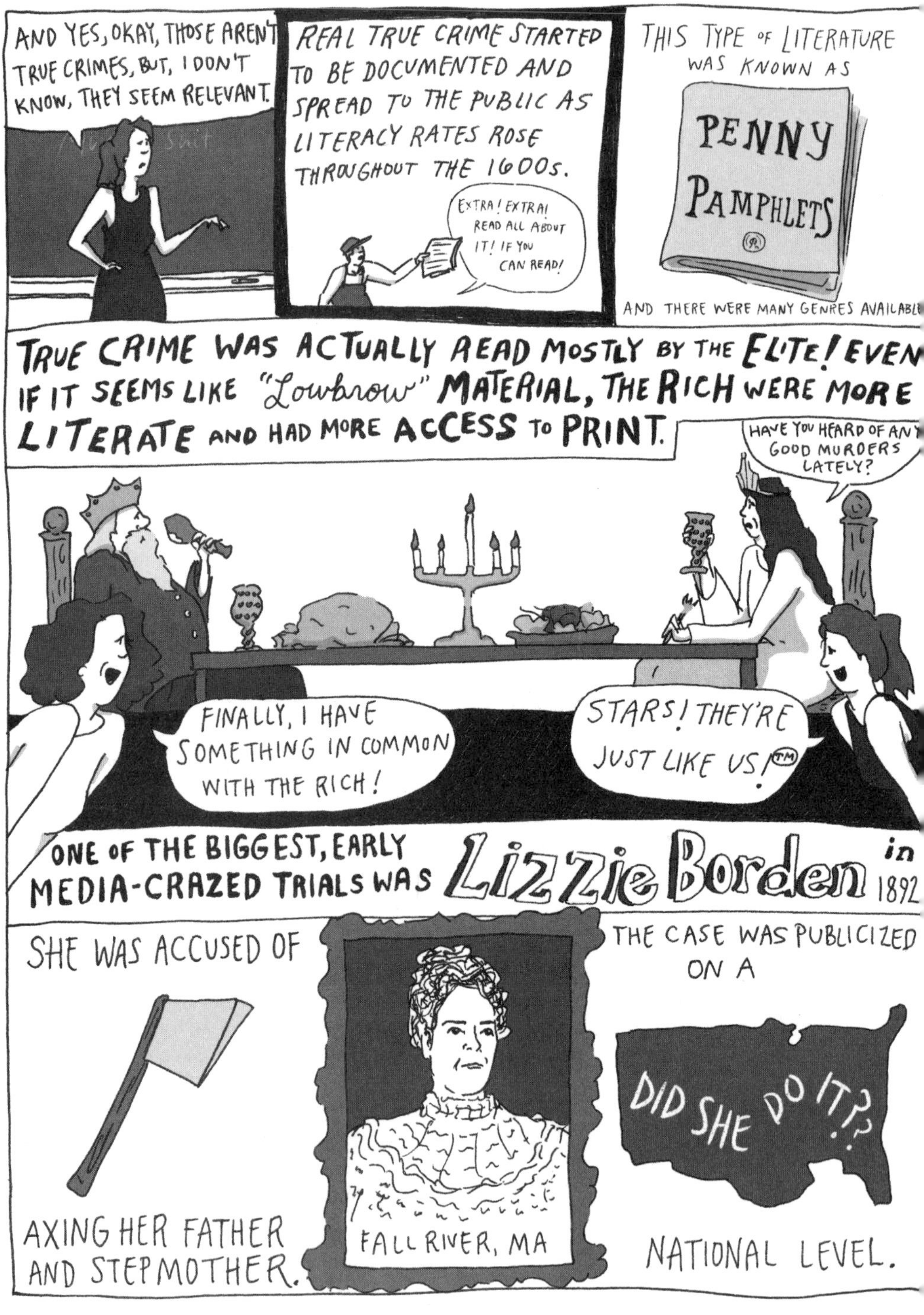
AND YES, OKAY, THOSE AREN'T TRUE CRIMES, BUT, I DON'T KNOW, THEY SEEM RELEVANT.
REAL TRUE CRIME STARTED TO BE DOCUMENTED AND SPREAD TO THE PUBLIC AS LITERACY RATES ROSE THROUGHOUT THE 1600s.
EXTRA! EXTRA! READ ALL ABOUT IT! IF YOU CAN READ!
THIS TYPE OF LITERATURE WAS KNOWN AS
PENNY PAMPHLETS
AND THERE WERE MANY GENRES AVAILABLE
TRUE CRIME WAS ACTUALLY READ MOSTLY BY THE ELITE! EVEN IF IT SEEMS LIKE "Lowbrow" MATERIAL, THE RICH WERE MORE LITERATE AND HAD MORE ACCESS TO PRINT.
HAVE YOU HEARD OF ANY GOOD MURDERS LATELY?
FINALLY, I HAVE SOMETHING IN COMMON WITH THE RICH!
STARS! THEY'RE JUST LIKE US!™
ONE OF THE BIGGEST, EARLY MEDIA-CRAZED TRIALS WAS Lizzie Borden in 1892
SHE WAS ACCUSED OF
AXING HER FATHER AND STEPMOTHER.
FALL RIVER, MA
THE CASE WAS PUBLICIZED ON A
DID SHE DO IT?!?
NATIONAL LEVEL.

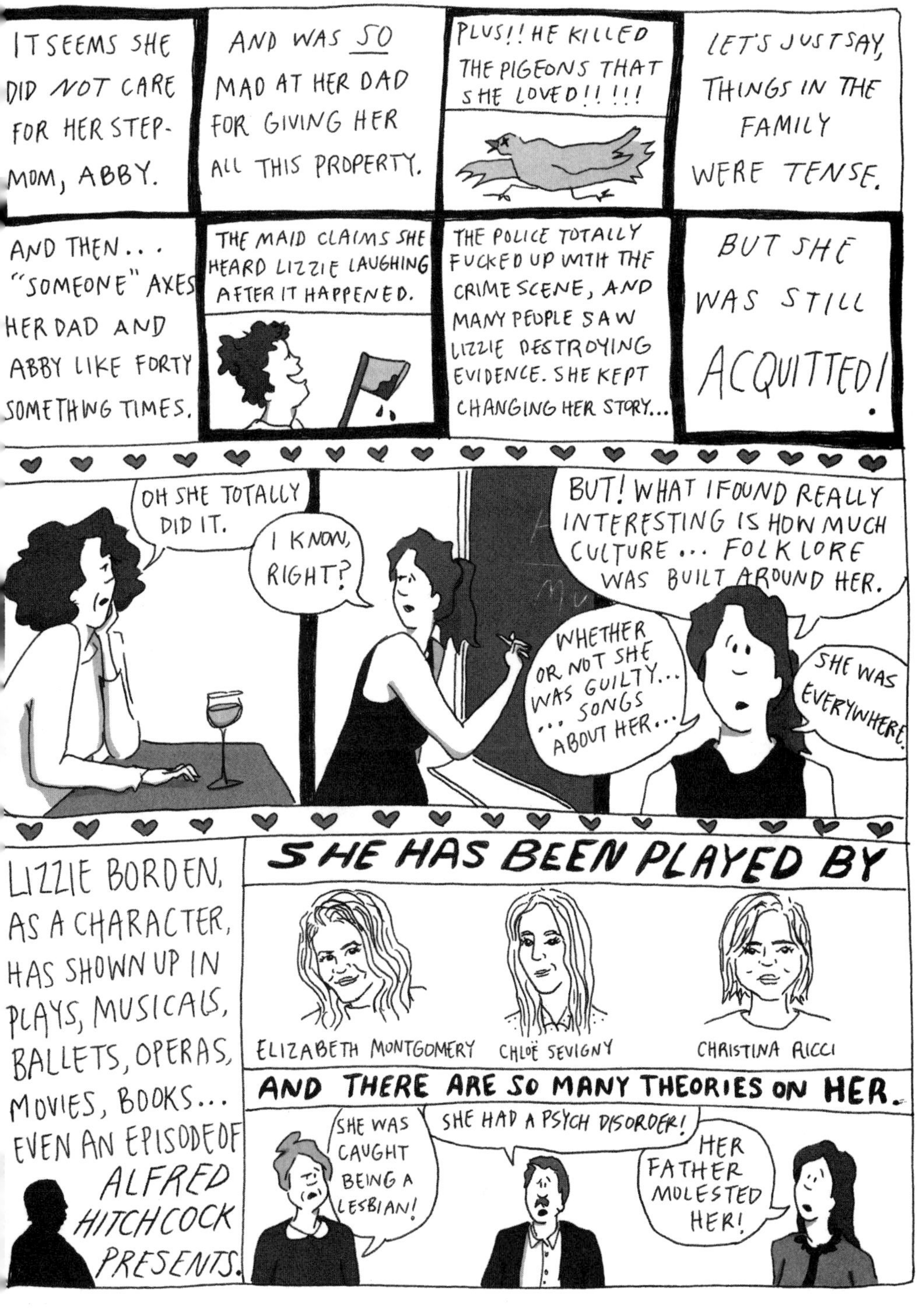
IT SEEMS SHE DID NOT CARE FOR HER STEP-MOM, ABBY.
AND WAS SO MAD AT HER DAD FOR GIVING HER ALL THIS PROPERTY.
PLUS!! HE KILLED THE PIGEONS THAT SHE LOVED!!!!!
LET'S JUST SAY, THINGS IN THE FAMILY WERE TENSE.
AND THEN... "SOMEONE" AXES HER DAD AND ABBY LIKE FORTY SOMETHING TIMES.
THE MAID CLAIMS SHE HEARD LIZZIE LAUGHING AFTER IT HAPPENED.
THE POLICE TOTALLY FUCKED UP WITH THE CRIME SCENE, AND MANY PEOPLE SAW LIZZIE DESTROYING EVIDENCE. SHE KEPT CHANGING HER STORY...
BUT SHE WAS STILL ACQUITTED!
OH SHE TOTALLY DID IT.
I KNOW, RIGHT?
BUT! WHAT I FOUND REALLY INTERESTING IS HOW MUCH CULTURE... FOLKLORE WAS BUILT AROUND HER.
WHETHER OR NOT SHE WAS GUILTY... ... SONGS ABOUT HER...
SHE WAS EVERYWHERE.
LIZZIE BORDEN, AS A CHARACTER, HAS SHOWN UP IN PLAYS, MUSICALS, BALLETS, OPERAS, MOVIES, BOOKS... EVEN AN EPISODE OF ALFRED HITCHCOCK PRESENTS.
SHE HAS BEEN PLAYED BY
ELIZABETH MONTGOMERY
CHLOË SEVIGNY
CHRISTINA RICCI
AND THERE ARE SO MANY THEORIES ON HER.
SHE WAS CAUGHT BEING A LESBIAN!
SHE HAD A PSYCH DISORDER!
HER FATHER MOLESTED HER!

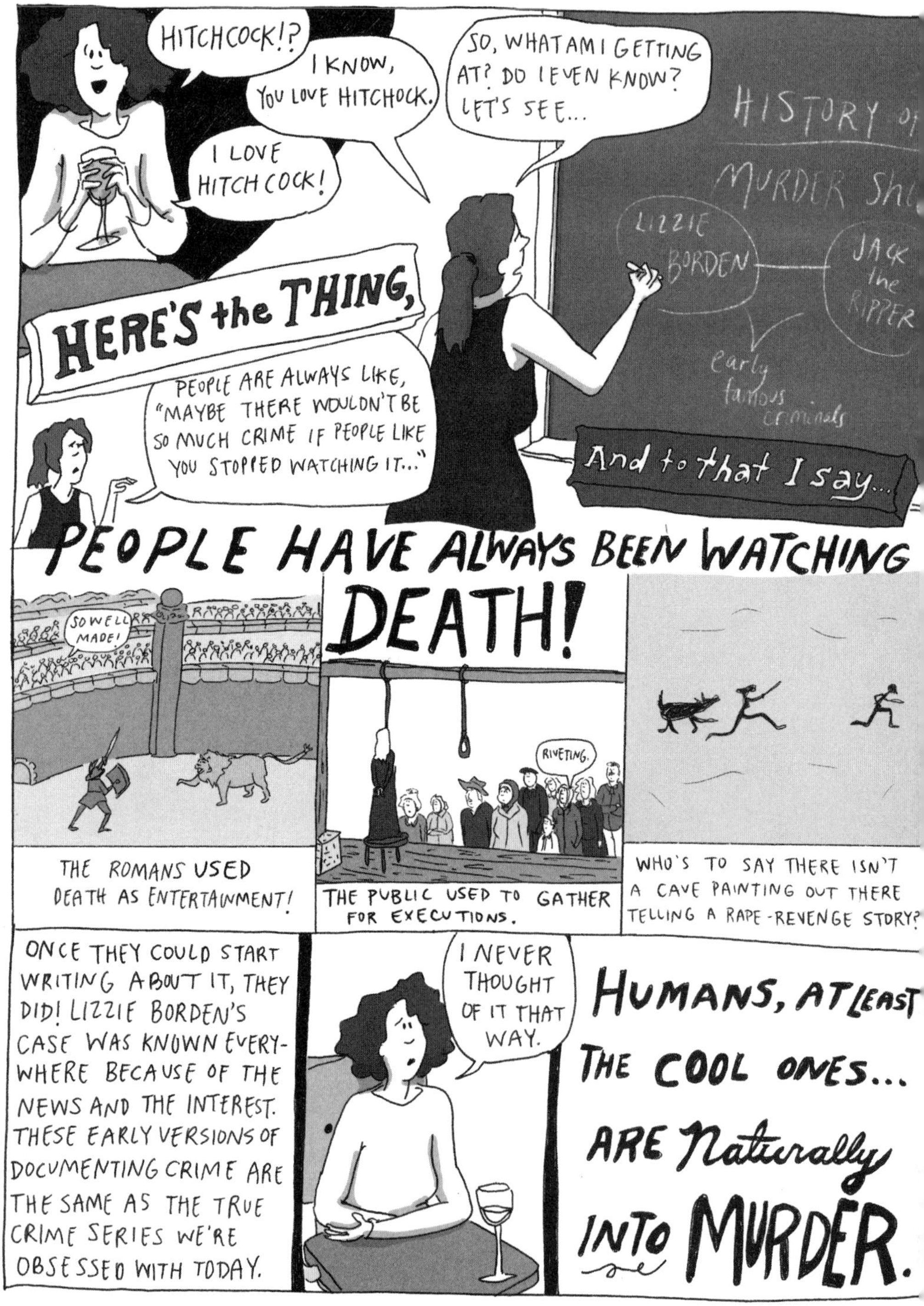
HITCHCOCK!?
I KNOW, YOU LOVE HITCHOCK.
I LOVE HITCHCOCK!
SO, WHAT AM I GETTING AT? DO I EVEN KNOW? LET'S SEE...
HISTORY OF MURDER SH
LIZZIE BORDEN
JACK the RIPPER
early famous criminals
HERE'S the THING,
PEOPLE ARE ALWAYS LIKE, "MAYBE THERE WOULDN'T BE SO MUCH CRIME IF PEOPLE LIKE YOU STOPPED WATCHING IT..."
And to that I say...
PEOPLE HAVE ALWAYS BEEN WATCHING DEATH!
SO WELL MADE!
THE ROMANS USED DEATH AS ENTERTAINMENT!
RIVETING.
THE PUBLIC USED TO GATHER FOR EXECUTIONS.
WHO'S TO SAY THERE ISN'T A CAVE PAINTING OUT THERE TELLING A RAPE-REVENGE STORY?
ONCE THEY COULD START WRITING ABOUT IT, THEY DID! LIZZIE BORDEN'S CASE WAS KNOWN EVERYWHERE BECAUSE OF THE NEWS AND THE INTEREST. THESE EARLY VERSIONS OF DOCUMENTING CRIME ARE THE SAME AS THE TRUE CRIME SERIES WE'RE OBSESSED WITH TODAY.
I NEVER THOUGHT OF IT THAT WAY.
HUMANS, AT LEAST THE COOL ONES... ARE Naturally INTO MURDER.

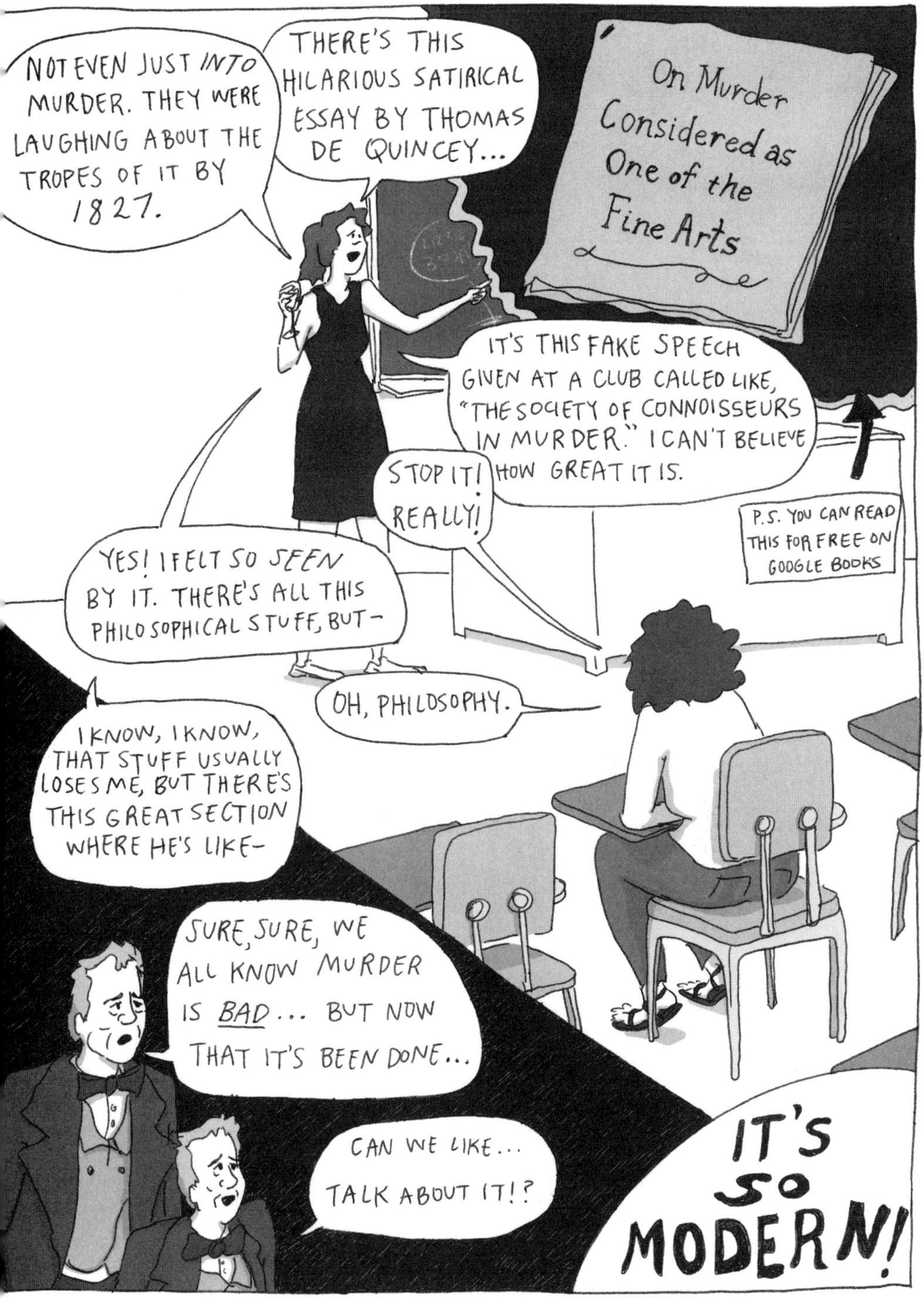
NOT EVEN JUST INTO MURDER. THEY WERE LAUGHING ABOUT THE TROPES OF IT BY 1827.
THERE'S THIS HILARIOUS SATIRICAL ESSAY BY THOMAS DE QUINCEY...
On Murder Considered as One of the Fine Arts
IT'S THIS FAKE SPEECH GIVEN AT A CLUB CALLED LIKE, "THE SOCIETY OF CONNOISSEURS IN MURDER." I CAN'T BELIEVE HOW GREAT IT IS.
STOP IT! REALLY!
P.S. YOU CAN READ THIS FOR FREE ON GOOGLE BOOKS
YES! I FELT SO SEEN BY IT. THERE'S ALL THIS PHILOSOPHICAL STUFF, BUT-
OH, PHILOSOPHY.
I KNOW, I KNOW, THAT STUFF USUALLY LOSES ME, BUT THERE'S THIS GREAT SECTION WHERE HE'S LIKE-
SURE, SURE, WE ALL KNOW MURDER IS BAD... BUT NOW THAT IT'S BEEN DONE...
CAN WE LIKE... TALK ABOUT IT!?
IT'S SO MODERN!

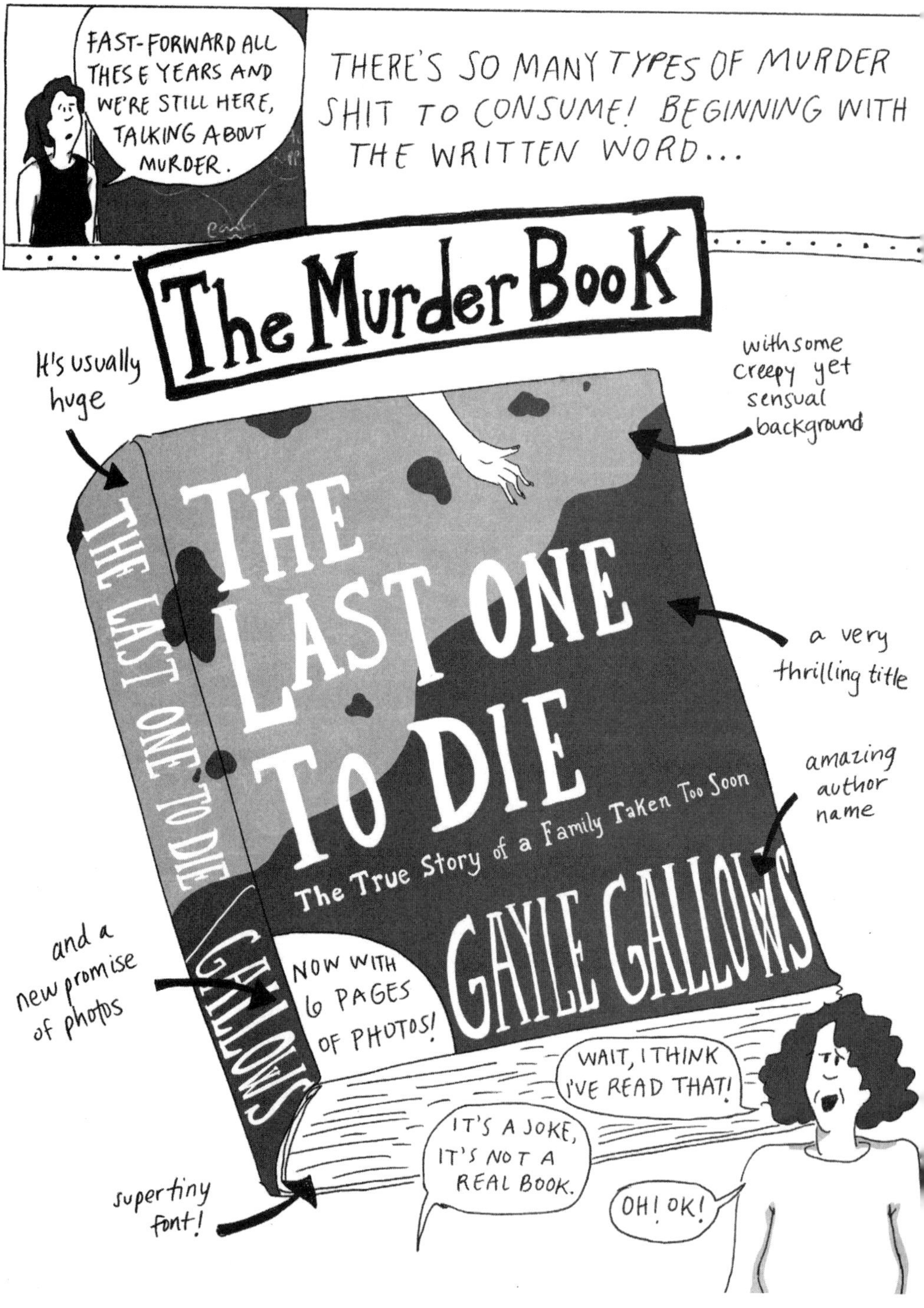
FAST-FORWARD ALL THESE YEARS AND WE'RE STILL HERE, TALKING ABOUT MURDER.
THERE'S SO MANY TYPES OF MURDER SHIT TO CONSUME! BEGINNING WITH THE WRITTEN WORD...
The Murder Book
It's usually huge
with some creepy yet sensual background
THE LAST ONE TO DIE
a very thrilling title
The True Story of a Family Taken Too Soon
amazing author name
GAYLE GALLOWS
and a new promise of photos
NOW WITH 6 PAGES OF PHOTOS!
THE LAST ONE TO DIE
GALLOWS
supertiny font!
WAIT, I THINK I'VE READ THAT!
IT'S A JOKE, IT'S NOT A REAL BOOK.
OH! OK!

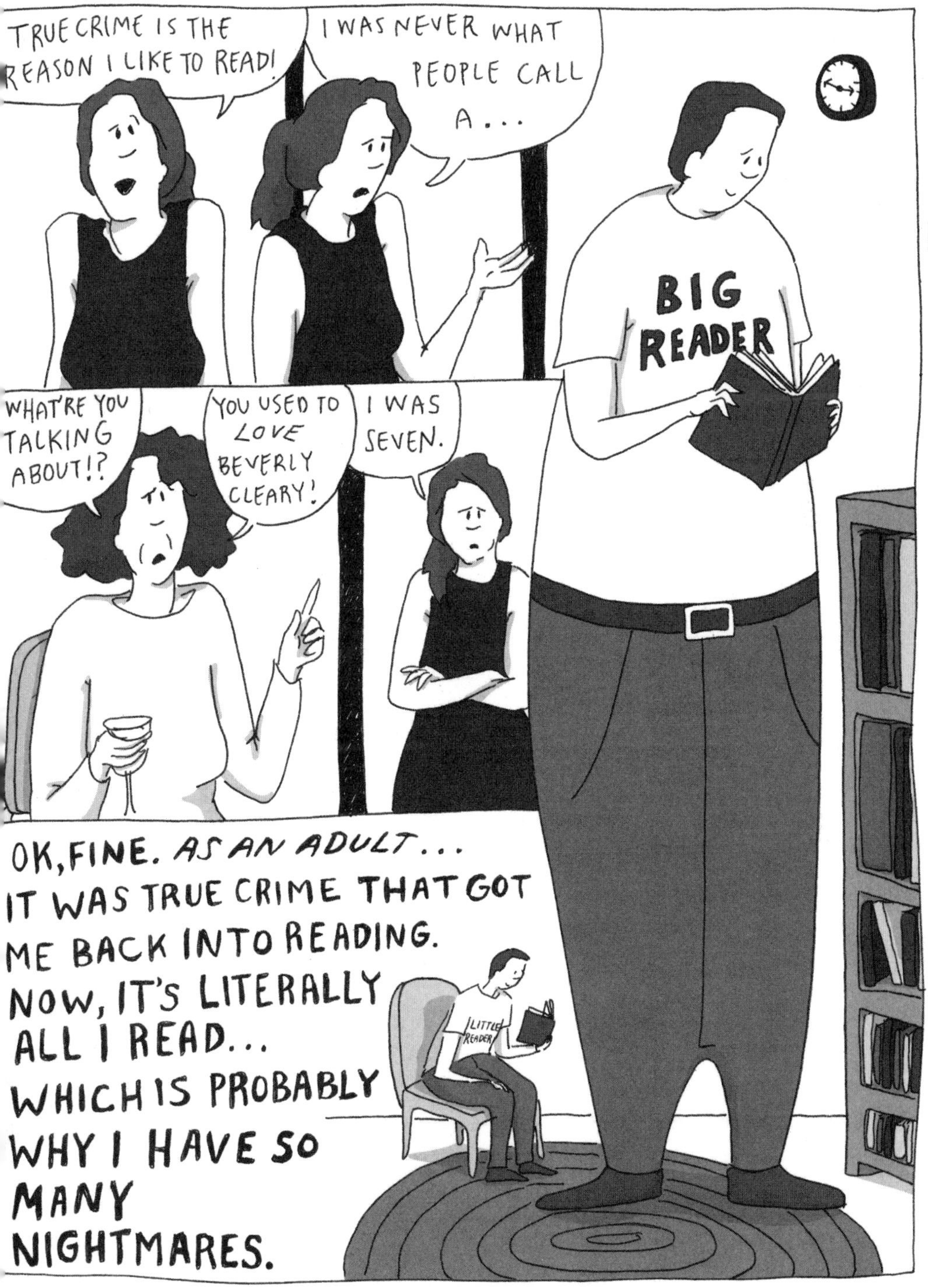
TRUE CRIME IS THE REASON I LIKE TO READ!
I WAS NEVER WHAT PEOPLE CALL A...
BIG READER
WHAT'RE YOU TALKING ABOUT!?
YOU USED TO LOVE BEVERLY CLEARY!
I WAS SEVEN.
OK, FINE. AS AN ADULT... IT WAS TRUE CRIME THAT GOT ME BACK INTO READING. NOW, IT'S LITERALLY ALL I READ... WHICH IS PROBABLY WHY I HAVE SO MANY NIGHTMARES.
LITTLE READER

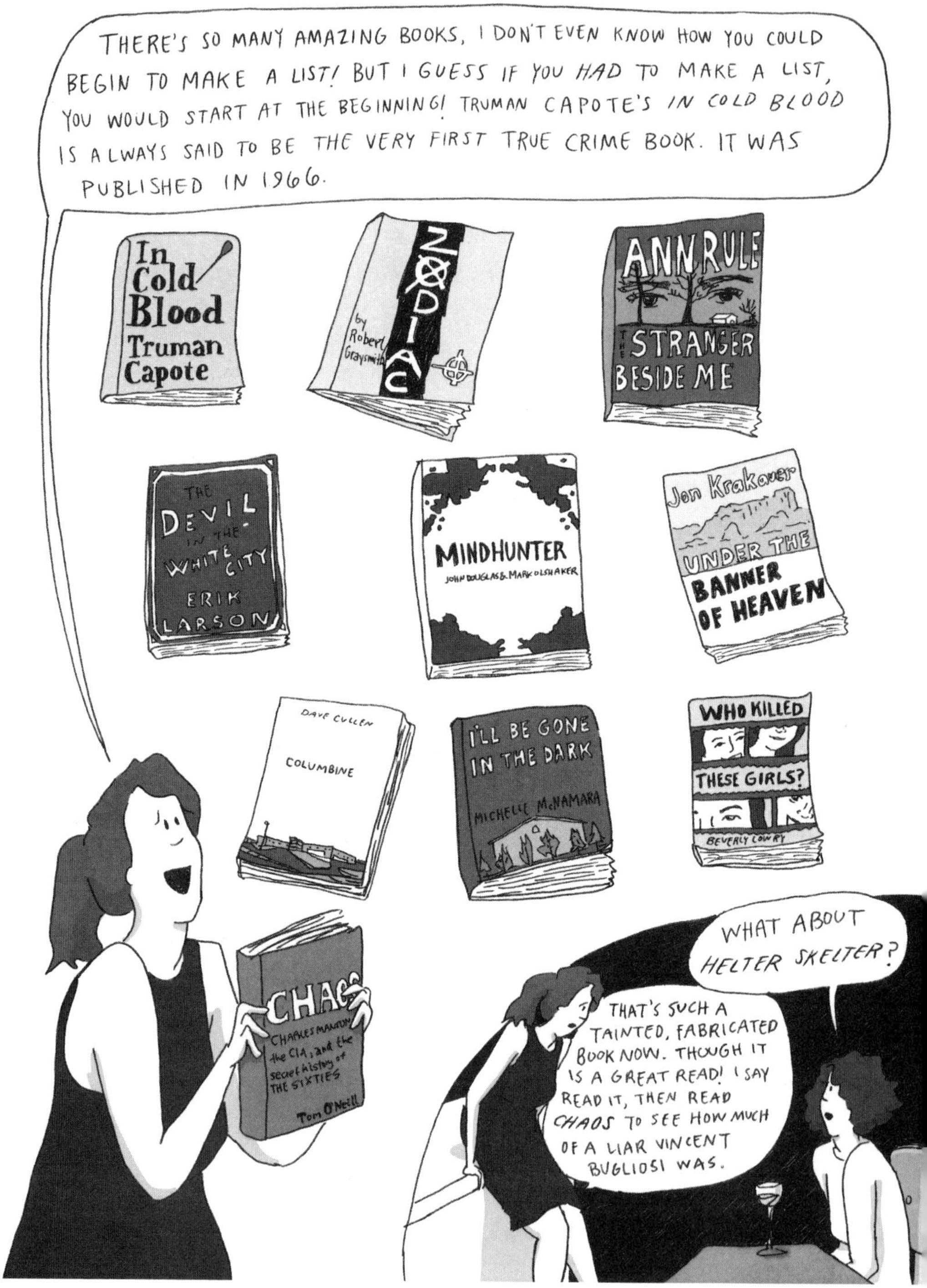
THERE'S SO MANY AMAZING BOOKS, I DON'T EVEN KNOW HOW YOU COULD BEGIN TO MAKE A LIST! BUT I GUESS IF YOU *HAD* TO MAKE A LIST, YOU WOULD START AT THE BEGINNING! TRUMAN CAPOTE'S *IN COLD BLOOD* IS ALWAYS SAID TO BE THE VERY FIRST TRUE CRIME BOOK. IT WAS PUBLISHED IN 1966.
In Cold Blood Truman Capote
ZODIAC by Robert Graysmith
ANN RULE THE STRANGER BESIDE ME
THE DEVIL IN THE WHITE CITY ERIK LARSON
MINDHUNTER JOHN DOUGLAS & MARK OLSHAKER
Jon Krakauer UNDER THE BANNER OF HEAVEN
DAVE CULLEN COLUMBINE
I'LL BE GONE IN THE DARK MICHELLE McNAMARA
WHO KILLED THESE GIRLS? BEVERLY LOWRY
CHAOS CHARLES MANSON, the CIA, and the secret history of THE SIXTIES Tom O'Neill
WHAT ABOUT *HELTER SKELTER*?
THAT'S SUCH A TAINTED, FABRICATED BOOK NOW. THOUGH IT IS A GREAT READ! I SAY READ IT, THEN READ *CHAOS* TO SEE HOW MUCH OF A LIAR VINCENT BUGLIOSI WAS.

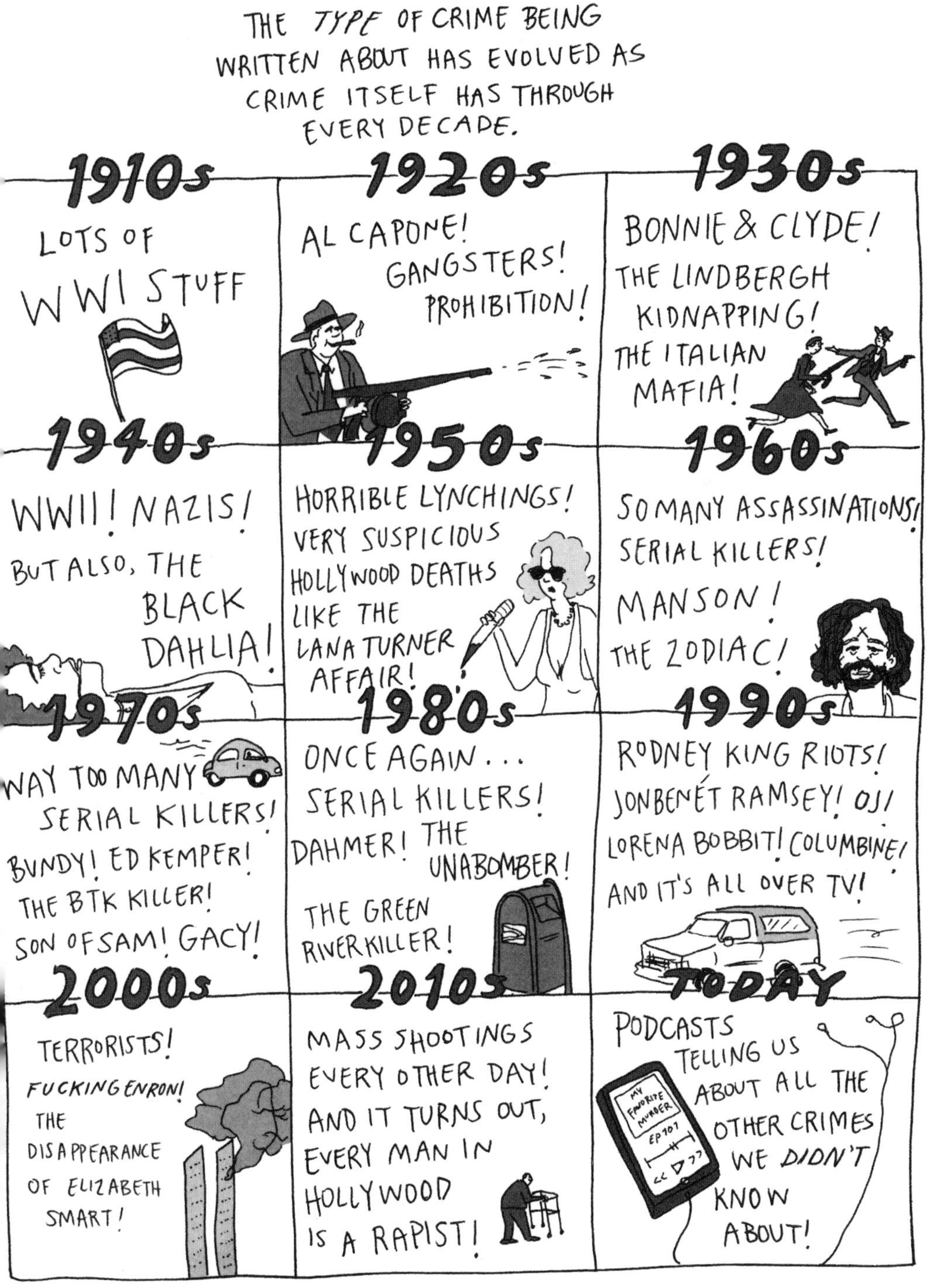
THE TYPE OF CRIME BEING WRITTEN ABOUT HAS EVOLVED AS CRIME ITSELF HAS THROUGH EVERY DECADE.
1910s
LOTS OF WWI STUFF
1920s
AL CAPONE! GANGSTERS! PROHIBITION!
1930s
BONNIE & CLYDE!
THE LINDBERGH KIDNAPPING!
THE ITALIAN MAFIA!
1940s
WWII! NAZIS!
BUT ALSO, THE BLACK DAHLIA!
1950s
HORRIBLE LYNCHINGS!
VERY SUSPICIOUS HOLLYWOOD DEATHS LIKE THE LANA TURNER AFFAIR!
1960s
SO MANY ASSASSINATIONS!
SERIAL KILLERS!
MANSON!
THE ZODIAC!
1970s
WAY TOO MANY SERIAL KILLERS!
BUNDY! ED KEMPER!
THE BTK KILLER!
SON OF SAM! GACY!
1980s
ONCE AGAIN... SERIAL KILLERS!
DAHMER! THE UNABOMBER!
THE GREEN RIVER KILLER!
1990s
RODNEY KING RIOTS!
JONBENÉT RAMSEY! OJ!
LORENA BOBBIT! COLUMBINE!
AND IT'S ALL OVER TV!
2000s
TERRORISTS!
FUCKING ENRON!
THE DISAPPEARANCE OF ELIZABETH SMART!
2010s
MASS SHOOTINGS EVERY OTHER DAY!
AND IT TURNS OUT, EVERY MAN IN HOLLYWOOD IS A RAPIST!
TODAY
PODCASTS TELLING US ABOUT ALL THE OTHER CRIMES WE DIDN'T KNOW ABOUT!
MY FAVORITE MURDER
EP 707

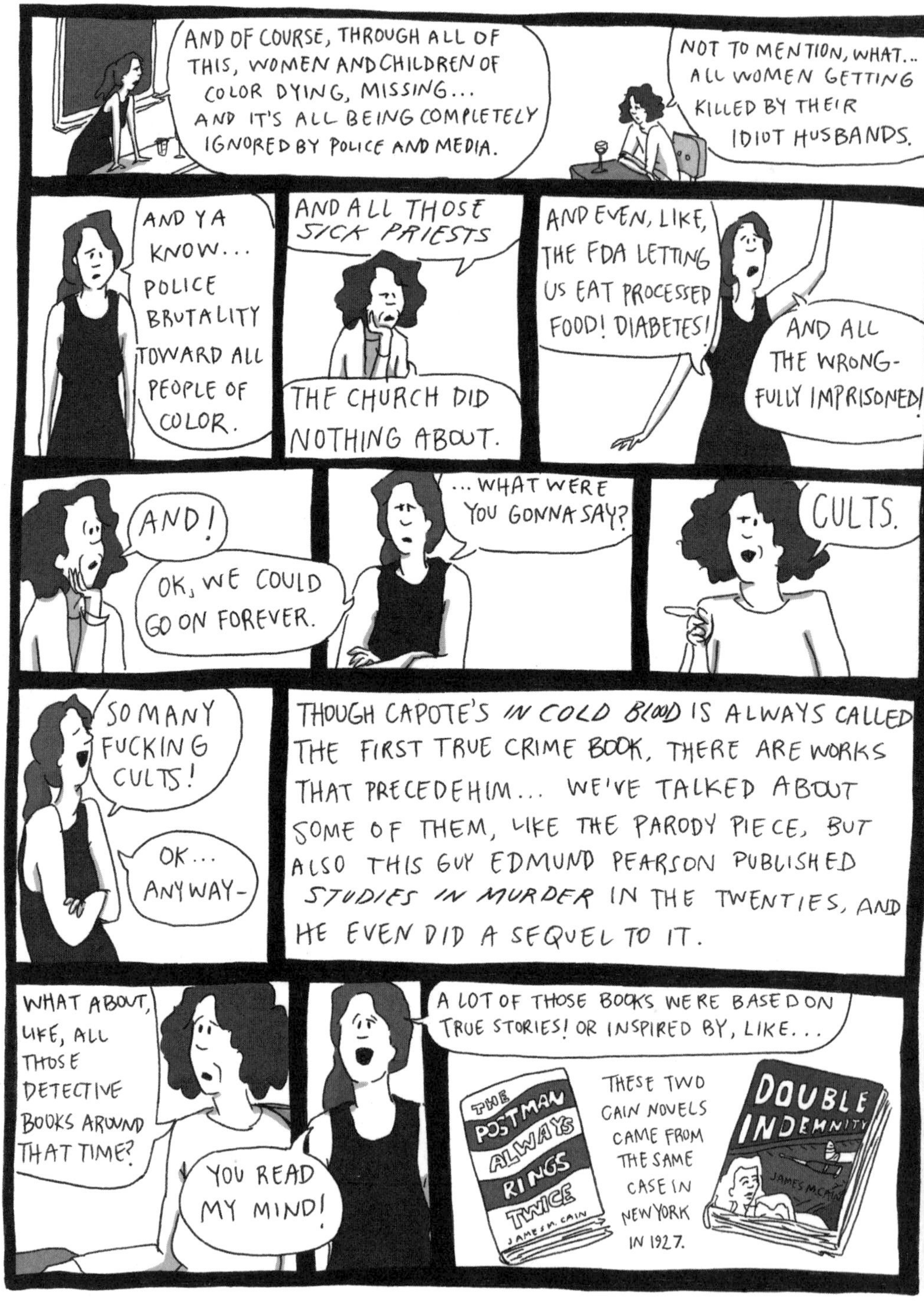
AND OF COURSE, THROUGH ALL OF THIS, WOMEN AND CHILDREN OF COLOR DYING, MISSING... AND IT'S ALL BEING COMPLETELY IGNORED BY POLICE AND MEDIA.
NOT TO MENTION, WHAT... ALL WOMEN GETTING KILLED BY THEIR IDIOT HUSBANDS.
AND YA KNOW... POLICE BRUTALITY TOWARD ALL PEOPLE OF COLOR.
AND ALL THOSE *SICK PRIESTS*
THE CHURCH DID NOTHING ABOUT.
AND EVEN, LIKE, THE FDA LETTING US EAT PROCESSED FOOD! DIABETES!
AND ALL THE WRONGFULLY IMPRISONED!
AND!
OK, WE COULD GO ON FOREVER.
...WHAT WERE YOU GONNA SAY?
CULTS.
SO MANY FUCKING CULTS!
OK... ANYWAY-
THOUGH CAPOTE'S *IN COLD BLOOD* IS ALWAYS CALLED THE FIRST TRUE CRIME BOOK, THERE ARE WORKS THAT PRECEDE HIM... WE'VE TALKED ABOUT SOME OF THEM, LIKE THE PARODY PIECE, BUT ALSO THIS GUY EDMUND PEARSON PUBLISHED *STUDIES IN MURDER* IN THE TWENTIES, AND HE EVEN DID A SEQUEL TO IT.
WHAT ABOUT, LIKE, ALL THOSE DETECTIVE BOOKS AROUND THAT TIME?
YOU READ MY MIND!
A LOT OF THOSE BOOKS WERE BASED ON TRUE STORIES! OR INSPIRED BY, LIKE...
THE POSTMAN ALWAYS RINGS TWICE
JAMES M. CAIN
THESE TWO CAIN NOVELS CAME FROM THE SAME CASE IN NEW YORK IN 1927.
DOUBLE INDEMNITY
JAMES M. CAIN

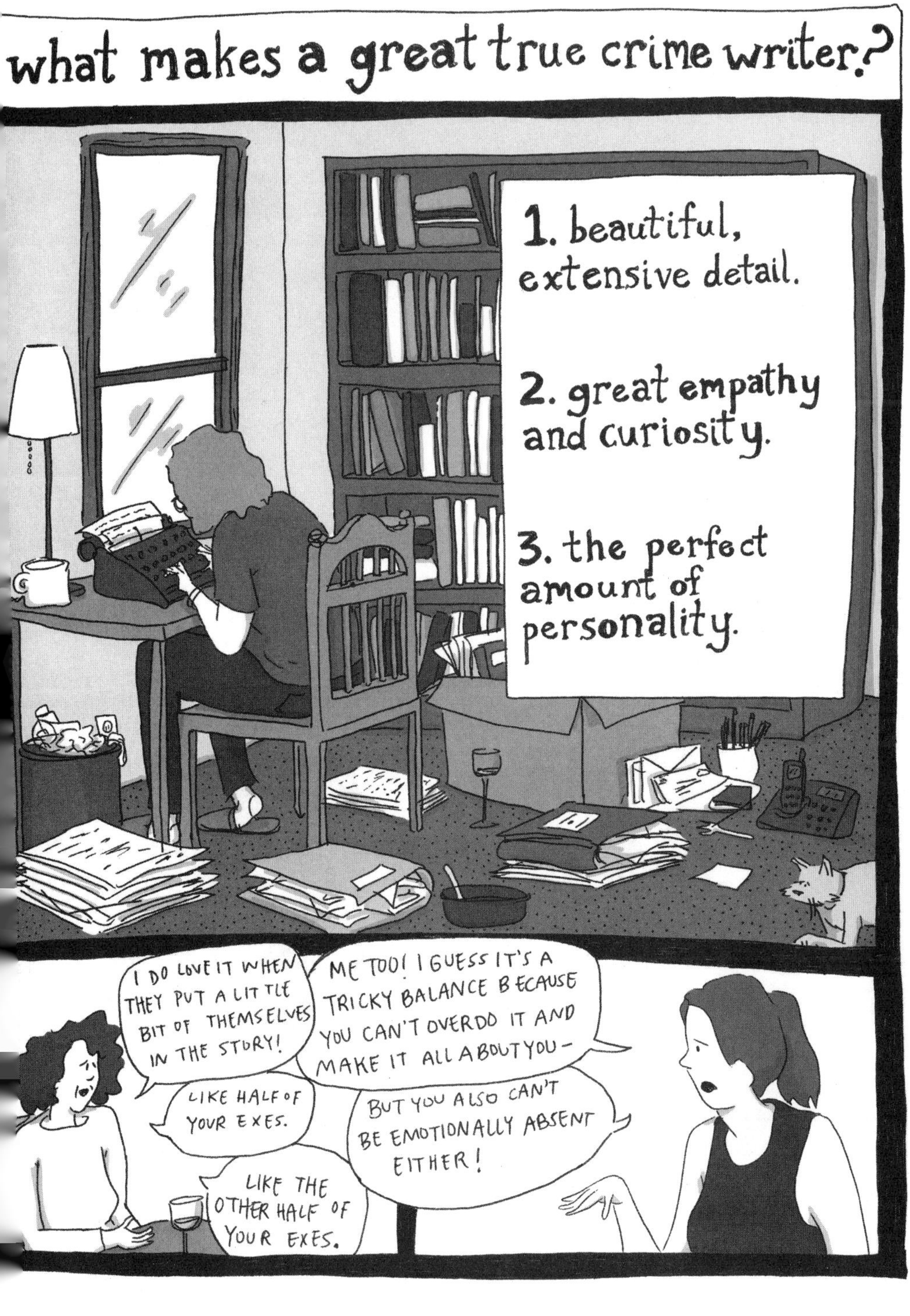
what makes a great true crime writer?
1. beautiful, extensive detail.
2. great empathy and curiosity.
3. the perfect amount of personality.
I DO LOVE IT WHEN THEY PUT A LITTLE BIT OF THEMSELVES IN THE STORY!
ME TOO! I GUESS IT'S A TRICKY BALANCE BECAUSE YOU CAN'T OVERDO IT AND MAKE IT ALL ABOUT YOU-
LIKE HALF OF YOUR EXES.
BUT YOU ALSO CAN'T BE EMOTIONALLY ABSENT EITHER!
LIKE THE OTHER HALF OF YOUR EXES.

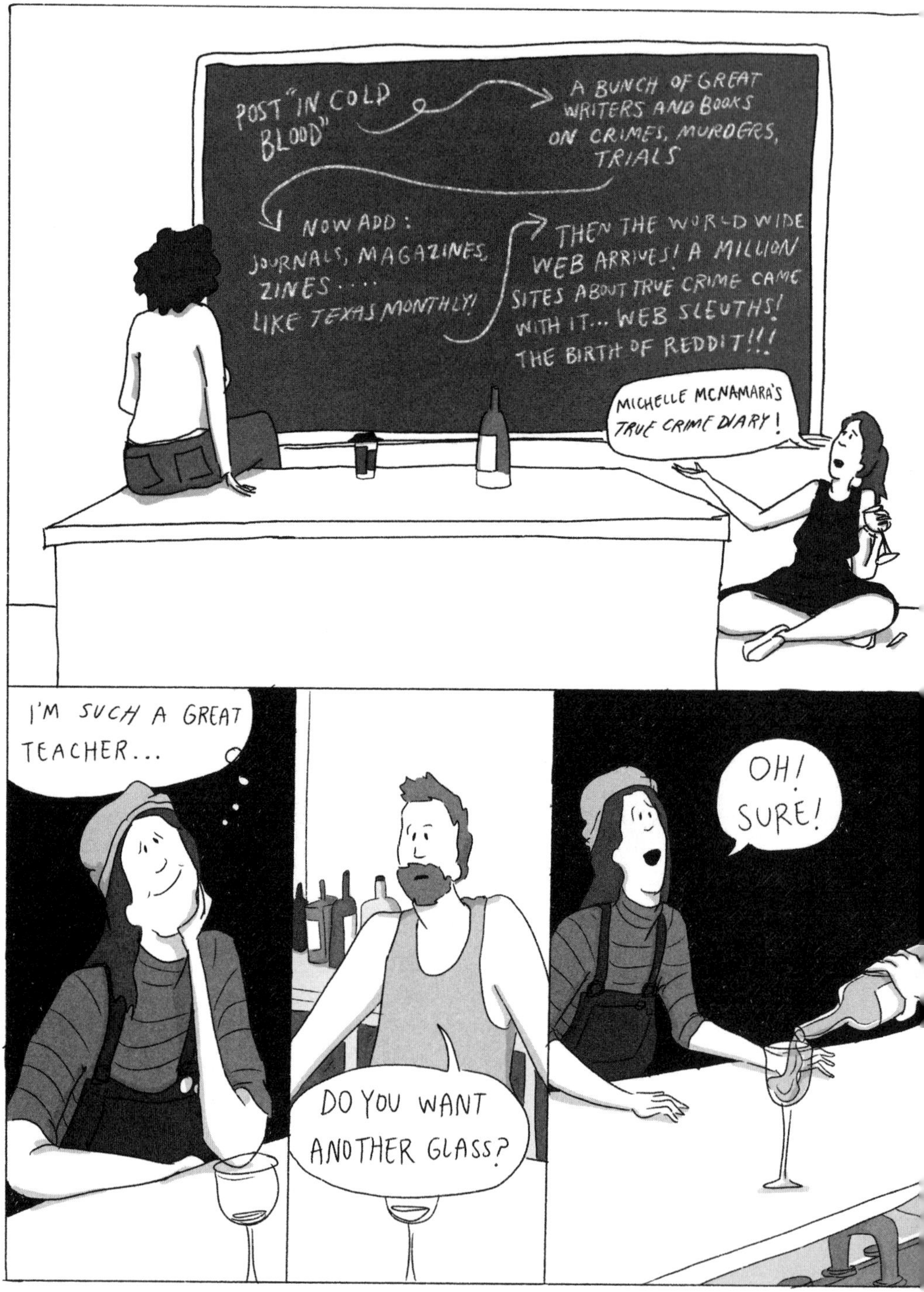
POST "IN COLD BLOOD"
A BUNCH OF GREAT WRITERS AND BOOKS ON CRIMES, MURDERS, TRIALS
NOW ADD: JOURNALS, MAGAZINES, ZINES.... LIKE TEXAS MONTHLY!
THEN THE WORLD WIDE WEB ARRIVES! A MILLION SITES ABOUT TRUE CRIME CAME WITH IT... WEB SLEUTHS! THE BIRTH OF REDDIT!!!
MICHELLE MCNAMARA'S TRUE CRIME DIARY!
I'M SUCH A GREAT TEACHER...
DO YOU WANT ANOTHER GLASS?
OH! SURE!

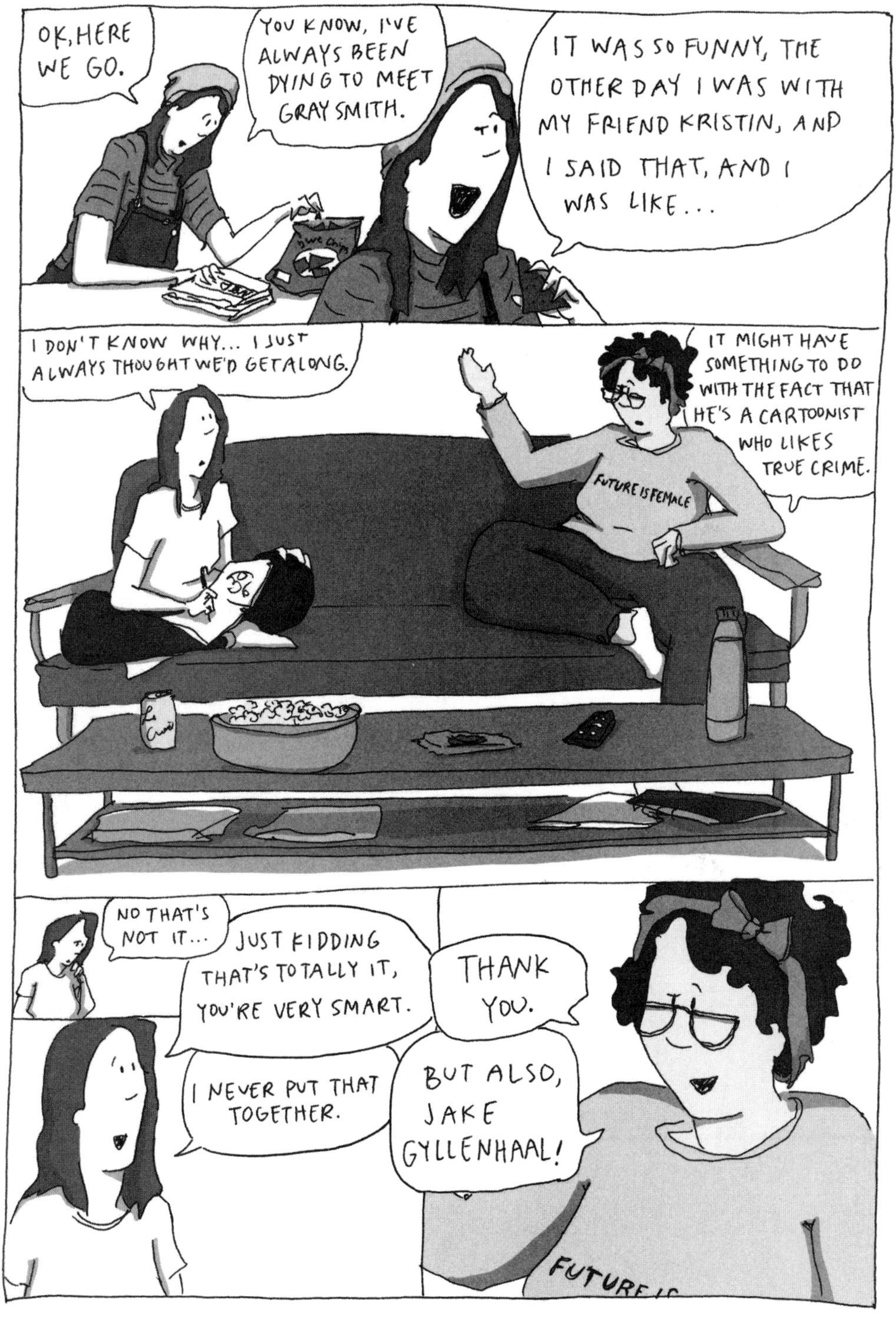
OK, HERE WE GO.
YOU KNOW, I'VE ALWAYS BEEN DYING TO MEET GRAY SMITH.
IT WAS SO FUNNY, THE OTHER DAY I WAS WITH MY FRIEND KRISTIN, AND I SAID THAT, AND I WAS LIKE...
I DON'T KNOW WHY... I JUST ALWAYS THOUGHT WE'D GET ALONG.
IT MIGHT HAVE SOMETHING TO DO WITH THE FACT THAT HE'S A CARTOONIST WHO LIKES TRUE CRIME.
FUTURE IS FEMALE
NO THAT'S NOT IT...
JUST KIDDING THAT'S TOTALLY IT, YOU'RE VERY SMART.
THANK YOU.
I NEVER PUT THAT TOGETHER.
BUT ALSO, JAKE GYLLENHAAL!

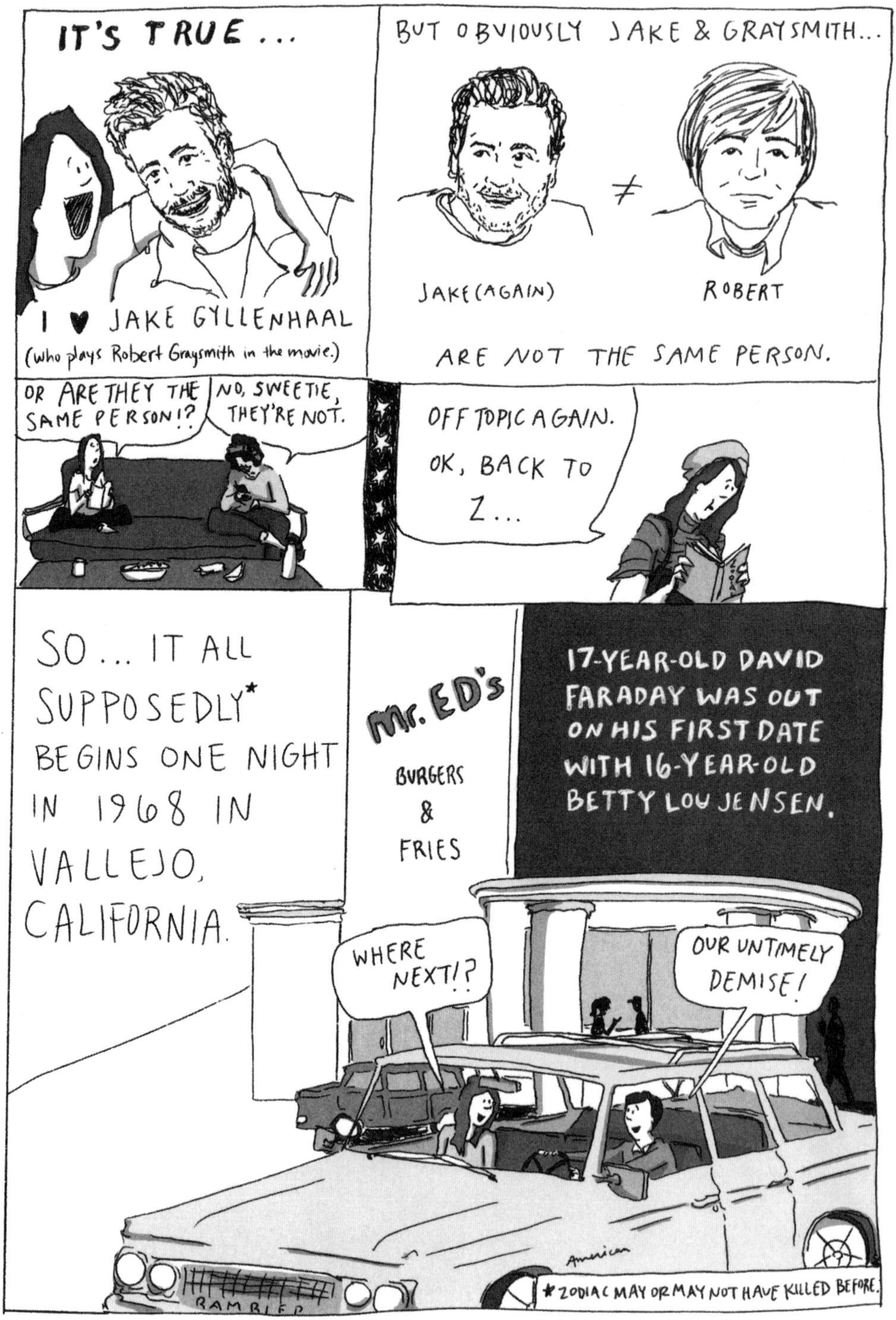
IT'S TRUE...
I ♥ JAKE GYLLENHAAL
(who plays Robert Graysmith in the movie.)
BUT OBVIOUSLY JAKE & GRAYSMITH...
JAKE (AGAIN)
≠
ROBERT
ARE NOT THE SAME PERSON.
OR ARE THEY THE SAME PERSON!?
NO, SWEETIE, THEY'RE NOT.
OFF TOPIC AGAIN. OK, BACK TO Z...
SO... IT ALL SUPPOSEDLY* BEGINS ONE NIGHT IN 1968 IN VALLEJO, CALIFORNIA.
Mr. ED's
BURGERS & FRIES
17-YEAR-OLD DAVID FARADAY WAS OUT ON HIS FIRST DATE WITH 16-YEAR-OLD BETTY LOU JENSEN.
WHERE NEXT!?
OUR UNTIMELY DEMISE!
*ZODIAC MAY OR MAY NOT HAVE KILLED BEFORE.

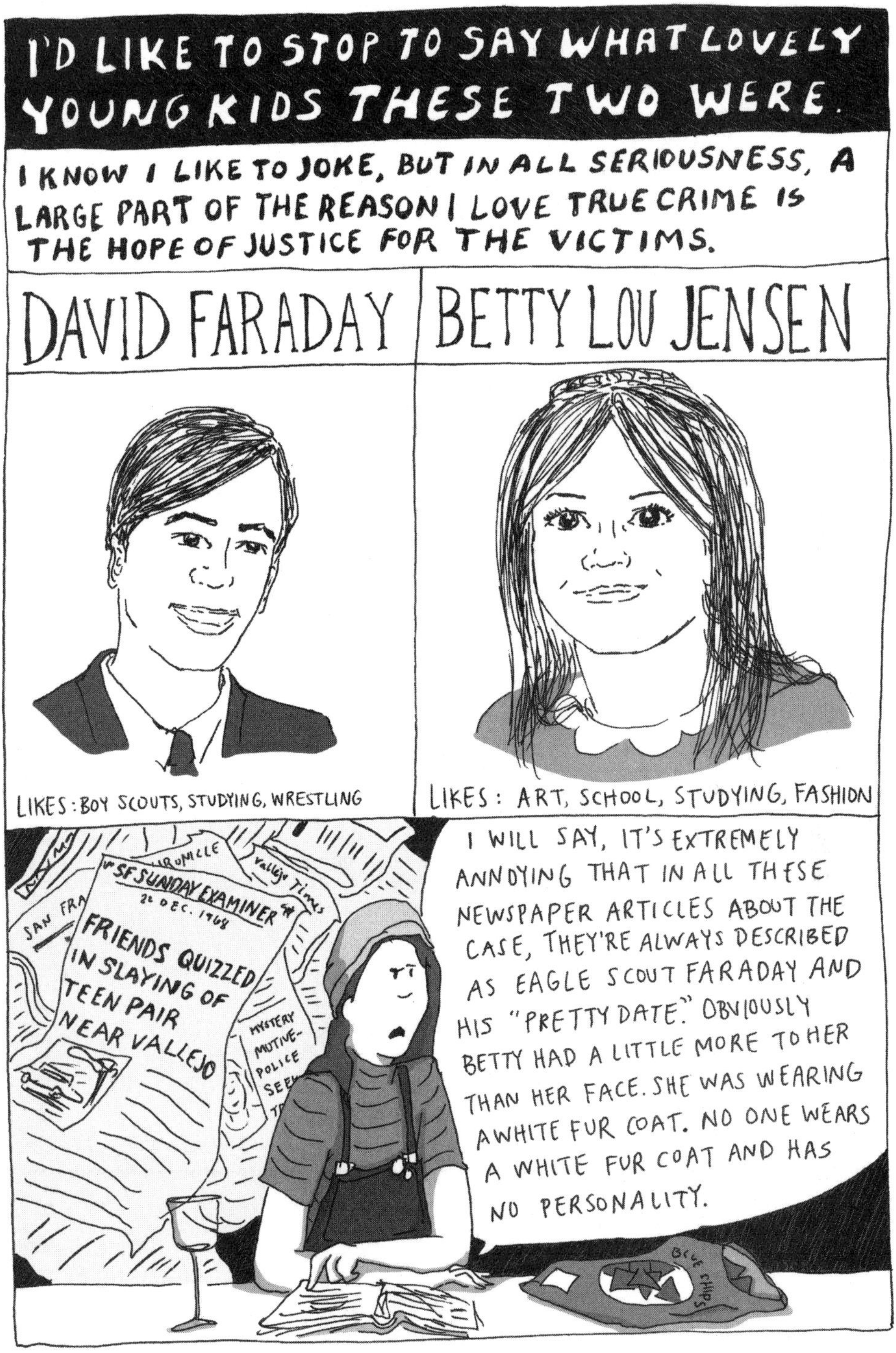
I'D LIKE TO STOP TO SAY WHAT LOVELY YOUNG KIDS THESE TWO WERE.
I KNOW I LIKE TO JOKE, BUT IN ALL SERIOUSNESS, A LARGE PART OF THE REASON I LOVE TRUE CRIME IS THE HOPE OF JUSTICE FOR THE VICTIMS.
DAVID FARADAY
BETTY LOU JENSEN
LIKES: BOY SCOUTS, STUDYING, WRESTLING
LIKES: ART, SCHOOL, STUDYING, FASHION
SF SUNDAY EXAMINER
FRIENDS QUIZZED IN SLAYING OF TEEN PAIR NEAR VALLEJO
MYSTERY MOTIVE- POLICE SEEK
I WILL SAY, IT'S EXTREMELY ANNOYING THAT IN ALL THESE NEWSPAPER ARTICLES ABOUT THE CASE, THEY'RE ALWAYS DESCRIBED AS EAGLE SCOUT FARADAY AND HIS "PRETTY DATE." OBVIOUSLY BETTY HAD A LITTLE MORE TO HER THAN HER FACE. SHE WAS WEARING A WHITE FUR COAT. NO ONE WEARS A WHITE FUR COAT AND HAS NO PERSONALITY.
BLUE CHIPS

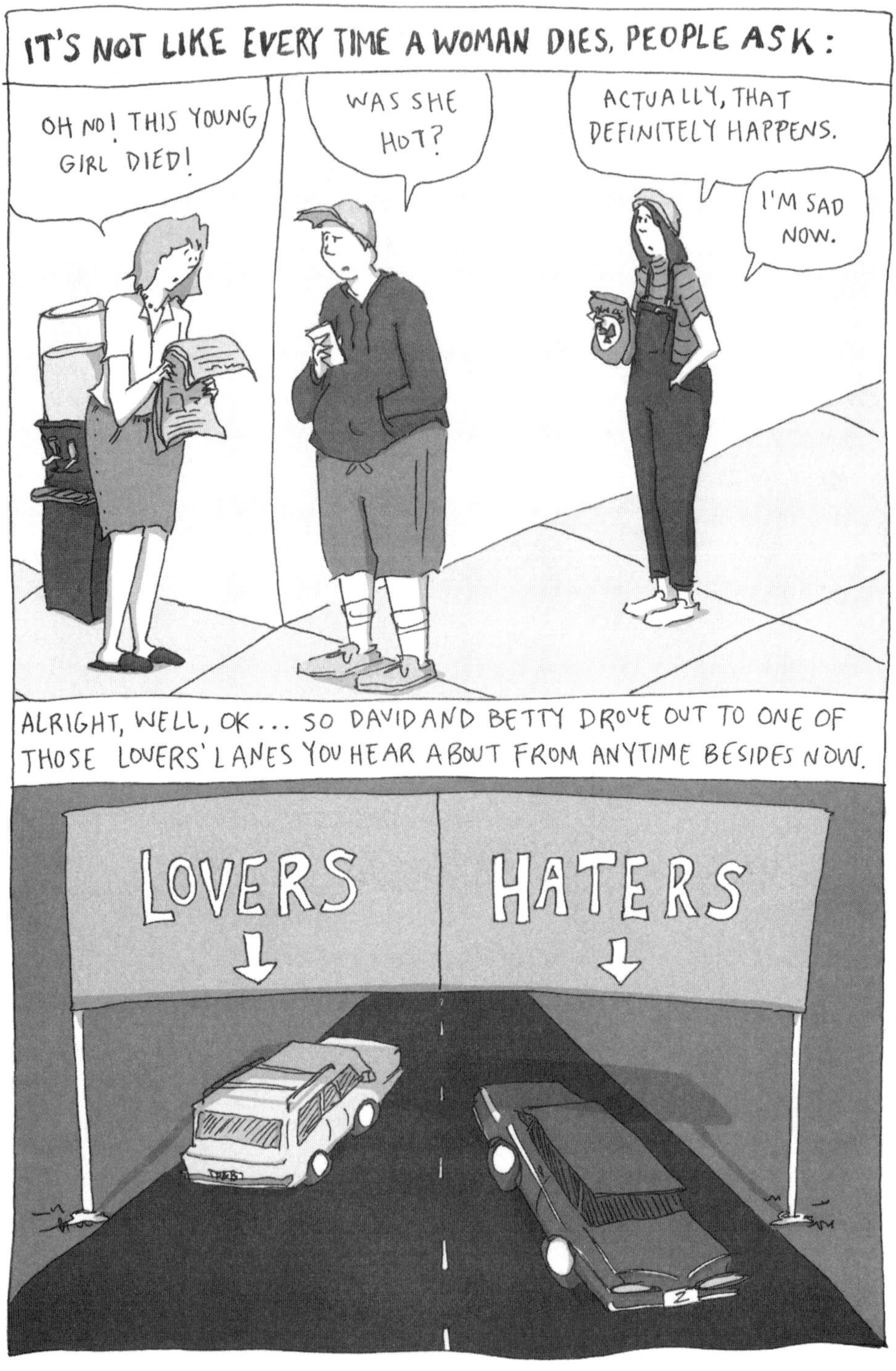
IT'S NOT LIKE EVERY TIME A WOMAN DIES, PEOPLE ASK:
OH NO! THIS YOUNG GIRL DIED!
WAS SHE HOT?
ACTUALLY, THAT DEFINITELY HAPPENS.
I'M SAD NOW.
ALRIGHT, WELL, OK... SO DAVID AND BETTY DROVE OUT TO ONE OF THOSE LOVERS' LANES YOU HEAR ABOUT FROM ANYTIME BESIDES NOW.
LOVERS
HATERS

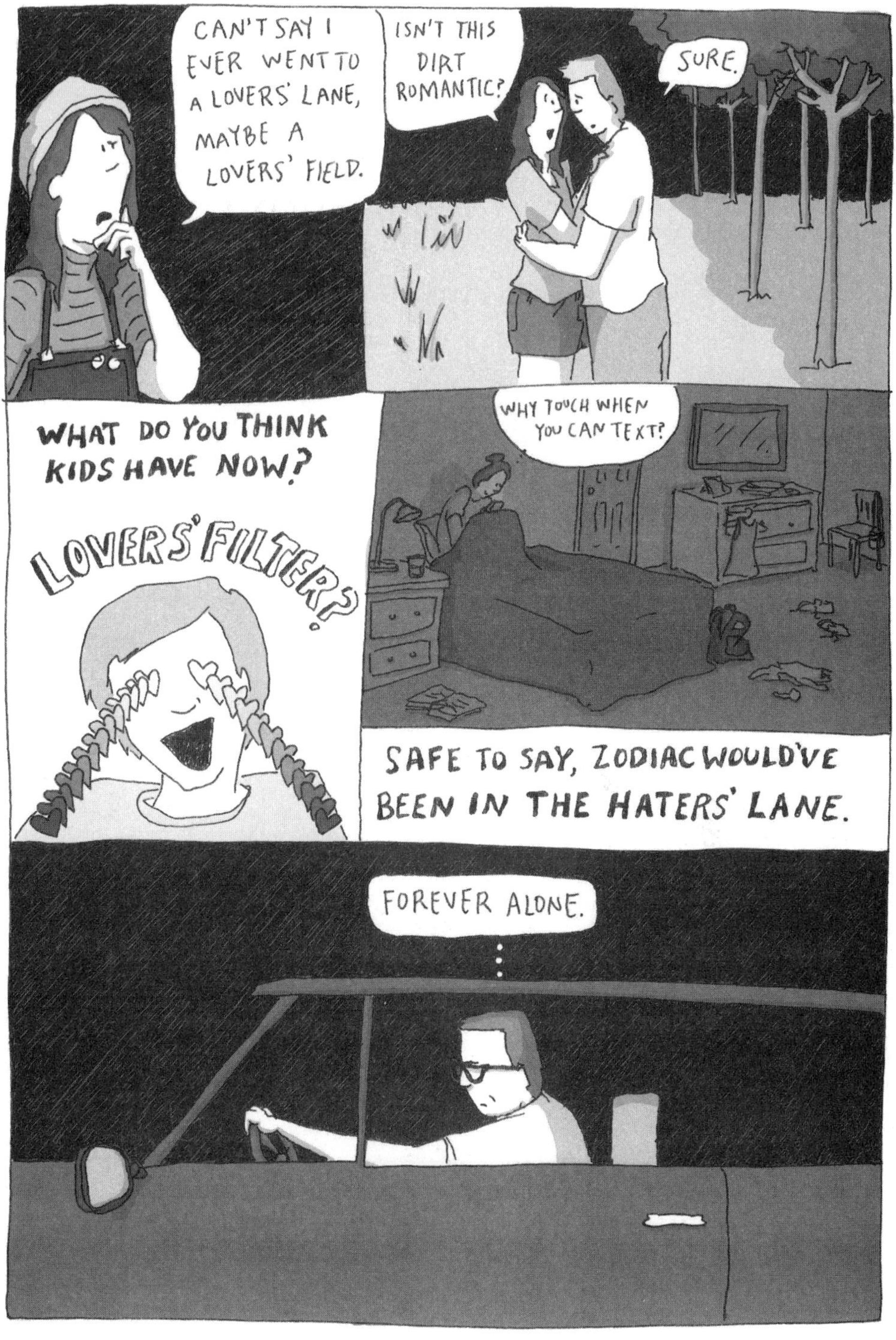
CAN'T SAY I EVER WENT TO A LOVERS' LANE, MAYBE A LOVERS' FIELD.
ISN'T THIS DIRT ROMANTIC?
SURE.
WHAT DO YOU THINK KIDS HAVE NOW?
LOVERS' FILTER?
WHY TOUCH WHEN YOU CAN TEXT?
SAFE TO SAY, ZODIAC WOULD'VE BEEN IN THE HATERS' LANE.
FOREVER ALONE.

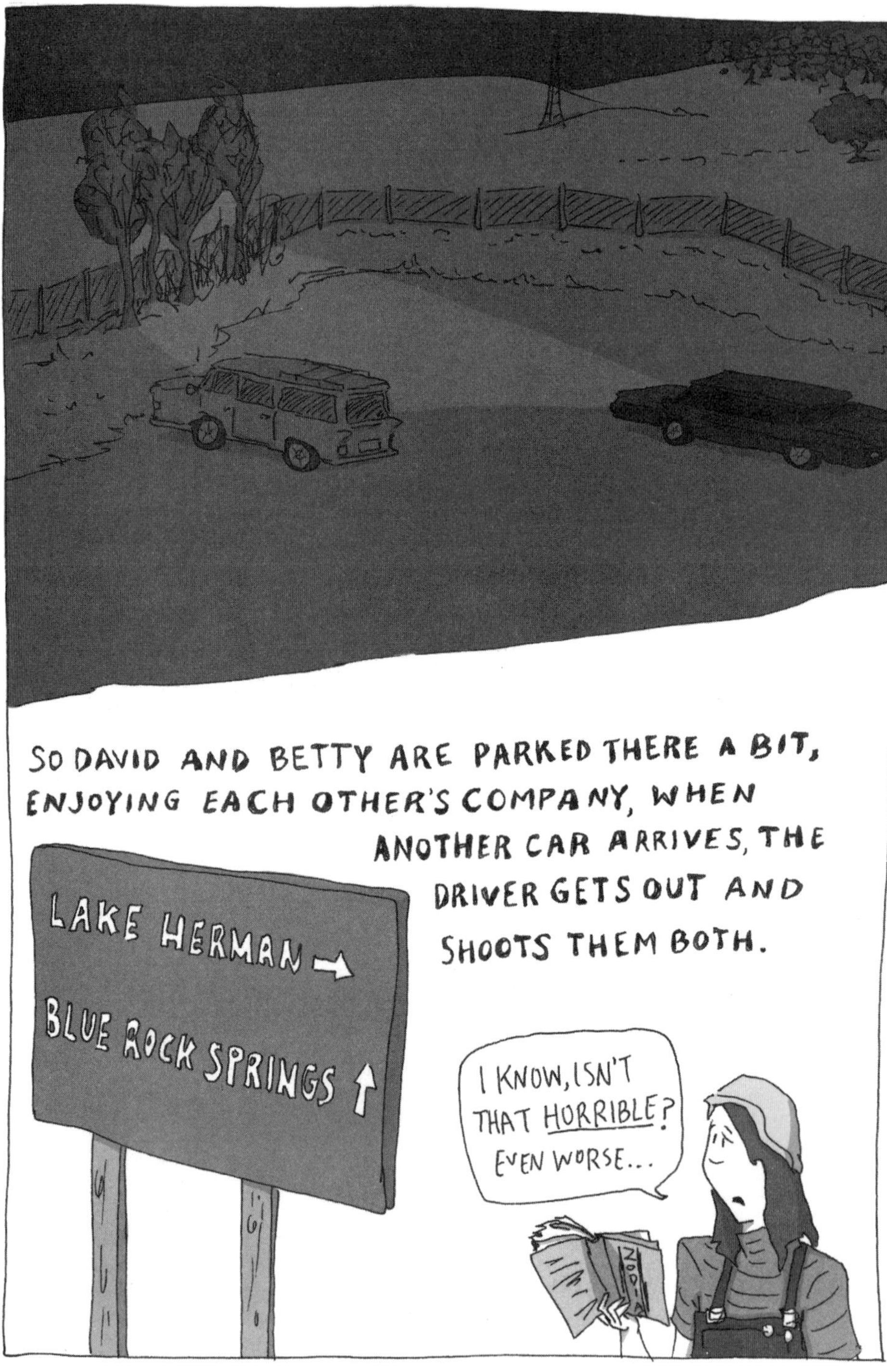
SO DAVID AND BETTY ARE PARKED THERE A BIT, ENJOYING EACH OTHER'S COMPANY, WHEN ANOTHER CAR ARRIVES, THE DRIVER GETS OUT AND SHOOTS THEM BOTH.
LAKE HERMAN →
BLUE ROCK SPRINGS ↑
I KNOW, ISN'T THAT HORRIBLE? EVEN WORSE...
ZODIA

THERE WAS BASICALLY NO EVIDENCE TO GO OFF OF, OTHER THAN, LIKE, A SHOE PRINT AND THE EMPTY SHELL CASES.

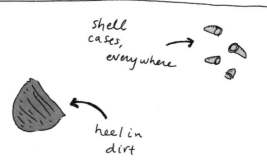

shell cases, everywhere

heel in dirt

THE POLICE, **THE DETECTIVES** AND THE COMMUNITY WERE RATTLED BY THE APPARENT

W.T.F.

LACK OF MOTIVE.

THEY WEREN'T ROBBED OR RAPED...

THAT IS SOMEHOW MORE DISTURBING.

IT SEEMED THE PERSON WAS KILLING FOR FUN.

CUT TO **6 MONTHS** LATER **& 4 MILES** THERE ARE NO REAL LEADS AND THE SAME SHIT HAPPENS ON THE **4th of JULY.**

THIS TIME IT'S THIS WOMAN WHO HONESTLY SOUNDS LIKE A GOD-DAMNED BLAST, AND THE GUY WITH HER, WHO, I DON'T KNOW, I'D SAY WAS LOW-KEY OBSESSED WITH HER, EVEN THOUGH SHE WAS MARRIED...

THIS IS ALSO WHEN ZODIAC STARTS DOING HIS WHOLE TAUNTING THE POLICE THING.

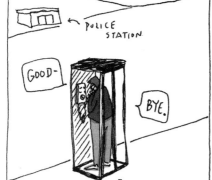

POLICE STATION

GOOD-

BYE.

2

DARLENE FERRIN

LIKES: DANCING, MOTHERHOOD, NEW PEOPLE

MICHAEL MAGEAU

SURVIVED

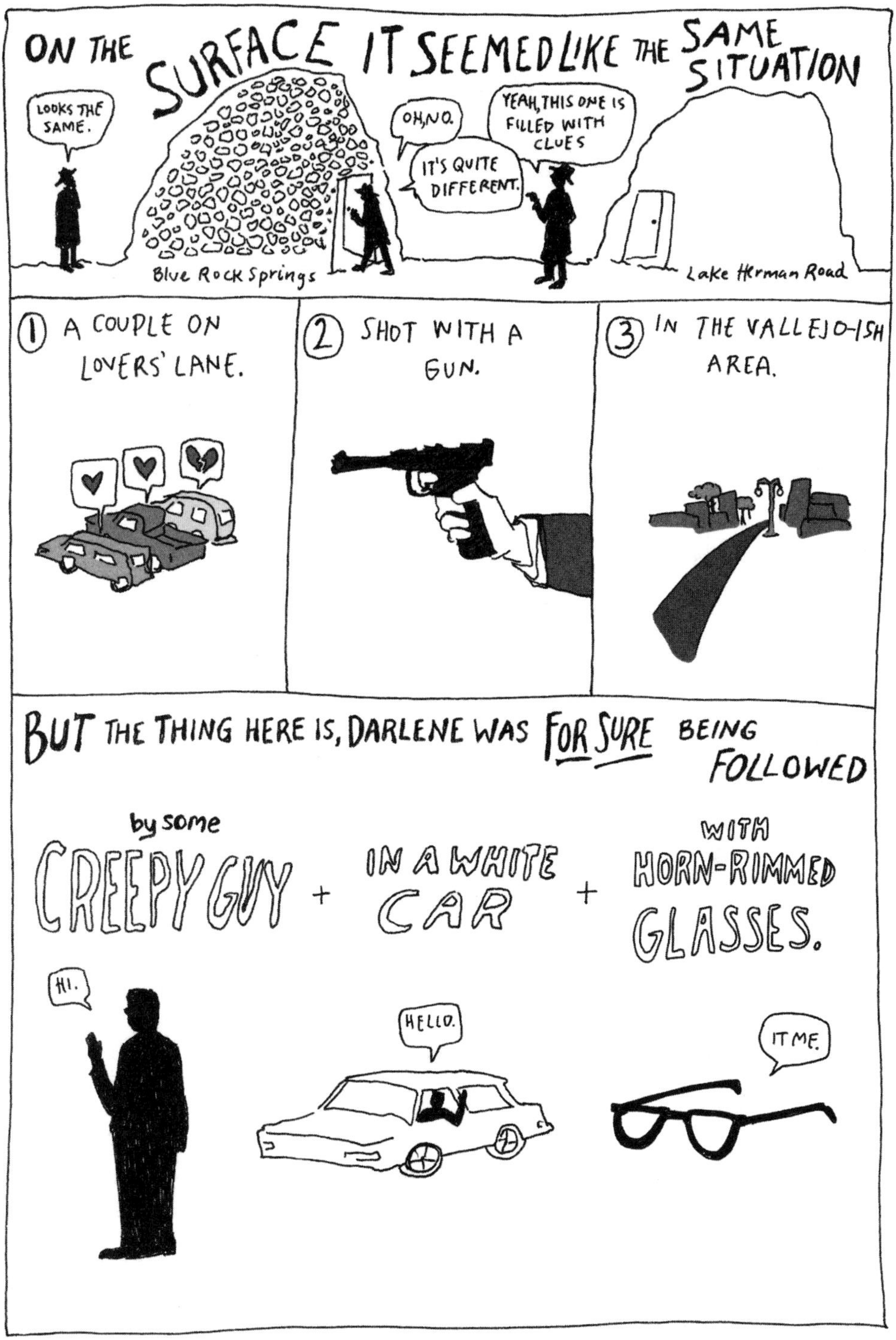
ON THE SURFACE IT SEEMED LIKE THE SAME SITUATION
LOOKS THE SAME.
OH, NO.
IT'S QUITE DIFFERENT.
YEAH, THIS ONE IS FILLED WITH CLUES
Blue Rock Springs
Lake Herman Road
① A COUPLE ON LOVERS' LANE.
② SHOT WITH A GUN.
③ IN THE VALLEJO-ISH AREA.
BUT THE THING HERE IS, DARLENE WAS FOR SURE BEING FOLLOWED
by some CREEPY GUY + IN A WHITE CAR + WITH HORN-RIMMED GLASSES.
HI.
HELLO.
IT ME.

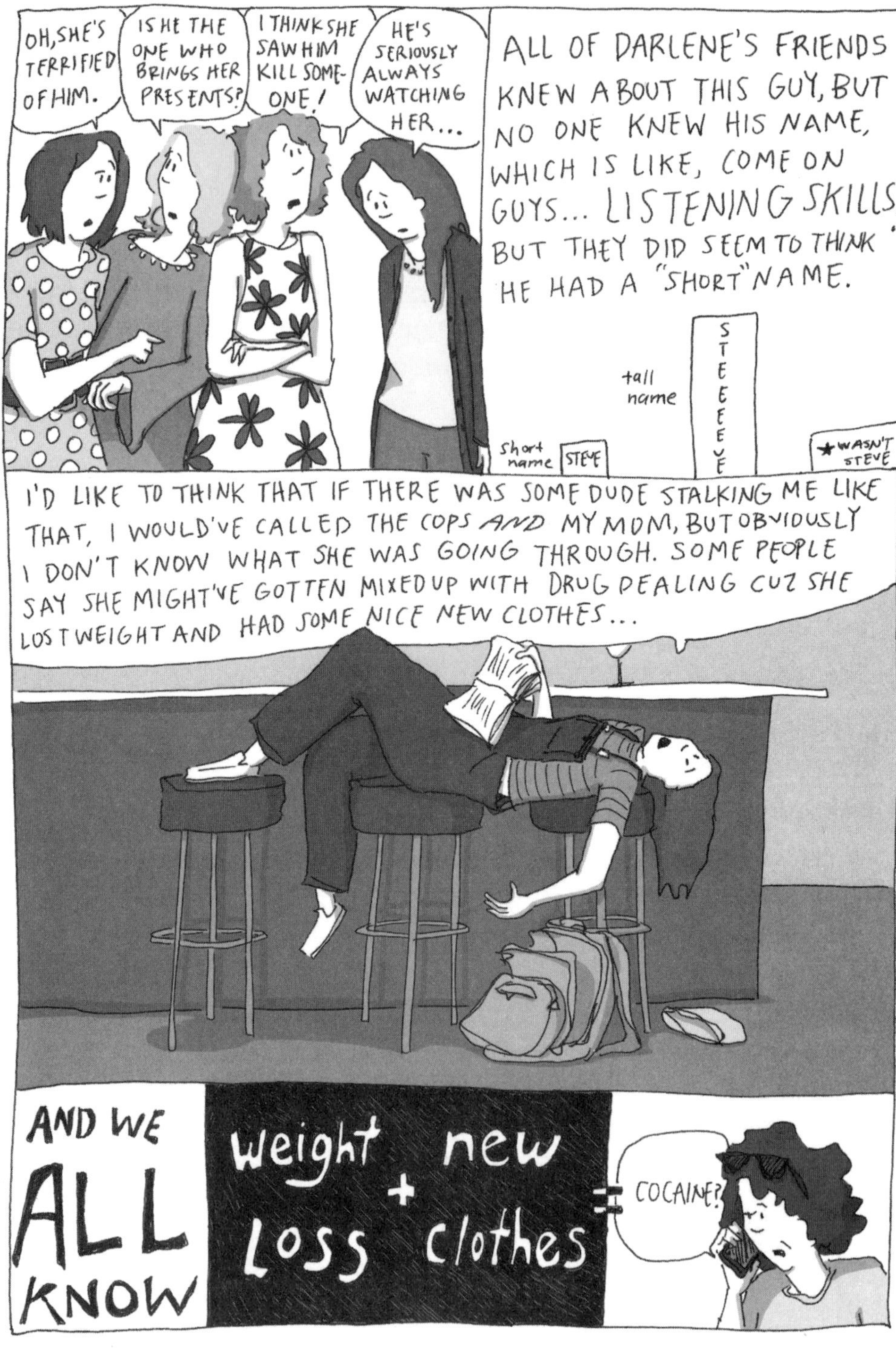
OH, SHE'S TERRIFIED OF HIM.
IS HE THE ONE WHO BRINGS HER PRESENTS?
I THINK SHE SAW HIM KILL SOME-ONE!
HE'S SERIOUSLY ALWAYS WATCHING HER...
ALL OF DARLENE'S FRIENDS KNEW ABOUT THIS GUY, BUT NO ONE KNEW HIS NAME, WHICH IS LIKE, COME ON GUYS... LISTENING SKILLS! BUT THEY DID SEEM TO THINK HE HAD A "SHORT" NAME.
short name
STEVE
tall name
STEEEEEVE
★WASN'T STEVE
I'D LIKE TO THINK THAT IF THERE WAS SOME DUDE STALKING ME LIKE THAT, I WOULD'VE CALLED THE COPS AND MY MOM, BUT OBVIOUSLY I DON'T KNOW WHAT SHE WAS GOING THROUGH. SOME PEOPLE SAY SHE MIGHT'VE GOTTEN MIXED UP WITH DRUG DEALING CUZ SHE LOST WEIGHT AND HAD SOME NICE NEW CLOTHES...
AND WE ALL KNOW
weight loss + new clothes =
COCAINE?

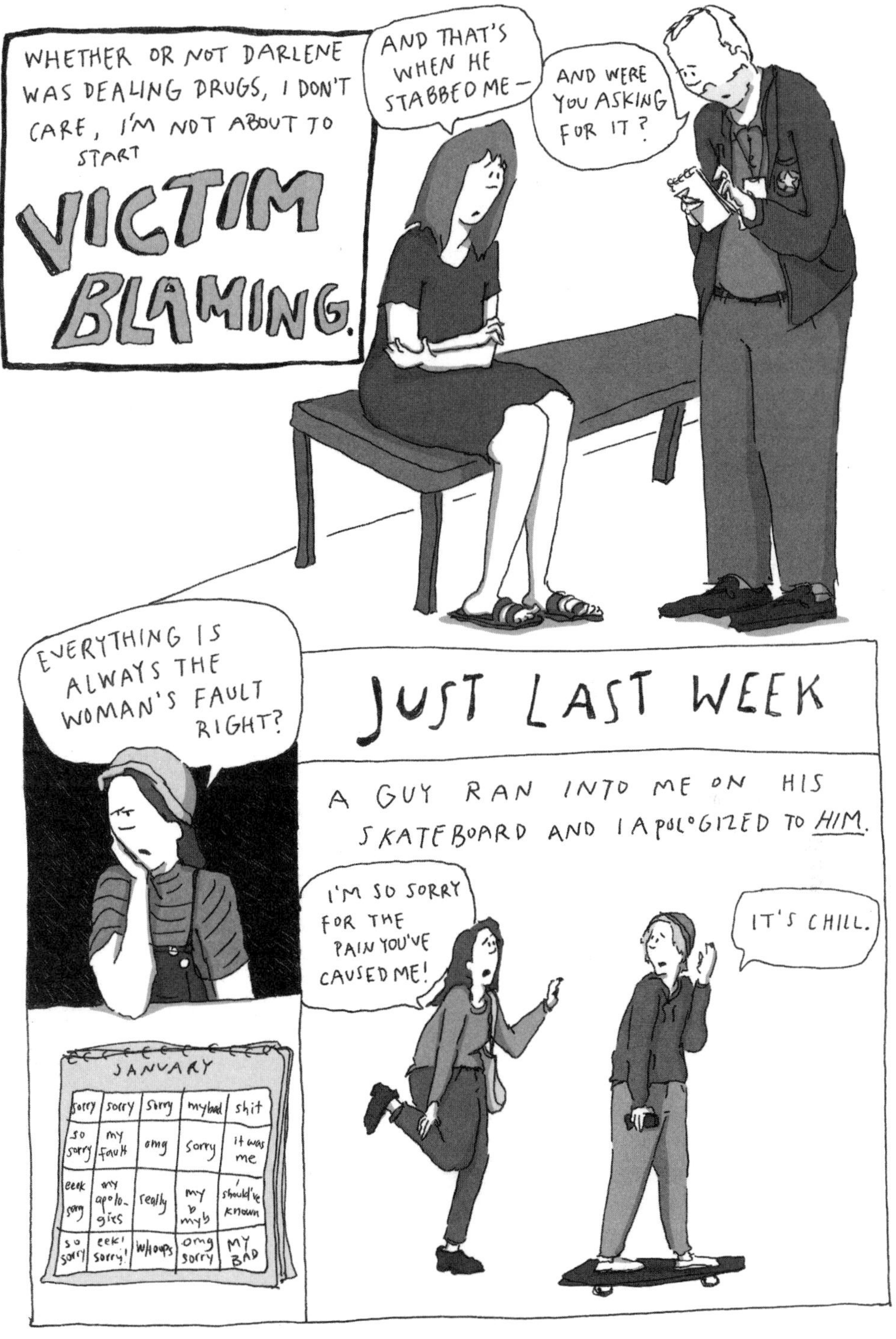
WHETHER OR NOT DARLENE WAS DEALING DRUGS, I DON'T CARE, I'M NOT ABOUT TO START
VICTIM BLAMING.
AND THAT'S WHEN HE STABBED ME—
AND WERE YOU ASKING FOR IT?
EVERYTHING IS ALWAYS THE WOMAN'S FAULT RIGHT?
JANUARY
sorry sorry sorry mybad shit
so sorry my fault omg sorry it was me
eeek sorry my apologies really my b myb I should've known
so sorry eek! sorry! whoops omg sorry MY BAD
JUST LAST WEEK
A GUY RAN INTO ME ON HIS SKATEBOARD AND I APOLOGIZED TO HIM.
I'M SO SORRY FOR THE PAIN YOU'VE CAUSED ME!
IT'S CHILL.

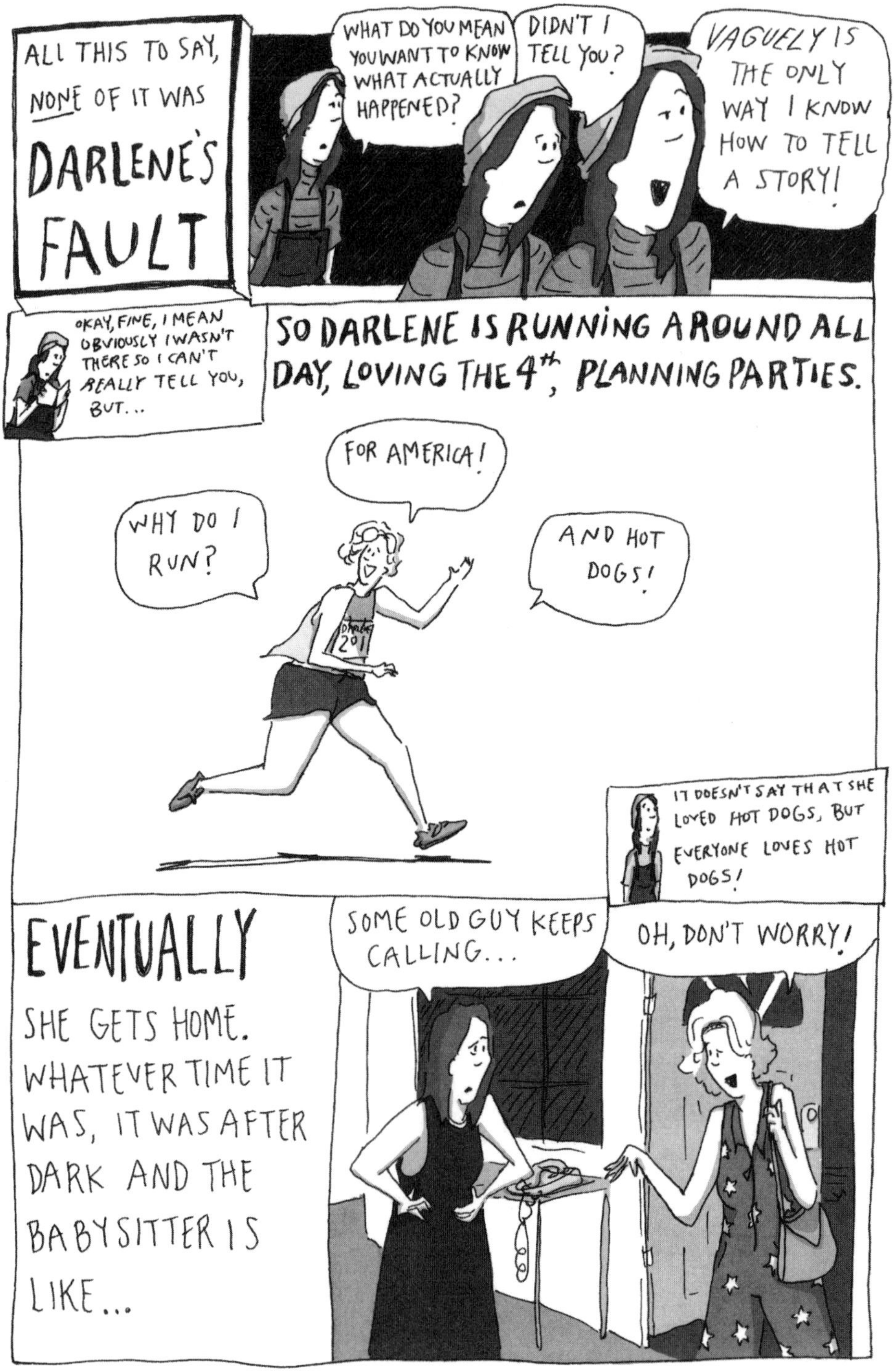

ALL THIS TO SAY, NONE OF IT WAS DARLENE'S FAULT
WHAT DO YOU MEAN YOU WANT TO KNOW WHAT ACTUALLY HAPPENED?
DIDN'T I TELL YOU?
VAGUELY IS THE ONLY WAY I KNOW HOW TO TELL A STORY!
OKAY, FINE, I MEAN OBVIOUSLY I WASN'T THERE SO I CAN'T REALLY TELL YOU, BUT...
SO DARLENE IS RUNNING AROUND ALL DAY, LOVING THE 4th, PLANNING PARTIES.
FOR AMERICA!
WHY DO I RUN?
AND HOT DOGS!
IT DOESN'T SAY THAT SHE LOVED HOT DOGS, BUT EVERYONE LOVES HOT DOGS!
EVENTUALLY SHE GETS HOME. WHATEVER TIME IT WAS, IT WAS AFTER DARK AND THE BABYSITTER IS LIKE...
SOME OLD GUY KEEPS CALLING...
OH, DON'T WORRY!

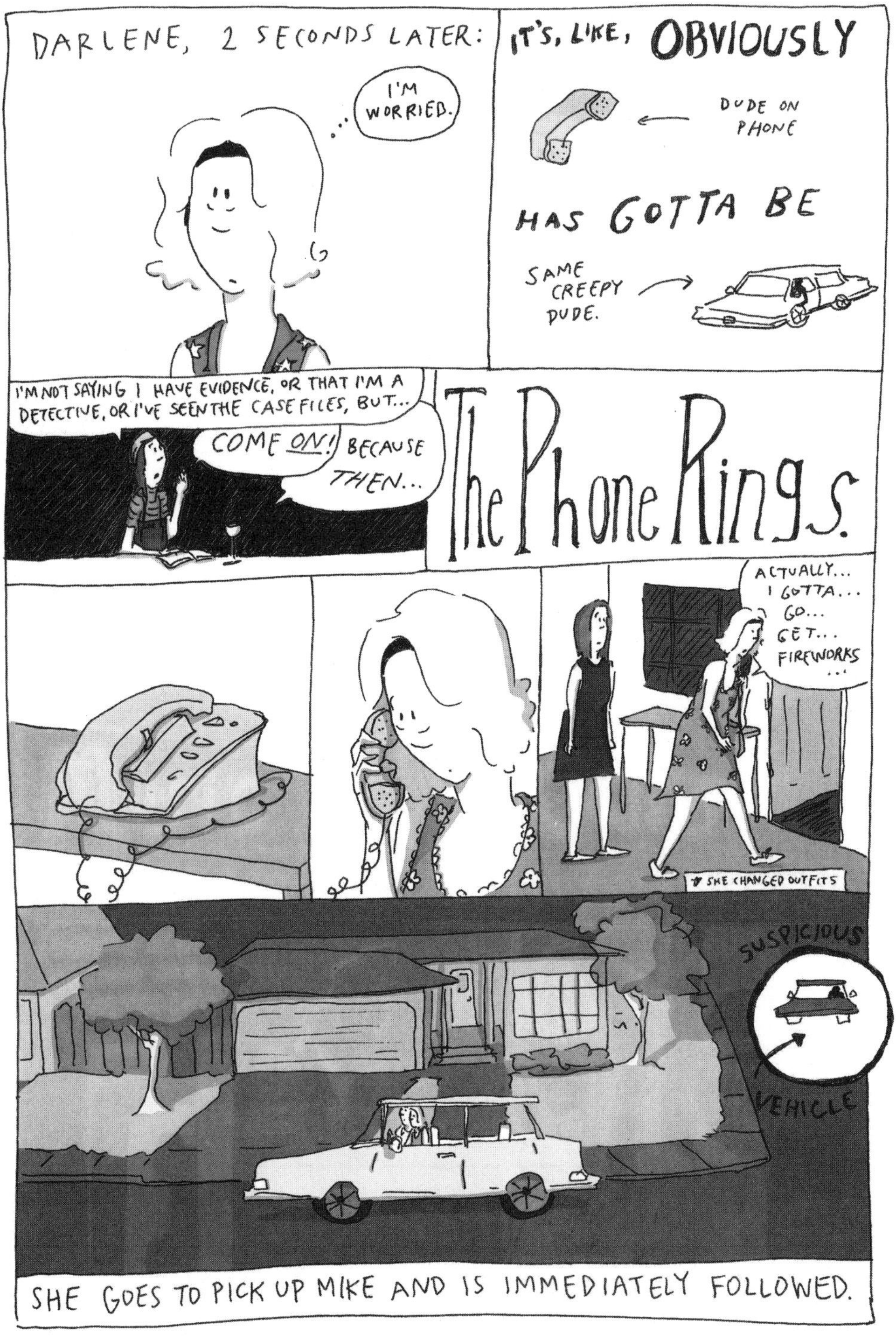

DARLENE, 2 SECONDS LATER:
... I'M WORRIED.
IT'S, LIKE, OBVIOUSLY
DUDE ON PHONE
HAS GOTTA BE
SAME CREEPY DUDE.
I'M NOT SAYING I HAVE EVIDENCE, OR THAT I'M A DETECTIVE, OR I'VE SEEN THE CASE FILES, BUT...
COME ON! BECAUSE THEN...
The Phone Rings.
ACTUALLY... I GOTTA... GO... GET... FIREWORKS ...
SHE CHANGED OUTFITS
SUSPICIOUS VEHICLE
SHE GOES TO PICK UP MIKE AND IS IMMEDIATELY FOLLOWED.

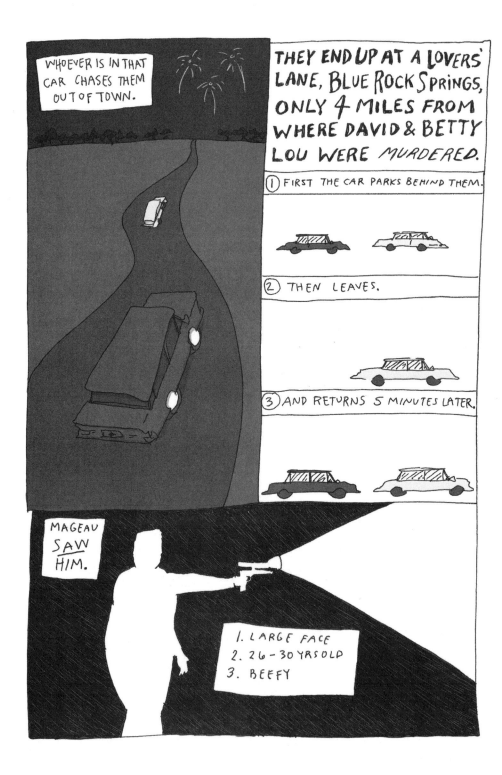

WHOEVER IS IN THAT CAR CHASES THEM OUT OF TOWN.

THEY END UP AT A LOVERS' LANE, BLUE ROCK SPRINGS, ONLY 4 MILES FROM WHERE DAVID & BETTY LOU WERE *MURDERED.*

1. FIRST THE CAR PARKS BEHIND THEM.

2. THEN LEAVES.

3. AND RETURNS 5 MINUTES LATER.

MAGEAU SAW HIM.

1. LARGE FACE
2. 26 - 30 YRS OLD
3. BEEFY

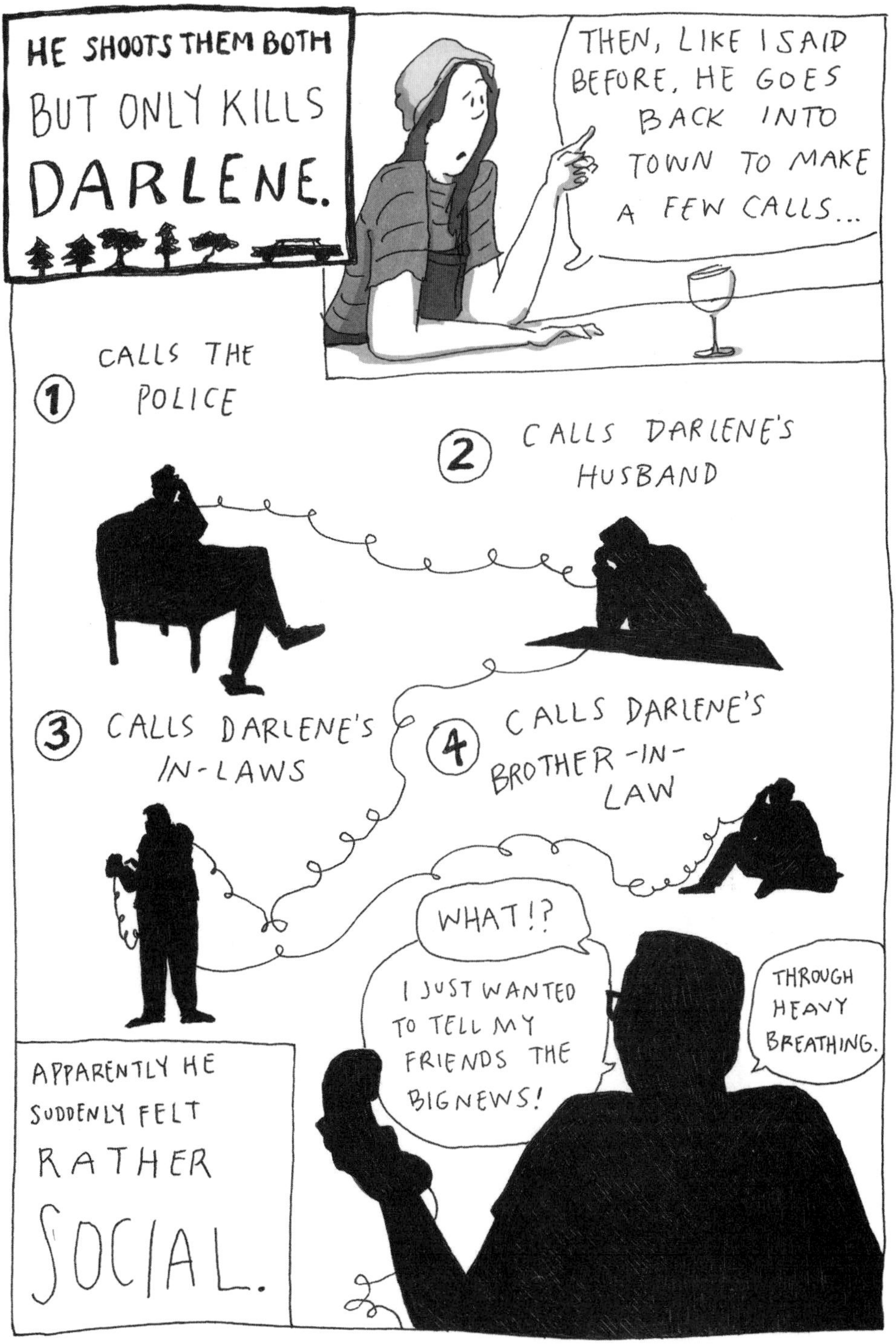
HE SHOOTS THEM BOTH BUT ONLY KILLS DARLENE.
THEN, LIKE I SAID BEFORE, HE GOES BACK INTO TOWN TO MAKE A FEW CALLS...
1 CALLS THE POLICE
2 CALLS DARLENE'S HUSBAND
3 CALLS DARLENE'S IN-LAWS
4 CALLS DARLENE'S BROTHER-IN-LAW
WHAT!?
I JUST WANTED TO TELL MY FRIENDS THE BIGNEWS!
THROUGH HEAVY BREATHING.
APPARENTLY HE SUDDENLY FELT RATHER SOCIAL.

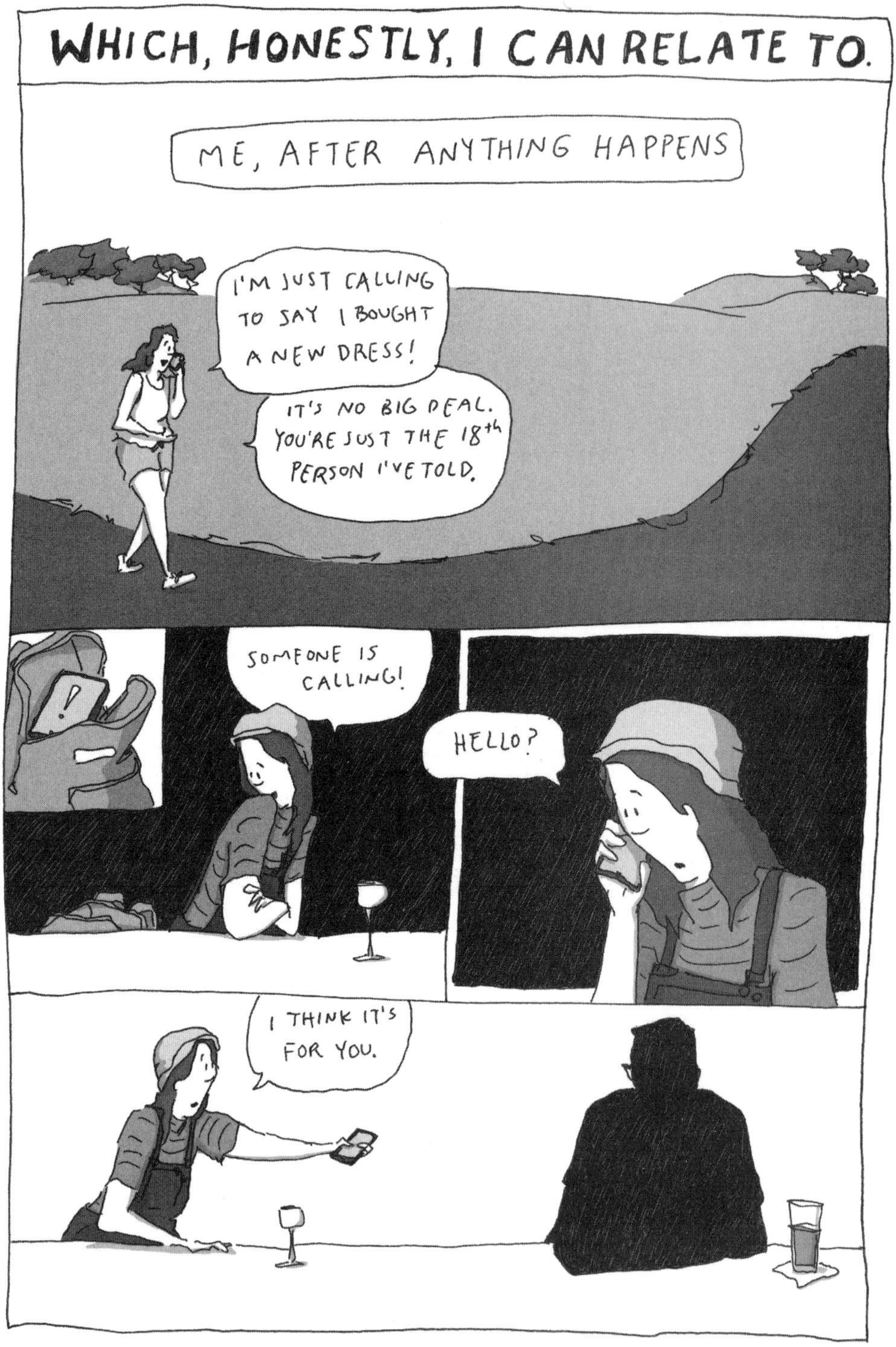
WHICH, HONESTLY, I CAN RELATE TO.
ME, AFTER ANYTHING HAPPENS
I'M JUST CALLING TO SAY I BOUGHT A NEW DRESS!
IT'S NO BIG DEAL. YOU'RE JUST THE 18th PERSON I'VE TOLD.
SOMEONE IS CALLING!
HELLO?
I THINK IT'S FOR YOU.

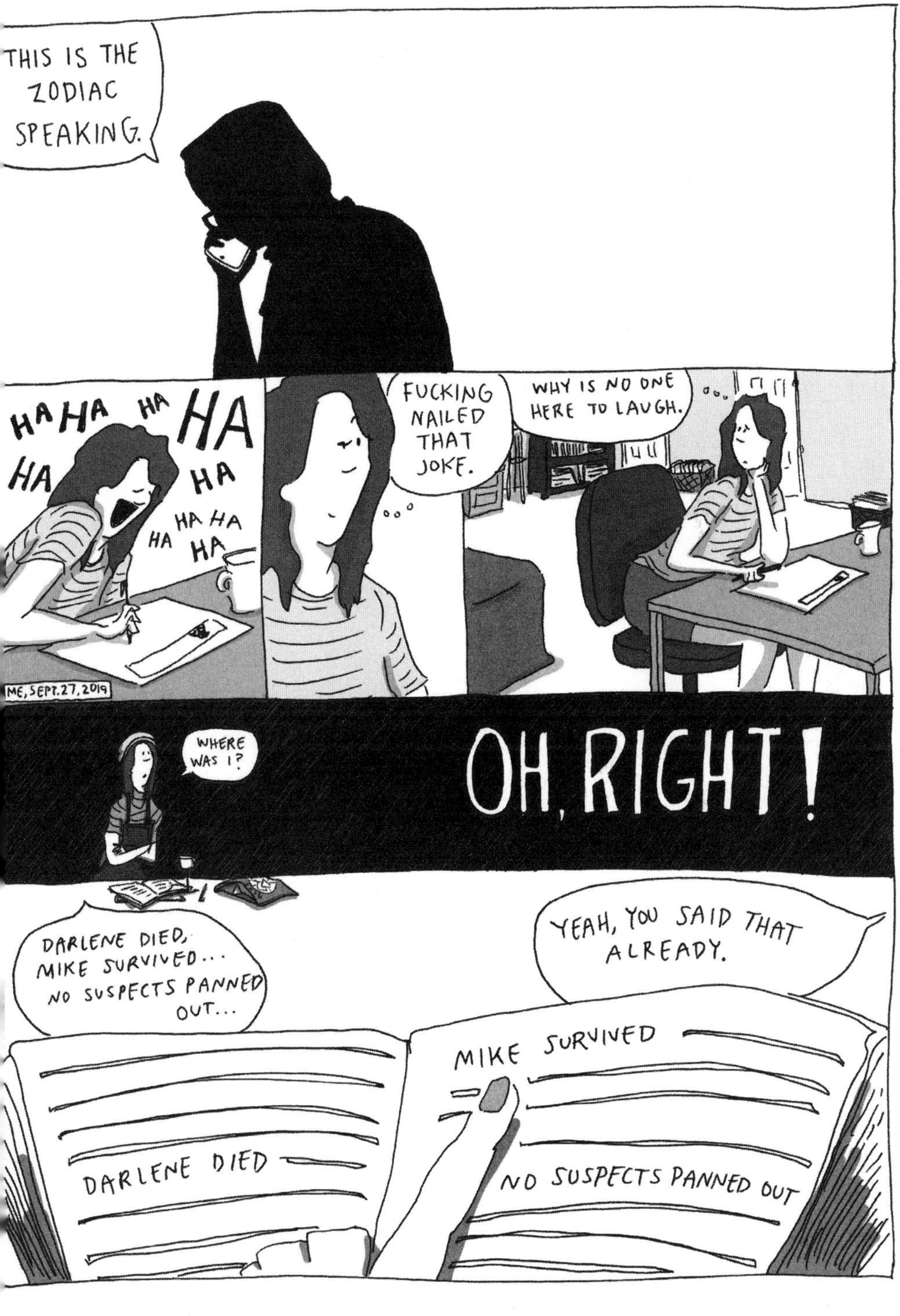
THIS IS THE ZODIAC SPEAKING.
HA HA HA HA HA HA HA HA HA HA
ME, SEPT. 27, 2019
FUCKING NAILED THAT JOKE.
WHY IS NO ONE HERE TO LAUGH.
WHERE WAS I?
OH, RIGHT!
DARLENE DIED, MIKE SURVIVED... NO SUSPECTS PANNED OUT...
YEAH, YOU SAID THAT ALREADY.
MIKE SURVIVED
DARLENE DIED
NO SUSPECTS PANNED OUT

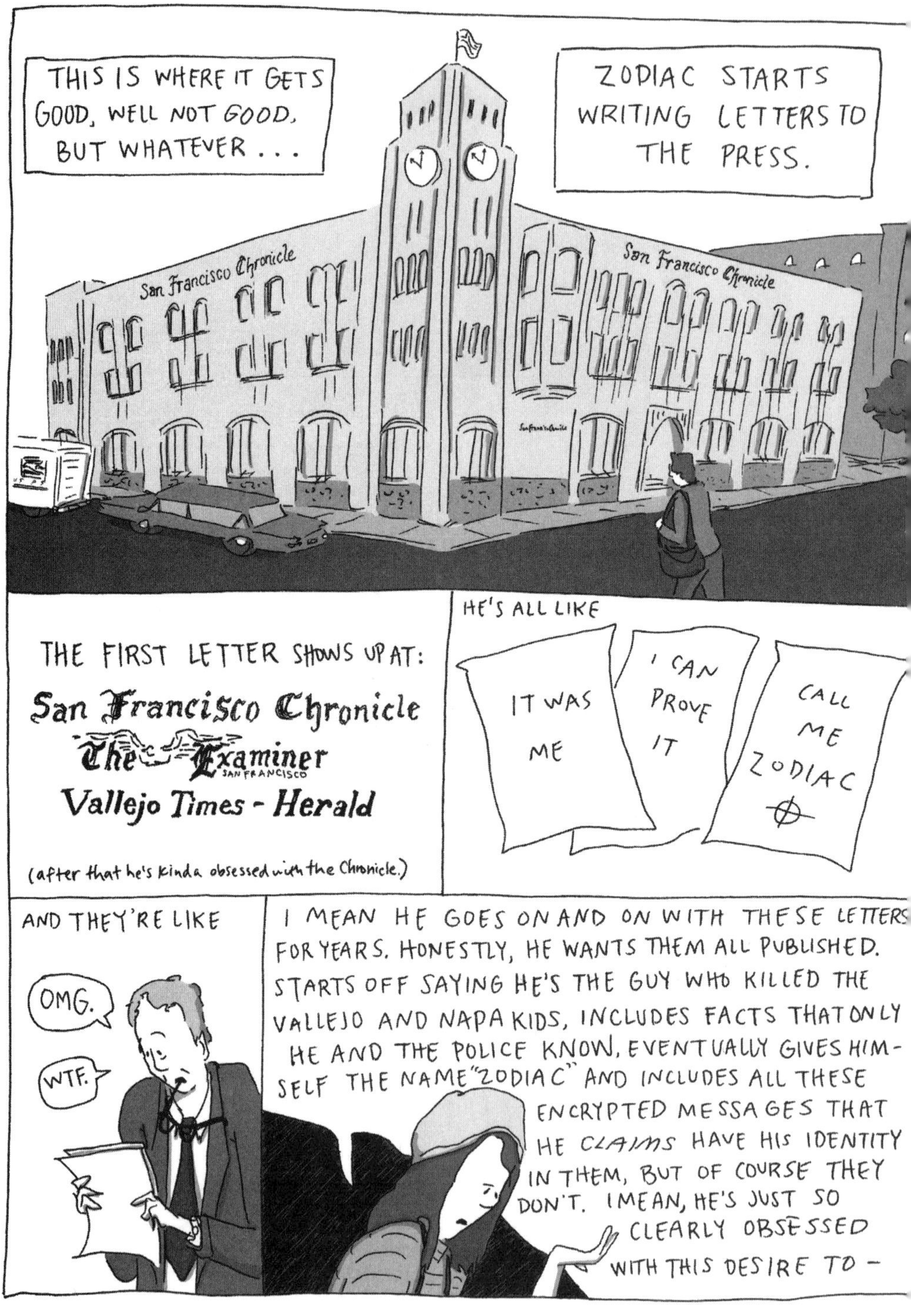
THIS IS WHERE IT GETS GOOD, WELL NOT GOOD, BUT WHATEVER...
ZODIAC STARTS WRITING LETTERS TO THE PRESS.
San Francisco Chronicle
San Francisco Chronicle
THE FIRST LETTER SHOWS UP AT:
San Francisco Chronicle
The Examiner SAN FRANCISCO
Vallejo Times - Herald
(after that he's kinda obsessed with the Chronicle.)
HE'S ALL LIKE
IT WAS ME
I CAN PROVE IT
CALL ME ZODIAC
AND THEY'RE LIKE
OMG.
WTF.
I MEAN HE GOES ON AND ON WITH THESE LETTERS FOR YEARS. HONESTLY, HE WANTS THEM ALL PUBLISHED. STARTS OFF SAYING HE'S THE GUY WHO KILLED THE VALLEJO AND NAPA KIDS, INCLUDES FACTS THAT ONLY HE AND THE POLICE KNOW, EVENTUALLY GIVES HIMSELF THE NAME "ZODIAC" AND INCLUDES ALL THESE ENCRYPTED MESSAGES THAT HE CLAIMS HAVE HIS IDENTITY IN THEM, BUT OF COURSE THEY DON'T. I MEAN, HE'S JUST SO CLEARLY OBSESSED WITH THIS DESIRE TO -

BE FRONT PAGE NEWS

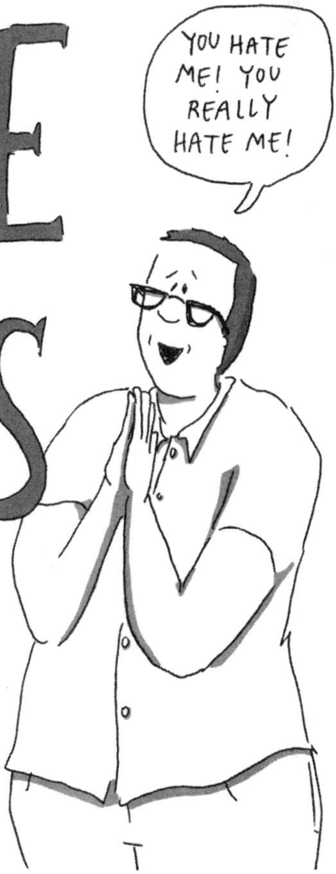
YOU HATE ME! YOU REALLY HATE ME!

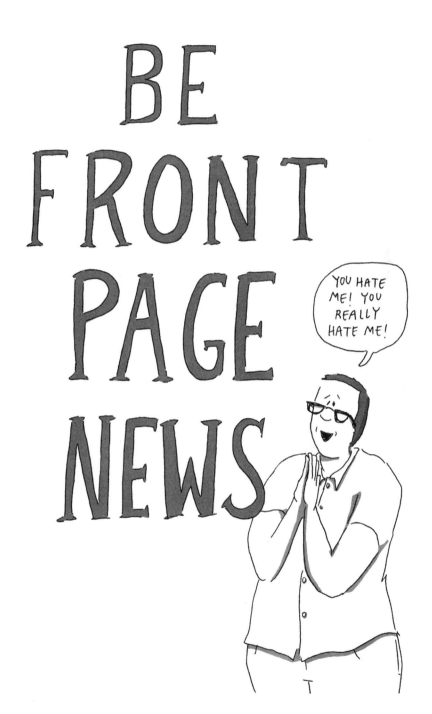

SUCH A

MILLENNIAL.

I NEED MORE WINE.

AND ICE.

THE FIRST ZODIAC CIPHER WAS *NOT* DECODED BY NAVAL INTELLIGENCE BUT BY A CUTE MARRIED COUPLE FROM SALINAS, CA.

DONALD HARDEN

BETTYE HARDEN

IT'S GOT ALL THIS CRAP ABOUT

COLLECTING SLAVES

Z'S COLLECTIBLES

FOR THE AFTERLIFE.

AND HE CAN'T SPELL TO SAVE HIS LIFE.

IN THE FOREST BECAUSE MAN IS THE MOST DANGEROUE ANAMAL OF ALL TO KILL SOMETHING GIVES ME THE MOST THRILLING EXPERENCE IT IS EVEN BETTER THAN GETTING YOUR ROCKS OFF WIT

PEOPLE IN SAN FRANCISCO AND THE BAY AREA, INCLUDING MY PARENTS, WHO DIDN'T KNOW EACH OTHER YET, ARE

SHOOK BY THIS.

WORSE THAN AN EARTHQUAKE.

SORT OF.

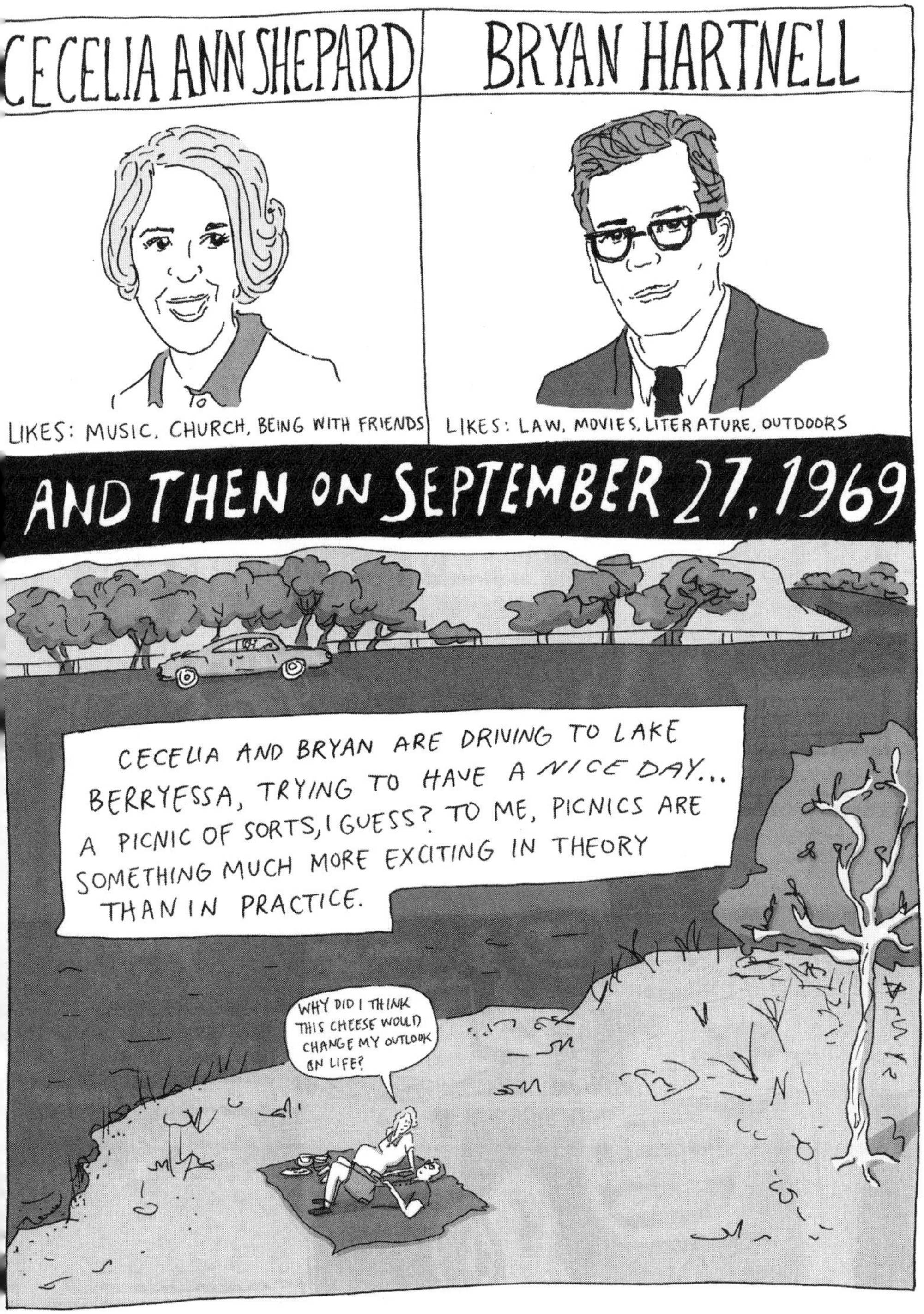

CECELIA ANN SHEPARD
BRYAN HARTNELL
LIKES: MUSIC, CHURCH, BEING WITH FRIENDS
LIKES: LAW, MOVIES, LITERATURE, OUTDOORS
AND THEN ON SEPTEMBER 27, 1969
CECELIA AND BRYAN ARE DRIVING TO LAKE BERRYESSA, TRYING TO HAVE A NICE DAY... A PICNIC OF SORTS, I GUESS? TO ME, PICNICS ARE SOMETHING MUCH MORE EXCITING IN THEORY THAN IN PRACTICE.
WHY DID I THINK THIS CHEESE WOULD CHANGE MY OUTLOOK ON LIFE?

WHEN THIS **CRAZY GUY** (2) APPEARS IN A TRULY *RIDICULOUS* OUTFIT.

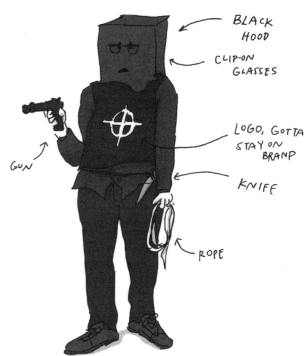

BLACK HOOD

CLIP-ON GLASSES

LOGO, GOTTA STAY ON BRAND

KNIFE

GUN

ROPE

HE'S LIKE MICHAEL CAIN IN *DRESSED TO KILL*.

HE SAYS HE'S GOING TO ROB THEM, BUT CLEARLY THAT'S A CRUEL JOKE TO HIM BECAUSE HE VERY MUCH PLANNED TO KILL. HE STABBED THE SHIT OUT OF THEM.

THEY'RE STUCK OUT THERE FOR HOURS. LUCKILY SOME GUY ON A BOAT HEARS THEM MOANING AND CALLS THE COPS.

I MEAN IT'S LIKE VERY MUCH TOO LATE.

BUT ALSO ...

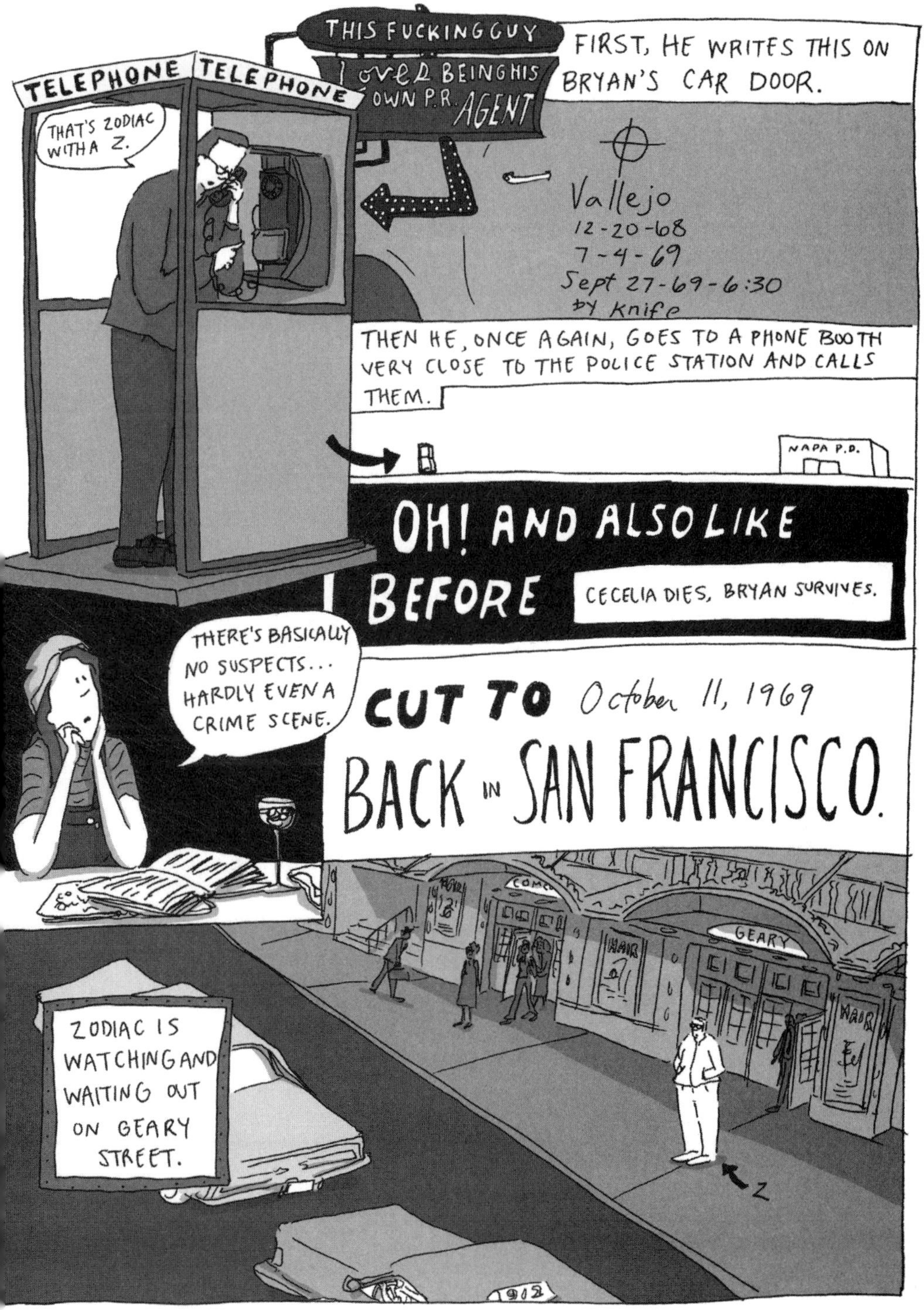

THIS FUCKING GUY
loves BEING HIS OWN P.R. AGENT
TELEPHONE
TELEPHONE
THAT'S ZODIAC WITH A Z.
FIRST, HE WRITES THIS ON BRYAN'S CAR DOOR.
Vallejo
12-20-68
7-4-69
Sept 27-69-6:30
by knife
THEN HE, ONCE AGAIN, GOES TO A PHONE BOOTH VERY CLOSE TO THE POLICE STATION AND CALLS THEM.
NAPA P.D.
OH! AND ALSO LIKE BEFORE
CECELIA DIES, BRYAN SURVIVES.
THERE'S BASICALLY NO SUSPECTS... HARDLY EVEN A CRIME SCENE.
CUT TO October 11, 1969
BACK IN SAN FRANCISCO.
GEARY
HAIR
ZODIAC IS WATCHING AND WAITING OUT ON GEARY STREET.
Z

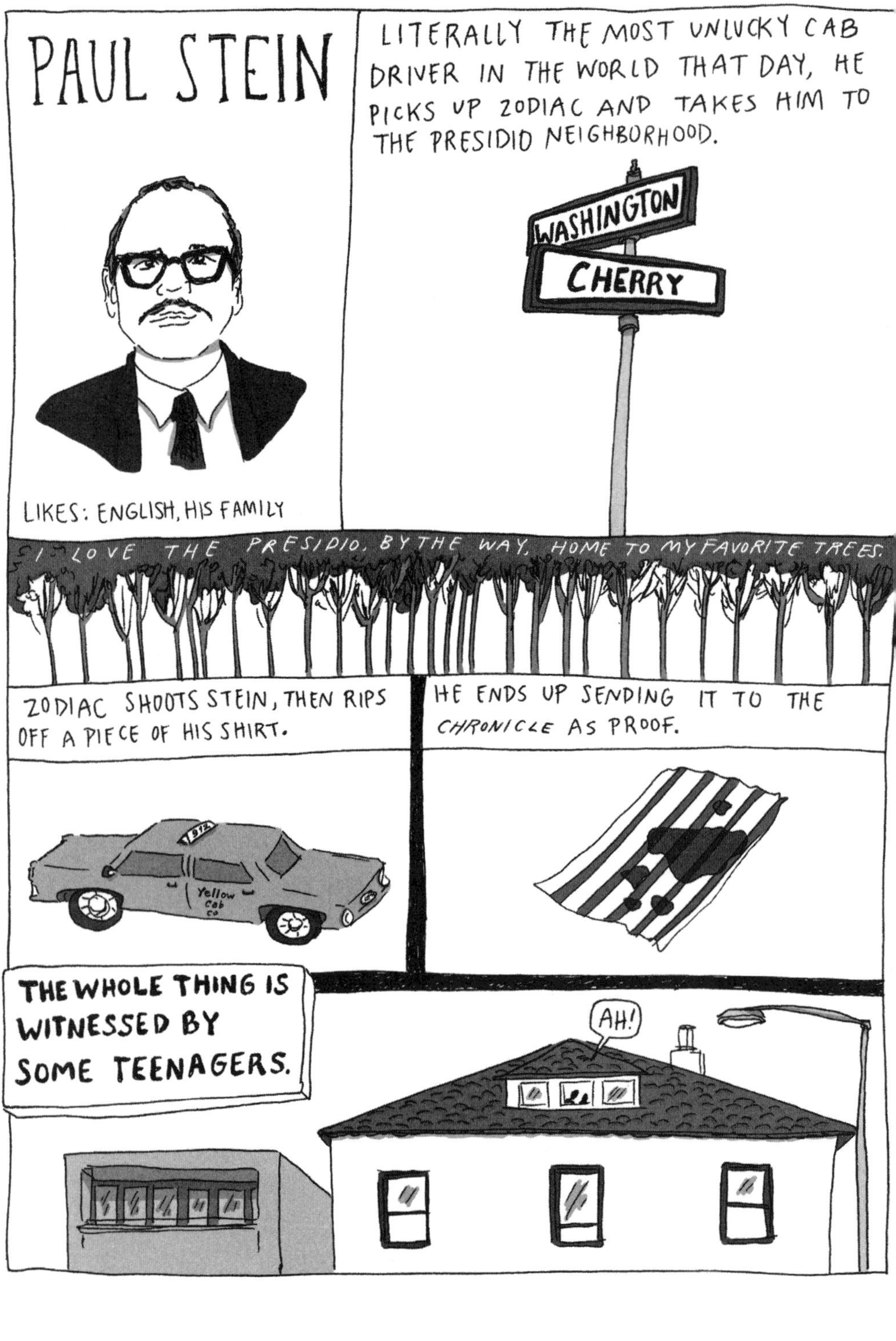
PAUL STEIN
LIKES: ENGLISH, HIS FAMILY
LITERALLY THE MOST UNLUCKY CAB DRIVER IN THE WORLD THAT DAY, HE PICKS UP ZODIAC AND TAKES HIM TO THE PRESIDIO NEIGHBORHOOD.
WASHINGTON
CHERRY
I LOVE THE PRESIDIO, BY THE WAY. HOME TO MY FAVORITE TREES.
ZODIAC SHOOTS STEIN, THEN RIPS OFF A PIECE OF HIS SHIRT.
Yellow Cab Co
HE ENDS UP SENDING IT TO THE *CHRONICLE* AS PROOF.
THE WHOLE THING IS WITNESSED BY SOME TEENAGERS.
AH!

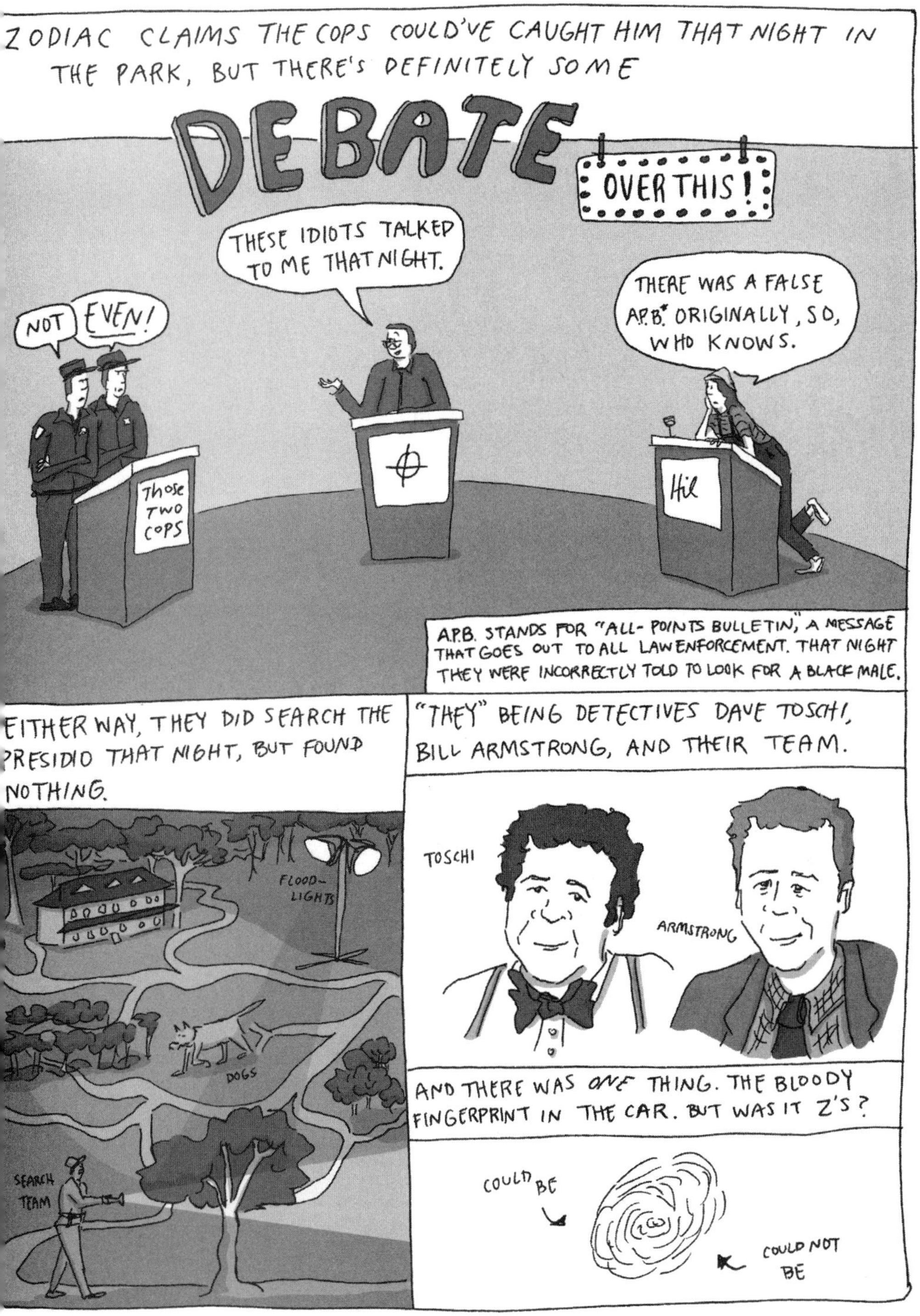

ZODIAC CLAIMS THE COPS COULD'VE CAUGHT HIM THAT NIGHT IN THE PARK, BUT THERE'S DEFINITELY SOME
DEBATE
OVER THIS!
THESE IDIOTS TALKED TO ME THAT NIGHT.
NOT
EVEN!
THERE WAS A FALSE A.P.B.* ORIGINALLY, SO, WHO KNOWS.
Those TWO COPS
Hil
A.P.B. STANDS FOR "ALL-POINTS BULLETIN," A MESSAGE THAT GOES OUT TO ALL LAW ENFORCEMENT. THAT NIGHT THEY WERE INCORRECTLY TOLD TO LOOK FOR A BLACK MALE.
EITHER WAY, THEY DID SEARCH THE PRESIDIO THAT NIGHT, BUT FOUND NOTHING.
FLOOD-LIGHTS
DOGS
SEARCH TEAM
"THEY" BEING DETECTIVES DAVE TOSCHI, BILL ARMSTRONG, AND THEIR TEAM.
TOSCHI
ARMSTRONG
AND THERE WAS ONE THING. THE BLOODY FINGERPRINT IN THE CAR. BUT WAS IT Z'S?
COULD BE
COULD NOT BE

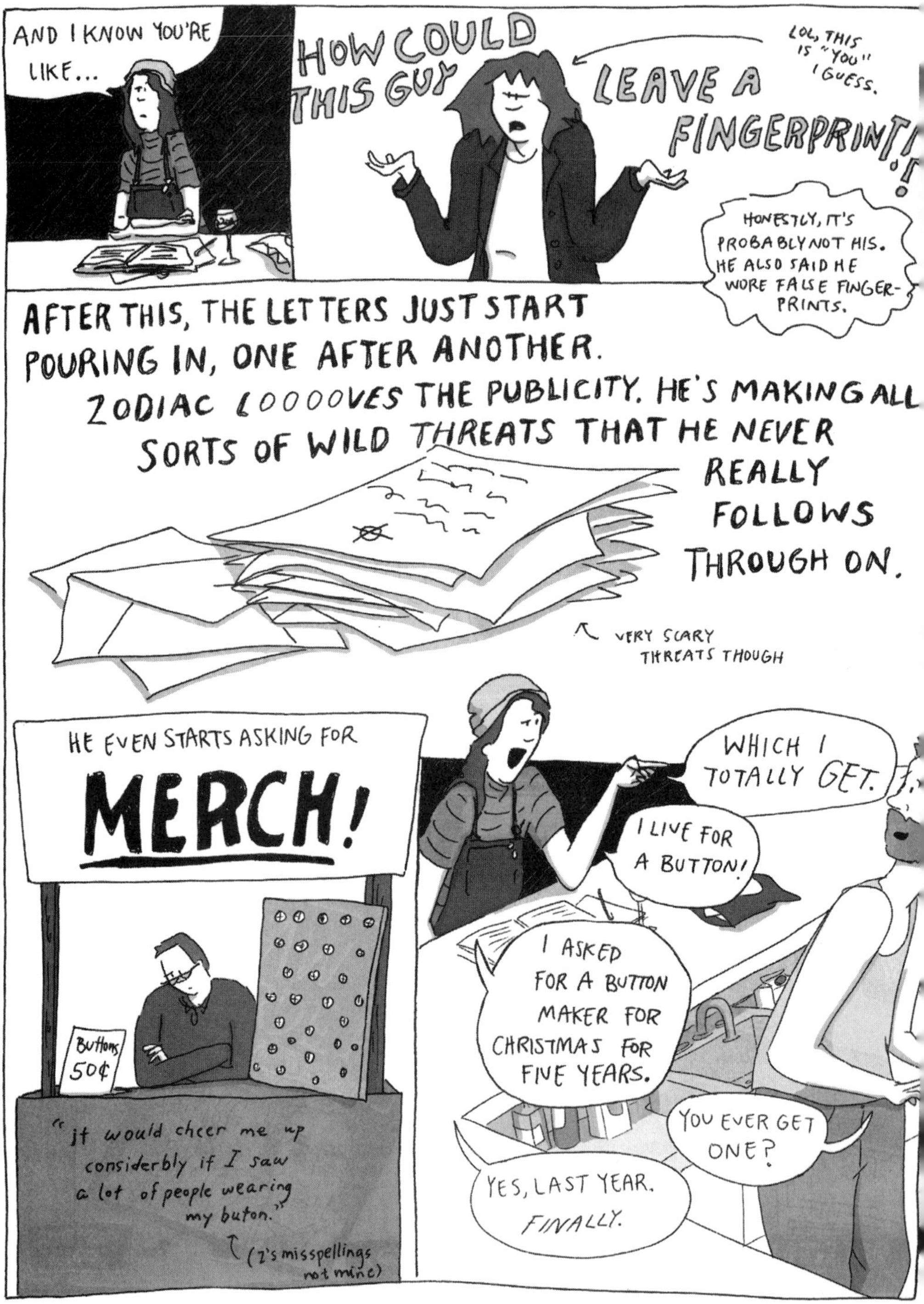

AND I KNOW YOU'RE LIKE...
HOW COULD THIS GUY LEAVE A FINGERPRINT?!
LOL, THIS IS "YOU" I GUESS.
HONESTLY, IT'S PROBABLY NOT HIS. HE ALSO SAID HE WORE FALSE FINGER-PRINTS.
AFTER THIS, THE LETTERS JUST START POURING IN, ONE AFTER ANOTHER.
ZODIAC LOOOOVES THE PUBLICITY. HE'S MAKING ALL SORTS OF WILD THREATS THAT HE NEVER REALLY FOLLOWS THROUGH ON.
VERY SCARY THREATS THOUGH
HE EVEN STARTS ASKING FOR
MERCH!
Buttons 50¢
"it would cheer me up considerbly if I saw a lot of people wearing my buton."
(Z's misspellings not mine)
WHICH I TOTALLY GET.
I LIVE FOR A BUTTON!
I ASKED FOR A BUTTON MAKER FOR CHRISTMAS FOR FIVE YEARS.
YOU EVER GET ONE?
YES, LAST YEAR. FINALLY.

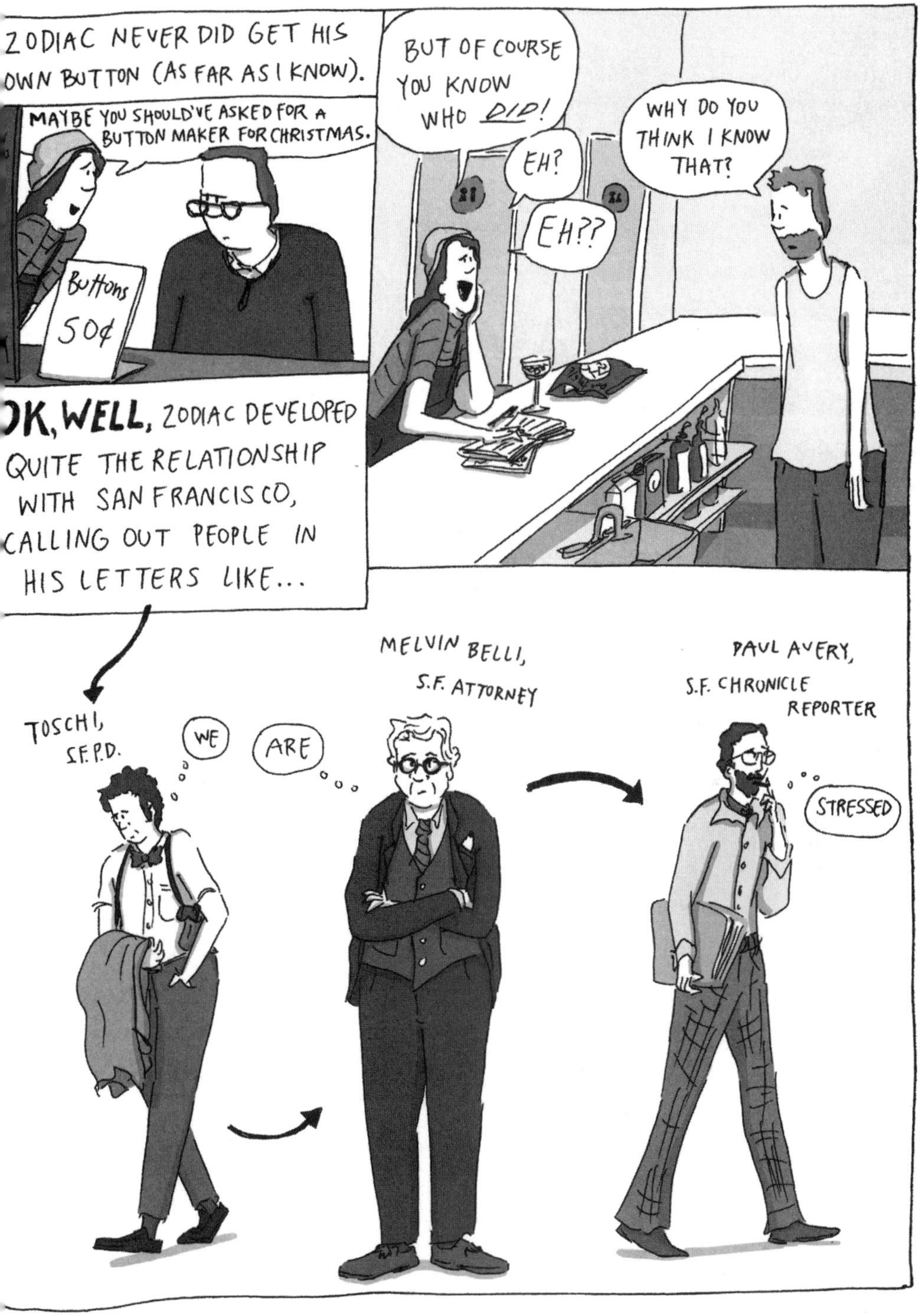
ZODIAC NEVER DID GET HIS OWN BUTTON (AS FAR AS I KNOW).
MAYBE YOU SHOULD'VE ASKED FOR A BUTTON MAKER FOR CHRISTMAS.
Buttons 50¢
BUT OF COURSE YOU KNOW WHO DID!
EH?
EH??
WHY DO YOU THINK I KNOW THAT?
OK, WELL, ZODIAC DEVELOPED QUITE THE RELATIONSHIP WITH SAN FRANCISCO, CALLING OUT PEOPLE IN HIS LETTERS LIKE...
TOSCHI, S.F.P.D.
WE
ARE
MELVIN BELLI, S.F. ATTORNEY
PAUL AVERY, S.F. CHRONICLE REPORTER
STRESSED

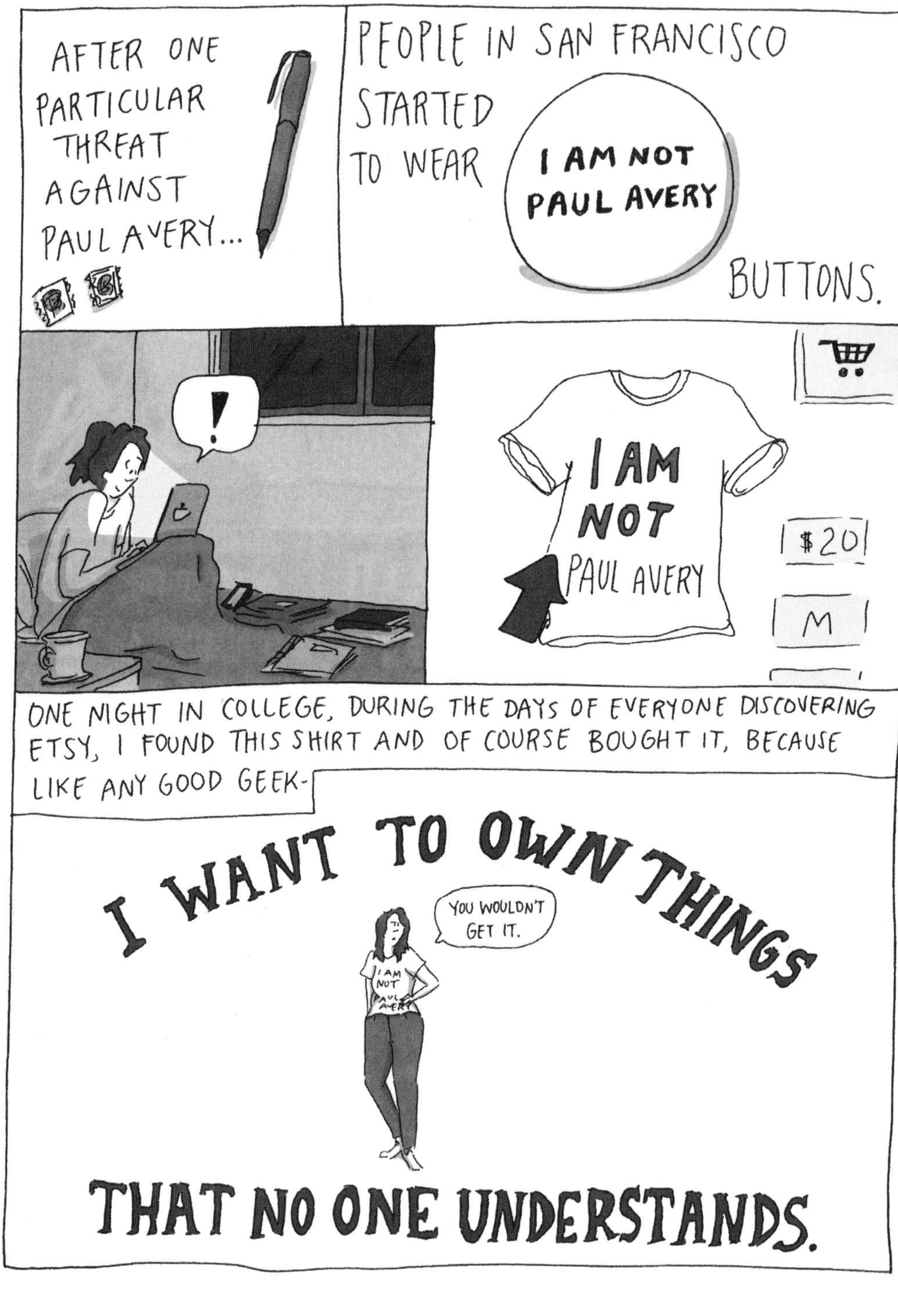

AFTER ONE PARTICULAR THREAT AGAINST PAUL AVERY...
PEOPLE IN SAN FRANCISCO STARTED TO WEAR
I AM NOT PAUL AVERY
BUTTONS.
!
I AM NOT PAUL AVERY
$20
M
ONE NIGHT IN COLLEGE, DURING THE DAYS OF EVERYONE DISCOVERING ETSY, I FOUND THIS SHIRT AND OF COURSE BOUGHT IT, BECAUSE LIKE ANY GOOD GEEK-
I WANT TO OWN THINGS
YOU WOULDN'T GET IT.
I AM NOT PAUL AVERY
THAT NO ONE UNDERSTANDS.

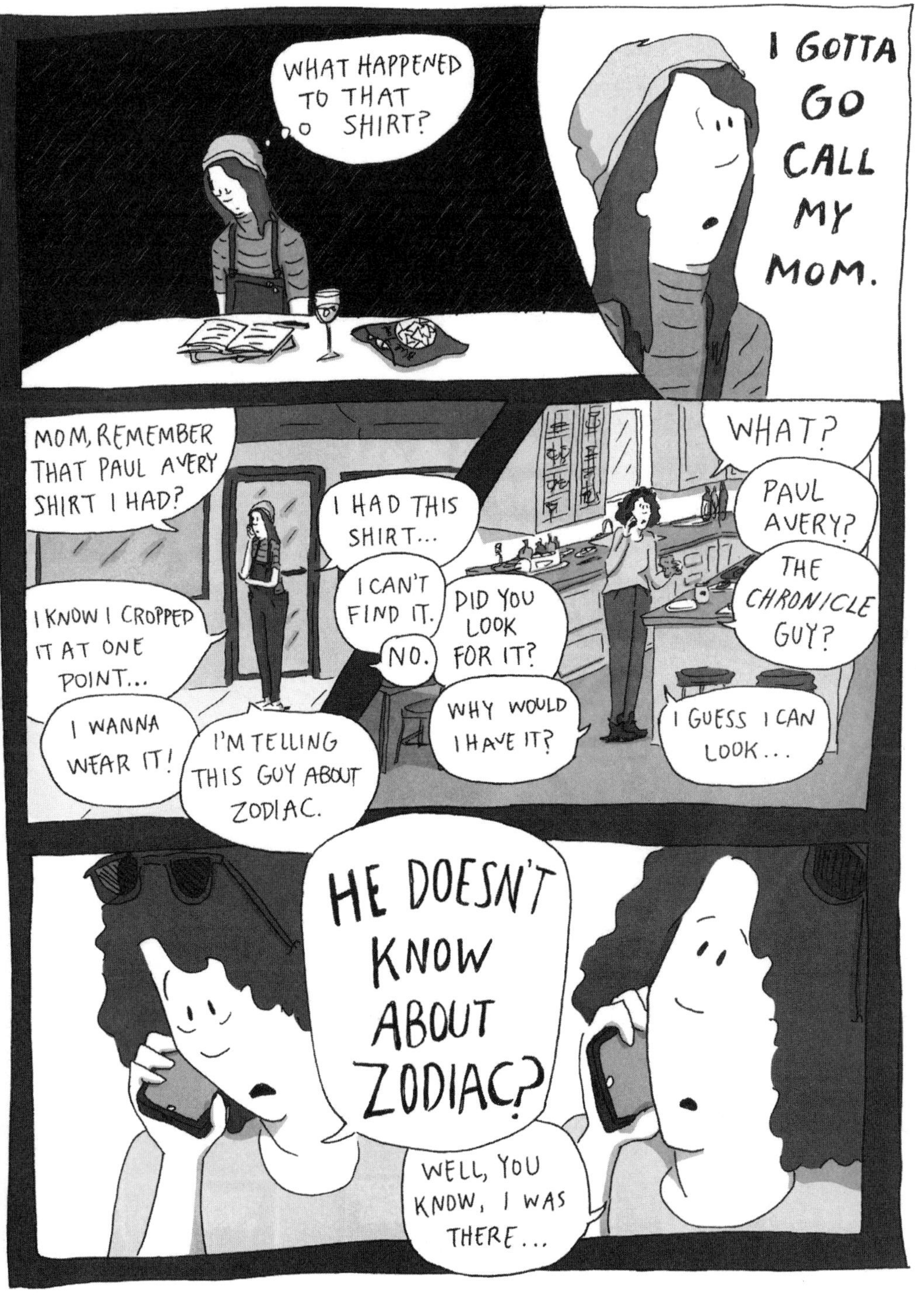
WHAT HAPPENED TO THAT SHIRT?
I GOTTA GO CALL MY MOM.
MOM, REMEMBER THAT PAUL AVERY SHIRT I HAD?
WHAT?
PAUL AVERY?
THE CHRONICLE GUY?
I HAD THIS SHIRT...
I CAN'T FIND IT.
DID YOU LOOK FOR IT?
NO.
I KNOW I CROPPED IT AT ONE POINT...
I WANNA WEAR IT!
WHY WOULD I HAVE IT?
I GUESS I CAN LOOK...
I'M TELLING THIS GUY ABOUT ZODIAC.
HE DOESN'T KNOW ABOUT ZODIAC?
WELL, YOU KNOW, I WAS THERE...

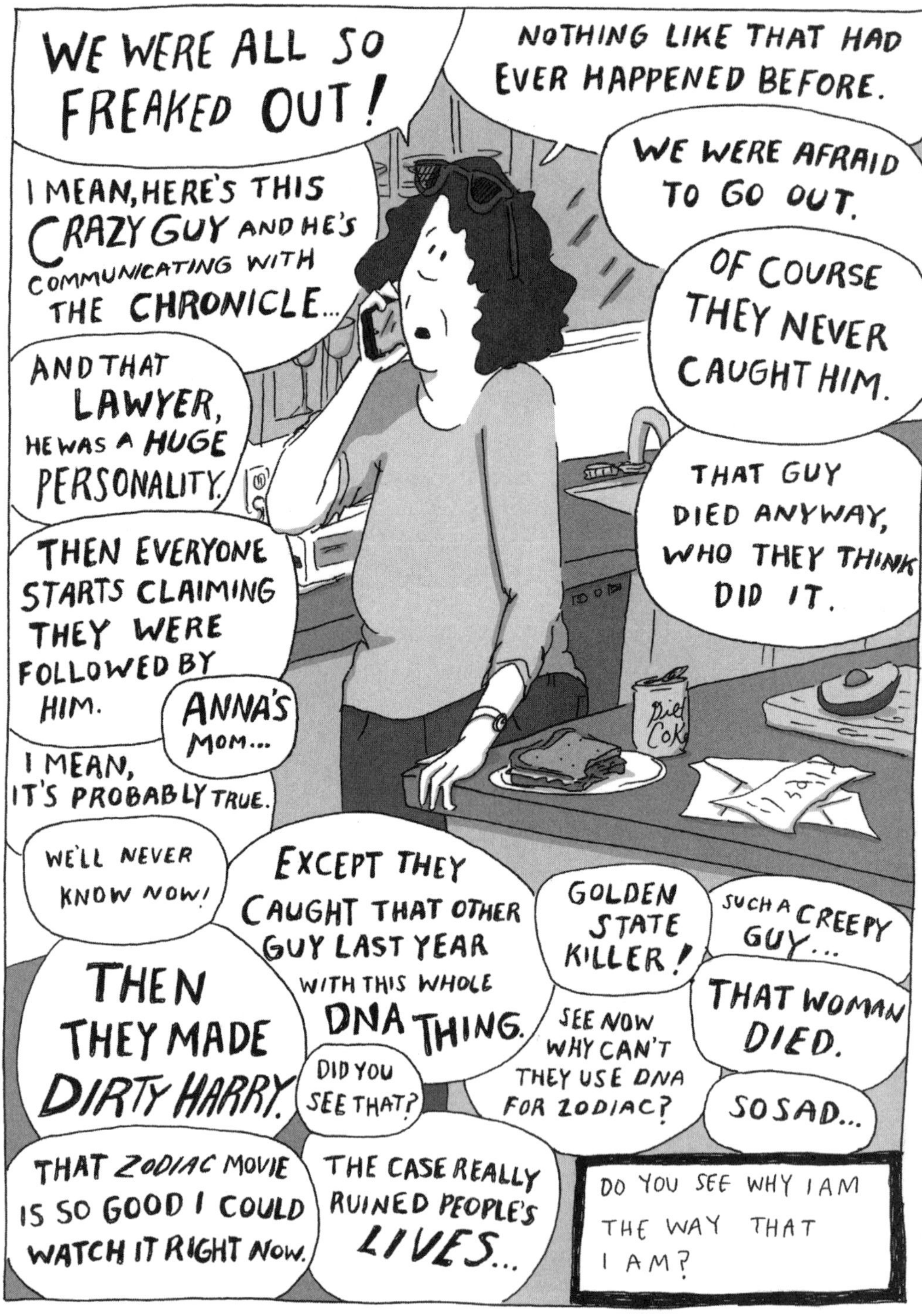
WE WERE ALL SO FREAKED OUT!
NOTHING LIKE THAT HAD EVER HAPPENED BEFORE.
WE WERE AFRAID TO GO OUT.
I MEAN, HERE'S THIS CRAZY GUY AND HE'S COMMUNICATING WITH THE CHRONICLE...
OF COURSE THEY NEVER CAUGHT HIM.
AND THAT LAWYER, HE WAS A HUGE PERSONALITY.
THAT GUY DIED ANYWAY, WHO THEY THINK DID IT.
THEN EVERYONE STARTS CLAIMING THEY WERE FOLLOWED BY HIM.
ANNA'S MOM...
I MEAN, IT'S PROBABLY TRUE.
WE'LL NEVER KNOW NOW!
EXCEPT THEY CAUGHT THAT OTHER GUY LAST YEAR WITH THIS WHOLE DNA THING.
GOLDEN STATE KILLER!
SUCH A CREEPY GUY...
THEN THEY MADE DIRTY HARRY.
DID YOU SEE THAT?
SEE NOW WHY CAN'T THEY USE DNA FOR ZODIAC?
THAT WOMAN DIED.
SO SAD...
THAT ZODIAC MOVIE IS SO GOOD I COULD WATCH IT RIGHT NOW.
THE CASE REALLY RUINED PEOPLE'S LIVES...
DO YOU SEE WHY I AM THE WAY THAT I AM?

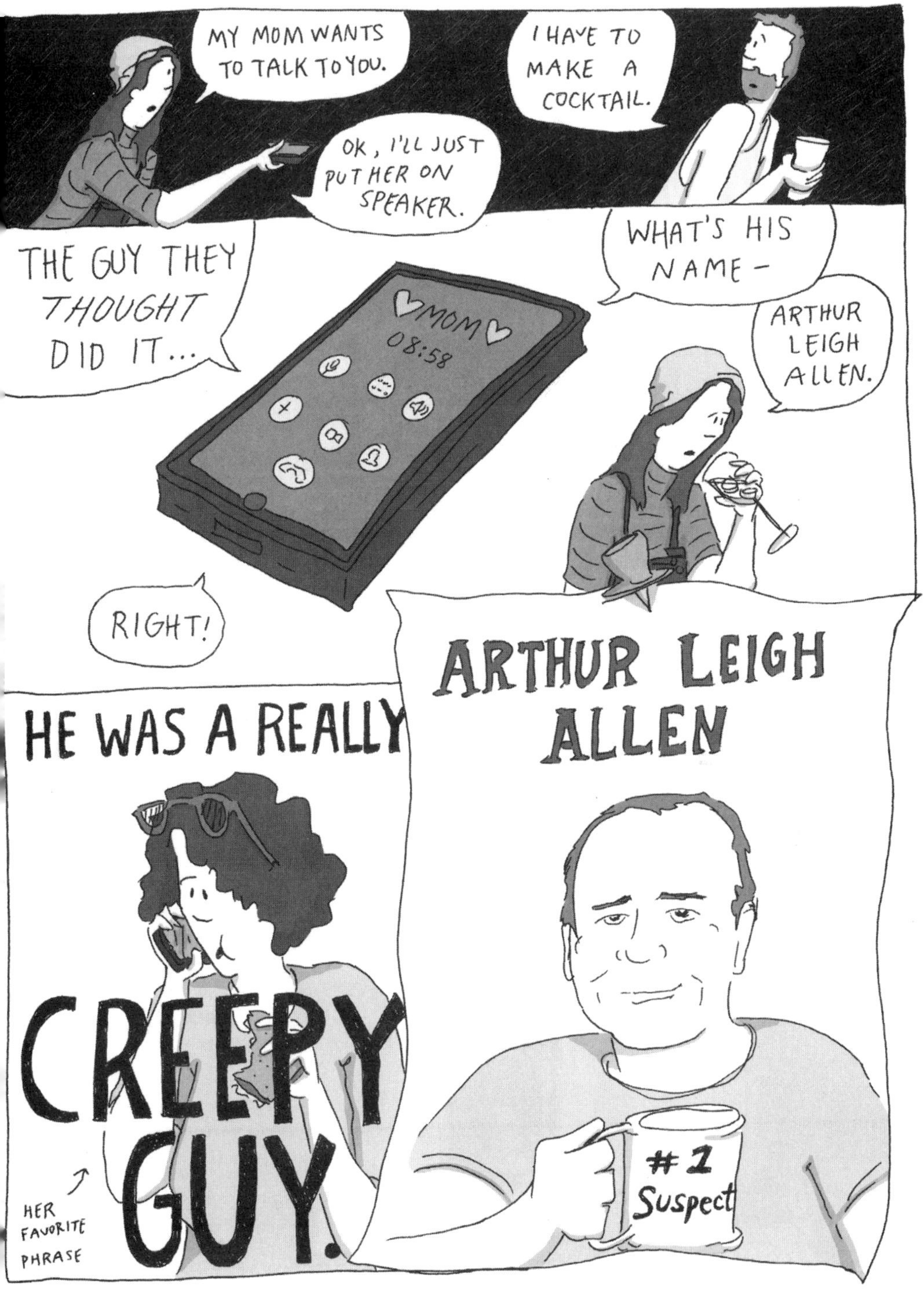
MY MOM WANTS TO TALK TO YOU.
I HAVE TO MAKE A COCKTAIL.
OK, I'LL JUST PUT HER ON SPEAKER.
THE GUY THEY THOUGHT DID IT...
MOM
08:58
WHAT'S HIS NAME-
ARTHUR LEIGH ALLEN.
RIGHT!
HE WAS A REALLY
ARTHUR LEIGH ALLEN
CREEPY GUY.
HER FAVORITE PHRASE
#1 Suspect

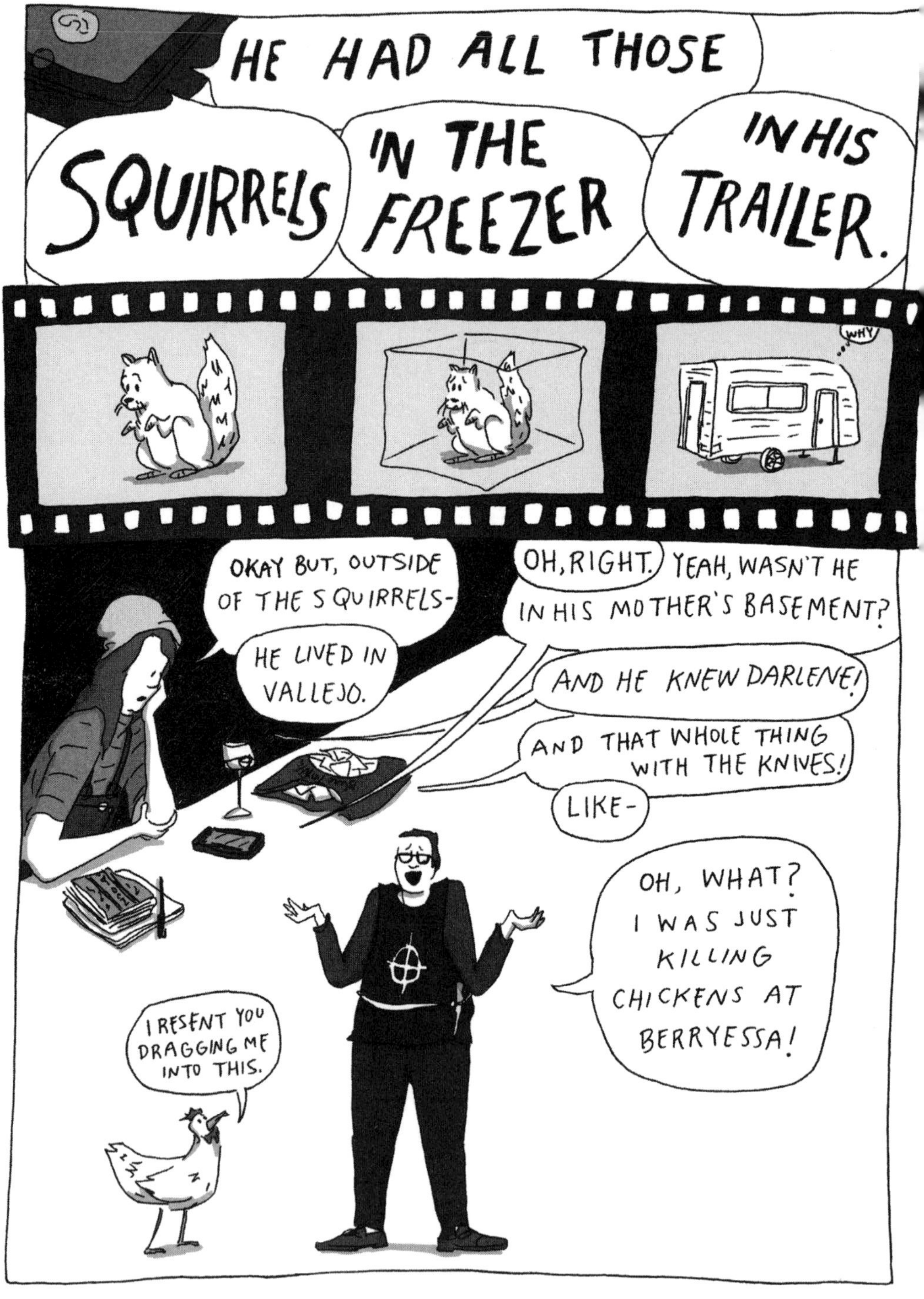
HE HAD ALL THOSE
SQUIRRELS
IN THE FREEZER
IN HIS TRAILER.
WHY
OKAY BUT, OUTSIDE OF THE SQUIRRELS-
HE LIVED IN VALLEJO.
OH, RIGHT.
YEAH, WASN'T HE IN HIS MOTHER'S BASEMENT?
AND HE KNEW DARLENE!
AND THAT WHOLE THING WITH THE KNIVES!
LIKE-
OH, WHAT? I WAS JUST KILLING CHICKENS AT BERRYESSA!
I RESENT YOU DRAGGING ME INTO THIS.

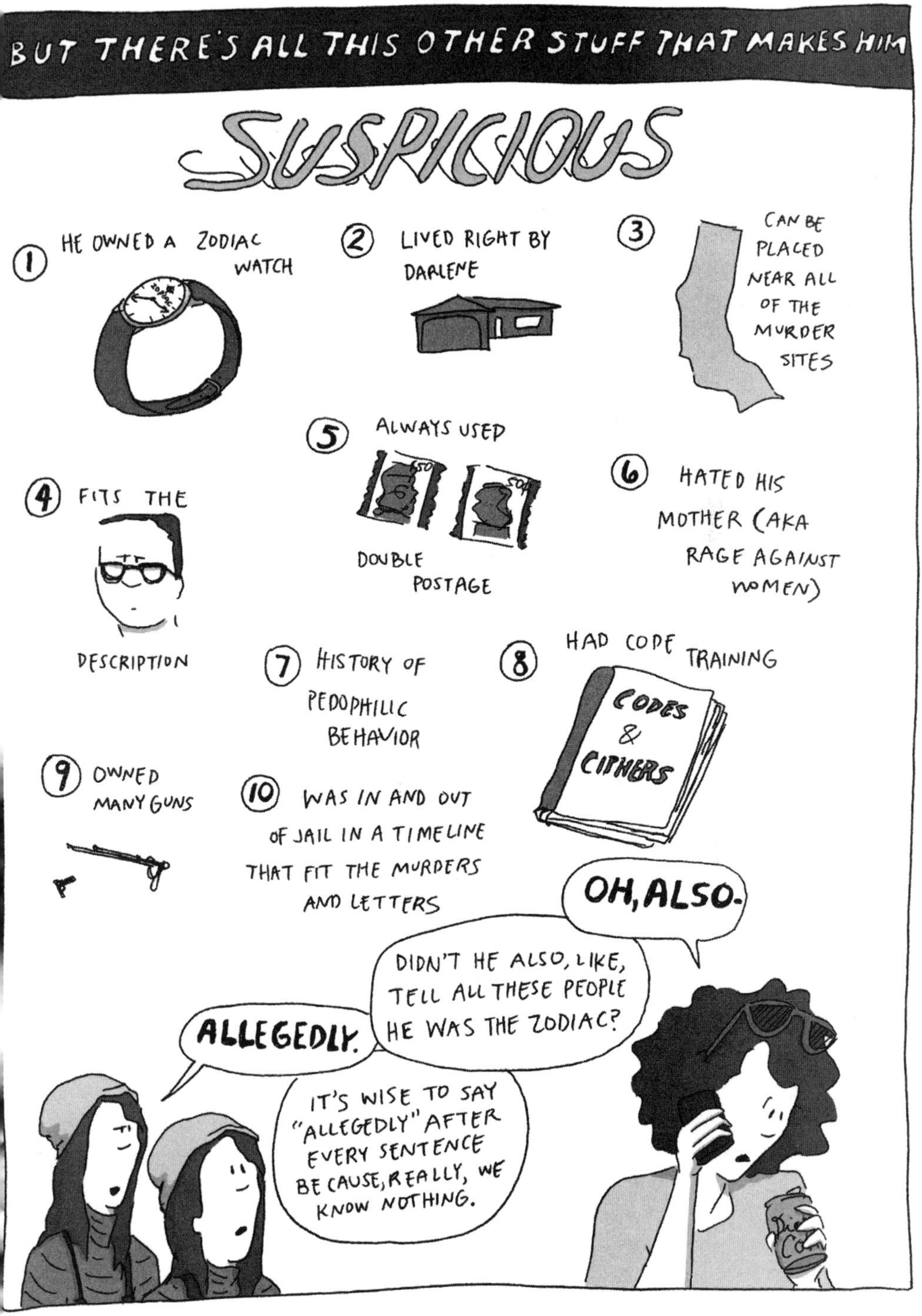
BUT THERE'S ALL THIS OTHER STUFF THAT MAKES HIM
SUSPICIOUS
1 HE OWNED A ZODIAC WATCH
2 LIVED RIGHT BY DARLENE
3 CAN BE PLACED NEAR ALL OF THE MURDER SITES
4 FITS THE DESCRIPTION
5 ALWAYS USED DOUBLE POSTAGE
6 HATED HIS MOTHER (AKA RAGE AGAINST WOMEN)
7 HISTORY OF PEDOPHILIC BEHAVIOR
8 HAD CODE TRAINING
CODES & CIPHERS
9 OWNED MANY GUNS
10 WAS IN AND OUT OF JAIL IN A TIMELINE THAT FIT THE MURDERS AND LETTERS
OH, ALSO-
DIDN'T HE ALSO, LIKE, TELL ALL THESE PEOPLE HE WAS THE ZODIAC?
ALLEGEDLY.
IT'S WISE TO SAY "ALLEGEDLY" AFTER EVERY SENTENCE BECAUSE, REALLY, WE KNOW NOTHING.

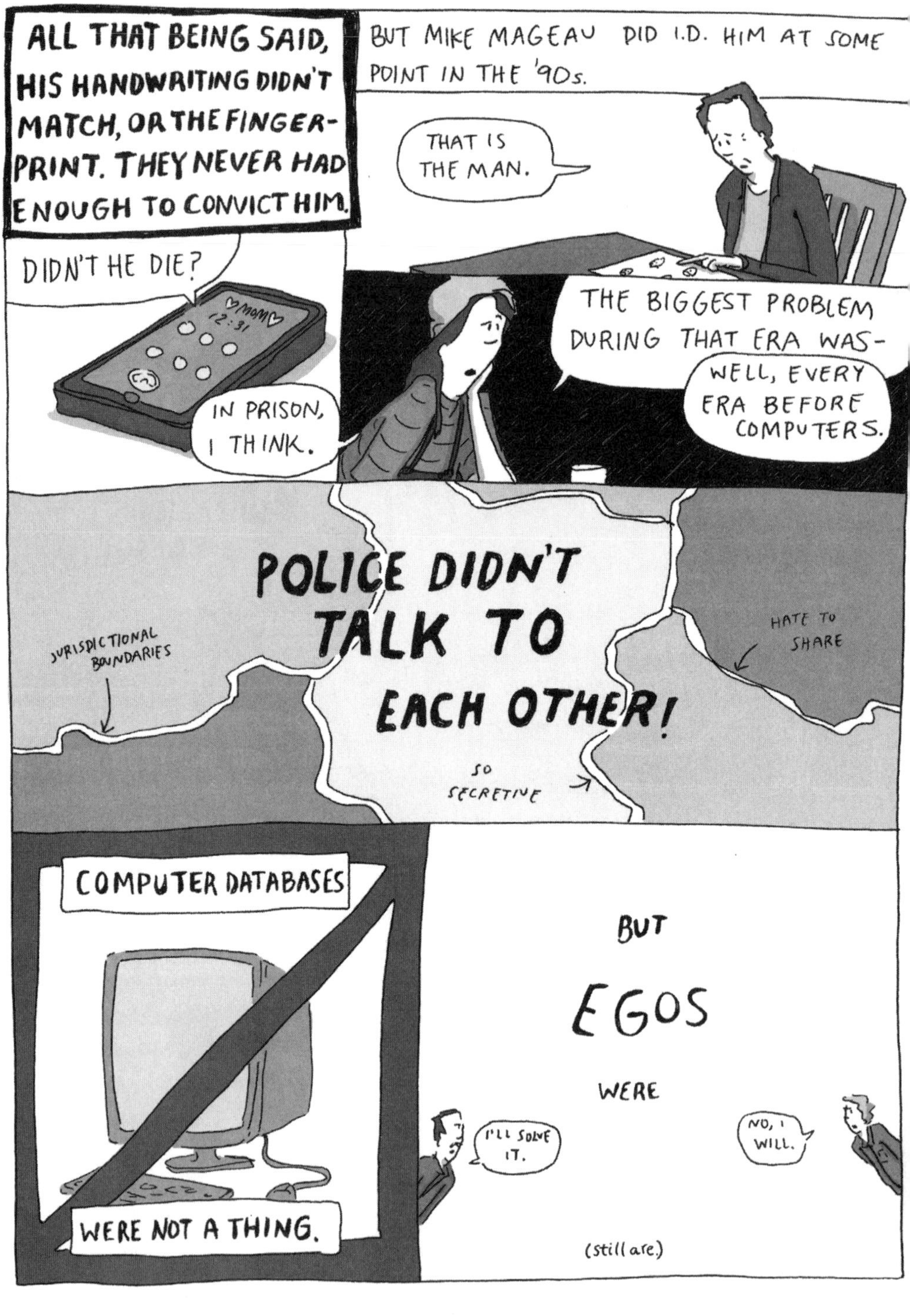
ALL THAT BEING SAID, HIS HANDWRITING DIDN'T MATCH, OR THE FINGERPRINT. THEY NEVER HAD ENOUGH TO CONVICT HIM.
BUT MIKE MAGEAU DID I.D. HIM AT SOME POINT IN THE '90s.
THAT IS THE MAN.
DIDN'T HE DIE?
MOM
12:31
IN PRISON, I THINK.
THE BIGGEST PROBLEM DURING THAT ERA WAS-
WELL, EVERY ERA BEFORE COMPUTERS.
POLICE DIDN'T TALK TO EACH OTHER!
JURISDICTIONAL BOUNDARIES
HATE TO SHARE
SO SECRETIVE
COMPUTER DATABASES
WERE NOT A THING.
BUT EGOS WERE
I'LL SOLVE IT.
NO, I WILL.
(still are.)

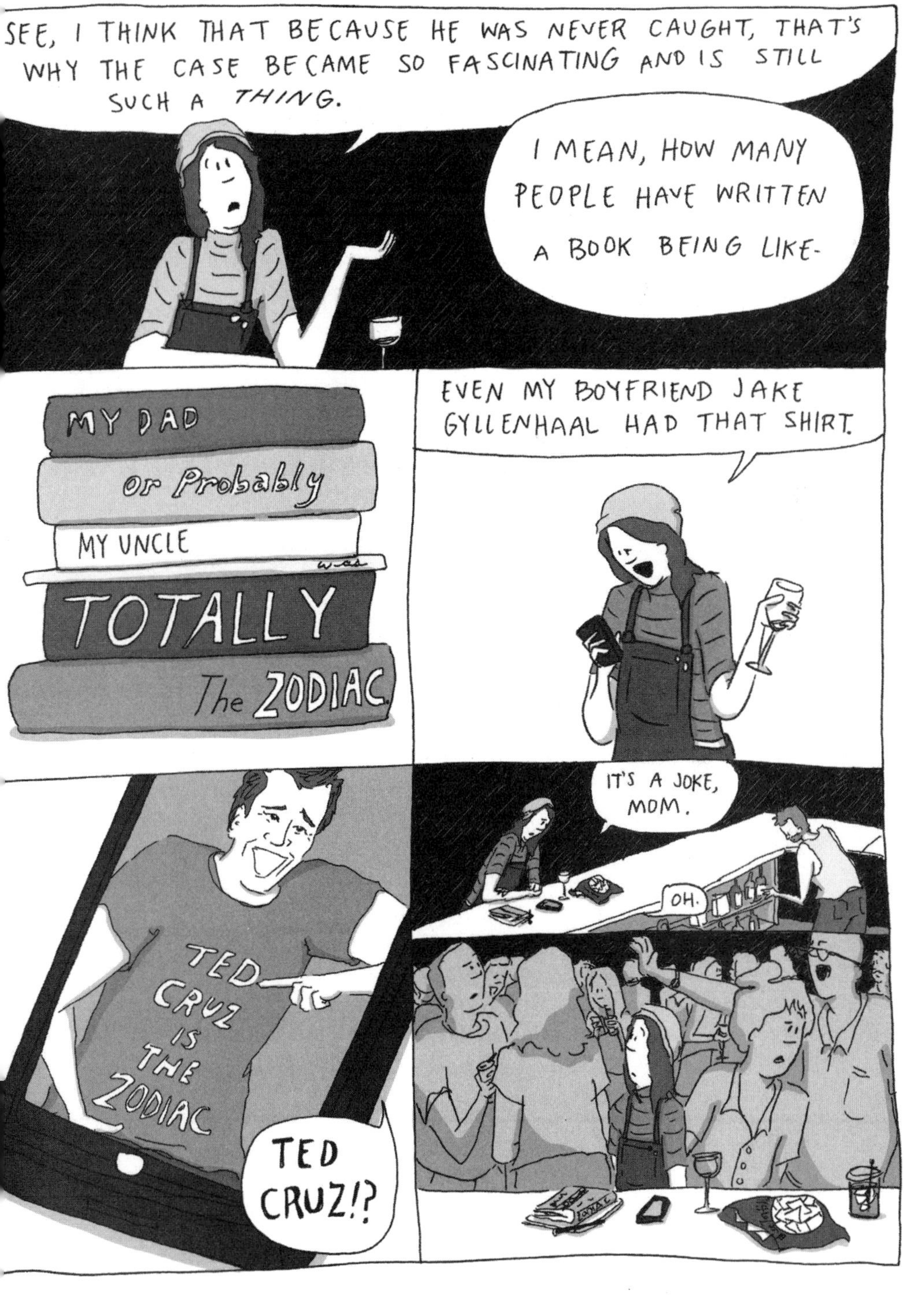
SEE, I THINK THAT BECAUSE HE WAS NEVER CAUGHT, THAT'S WHY THE CASE BECAME SO FASCINATING AND IS STILL SUCH A *THING.*
I MEAN, HOW MANY PEOPLE HAVE WRITTEN A BOOK BEING LIKE-
MY DAD
or Probably
MY UNCLE
was
TOTALLY
The ZODIAC
EVEN MY BOYFRIEND JAKE GYLLENHAAL HAD THAT SHIRT.
TED CRUZ IS THE ZODIAC
TED CRUZ!?
IT'S A JOKE, MOM.
OH.

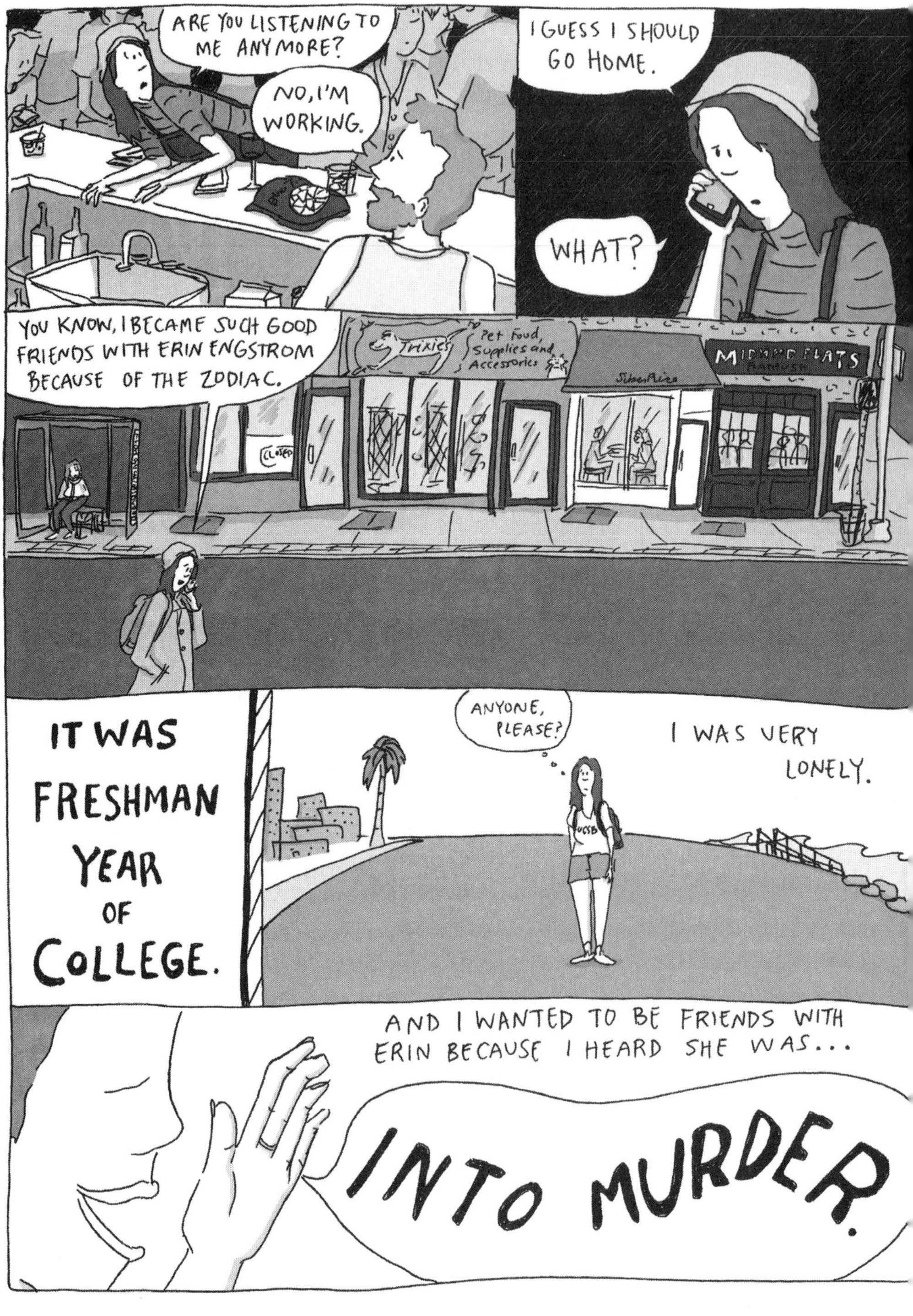
ARE YOU LISTENING TO ME ANYMORE?
NO, I'M WORKING.
I GUESS I SHOULD GO HOME.
WHAT?
YOU KNOW, I BECAME SUCH GOOD FRIENDS WITH ERIN ENGSTROM BECAUSE OF THE ZODIAC.
Trixie's
Pet Food, Supplies and Accessories
IT WAS FRESHMAN YEAR OF COLLEGE.
ANYONE, PLEASE?
I WAS VERY LONELY.
UCSB
AND I WANTED TO BE FRIENDS WITH ERIN BECAUSE I HEARD SHE WAS...
INTO MURDER.

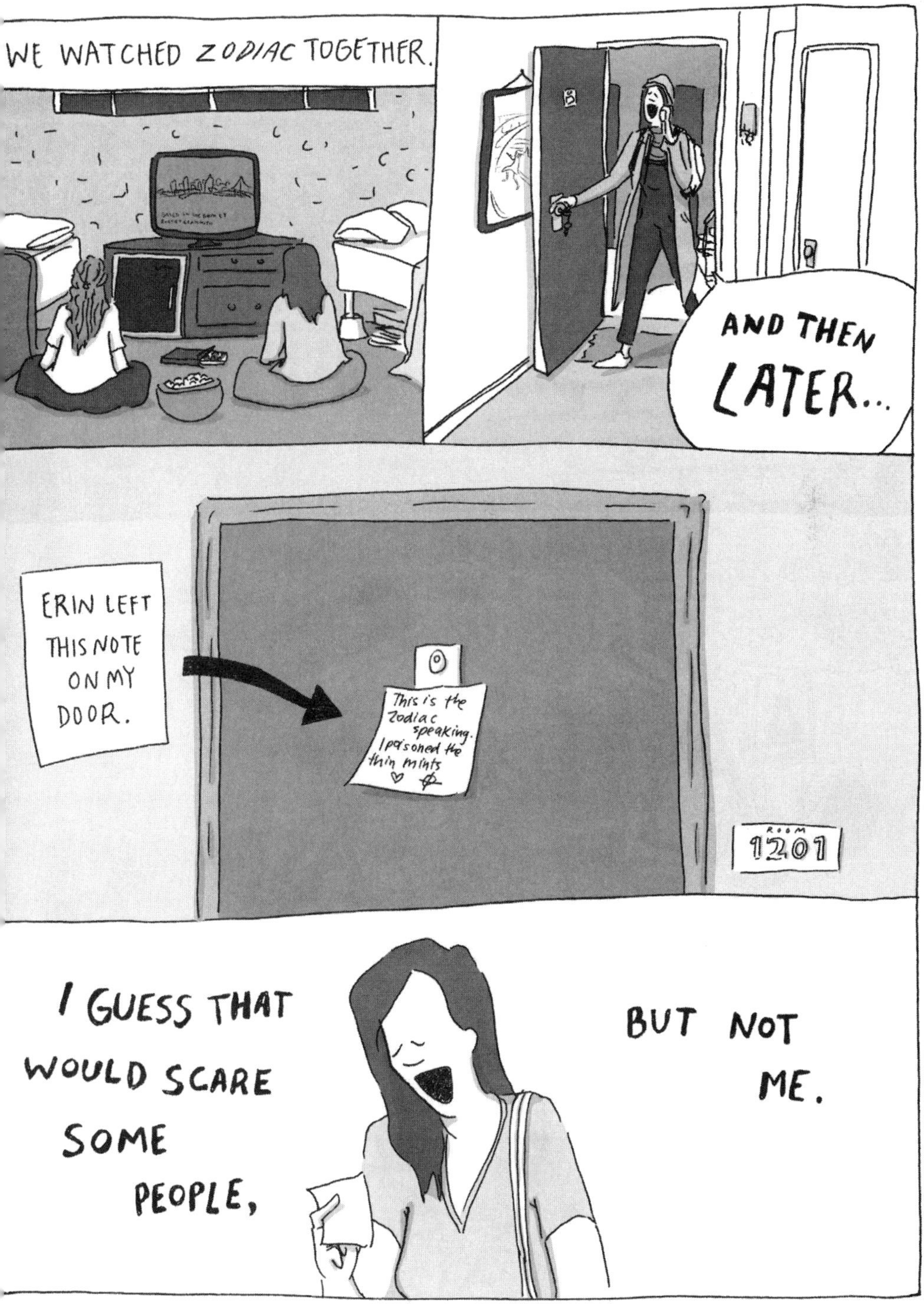
WE WATCHED ZODIAC TOGETHER.
AND THEN LATER...
ERIN LEFT THIS NOTE ON MY DOOR.
This is the Zodiac speaking. I poisoned the thin mints
ROOM 1201
I GUESS THAT WOULD SCARE SOME PEOPLE,
BUT NOT ME.

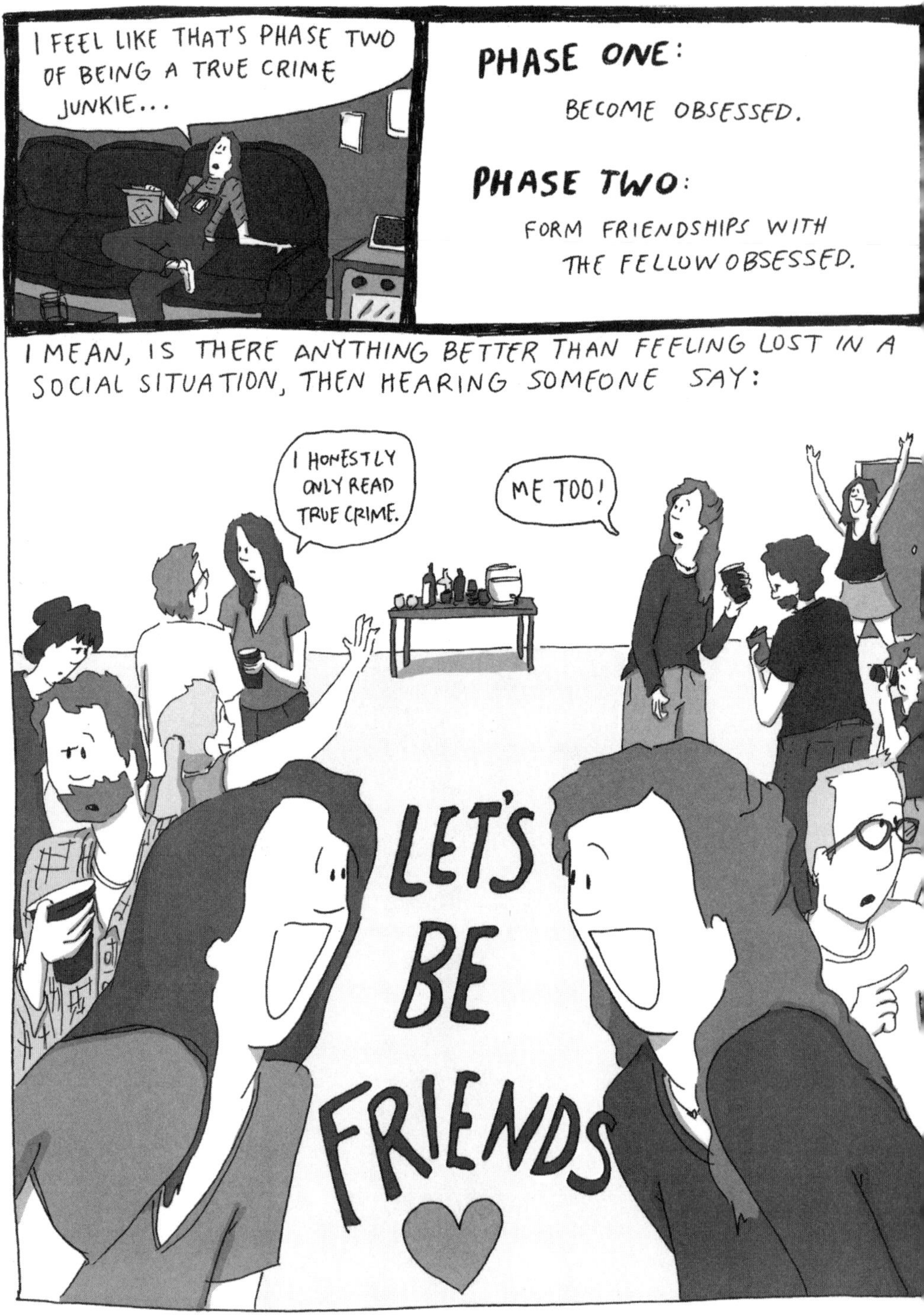
I FEEL LIKE THAT'S PHASE TWO OF BEING A TRUE CRIME JUNKIE...
PHASE ONE:
BECOME OBSESSED.
PHASE TWO:
FORM FRIENDSHIPS WITH THE FELLOW OBSESSED.
I MEAN, IS THERE ANYTHING BETTER THAN FEELING LOST IN A SOCIAL SITUATION, THEN HEARING SOMEONE SAY:
I HONESTLY ONLY READ TRUE CRIME.
ME TOO!
LET'S BE FRIENDS

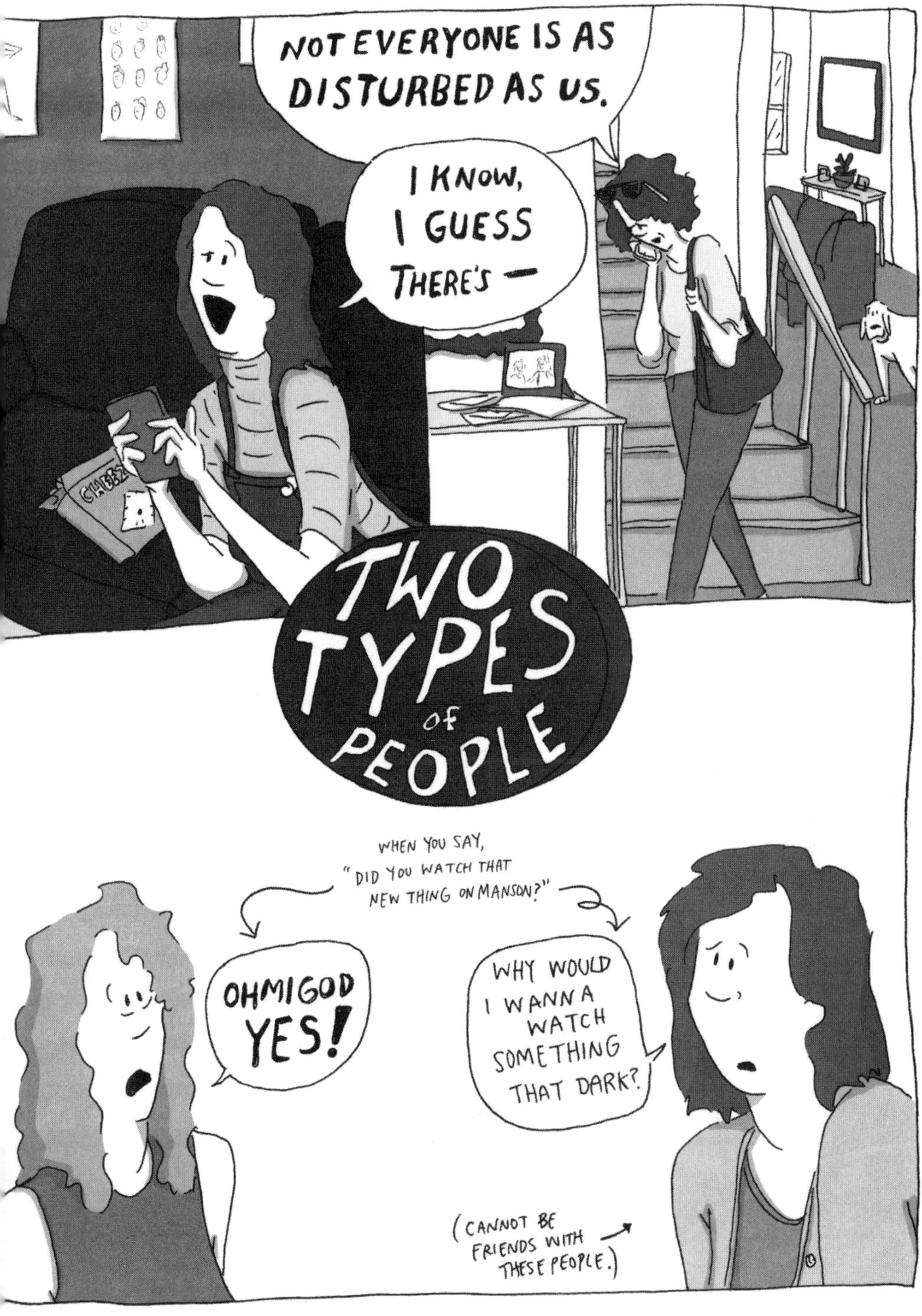
NOT EVERYONE IS AS DISTURBED AS US.
I KNOW, I GUESS THERE'S —
CHEEZ
TWO TYPES of PEOPLE
WHEN YOU SAY, "DID YOU WATCH THAT NEW THING ON MANSON?"
OHMIGOD YES!
WHY WOULD I WANNA WATCH SOMETHING THAT DARK?
(CANNOT BE FRIENDS WITH THESE PEOPLE.)

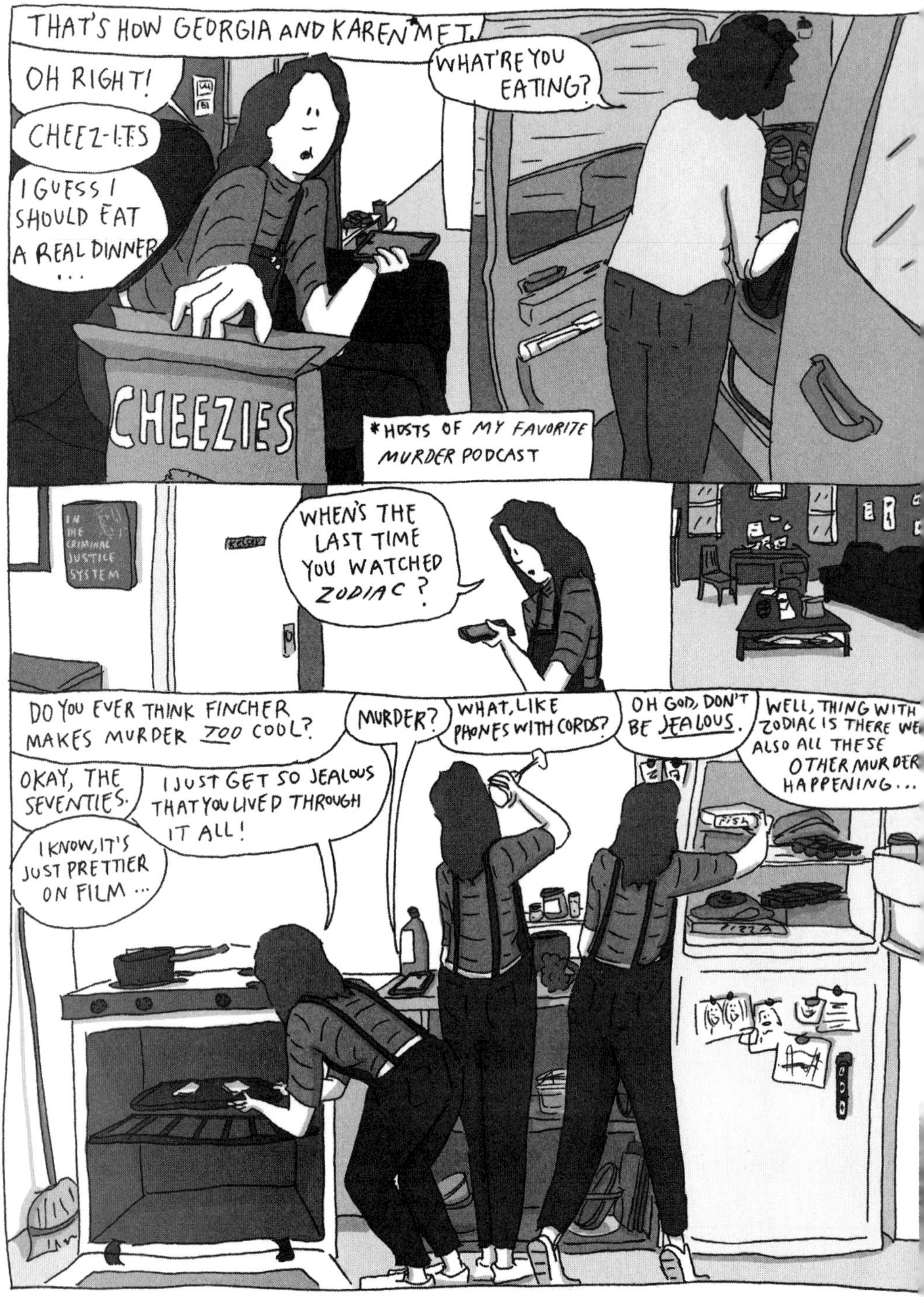
THAT'S HOW GEORGIA AND KAREN* MET.
OH RIGHT!
CHEEZ-ITS
I GUESS I SHOULD EAT A REAL DINNER...
WHAT'RE YOU EATING?
CHEEZIES
*HOSTS OF MY FAVORITE MURDER PODCAST
IN THE CRIMINAL JUSTICE SYSTEM
WHEN'S THE LAST TIME YOU WATCHED ZODIAC?
DO YOU EVER THINK FINCHER MAKES MURDER TOO COOL?
MURDER?
WHAT, LIKE PHONES WITH CORDS?
OH GOD, DON'T BE JEALOUS.
WELL, THING WITH ZODIAC IS THERE WE ALSO ALL THESE OTHER MURDER HAPPENING...
OKAY, THE SEVENTIES.
I JUST GET SO JEALOUS THAT YOU LIVED THROUGH IT ALL!
I KNOW, IT'S JUST PRETTIER ON FILM...
FISH
PIZZA

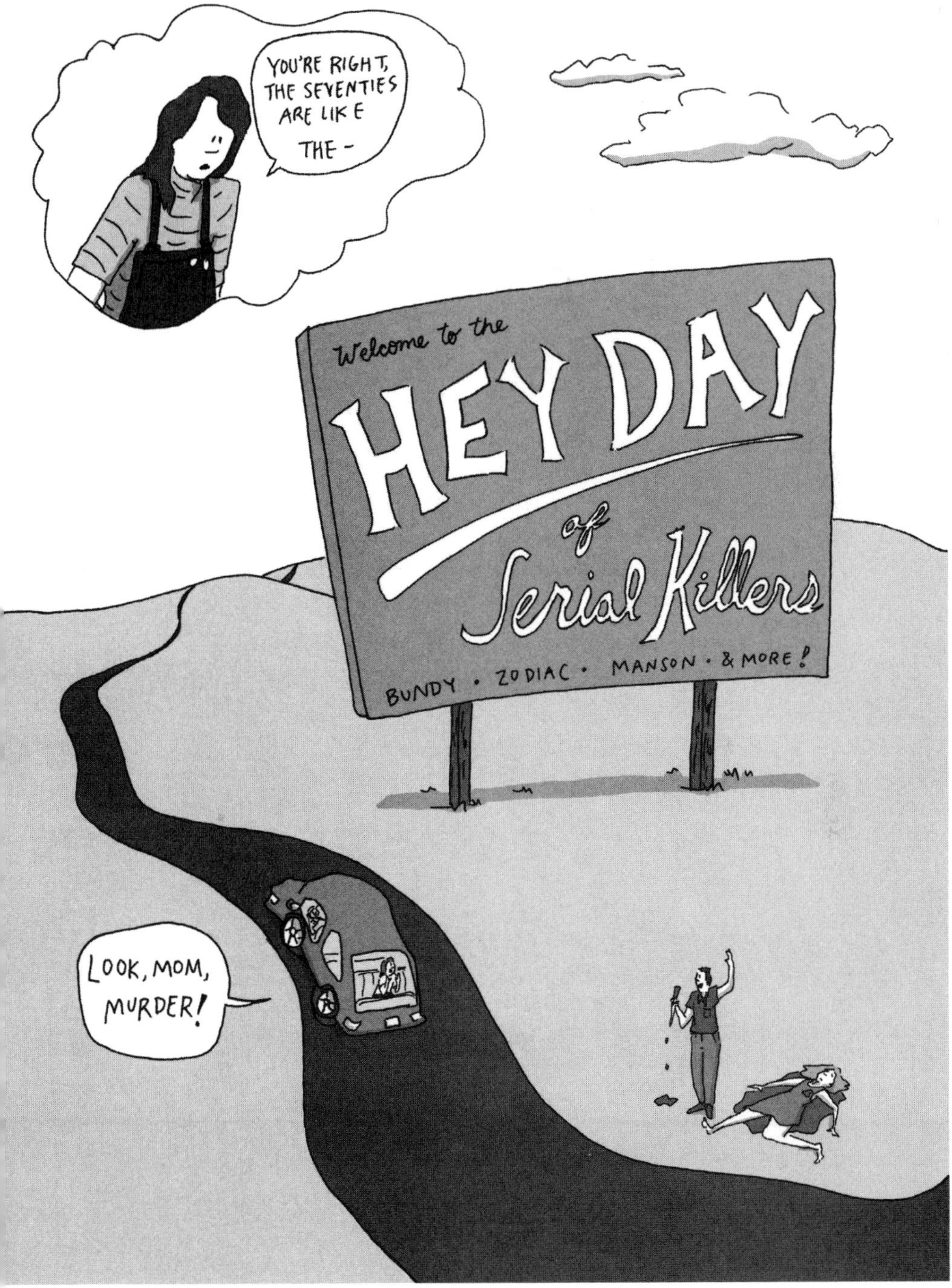
YOU'RE RIGHT, THE SEVENTIES ARE LIKE THE -
Welcome to the
HEY DAY
of
Serial Killers
BUNDY • ZODIAC • MANSON • & MORE!
LOOK, MOM, MURDER!

Let's Think (again)

This '70s Thing

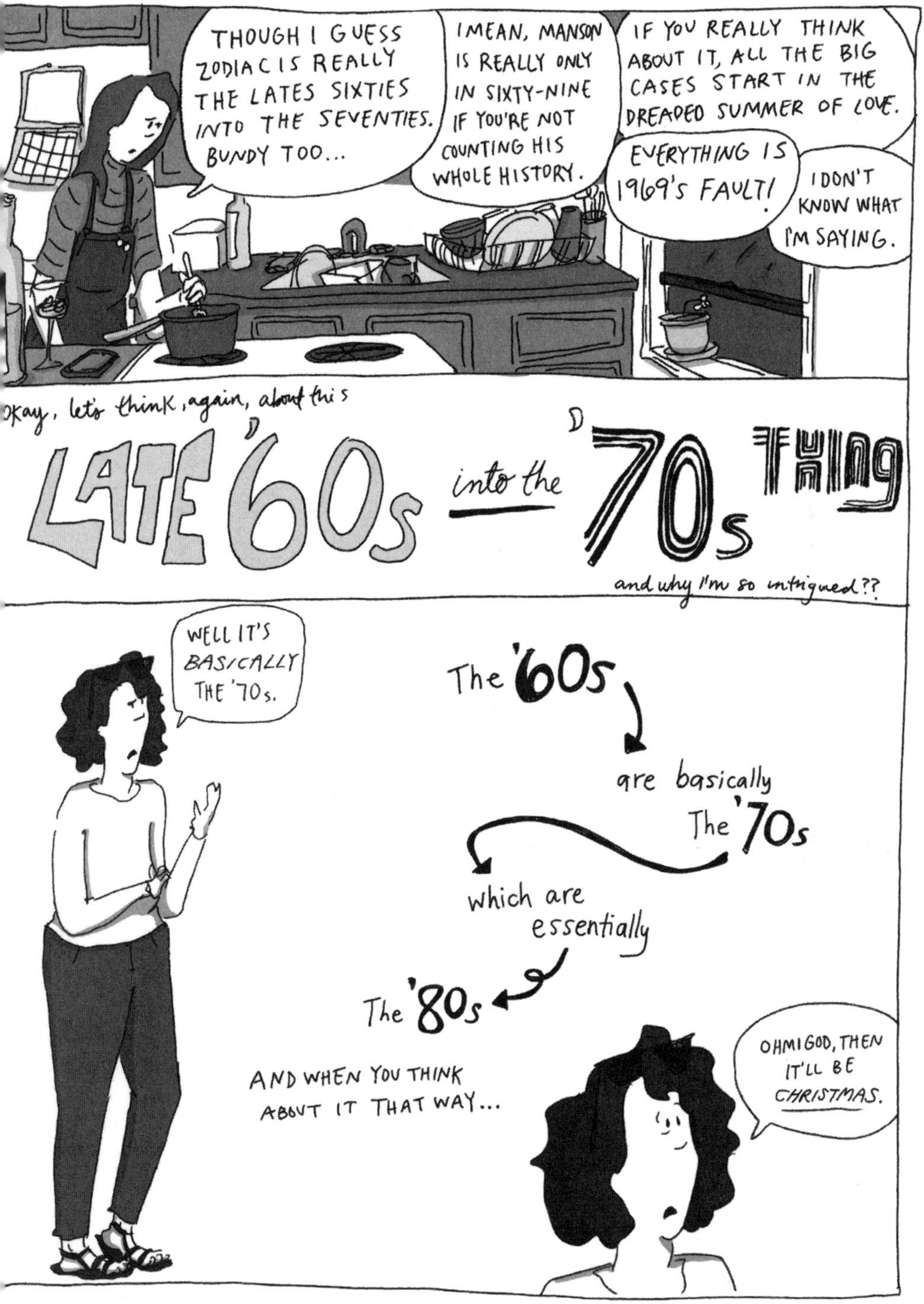
THOUGH I GUESS ZODIAC IS REALLY THE LATES SIXTIES INTO THE SEVENTIES. BUNDY TOO...
I MEAN, MANSON IS REALLY ONLY IN SIXTY-NINE IF YOU'RE NOT COUNTING HIS WHOLE HISTORY.
IF YOU REALLY THINK ABOUT IT, ALL THE BIG CASES START IN THE DREADED SUMMER OF LOVE.
EVERYTHING IS 1969's FAULT!
I DON'T KNOW WHAT I'M SAYING.
okay, let's think, again, about this
LATE '60s into the '70s THING
and why I'm so intrigued??
WELL IT'S BASICALLY THE '70s.
The '60s
are basically
The '70s
which are essentially
The '80s
AND WHEN YOU THINK ABOUT IT THAT WAY...
OHMIGOD, THEN IT'LL BE CHRISTMAS.

I WAS SO ATTRACTED BECAUSE
THE CLOTHING WAS SO ATTRACTIVE.

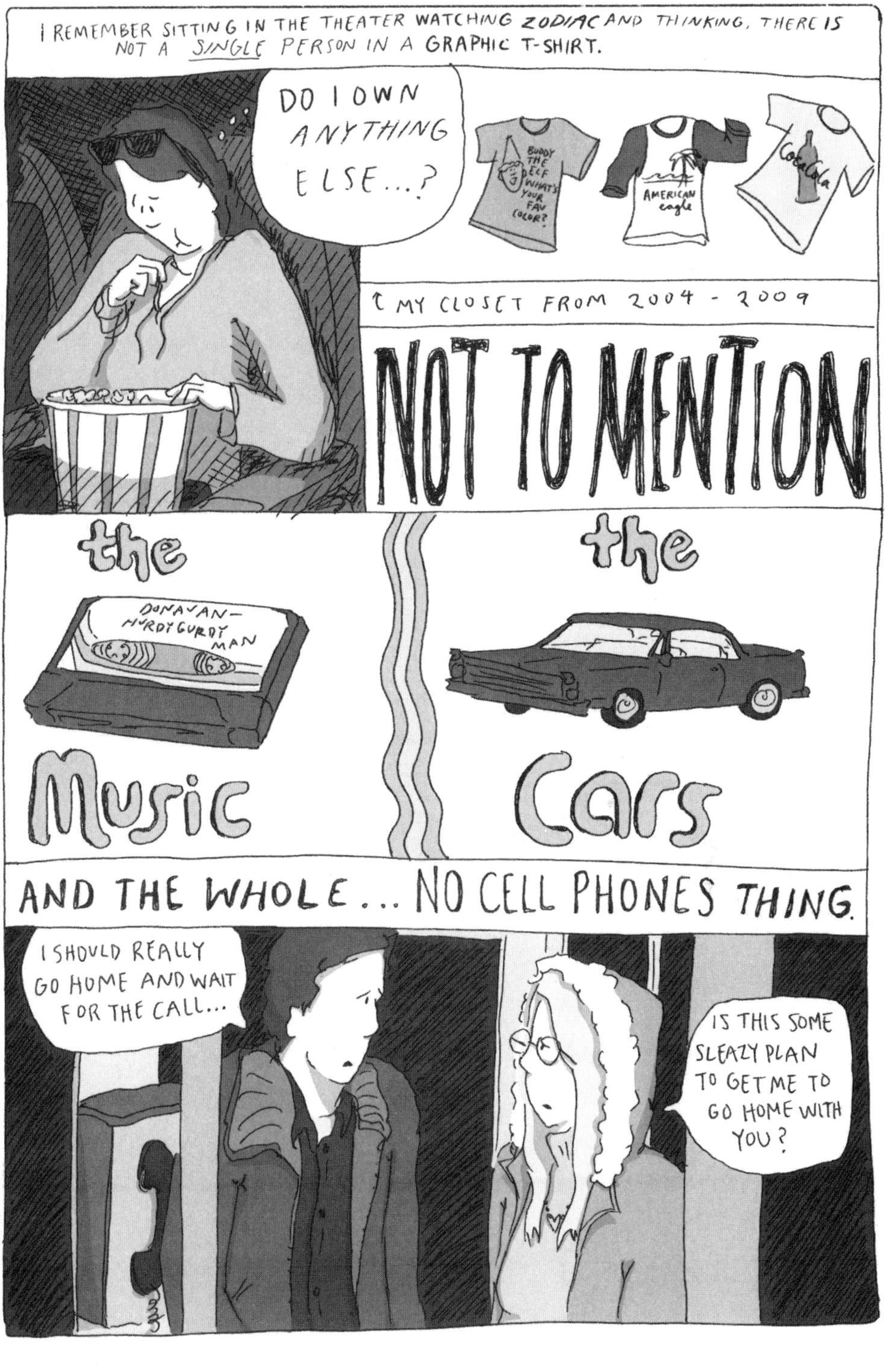
I REMEMBER SITTING IN THE THEATER WATCHING ZODIAC AND THINKING, THERE IS NOT A SINGLE PERSON IN A GRAPHIC T-SHIRT.
DO I OWN ANYTHING ELSE...?
BUDDY THE ELF WHAT'S YOUR FAV COLOR?
AMERICAN eagle
CocaCola
↑ MY CLOSET FROM 2004 - 2009
NOT TO MENTION
the
DONAVAN- HURDY GURDY MAN
Music
the
Cars
AND THE WHOLE... NO CELL PHONES THING.
I SHOULD REALLY GO HOME AND WAIT FOR THE CALL...
IS THIS SOME SLEAZY PLAN TO GET ME TO GO HOME WITH YOU?

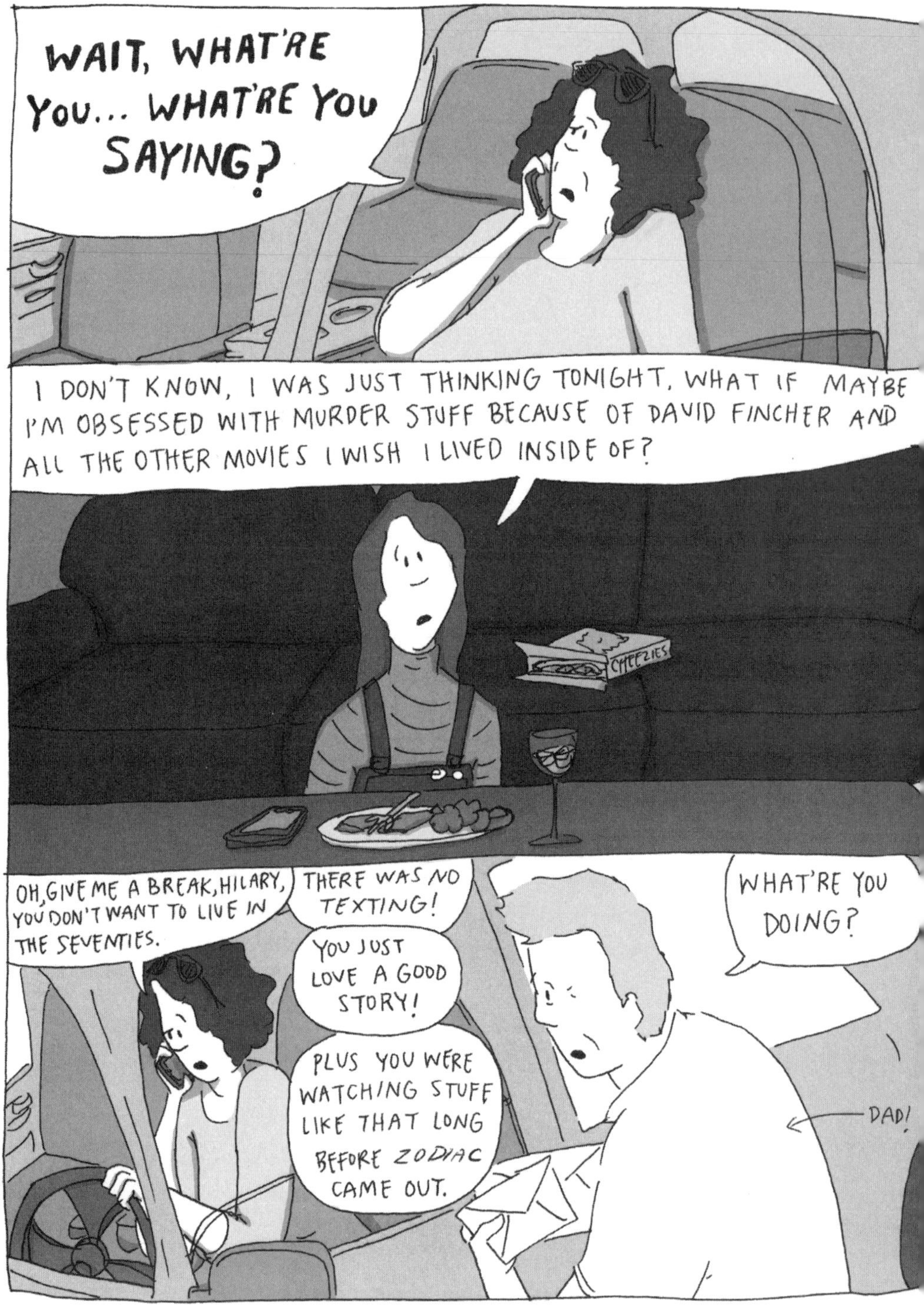
WAIT, WHAT'RE YOU... WHAT'RE YOU SAYING?
I DON'T KNOW, I WAS JUST THINKING TONIGHT, WHAT IF MAYBE I'M OBSESSED WITH MURDER STUFF BECAUSE OF DAVID FINCHER AND ALL THE OTHER MOVIES I WISH I LIVED INSIDE OF?
CHEEZIES
OH, GIVE ME A BREAK, HILARY, YOU DON'T WANT TO LIVE IN THE SEVENTIES.
THERE WAS NO TEXTING!
YOU JUST LOVE A GOOD STORY!
PLUS YOU WERE WATCHING STUFF LIKE THAT LONG BEFORE ZODIAC CAME OUT.
WHAT'RE YOU DOING?
DAD!

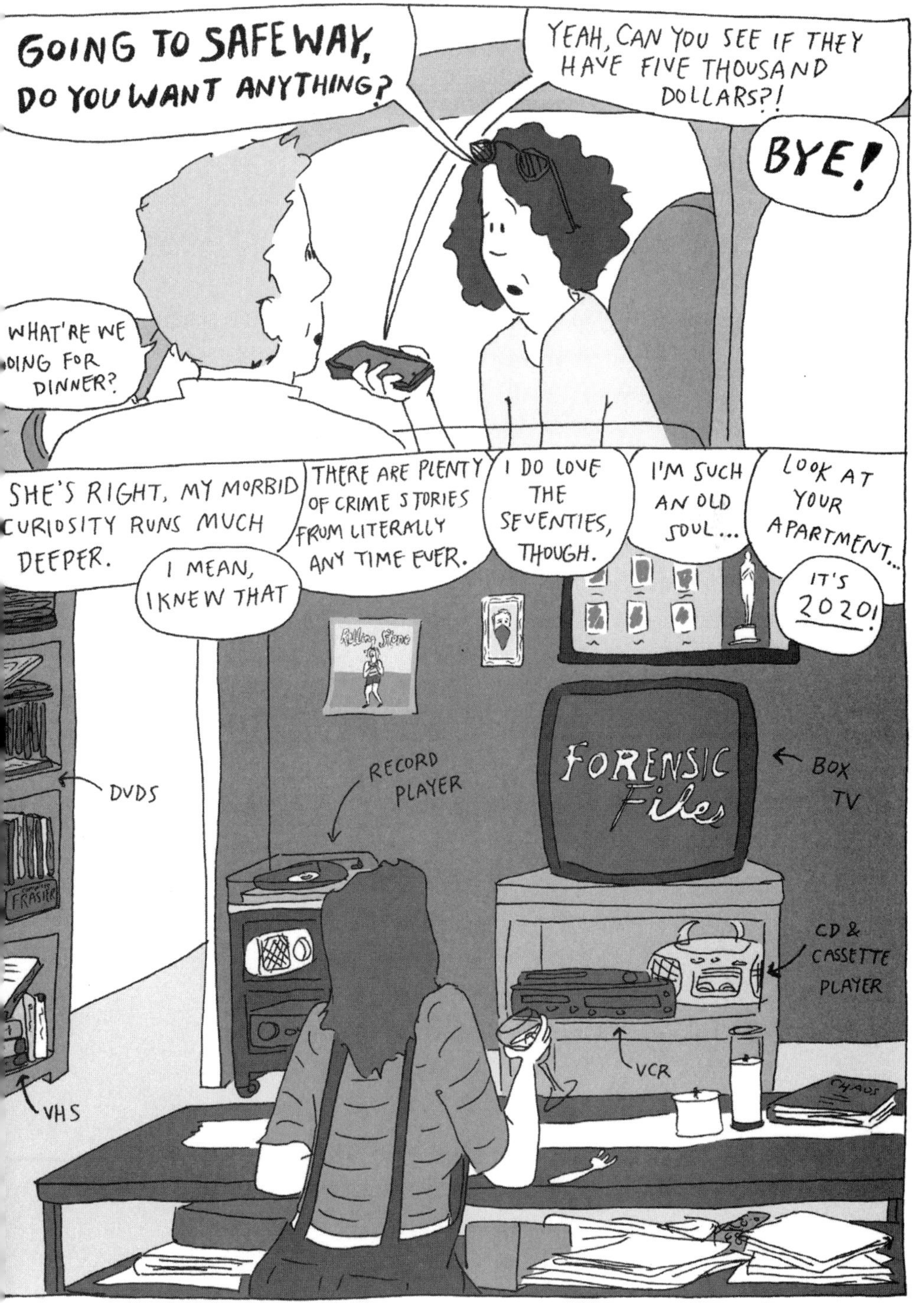
GOING TO SAFEWAY, DO YOU WANT ANYTHING?
YEAH, CAN YOU SEE IF THEY HAVE FIVE THOUSAND DOLLARS?!
BYE!
WHAT'RE WE DOING FOR DINNER?
SHE'S RIGHT, MY MORBID CURIOSITY RUNS MUCH DEEPER.
I MEAN, I KNEW THAT
THERE ARE PLENTY OF CRIME STORIES FROM LITERALLY ANY TIME EVER.
I DO LOVE THE SEVENTIES, THOUGH.
I'M SUCH AN OLD SOUL...
LOOK AT YOUR APARTMENT...
IT'S 2020!
Rolling Stone
FORENSIC Files
BOX TV
RECORD PLAYER
DVDS
FRASIER
CD & CASSETTE PLAYER
VCR
VHS
CHAOS

BLAME THE MOVIES

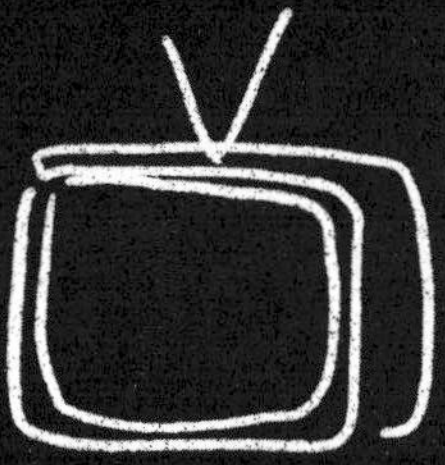

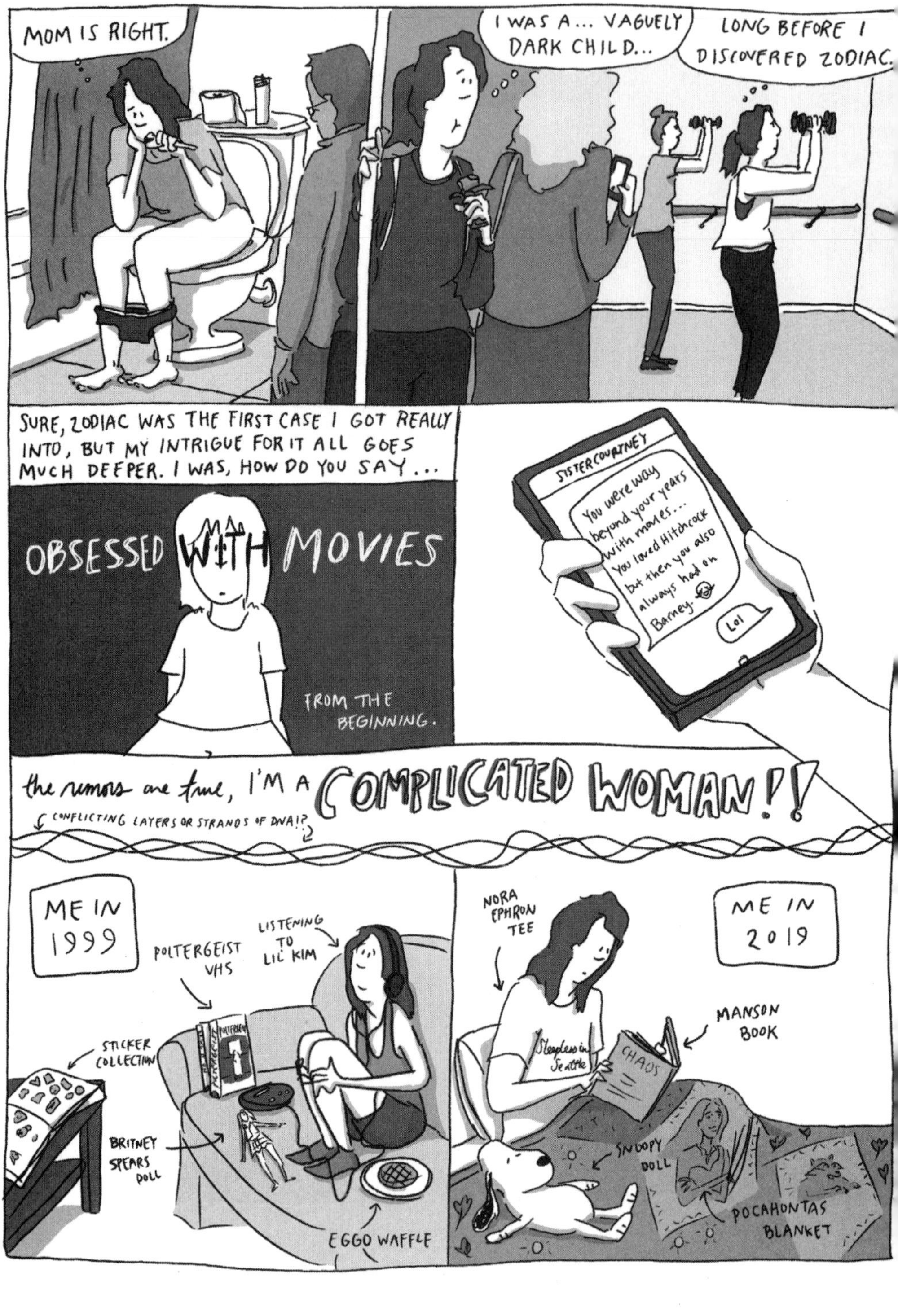

MOM IS RIGHT.
I WAS A... VAGUELY DARK CHILD...
LONG BEFORE I DISCOVERED ZODIAC.
SURE, ZODIAC WAS THE FIRST CASE I GOT REALLY INTO, BUT MY INTRIGUE FOR IT ALL GOES MUCH DEEPER. I WAS, HOW DO YOU SAY...
OBSESSED WITH MOVIES
FROM THE BEGINNING.
SISTER COURTNEY
You were way beyond your years with movies... You loved Hitchcock but then you also always had on Barney.
Lol
the rumors are true, I'M A COMPLICATED WOMAN!!
CONFLICTING LAYERS OR STRANDS OF DNA!?
ME IN 1999
POLTERGEIST VHS
LISTENING TO LIL' KIM
STICKER COLLECTION
BRITNEY SPEARS DOLL
EGGO WAFFLE
NORA EPHRON TEE
ME IN 2019
Sleepless in Seattle
CHAOS
MANSON BOOK
SNOOPY DOLL
POCAHONTAS BLANKET

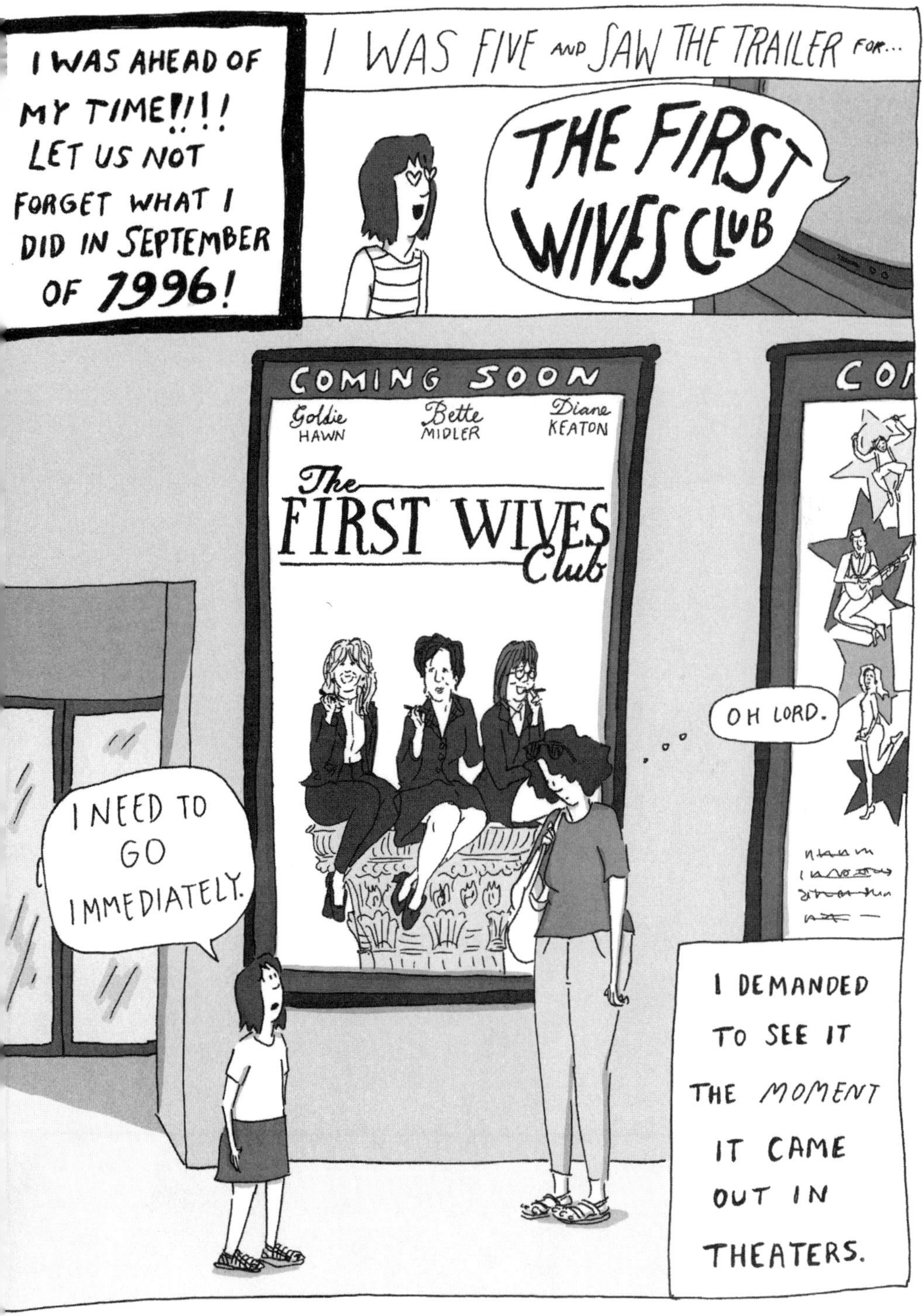
I WAS AHEAD OF MY TIME!!!! LET US NOT FORGET WHAT I DID IN SEPTEMBER OF 1996!
I WAS FIVE AND SAW THE TRAILER FOR...
THE FIRST WIVES CLUB
COMING SOON
Goldie HAWN
Bette MIDLER
Diane KEATON
The FIRST WIVES Club
I NEED TO GO IMMEDIATELY.
OH LORD.
I DEMANDED TO SEE IT THE MOMENT IT CAME OUT IN THEATERS.

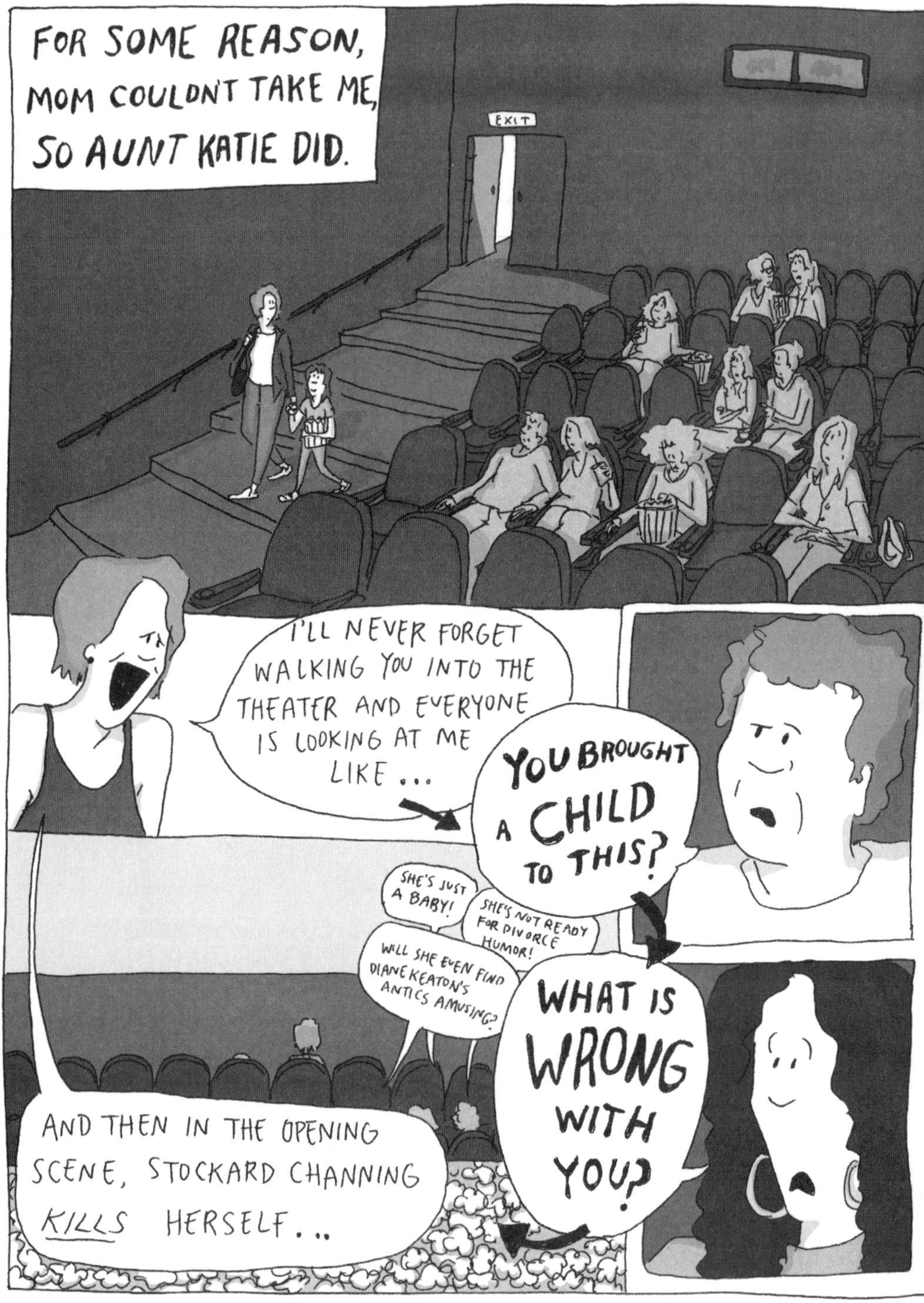
FOR SOME REASON, MOM COULDN'T TAKE ME, SO AUNT KATIE DID.
EXIT
I'LL NEVER FORGET WALKING YOU INTO THE THEATER AND EVERYONE IS LOOKING AT ME LIKE...
YOU BROUGHT A CHILD TO THIS?
SHE'S JUST A BABY!
SHE'S NOT READY FOR DIVORCE HUMOR!
WILL SHE EVEN FIND DIANE KEATON'S ANTICS AMUSING?
WHAT IS WRONG WITH YOU?
AND THEN IN THE OPENING SCENE, STOCKARD CHANNING KILLS HERSELF...

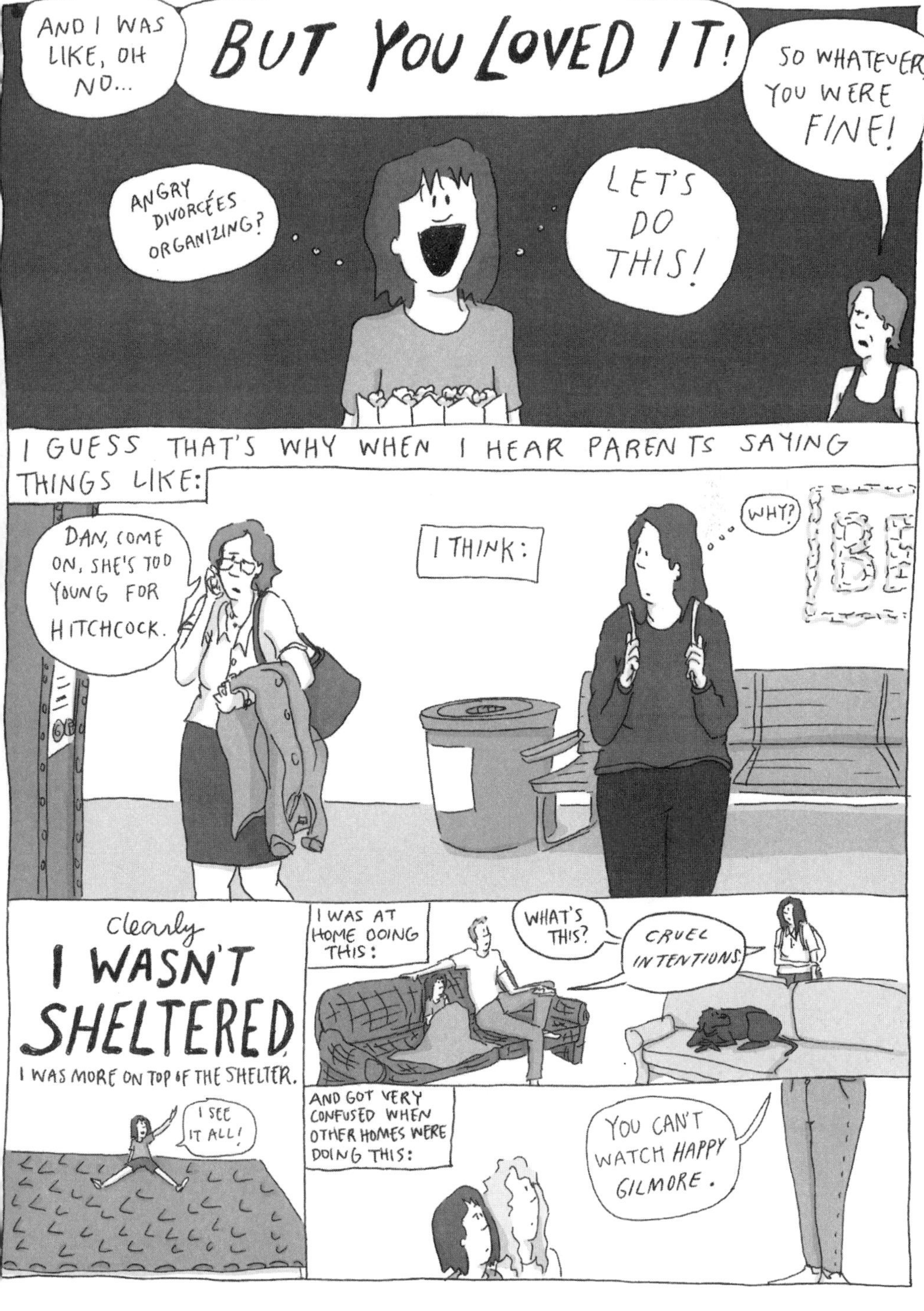
AND I WAS LIKE, OH NO...
BUT YOU LOVED IT!
SO WHATEVER, YOU WERE FINE!
ANGRY DIVORCÉES ORGANIZING?
LET'S DO THIS!
I GUESS THAT'S WHY WHEN I HEAR PARENTS SAYING THINGS LIKE:
DAN, COME ON, SHE'S TOO YOUNG FOR HITCHCOCK.
I THINK:
WHY?
Clearly I WASN'T SHELTERED, I WAS MORE ON TOP OF THE SHELTER.
I SEE IT ALL!
I WAS AT HOME DOING THIS:
WHAT'S THIS?
CRUEL INTENTIONS.
AND GOT VERY CONFUSED WHEN OTHER HOMES WERE DOING THIS:
YOU CAN'T WATCH HAPPY GILMORE.

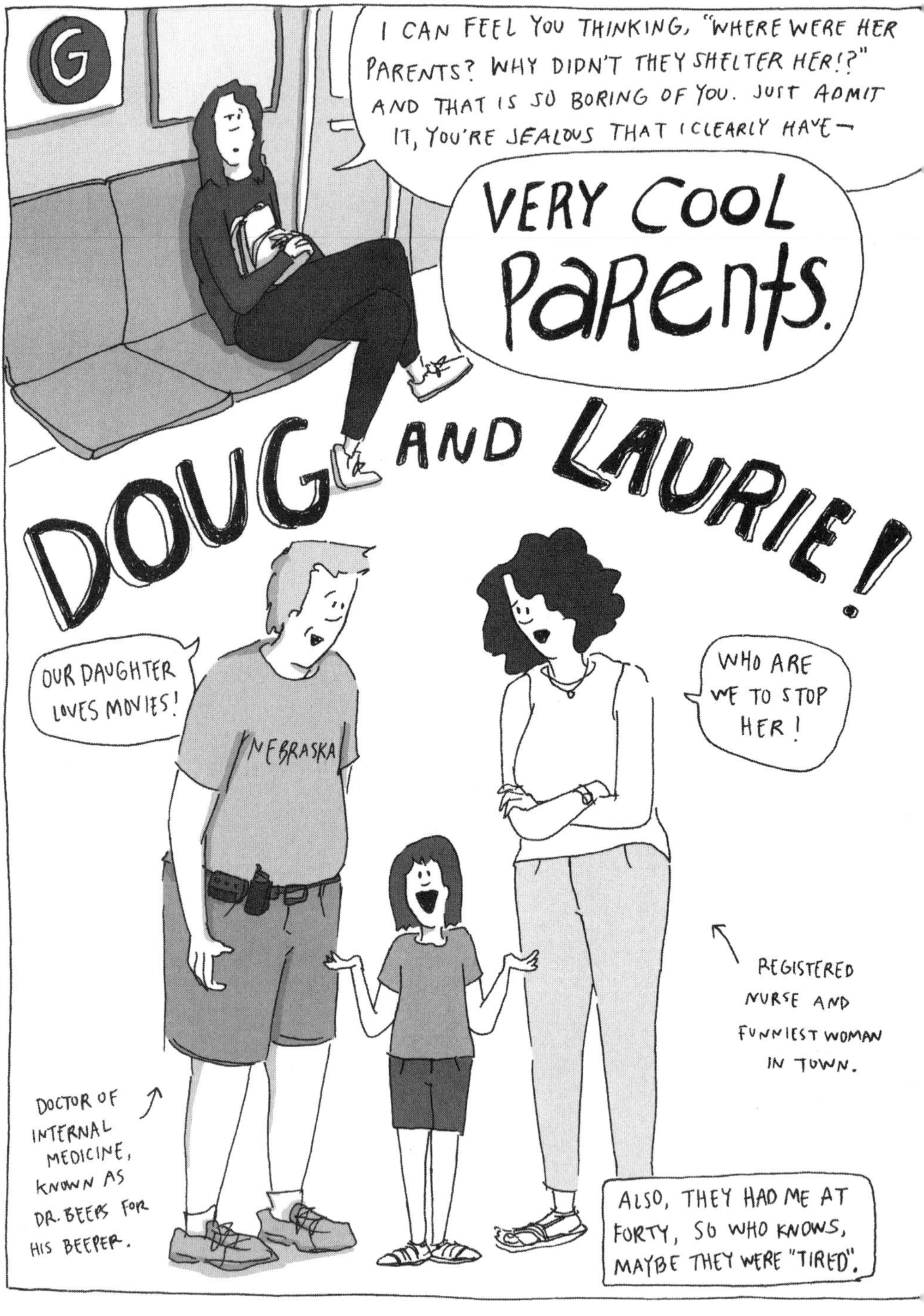
G
I CAN FEEL YOU THINKING, "WHERE WERE HER PARENTS? WHY DIDN'T THEY SHELTER HER!?" AND THAT IS SO BORING OF YOU. JUST ADMIT IT, YOU'RE JEALOUS THAT I CLEARLY HAVE—
VERY COOL Parents.
DOUG AND LAURIE!
OUR DAUGHTER LOVES MOVIES!
WHO ARE WE TO STOP HER!
NEBRASKA
REGISTERED NURSE AND FUNNIEST WOMAN IN TOWN.
DOCTOR OF INTERNAL MEDICINE, KNOWN AS DR. BEEPS FOR HIS BEEPER.
ALSO, THEY HAD ME AT FORTY, SO WHO KNOWS, MAYBE THEY WERE "TIRED".

IT WASN'T THAT I WASN'T *Wholesome*, I JUST WANTED TO SEE IT **ALL** ... I WENT BOTH WAYS, IF YOU WILL.

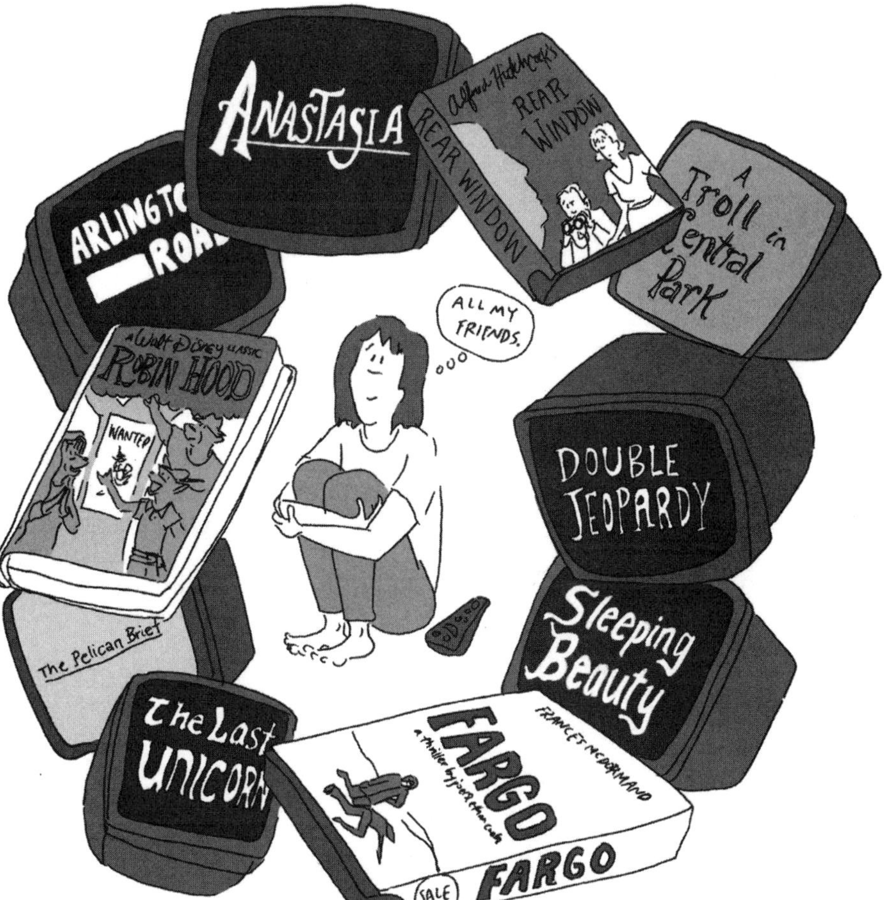
ANASTASIA
Alfred Hitchcock's
REAR WINDOW
REAR WINDOW
A Troll in Central Park
ARLINGTO
ROA
A Walt Disney Classic
ROBIN HOOD
WANTED
ALL MY FRIENDS.
DOUBLE JEOPARDY
Sleeping Beauty
The Pelican Brief
The Last Unicorn
FARGO
FRANCES MCDORMAND
SALE
FARGO

THE DISNEY MOVIES MAKE SENSE, BUT THE JOHN GRISHAM STANDS OUT (TO SOME, LESS INTERESTING, HUMANS...).

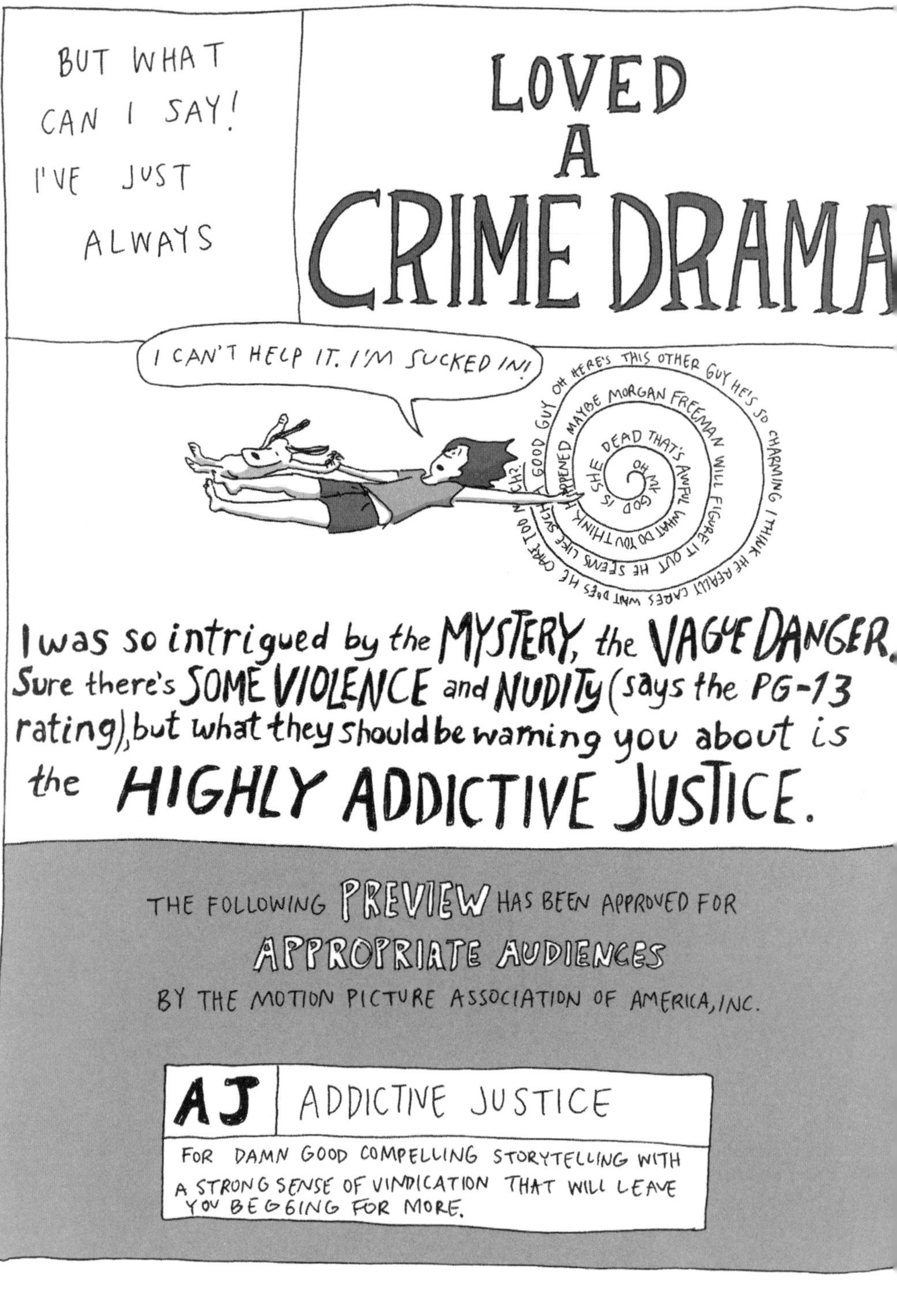
BUT WHAT CAN I SAY! I'VE JUST ALWAYS
LOVED A CRIME DRAMA
I CAN'T HELP IT. I'M SUCKED IN!
OH MY GOD IS SHE DEAD THAT'S AWFUL WHAT DO YOU THINK HAPPENED MAYBE MORGAN FREEMAN WILL FIGURE IT OUT HE SEEMS LIKE SUCH A GOOD GUY OH HERE'S THIS OTHER GUY HE'S SO CHARMING I THINK HE REALLY CARES WHAT DOES HE CARE TOO MUCH?
I was so intrigued by the MYSTERY, the VAGUE DANGER. Sure there's SOME VIOLENCE and NUDITY (says the PG-13 rating), but what they should be warning you about is the HIGHLY ADDICTIVE JUSTICE.
THE FOLLOWING PREVIEW HAS BEEN APPROVED FOR APPROPRIATE AUDIENCES BY THE MOTION PICTURE ASSOCIATION OF AMERICA, INC.
AJ
ADDICTIVE JUSTICE
FOR DAMN GOOD COMPELLING STORYTELLING WITH A STRONG SENSE OF VINDICATION THAT WILL LEAVE YOU BEGGING FOR MORE.

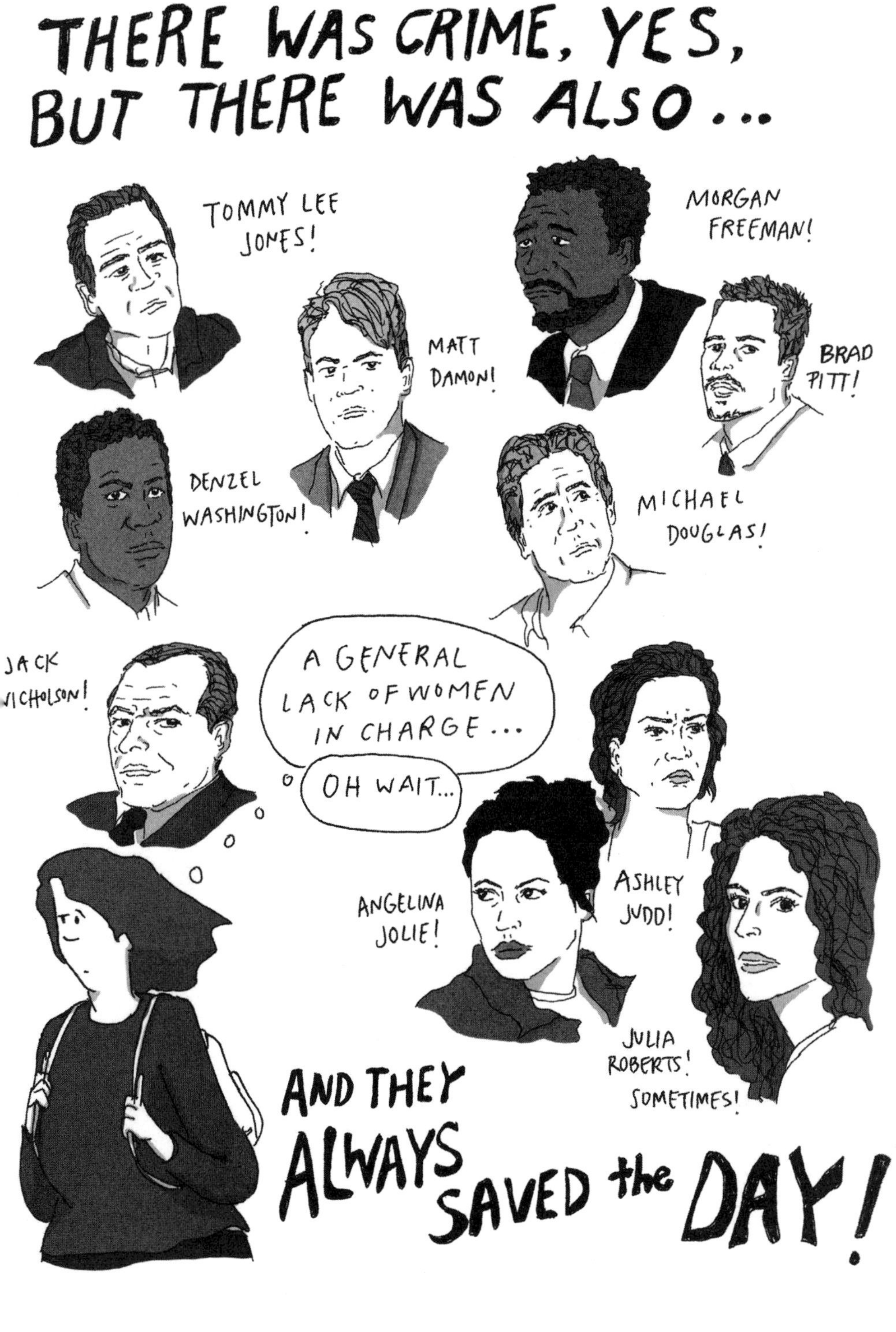
THERE WAS CRIME, YES, BUT THERE WAS ALSO...
TOMMY LEE JONES!
MORGAN FREEMAN!
MATT DAMON!
BRAD PITT!
DENZEL WASHINGTON!
MICHAEL DOUGLAS!
JACK ICHOLSON!
A GENERAL LACK OF WOMEN IN CHARGE...
OH WAIT...
ANGELINA JOLIE!
ASHLEY JUDD!
JULIA ROBERTS!
SOMETIMES!
AND THEY ALWAYS SAVED the DAY!

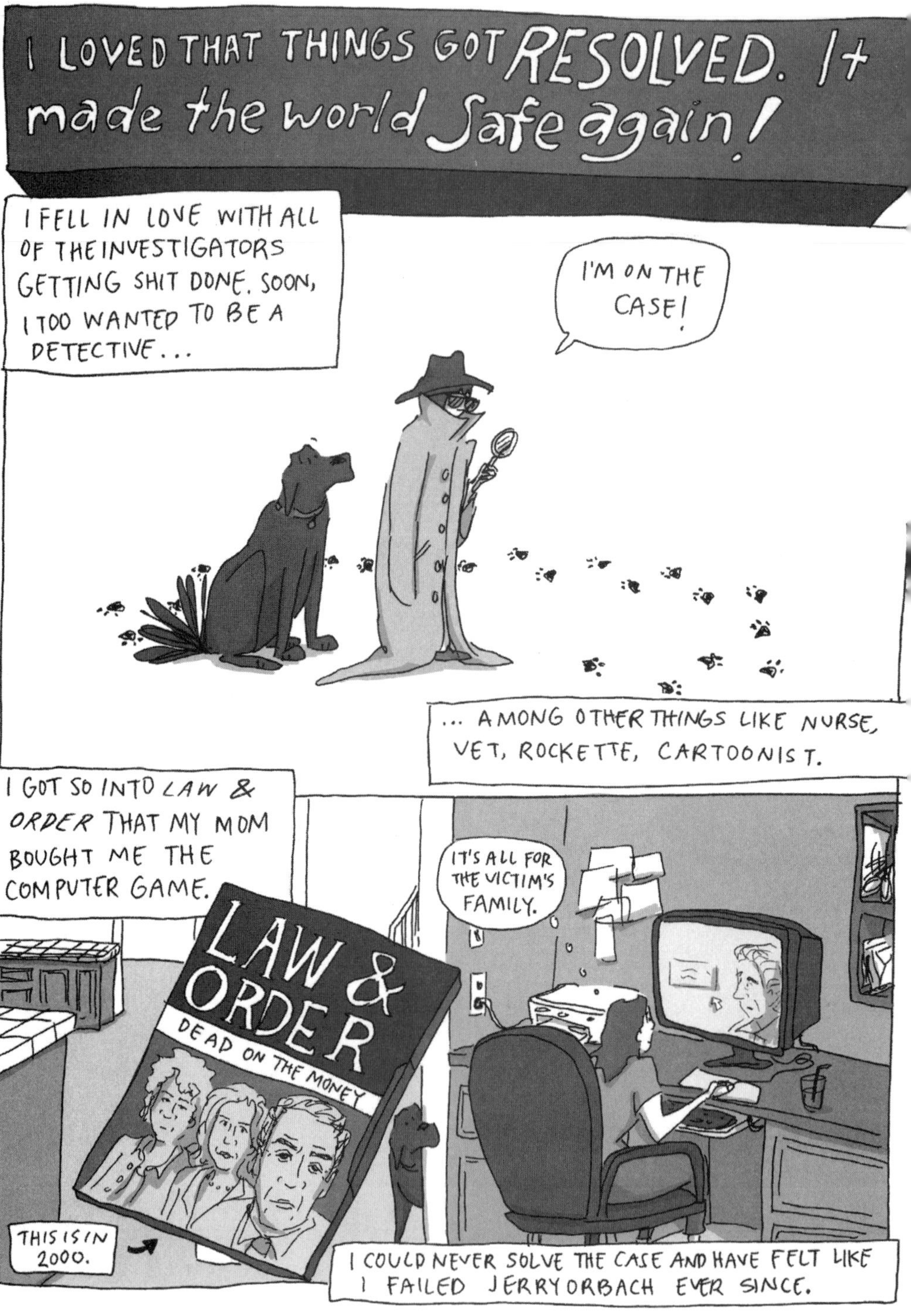
I LOVED THAT THINGS GOT RESOLVED. It made the world safe again!
I FELL IN LOVE WITH ALL OF THE INVESTIGATORS GETTING SHIT DONE. SOON, I TOO WANTED TO BE A DETECTIVE...
I'M ON THE CASE!
... AMONG OTHER THINGS LIKE NURSE, VET, ROCKETTE, CARTOONIST.
I GOT SO INTO LAW & ORDER THAT MY MOM BOUGHT ME THE COMPUTER GAME.
LAW & ORDER
DEAD ON THE MONEY
IT'S ALL FOR THE VICTIM'S FAMILY.
THIS IS IN 2000.
I COULD NEVER SOLVE THE CASE AND HAVE FELT LIKE I FAILED JERRY ORBACH EVER SINCE.

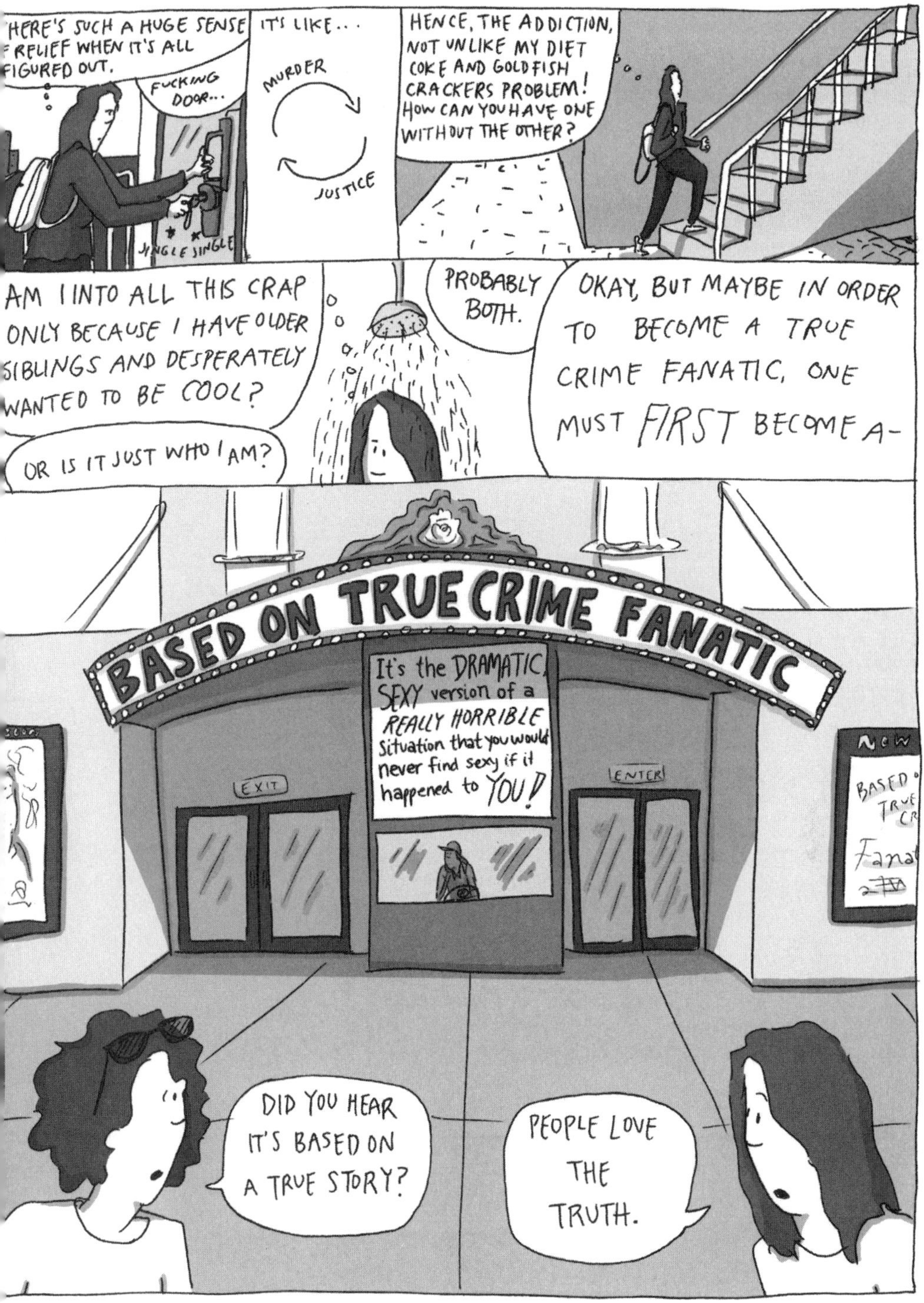
HERE'S SUCH A HUGE SENSE OF RELIEF WHEN IT'S ALL FIGURED OUT.
FUCKING DOOR...
JINGLE JINGLE
IT'S LIKE...
MURDER
JUSTICE
HENCE, THE ADDICTION, NOT UNLIKE MY DIET COKE AND GOLDFISH CRACKERS PROBLEM! HOW CAN YOU HAVE ONE WITHOUT THE OTHER?
AM I INTO ALL THIS CRAP ONLY BECAUSE I HAVE OLDER SIBLINGS AND DESPERATELY WANTED TO BE COOL?
OR IS IT JUST WHO I AM?
PROBABLY BOTH.
OKAY, BUT MAYBE IN ORDER TO BECOME A TRUE CRIME FANATIC, ONE MUST FIRST BECOME A-
BASED ON TRUE CRIME FANATIC
It's the DRAMATIC, SEXY version of a REALLY HORRIBLE situation that you would never find sexy if it happened to YOU!
EXIT
ENTER
DID YOU HEAR IT'S BASED ON A TRUE STORY?
PEOPLE LOVE THE TRUTH.

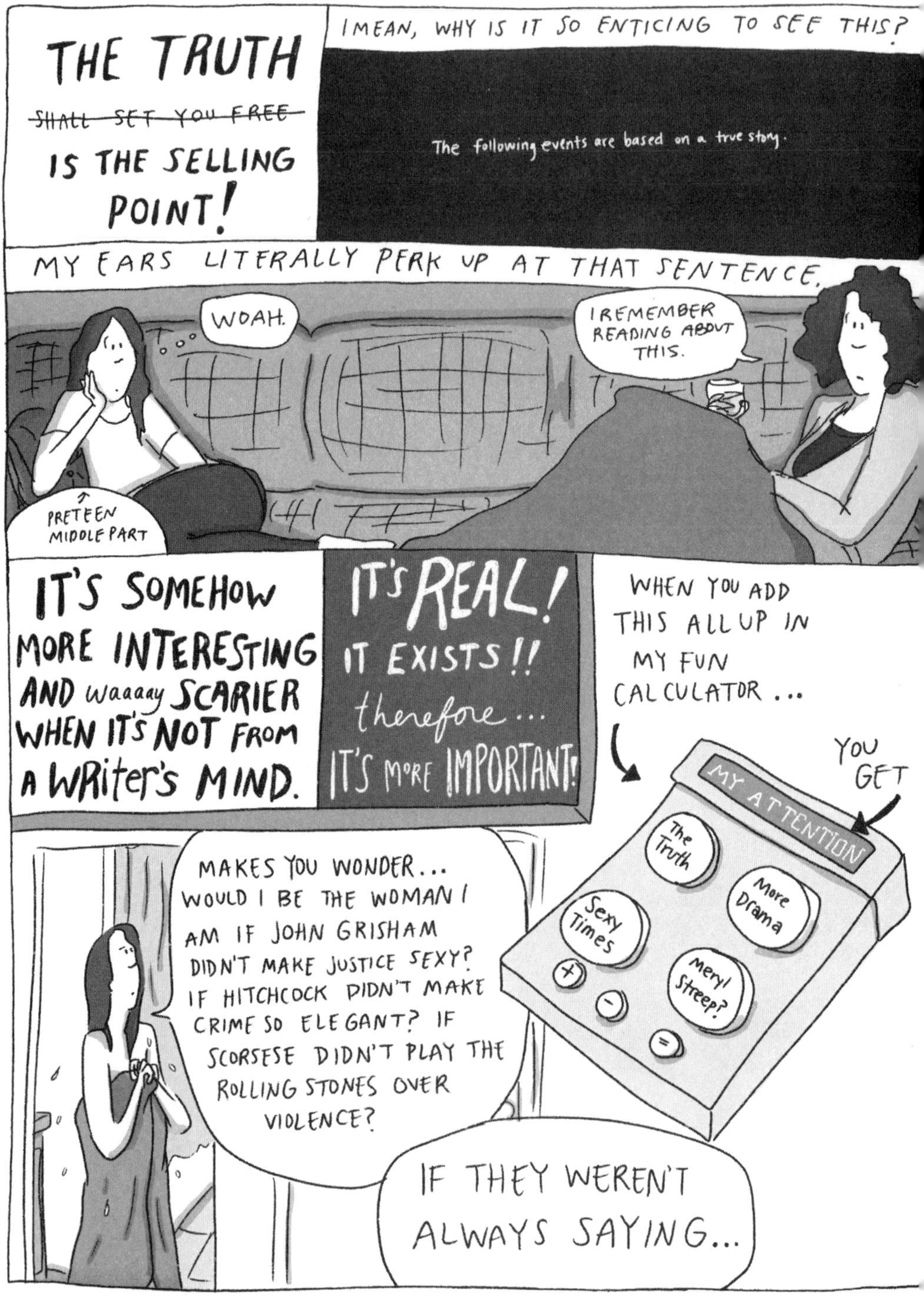
THE TRUTH
SHALL SET YOU FREE
IS THE SELLING POINT!
I MEAN, WHY IS IT SO ENTICING TO SEE THIS?
The following events are based on a true story.
MY EARS LITERALLY PERK UP AT THAT SENTENCE.
WOAH.
I REMEMBER READING ABOUT THIS.
PRETEEN MIDDLE PART
IT'S SOMEHOW MORE INTERESTING AND waaaay SCARIER WHEN IT'S NOT FROM A WRITER'S MIND.
IT'S REAL! IT EXISTS!! therefore... IT'S MORE IMPORTANT!
WHEN YOU ADD THIS ALL UP IN MY FUN CALCULATOR...
YOU GET
MY ATTENTION
The Truth
More Drama
Sexy Times
Meryl Streep?
+
-
=
MAKES YOU WONDER... WOULD I BE THE WOMAN I AM IF JOHN GRISHAM DIDN'T MAKE JUSTICE SEXY? IF HITCHCOCK DIDN'T MAKE CRIME SO ELEGANT? IF SCORSESE DIDN'T PLAY THE ROLLING STONES OVER VIOLENCE?
IF THEY WEREN'T ALWAYS SAYING...

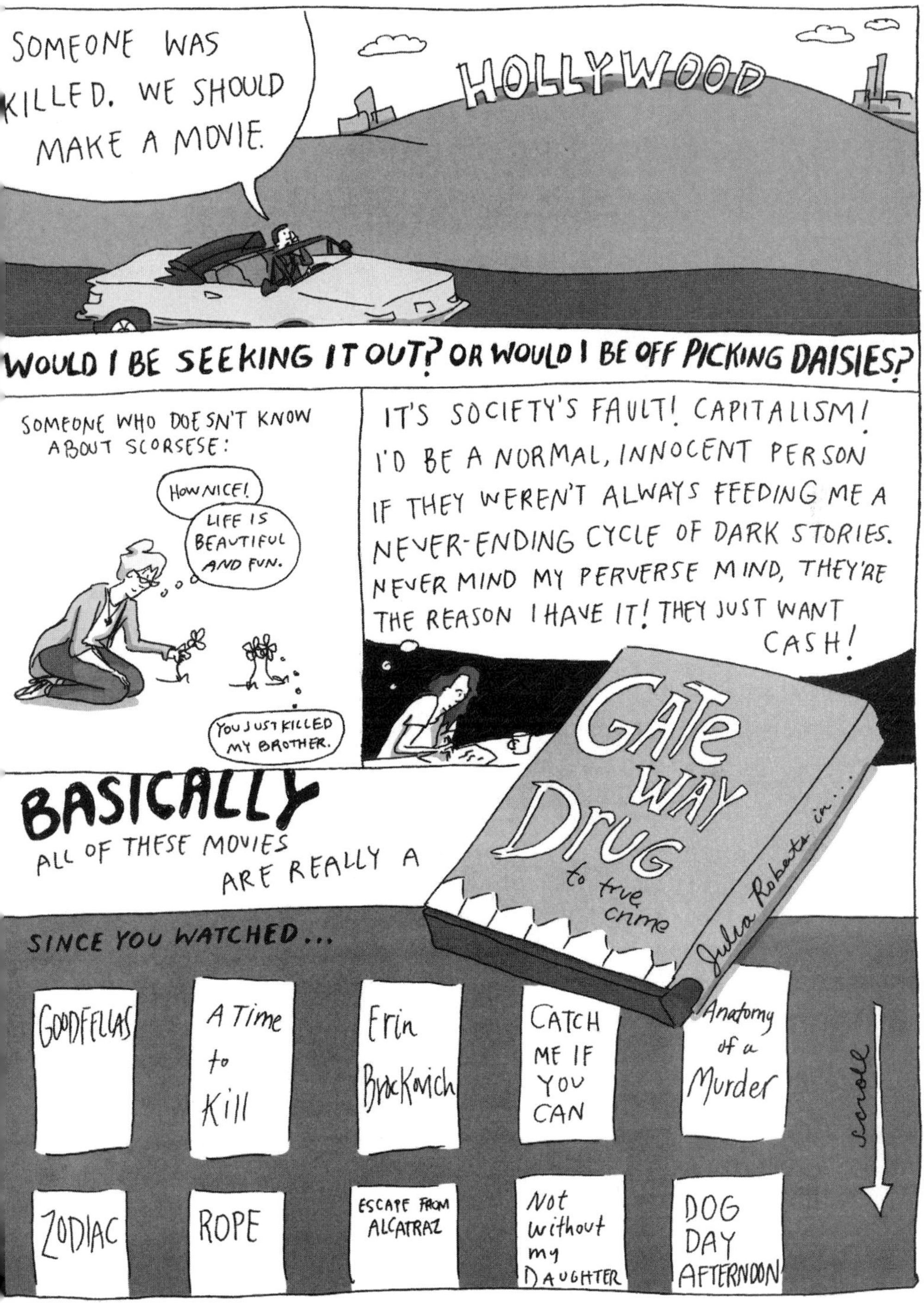
SOMEONE WAS KILLED. WE SHOULD MAKE A MOVIE.
HOLLYWOOD
WOULD I BE SEEKING IT OUT? OR WOULD I BE OFF PICKING DAISIES?
SOMEONE WHO DOESN'T KNOW ABOUT SCORSESE:
HOW NICE!
LIFE IS BEAUTIFUL AND FUN.
YOU JUST KILLED MY BROTHER.
IT'S SOCIETY'S FAULT! CAPITALISM! I'D BE A NORMAL, INNOCENT PERSON IF THEY WEREN'T ALWAYS FEEDING ME A NEVER-ENDING CYCLE OF DARK STORIES. NEVER MIND MY PERVERSE MIND, THEY'RE THE REASON I HAVE IT! THEY JUST WANT CASH!
BASICALLY
ALL OF THESE MOVIES ARE REALLY A
GATEWAY DRUG to true crime
Julia Roberts in...
SINCE YOU WATCHED...
GOODFELLAS
A Time to Kill
Erin Brockovich
CATCH ME IF YOU CAN
Anatomy of a Murder
scroll
ZODIAC
ROPE
ESCAPE FROM ALCATRAZ
Not without my DAUGHTER
DOG DAY AFTERNOON

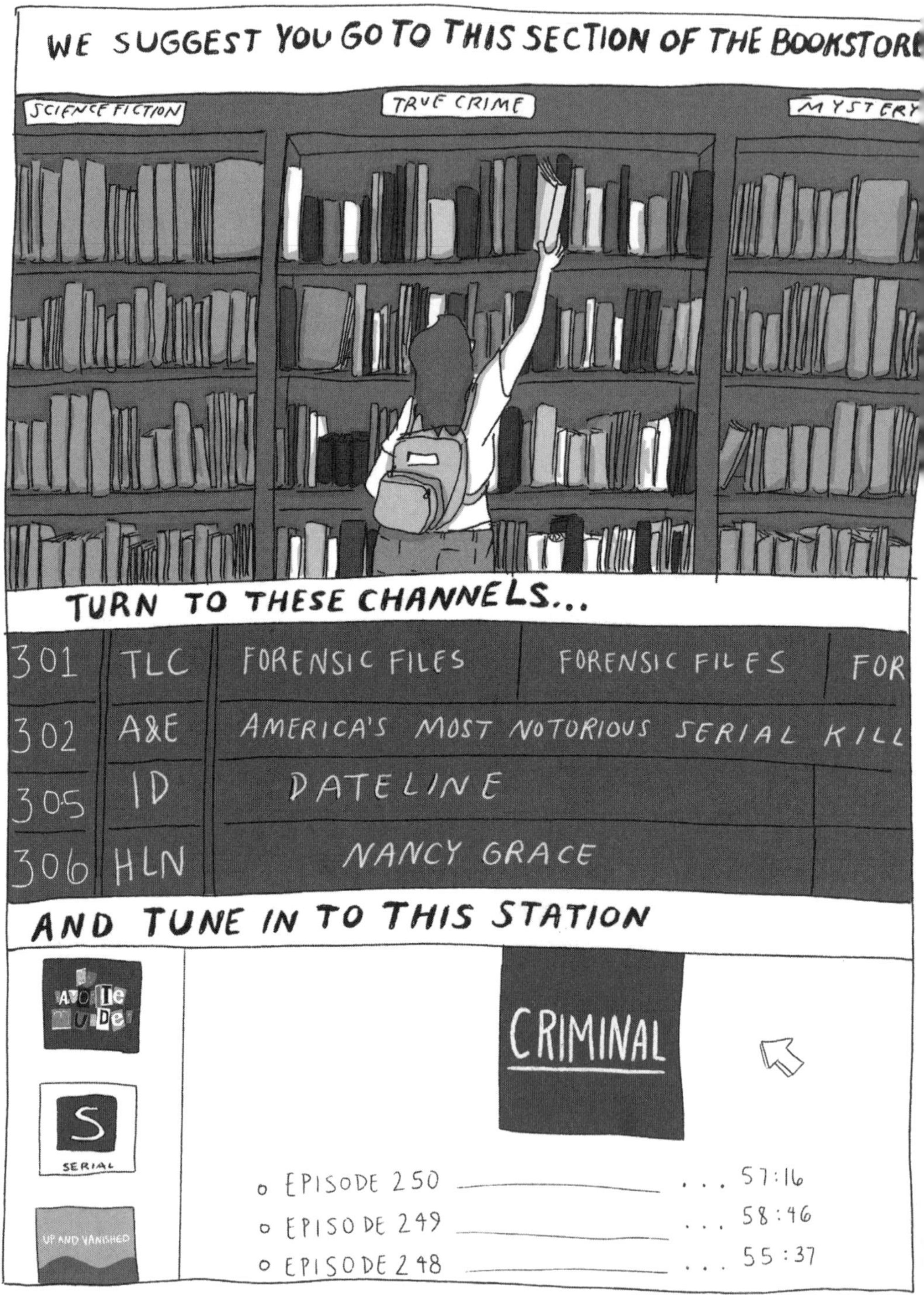
WE SUGGEST YOU GO TO THIS SECTION OF THE BOOKSTORE
SCIENCE FICTION
TRUE CRIME
MYSTERY
TURN TO THESE CHANNELS...
301 TLC FORENSIC FILES FORENSIC FILES FOR
302 A&E AMERICA'S MOST NOTORIOUS SERIAL KILL
305 ID DATELINE
306 HLN NANCY GRACE
AND TUNE IN TO THIS STATION
S
SERIAL
UP AND VANISHED
CRIMINAL
EPISODE 250 ... 57:16
EPISODE 249 ... 58:46
EPISODE 248 ... 55:37

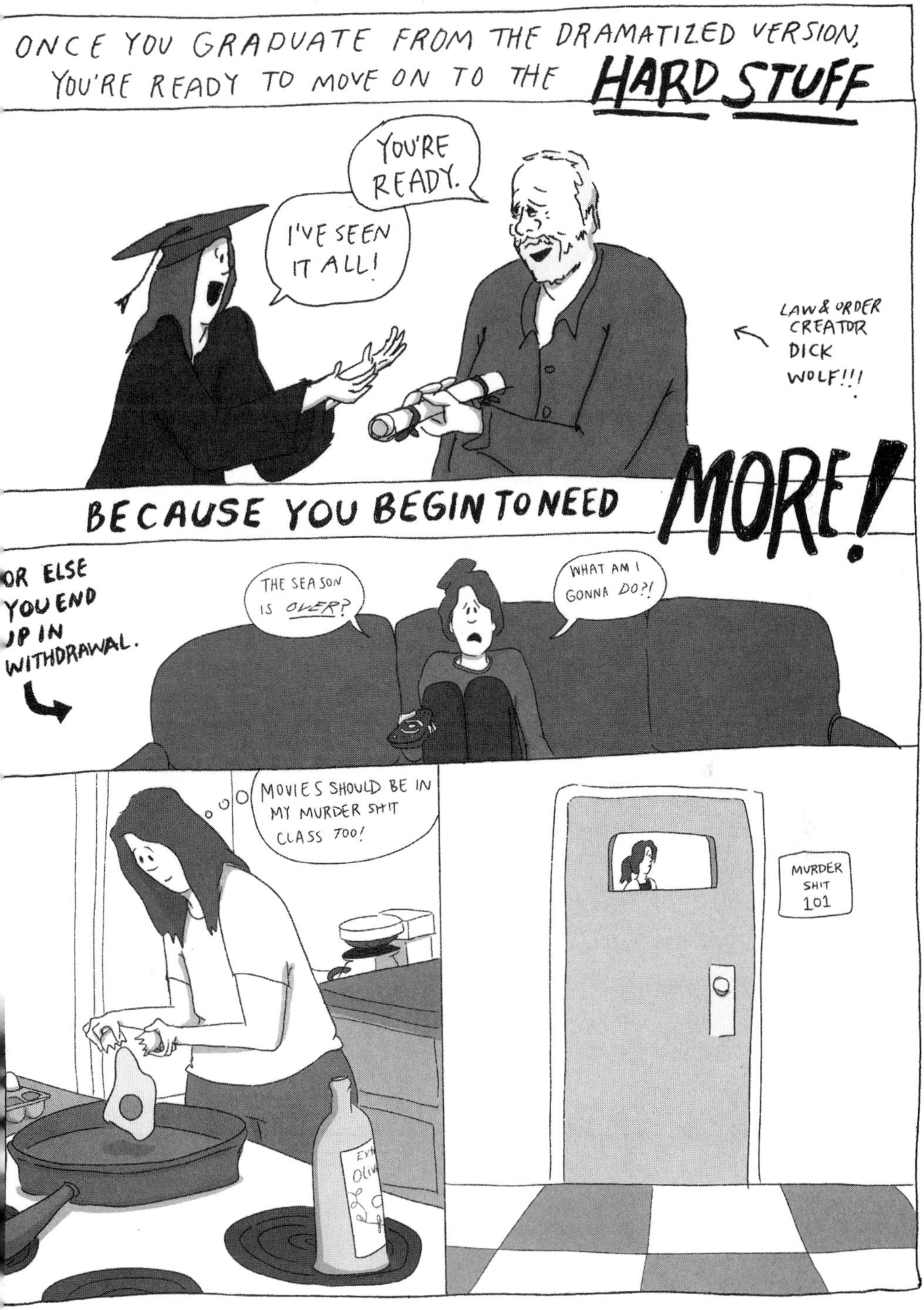
ONCE YOU GRADUATE FROM THE DRAMATIZED VERSION, YOU'RE READY TO MOVE ON TO THE HARD STUFF
I'VE SEEN IT ALL!
YOU'RE READY.
LAW & ORDER CREATOR DICK WOLF!!!
BECAUSE YOU BEGIN TO NEED MORE!
OR ELSE YOU END UP IN WITHDRAWAL.
THE SEASON IS OVER?
WHAT AM I GONNA DO?!
MOVIES SHOULD BE IN MY MURDER SHIT CLASS TOO!
MURDER SHIT 101

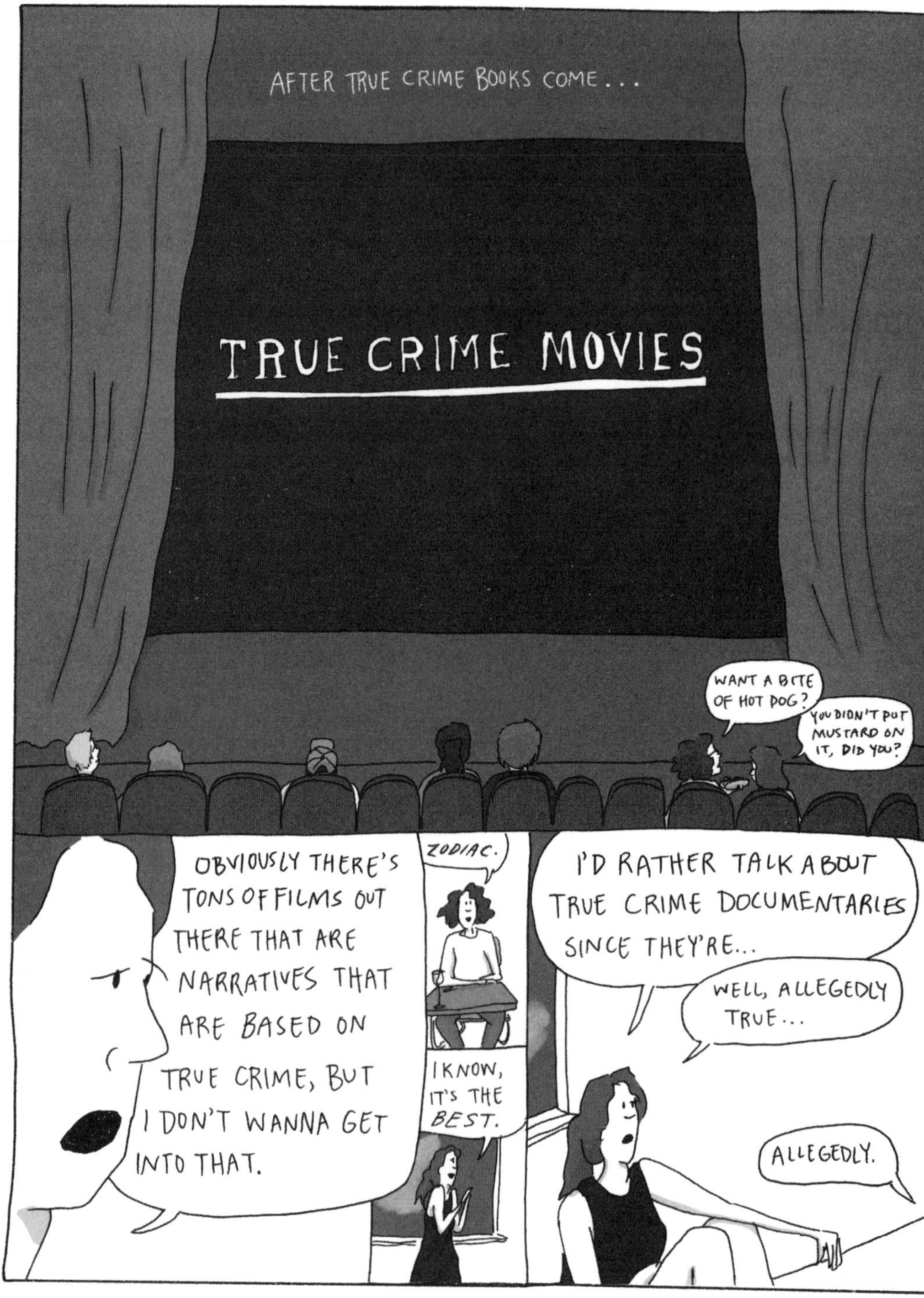

AFTER TRUE CRIME BOOKS COME...
TRUE CRIME MOVIES
WANT A BITE OF HOT DOG?
YOU DIDN'T PUT MUSTARD ON IT, DID YOU?
OBVIOUSLY THERE'S TONS OF FILMS OUT THERE THAT ARE NARRATIVES THAT ARE BASED ON TRUE CRIME, BUT I DON'T WANNA GET INTO THAT.
ZODIAC.
I KNOW, IT'S THE BEST.
I'D RATHER TALK ABOUT TRUE CRIME DOCUMENTARIES SINCE THEY'RE...
WELL, ALLEGEDLY TRUE...
ALLEGEDLY.

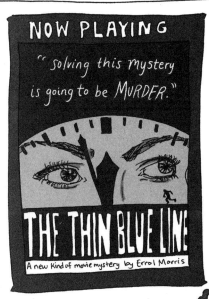

NOW PLAYING

"Solving this mystery is going to be MURDER."

THE THIN BLUE LINE

A new Kind of movie mystery by Errol Morris

THE "FIRST"* BIG, POPULAR DOCUMENTARY ABOUT A CRIME WAS ERROL MORRIS' 1988 FILM *THE THIN BLUE LINE.* IT WAS A GROUNDBREAKING PIECE. IT PROVED THE GUY WAS INNOCENT— IT GOT HIM ACQUITTED!

FREE, BITCH!

* IN AMERICA, I'M SURE EUROPE WAS AHEAD OF US.

AFTER that came MORE FILMS from MEN.

COMING SOON

BROTHER'S KEEPER

1992

COMING SOON

PARADISE LOST

THE CHILD MURDERS AT ROBIN HOOD HILLS

1996

COMING SOON

Capturing the Friedmans

who do you believe?

2003

MICHAEL MOORE

BOWLING for COLUMBINE

WACO

THE RULES OF ENGAGEMENT

CRAZYLOVE
HE HAD TO HAVE HER

TAXI TO THE DARKSIDE

INTO THE ABYSS

THE CENTRAL PARK FIVE

* AND MANY MANY MORE FILMS FROM MEN.

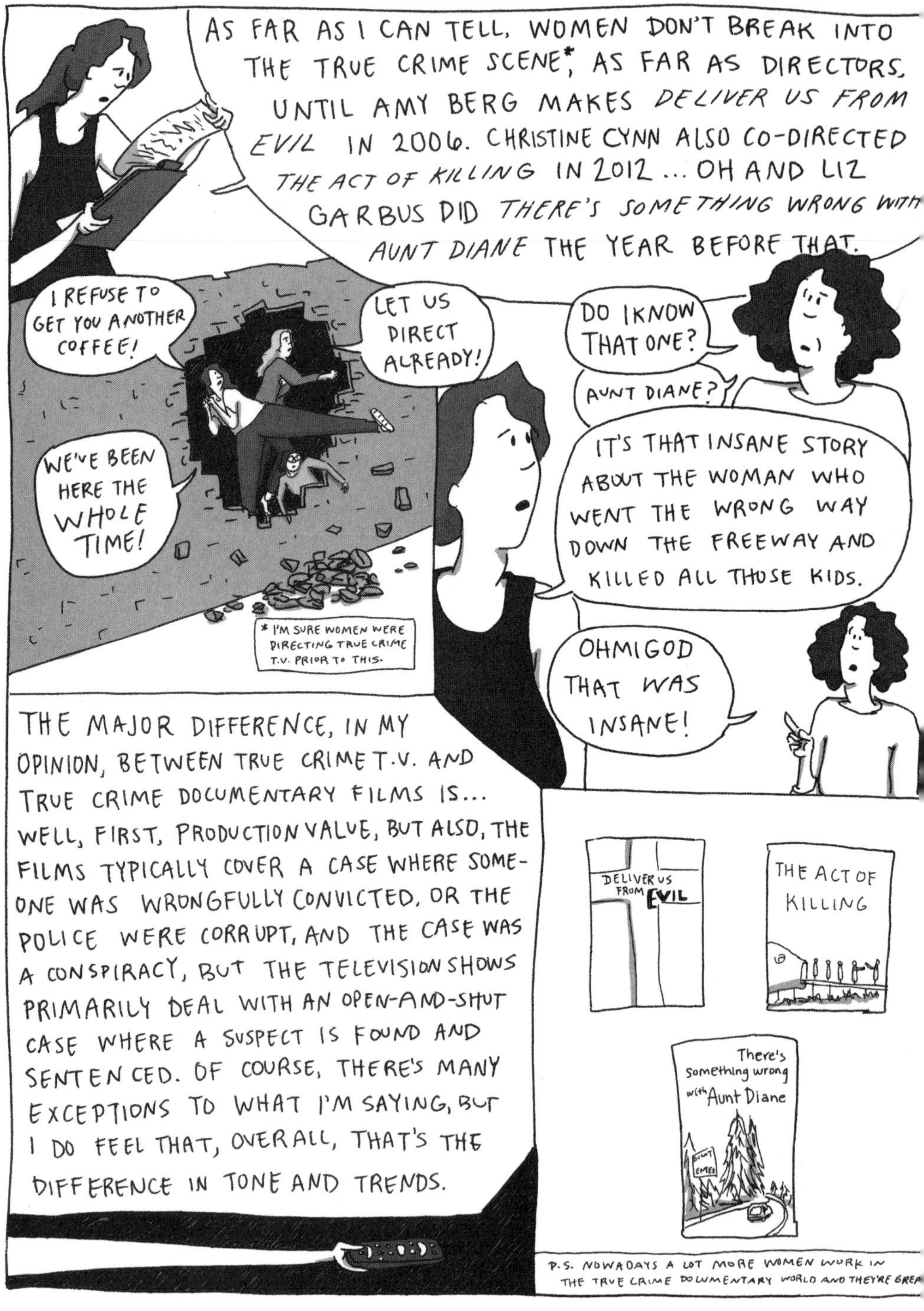
AS FAR AS I CAN TELL, WOMEN DON'T BREAK INTO THE TRUE CRIME SCENE*, AS FAR AS DIRECTORS, UNTIL AMY BERG MAKES *DELIVER US FROM EVIL* IN 2006. CHRISTINE CYNN ALSO CO-DIRECTED *THE ACT OF KILLING* IN 2012 ... OH AND LIZ GARBUS DID *THERE'S SOMETHING WRONG WITH AUNT DIANE* THE YEAR BEFORE THAT.
I REFUSE TO GET YOU ANOTHER COFFEE!
LET US DIRECT ALREADY!
WE'VE BEEN HERE THE WHOLE TIME!
* I'M SURE WOMEN WERE DIRECTING TRUE CRIME T.V. PRIOR TO THIS.
DO I KNOW THAT ONE?
AUNT DIANE?
IT'S THAT INSANE STORY ABOUT THE WOMAN WHO WENT THE WRONG WAY DOWN THE FREEWAY AND KILLED ALL THOSE KIDS.
OHMIGOD THAT WAS INSANE!
THE MAJOR DIFFERENCE, IN MY OPINION, BETWEEN TRUE CRIME T.V. AND TRUE CRIME DOCUMENTARY FILMS IS... WELL, FIRST, PRODUCTION VALUE, BUT ALSO, THE FILMS TYPICALLY COVER A CASE WHERE SOMEONE WAS WRONGFULLY CONVICTED, OR THE POLICE WERE CORRUPT, AND THE CASE WAS A CONSPIRACY, BUT THE TELEVISION SHOWS PRIMARILY DEAL WITH AN OPEN-AND-SHUT CASE WHERE A SUSPECT IS FOUND AND SENTENCED. OF COURSE, THERE'S MANY EXCEPTIONS TO WHAT I'M SAYING, BUT I DO FEEL THAT, OVERALL, THAT'S THE DIFFERENCE IN TONE AND TRENDS.
DELIVER US FROM EVIL
THE ACT OF KILLING
There's Something wrong with Aunt Diane
P.S. NOWADAYS A LOT MORE WOMEN WORK IN THE TRUE CRIME DOCUMENTARY WORLD AND THEY'RE GREA

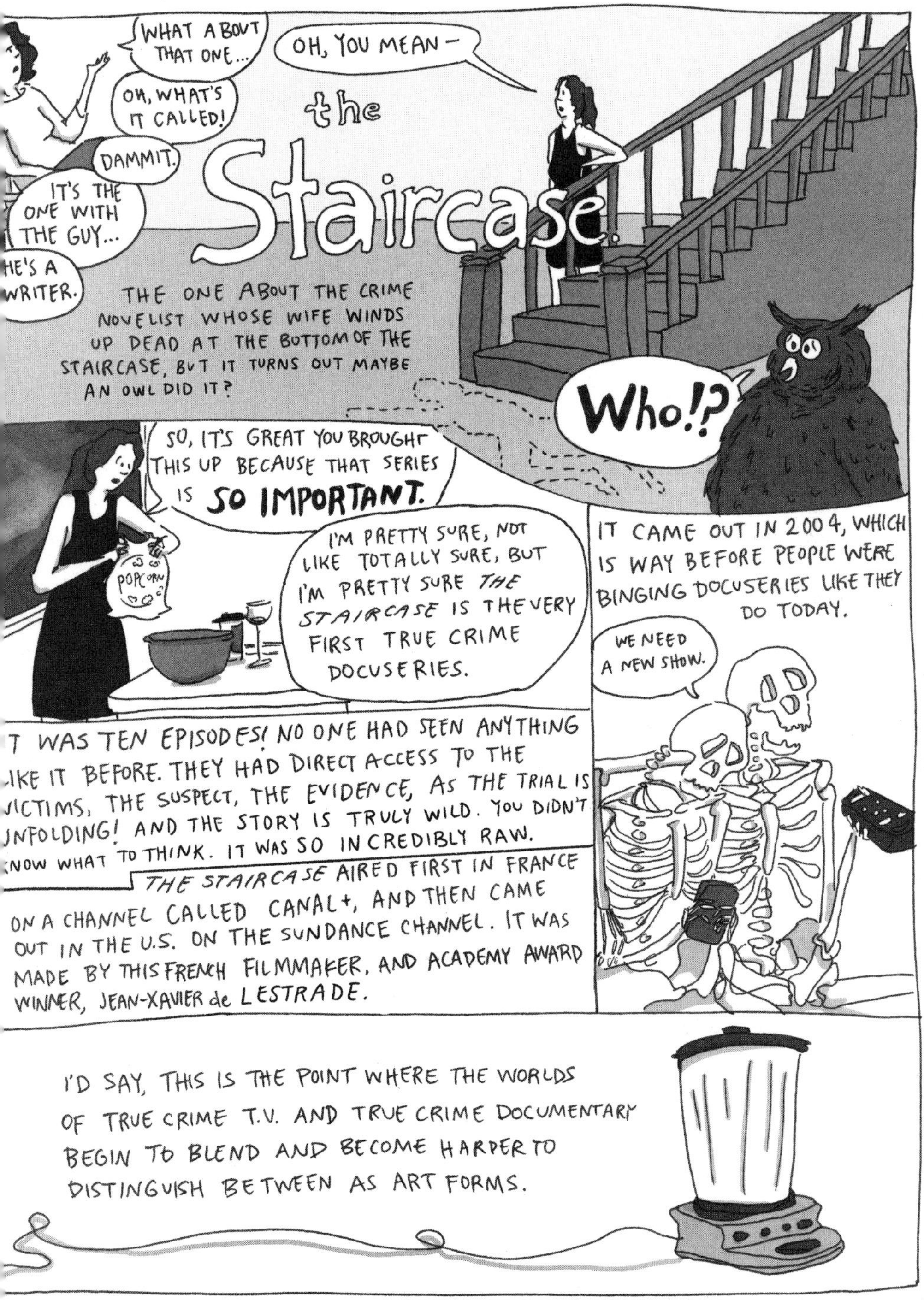
WHAT ABOUT THAT ONE...
OH, YOU MEAN—
OH, WHAT'S IT CALLED!
DAMMIT.
IT'S THE ONE WITH THE GUY...
HE'S A WRITER.
the Staircase!
THE ONE ABOUT THE CRIME NOVELIST WHOSE WIFE WINDS UP DEAD AT THE BOTTOM OF THE STAIRCASE, BUT IT TURNS OUT MAYBE AN OWL DID IT?
Who!?
SO, IT'S GREAT YOU BROUGHT THIS UP BECAUSE THAT SERIES IS SO IMPORTANT.
POPCORN
I'M PRETTY SURE, NOT LIKE TOTALLY SURE, BUT I'M PRETTY SURE THE STAIRCASE IS THE VERY FIRST TRUE CRIME DOCUSERIES.
IT CAME OUT IN 2004, WHICH IS WAY BEFORE PEOPLE WERE BINGING DOCUSERIES LIKE THEY DO TODAY.
WE NEED A NEW SHOW.
T WAS TEN EPISODES! NO ONE HAD SEEN ANYTHING
IKE IT BEFORE. THEY HAD DIRECT ACCESS TO THE
ICTIMS, THE SUSPECT, THE EVIDENCE, AS THE TRIAL IS
JNFOLDING! AND THE STORY IS TRULY WILD. YOU DIDN'T
NOW WHAT TO THINK. IT WAS SO INCREDIBLY RAW.
THE STAIRCASE AIRED FIRST IN FRANCE ON A CHANNEL CALLED CANAL+, AND THEN CAME OUT IN THE U.S. ON THE SUNDANCE CHANNEL. IT WAS MADE BY THIS FRENCH FILMMAKER, AND ACADEMY AWARD WINNER, JEAN-XAVIER de LESTRADE.
I'D SAY, THIS IS THE POINT WHERE THE WORLDS OF TRUE CRIME T.V. AND TRUE CRIME DOCUMENTARY BEGIN TO BLEND AND BECOME HARDER TO DISTINGUISH BETWEEN AS ART FORMS.

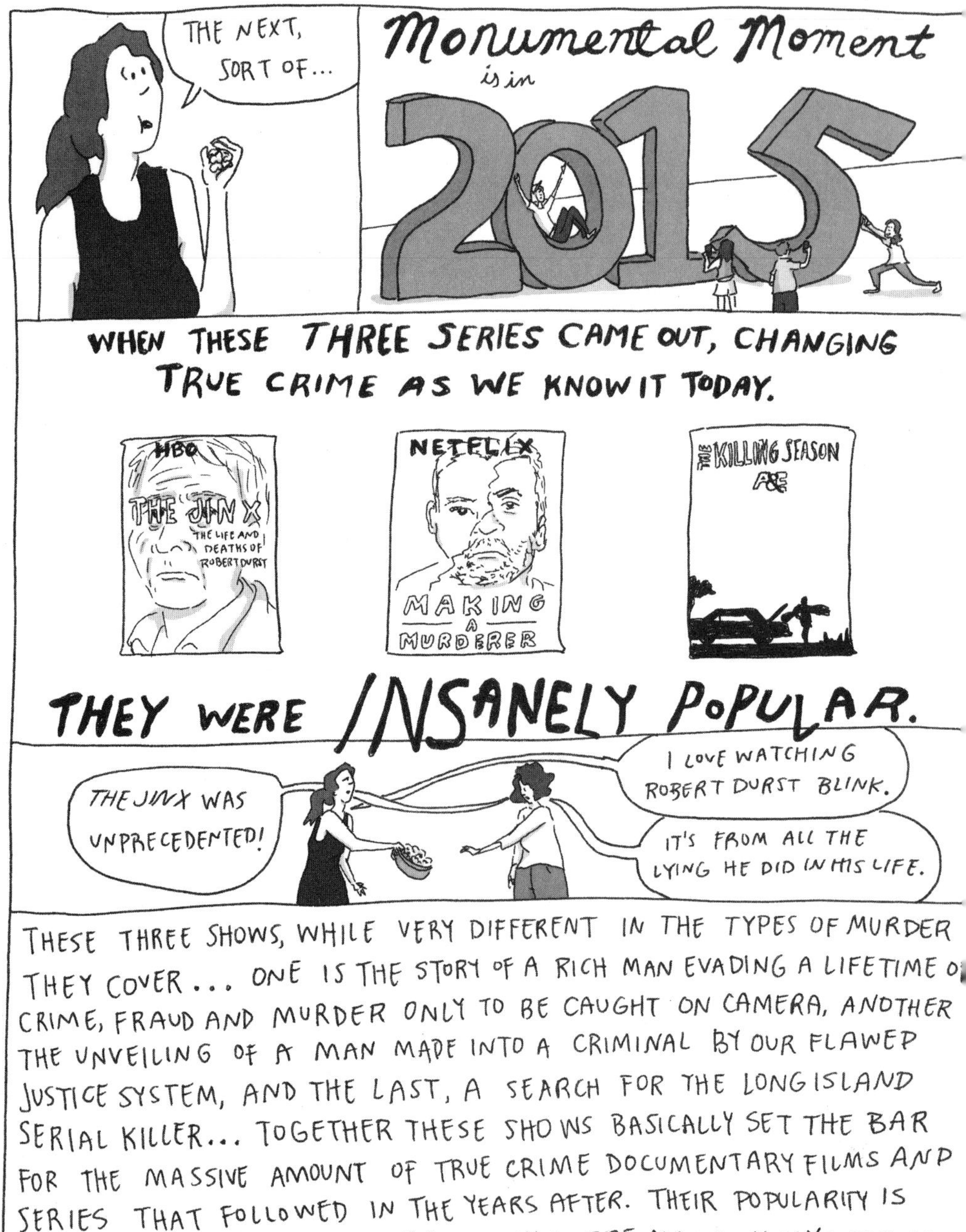
THE NEXT, SORT OF...
Monumental Moment is in 2015
WHEN THESE THREE SERIES CAME OUT, CHANGING TRUE CRIME AS WE KNOW IT TODAY.
HBO
THE JINX
THE LIFE AND DEATHS OF ROBERT DURST
NETFLIX
MAKING A MURDERER
THE KILLING SEASON
A&E
THEY WERE INSANELY POPULAR.
THE JINX WAS UNPRECEDENTED!
I LOVE WATCHING ROBERT DURST BLINK.
IT'S FROM ALL THE LYING HE DID IN HIS LIFE.
THESE THREE SHOWS, WHILE VERY DIFFERENT IN THE TYPES OF MURDER THEY COVER... ONE IS THE STORY OF A RICH MAN EVADING A LIFETIME OF CRIME, FRAUD AND MURDER ONLY TO BE CAUGHT ON CAMERA, ANOTHER THE UNVEILING OF A MAN MADE INTO A CRIMINAL BY OUR FLAWED JUSTICE SYSTEM, AND THE LAST, A SEARCH FOR THE LONG ISLAND SERIAL KILLER... TOGETHER THESE SHOWS BASICALLY SET THE BAR FOR THE MASSIVE AMOUNT OF TRUE CRIME DOCUMENTARY FILMS AND SERIES THAT FOLLOWED IN THE YEARS AFTER. THEIR POPULARITY IS WHY SO MANY SHOWS SUBSEQUENTLY WERE MADE. HOLLYWOOD SAW THE MARKET AND FLOODED THE GATES WITH CONTENT. THIS ALSO MARKS A TIME WHEN AMERICANS WERE CHANGING HOW THEY CONSUMED T.V.

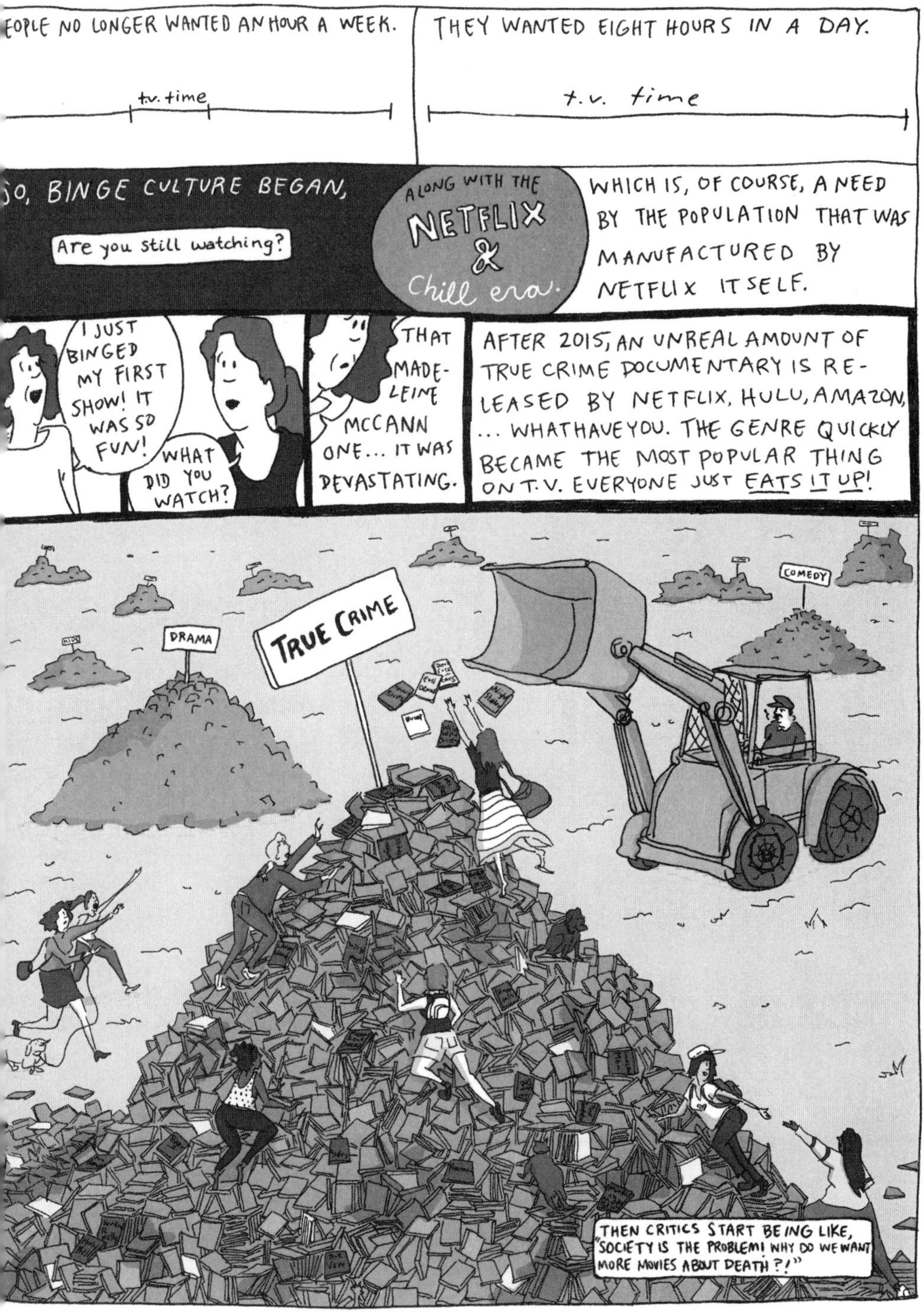

EOPLE NO LONGER WANTED AN HOUR A WEEK.
t.v. time
THEY WANTED EIGHT HOURS IN A DAY.
t.v. time
O, BINGE CULTURE BEGAN,
Are you still watching?
ALONG WITH THE NETFLIX & Chill era.
WHICH IS, OF COURSE, A NEED BY THE POPULATION THAT WAS MANUFACTURED BY NETFLIX ITSELF.
I JUST BINGED MY FIRST SHOW! IT WAS SO FUN!
WHAT DID YOU WATCH?
THAT MADELEINE MCCANN ONE... IT WAS DEVASTATING.
AFTER 2015, AN UNREAL AMOUNT OF TRUE CRIME DOCUMENTARY IS RELEASED BY NETFLIX, HULU, AMAZON, ... WHATHAVEYOU. THE GENRE QUICKLY BECAME THE MOST POPULAR THING ON T.V. EVERYONE JUST EATS IT UP!
DRAMA
TRUE CRIME
COMEDY
THEN CRITICS START BEING LIKE, "SOCIETY IS THE PROBLEM! WHY DO WE WANT MORE MOVIES ABOUT DEATH?!"

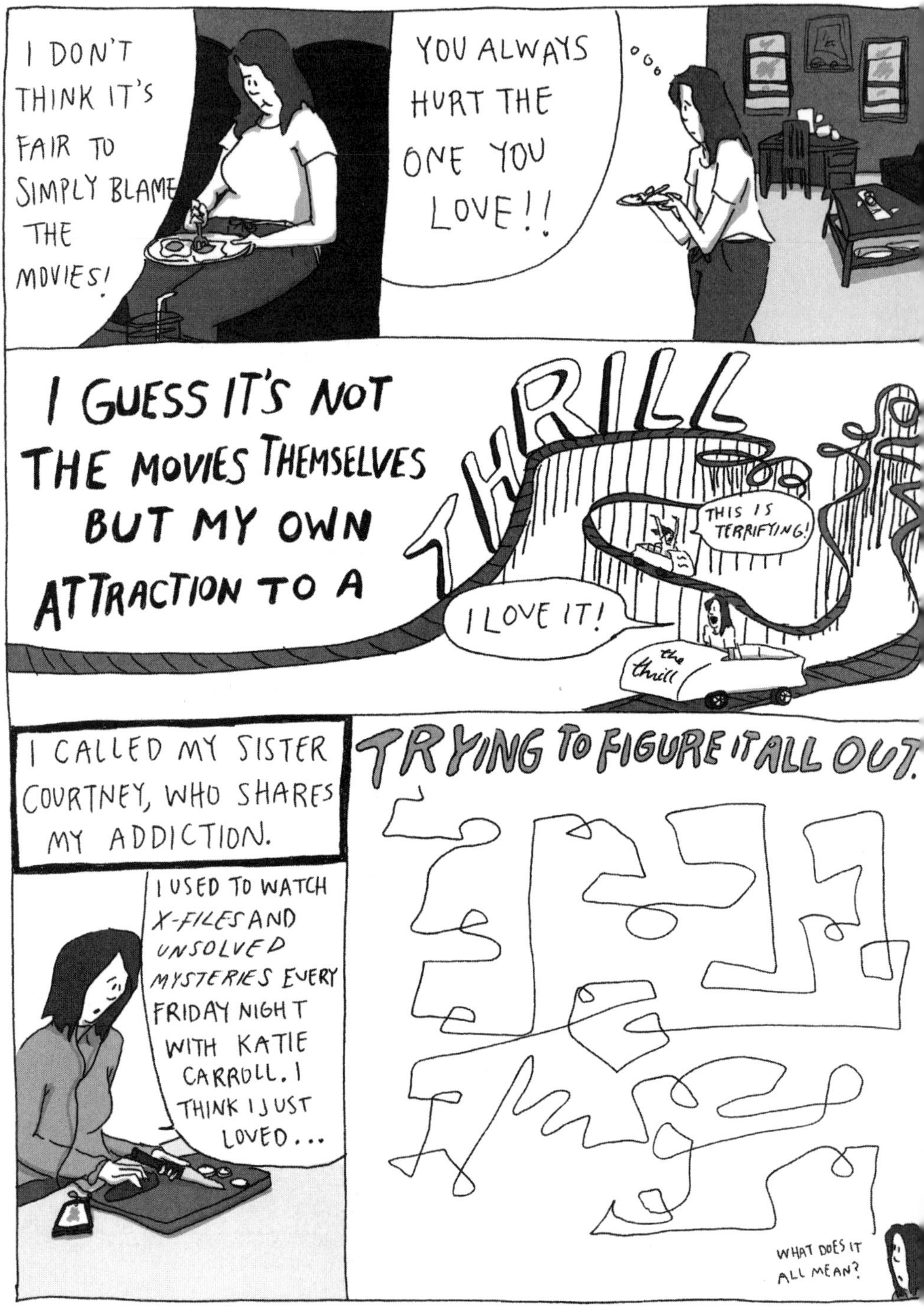
I DON'T THINK IT'S FAIR TO SIMPLY BLAME THE MOVIES!
YOU ALWAYS HURT THE ONE YOU LOVE!!
I GUESS IT'S NOT THE MOVIES THEMSELVES BUT MY OWN ATTRACTION TO A
THRILL
THIS IS TERRIFYING!
I LOVE IT!
the thrill
I CALLED MY SISTER COURTNEY, WHO SHARES MY ADDICTION.
I USED TO WATCH X-FILES AND UNSOLVED MYSTERIES EVERY FRIDAY NIGHT WITH KATIE CARROLL. I THINK I JUST LOVED...
TRYING TO FIGURE IT ALL OUT.
WHAT DOES IT ALL MEAN?

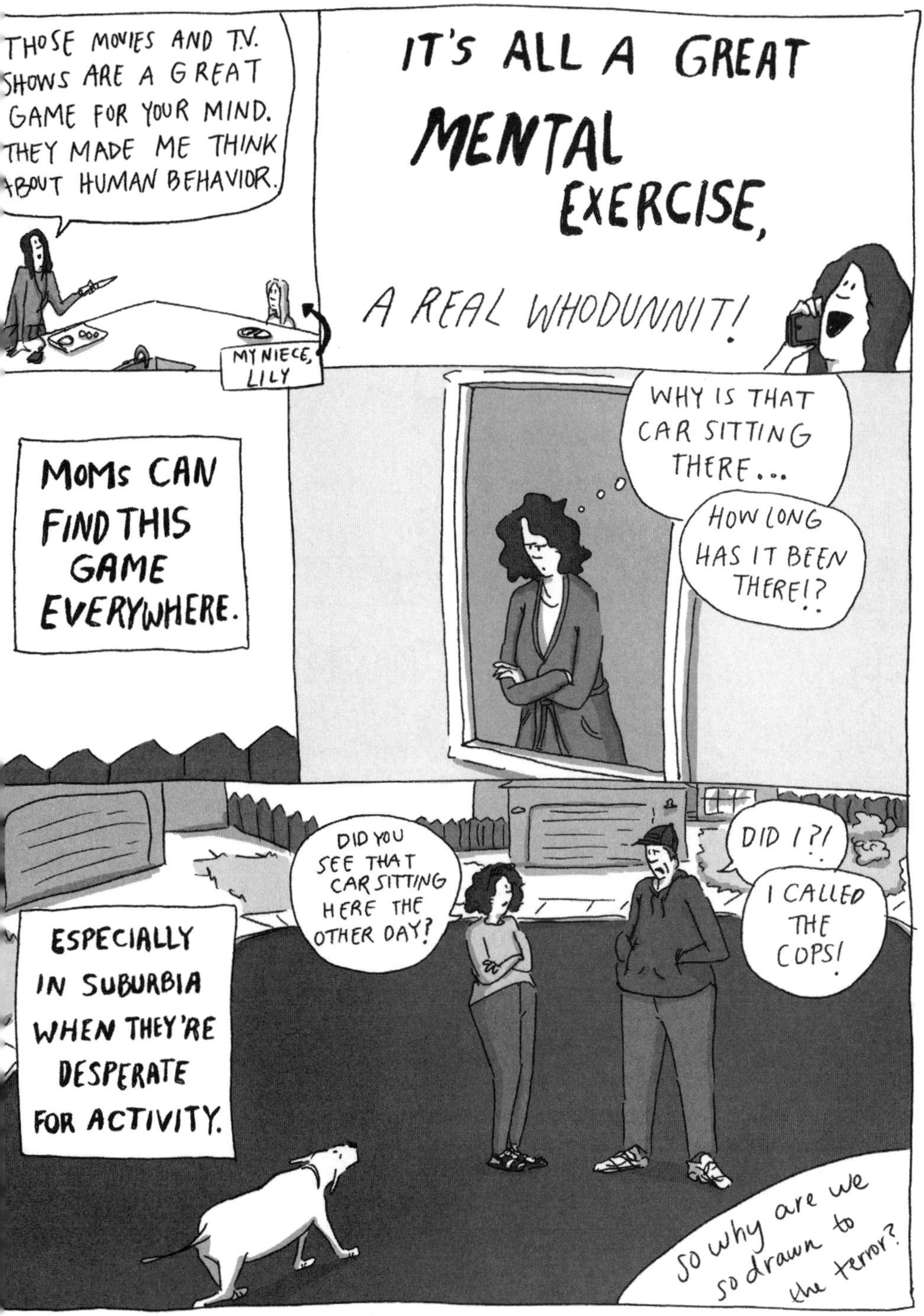
THOSE MOVIES AND T.V. SHOWS ARE A GREAT GAME FOR YOUR MIND. THEY MADE ME THINK ABOUT HUMAN BEHAVIOR.
MY NIECE, LILY
IT'S ALL A GREAT MENTAL EXERCISE,
A REAL WHODUNNIT!
MOMS CAN FIND THIS GAME EVERYWHERE.
WHY IS THAT CAR SITTING THERE...
HOW LONG HAS IT BEEN THERE!?
ESPECIALLY IN SUBURBIA WHEN THEY'RE DESPERATE FOR ACTIVITY.
DID YOU SEE THAT CAR SITTING HERE THE OTHER DAY?
DID I?!
I CALLED THE COPS!
So why are we so drawn to the terror?

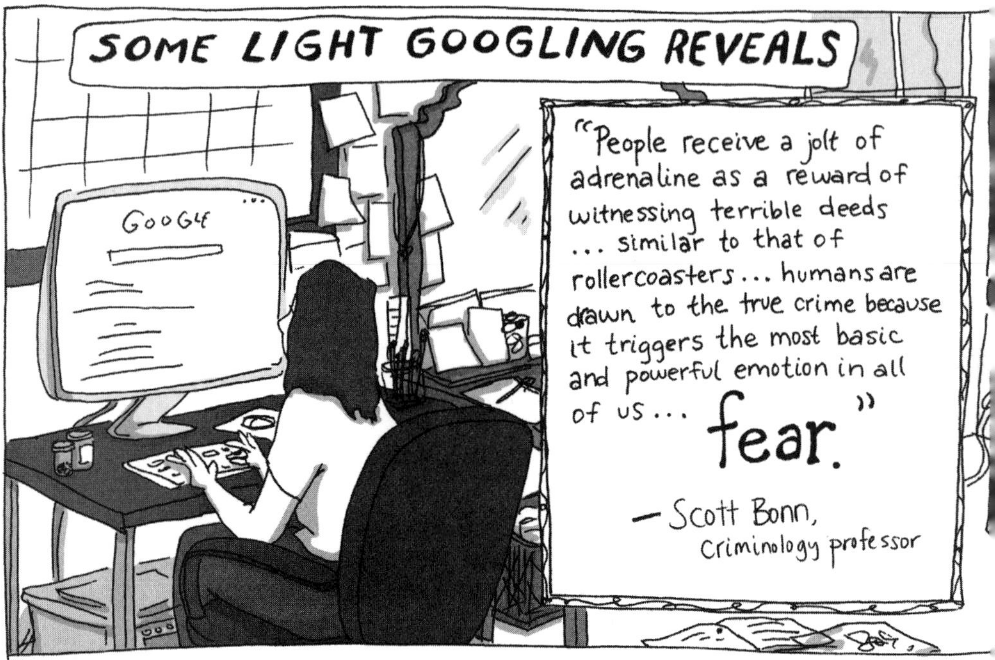
SOME LIGHT GOOGLING REVEALS
GOOGLE
"People receive a jolt of adrenaline as a reward of witnessing terrible deeds ... similar to that of rollercoasters ... humans are drawn to the true crime because it triggers the most basic and powerful emotion in all of us ... fear."
— Scott Bonn, Criminology professor

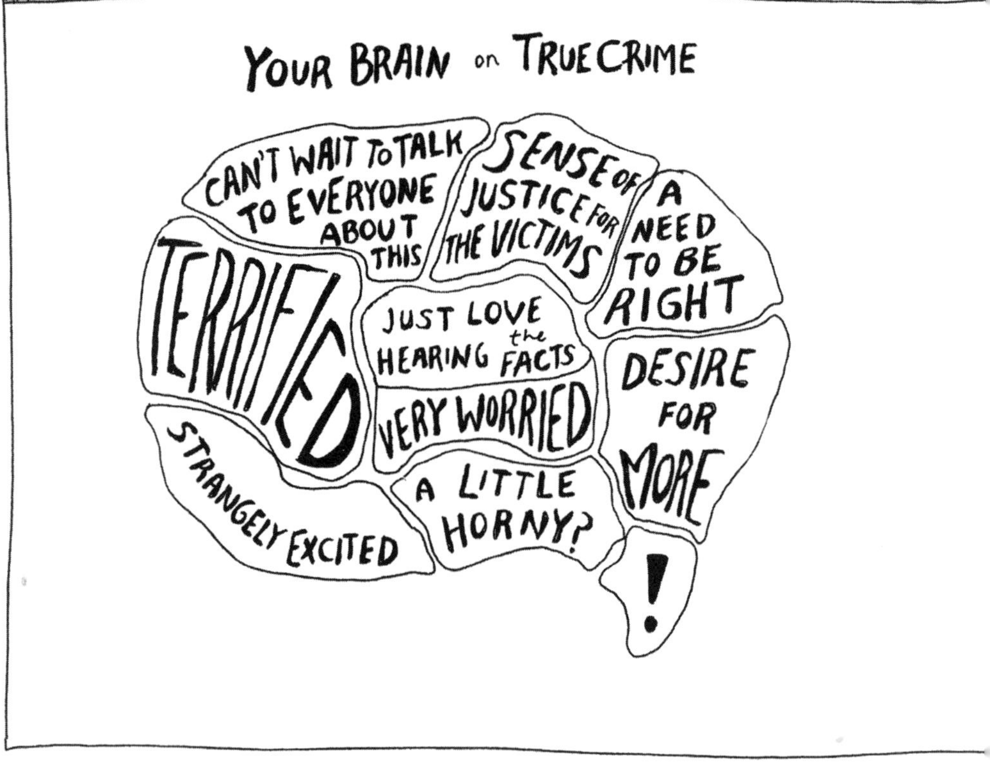
YOUR BRAIN on TRUE CRIME
CAN'T WAIT TO TALK TO EVERYONE ABOUT THIS
SENSE OF JUSTICE FOR THE VICTIMS
A NEED TO BE RIGHT
TERRIFIED
JUST LOVE HEARING the FACTS
DESIRE FOR MORE
VERY WORRIED
STRANGELY EXCITED
A LITTLE HORNY?
!

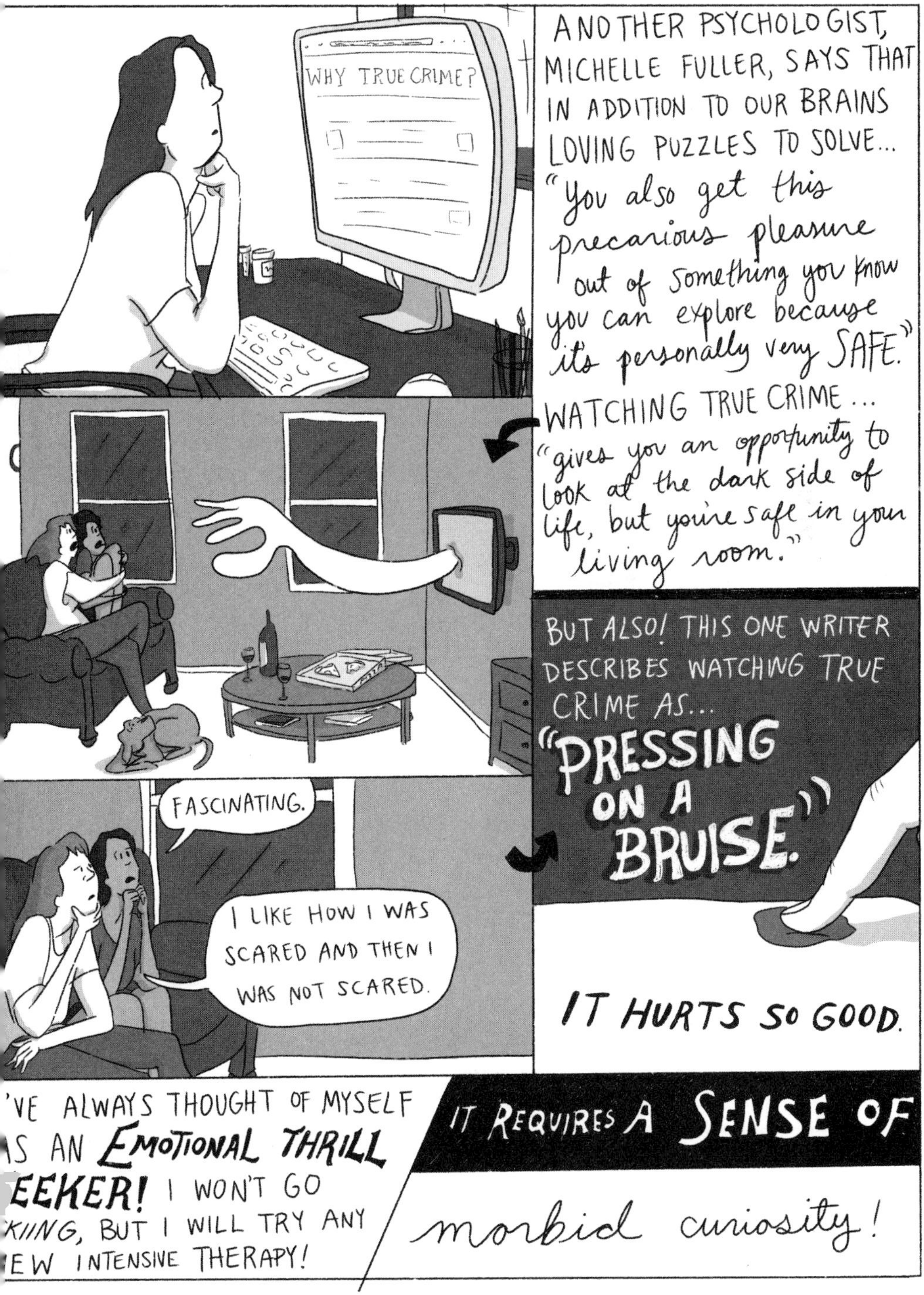
WHY TRUE CRIME?
ANOTHER PSYCHOLOGIST, MICHELLE FULLER, SAYS THAT IN ADDITION TO OUR BRAINS LOVING PUZZLES TO SOLVE...
"You also get this precarious pleasure out of something you know you can explore because it's personally very SAFE."
WATCHING TRUE CRIME...
"gives you an opportunity to look at the dark side of life, but you're safe in your living room."
BUT ALSO! THIS ONE WRITER DESCRIBES WATCHING TRUE CRIME AS...
"PRESSING ON A BRUISE."
FASCINATING.
I LIKE HOW I WAS SCARED AND THEN I WAS NOT SCARED.
IT HURTS SO GOOD.
'VE ALWAYS THOUGHT OF MYSELF S AN EMOTIONAL THRILL EEKER! I WON'T GO KIING, BUT I WILL TRY ANY EW INTENSIVE THERAPY!
IT REQUIRES A SENSE OF
morbid curiosity!

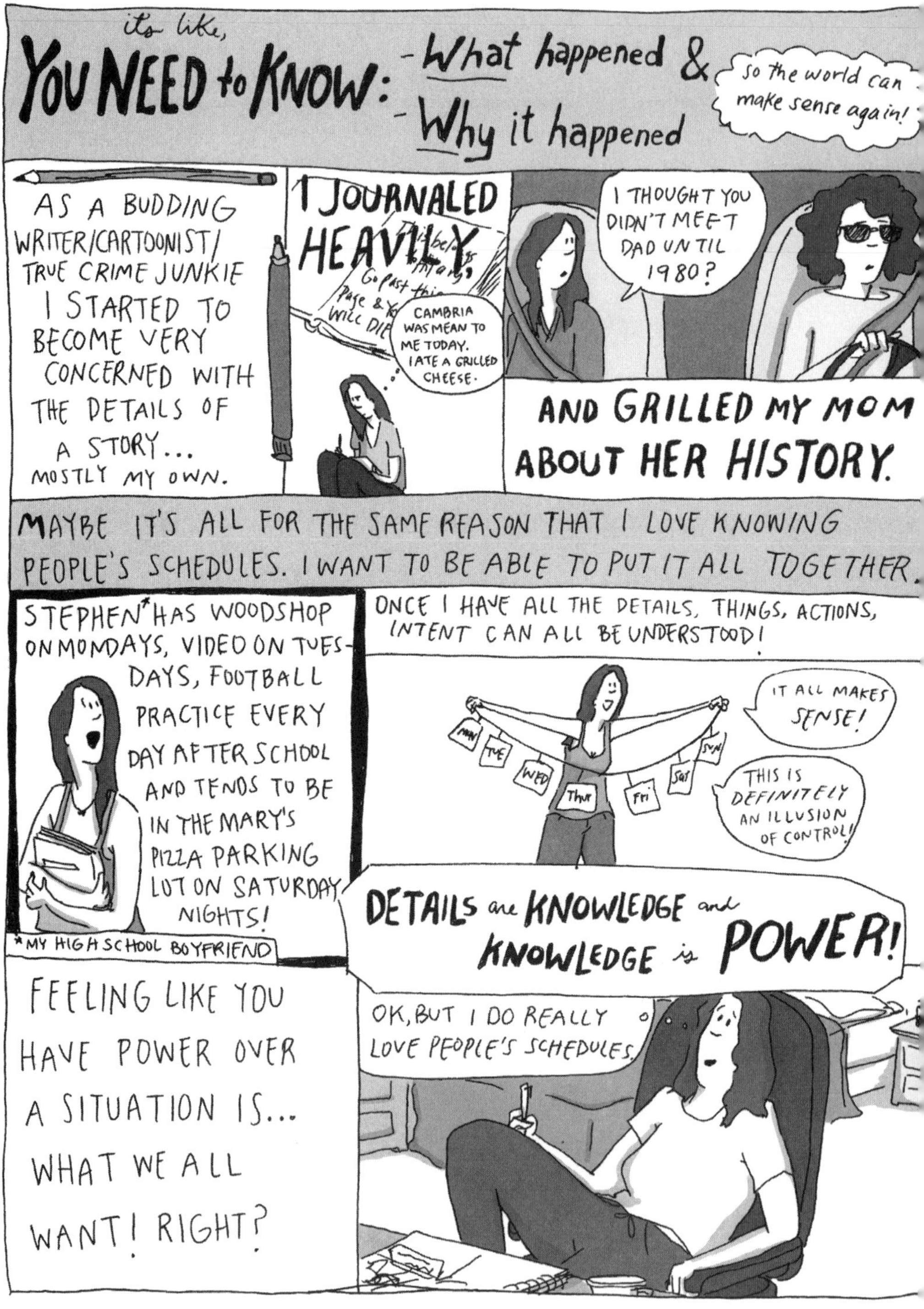

it's like, YOU NEED to KNOW: - What happened & - Why it happened
so the world can make sense again!
AS A BUDDING WRITER/CARTOONIST/ TRUE CRIME JUNKIE I STARTED TO BECOME VERY CONCERNED WITH THE DETAILS OF A STORY... MOSTLY MY OWN.
I JOURNALED HEAVILY,
CAMBRIA WAS MEAN TO ME TODAY. I ATE A GRILLED CHEESE.
I THOUGHT YOU DIDN'T MEET DAD UNTIL 1980?
AND GRILLED MY MOM ABOUT HER HISTORY.
MAYBE IT'S ALL FOR THE SAME REASON THAT I LOVE KNOWING PEOPLE'S SCHEDULES. I WANT TO BE ABLE TO PUT IT ALL TOGETHER.
STEPHEN* HAS WOODSHOP ON MONDAYS, VIDEO ON TUESDAYS, FOOTBALL PRACTICE EVERY DAY AFTER SCHOOL AND TENDS TO BE IN THE MARY'S PIZZA PARKING LOT ON SATURDAY NIGHTS!
*MY HIGH SCHOOL BOYFRIEND
ONCE I HAVE ALL THE DETAILS, THINGS, ACTIONS, INTENT CAN ALL BE UNDERSTOOD!
MON
TUE
WED
Thur
Fri
Sat
SUN
IT ALL MAKES SENSE!
THIS IS DEFINITELY AN ILLUSION OF CONTROL!
DETAILS are KNOWLEDGE and KNOWLEDGE is POWER!
FEELING LIKE YOU HAVE POWER OVER A SITUATION IS... WHAT WE ALL WANT! RIGHT?
OK, BUT I DO REALLY LOVE PEOPLE'S SCHEDULES.

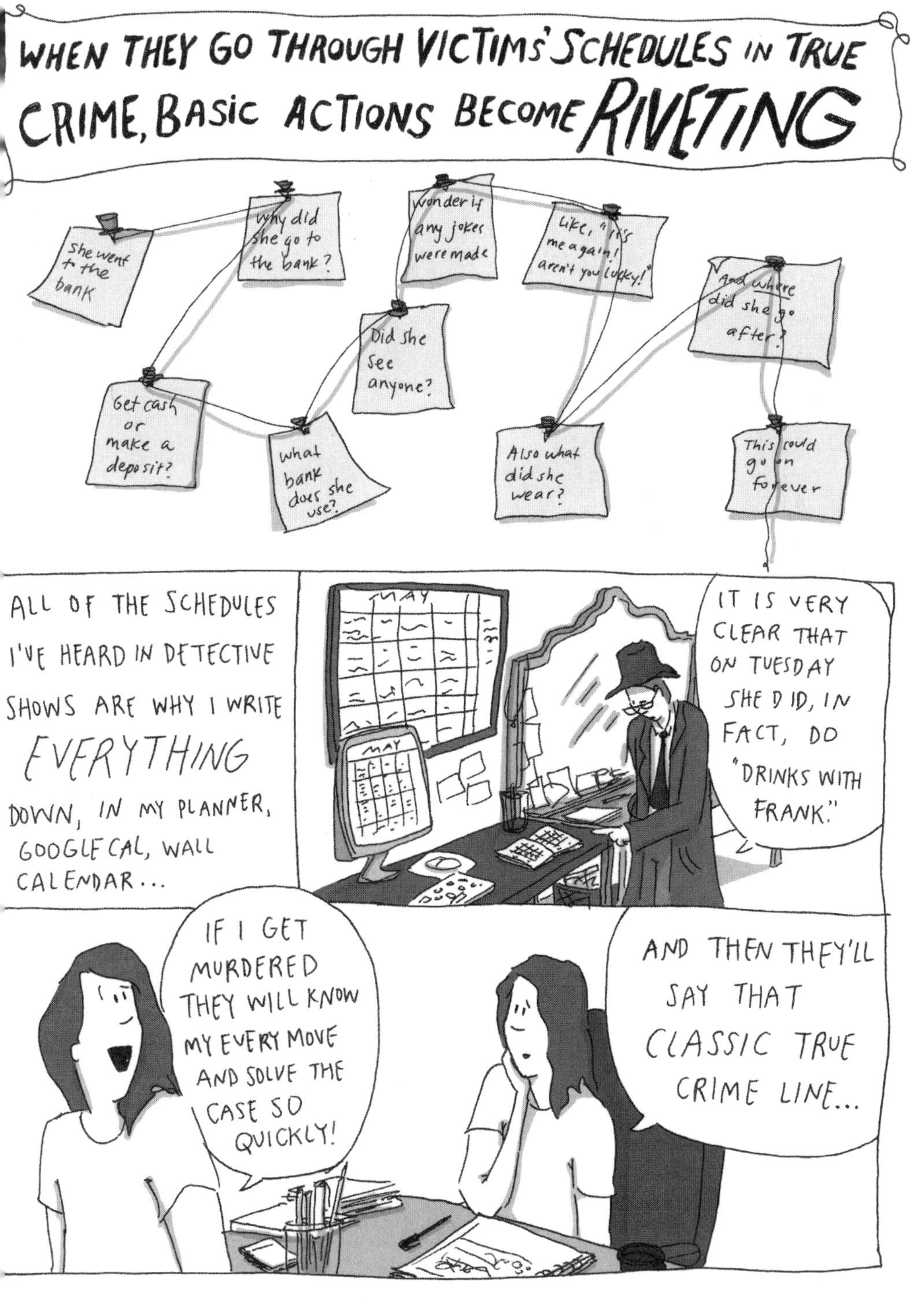
WHEN THEY GO THROUGH VICTIMS' SCHEDULES IN TRUE CRIME, BASIC ACTIONS BECOME RIVETING
She went to the bank
Why did she go to the bank?
Get cash or make a deposit?
What bank does she use?
Did she see anyone?
Wonder if any jokes were made
Like, "It's me again! aren't you lucky!"
And where did she go after?
Also what did she wear?
This could go on forever
ALL OF THE SCHEDULES I'VE HEARD IN DETECTIVE SHOWS ARE WHY I WRITE EVERYTHING DOWN, IN MY PLANNER, GOOGLE CAL, WALL CALENDAR...
MAY
MAY
IT IS VERY CLEAR THAT ON TUESDAY SHE DID, IN FACT, DO "DRINKS WITH FRANK."
IF I GET MURDERED THEY WILL KNOW MY EVERY MOVE AND SOLVE THE CASE SO QUICKLY!
AND THEN THEY'LL SAY THAT CLASSIC TRUE CRIME LINE...

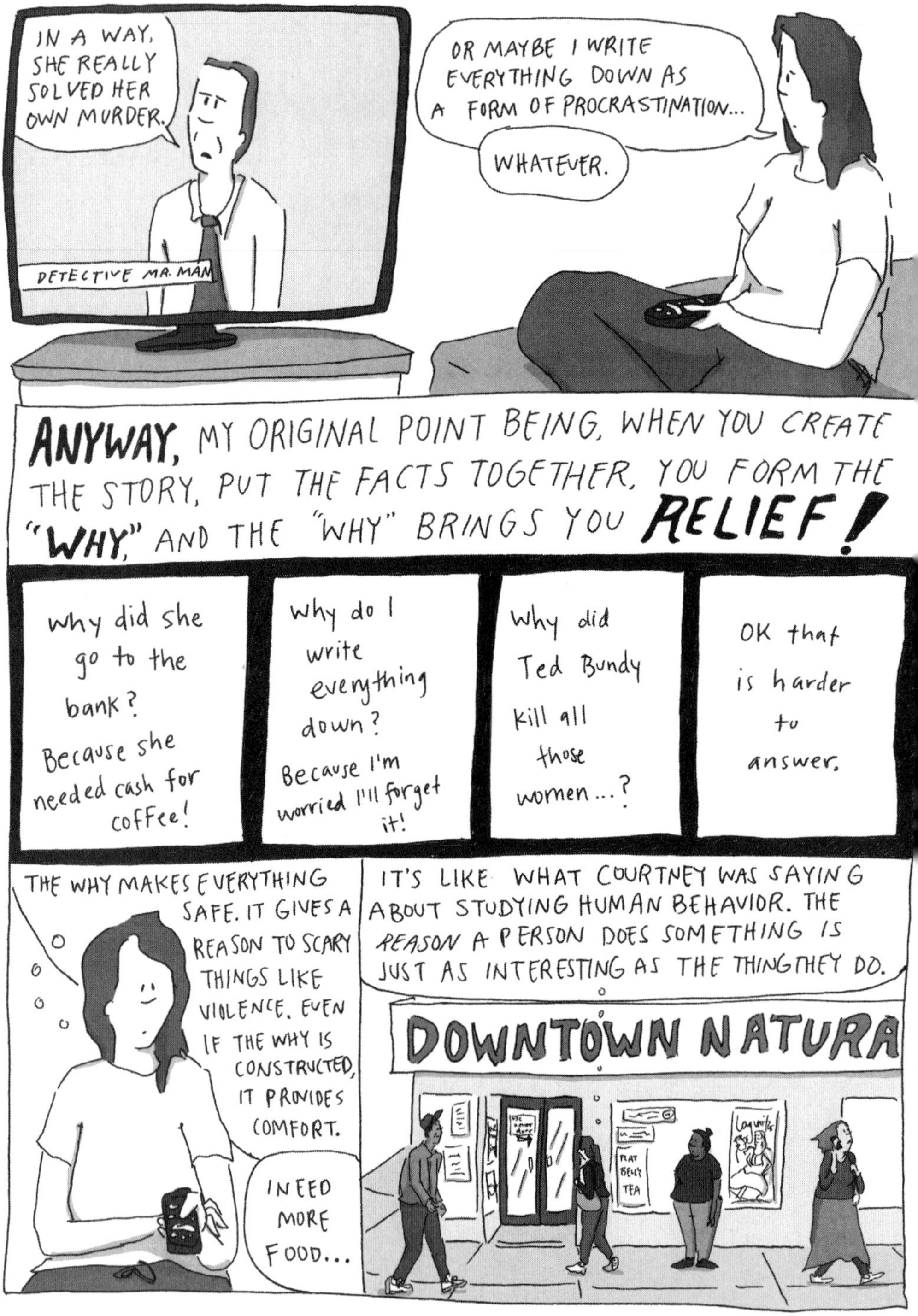
IN A WAY, SHE REALLY SOLVED HER OWN MURDER.
DETECTIVE MR. MAN
OR MAYBE I WRITE EVERYTHING DOWN AS A FORM OF PROCRASTINATION...
WHATEVER.
ANYWAY, MY ORIGINAL POINT BEING, WHEN YOU CREATE THE STORY, PUT THE FACTS TOGETHER, YOU FORM THE "WHY," AND THE "WHY" BRINGS YOU RELIEF!
why did she go to the bank? Because she needed cash for coffee!
why do I write everything down? Because I'm worried I'll forget it!
Why did Ted Bundy kill all those women...?
OK that is harder to answer.
THE WHY MAKES EVERYTHING SAFE. IT GIVES A REASON TO SCARY THINGS LIKE VIOLENCE. EVEN IF THE WHY IS CONSTRUCTED, IT PROVIDES COMFORT.
I NEED MORE FOOD...
IT'S LIKE WHAT COURTNEY WAS SAYING ABOUT STUDYING HUMAN BEHAVIOR. THE REASON A PERSON DOES SOMETHING IS JUST AS INTERESTING AS THE THING THEY DO.
DOWNTOWN NATURA
FLAT BELLY TEA

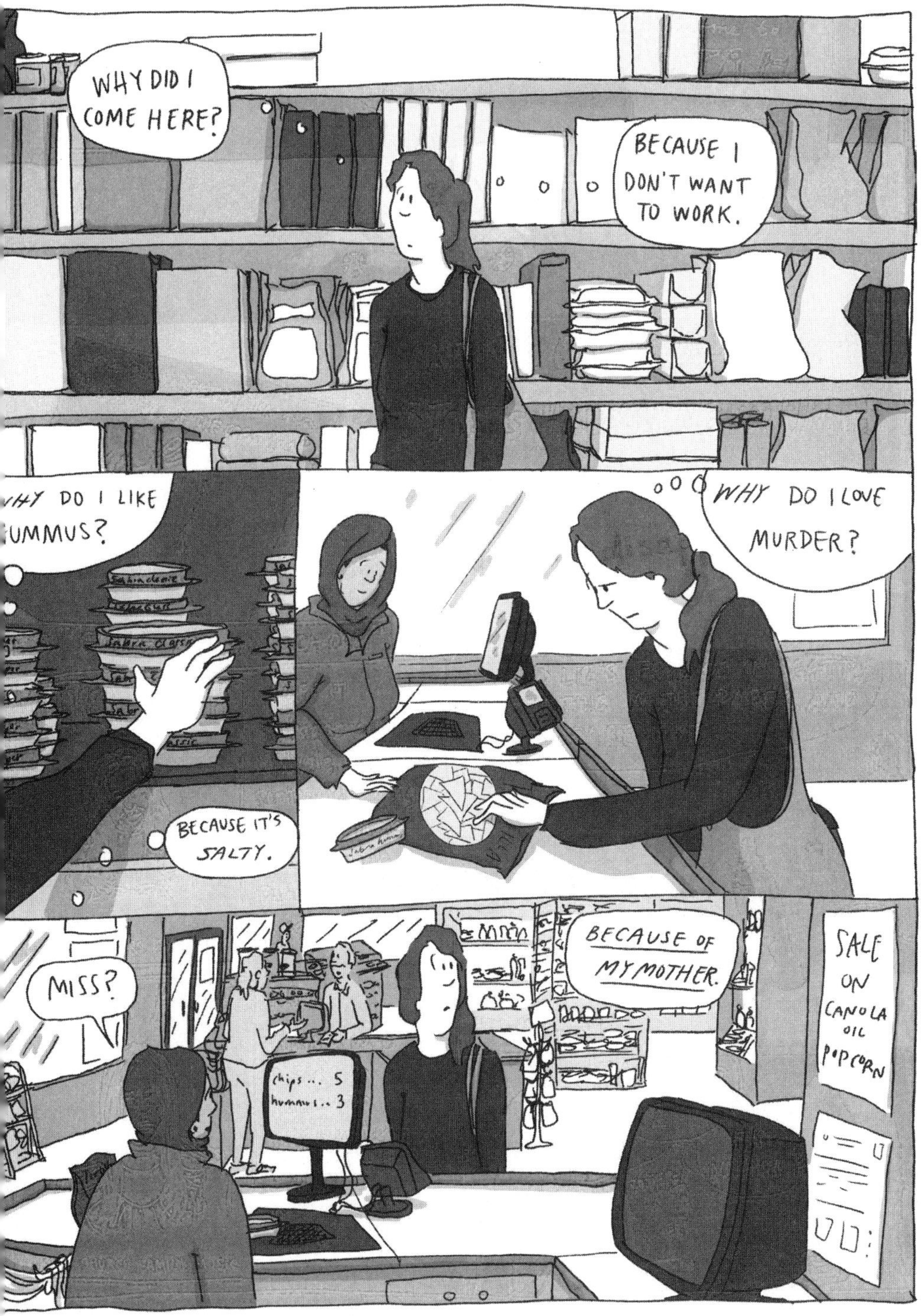
WHY DID I COME HERE?
BECAUSE I DON'T WANT TO WORK.
HY DO I LIKE UMMUS?
BECAUSE IT'S SALTY.
WHY DO I LOVE MURDER?
MISS?
chips... 5
hummus.. 3
BECAUSE OF MY MOTHER.
SALE ON CANOLA OIL POPCORN

TED BUNDY

IS NOT

AN AVERAGE

GUY

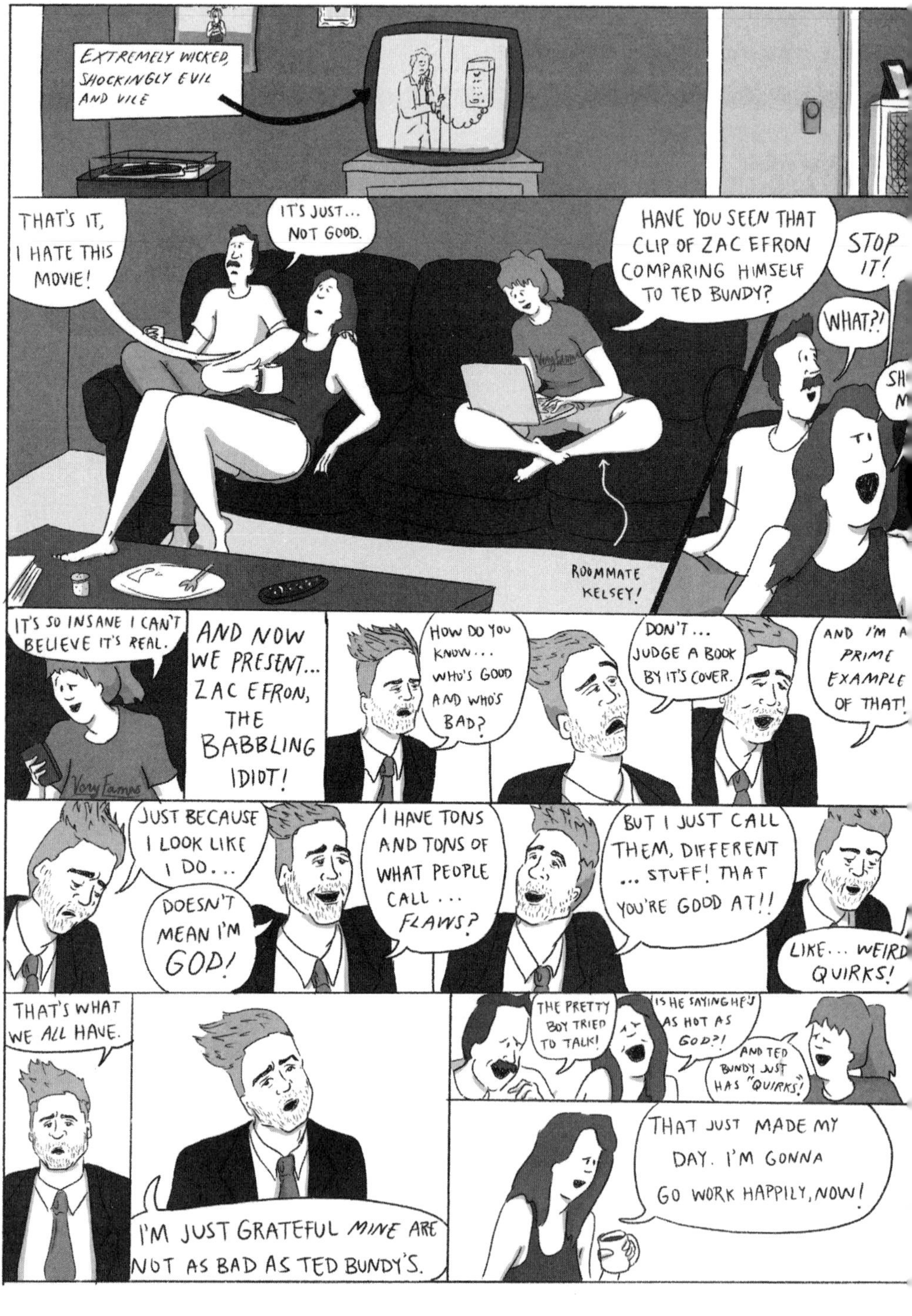
EXTREMELY WICKED, SHOCKINGLY EVIL AND VILE
THAT'S IT, I HATE THIS MOVIE!
IT'S JUST... NOT GOOD.
HAVE YOU SEEN THAT CLIP OF ZAC EFRON COMPARING HIMSELF TO TED BUNDY?
ROOMMATE KELSEY!
STOP IT!
WHAT?!
IT'S SO INSANE I CAN'T BELIEVE IT'S REAL.
AND NOW WE PRESENT... ZAC EFRON, THE BABBLING IDIOT!
HOW DO YOU KNOW... WHO'S GOOD AND WHO'S BAD?
DON'T... JUDGE A BOOK BY IT'S COVER.
AND I'M A PRIME EXAMPLE OF THAT!
JUST BECAUSE I LOOK LIKE I DO...
DOESN'T MEAN I'M GOD!
I HAVE TONS AND TONS OF WHAT PEOPLE CALL... FLAWS?
BUT I JUST CALL THEM, DIFFERENT ... STUFF! THAT YOU'RE GOOD AT!!
LIKE... WEIRD QUIRKS!
THAT'S WHAT WE ALL HAVE.
I'M JUST GRATEFUL MINE ARE NOT AS BAD AS TED BUNDY'S.
THE PRETTY BOY TRIED TO TALK!
IS HE SAYING HE'S AS HOT AS GOD?!
AND TED BUNDY JUST HAS "QUIRKS"!
THAT JUST MADE MY DAY. I'M GONNA GO WORK HAPPILY, NOW!

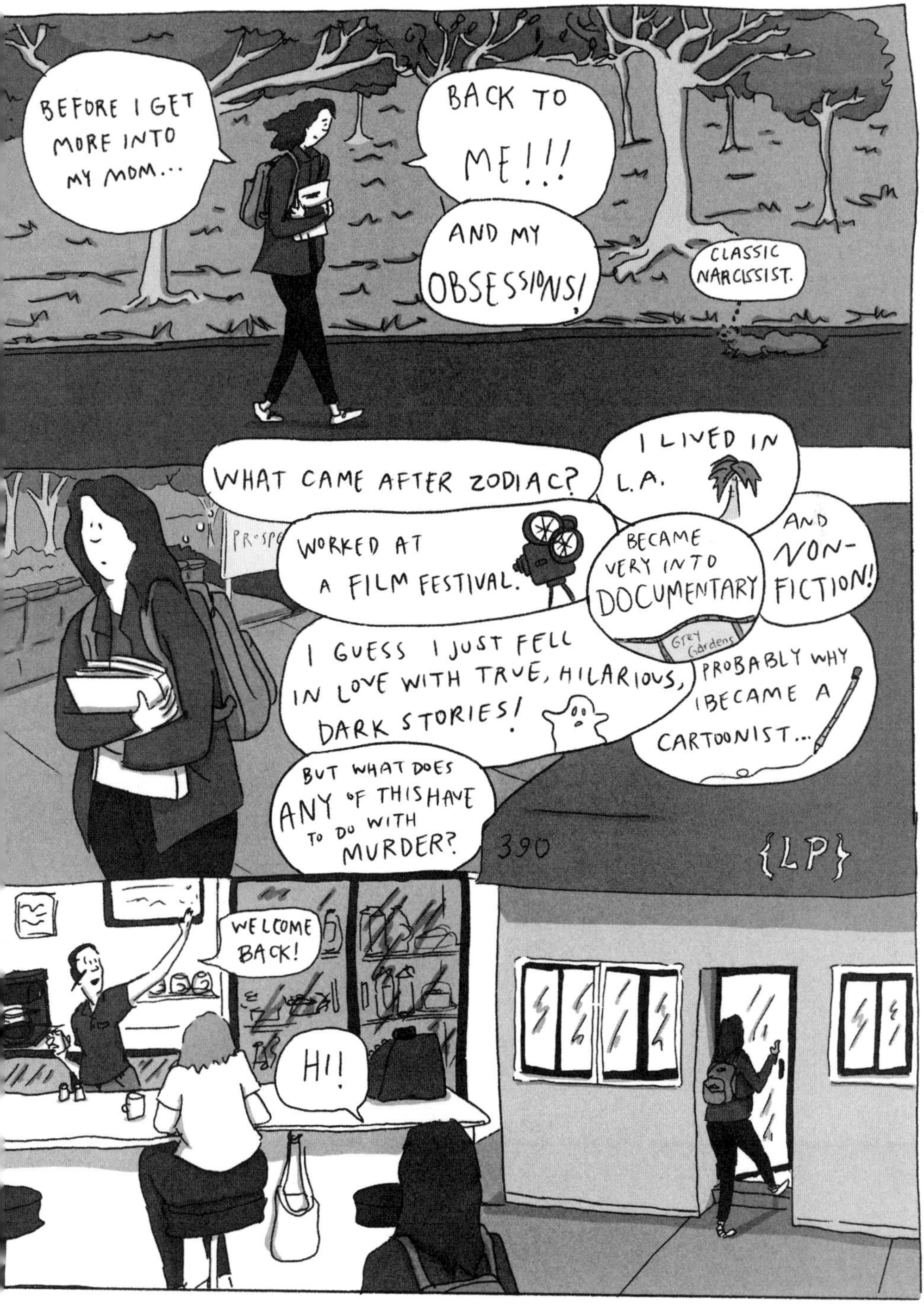
BEFORE I GET MORE INTO MY MOM...
BACK TO ME!!!
AND MY OBSESSIONS!
CLASSIC NARCISSIST.
WHAT CAME AFTER ZODIAC?
I LIVED IN L.A.
WORKED AT A FILM FESTIVAL.
BECAME VERY INTO DOCUMENTARY
Grey Gardens
AND NON-FICTION!
I GUESS I JUST FELL IN LOVE WITH TRUE, HILARIOUS, DARK STORIES!
PROBABLY WHY I BECAME A CARTOONIST...
BUT WHAT DOES ANY OF THIS HAVE TO DO WITH MURDER?
390
{LP}
WELCOME BACK!
HI!

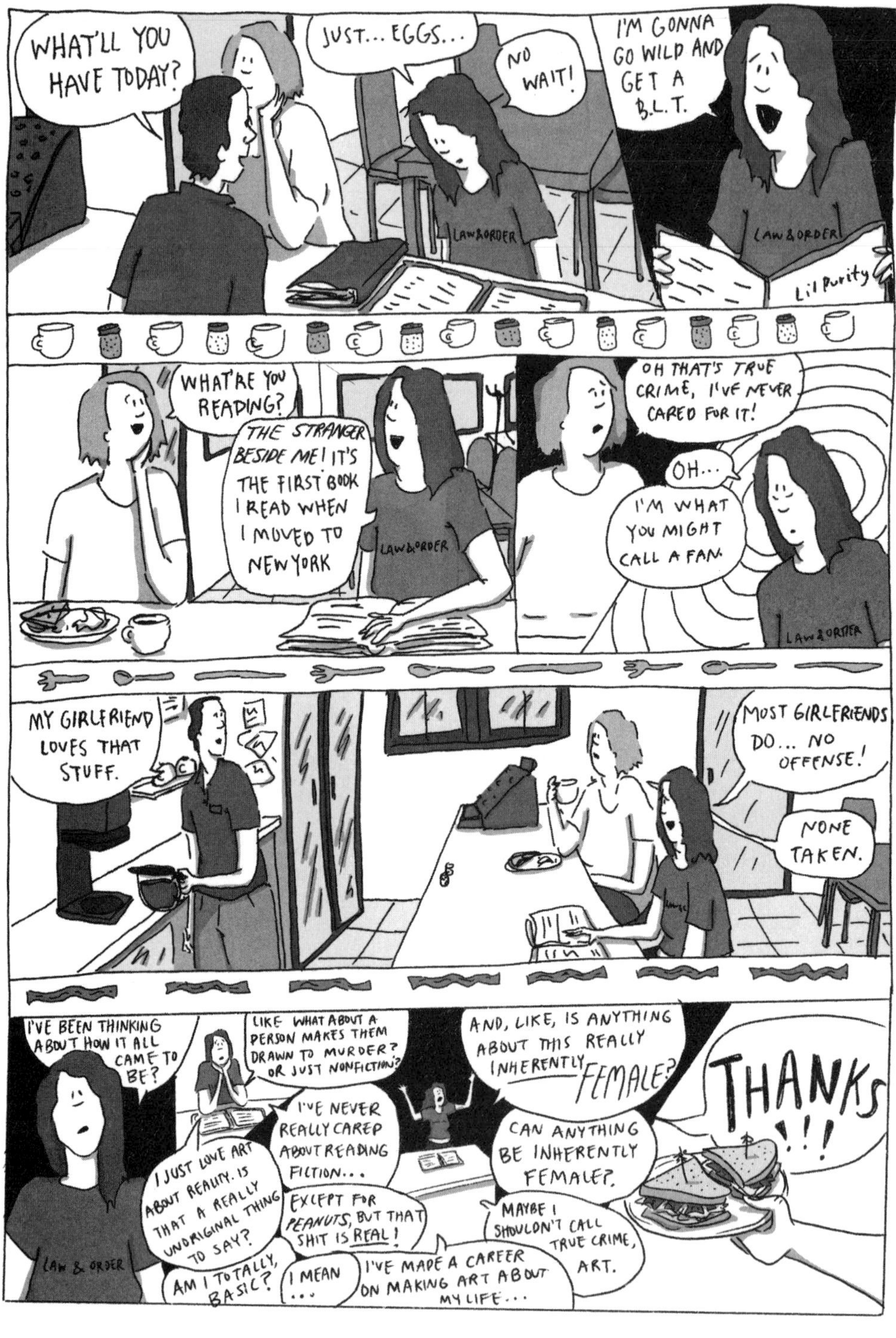
WHAT'LL YOU HAVE TODAY?
JUST... EGGS...
NO WAIT!
I'M GONNA GO WILD AND GET A B.L.T.
LAW&ORDER
Lil Purity
WHAT'RE YOU READING?
THE STRANGER BESIDE ME! IT'S THE FIRST BOOK I READ WHEN I MOVED TO NEW YORK
OH THAT'S TRUE CRIME, I'VE NEVER CARED FOR IT!
OH...
I'M WHAT YOU MIGHT CALL A FAN.
MY GIRLFRIEND LOVES THAT STUFF.
MOST GIRLFRIENDS DO... NO OFFENSE!
NONE TAKEN.
I'VE BEEN THINKING ABOUT HOW IT ALL CAME TO BE?
LIKE WHAT ABOUT A PERSON MAKES THEM DRAWN TO MURDER? OR JUST NONFICTION?
I'VE NEVER REALLY CARED ABOUT READING FICTION...
EXCEPT FOR PEANUTS, BUT THAT SHIT IS REAL!
I JUST LOVE ART ABOUT REALITY. IS THAT A REALLY UNORIGINAL THING TO SAY?
AM I TOTALLY BASIC?
I MEAN ...
I'VE MADE A CAREER ON MAKING ART ABOUT MY LIFE...
AND, LIKE, IS ANYTHING ABOUT THIS REALLY INHERENTLY FEMALE?
CAN ANYTHING BE INHERENTLY FEMALE?
MAYBE I SHOULDN'T CALL TRUE CRIME, ART.
THANKS!!!
LAW & ORDER

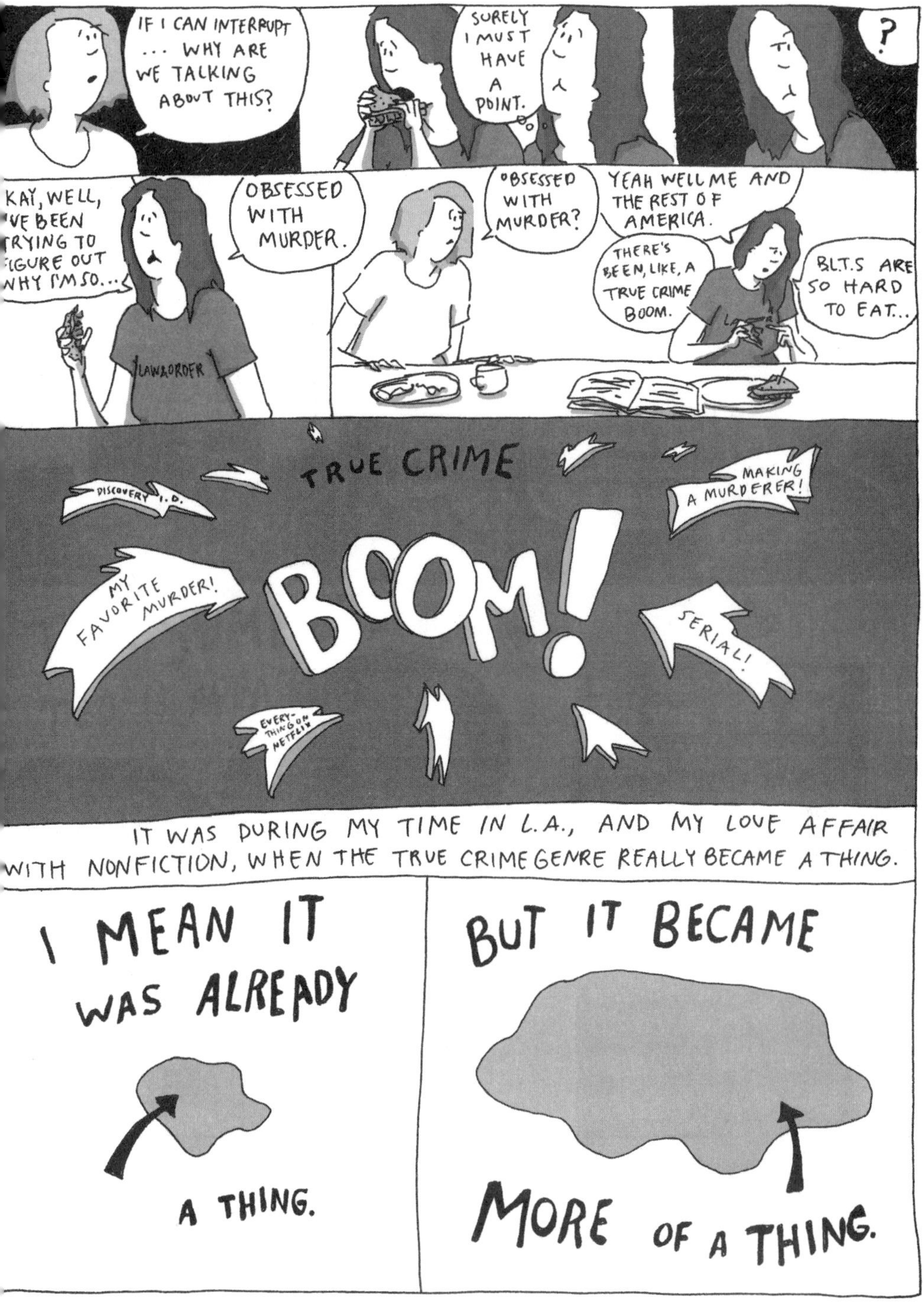
IF I CAN INTERRUPT ... WHY ARE WE TALKING ABOUT THIS?
SURELY I MUST HAVE A POINT.
?
KAY, WELL, 'VE BEEN TRYING TO IGURE OUT NHY I'M SO...
OBSESSED WITH MURDER.
LAW&ORDER
OBSESSED WITH MURDER?
YEAH WELL ME AND THE REST OF AMERICA.
THERE'S BEEN, LIKE, A TRUE CRIME BOOM.
BLT.S ARE SO HARD TO EAT...
TRUE CRIME
DISCOVERY I.D.
MAKING A MURDERER!
MY FAVORITE MURDER!
BOOM!
SERIAL!
EVERY-THING ON NETFLIX
IT WAS DURING MY TIME IN L.A., AND MY LOVE AFFAIR WITH NONFICTION, WHEN THE TRUE CRIME GENRE REALLY BECAME A THING.
I MEAN IT WAS ALREADY
A THING.
BUT IT BECAME
MORE OF A THING.

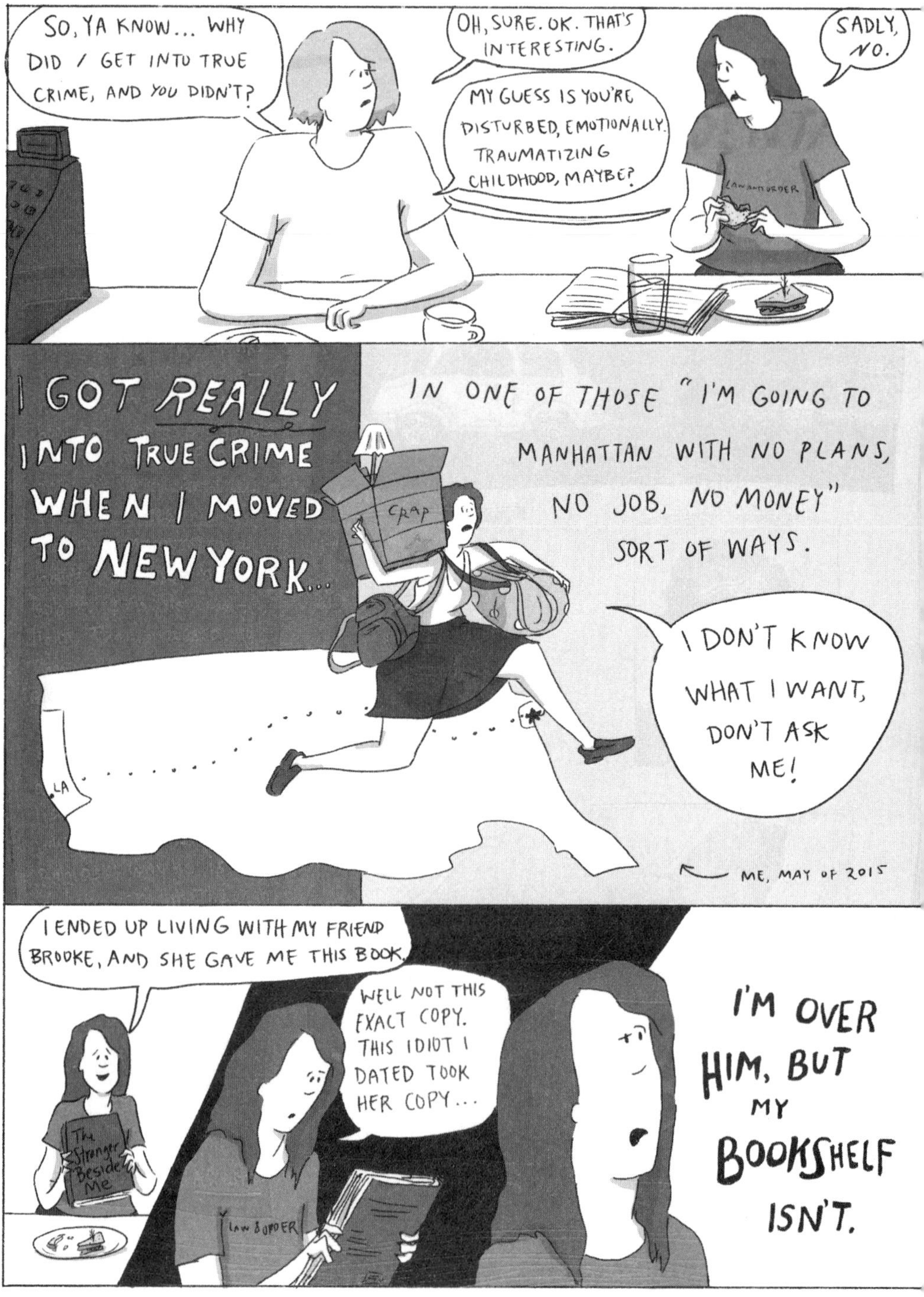
SO, YA KNOW... WHY DID I GET INTO TRUE CRIME, AND YOU DIDN'T?
OH, SURE. OK. THAT'S INTERESTING.
MY GUESS IS YOU'RE DISTURBED, EMOTIONALLY. TRAUMATIZING CHILDHOOD, MAYBE?
SADLY, NO.
I GOT REALLY INTO TRUE CRIME WHEN I MOVED TO NEW YORK...
IN ONE OF THOSE "I'M GOING TO MANHATTAN WITH NO PLANS, NO JOB, NO MONEY" SORT OF WAYS.
CRAP
LA
I DON'T KNOW WHAT I WANT, DON'T ASK ME!
ME, MAY OF 2015
I ENDED UP LIVING WITH MY FRIEND BROOKE, AND SHE GAVE ME THIS BOOK.
The Stranger Beside Me
WELL NOT THIS EXACT COPY. THIS IDIOT I DATED TOOK HER COPY...
LAW & ORDER
I'M OVER HIM, BUT MY BOOKSHELF ISN'T.

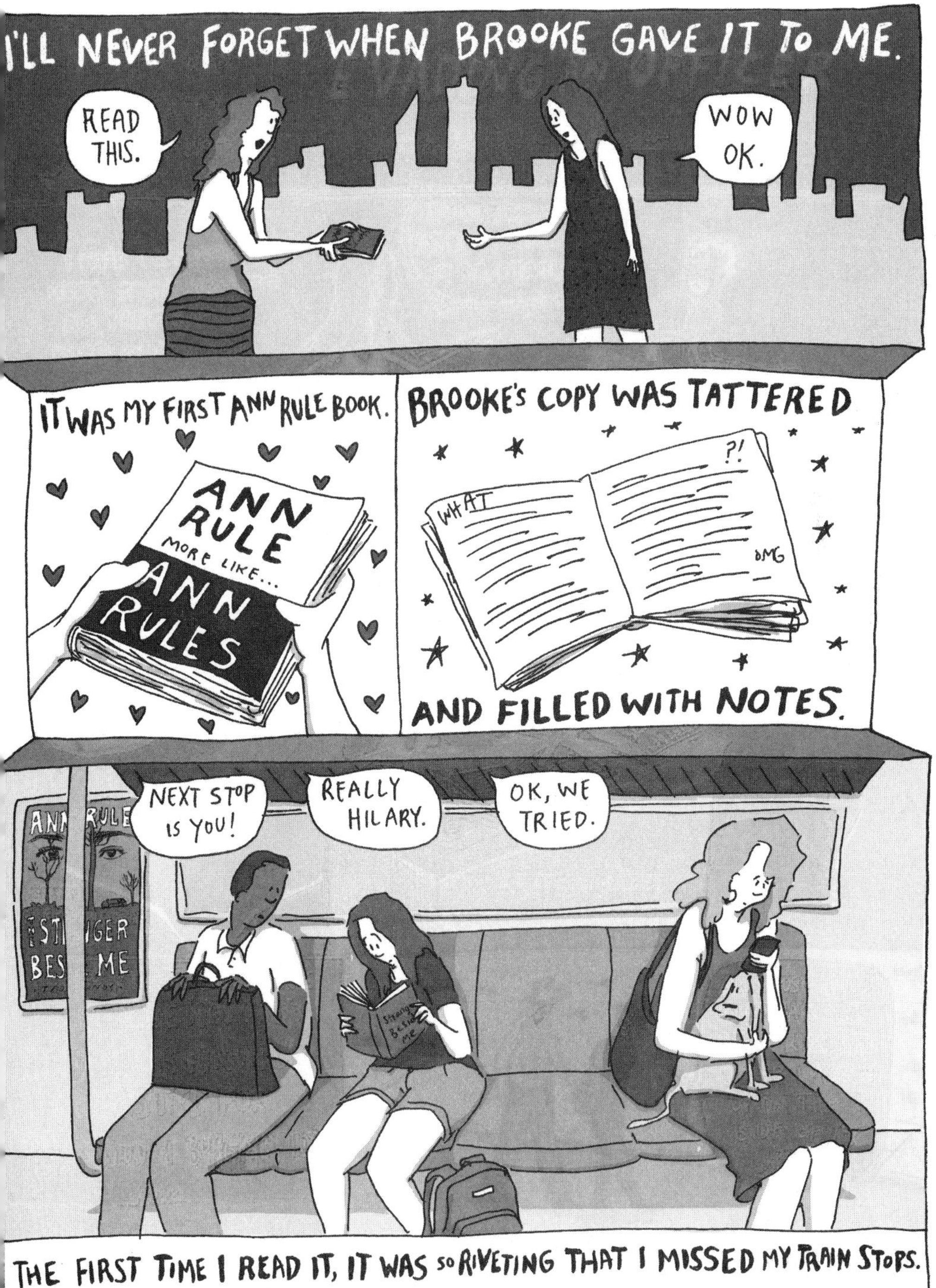
I'LL NEVER FORGET WHEN BROOKE GAVE IT TO ME.
READ THIS.
WOW OK.
IT WAS MY FIRST ANN RULE BOOK.
ANN RULE MORE LIKE... ANN RULES
BROOKE'S COPY WAS TATTERED
WHAT
?!
OMG
AND FILLED WITH NOTES.
ANN RULE
NEXT STOP IS YOU!
REALLY HILARY.
OK, WE TRIED.
THE FIRST TIME I READ IT, IT WAS SO RIVETING THAT I MISSED MY TRAIN STOPS.

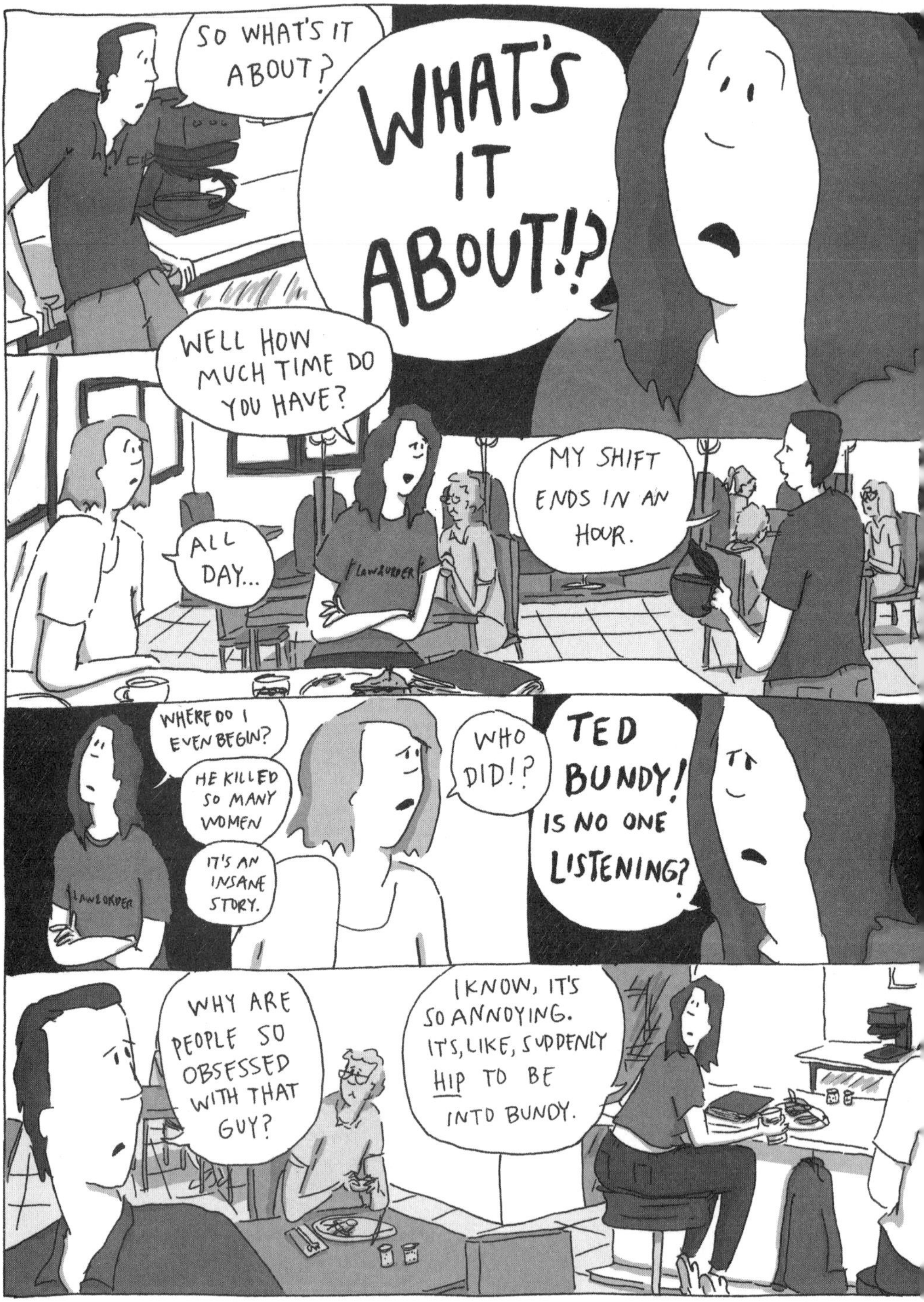
SO WHAT'S IT ABOUT?
WHAT'S IT ABOUT!?
WELL HOW MUCH TIME DO YOU HAVE?
ALL DAY...
MY SHIFT ENDS IN AN HOUR.
LAW&ORDER
WHERE DO I EVEN BEGIN?
HE KILLED SO MANY WOMEN
IT'S AN INSANE STORY.
WHO DID!?
TED BUNDY! IS NO ONE LISTENING?
WHY ARE PEOPLE SO OBSESSED WITH THAT GUY?
I KNOW, IT'S SO ANNOYING. IT'S, LIKE, SUDDENLY HIP TO BE INTO BUNDY.

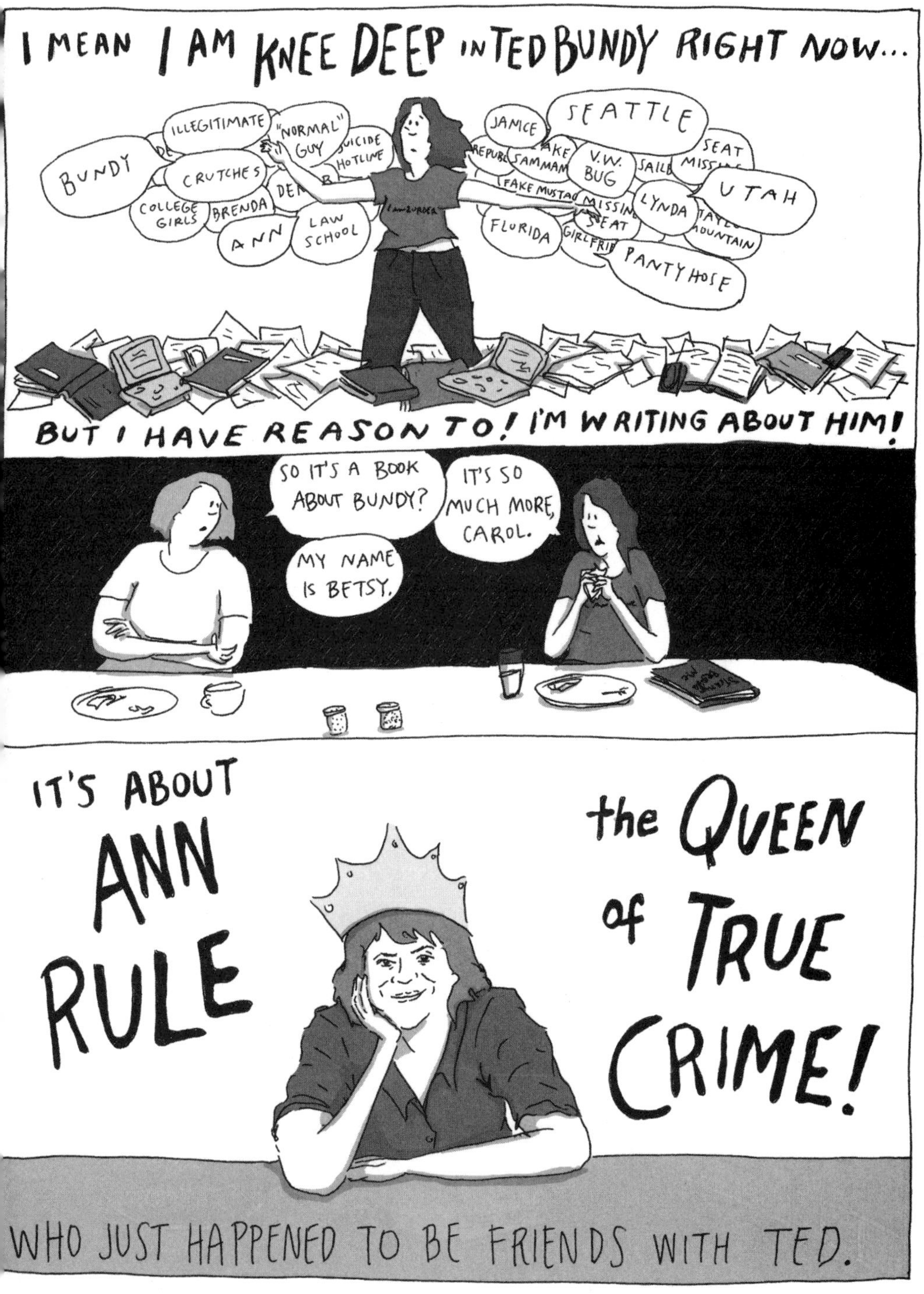
I MEAN I AM KNEE DEEP IN TED BUNDY RIGHT NOW...
BUNDY
ILLEGITIMATE
"NORMAL" GUY
CRUTCHES
COLLEGE GIRLS
BRENDA
ANN
LAW SCHOOL
JANICE
SEATTLE
V.W. BUG
LYNDA
UTAH
FLORIDA
PANTYHOSE
BUT I HAVE REASON TO! I'M WRITING ABOUT HIM!
SO IT'S A BOOK ABOUT BUNDY?
IT'S SO MUCH MORE, CAROL.
MY NAME IS BETSY.
IT'S ABOUT ANN RULE
the QUEEN of TRUE CRIME!
WHO JUST HAPPENED TO BE FRIENDS WITH TED.

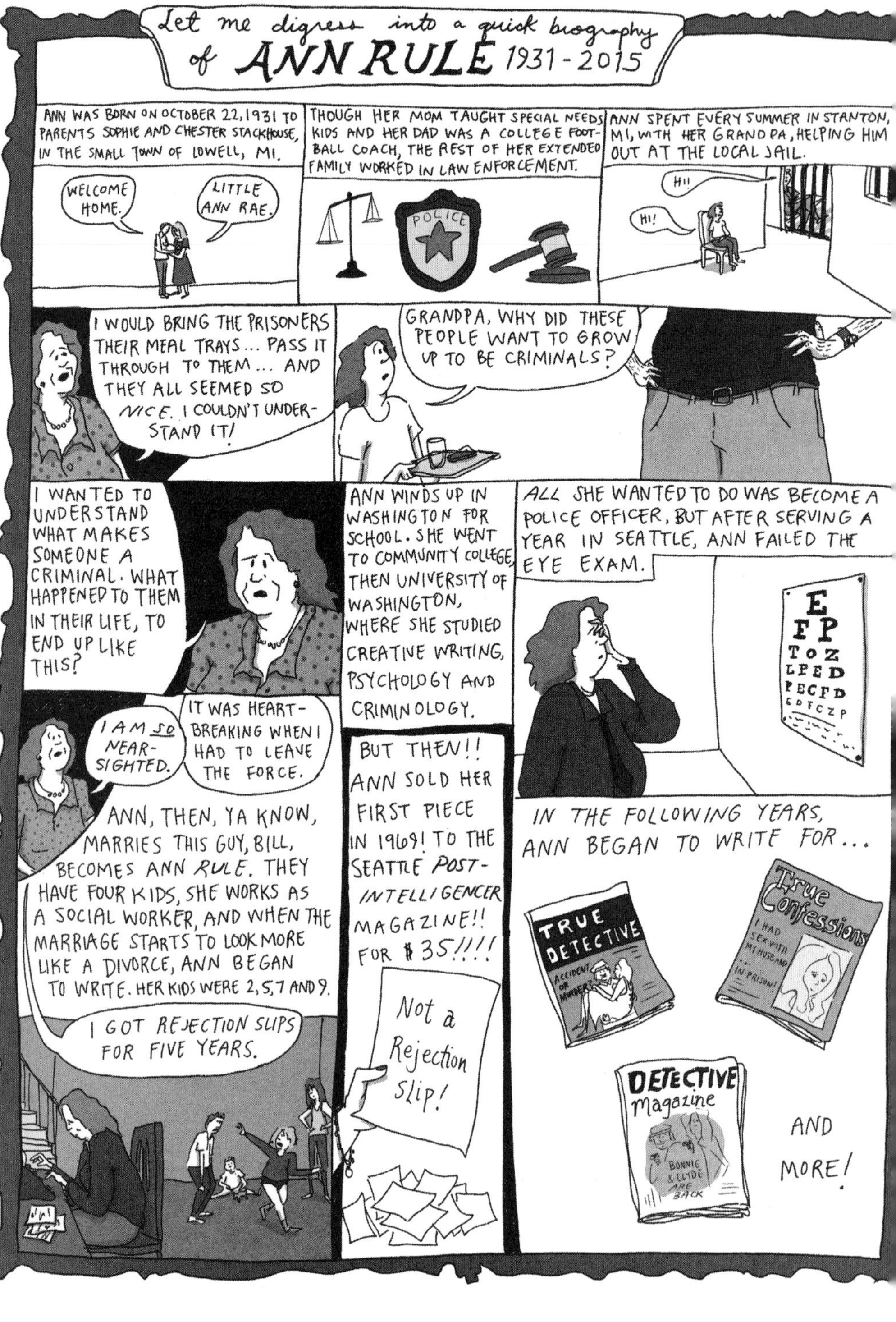
Let me digress into a quick biography of ANN RULE 1931 - 2015
ANN WAS BORN ON OCTOBER 22, 1931 TO PARENTS SOPHIE AND CHESTER STACKHOUSE, IN THE SMALL TOWN OF LOWELL, MI.
WELCOME HOME.
LITTLE ANN RAE.
THOUGH HER MOM TAUGHT SPECIAL NEEDS KIDS AND HER DAD WAS A COLLEGE FOOTBALL COACH, THE REST OF HER EXTENDED FAMILY WORKED IN LAW ENFORCEMENT.
POLICE
ANN SPENT EVERY SUMMER IN STANTON, MI, WITH HER GRANDPA, HELPING HIM OUT AT THE LOCAL JAIL.
HI!
HI!
I WOULD BRING THE PRISONERS THEIR MEAL TRAYS... PASS IT THROUGH TO THEM... AND THEY ALL SEEMED SO NICE. I COULDN'T UNDERSTAND IT!
GRANDPA, WHY DID THESE PEOPLE WANT TO GROW UP TO BE CRIMINALS?
I WANTED TO UNDERSTAND WHAT MAKES SOMEONE A CRIMINAL. WHAT HAPPENED TO THEM IN THEIR LIFE, TO END UP LIKE THIS?
ANN WINDS UP IN WASHINGTON FOR SCHOOL. SHE WENT TO COMMUNITY COLLEGE, THEN UNIVERSITY OF WASHINGTON, WHERE SHE STUDIED CREATIVE WRITING, PSYCHOLOGY AND CRIMINOLOGY.
ALL SHE WANTED TO DO WAS BECOME A POLICE OFFICER, BUT AFTER SERVING A YEAR IN SEATTLE, ANN FAILED THE EYE EXAM.
E
F P
T O Z
L P E D
P E C F D
E D F C Z P
I AM SO NEAR-SIGHTED.
IT WAS HEART-BREAKING WHEN I HAD TO LEAVE THE FORCE.
ANN, THEN, YA KNOW, MARRIES THIS GUY, BILL, BECOMES ANN RULE. THEY HAVE FOUR KIDS, SHE WORKS AS A SOCIAL WORKER, AND WHEN THE MARRIAGE STARTS TO LOOK MORE LIKE A DIVORCE, ANN BEGAN TO WRITE. HER KIDS WERE 2, 5, 7 AND 9.
I GOT REJECTION SLIPS FOR FIVE YEARS.
BUT THEN!! ANN SOLD HER FIRST PIECE IN 1969! TO THE SEATTLE POST-INTELLIGENCER MAGAZINE!! FOR $35!!!!
Not a Rejection Slip!
IN THE FOLLOWING YEARS, ANN BEGAN TO WRITE FOR...
TRUE DETECTIVE
ACCIDENT OR MURDER?
True Confessions
I HAD SEX WITH MY HUSBAND ... IN PRISON!
DETECTIVE Magazine
BONNIE & CLYDE ARE BACK
AND MORE!

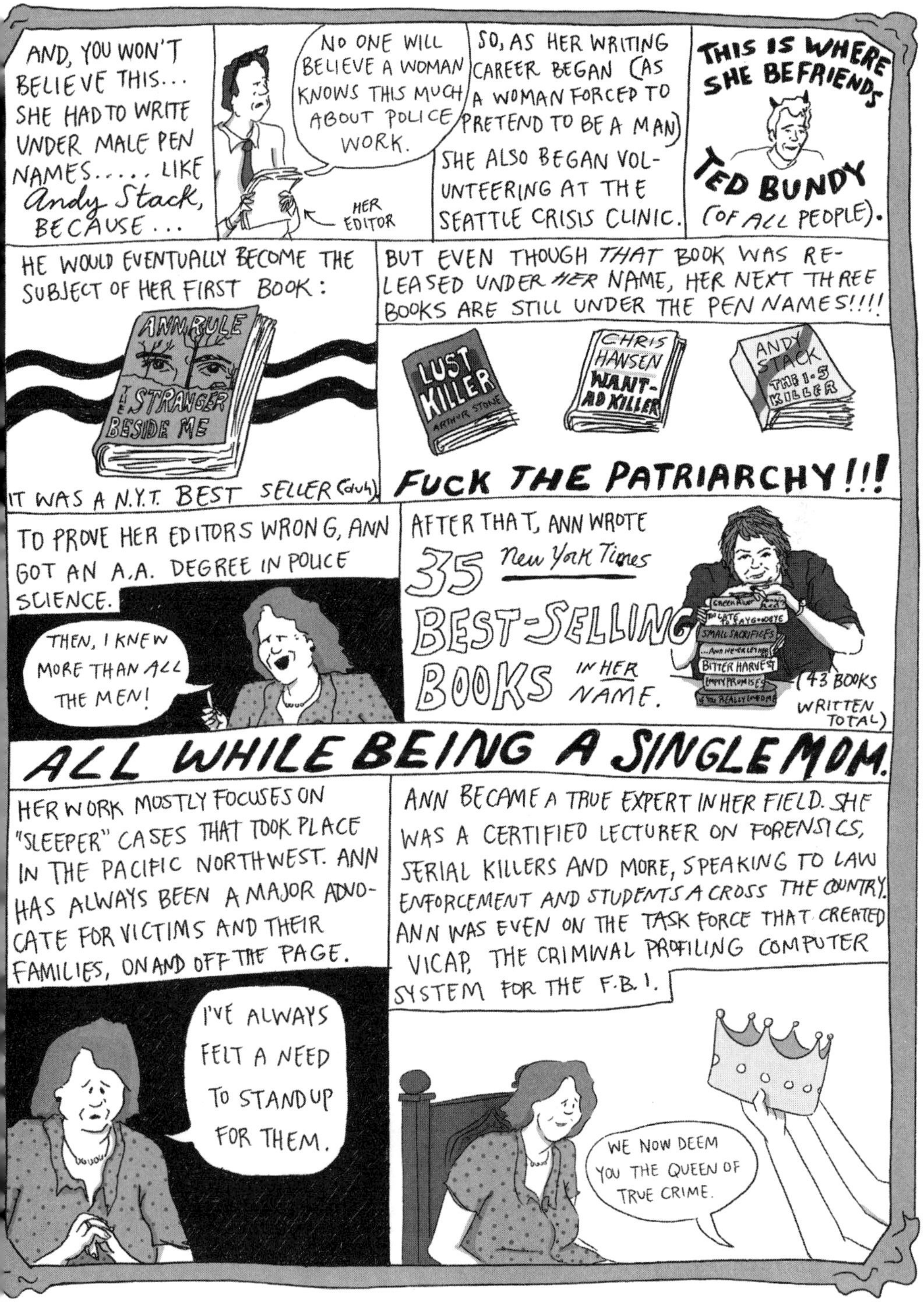
AND, YOU WON'T BELIEVE THIS... SHE HAD TO WRITE UNDER MALE PEN NAMES..... LIKE Andy Stack, BECAUSE...
NO ONE WILL BELIEVE A WOMAN KNOWS THIS MUCH ABOUT POLICE WORK.
HER EDITOR
SO, AS HER WRITING CAREER BEGAN (AS A WOMAN FORCED TO PRETEND TO BE A MAN) SHE ALSO BEGAN VOLUNTEERING AT THE SEATTLE CRISIS CLINIC.
THIS IS WHERE SHE BEFRIENDS TED BUNDY (OF ALL PEOPLE).
HE WOULD EVENTUALLY BECOME THE SUBJECT OF HER FIRST BOOK:
ANN RULE
THE STRANGER BESIDE ME
IT WAS A N.Y.T. BEST SELLER (duh)
BUT EVEN THOUGH THAT BOOK WAS RELEASED UNDER HER NAME, HER NEXT THREE BOOKS ARE STILL UNDER THE PEN NAMES!!!!
LUST KILLER
ARTHUR STONE
CHRIS HANSEN
WANT-AD KILLER
ANDY STACK
THE I-5 KILLER
FUCK THE PATRIARCHY!!!
TO PROVE HER EDITORS WRONG, ANN GOT AN A.A. DEGREE IN POLICE SCIENCE.
THEN, I KNEW MORE THAN ALL THE MEN!
AFTER THAT, ANN WROTE 35 New York Times BEST-SELLING BOOKS IN HER NAME.
BITTER HARVEST
(43 BOOKS WRITTEN TOTAL)
ALL WHILE BEING A SINGLE MOM.
HER WORK MOSTLY FOCUSES ON "SLEEPER" CASES THAT TOOK PLACE IN THE PACIFIC NORTHWEST. ANN HAS ALWAYS BEEN A MAJOR ADVOCATE FOR VICTIMS AND THEIR FAMILIES, ON AND OFF THE PAGE.
I'VE ALWAYS FELT A NEED TO STAND UP FOR THEM.
ANN BECAME A TRUE EXPERT IN HER FIELD. SHE WAS A CERTIFIED LECTURER ON FORENSICS, SERIAL KILLERS AND MORE, SPEAKING TO LAW ENFORCEMENT AND STUDENTS ACROSS THE COUNTRY. ANN WAS EVEN ON THE TASK FORCE THAT CREATED VICAP, THE CRIMINAL PROFILING COMPUTER SYSTEM FOR THE F.B.I.
WE NOW DEEM YOU THE QUEEN OF TRUE CRIME.

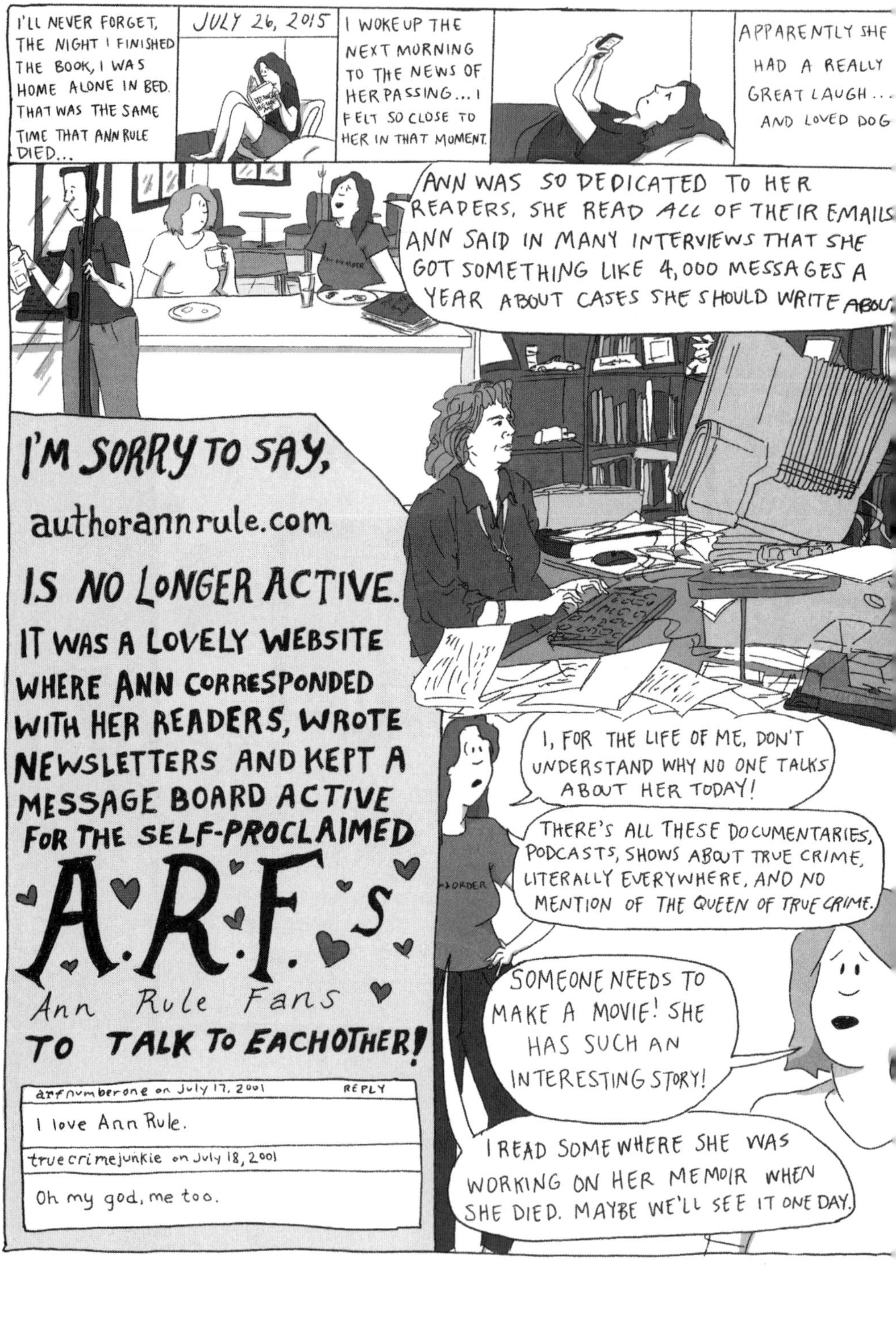
I'LL NEVER FORGET, THE NIGHT I FINISHED THE BOOK, I WAS HOME ALONE IN BED. THAT WAS THE SAME TIME THAT ANN RULE DIED...
JULY 26, 2015
I WOKE UP THE NEXT MORNING TO THE NEWS OF HER PASSING... I FELT SO CLOSE TO HER IN THAT MOMENT.
APPARENTLY SHE HAD A REALLY GREAT LAUGH... AND LOVED DOG
ANN WAS SO DEDICATED TO HER READERS, SHE READ ALL OF THEIR EMAILS. ANN SAID IN MANY INTERVIEWS THAT SHE GOT SOMETHING LIKE 4,000 MESSAGES A YEAR ABOUT CASES SHE SHOULD WRITE ABOUT.
I'M SORRY TO SAY, authorannrule.com IS NO LONGER ACTIVE.
IT WAS A LOVELY WEBSITE WHERE ANN CORRESPONDED WITH HER READERS, WROTE NEWSLETTERS AND KEPT A MESSAGE BOARD ACTIVE FOR THE SELF-PROCLAIMED
A.R.F.s
Ann Rule Fans
TO TALK TO EACHOTHER!
arfnumberone on July 17, 2001 REPLY
I love Ann Rule.
truecrimejunkie on July 18, 2001
Oh my god, me too.
I, FOR THE LIFE OF ME, DON'T UNDERSTAND WHY NO ONE TALKS ABOUT HER TODAY!
THERE'S ALL THESE DOCUMENTARIES, PODCASTS, SHOWS ABOUT TRUE CRIME, LITERALLY EVERYWHERE, AND NO MENTION OF THE QUEEN OF TRUE CRIME.
SOMEONE NEEDS TO MAKE A MOVIE! SHE HAS SUCH AN INTERESTING STORY!
I READ SOMEWHERE SHE WAS WORKING ON HER MEMOIR WHEN SHE DIED. MAYBE WE'LL SEE IT ONE DAY.

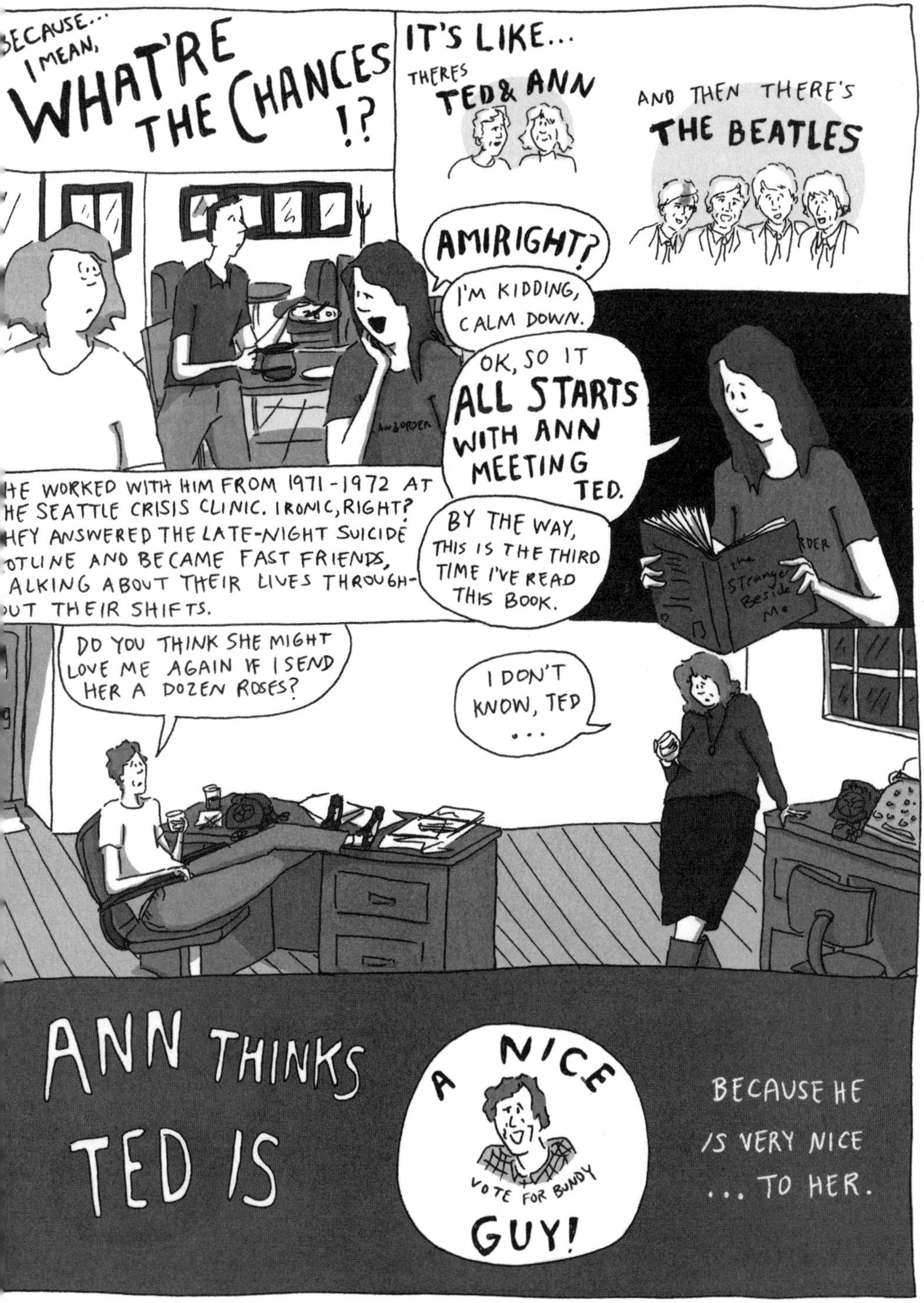
BECAUSE... I MEAN, WHAT'RE THE CHANCES !?
IT'S LIKE...
THERES TED & ANN
AND THEN THERE'S THE BEATLES
AMIRIGHT?
I'M KIDDING, CALM DOWN.
OK, SO IT ALL STARTS WITH ANN MEETING TED.
HE WORKED WITH HIM FROM 1971-1972 AT HE SEATTLE CRISIS CLINIC. IRONIC, RIGHT? HEY ANSWERED THE LATE-NIGHT SUICIDE OTLINE AND BECAME FAST FRIENDS, ALKING ABOUT THEIR LIVES THROUGH-UT THEIR SHIFTS.
BY THE WAY, THIS IS THE THIRD TIME I'VE READ THIS BOOK.
the Stranger Beside Me
DO YOU THINK SHE MIGHT LOVE ME AGAIN IF I SEND HER A DOZEN ROSES?
I DON'T KNOW, TED ...
ANN THINKS TED IS
A NICE GUY!
VOTE FOR BUNDY
BECAUSE HE IS VERY NICE ... TO HER.

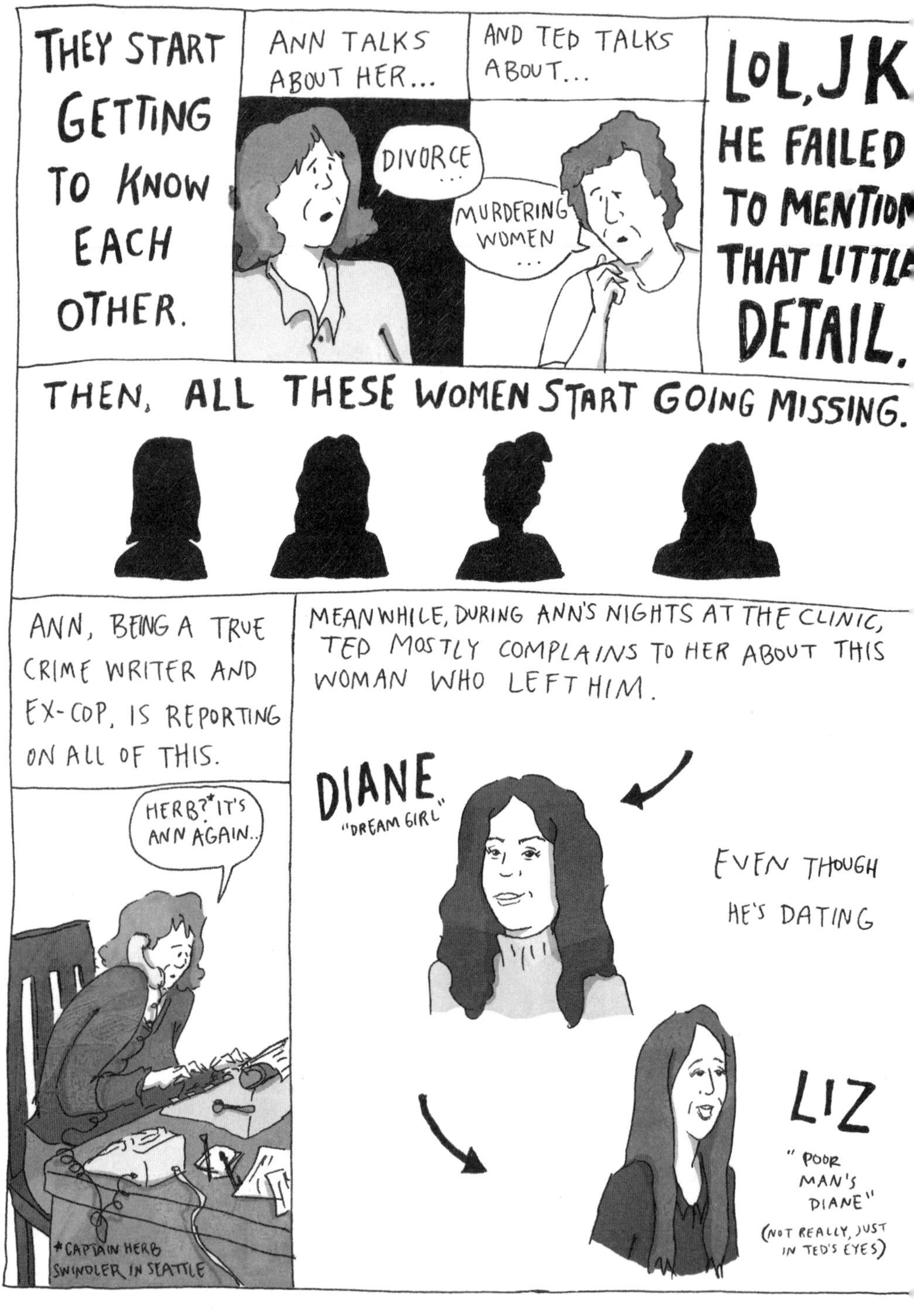
THEY START GETTING TO KNOW EACH OTHER.
ANN TALKS ABOUT HER...
DIVORCE...
AND TED TALKS ABOUT...
MURDERING WOMEN...
LOL, JK HE FAILED TO MENTION THAT LITTLE DETAIL.
THEN, ALL THESE WOMEN START GOING MISSING.
ANN, BEING A TRUE CRIME WRITER AND EX-COP, IS REPORTING ON ALL OF THIS.
HERB?* IT'S ANN AGAIN...
*CAPTAIN HERB SWINDLER IN SEATTLE
MEANWHILE, DURING ANN'S NIGHTS AT THE CLINIC, TED MOSTLY COMPLAINS TO HER ABOUT THIS WOMAN WHO LEFT HIM.
DIANE
"DREAM GIRL"
EVEN THOUGH HE'S DATING
LIZ
"POOR MAN'S DIANE"
(NOT REALLY, JUST IN TED'S EYES)

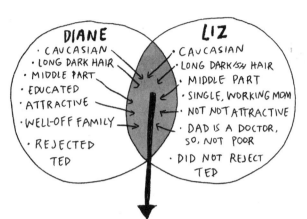

SO, WHAT'S IN COMMON BETWEEN THEM?

DIANE
· CAUCASIAN
· LONG DARK HAIR
· MIDDLE PART
· EDUCATED
· ATTRACTIVE
· WELL-OFF FAMILY
· REJECTED TED
LIZ
· CAUCASIAN
· LONG DARK-ISH HAIR
· MIDDLE PART
· SINGLE, WORKING MOM
· NOT NOT ATTRACTIVE
· DAD IS A DOCTOR, SO, NOT POOR
· DID NOT REJECT TED

AND... WHO ARE THE VICTIMS, you ask?

EDU-CATED
YOUNG
WHITE
WOMEN
WITH LONG
DARK HAIR
PARTED DOWN
THE
MIDDLE

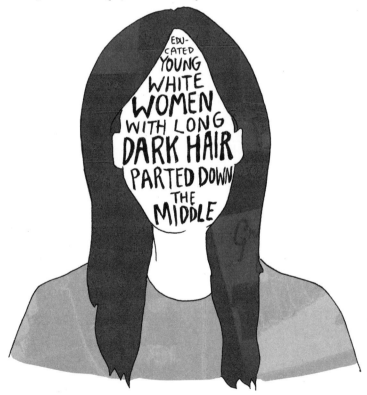

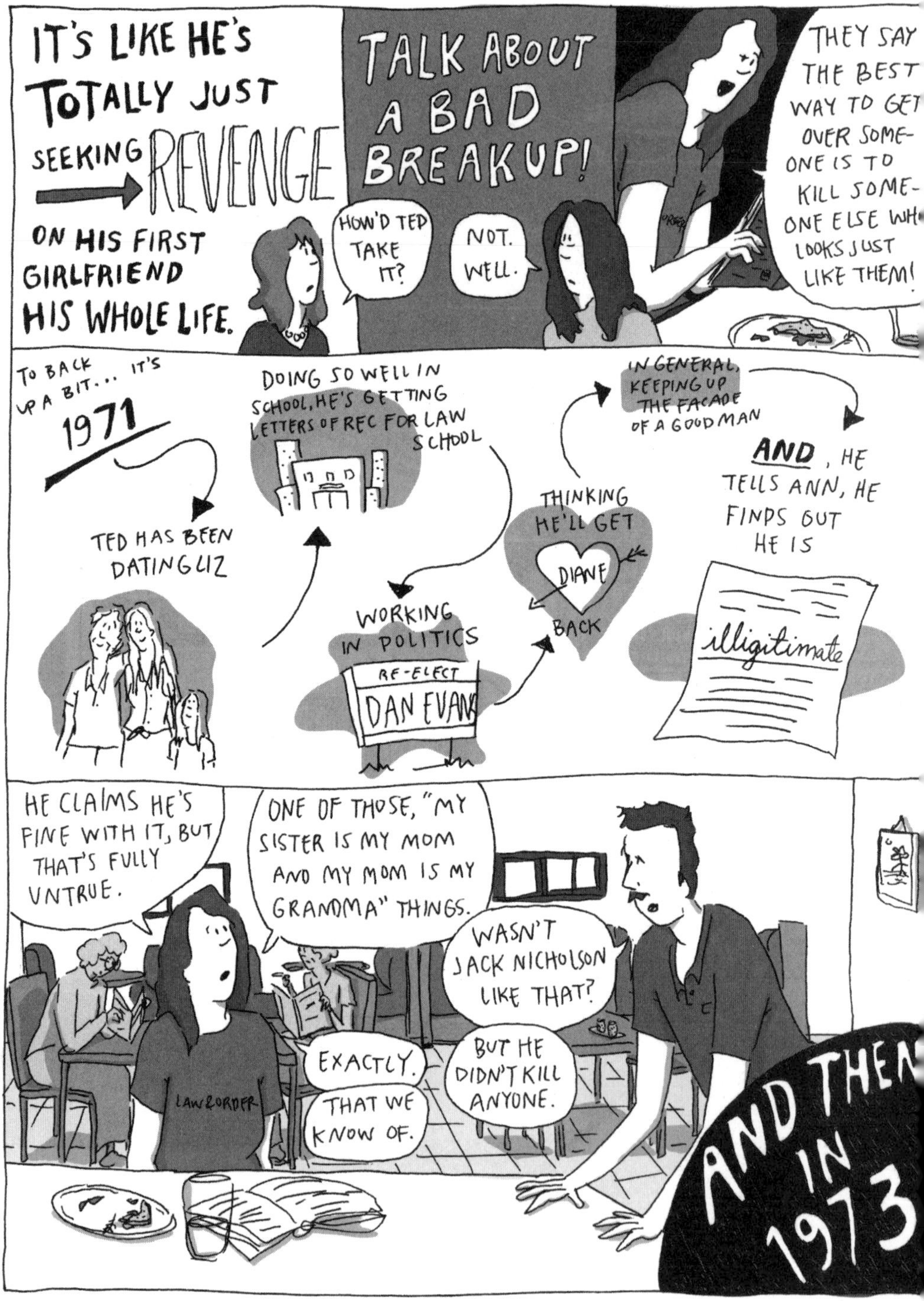

IT'S LIKE HE'S TOTALLY JUST SEEKING → REVENGE ON HIS FIRST GIRLFRIEND HIS WHOLE LIFE.
TALK ABOUT A BAD BREAKUP!
HOW'D TED TAKE IT?
NOT. WELL.
THEY SAY THE BEST WAY TO GET OVER SOME-ONE IS TO KILL SOME-ONE ELSE WHO LOOKS JUST LIKE THEM!
TO BACK UP A BIT... IT'S 1971
TED HAS BEEN DATING LIZ
DOING SO WELL IN SCHOOL, HE'S GETTING LETTERS OF REC FOR LAW SCHOOL
WORKING IN POLITICS
RE-ELECT DAN EVANS
THINKING HE'LL GET DIANE BACK
IN GENERAL, KEEPING UP THE FACADE OF A GOOD MAN
AND, HE TELLS ANN, HE FINDS OUT HE IS
illigitimate
HE CLAIMS HE'S FINE WITH IT, BUT THAT'S FULLY UNTRUE.
ONE OF THOSE, "MY SISTER IS MY MOM AND MY MOM IS MY GRANDMA" THINGS.
WASN'T JACK NICHOLSON LIKE THAT?
EXACTLY.
BUT HE DIDN'T KILL ANYONE.
THAT WE KNOW OF.
LAW&ORDER
AND THEN IN 1973

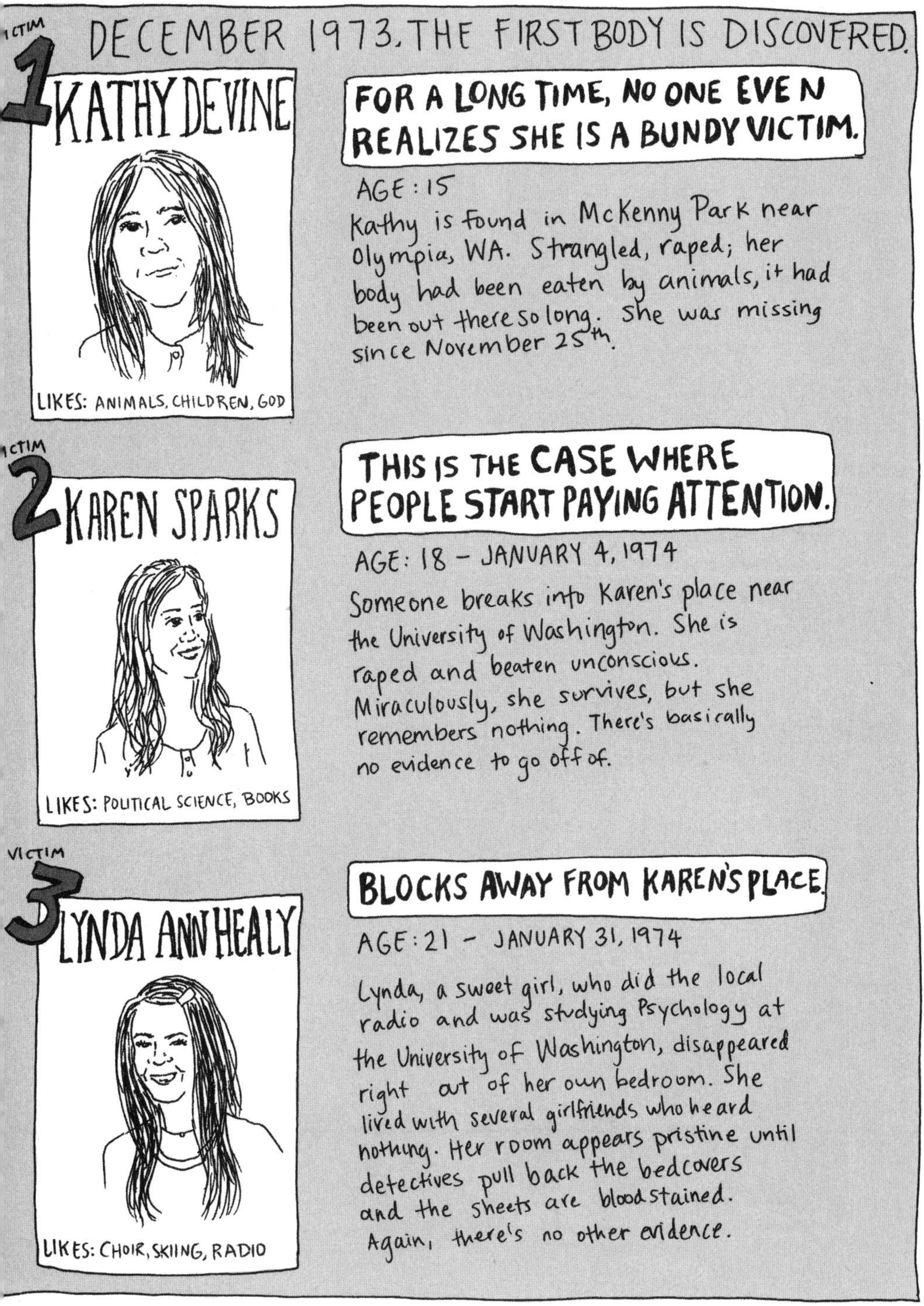
DECEMBER 1973. THE FIRST BODY IS DISCOVERED.
VICTIM 1
KATHY DEVINE
LIKES: ANIMALS, CHILDREN, GOD
FOR A LONG TIME, NO ONE EVEN REALIZES SHE IS A BUNDY VICTIM.
AGE: 15
Kathy is found in McKenny Park near Olympia, WA. Strangled, raped; her body had been eaten by animals, it had been out there so long. She was missing since November 25th.
VICTIM 2
KAREN SPARKS
LIKES: POLITICAL SCIENCE, BOOKS
THIS IS THE CASE WHERE PEOPLE START PAYING ATTENTION.
AGE: 18 - JANUARY 4, 1974
Someone breaks into Karen's place near the University of Washington. She is raped and beaten unconscious. Miraculously, she survives, but she remembers nothing. There's basically no evidence to go off of.
VICTIM 3
LYNDA ANN HEALY
LIKES: CHOIR, SKIING, RADIO
BLOCKS AWAY FROM KAREN'S PLACE.
AGE: 21 - JANUARY 31, 1974
Lynda, a sweet girl, who did the local radio and was studying Psychology at the University of Washington, disappeared right out of her own bedroom. She lived with several girlfriends who heard nothing. Her room appears pristine until detectives pull back the bedcovers and the sheets are bloodstained. Again, there's no other evidence.

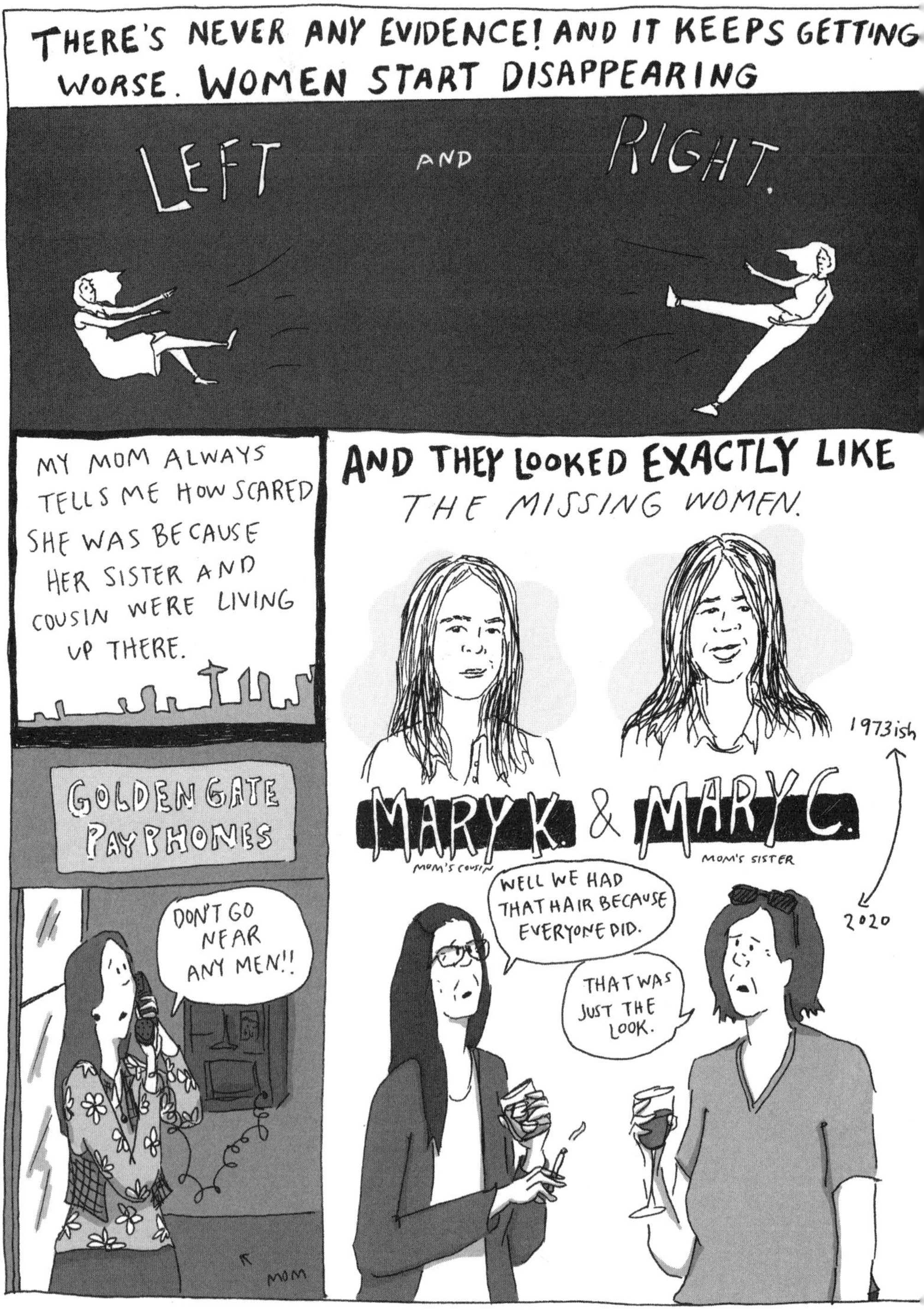
THERE'S NEVER ANY EVIDENCE! AND IT KEEPS GETTING WORSE. WOMEN START DISAPPEARING
LEFT AND RIGHT.
MY MOM ALWAYS TELLS ME HOW SCARED SHE WAS BECAUSE HER SISTER AND COUSIN WERE LIVING UP THERE.
AND THEY LOOKED EXACTLY LIKE THE MISSING WOMEN.
1973ish
MARY K. & MARY C.
MOM'S COUSIN
MOM'S SISTER
2020
GOLDEN GATE PAYPHONES
DON'T GO NEAR ANY MEN!!
MOM
WELL WE HAD THAT HAIR BECAUSE EVERYONE DID.
THAT WAS JUST THE LOOK.

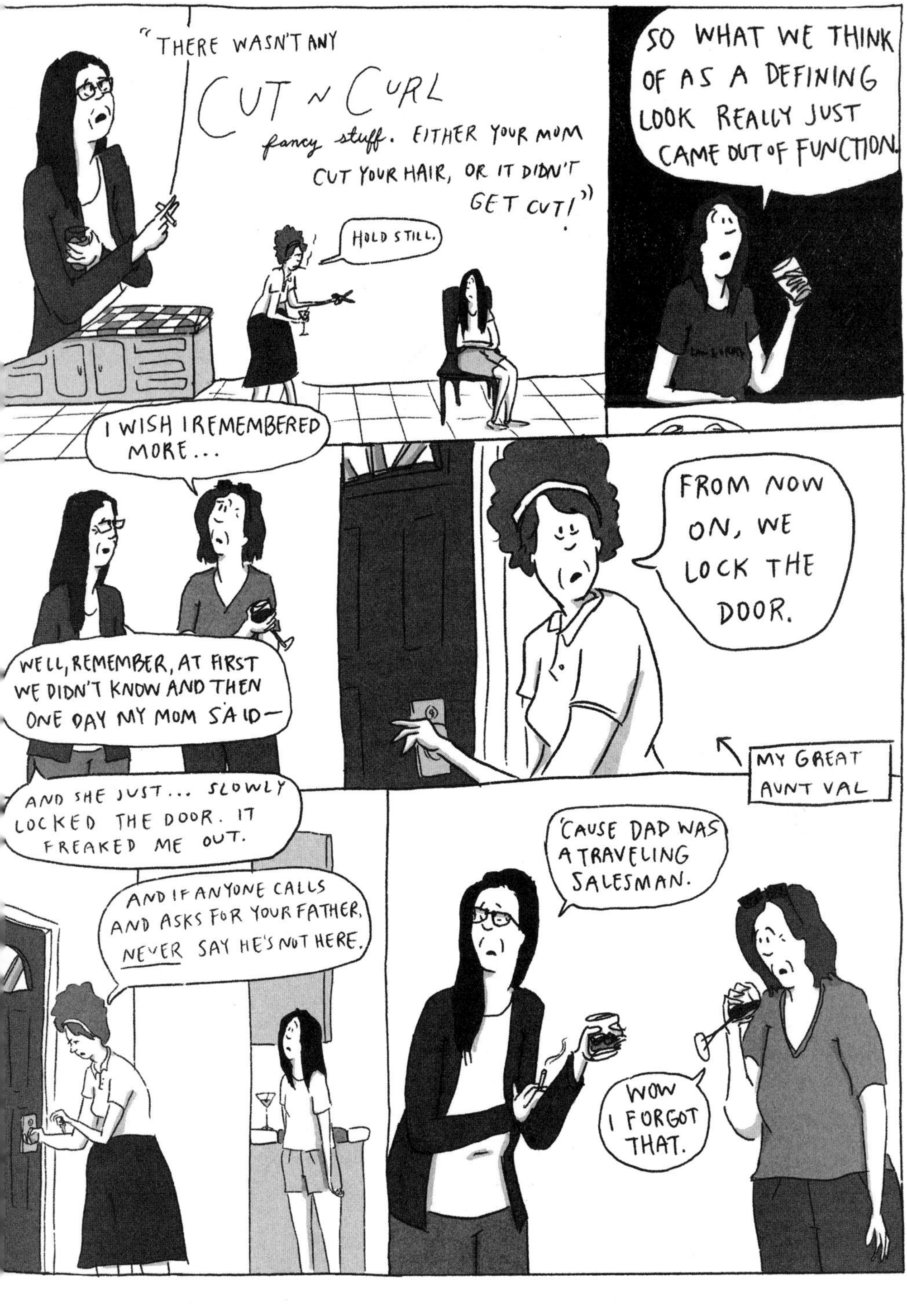
"THERE WASN'T ANY CUT N CURL fancy stuff. EITHER YOUR MOM CUT YOUR HAIR, OR IT DIDN'T GET CUT!"
HOLD STILL.
SO WHAT WE THINK OF AS A DEFINING LOOK REALLY JUST CAME OUT OF FUNCTION.
I WISH I REMEMBERED MORE...
WELL, REMEMBER, AT FIRST WE DIDN'T KNOW AND THEN ONE DAY MY MOM SAID—
FROM NOW ON, WE LOCK THE DOOR.
MY GREAT AUNT VAL
AND SHE JUST... SLOWLY LOCKED THE DOOR. IT FREAKED ME OUT.
AND IF ANYONE CALLS AND ASKS FOR YOUR FATHER, NEVER SAY HE'S NOT HERE.
'CAUSE DAD WAS A TRAVELING SALESMAN.
WOW I FORGOT THAT.

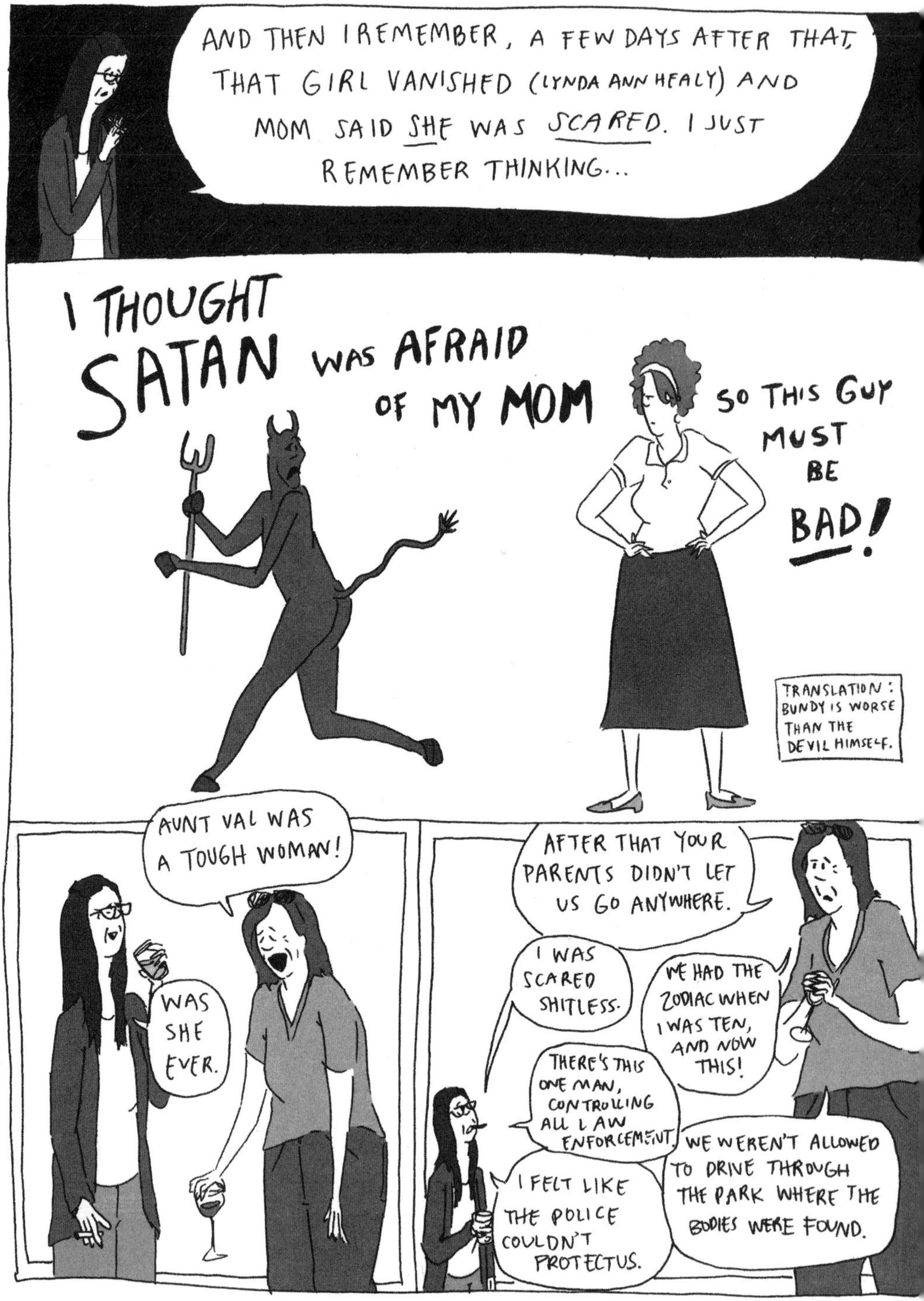
AND THEN I REMEMBER, A FEW DAYS AFTER THAT, THAT GIRL VANISHED (LYNDA ANN HEALY) AND MOM SAID SHE WAS SCARED. I JUST REMEMBER THINKING...
I THOUGHT SATAN WAS AFRAID OF MY MOM
SO THIS GUY MUST BE BAD!
TRANSLATION: BUNDY IS WORSE THAN THE DEVIL HIMSELF.
AUNT VAL WAS A TOUGH WOMAN!
WAS SHE EVER.
AFTER THAT YOUR PARENTS DIDN'T LET US GO ANYWHERE.
I WAS SCARED SHITLESS.
WE HAD THE ZODIAC WHEN I WAS TEN, AND NOW THIS!
THERE'S THIS ONE MAN, CONTROLLING ALL LAW ENFORCEMENT.
WE WEREN'T ALLOWED TO DRIVE THROUGH THE PARK WHERE THE BODIES WERE FOUND.
I FELT LIKE THE POLICE COULDN'T PROTECT US.

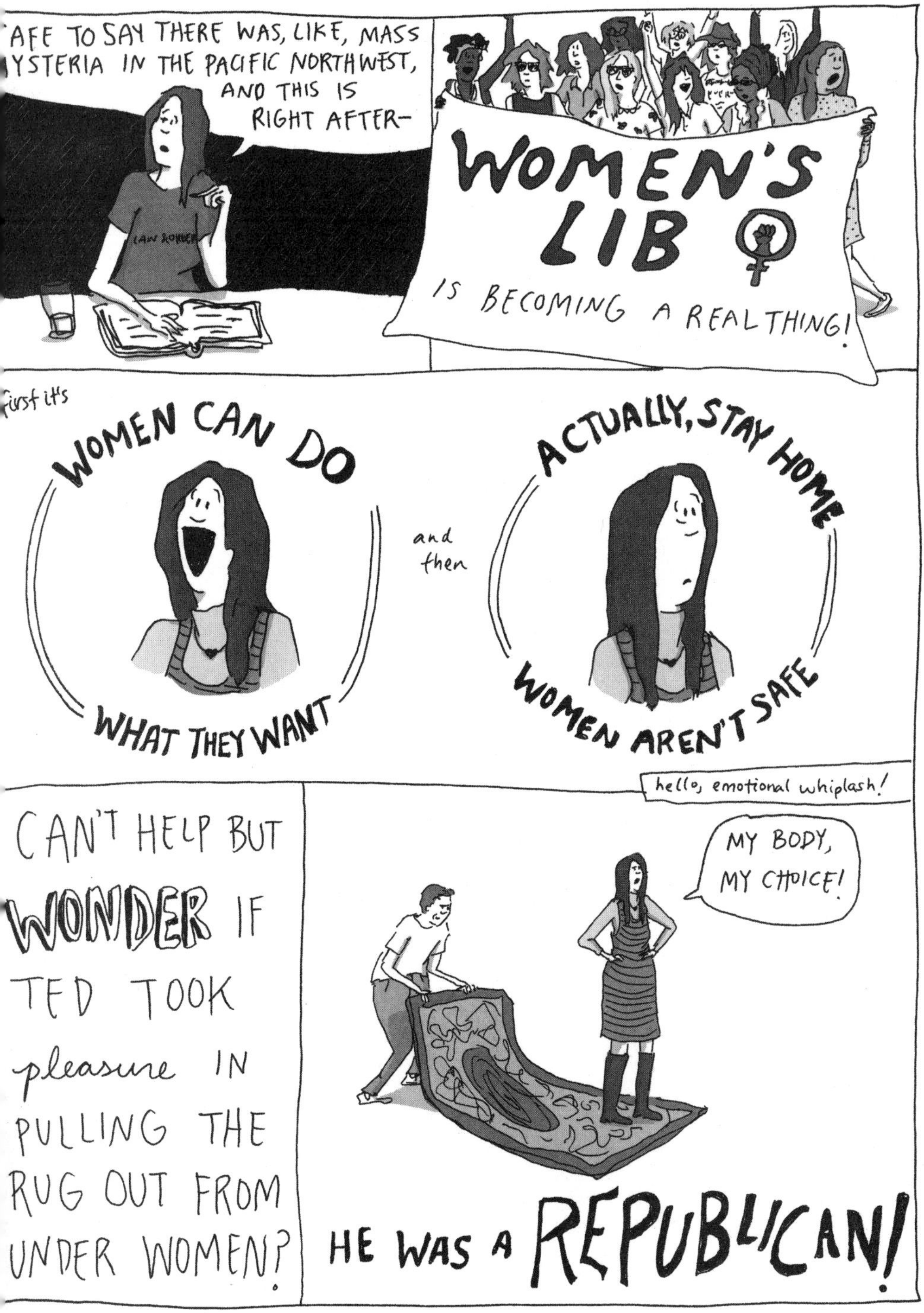
AFE TO SAY THERE WAS, LIKE, MASS YSTERIA IN THE PACIFIC NORTHWEST, AND THIS IS RIGHT AFTER-
WOMEN'S LIB IS BECOMING A REAL THING!
first it's
WOMEN CAN DO WHAT THEY WANT
and then
ACTUALLY, STAY HOME WOMEN AREN'T SAFE
hello, emotional whiplash!
CAN'T HELP BUT WONDER IF TED TOOK pleasure IN PULLING THE RUG OUT FROM UNDER WOMEN?
MY BODY, MY CHOICE!
HE WAS A REPUBLICAN!

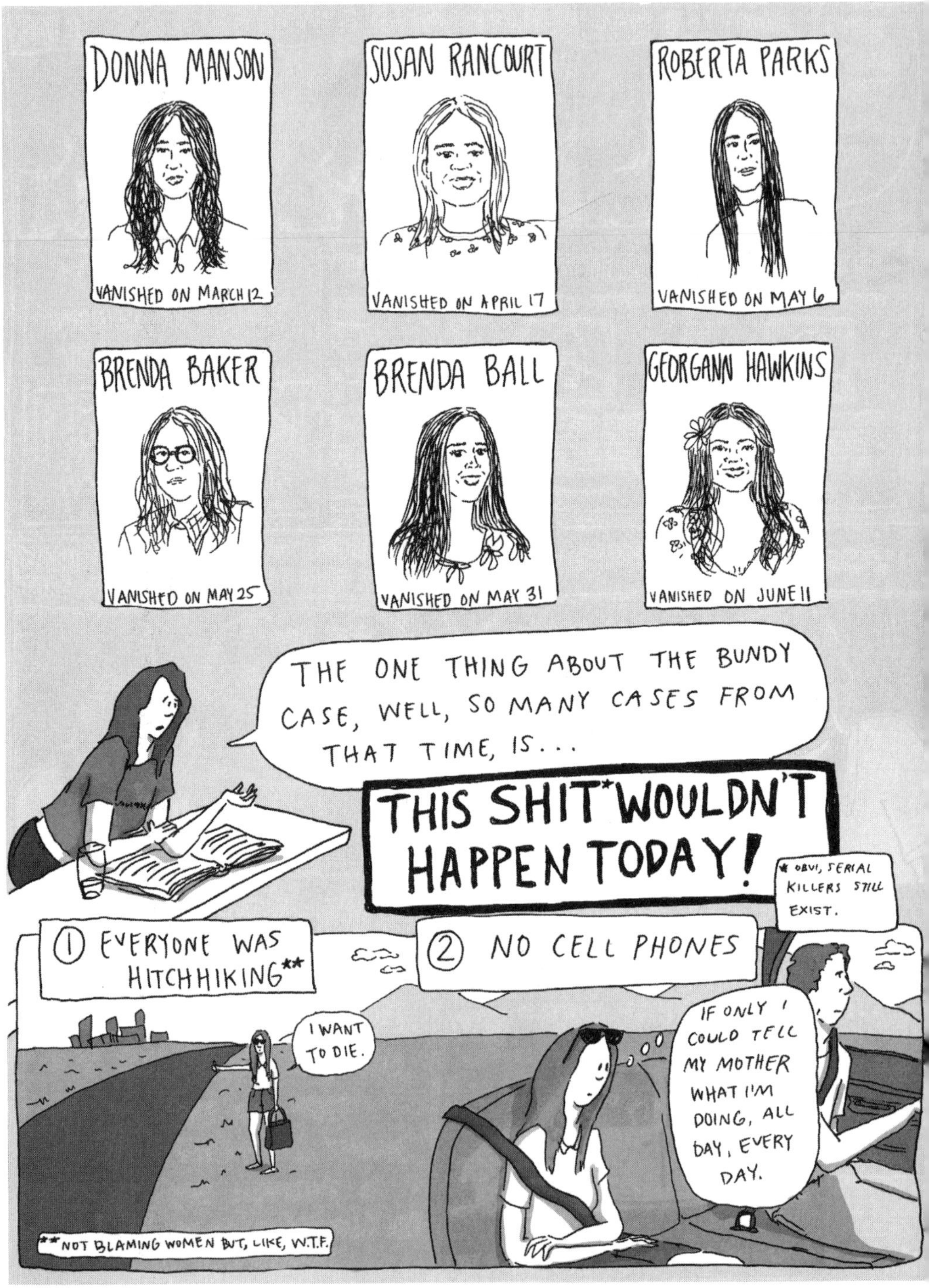
DONNA MANSON
VANISHED ON MARCH 12
SUSAN RANCOURT
VANISHED ON APRIL 17
ROBERTA PARKS
VANISHED ON MAY 6
BRENDA BAKER
VANISHED ON MAY 25
BRENDA BALL
VANISHED ON MAY 31
GEORGANN HAWKINS
VANISHED ON JUNE 11
THE ONE THING ABOUT THE BUNDY CASE, WELL, SO MANY CASES FROM THAT TIME, IS...
THIS SHIT* WOULDN'T HAPPEN TODAY!
* OBVI, SERIAL KILLERS STILL EXIST.
① EVERYONE WAS HITCHHIKING**
② NO CELL PHONES
I WANT TO DIE.
IF ONLY I COULD TELL MY MOTHER WHAT I'M DOING, ALL DAY, EVERY DAY.
** NOT BLAMING WOMEN BUT, LIKE, W.T.F.

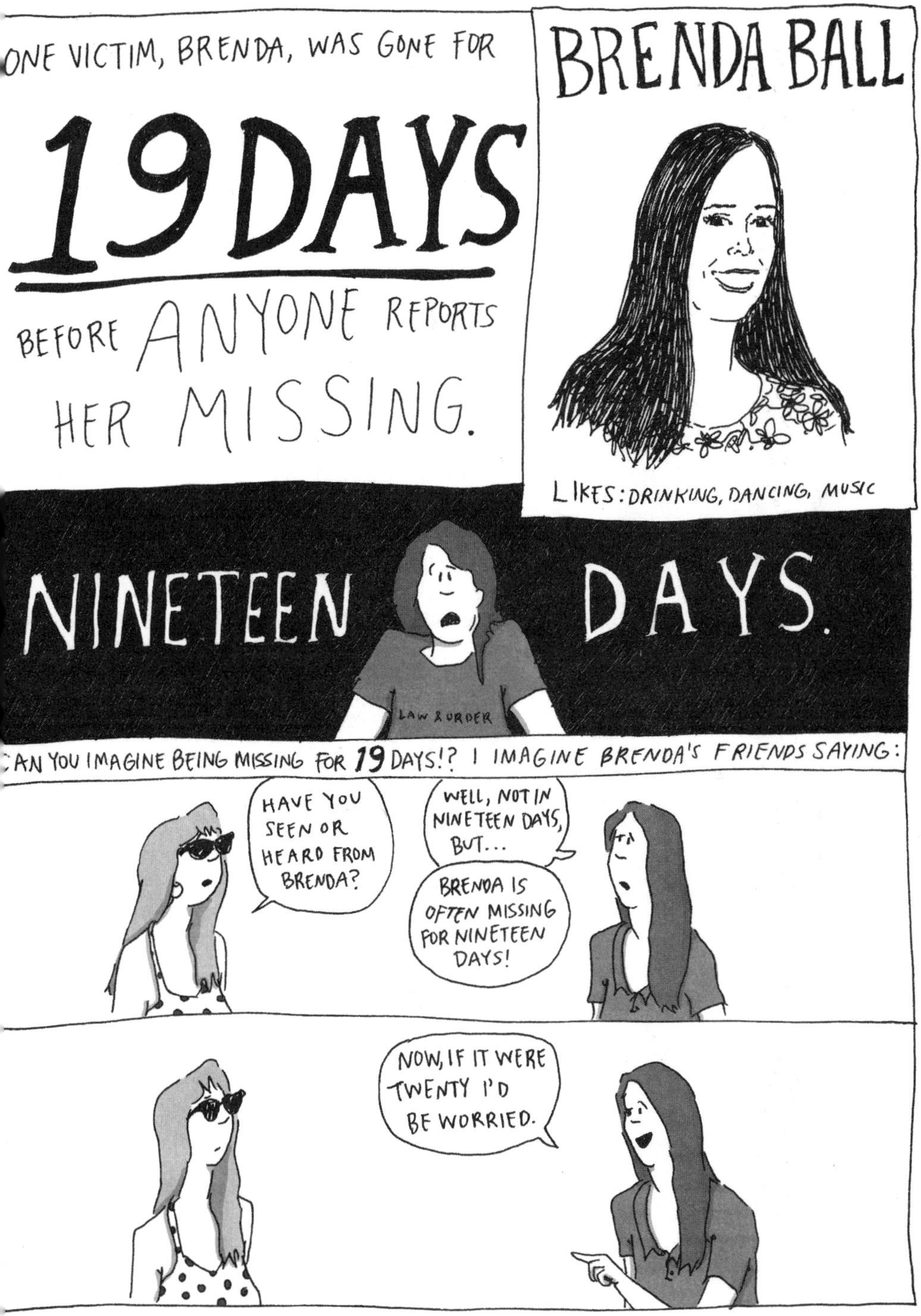
ONE VICTIM, BRENDA, WAS GONE FOR
19 DAYS
BEFORE ANYONE REPORTS HER MISSING.
BRENDA BALL
LIKES: DRINKING, DANCING, MUSIC
NINETEEN DAYS.
LAW & ORDER
CAN YOU IMAGINE BEING MISSING FOR 19 DAYS!? I IMAGINE BRENDA'S FRIENDS SAYING:
HAVE YOU SEEN OR HEARD FROM BRENDA?
WELL, NOT IN NINETEEN DAYS, BUT...
BRENDA IS OFTEN MISSING FOR NINETEEN DAYS!
NOW, IF IT WERE TWENTY I'D BE WORRIED.

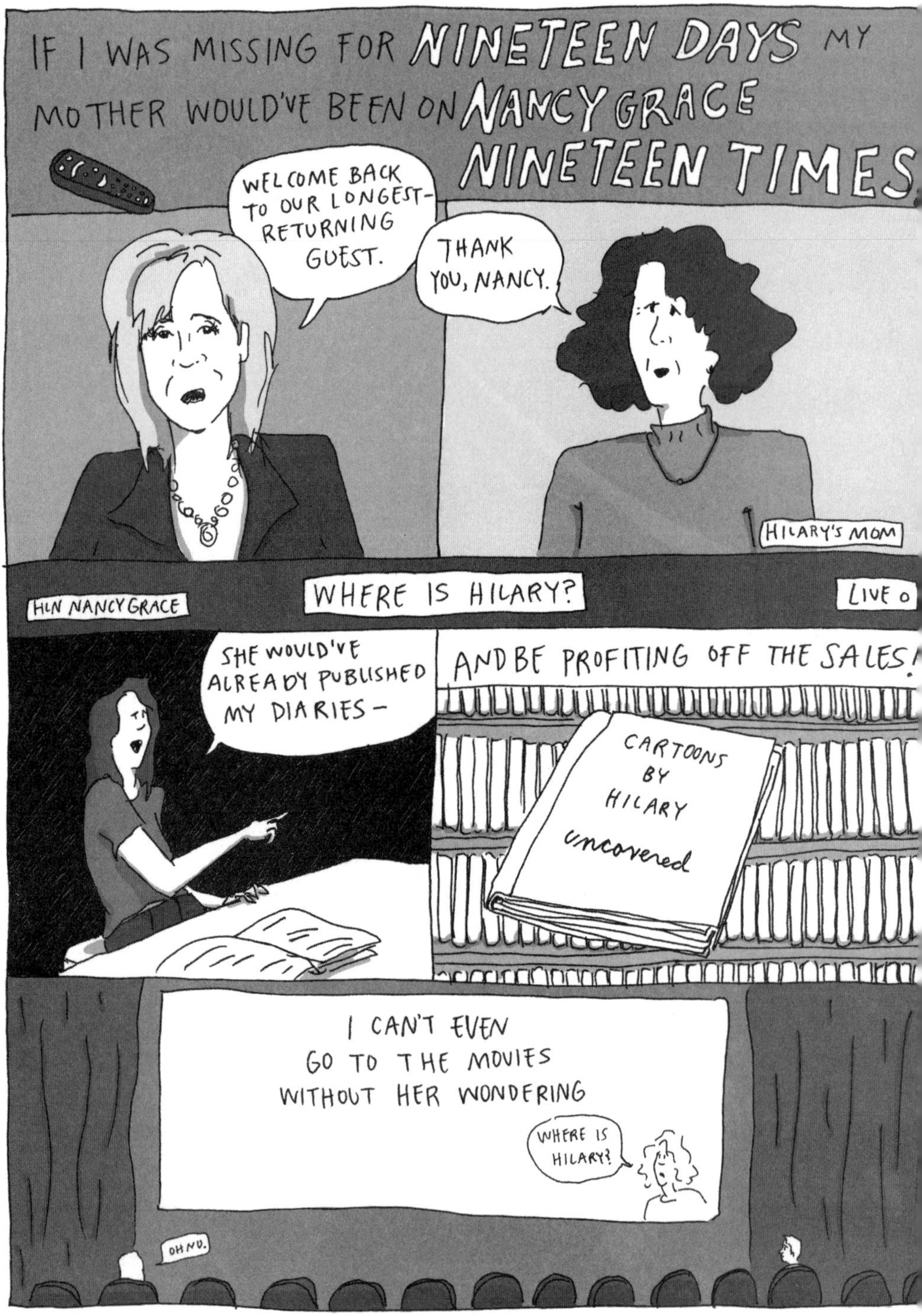
IF I WAS MISSING FOR NINETEEN DAYS MY MOTHER WOULD'VE BEEN ON NANCY GRACE NINETEEN TIMES.
WELCOME BACK TO OUR LONGEST-RETURNING GUEST.
THANK YOU, NANCY.
HILARY'S MOM
HLN NANCY GRACE
WHERE IS HILARY?
LIVE
SHE WOULD'VE ALREADY PUBLISHED MY DIARIES -
AND BE PROFITING OFF THE SALES!
CARTOONS BY HILARY uncovered
I CAN'T EVEN GO TO THE MOVIES WITHOUT HER WONDERING
WHERE IS HILARY?
OH NO.

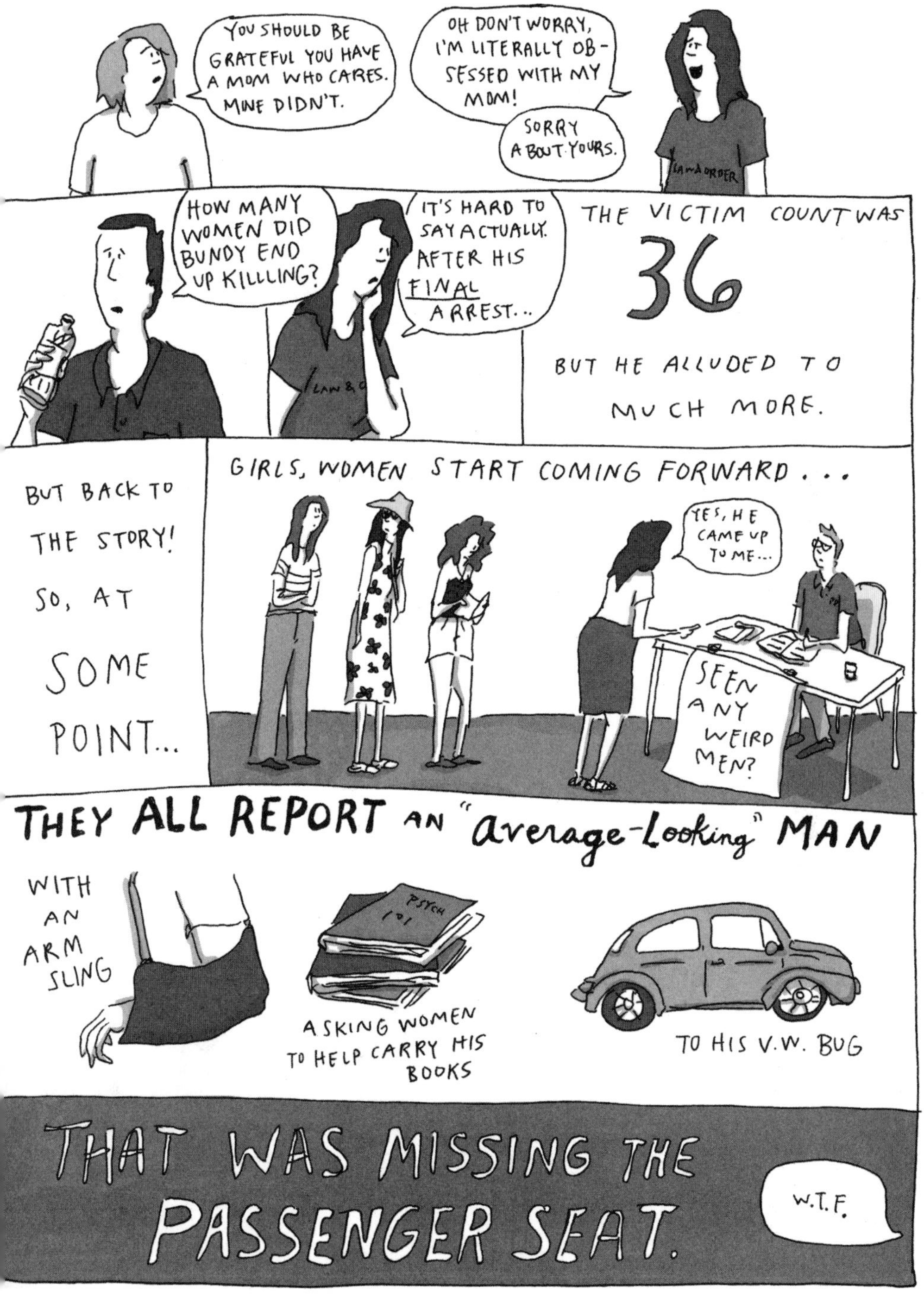
YOU SHOULD BE GRATEFUL YOU HAVE A MOM WHO CARES. MINE DIDN'T.
OH DON'T WORRY, I'M LITERALLY OB-SESSED WITH MY MOM!
SORRY ABOUT YOURS.
LAW & ORDER
HOW MANY WOMEN DID BUNDY END UP KILLLING?
IT'S HARD TO SAY ACTUALLY. AFTER HIS FINAL ARREST...
THE VICTIM COUNT WAS
36
BUT HE ALLUDED TO MUCH MORE.
BUT BACK TO THE STORY! SO, AT SOME POINT...
GIRLS, WOMEN START COMING FORWARD...
YES, HE CAME UP TO ME...
SEEN ANY WEIRD MEN?
THEY ALL REPORT AN "Average-Looking" MAN
WITH AN ARM SLING
PSYCH 101
ASKING WOMEN TO HELP CARRY HIS BOOKS
TO HIS V.W. BUG
THAT WAS MISSING THE PASSENGER SEAT.
W.T.F.

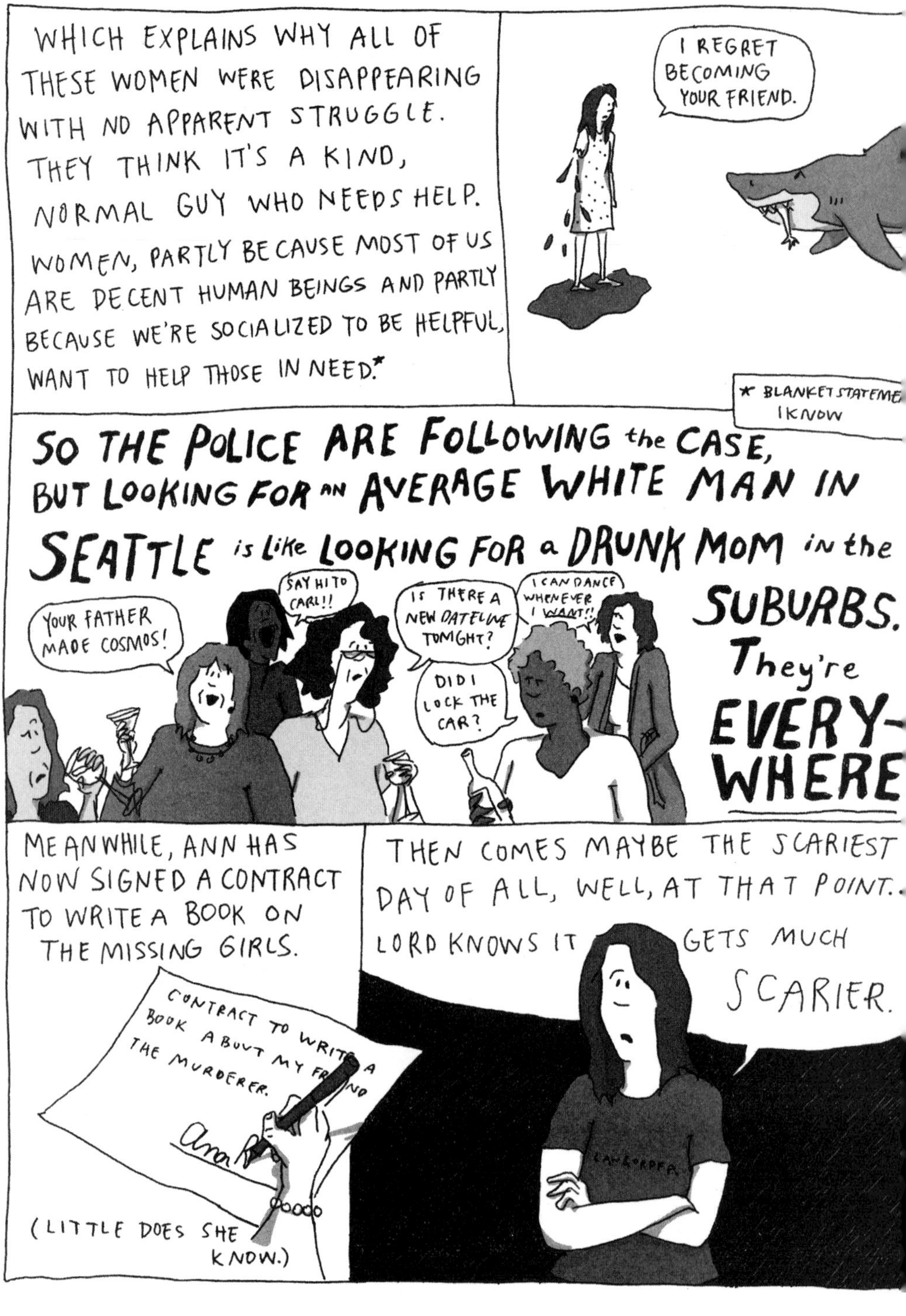
WHICH EXPLAINS WHY ALL OF THESE WOMEN WERE DISAPPEARING WITH NO APPARENT STRUGGLE. THEY THINK IT'S A KIND, NORMAL GUY WHO NEEDS HELP.
WOMEN, PARTLY BECAUSE MOST OF US ARE DECENT HUMAN BEINGS AND PARTLY BECAUSE WE'RE SOCIALIZED TO BE HELPFUL, WANT TO HELP THOSE IN NEED.*
I REGRET BECOMING YOUR FRIEND.
* BLANKET STATEME
I KNOW
SO THE POLICE ARE FOLLOWING the CASE, BUT LOOKING FOR AN AVERAGE WHITE MAN IN SEATTLE is like LOOKING FOR a DRUNK MOM in the SUBURBS. They're EVERY-WHERE
YOUR FATHER MADE COSMOS!
SAY HI TO CARL!!
IS THERE A NEW DATELINE TONIGHT?
DID I LOCK THE CAR?
I CAN DANCE WHENEVER I WANT!!
MEANWHILE, ANN HAS NOW SIGNED A CONTRACT TO WRITE A BOOK ON THE MISSING GIRLS.
CONTRACT TO WRIT A
BOOK ABUVT MY FR ND
THE MURDERER.
(LITTLE DOES SHE KNOW.)
THEN COMES MAYBE THE SCARIEST DAY OF ALL, WELL, AT THAT POINT... LORD KNOWS IT GETS MUCH SCARIER.

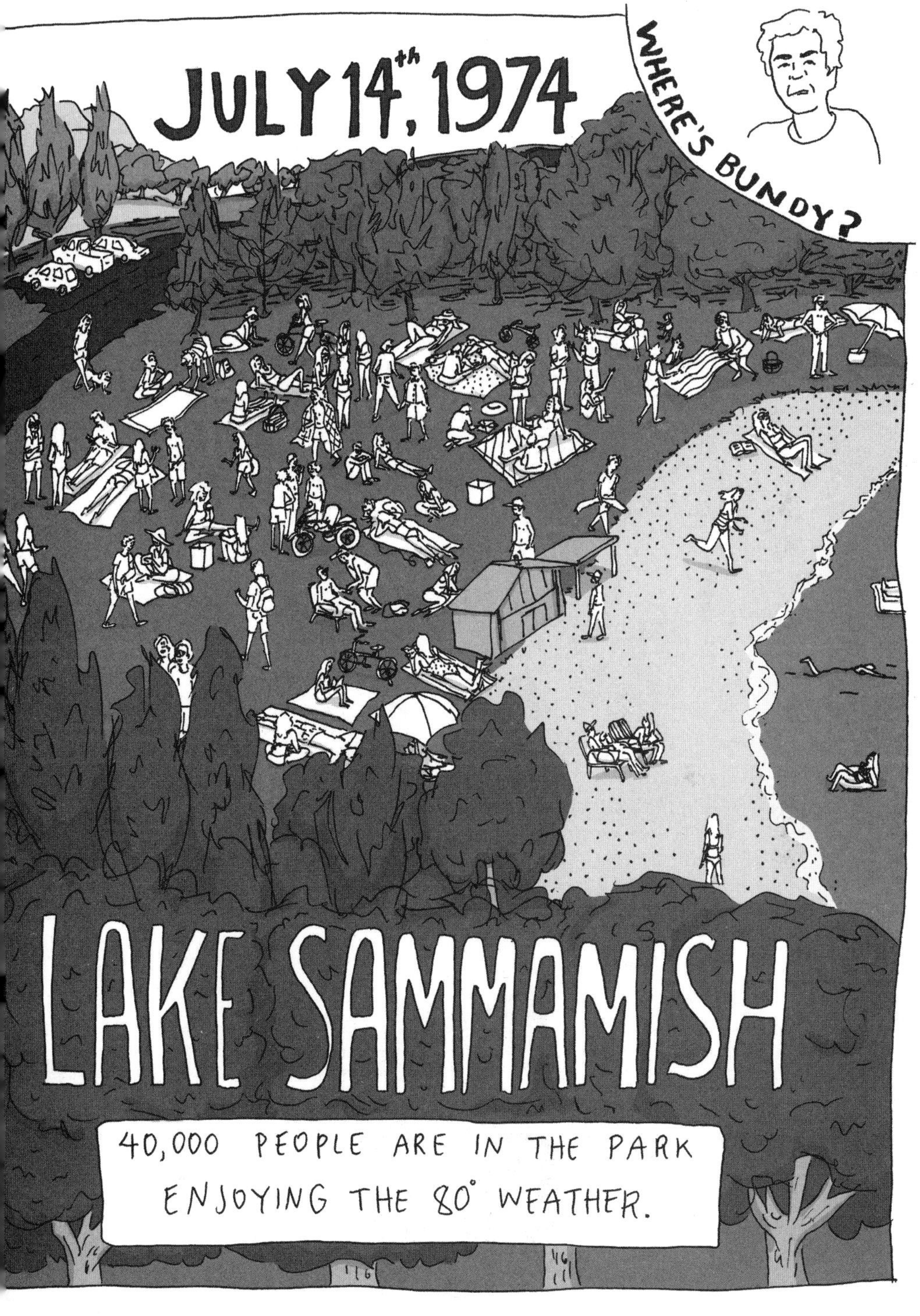
JULY 14th, 1974
WHERE'S BUNDY?
LAKE SAMMAMISH
40,000 PEOPLE ARE IN THE PARK ENJOYING THE 80° WEATHER.

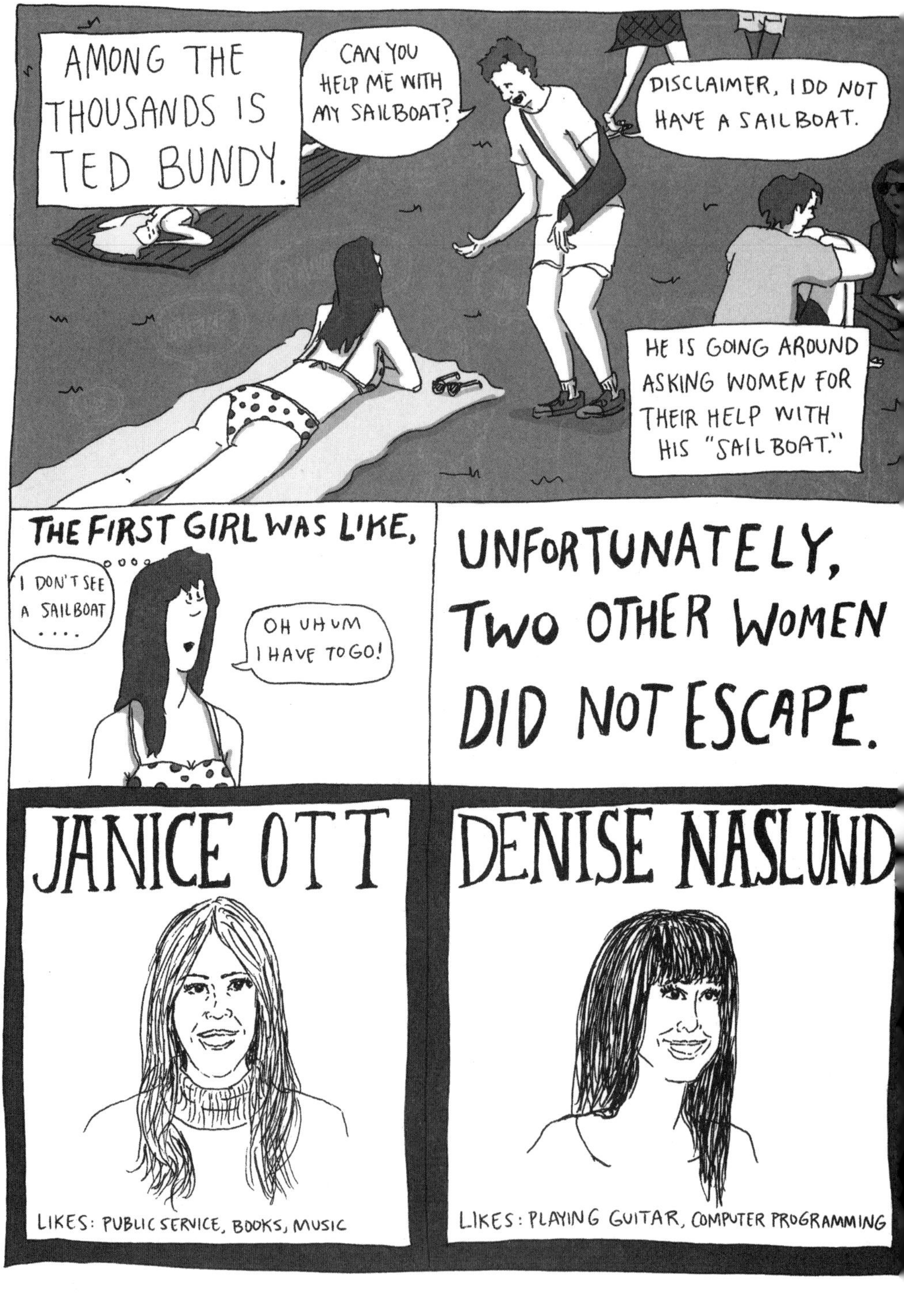
AMONG THE THOUSANDS IS TED BUNDY.
CAN YOU HELP ME WITH MY SAILBOAT?
DISCLAIMER, I DO NOT HAVE A SAILBOAT.
HE IS GOING AROUND ASKING WOMEN FOR THEIR HELP WITH HIS "SAILBOAT."
THE FIRST GIRL WAS LIKE,
I DON'T SEE A SAILBOAT ....
OH UH UM I HAVE TO GO!
UNFORTUNATELY, TWO OTHER WOMEN DID NOT ESCAPE.
JANICE OTT
LIKES: PUBLIC SERVICE, BOOKS, MUSIC
DENISE NASLUND
LIKES: PLAYING GUITAR, COMPUTER PROGRAMMING

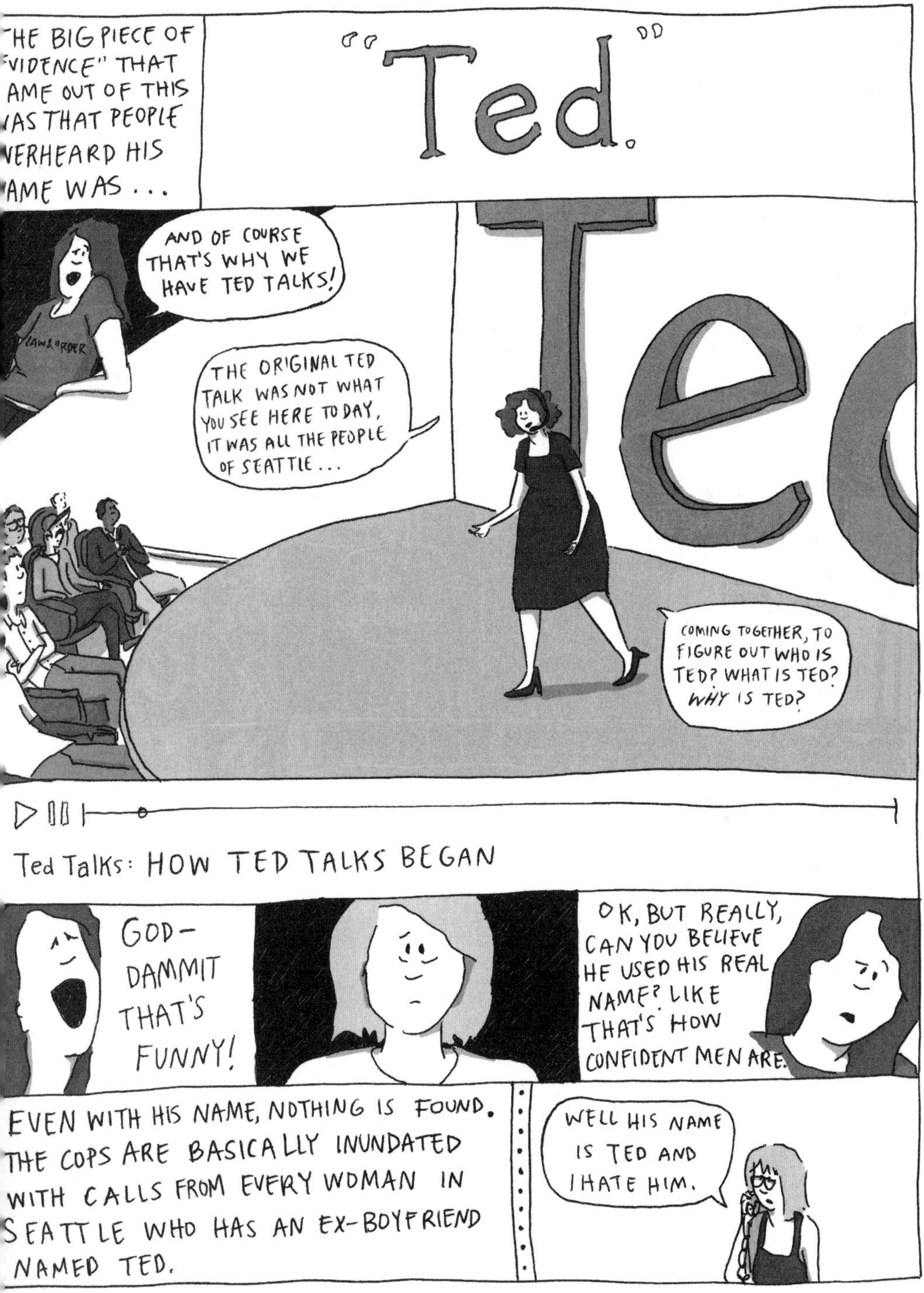
THE BIG PIECE OF EVIDENCE" THAT CAME OUT OF THIS WAS THAT PEOPLE OVERHEARD HIS NAME WAS . . .
"Ted."
AND OF COURSE THAT'S WHY WE HAVE TED TALKS!
LAW & ORDER
THE ORIGINAL TED TALK WAS NOT WHAT YOU SEE HERE TODAY, IT WAS ALL THE PEOPLE OF SEATTLE . . .
Ted
COMING TOGETHER, TO FIGURE OUT WHO IS TED? WHAT IS TED? WHY IS TED?
Ted Talks: HOW TED TALKS BEGAN
GOD-DAMMIT THAT'S FUNNY!
OK, BUT REALLY, CAN YOU BELIEVE HE USED HIS REAL NAME? LIKE THAT'S HOW CONFIDENT MEN ARE.
EVEN WITH HIS NAME, NOTHING IS FOUND. THE COPS ARE BASICALLY INUNDATED WITH CALLS FROM EVERY WOMAN IN SEATTLE WHO HAS AN EX-BOYFRIEND NAMED TED.
WELL HIS NAME IS TED AND I HATE HIM.

THIS IS WHEN ANN & TED'S GIRLFRIEND START THINKING
A MAN... NAMED TED... WITH A V.W. BUG...
IT COULDN'T BE MY TED!
BUT THEY COULDN'T FACE THEIR FEARS.
EVEN THOUGH LIZ
I FOUND THOSE CRUTCHES.
I CAUGHT HIM STARING AT MY BODY WITH A FLASH-LIGHT IN THE NIGHT.
HE HAS A FAKE MUSTACHE.
WE'RE NOT HAVING SEX ANYMORE.
AND THAT CROWBAR.
AND THE PLASTER OF PARIS.
AND THE WOMEN'S CLOTHES.
HE'S MISSING ALL THE TIME.
ONE TIME HE SAT OUTSIDE MY HOUSE ALL NIGHT IN HIS CAR.
WHO DOES THAT?
HAS A LITTLE MORE TO THINK ABOUT.
AND THEN, IT ALL ... JUST... STOPS.
THE TERROR!
WAIT, WHERE DID THE TERROR GO?

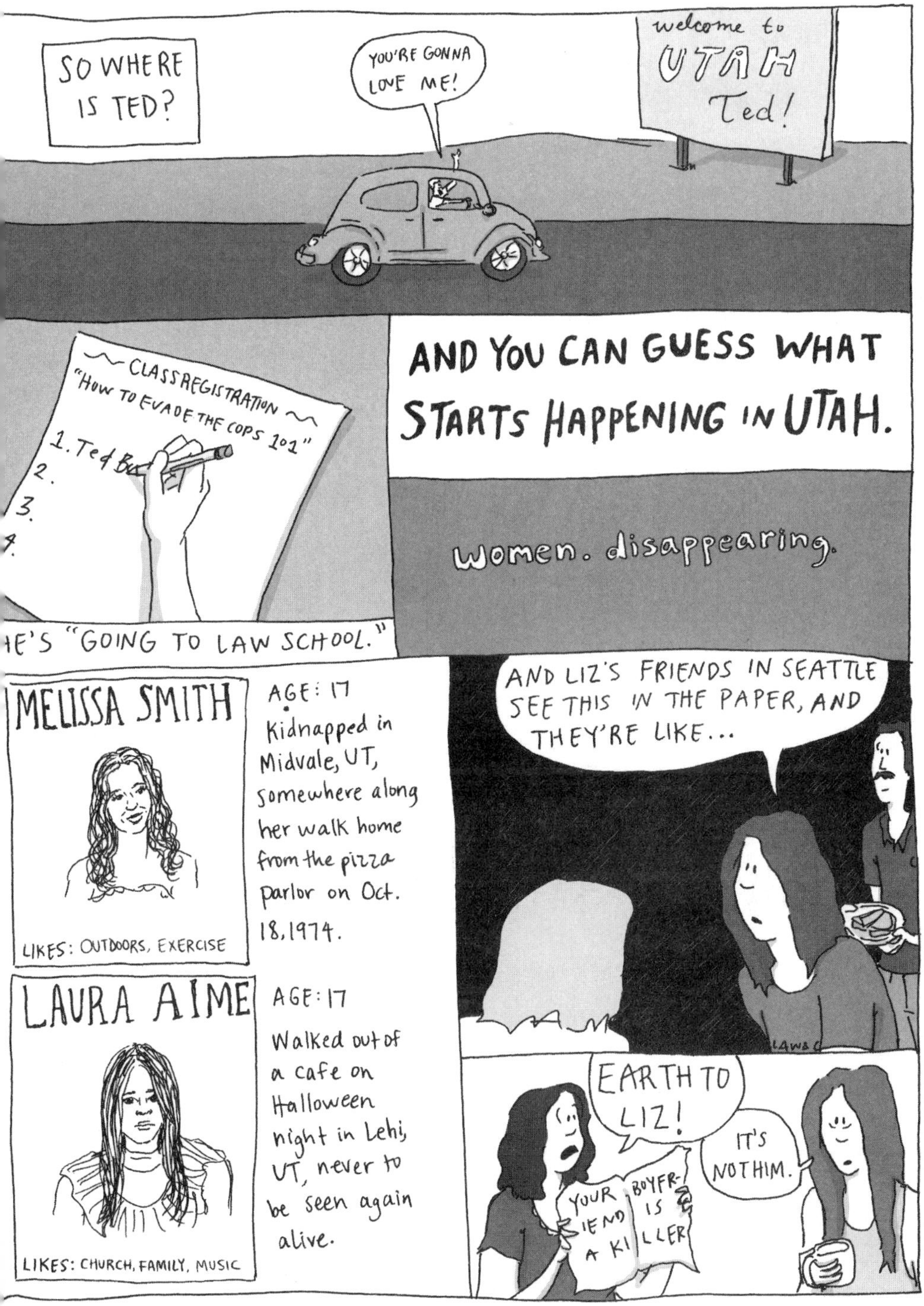

SO WHERE IS TED?
YOU'RE GONNA LOVE ME!
welcome to UTAH Ted!
CLASS REGISTRATION
"HOW TO EVADE THE COPS 101"
1. Ted Bu
2.
3.
4.
HE'S "GOING TO LAW SCHOOL."
AND YOU CAN GUESS WHAT STARTS HAPPENING IN UTAH.
women. disappearing.
MELISSA SMITH
LIKES: OUTDOORS, EXERCISE
AGE: 17
Kidnapped in Midvale, UT, somewhere along her walk home from the pizza parlor on Oct. 18, 1974.
LAURA AIME
LIKES: CHURCH, FAMILY, MUSIC
AGE: 17
Walked out of a cafe on Halloween night in Lehi, UT, never to be seen again alive.
AND LIZ'S FRIENDS IN SEATTLE SEE THIS IN THE PAPER, AND THEY'RE LIKE...
EARTH TO LIZ!
YOUR BOYFR- IEND IS A KILLER
IT'S NOT HIM.

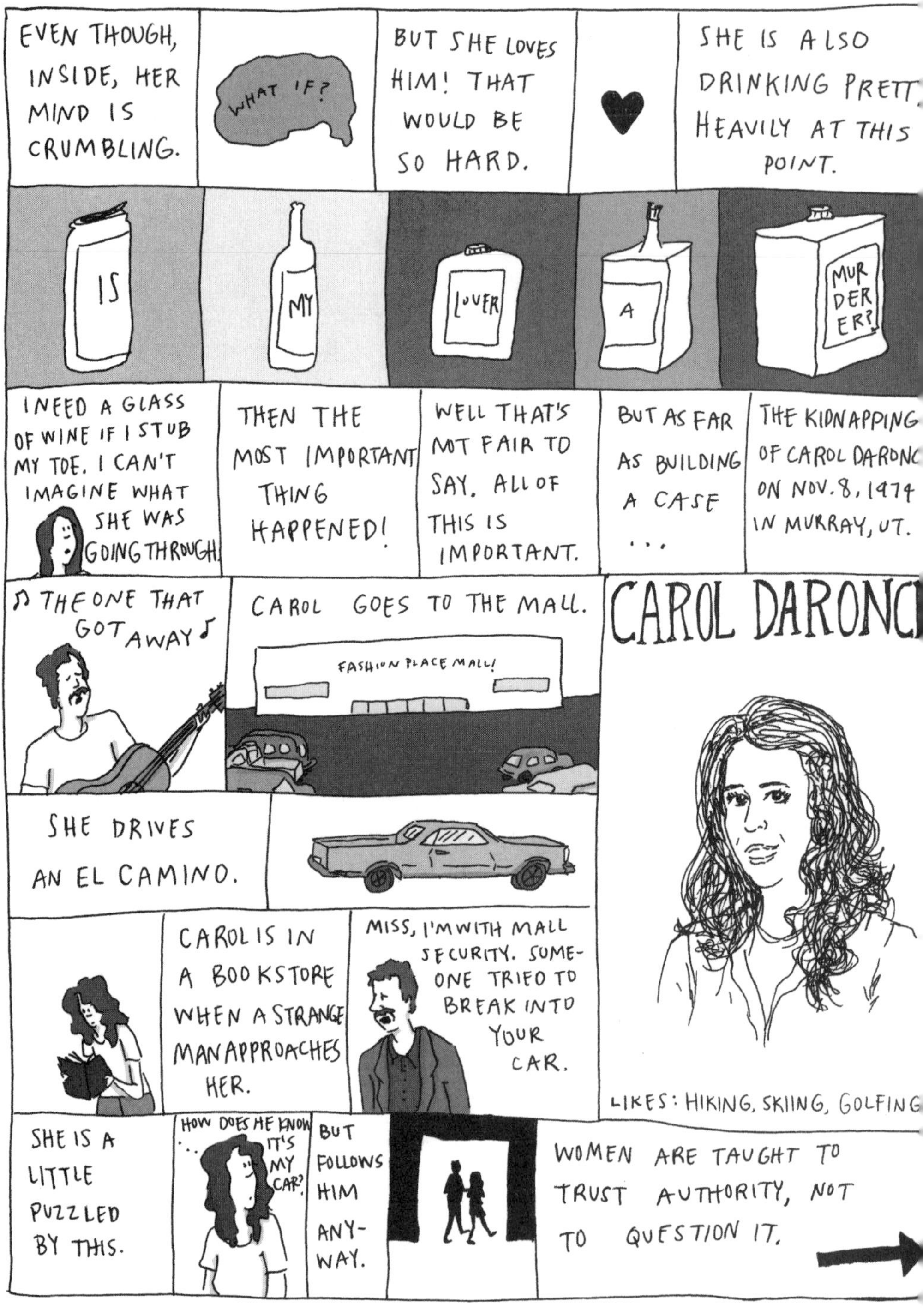
EVEN THOUGH, INSIDE, HER MIND IS CRUMBLING.
WHAT IF?
BUT SHE LOVES HIM! THAT WOULD BE SO HARD.
SHE IS ALSO DRINKING PRETT[Y] HEAVILY AT THIS POINT.
IS
MY
LOVER
A
MURDERER?
I NEED A GLASS OF WINE IF I STUB MY TOE. I CAN'T IMAGINE WHAT SHE WAS GOING THROUGH!
THEN THE MOST IMPORTANT THING HAPPENED!
WELL THAT'S NOT FAIR TO SAY. ALL OF THIS IS IMPORTANT.
BUT AS FAR AS BUILDING A CASE ...
THE KIDNAPPING OF CAROL DARONC[H] ON NOV. 8, 1974 IN MURRAY, UT.
♫ THE ONE THAT GOT AWAY ♪
CAROL GOES TO THE MALL.
FASHION PLACE MALL!
CAROL DARONC[H]
LIKES: HIKING, SKIING, GOLFING
SHE DRIVES AN EL CAMINO.
CAROL IS IN A BOOKSTORE WHEN A STRANGE MAN APPROACHES HER.
MISS, I'M WITH MALL SECURITY. SOMEONE TRIED TO BREAK INTO YOUR CAR.
SHE IS A LITTLE PUZZLED BY THIS.
HOW DOES HE KNOW IT'S MY CAR?
BUT FOLLOWS HIM ANYWAY.
WOMEN ARE TAUGHT TO TRUST AUTHORITY, NOT TO QUESTION IT.

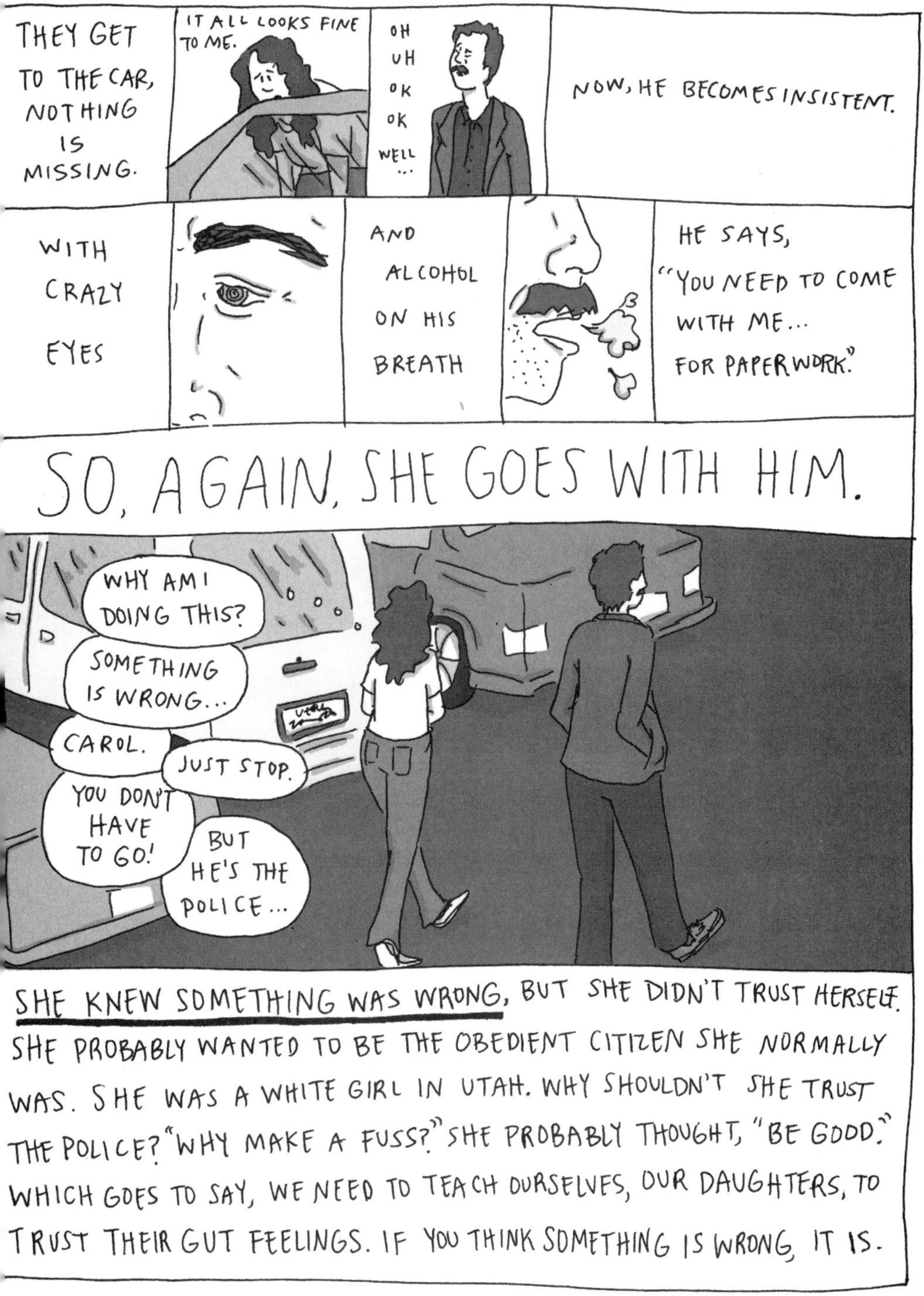
THEY GET TO THE CAR, NOTHING IS MISSING.
IT ALL LOOKS FINE TO ME.
OH UH OK OK WELL...
NOW, HE BECOMES INSISTENT.
WITH CRAZY EYES
AND ALCOHOL ON HIS BREATH
HE SAYS, "YOU NEED TO COME WITH ME... FOR PAPERWORK."
SO, AGAIN, SHE GOES WITH HIM.
WHY AM I DOING THIS?
SOMETHING IS WRONG...
CAROL.
JUST STOP.
YOU DON'T HAVE TO GO!
BUT HE'S THE POLICE...
SHE KNEW SOMETHING WAS WRONG, BUT SHE DIDN'T TRUST HERSELF. SHE PROBABLY WANTED TO BE THE OBEDIENT CITIZEN SHE NORMALLY WAS. SHE WAS A WHITE GIRL IN UTAH. WHY SHOULDN'T SHE TRUST THE POLICE? "WHY MAKE A FUSS?" SHE PROBABLY THOUGHT, "BE GOOD." WHICH GOES TO SAY, WE NEED TO TEACH OURSELVES, OUR DAUGHTERS, TO TRUST THEIR GUT FEELINGS. IF YOU THINK SOMETHING IS WRONG, IT IS.

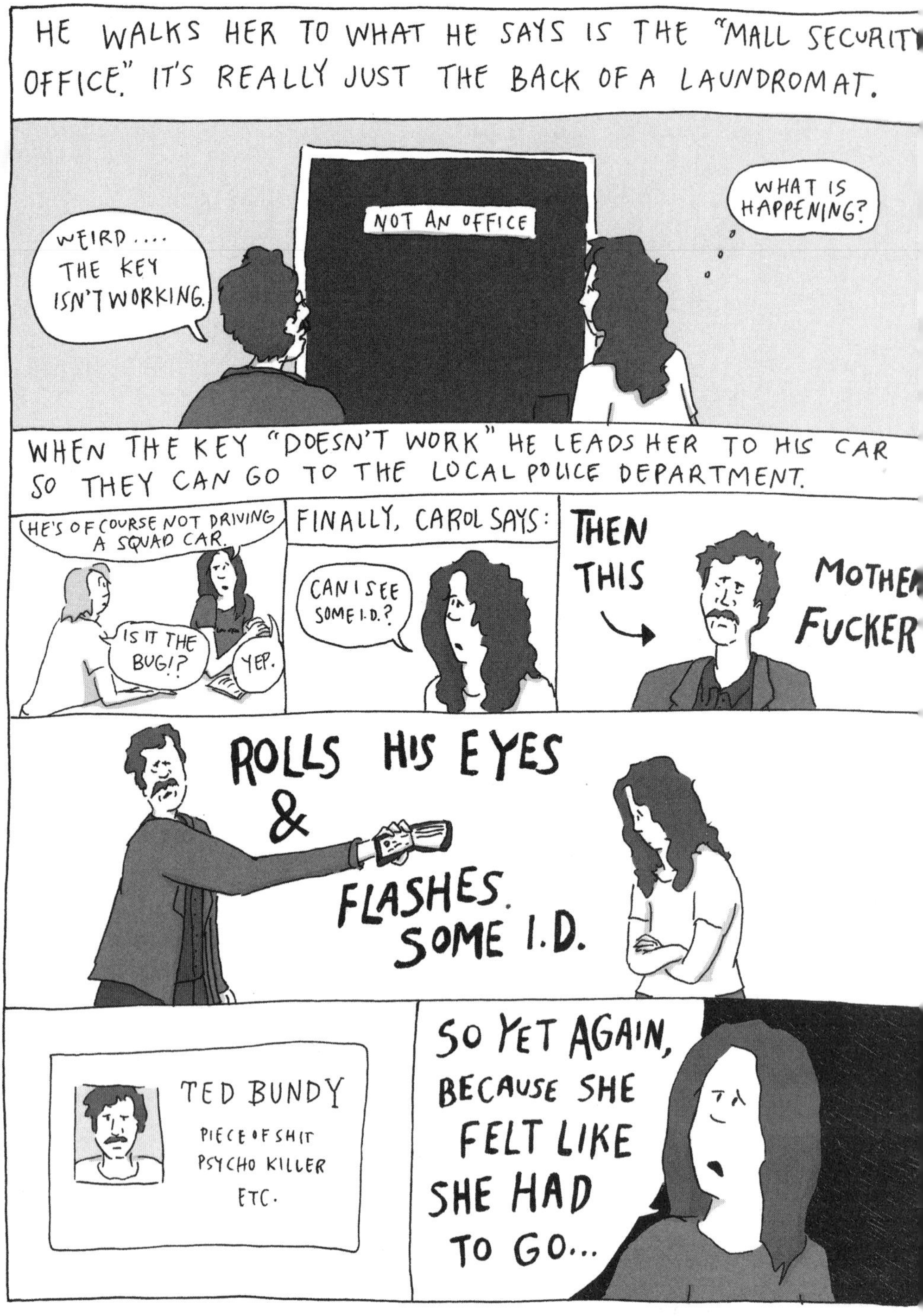

HE WALKS HER TO WHAT HE SAYS IS THE "MALL SECURITY OFFICE." IT'S REALLY JUST THE BACK OF A LAUNDROMAT.
WEIRD.... THE KEY ISN'T WORKING.
NOT AN OFFICE
WHAT IS HAPPENING?
WHEN THE KEY "DOESN'T WORK" HE LEADS HER TO HIS CAR SO THEY CAN GO TO THE LOCAL POLICE DEPARTMENT.
(HE'S OF COURSE NOT DRIVING A SQUAD CAR.)
IS IT THE BUG!?
YEP.
FINALLY, CAROL SAYS:
CAN I SEE SOME I.D.?
THEN THIS
MOTHER FUCKER
ROLLS HIS EYES & FLASHES SOME I.D.
TED BUNDY
PIECE OF SHIT
PSYCHO KILLER
ETC.
SO YET AGAIN, BECAUSE SHE FELT LIKE SHE HAD TO GO...

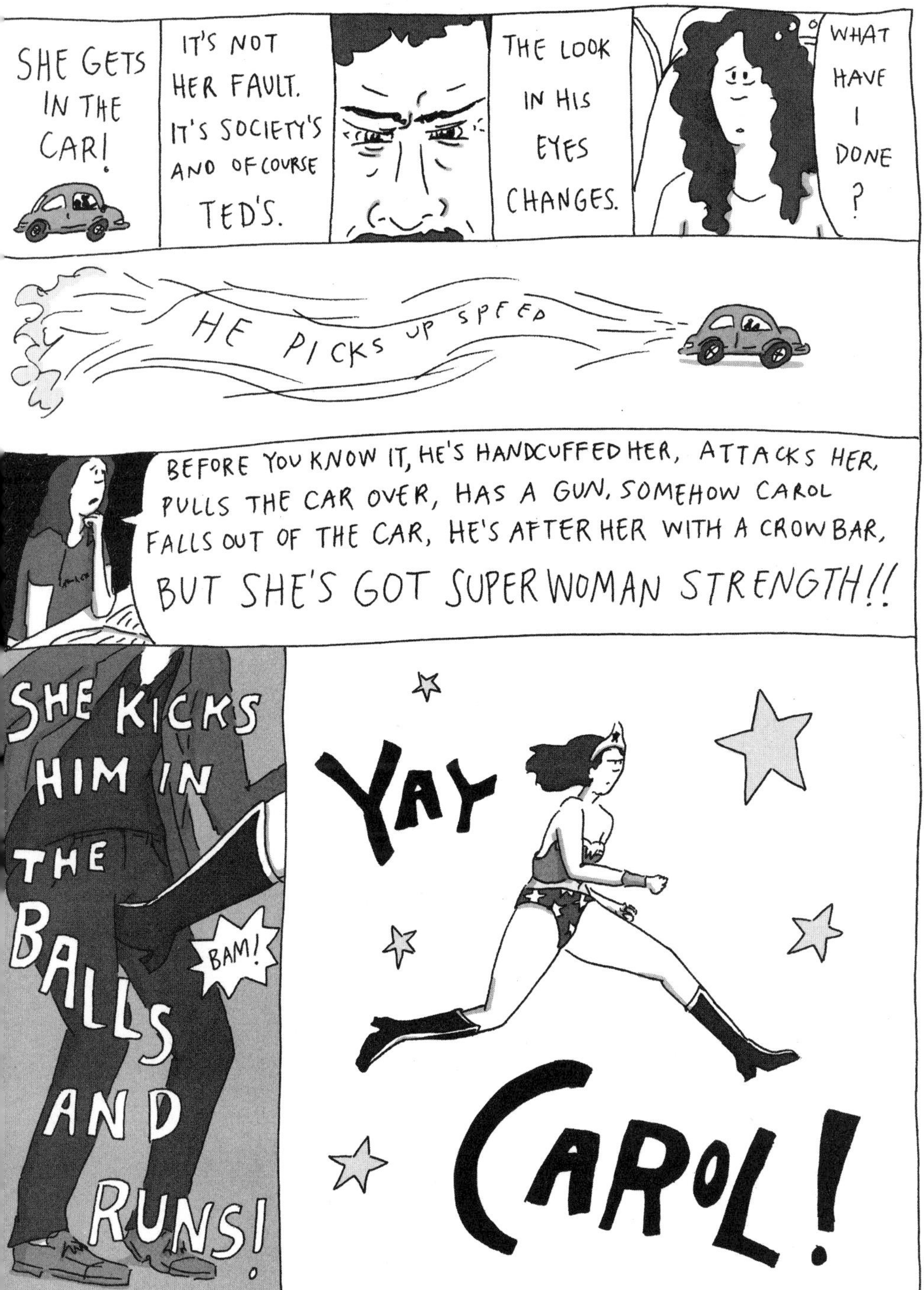
SHE GETS IN THE CAR!
IT'S NOT HER FAULT. IT'S SOCIETY'S AND OF COURSE TED'S.
THE LOOK IN HIS EYES CHANGES.
WHAT HAVE I DONE ?
HE PICKS UP SPEED
BEFORE YOU KNOW IT, HE'S HANDCUFFED HER, ATTACKS HER, PULLS THE CAR OVER, HAS A GUN, SOMEHOW CAROL FALLS OUT OF THE CAR, HE'S AFTER HER WITH A CROWBAR, BUT SHE'S GOT SUPERWOMAN STRENGTH!!
SHE KICKS HIM IN THE BALLS AND RUNS!
BAM!
YAY CAROL!

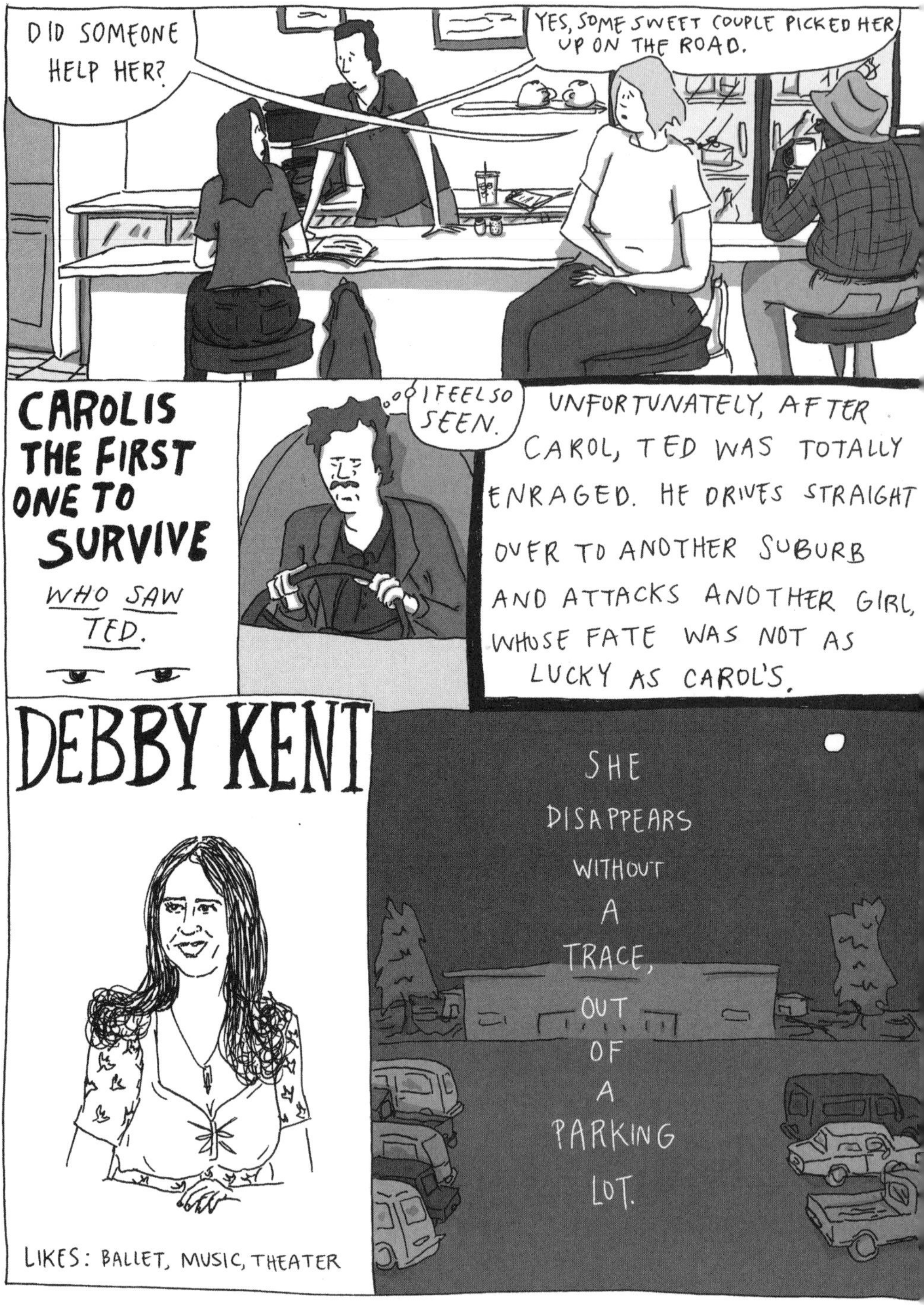
DID SOMEONE HELP HER?
YES, SOME SWEET COUPLE PICKED HER UP ON THE ROAD.
CAROL IS THE FIRST ONE TO SURVIVE WHO SAW TED.
I FEEL SO SEEN.
UNFORTUNATELY, AFTER CAROL, TED WAS TOTALLY ENRAGED. HE DRIVES STRAIGHT OVER TO ANOTHER SUBURB AND ATTACKS ANOTHER GIRL, WHOSE FATE WAS NOT AS LUCKY AS CAROL'S.
DEBBY KENT
LIKES: BALLET, MUSIC, THEATER
SHE DISAPPEARS WITHOUT A TRACE, OUT OF A PARKING LOT.

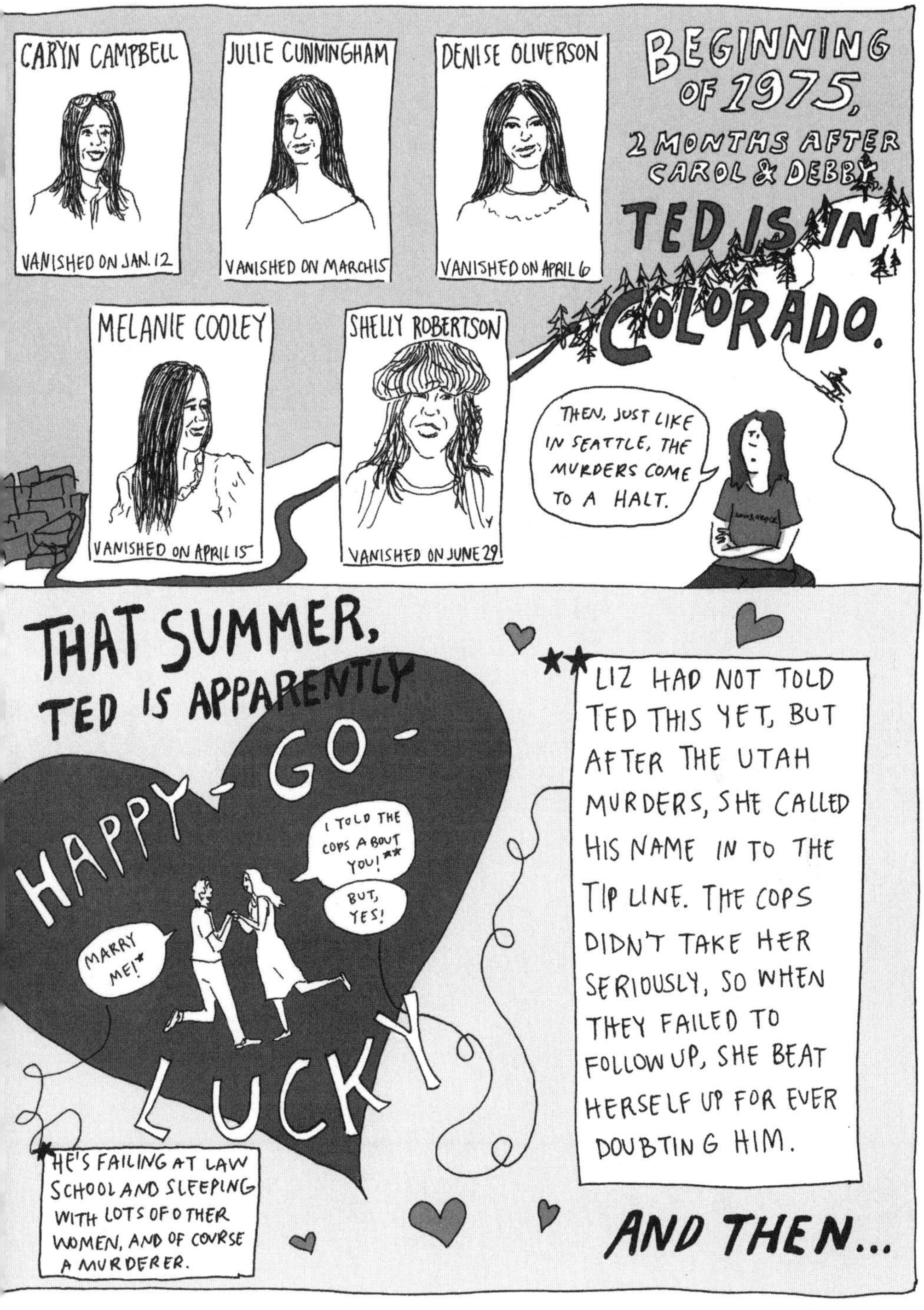

CARYN CAMPBELL
VANISHED ON JAN. 12
JULIE CUNNINGHAM
VANISHED ON MARCH 15
DENISE OLIVERSON
VANISHED ON APRIL 6
BEGINNING OF 1975, 2 MONTHS AFTER CAROL & DEBBY,
TED IS IN COLORADO.
MELANIE COOLEY
VANISHED ON APRIL 15
SHELLY ROBERTSON
VANISHED ON JUNE 29
THEN, JUST LIKE IN SEATTLE, THE MURDERS COME TO A HALT.
THAT SUMMER, TED IS APPARENTLY
HAPPY-GO-LUCKY
MARRY ME!*
I TOLD THE COPS ABOUT YOU!**
BUT, YES!
*HE'S FAILING AT LAW SCHOOL AND SLEEPING WITH LOTS OF OTHER WOMEN, AND OF COURSE A MURDERER.
**LIZ HAD NOT TOLD TED THIS YET, BUT AFTER THE UTAH MURDERS, SHE CALLED HIS NAME IN TO THE TIP LINE. THE COPS DIDN'T TAKE HER SERIOUSLY, SO WHEN THEY FAILED TO FOLLOW UP, SHE BEAT HERSELF UP FOR EVER DOUBTING HIM.
AND THEN...

the UTAH Daily

THE POLICE FINALLY, ACCIDENTALLY, CATCH A BREAK!

Sergeant Bob Hayward notices what he thinks is a suspicious vehicle — he lives in the neighborhood and knows everyone's car. Reminds me of my neighbor Kray. Anyway, so when he sees this V.W. Bug loitering outside a house, he's like "huh." Bob turns on his headlights. The Bug races away! They end up in a little car chase, but the Bug eventually pulls into a gas station. The man driving the Bug is all like, "I guess I was lost!" which is the worst excuse. Bob asks why he is out so late at night. The man gives a vague, unreliable answer. Then Bob sees in the Bug:

1. crowbar
2. ski mask
3. ice pick
4. rope

Suspicious much? <u>Arrested.</u>

BOB HAYWARD

THEODORE BUNDY

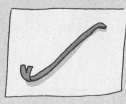

A1

162

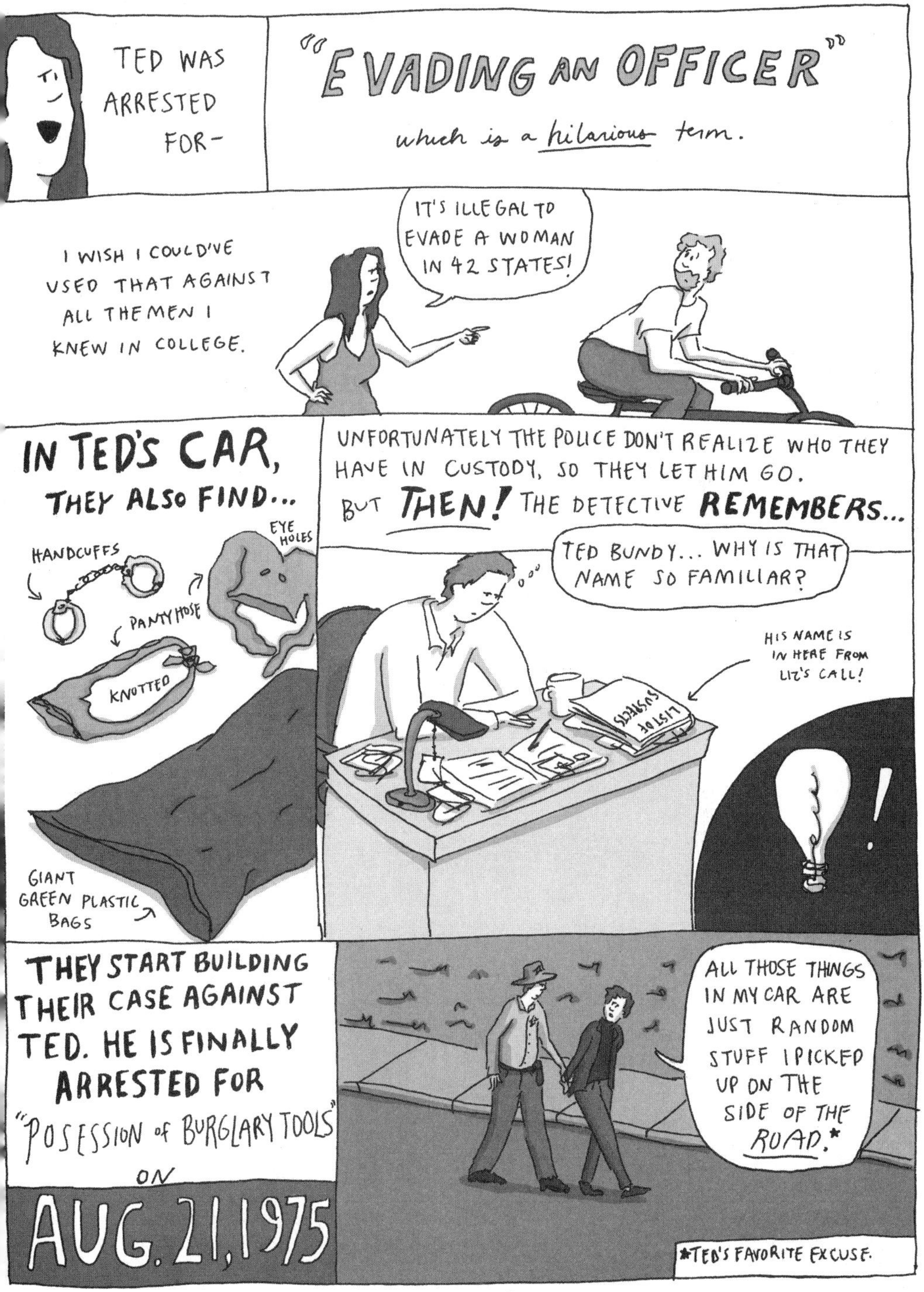
TED WAS ARRESTED FOR-
"EVADING AN OFFICER"
which is a hilarious term.
I WISH I COULD'VE USED THAT AGAINST ALL THE MEN I KNEW IN COLLEGE.
IT'S ILLEGAL TO EVADE A WOMAN IN 42 STATES!
IN TED'S CAR, THEY ALSO FIND...
HANDCUFFS
EYE HOLES
PANTY HOSE
KNOTTED
GIANT GREEN PLASTIC BAGS
UNFORTUNATELY THE POLICE DON'T REALIZE WHO THEY HAVE IN CUSTODY, SO THEY LET HIM GO.
BUT THEN! THE DETECTIVE REMEMBERS...
TED BUNDY... WHY IS THAT NAME SO FAMILIAR?
HIS NAME IS IN HERE FROM LIZ'S CALL!
LIST OF SUSPECTS
!
THEY START BUILDING THEIR CASE AGAINST TED. HE IS FINALLY ARRESTED FOR "POSESSION OF BURGLARY TOOLS" ON
AUG. 21, 1975
ALL THOSE THINGS IN MY CAR ARE JUST RANDOM STUFF I PICKED UP ON THE SIDE OF THE ROAD.*
*TED'S FAVORITE EXCUSE.

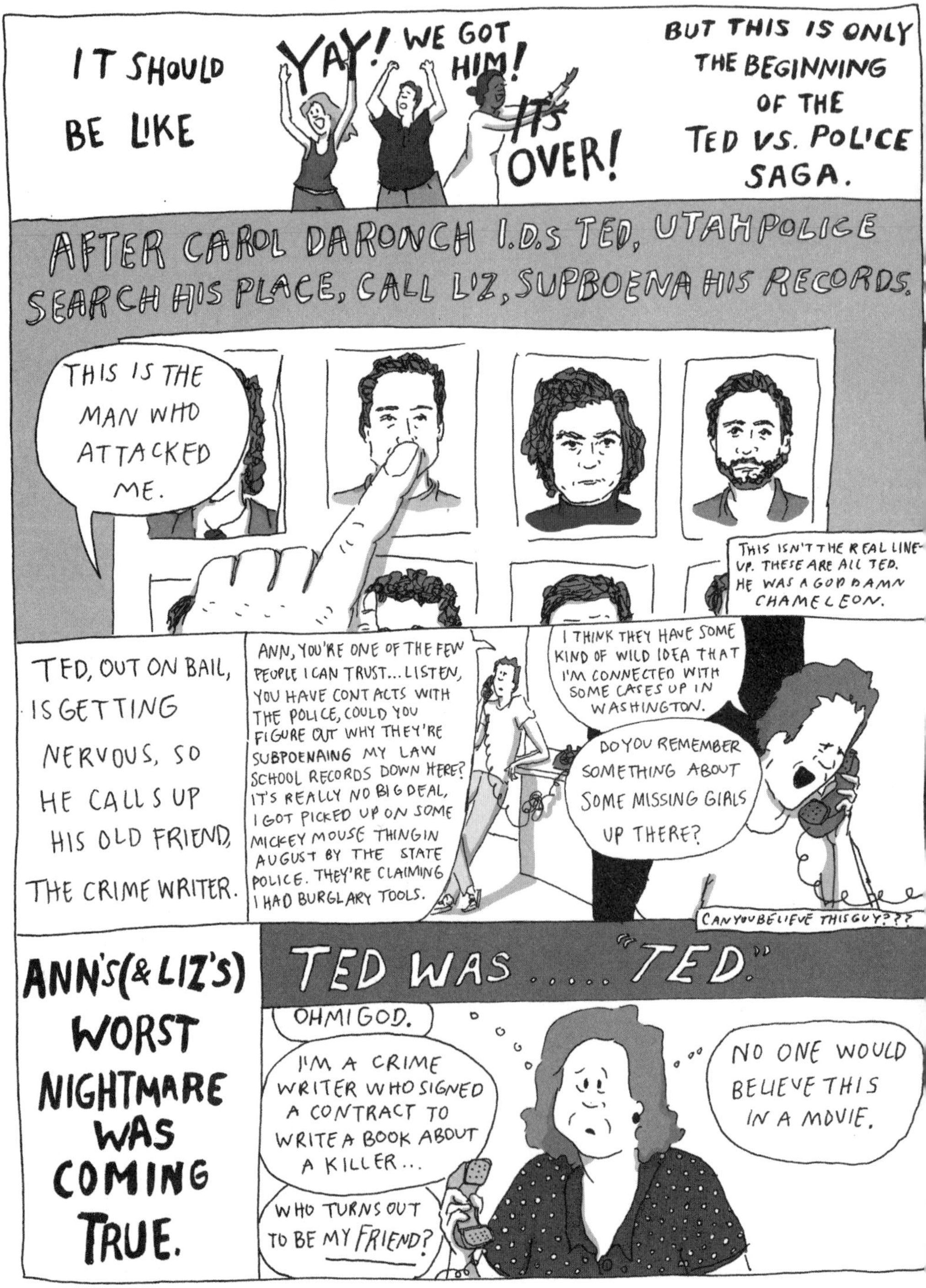
IT SHOULD BE LIKE
YAY! WE GOT HIM!
IT'S OVER!
BUT THIS IS ONLY THE BEGINNING OF THE TED VS. POLICE SAGA.
AFTER CAROL DARONCH I.D.S TED, UTAH POLICE SEARCH HIS PLACE, CALL LIZ, SUPBOENA HIS RECORDS.
THIS IS THE MAN WHO ATTACKED ME.
THIS ISN'T THE REAL LINE-UP. THESE ARE ALL TED. HE WAS A GOD DAMN CHAMELEON.
TED, OUT ON BAIL, IS GETTING NERVOUS, SO HE CALLS UP HIS OLD FRIEND, THE CRIME WRITER.
ANN, YOU'RE ONE OF THE FEW PEOPLE I CAN TRUST... LISTEN, YOU HAVE CONTACTS WITH THE POLICE, COULD YOU FIGURE OUT WHY THEY'RE SUBPOENAING MY LAW SCHOOL RECORDS DOWN HERE? IT'S REALLY NO BIG DEAL, I GOT PICKED UP ON SOME MICKEY MOUSE THING IN AUGUST BY THE STATE POLICE. THEY'RE CLAIMING I HAD BURGLARY TOOLS.
I THINK THEY HAVE SOME KIND OF WILD IDEA THAT I'M CONNECTED WITH SOME CASES UP IN WASHINGTON.
DO YOU REMEMBER SOMETHING ABOUT SOME MISSING GIRLS UP THERE?
CAN YOU BELIEVE THIS GUY???
ANN'S (& LIZ'S) WORST NIGHTMARE WAS COMING TRUE.
TED WAS ...."TED."
OHMIGOD.
I'M A CRIME WRITER WHO SIGNED A CONTRACT TO WRITE A BOOK ABOUT A KILLER...
WHO TURNS OUT TO BE MY FRIEND?
NO ONE WOULD BELIEVE THIS IN A MOVIE.

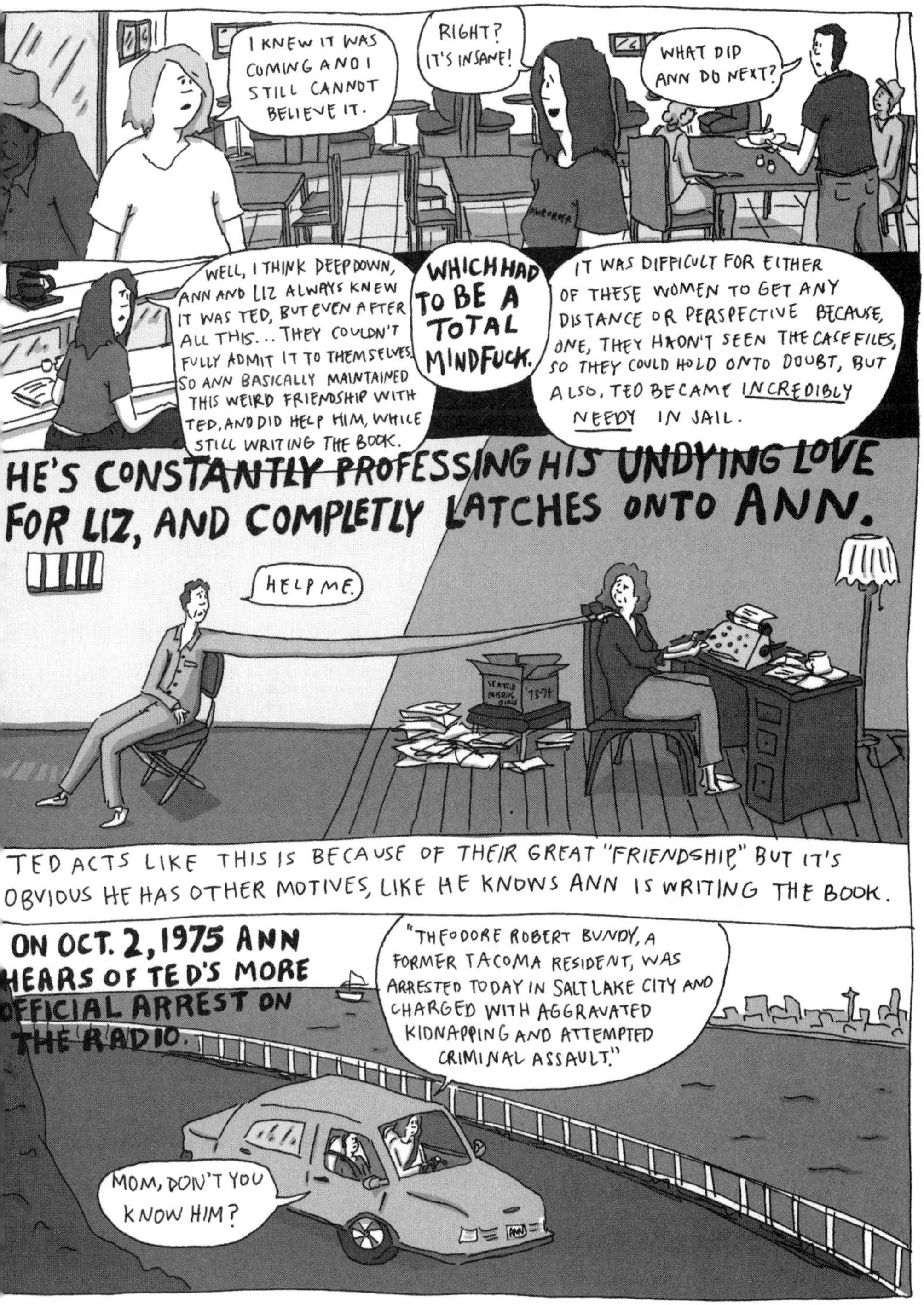
I KNEW IT WAS COMING AND I STILL CANNOT BELIEVE IT.
RIGHT? IT'S INSANE!
WHAT DID ANN DO NEXT?
WELL, I THINK DEEPDOWN, ANN AND LIZ ALWAYS KNEW IT WAS TED, BUT EVEN AFTER ALL THIS... THEY COULDN'T FULLY ADMIT IT TO THEMSELVES. SO ANN BASICALLY MAINTAINED THIS WEIRD FRIENDSHIP WITH TED, AND DID HELP HIM, WHILE STILL WRITING THE BOOK.
WHICH HAD TO BE A TOTAL MINDFUCK.
IT WAS DIFFICULT FOR EITHER OF THESE WOMEN TO GET ANY DISTANCE OR PERSPECTIVE BECAUSE, ONE, THEY HADN'T SEEN THE CASE FILES, SO THEY COULD HOLD ONTO DOUBT, BUT ALSO, TED BECAME INCREDIBLY NEEDY IN JAIL.
HE'S CONSTANTLY PROFESSING HIS UNDYING LOVE FOR LIZ, AND COMPLETLY LATCHES ONTO ANN.
HELP ME.
TED ACTS LIKE THIS IS BECAUSE OF THEIR GREAT "FRIENDSHIP," BUT IT'S OBVIOUS HE HAS OTHER MOTIVES, LIKE HE KNOWS ANN IS WRITING THE BOOK.
ON OCT. 2, 1975 ANN HEARS OF TED'S MORE OFFICIAL ARREST ON THE RADIO.
"THEODORE ROBERT BUNDY, A FORMER TACOMA RESIDENT, WAS ARRESTED TODAY IN SALT LAKE CITY AND CHARGED WITH AGGRAVATED KIDNAPPING AND ATTEMPTED CRIMINAL ASSAULT."
MOM, DON'T YOU KNOW HIM?

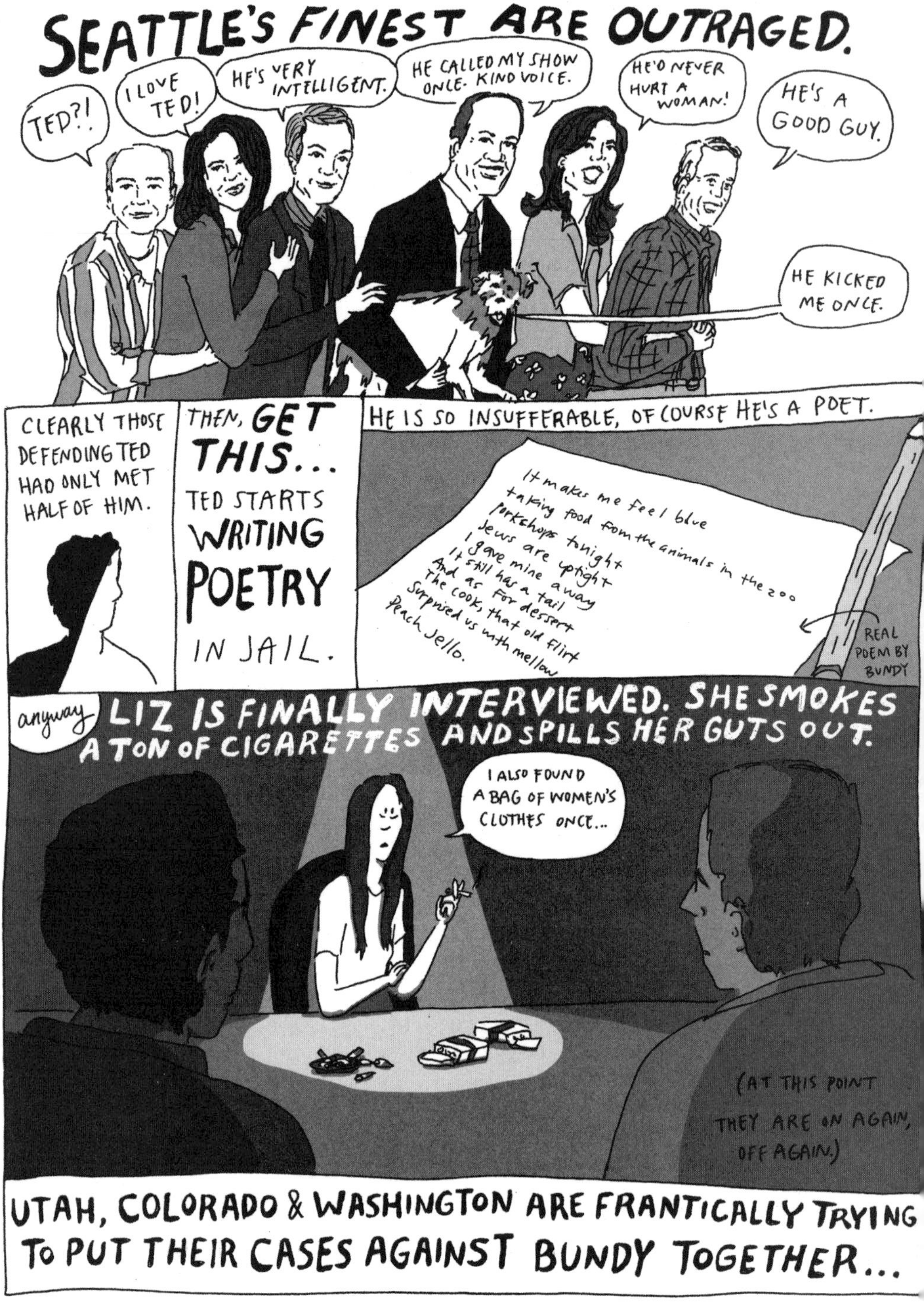
SEATTLE'S FINEST ARE OUTRAGED.
TED?!
I LOVE TED!
HE'S VERY INTELLIGENT.
HE CALLED MY SHOW ONCE. KIND VOICE.
HE'D NEVER HURT A WOMAN!
HE'S A GOOD GUY.
HE KICKED ME ONCE.
CLEARLY THOSE DEFENDING TED HAD ONLY MET HALF OF HIM.
THEN, GET THIS... TED STARTS WRITING POETRY IN JAIL.
HE IS SO INSUFFERABLE, OF COURSE HE'S A POET.
It makes me feel blue
taking food from the animals in the zoo
porkchops tonight
Jews are uptight
I gave mine away
It still has a tail
And as for dessert
The cook, that old flirt
Surprised us with mellow
Peach Jello.
REAL POEM BY BUNDY
anyway LIZ IS FINALLY INTERVIEWED. SHE SMOKES A TON OF CIGARETTES AND SPILLS HER GUTS OUT.
I ALSO FOUND A BAG OF WOMEN'S CLOTHES ONCE...
(AT THIS POINT THEY ARE ON AGAIN, OFF AGAIN.)
UTAH, COLORADO & WASHINGTON ARE FRANTICALLY TRYING TO PUT THEIR CASES AGAINST BUNDY TOGETHER...

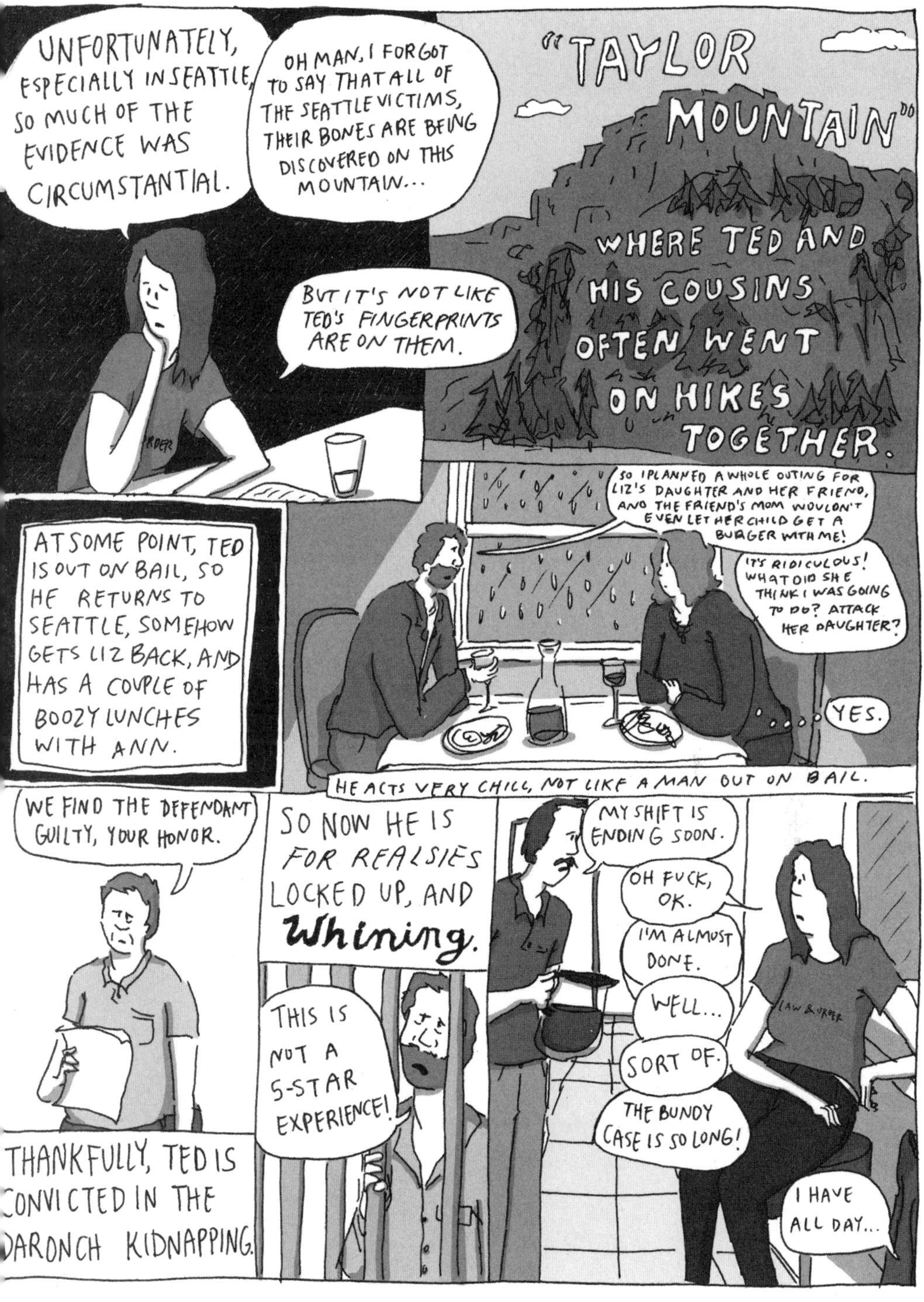
UNFORTUNATELY, ESPECIALLY IN SEATTLE, SO MUCH OF THE EVIDENCE WAS CIRCUMSTANTIAL.
OH MAN, I FORGOT TO SAY THAT ALL OF THE SEATTLE VICTIMS, THEIR BONES ARE BEING DISCOVERED ON THIS MOUNTAIN...
BUT IT'S NOT LIKE TED'S FINGERPRINTS ARE ON THEM.
"TAYLOR MOUNTAIN"
WHERE TED AND HIS COUSINS OFTEN WENT ON HIKES TOGETHER.
AT SOME POINT, TED IS OUT ON BAIL, SO HE RETURNS TO SEATTLE, SOMEHOW GETS LIZ BACK, AND HAS A COUPLE OF BOOZY LUNCHES WITH ANN.
SO I PLANNED A WHOLE OUTING FOR LIZ'S DAUGHTER AND HER FRIEND, AND THE FRIEND'S MOM WOULDN'T EVEN LET HER CHILD GET A BURGER WITH ME!
IT'S RIDICULOUS! WHAT DID SHE THINK I WAS GOING TO DO? ATTACK HER DAUGHTER?
....YES.
HE ACTS VERY CHILL, NOT LIKE A MAN OUT ON BAIL.
WE FIND THE DEFENDANT GUILTY, YOUR HONOR.
THANKFULLY, TED IS CONVICTED IN THE DARONCH KIDNAPPING.
SO NOW HE IS FOR REALSIES LOCKED UP, AND Whining.
THIS IS NOT A 5-STAR EXPERIENCE!
MY SHIFT IS ENDING SOON.
OH FUCK, OK.
I'M ALMOST DONE.
WELL...
SORT OF.
THE BUNDY CASE IS SO LONG!
I HAVE ALL DAY...

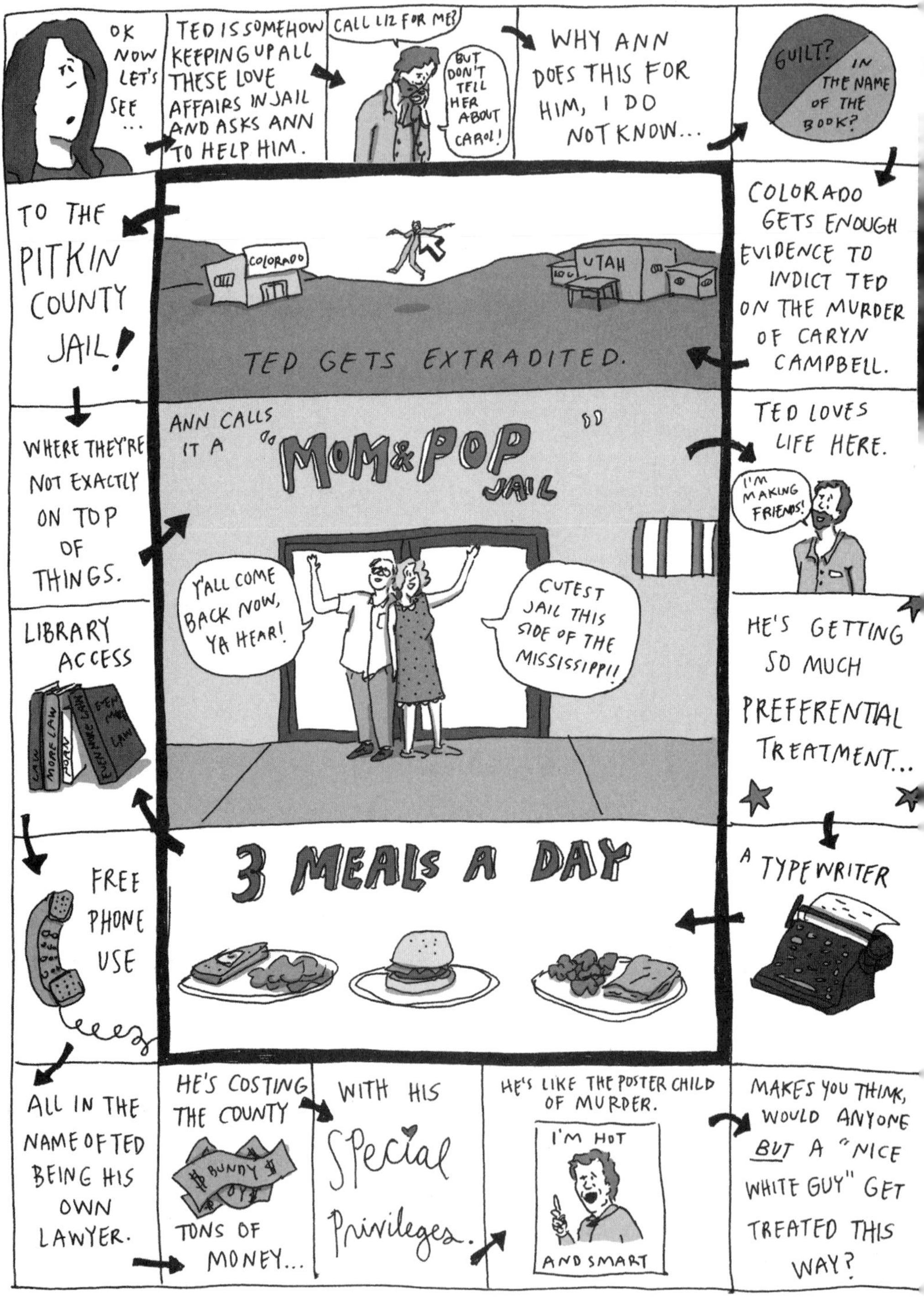

OK NOW LET'S SEE...
TED IS SOMEHOW KEEPING UP ALL THESE LOVE AFFAIRS IN JAIL AND ASKS ANN TO HELP HIM.
CALL LIZ FOR ME?
BUT DON'T TELL HER ABOUT CAROL!
WHY ANN DOES THIS FOR HIM, I DO NOT KNOW...
GUILT?
IN THE NAME OF THE BOOK?
COLORADO GETS ENOUGH EVIDENCE TO INDICT TED ON THE MURDER OF CARYN CAMPBELL.
COLORADO
UTAH
TED GETS EXTRADITED.
TO THE PITKIN COUNTY JAIL!
WHERE THEY'RE NOT EXACTLY ON TOP OF THINGS.
ANN CALLS IT A "MOM & POP JAIL"
Y'ALL COME BACK NOW, YA HEAR!
CUTEST JAIL THIS SIDE OF THE MISSISSIPPI!
TED LOVES LIFE HERE.
I'M MAKING FRIENDS!
LIBRARY ACCESS
LAW
MORE LAW
PORN
EVEN MORE LAW
EVEN MORE LAW
HE'S GETTING SO MUCH PREFERENTIAL TREATMENT...
3 MEALS A DAY
A TYPEWRITER
FREE PHONE USE
ALL IN THE NAME OF TED BEING HIS OWN LAWYER.
HE'S COSTING THE COUNTY
BUNDY $
TONS OF MONEY...
WITH HIS Special Privileges.
HE'S LIKE THE POSTER CHILD OF MURDER.
I'M HOT
AND SMART
MAKES YOU THINK, WOULD ANYONE BUT A "NICE WHITE GUY" GET TREATED THIS WAY?

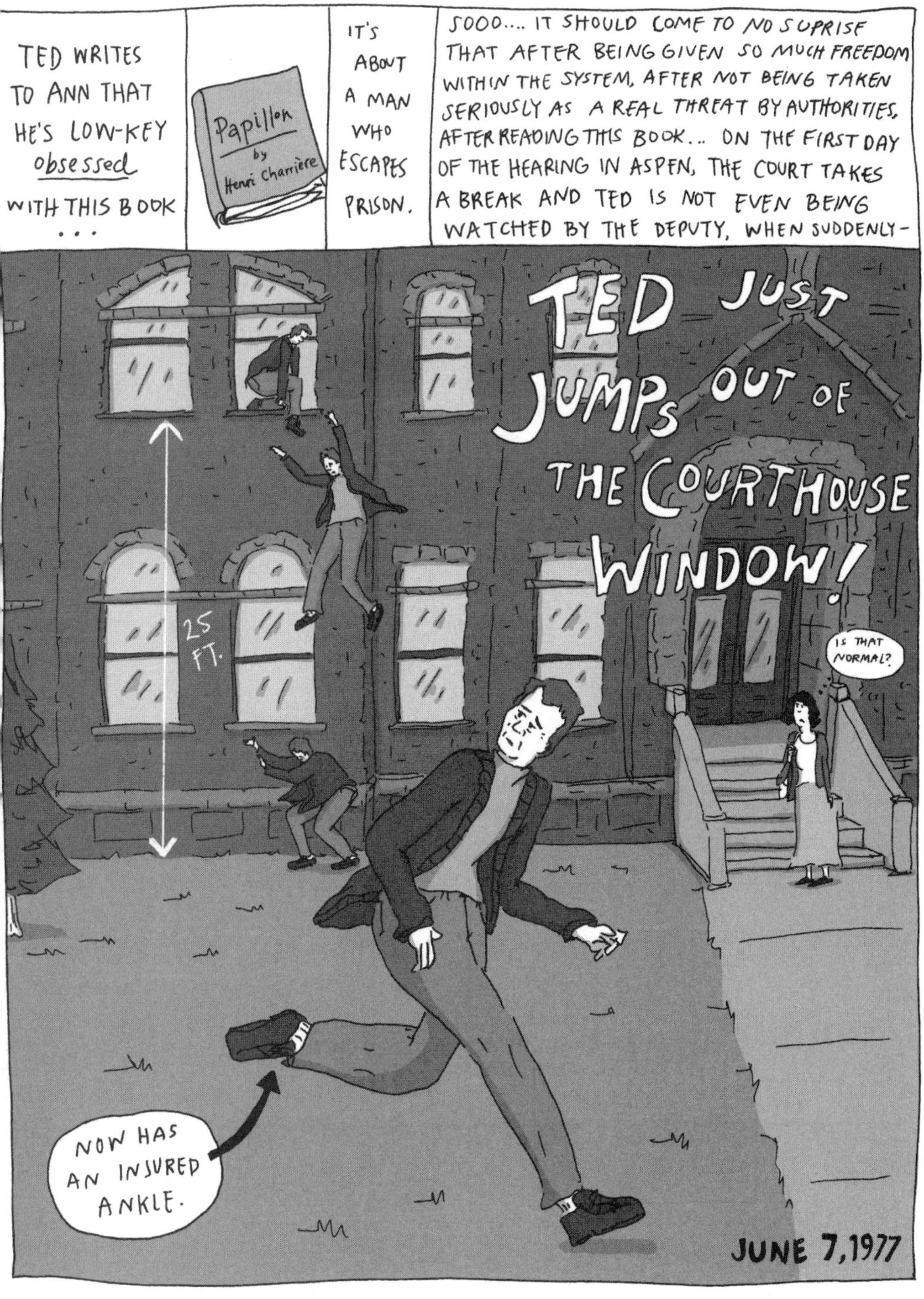
TED WRITES TO ANN THAT HE'S LOW-KEY obsessed WITH THIS BOOK . . .
Papillon by Henri Charrière
IT'S ABOUT A MAN WHO ESCAPES PRISON.
SOOO.... IT SHOULD COME TO NO SUPRISE THAT AFTER BEING GIVEN SO MUCH FREEDOM WITHIN THE SYSTEM, AFTER NOT BEING TAKEN SERIOUSLY AS A REAL THREAT BY AUTHORITIES, AFTER READING THIS BOOK... ON THE FIRST DAY OF THE HEARING IN ASPEN, THE COURT TAKES A BREAK AND TED IS NOT EVEN BEING WATCHED BY THE DEPUTY, WHEN SUDDENLY-
TED JUST JUMPS OUT OF THE COURTHOUSE WINDOW!
25 FT.
IS THAT NORMAL?
NOW HAS AN INJURED ANKLE.
JUNE 7, 1977

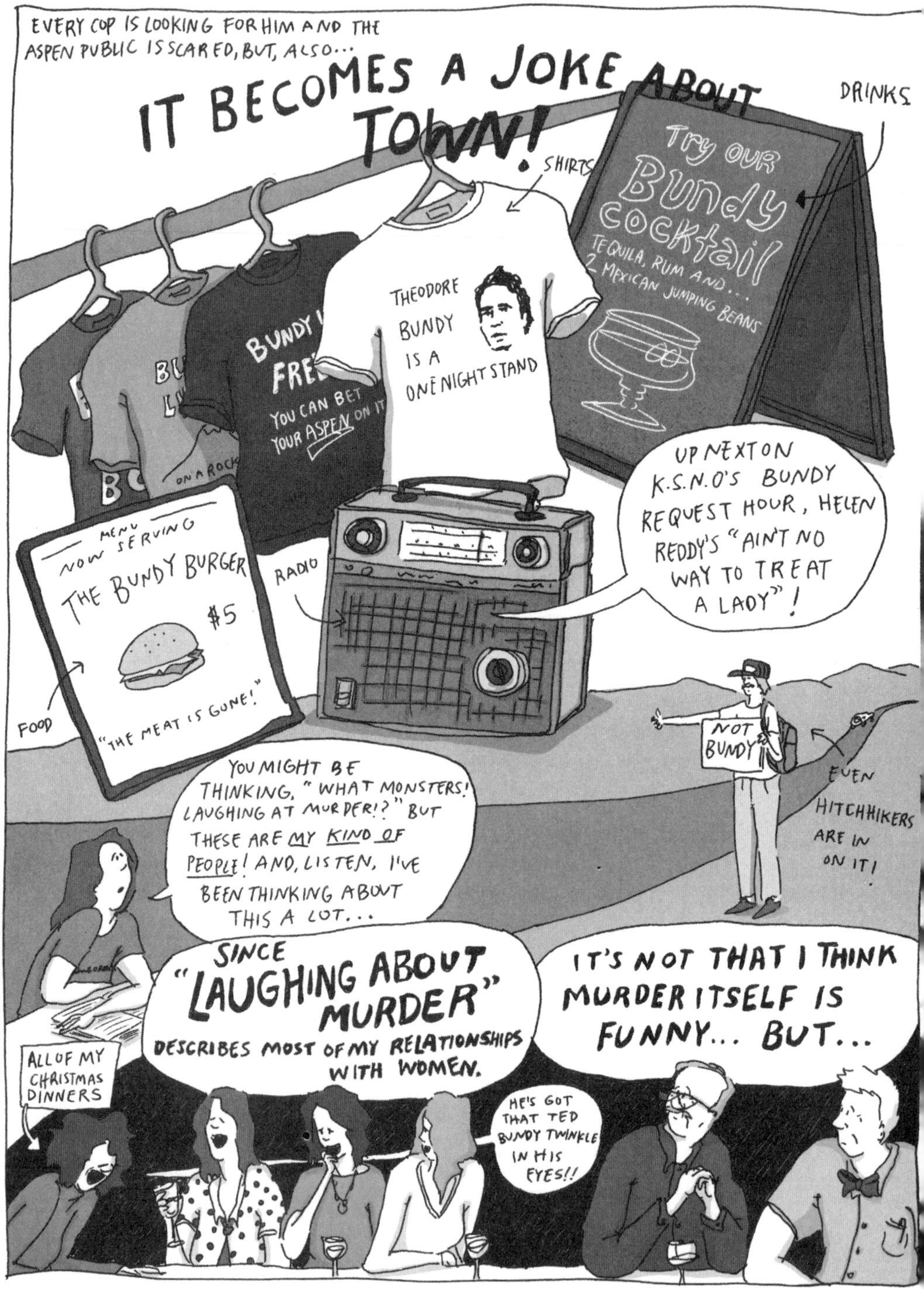
EVERY COP IS LOOKING FOR HIM AND THE ASPEN PUBLIC IS SCARED, BUT, ALSO...
IT BECOMES A JOKE ABOUT TOWN!
SHIRTS
DRINKS
Try our Bundy cocktail
TEQUILA, RUM AND... 2 MEXICAN JUMPING BEANS
THEODORE BUNDY IS A ONE NIGHT STAND
YOU CAN BET YOUR ASPEN ON IT
ON A ROCK
MENU
NOW SERVING
THE BUNDY BURGER
$5
"THE MEAT IS GONE!"
FOOD
RADIO
UP NEXT ON K.S.N.O'S BUNDY REQUEST HOUR, HELEN REDDY'S "AIN'T NO WAY TO TREAT A LADY"!
NOT BUNDY
EVEN HITCHHIKERS ARE IN ON IT!
YOU MIGHT BE THINKING, "WHAT MONSTERS! LAUGHING AT MURDER!?" BUT THESE ARE MY KIND OF PEOPLE! AND, LISTEN, I'VE BEEN THINKING ABOUT THIS A LOT...
SINCE "LAUGHING ABOUT MURDER" DESCRIBES MOST OF MY RELATIONSHIPS WITH WOMEN.
IT'S NOT THAT I THINK MURDER ITSELF IS FUNNY... BUT...
ALL OF MY CHRISTMAS DINNERS
HE'S GOT THAT TED BUNDY TWINKLE IN HIS EYES!!

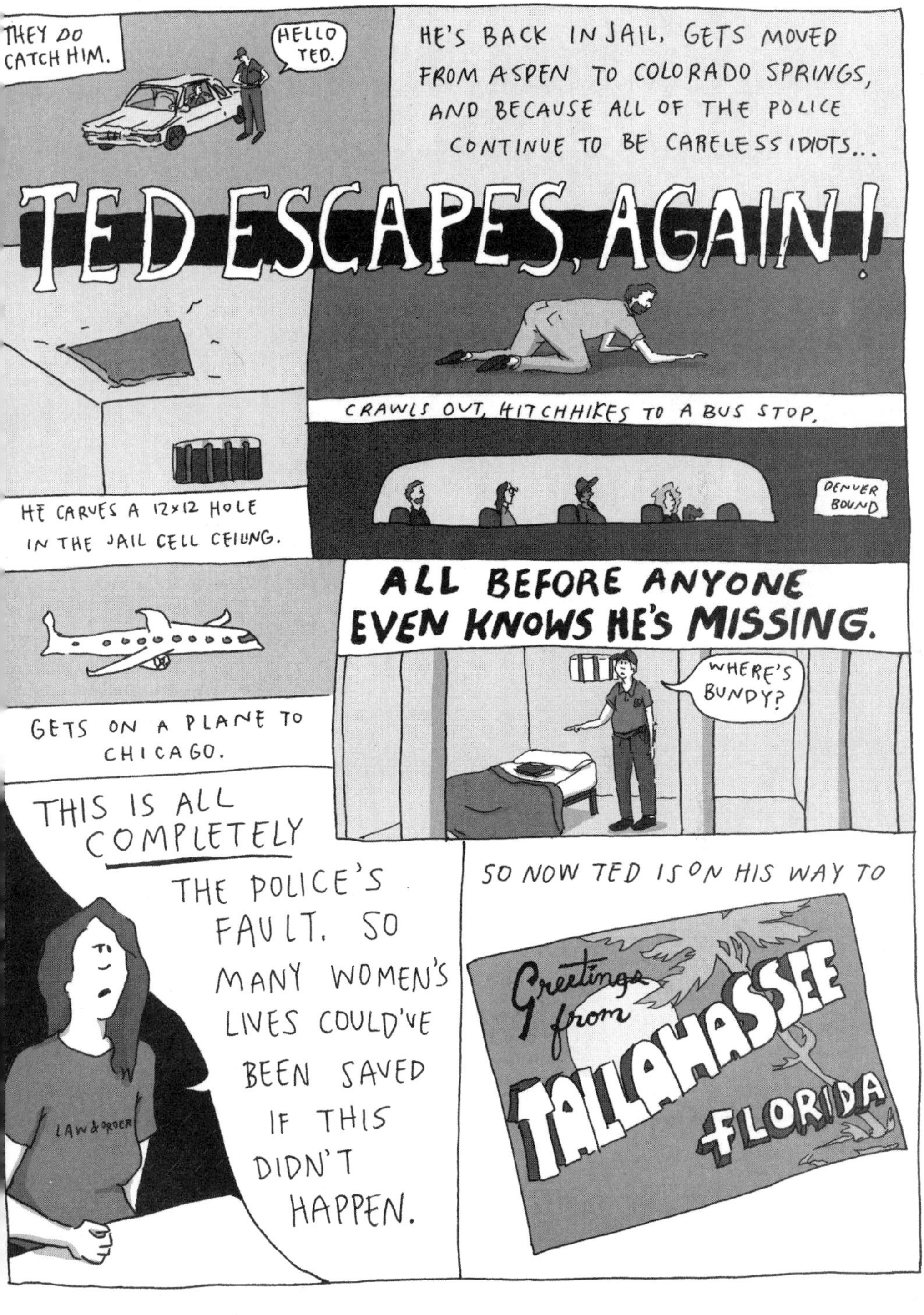

THEY DO CATCH HIM.
HELLO TED.
HE'S BACK IN JAIL, GETS MOVED FROM ASPEN TO COLORADO SPRINGS, AND BECAUSE ALL OF THE POLICE CONTINUE TO BE CARELESS IDIOTS...
TED ESCAPES, AGAIN!
HE CARVES A 12×12 HOLE IN THE JAIL CELL CEILING.
CRAWLS OUT, HITCHHIKES TO A BUS STOP.
DENVER BOUND
GETS ON A PLANE TO CHICAGO.
ALL BEFORE ANYONE EVEN KNOWS HE'S MISSING.
WHERE'S BUNDY?
THIS IS ALL COMPLETELY THE POLICE'S FAULT. SO MANY WOMEN'S LIVES COULD'VE BEEN SAVED IF THIS DIDN'T HAPPEN.
LAW & ORDER
SO NOW TED IS ON HIS WAY TO
Greetings from TALLAHASSEE FLORIDA

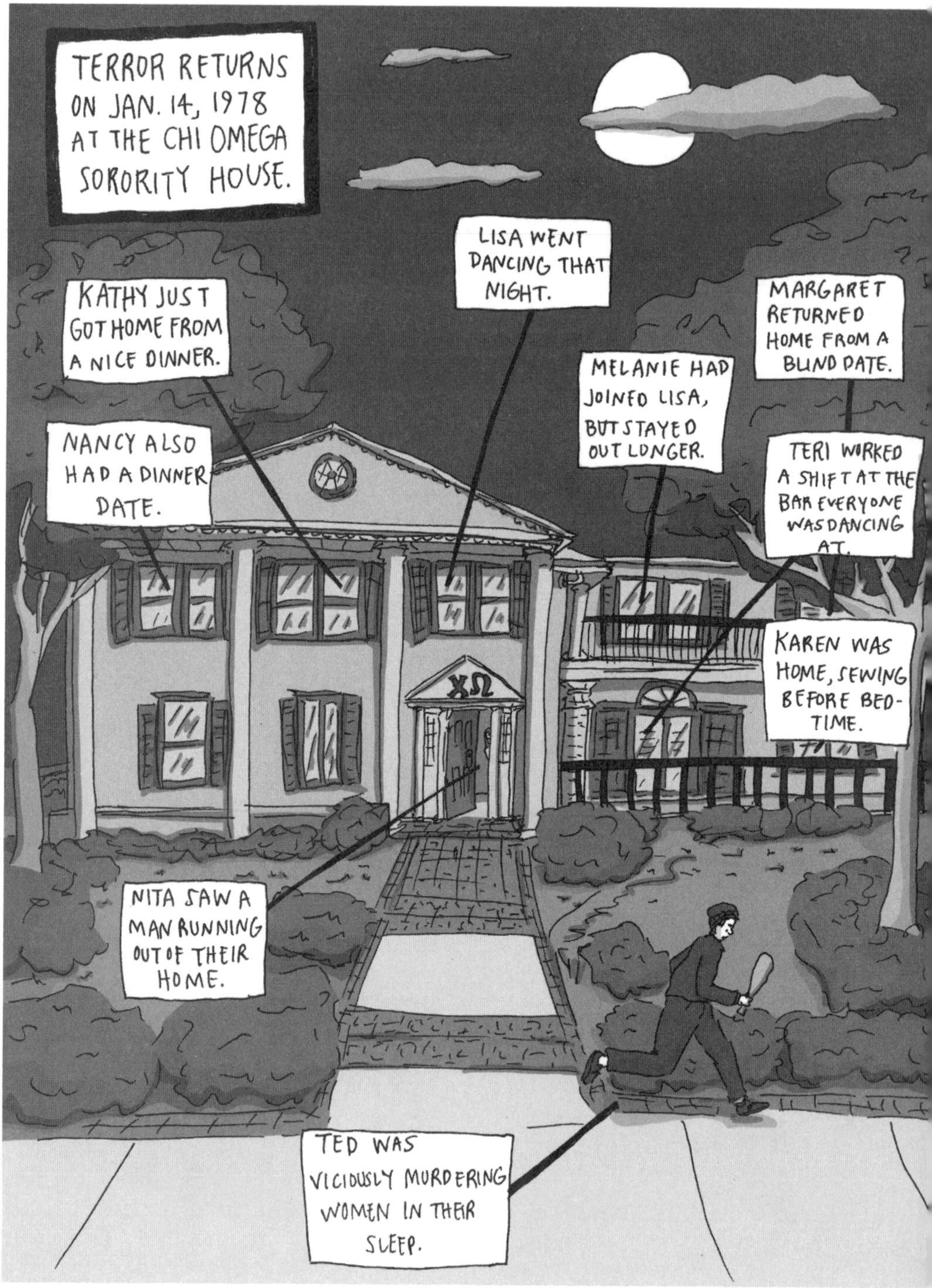
TERROR RETURNS ON JAN. 14, 1978 AT THE CHI OMEGA SORORITY HOUSE.
LISA WENT DANCING THAT NIGHT.
KATHY JUST GOT HOME FROM A NICE DINNER.
MARGARET RETURNED HOME FROM A BLIND DATE.
MELANIE HAD JOINED LISA, BUT STAYED OUT LONGER.
NANCY ALSO HAD A DINNER DATE.
TERI WORKED A SHIFT AT THE BAR EVERYONE WAS DANCING AT.
XΩ
KAREN WAS HOME, SEWING BEFORE BED-TIME.
NITA SAW A MAN RUNNING OUT OF THEIR HOME.
TED WAS VICIOUSLY MURDERING WOMEN IN THEIR SLEEP.

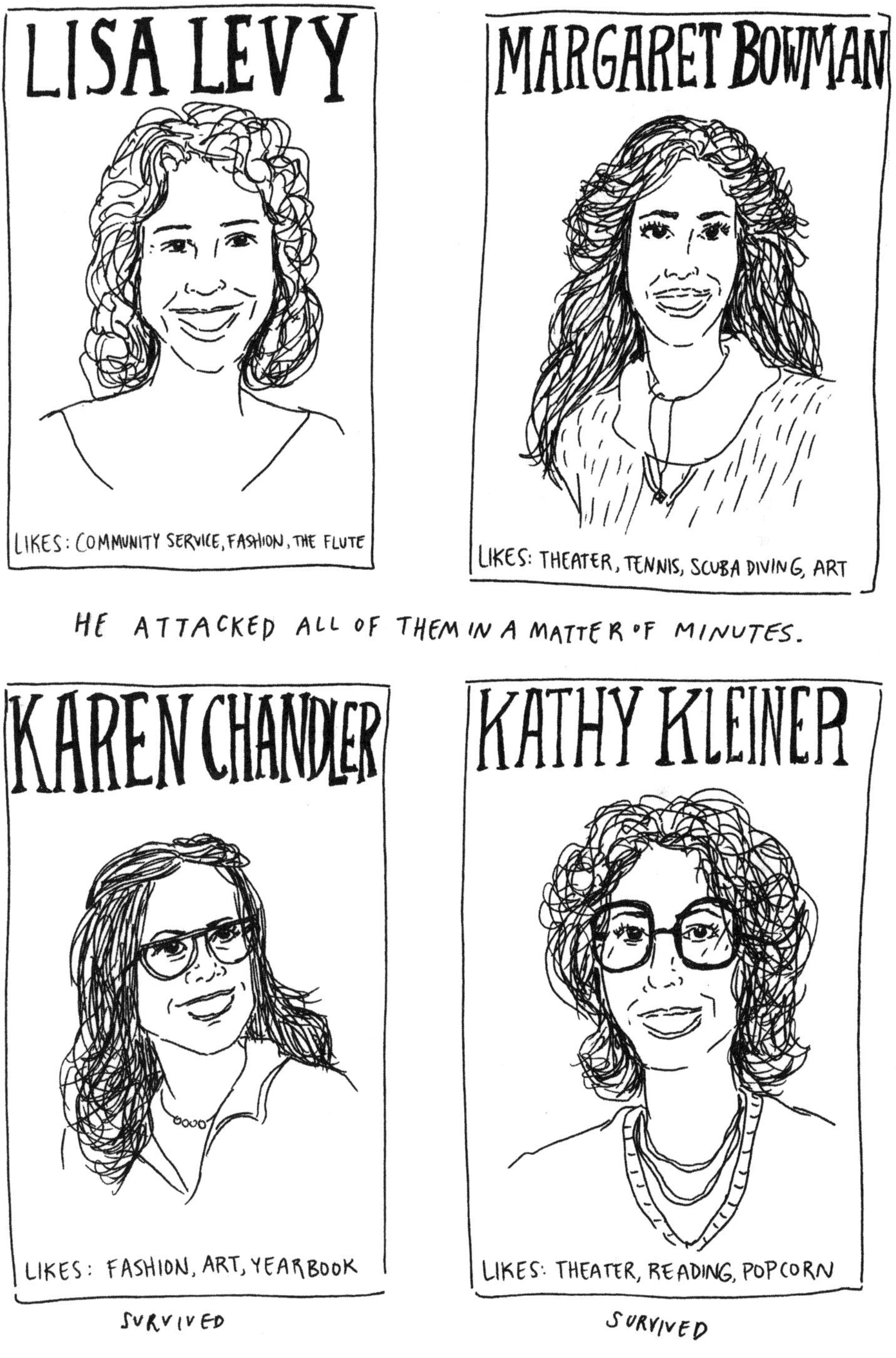
LISA LEVY
LIKES: COMMUNITY SERVICE, FASHION, THE FLUTE
MARGARET BOWMAN
LIKES: THEATER, TENNIS, SCUBA DIVING, ART
HE ATTACKED ALL OF THEM IN A MATTER OF MINUTES.
KAREN CHANDLER
LIKES: FASHION, ART, YEARBOOK
SURVIVED
KATHY KLEINER
LIKES: THEATER, READING, POPCORN
SURVIVED

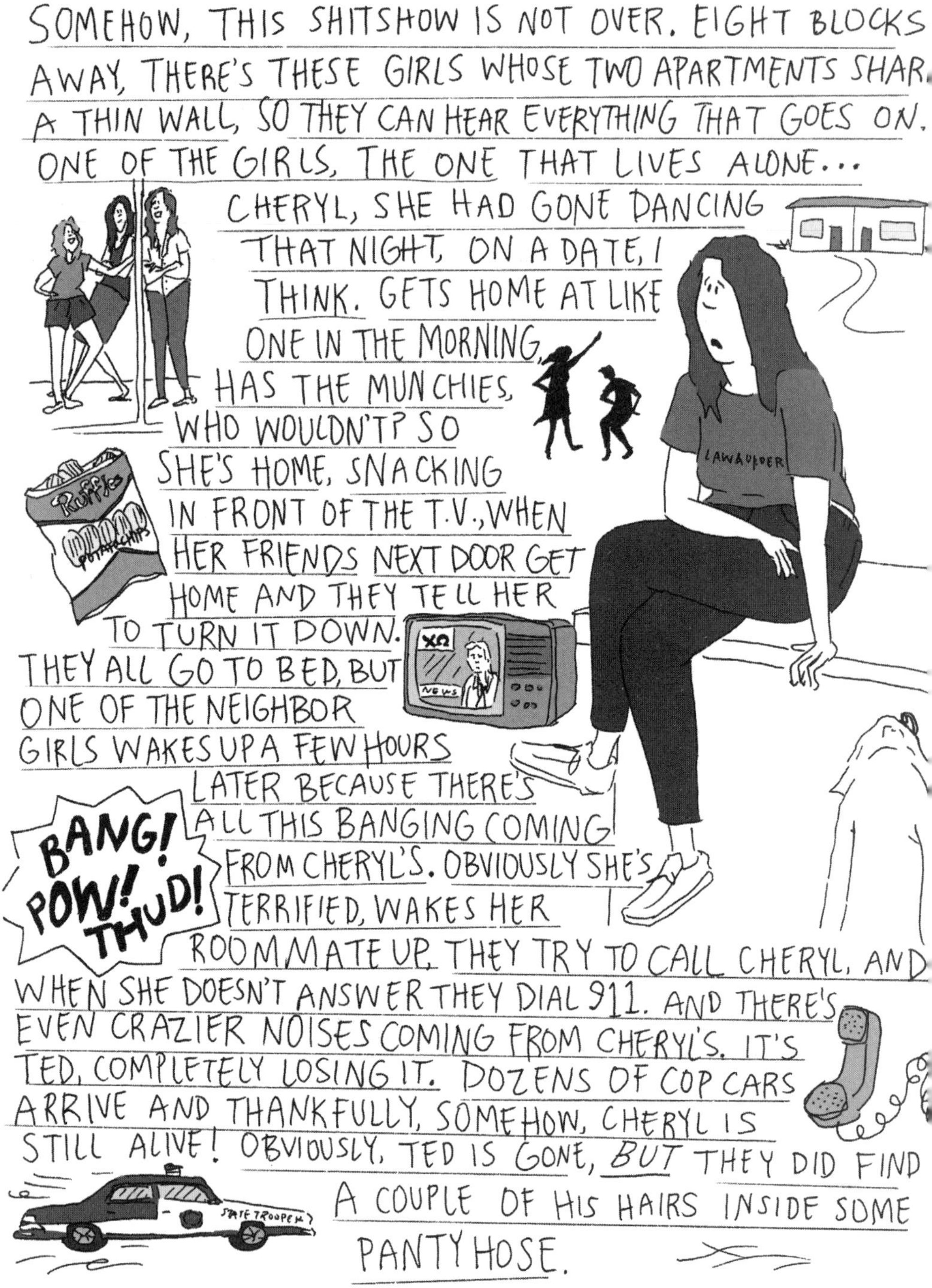
SOMEHOW, THIS SHITSHOW IS NOT OVER. EIGHT BLOCKS AWAY, THERE'S THESE GIRLS WHOSE TWO APARTMENTS SHARE A THIN WALL, SO THEY CAN HEAR EVERYTHING THAT GOES ON. ONE OF THE GIRLS, THE ONE THAT LIVES ALONE... CHERYL, SHE HAD GONE DANCING THAT NIGHT, ON A DATE, I THINK. GETS HOME AT LIKE ONE IN THE MORNING, HAS THE MUNCHIES, WHO WOULDN'T? SO SHE'S HOME, SNACKING IN FRONT OF THE T.V., WHEN HER FRIENDS NEXT DOOR GET HOME AND THEY TELL HER TO TURN IT DOWN. THEY ALL GO TO BED, BUT ONE OF THE NEIGHBOR GIRLS WAKES UP A FEW HOURS LATER BECAUSE THERE'S ALL THIS BANGING COMING FROM CHERYL'S. OBVIOUSLY SHE'S TERRIFIED, WAKES HER ROOMMATE UP, THEY TRY TO CALL CHERYL, AND WHEN SHE DOESN'T ANSWER THEY DIAL 911. AND THERE'S EVEN CRAZIER NOISES COMING FROM CHERYL'S. IT'S TED, COMPLETELY LOSING IT. DOZENS OF COP CARS ARRIVE AND THANKFULLY, SOMEHOW, CHERYL IS STILL ALIVE! OBVIOUSLY, TED IS GONE, BUT THEY DID FIND A COUPLE OF HIS HAIRS INSIDE SOME PANTY HOSE.
Ruffles
POTATO CHIPS
LAW & ORDER
XΩ
NEWS
BANG! POW! THUD!
STATE TROOPER

CHERYL THOMAS

SURVIVOR

TED WAS IN FLORIDA
ONE WEEK
AND THIS IS THE AMOUNT OF
DAMAGE
HE CAUSED.

TED'S TO-DO LIST
☑ Be as horrible as possible as fast as possible
☑ Drink beer

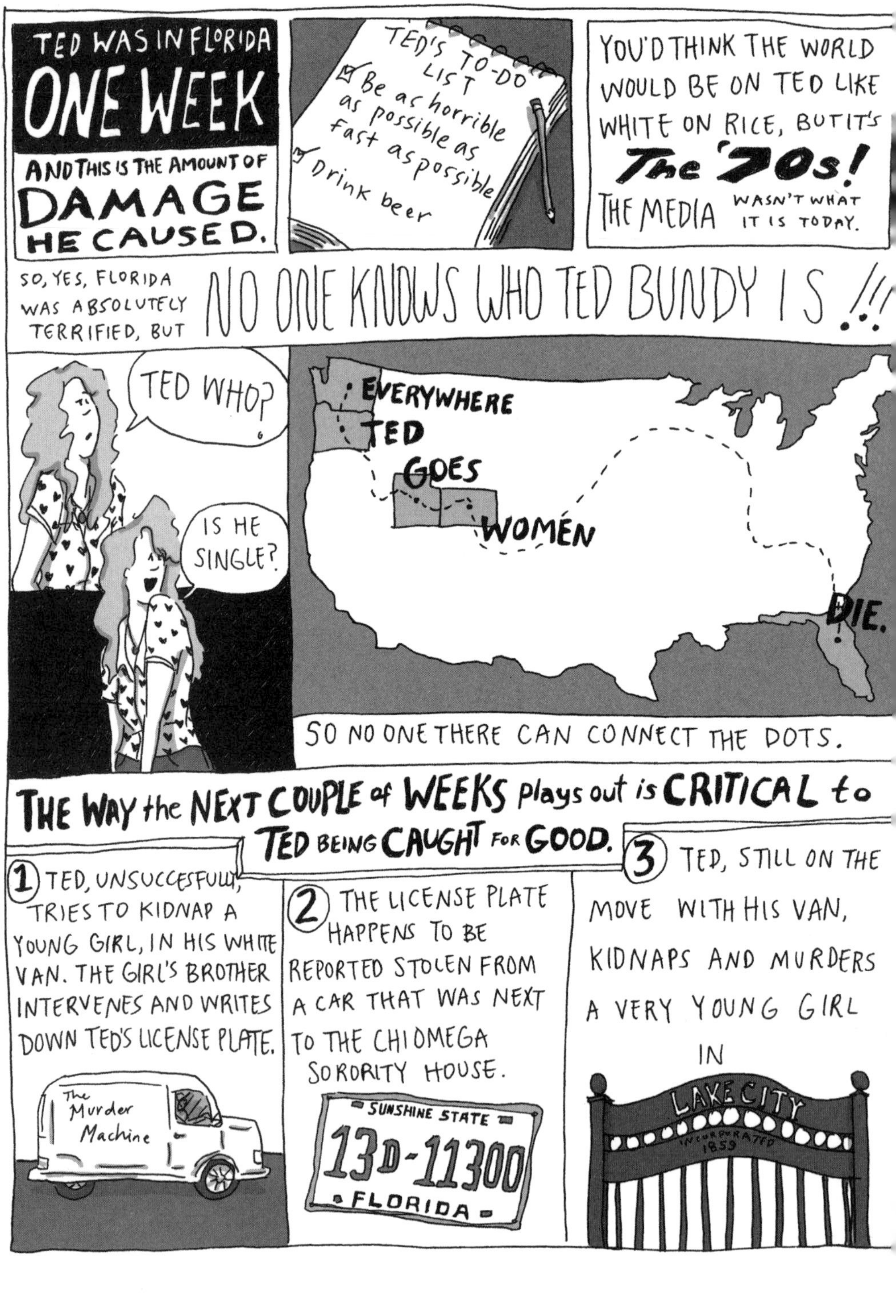

YOU'D THINK THE WORLD WOULD BE ON TED LIKE WHITE ON RICE, BUT IT'S *The '70s!* THE MEDIA WASN'T WHAT IT IS TODAY.

SO, YES, FLORIDA WAS ABSOLUTELY TERRIFIED, BUT **NO ONE KNOWS WHO TED BUNDY IS !!!**

TED WHO?

IS HE SINGLE?

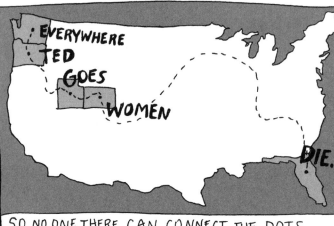
EVERYWHERE TED GOES WOMEN DIE.

SO NO ONE THERE CAN CONNECT THE DOTS.

THE WAY the NEXT COUPLE of WEEKS plays out is CRITICAL to TED BEING CAUGHT FOR GOOD.

① TED, UNSUCCESSFULLY, TRIES TO KIDNAP A YOUNG GIRL, IN HIS WHITE VAN. THE GIRL'S BROTHER INTERVENES AND WRITES DOWN TED'S LICENSE PLATE.

The Murder Machine

② THE LICENSE PLATE HAPPENS TO BE REPORTED STOLEN FROM A CAR THAT WAS NEXT TO THE CHI OMEGA SORORITY HOUSE.

SUNSHINE STATE
13D-11300
FLORIDA

③ TED, STILL ON THE MOVE WITH HIS VAN, KIDNAPS AND MURDERS A VERY YOUNG GIRL IN

LAKE CITY
INCORPORATED 1859

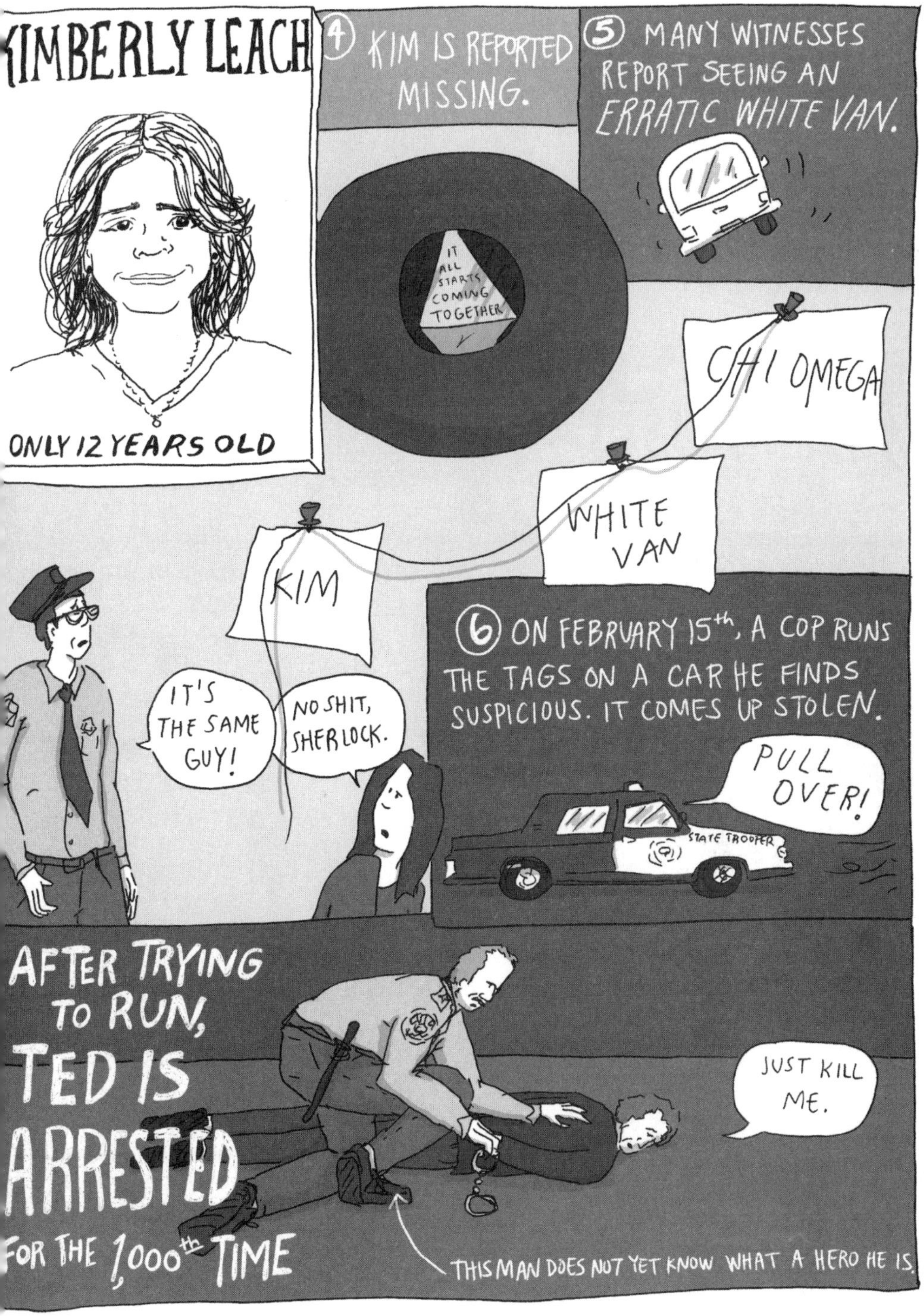
KIMBERLY LEACH
ONLY 12 YEARS OLD
4 KIM IS REPORTED MISSING.
IT ALL STARTS COMING TOGETHER
5 MANY WITNESSES REPORT SEEING AN ERRATIC WHITE VAN.
CHI OMEGA
WHITE VAN
KIM
IT'S THE SAME GUY!
NO SHIT, SHERLOCK.
6 ON FEBRUARY 15th, A COP RUNS THE TAGS ON A CAR HE FINDS SUSPICIOUS. IT COMES UP STOLEN.
PULL OVER!
STATE TROOPER
AFTER TRYING TO RUN, TED IS ARRESTED FOR THE 1,000th TIME
JUST KILL ME.
THIS MAN DOES NOT YET KNOW WHAT A HERO HE IS.

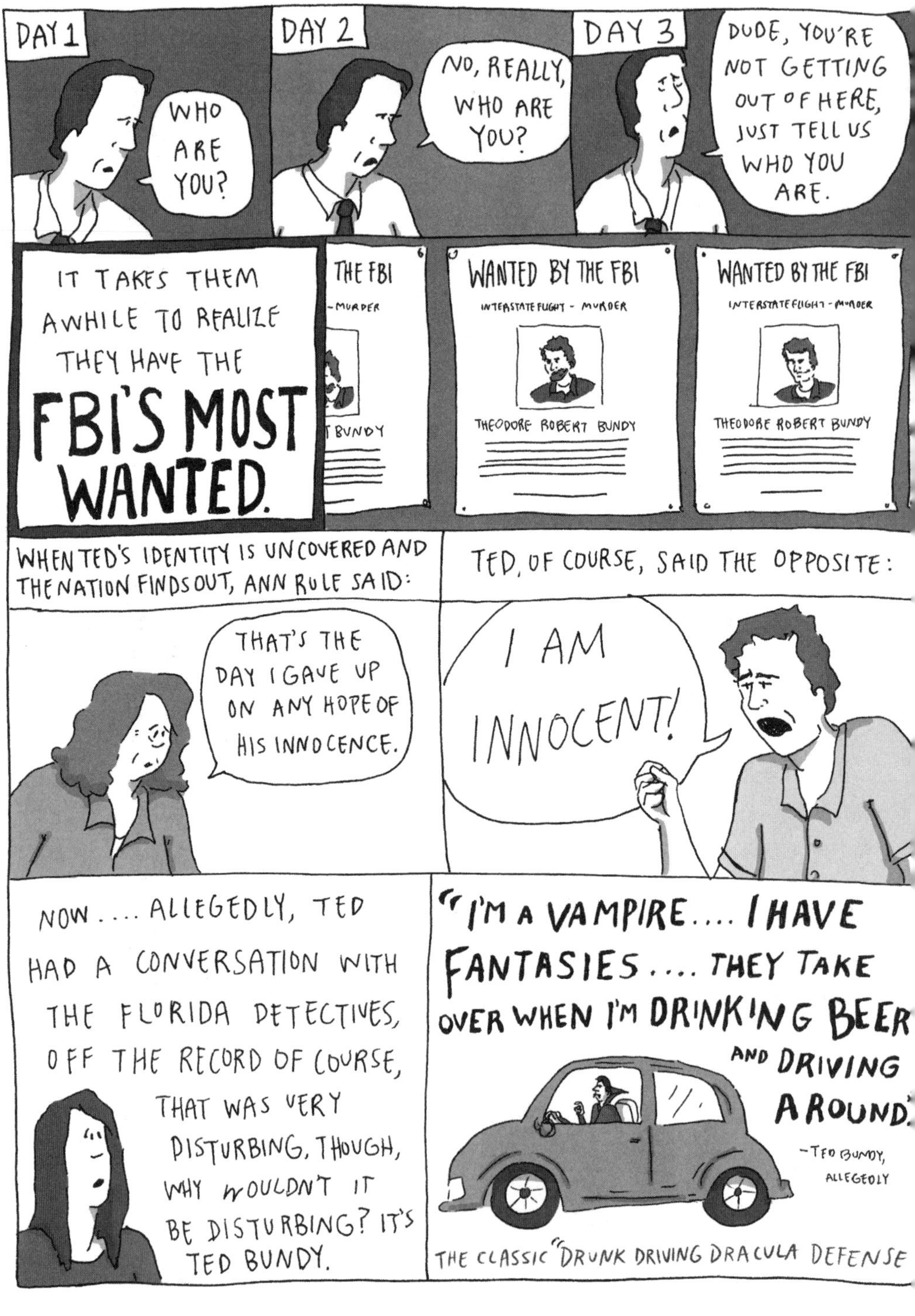
DAY 1
WHO ARE YOU?
DAY 2
NO, REALLY, WHO ARE YOU?
DAY 3
DUDE, YOU'RE NOT GETTING OUT OF HERE, JUST TELL US WHO YOU ARE.
IT TAKES THEM AWHILE TO REALIZE THEY HAVE THE FBI'S MOST WANTED.
WANTED BY THE FBI
INTERSTATE FLIGHT - MURDER
THEODORE ROBERT BUNDY
WANTED BY THE FBI
INTERSTATE FLIGHT - MURDER
THEODORE ROBERT BUNDY
WHEN TED'S IDENTITY IS UNCOVERED AND THE NATION FINDS OUT, ANN RULE SAID:
THAT'S THE DAY I GAVE UP ON ANY HOPE OF HIS INNOCENCE.
TED, OF COURSE, SAID THE OPPOSITE:
I AM INNOCENT!
NOW.... ALLEGEDLY, TED HAD A CONVERSATION WITH THE FLORIDA DETECTIVES, OFF THE RECORD OF COURSE, THAT WAS VERY DISTURBING, THOUGH, WHY WOULDN'T IT BE DISTURBING? IT'S TED BUNDY.
"I'M A VAMPIRE.... I HAVE FANTASIES.... THEY TAKE OVER WHEN I'M DRINKING BEER AND DRIVING AROUND."
-TED BUNDY, ALLEGEDLY
THE CLASSIC "DRUNK DRIVING DRACULA DEFENSE"

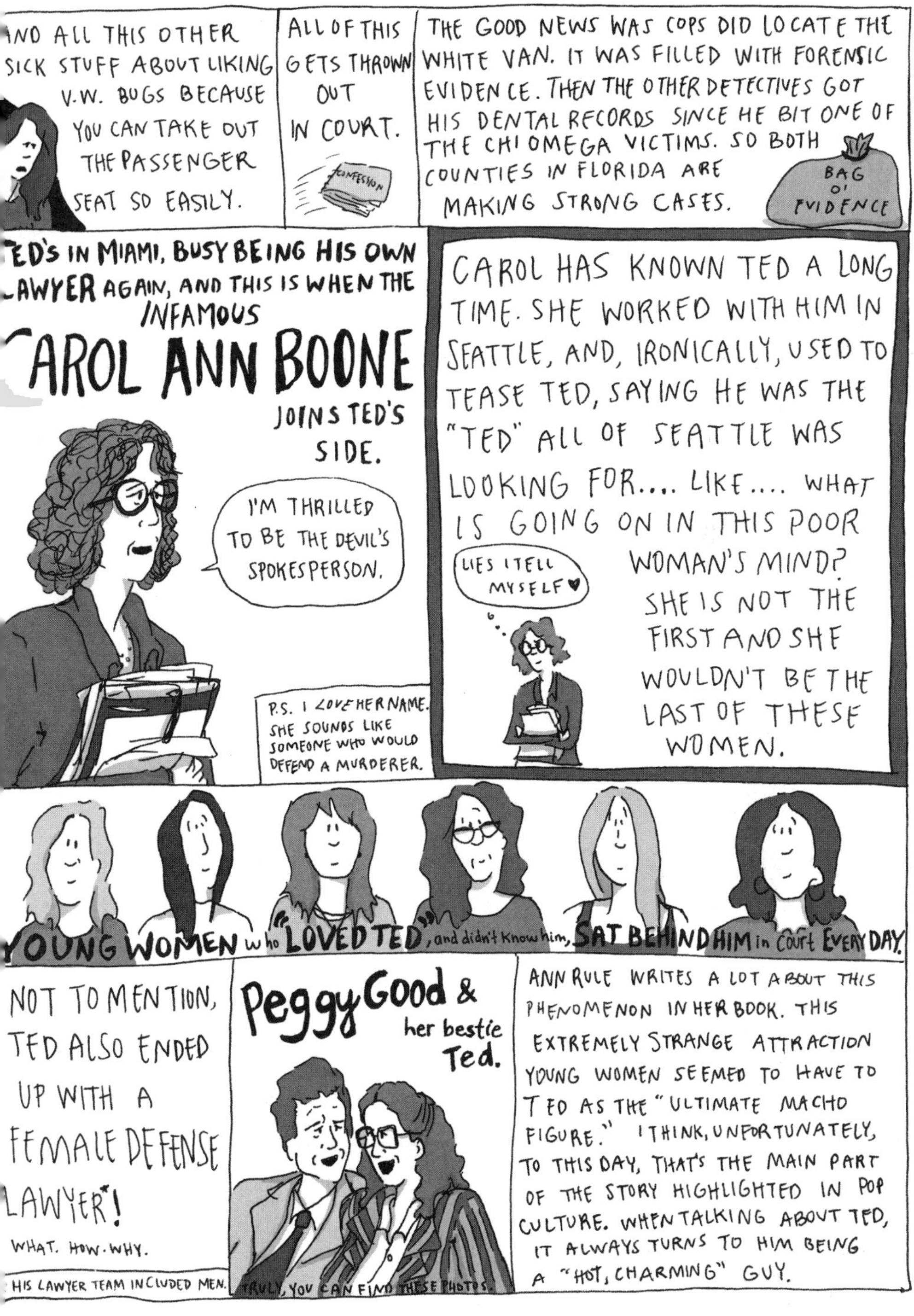
AND ALL THIS OTHER SICK STUFF ABOUT LIKING V.W. BUGS BECAUSE YOU CAN TAKE OUT THE PASSENGER SEAT SO EASILY.
ALL OF THIS GETS THROWN OUT IN COURT.
CONFESSION
THE GOOD NEWS WAS COPS DID LOCATE THE WHITE VAN. IT WAS FILLED WITH FORENSIC EVIDENCE. THEN THE OTHER DETECTIVES GOT HIS DENTAL RECORDS SINCE HE BIT ONE OF THE CHI OMEGA VICTIMS. SO BOTH COUNTIES IN FLORIDA ARE MAKING STRONG CASES.
BAG O' EVIDENCE
TED'S IN MIAMI, BUSY BEING HIS OWN LAWYER AGAIN, AND THIS IS WHEN THE INFAMOUS
CAROL ANN BOONE
JOINS TED'S SIDE.
I'M THRILLED TO BE THE DEVIL'S SPOKESPERSON.
P.S. I LOVE HER NAME. SHE SOUNDS LIKE SOMEONE WHO WOULD DEFEND A MURDERER.
CAROL HAS KNOWN TED A LONG TIME. SHE WORKED WITH HIM IN SEATTLE, AND, IRONICALLY, USED TO TEASE TED, SAYING HE WAS THE "TED" ALL OF SEATTLE WAS LOOKING FOR.... LIKE.... WHAT IS GOING ON IN THIS POOR WOMAN'S MIND? SHE IS NOT THE FIRST AND SHE WOULDN'T BE THE LAST OF THESE WOMEN.
LIES I TELL MYSELF ♥
YOUNG WOMEN who "LOVED TED", and didn't know him, SAT BEHIND HIM in court EVERY DAY.
NOT TO MENTION, TED ALSO ENDED UP WITH A FEMALE DEFENSE LAWYER*!
WHAT. HOW. WHY.
*HIS LAWYER TEAM INCLUDED MEN.
Peggy Good & her bestie Ted.
TRULY, YOU CAN FIND THESE PHOTOS.
ANN RULE WRITES A LOT ABOUT THIS PHENOMENON IN HER BOOK. THIS EXTREMELY STRANGE ATTRACTION YOUNG WOMEN SEEMED TO HAVE TO TED AS THE "ULTIMATE MACHO FIGURE." I THINK, UNFORTUNATELY, TO THIS DAY, THAT'S THE MAIN PART OF THE STORY HIGHLIGHTED IN POP CULTURE. WHEN TALKING ABOUT TED, IT ALWAYS TURNS TO HIM BEING A "HOT, CHARMING" GUY.

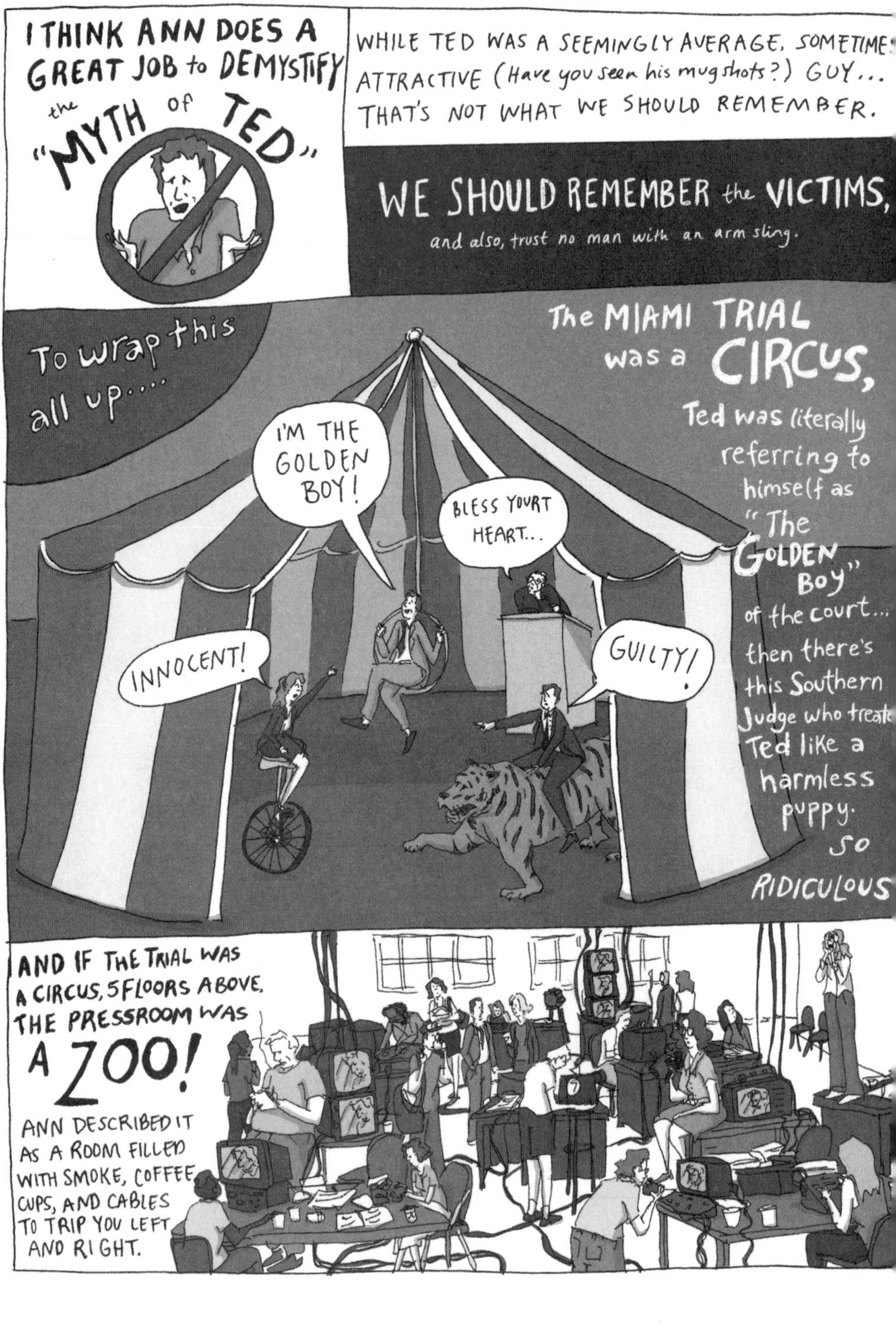

I THINK ANN DOES A GREAT JOB to DEMYSTIFY the "MYTH OF TED"
WHILE TED WAS A SEEMINGLY AVERAGE, SOMETIME
ATTRACTIVE (Have you seen his mugshots?) GUY... THAT'S NOT WHAT WE SHOULD REMEMBER.
WE SHOULD REMEMBER the VICTIMS,
and also, trust no man with an arm sling.
To wrap this all up....
The MIAMI TRIAL was a CIRCUS,
Ted was literally referring to himself as "The GOLDEN Boy" of the court... then there's this Southern Judge who treat
Ted like a harmless puppy.
SO RIDICULOUS
I'M THE GOLDEN BOY!
BLESS YOURT HEART...
INNOCENT!
GUILTY!
AND IF THE TRIAL WAS A CIRCUS, 5 FLOORS ABOVE, THE PRESSROOM WAS A ZOO!
ANN DESCRIBED IT AS A ROOM FILLED WITH SMOKE, COFFEE CUPS, AND CABLES TO TRIP YOU LEFT AND RIGHT.

THE TRIAL IS NUTS, AND THOUGH TED TRIES TO PULL EVERY TRICK IN THE BOOK, THE PEOPLE OF FLORIDA DESPISE HIM.

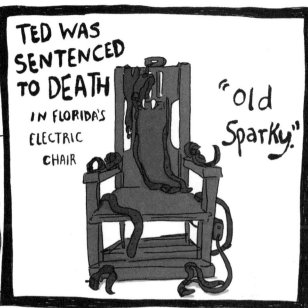

TED WAS SENTENCED TO DEATH IN FLORIDA'S ELECTRIC CHAIR

"Old Sparky."

Why on earth did Ted flee to a hardcore death penalty state? Did he.... want to die?

IN ORLANDO, BUNDY IS SENTENCED TO DEATH AGAIN IN THE KIMBERLY LEACH TRIAL, BUT NOT BEFORE HE COULD SNEAK IN A MARRIAGE PROPOSAL TO CAROL ANN.

WILL YOU MARRY ME?

YOU'VE GOT TO BE KIDDING ME...

YES, I WILL.

THEN I DO HEREBY MARRY YOU.

DON'T YOU JUST HATE THAT TED GETS TO TECHNICALLY GET MARRIED, AFTER HE'S TAKEN AWAY THE FUTURES OF ALL THOSE INNOCENT GIRLS?

MARRIAGE ISN'T ALL IT'S CRACKED UP TO BE.

I THINK YOU MISSED MY POINT.

IT'S YEARS BEFORE TED ACTUALLY REACHES "OLD SPARKY." IN THE MEANTIME, ANN FINISHES THE BOOK. TED GETS MAD AT HER, THEN FORGIVES HER. CAROL ANN HAS TED'S BABY AND EVENTUALLY STOPS VISITING TED IN JAIL.

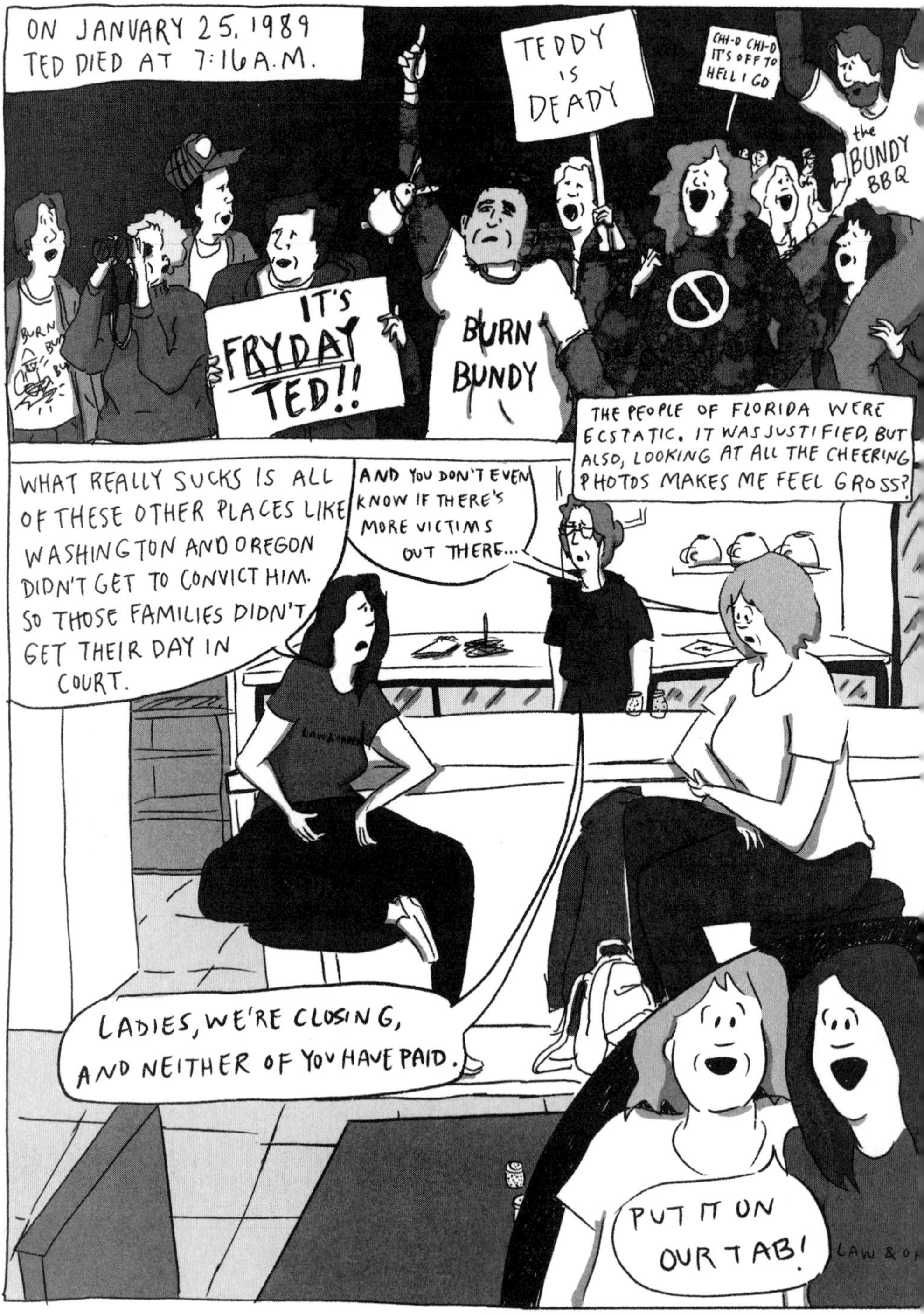
ON JANUARY 25, 1989 TED DIED AT 7:16 A.M.
TEDDY IS DEADY
CHI-O CHI-O IT'S OFF TO HELL I GO
the BUNDY BBQ
IT'S FRYDAY TED!!
BURN BUNDY
THE PEOPLE OF FLORIDA WERE ECSTATIC. IT WAS JUSTIFIED, BUT ALSO, LOOKING AT ALL THE CHEERING PHOTOS MAKES ME FEEL GROSS?
WHAT REALLY SUCKS IS ALL OF THESE OTHER PLACES LIKE WASHINGTON AND OREGON DIDN'T GET TO CONVICT HIM. SO THOSE FAMILIES DIDN'T GET THEIR DAY IN COURT.
AND YOU DON'T EVEN KNOW IF THERE'S MORE VICTIMS OUT THERE...
LADIES, WE'RE CLOSING, AND NEITHER OF YOU HAVE PAID.
PUT IT ON OUR TAB!

BECAUSE

OF

MOM?

SO HOW DOES IT REALLY HAPPEN? HOW DOES ONE BECOME A TRUE CRIME JUNKIE OVER TIME?
IS
THERE
MURDER
IN
IT?
THERE IS MURDER IN IT.
HOW DOES ONE GET FROM
A
B?
MOMMY!
MOM, DID YOU HEAR THEY CAUGHT THE GOLDEN STATE KILLER?!
is it the
"MOTHER?!"

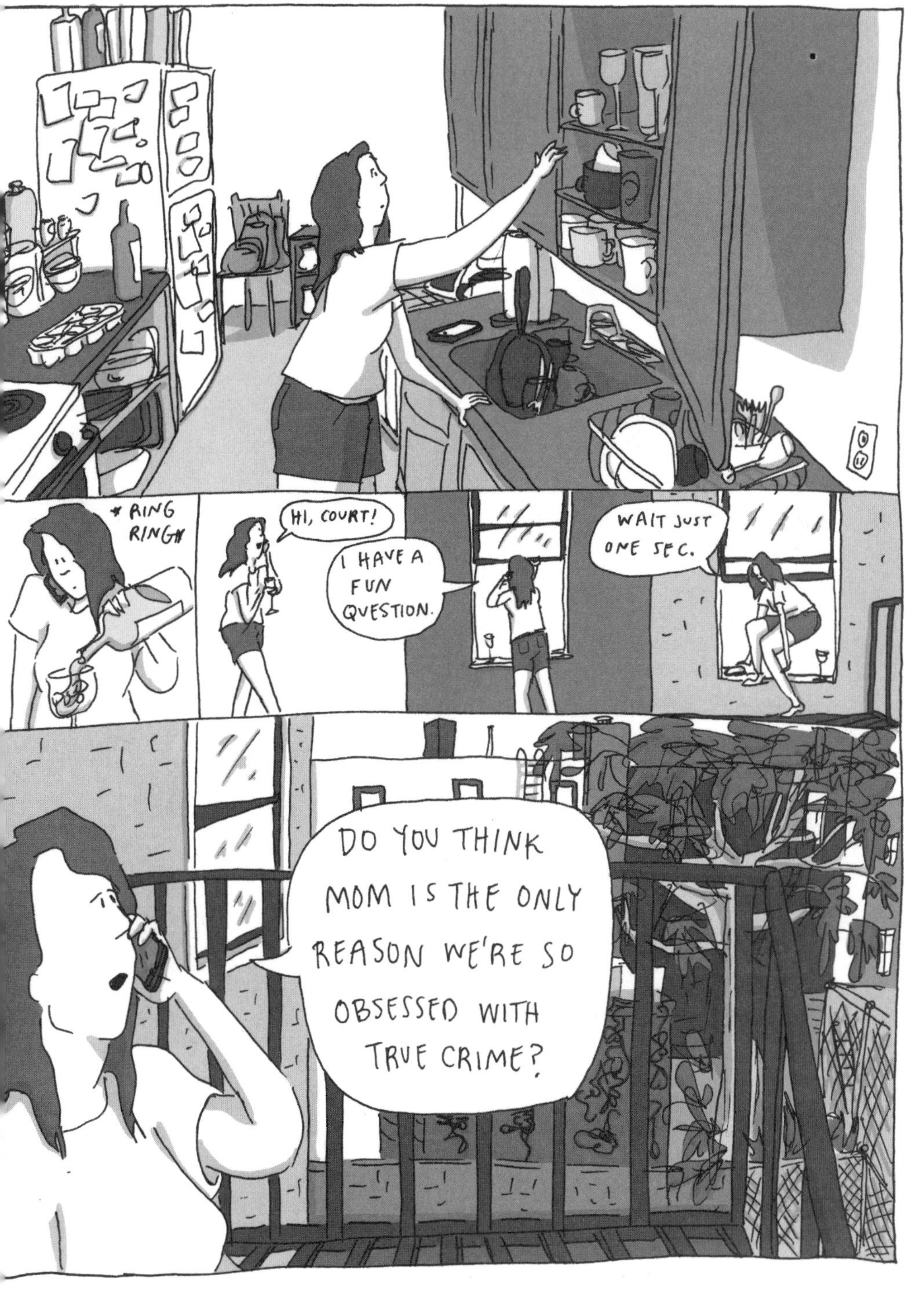
RING RING
HI, COURT!
I HAVE A FUN QUESTION.
WAIT JUST ONE SEC.
DO YOU THINK MOM IS THE ONLY REASON WE'RE SO OBSESSED WITH TRUE CRIME?

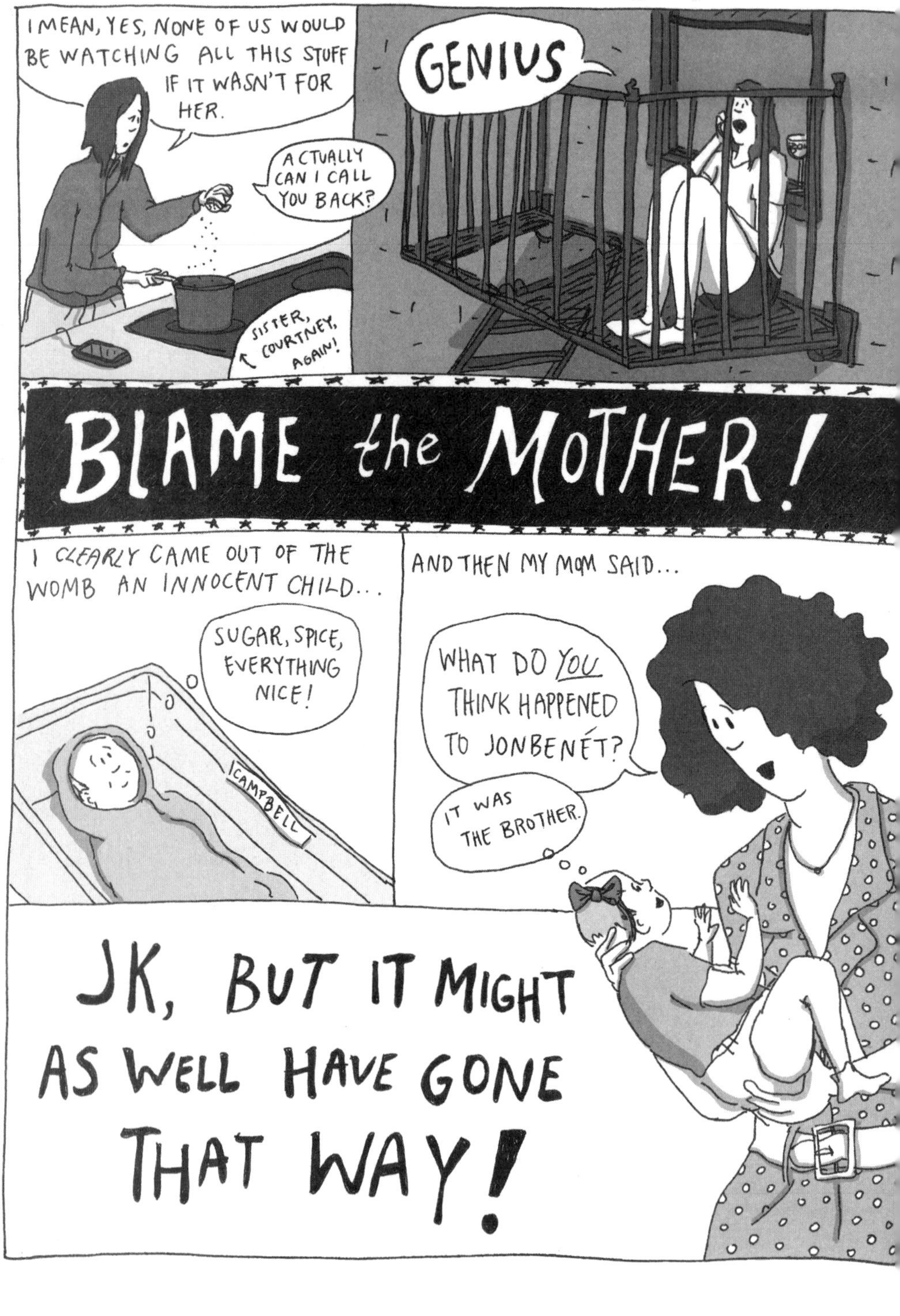

I MEAN, YES, NONE OF US WOULD BE WATCHING ALL THIS STUFF IF IT WASN'T FOR HER.
ACTUALLY CAN I CALL YOU BACK?
SISTER, COURTNEY, AGAIN!
GENIUS
BLAME the MOTHER!
I CLEARLY CAME OUT OF THE WOMB AN INNOCENT CHILD...
SUGAR, SPICE, EVERYTHING NICE!
CAMPBELL
AND THEN MY MOM SAID...
WHAT DO YOU THINK HAPPENED TO JONBENÉT?
IT WAS THE BROTHER.
JK, BUT IT MIGHT AS WELL HAVE GONE THAT WAY!

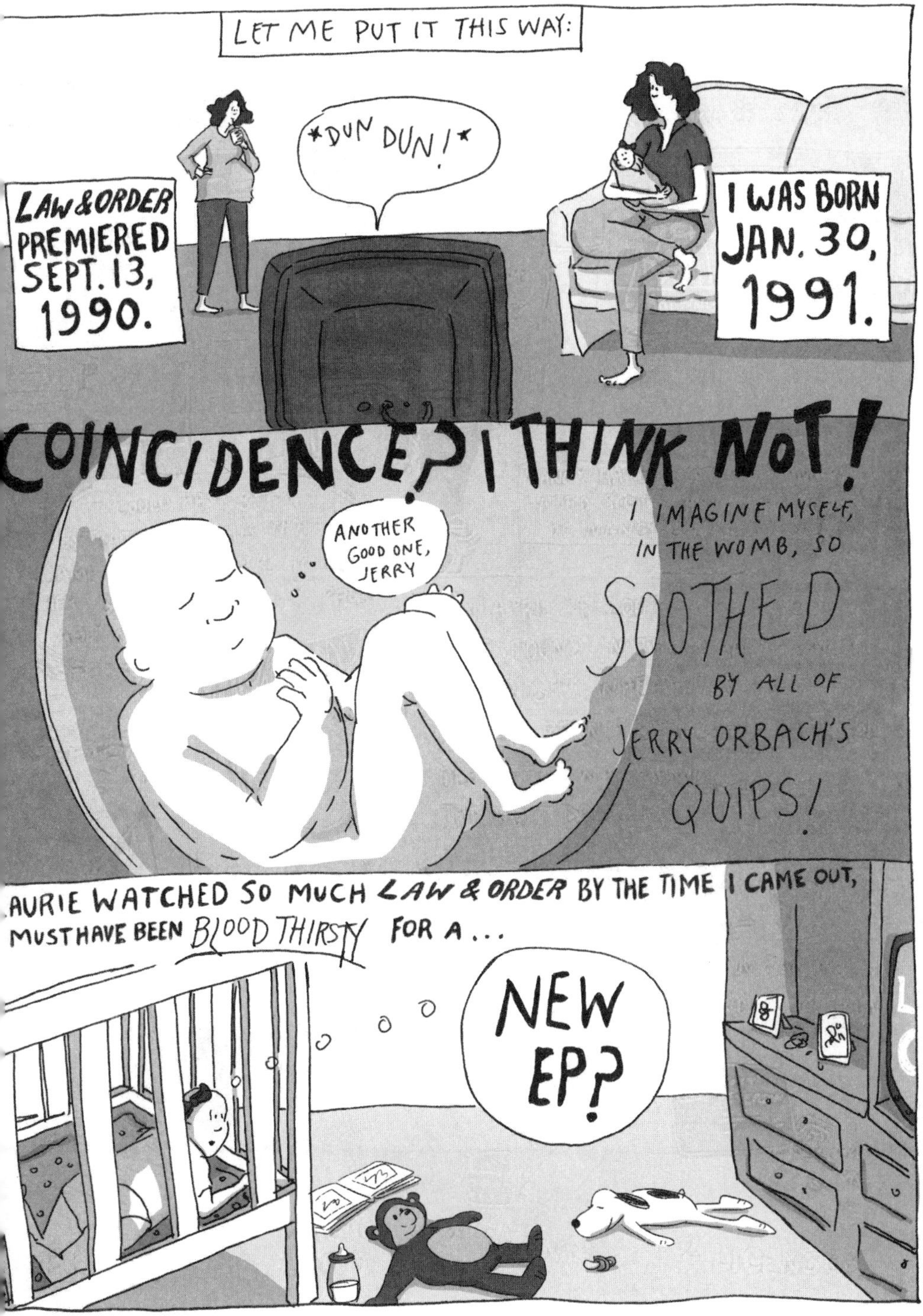
LET ME PUT IT THIS WAY:
LAW & ORDER PREMIERED SEPT. 13, 1990.
DUN DUN!
I WAS BORN JAN. 30, 1991.
COINCIDENCE? I THINK NOT!
ANOTHER GOOD ONE, JERRY
I IMAGINE MYSELF, IN THE WOMB, SO SOOTHED BY ALL OF JERRY ORBACH'S QUIPS!
AURIE WATCHED SO MUCH LAW & ORDER BY THE TIME I CAME OUT,
MUST HAVE BEEN BLOOD THIRSTY FOR A...
NEW EP?

THAT REMINDS ME! WE HAVEN'T TALKED ABOUT THIS IN CLASS!
IT'S MURDER MOVIES BUT JUST... BETTER.

MURDER T.V.

THERE'S TWO TYPES:

TRUE CRIME
TNT MORE DRAMA
CRIME DRAMA PROCEDURALS

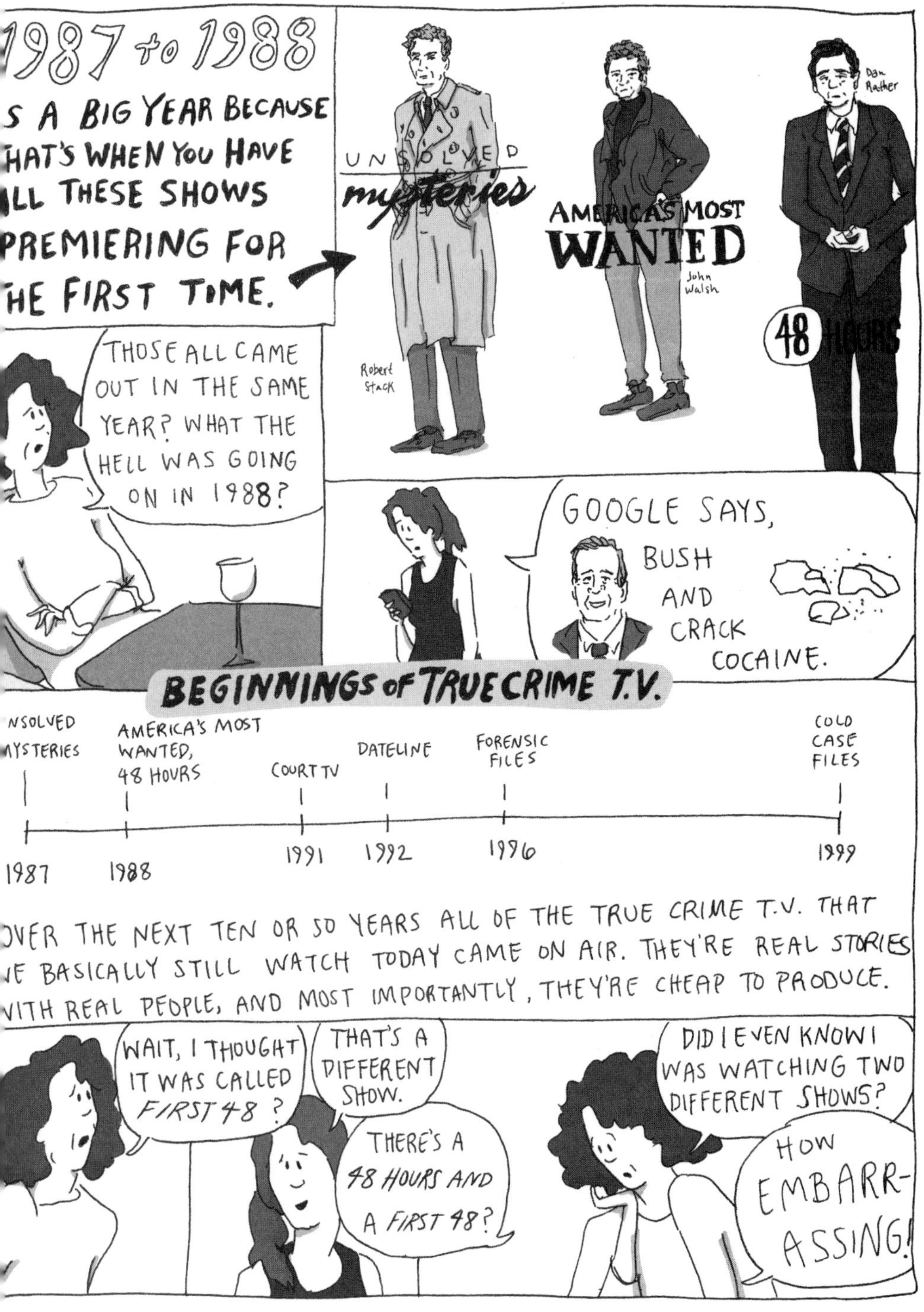

1987 to 1988
S A BIG YEAR BECAUSE HAT'S WHEN YOU HAVE LL THESE SHOWS PREMIERING FOR HE FIRST TIME.
UNSOLVED mysteries
Robert Stack
AMERICA'S MOST WANTED
John Walsh
Dan Rather
48 HOURS
THOSE ALL CAME OUT IN THE SAME YEAR? WHAT THE HELL WAS GOING ON IN 1988?
GOOGLE SAYS, BUSH AND CRACK COCAINE.
BEGINNINGS OF TRUE CRIME T.V.
NSOLVED MYSTERIES
AMERICA'S MOST WANTED, 48 HOURS
COURT TV
DATELINE
FORENSIC FILES
COLD CASE FILES
1987
1988
1991
1992
1996
1999
OVER THE NEXT TEN OR SO YEARS ALL OF THE TRUE CRIME T.V. THAT WE BASICALLY STILL WATCH TODAY CAME ON AIR. THEY'RE REAL STORIES WITH REAL PEOPLE, AND MOST IMPORTANTLY, THEY'RE CHEAP TO PRODUCE.
WAIT, I THOUGHT IT WAS CALLED FIRST 48?
THAT'S A DIFFERENT SHOW.
THERE'S A 48 HOURS AND A FIRST 48?
DID I EVEN KNOW I WAS WATCHING TWO DIFFERENT SHOWS?
HOW EMBARR-ASSING!

HOW CAN YOU EVEN KNOW WHICH TRUE CRIME SHOW YOU'RE WATCHING?

a flowchart

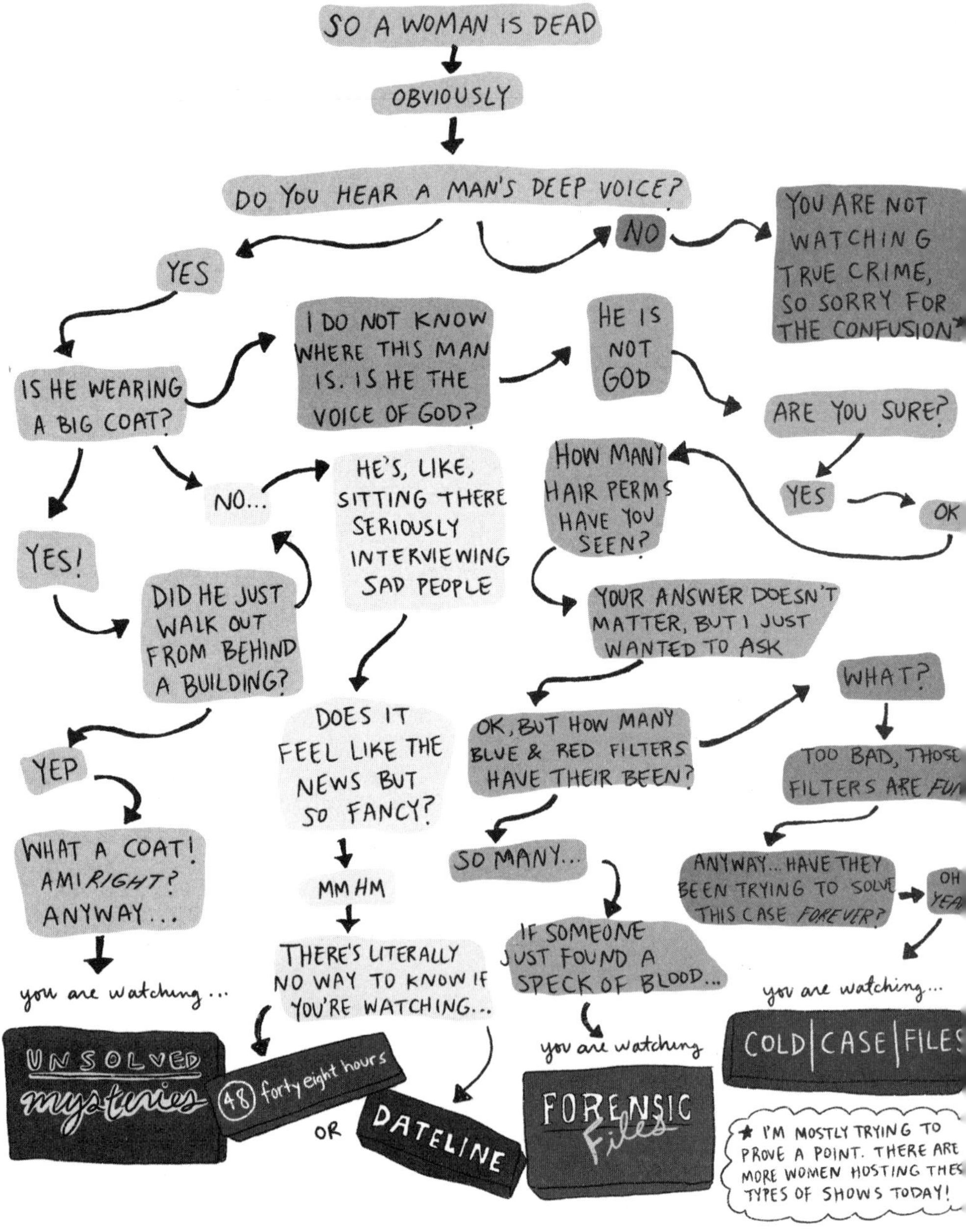
SO A WOMAN IS DEAD
OBVIOUSLY
DO YOU HEAR A MAN'S DEEP VOICE?
NO
YOU ARE NOT WATCHING TRUE CRIME, SO SORRY FOR THE CONFUSION*
YES
IS HE WEARING A BIG COAT?
I DO NOT KNOW WHERE THIS MAN IS. IS HE THE VOICE OF GOD?
HE IS NOT GOD
ARE YOU SURE?
YES
OK
HOW MANY HAIR PERMS HAVE YOU SEEN?
YOUR ANSWER DOESN'T MATTER, BUT I JUST WANTED TO ASK
NO...
HE'S, LIKE, SITTING THERE SERIOUSLY INTERVIEWING SAD PEOPLE
YES!
DID HE JUST WALK OUT FROM BEHIND A BUILDING?
YEP
WHAT A COAT! AM I RIGHT? ANYWAY...
you are watching...
DOES IT FEEL LIKE THE NEWS BUT SO FANCY?
MM HM
THERE'S LITERALLY NO WAY TO KNOW IF YOU'RE WATCHING...
OK, BUT HOW MANY BLUE & RED FILTERS HAVE THEIR BEEN?
WHAT?
TOO BAD, THOSE FILTERS ARE FU
SO MANY...
IF SOMEONE JUST FOUND A SPECK OF BLOOD...
you are watching
ANYWAY... HAVE THEY BEEN TRYING TO SOLVE THIS CASE FOREVER?
OH YEA
you are watching...
UNSOLVED mysteries
48 forty eight hours
OR
DATELINE
FORENSIC Files
COLD CASE FILES
★ I'M MOSTLY TRYING TO PROVE A POINT. THERE ARE MORE WOMEN HOSTING THES TYPES OF SHOWS TODAY!

I KNOW THERE'S ABOUT 5,000 TRUE CRIME SHOWS NOW...

thanks to ID INVESTIGATION DISCOVERY ...

or what my mom calls THE ALL MURDER CHANNEL

I DID SAY THAT DIDN'T I!?

A.M.A.T.T.
All Murder
All The Time
I.D.

... There's 24 HOURS of it!

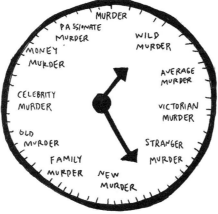

MURDER
PASSIONATE MURDER
WILD MURDER
MONEY MURDER
AVERAGE MURDER
CELEBRITY MURDER
VICTORIAN MURDER
OLD MURDER
STRANGER MURDER
FAMILY MURDER
NEW MURDER

BUT AS FAR AS I'M CONCERNED...

FORENSIC Files

IS ALL THAT MATTERS! BUT WHY??

SO MANY REASONS AND THEY'RE ALL SUBJECTIVE AND PERSONAL.

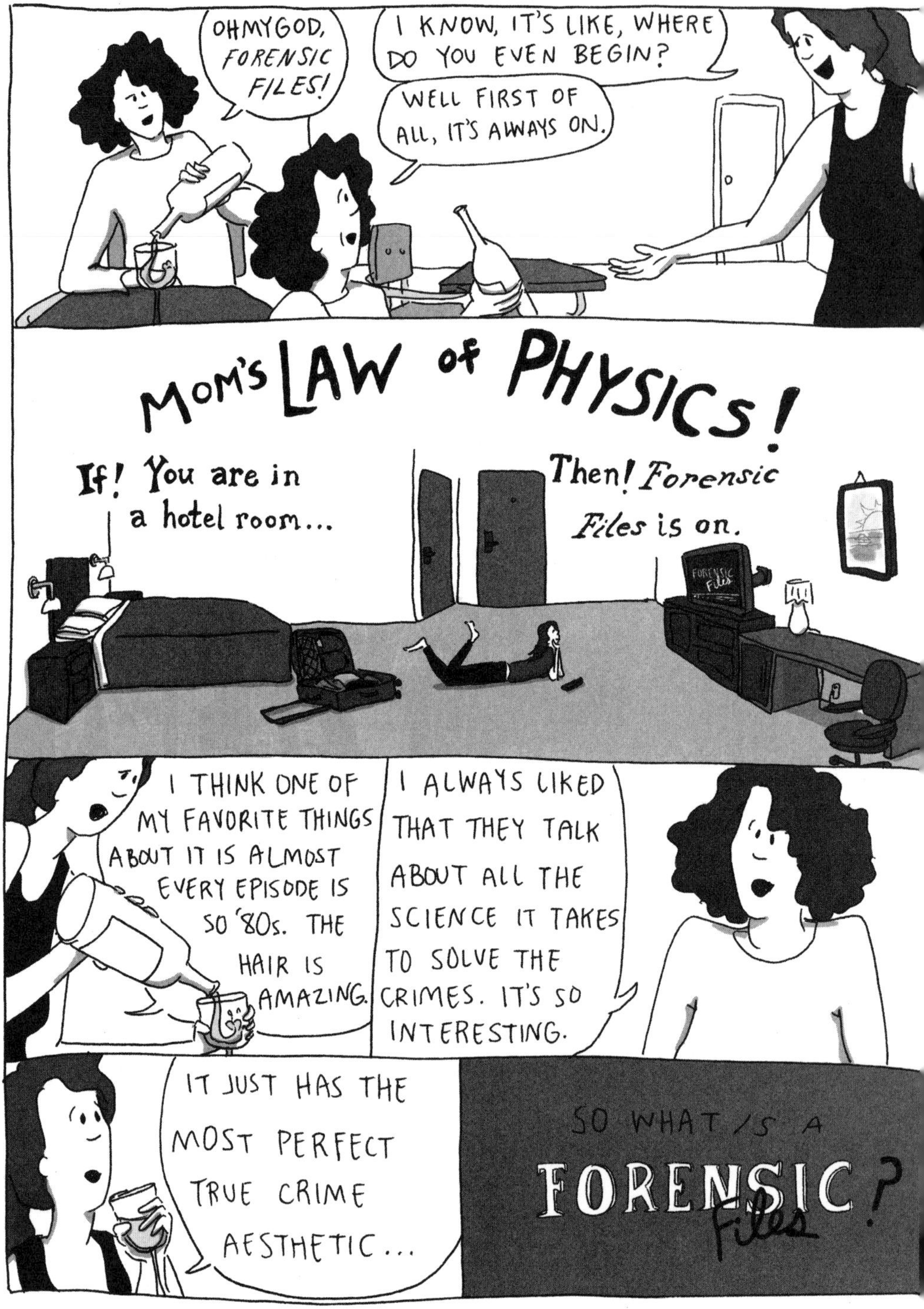
OHMYGOD, FORENSIC FILES!
I KNOW, IT'S LIKE, WHERE DO YOU EVEN BEGIN?
WELL FIRST OF ALL, IT'S ALWAYS ON.
MOM'S LAW of PHYSICS!
If! You are in a hotel room...
Then! Forensic Files is on.
FORENSIC Files
I THINK ONE OF MY FAVORITE THINGS ABOUT IT IS ALMOST EVERY EPISODE IS SO '80s. THE HAIR IS AMAZING.
I ALWAYS LIKED THAT THEY TALK ABOUT ALL THE SCIENCE IT TAKES TO SOLVE THE CRIMES. IT'S SO INTERESTING.
IT JUST HAS THE MOST PERFECT TRUE CRIME AESTHETIC...
SO WHAT IS A FORENSIC Files?

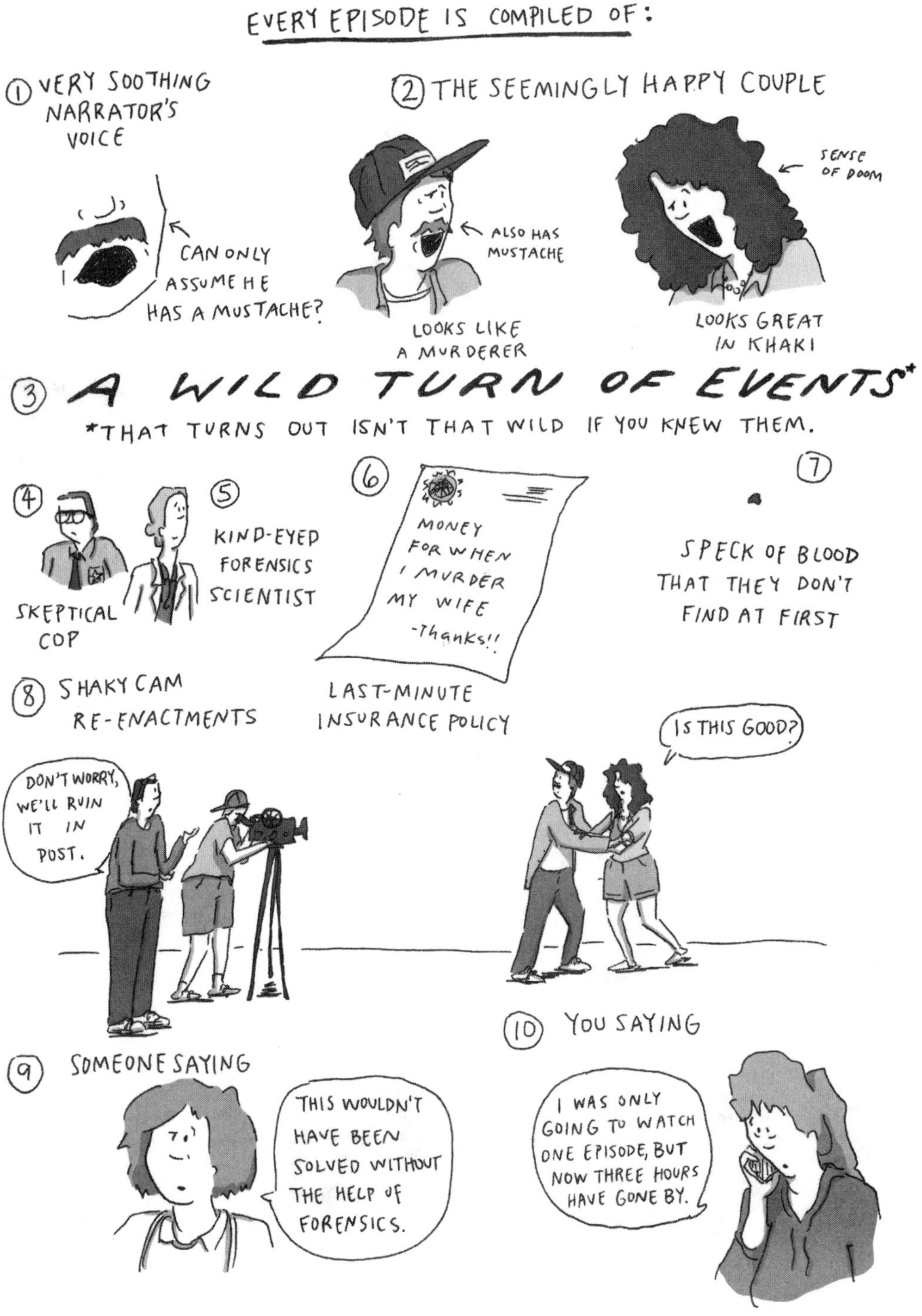
EVERY EPISODE IS COMPILED OF:
1 VERY SOOTHING NARRATOR'S VOICE
CAN ONLY ASSUME HE HAS A MUSTACHE?
2 THE SEEMINGLY HAPPY COUPLE
ALSO HAS MUSTACHE
LOOKS LIKE A MURDERER
SENSE OF DOOM
LOOKS GREAT IN KHAKI
3 A WILD TURN OF EVENTS*
*THAT TURNS OUT ISN'T THAT WILD IF YOU KNEW THEM.
4 SKEPTICAL COP
5 KIND-EYED FORENSICS SCIENTIST
6 MONEY FOR WHEN I MURDER MY WIFE -thanks!!
LAST-MINUTE INSURANCE POLICY
7 SPECK OF BLOOD THAT THEY DON'T FIND AT FIRST
8 SHAKY CAM RE-ENACTMENTS
DON'T WORRY, WE'LL RUIN IT IN POST.
IS THIS GOOD?
9 SOMEONE SAYING
THIS WOULDN'T HAVE BEEN SOLVED WITHOUT THE HELP OF FORENSICS.
10 YOU SAYING
I WAS ONLY GOING TO WATCH ONE EPISODE, BUT NOW THREE HOURS HAVE GONE BY.

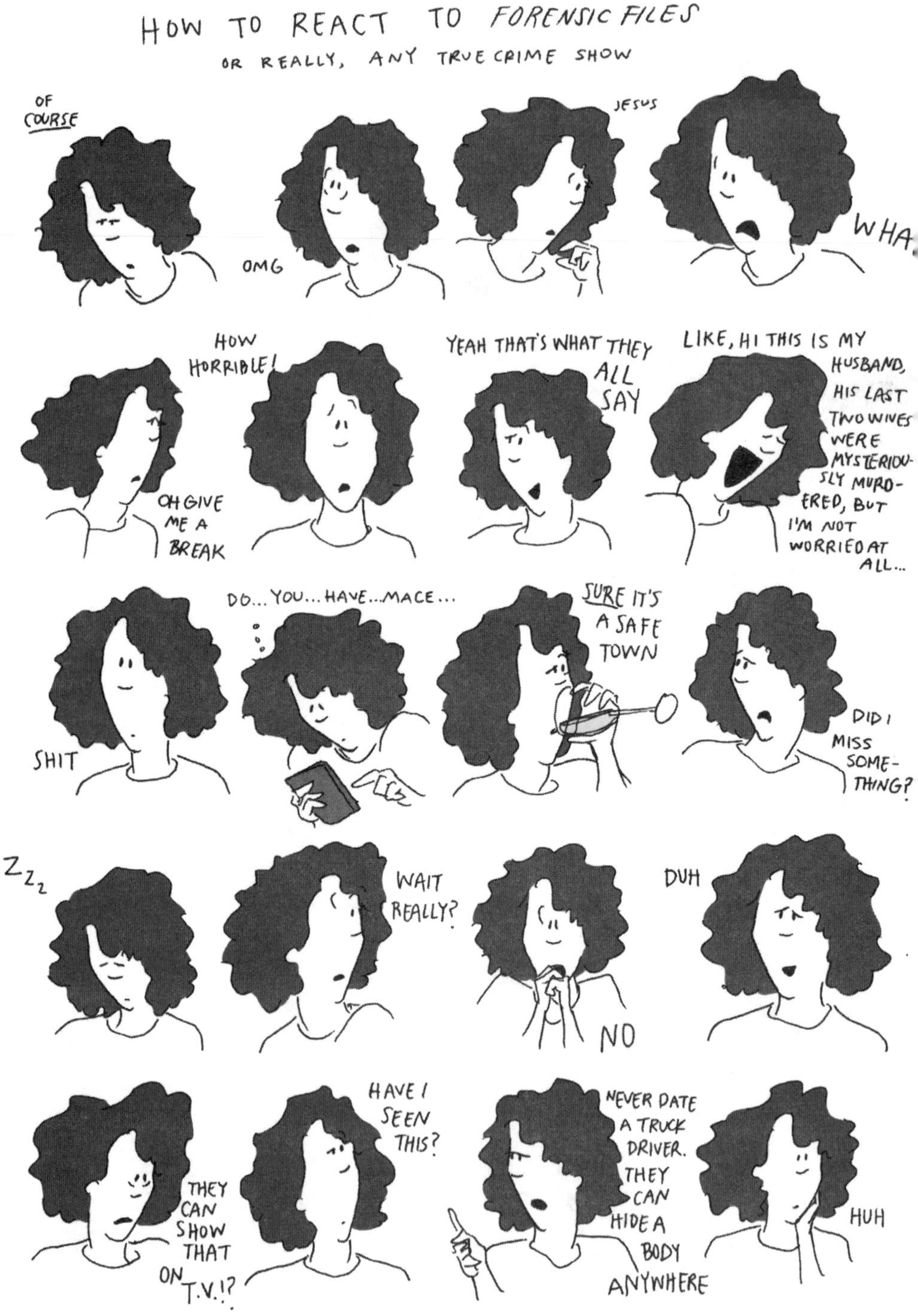

HOW TO REACT TO FORENSIC FILES
OR REALLY, ANY TRUE CRIME SHOW
OF COURSE
OMG
JESUS
WHA
HOW HORRIBLE!
OH GIVE ME A BREAK
YEAH THAT'S WHAT THEY ALL SAY
LIKE, HI THIS IS MY HUSBAND, HIS LAST TWO WIVES WERE MYSTERIOUSLY MURDERED, BUT I'M NOT WORRIED AT ALL...
SHIT
DO... YOU... HAVE... MACE...
SURE IT'S A SAFE TOWN
DID I MISS SOMETHING?
Z Z Z
WAIT REALLY?
NO
DUH
THEY CAN SHOW THAT ON T.V.!?
HAVE I SEEN THIS?
NEVER DATE A TRUCK DRIVER. THEY CAN HIDE A BODY ANYWHERE
HUH

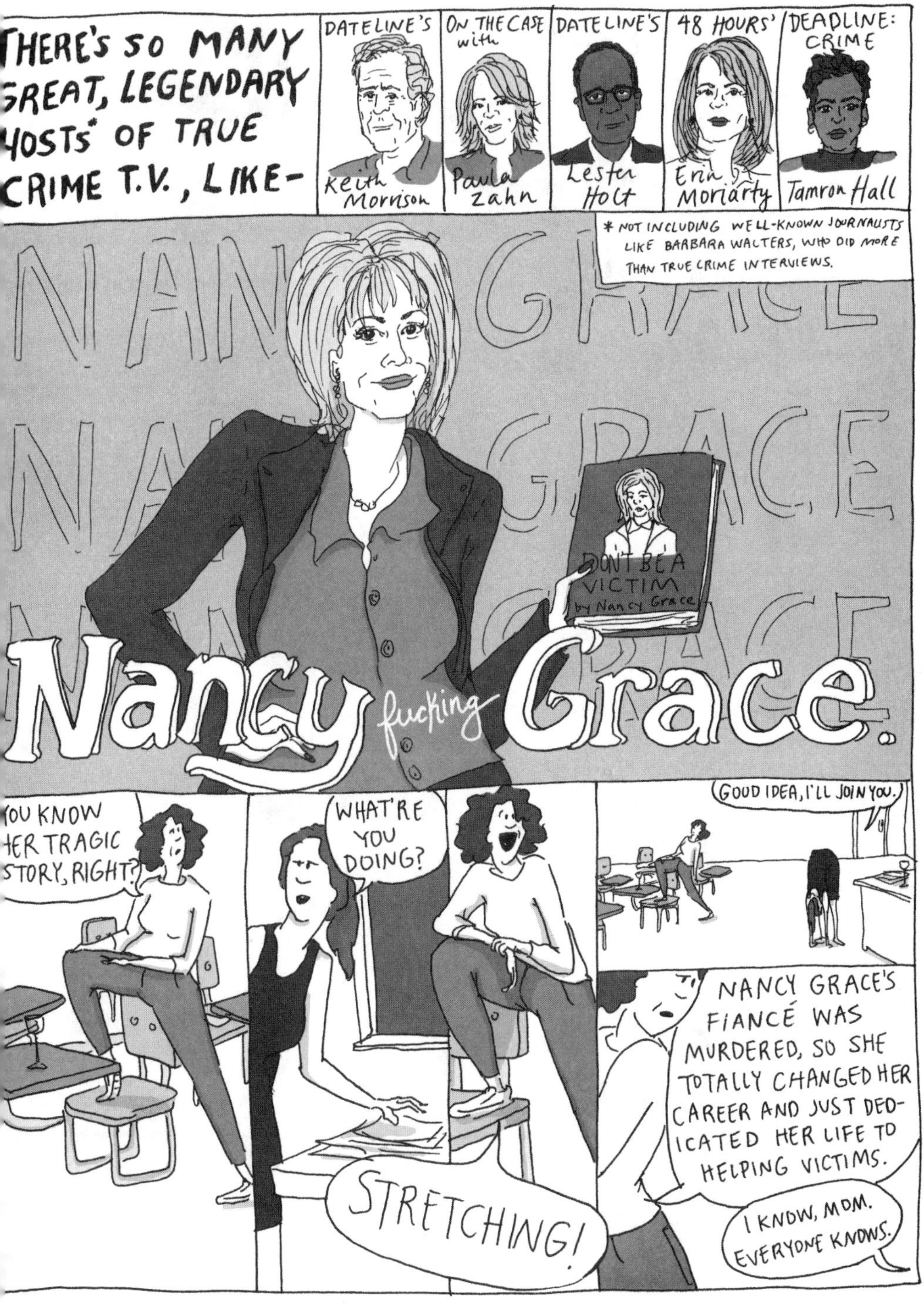

THERE'S SO MANY GREAT, LEGENDARY HOSTS* OF TRUE CRIME T.V., LIKE-
DATELINE'S
Keith Morrison
ON THE CASE with
Paula Zahn
DATELINE'S
Lester Holt
48 HOURS'
Erin Moriarty
DEADLINE: CRIME
Tamron Hall
* NOT INCLUDING WELL-KNOWN JOURNALISTS LIKE BARBARA WALTERS, WHO DID MORE THAN TRUE CRIME INTERVIEWS.
DON'T BE A VICTIM by Nancy Grace
Nancy fucking Grace.
YOU KNOW HER TRAGIC STORY, RIGHT?
WHAT'RE YOU DOING?
STRETCHING!
GOOD IDEA, I'LL JOIN YOU.
NANCY GRACE'S FIANCÉ WAS MURDERED, SO SHE TOTALLY CHANGED HER CAREER AND JUST DEDICATED HER LIFE TO HELPING VICTIMS.
I KNOW, MOM. EVERYONE KNOWS.

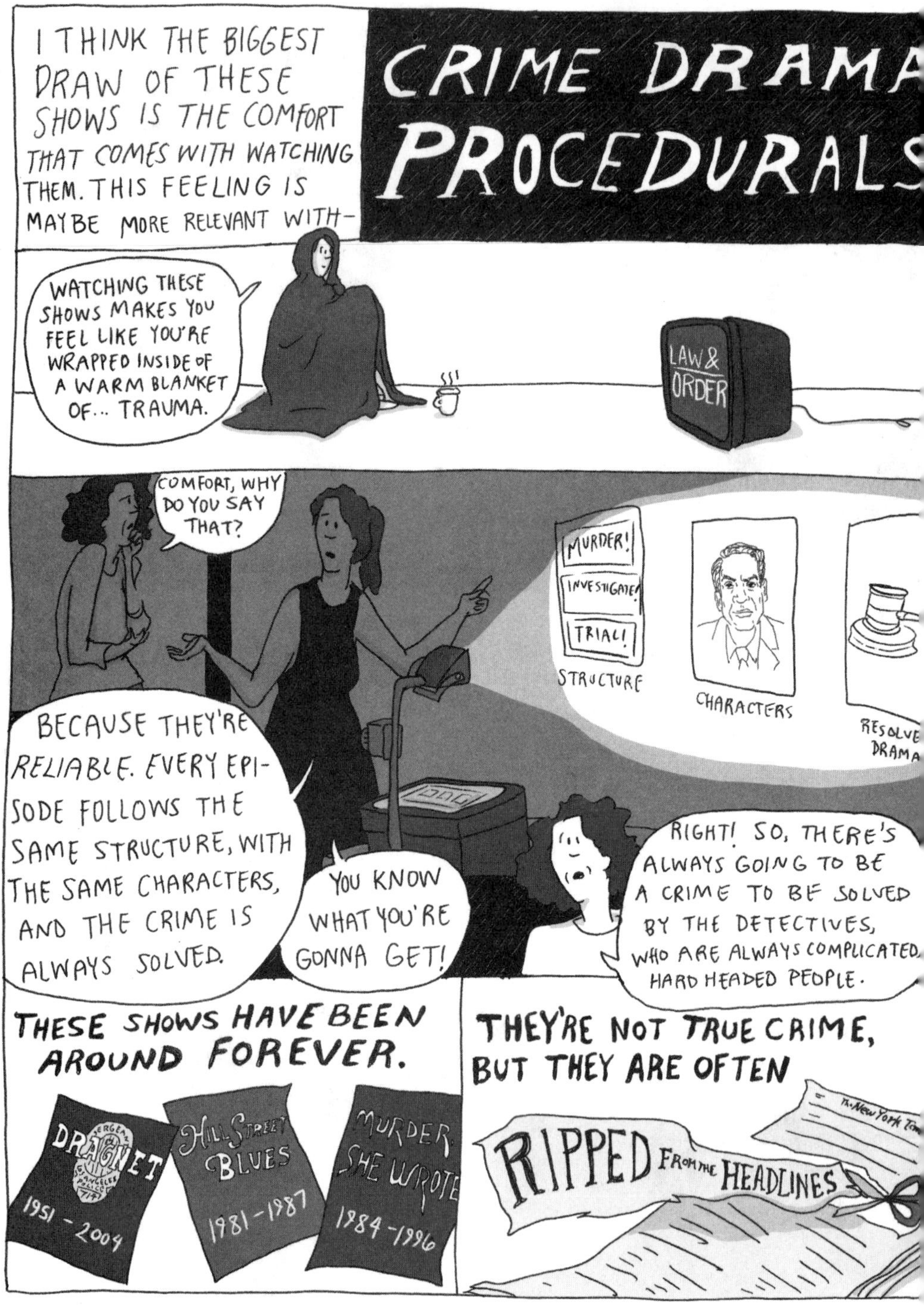
I THINK THE BIGGEST DRAW OF THESE SHOWS IS THE COMFORT THAT COMES WITH WATCHING THEM. THIS FEELING IS MAYBE MORE RELEVANT WITH-
CRIME DRAMA PROCEDURALS
WATCHING THESE SHOWS MAKES YOU FEEL LIKE YOU'RE WRAPPED INSIDE OF A WARM BLANKET OF... TRAUMA.
LAW & ORDER
COMFORT, WHY DO YOU SAY THAT?
MURDER!
INVESTIGATE!
TRIAL!
STRUCTURE
CHARACTERS
RESOLVE DRAMA
BECAUSE THEY'RE RELIABLE. EVERY EPISODE FOLLOWS THE SAME STRUCTURE, WITH THE SAME CHARACTERS, AND THE CRIME IS ALWAYS SOLVED.
YOU KNOW WHAT YOU'RE GONNA GET!
RIGHT! SO, THERE'S ALWAYS GOING TO BE A CRIME TO BE SOLVED BY THE DETECTIVES, WHO ARE ALWAYS COMPLICATED, HARD HEADED PEOPLE.
THESE SHOWS HAVE BEEN AROUND FOREVER.
DRAGNET
1951 - 2004
HILL STREET BLUES
1981 - 1987
MURDER, SHE WROTE
1984 - 1996
THEY'RE NOT TRUE CRIME, BUT THEY ARE OFTEN
The New York Times
RIPPED FROM THE HEADLINES

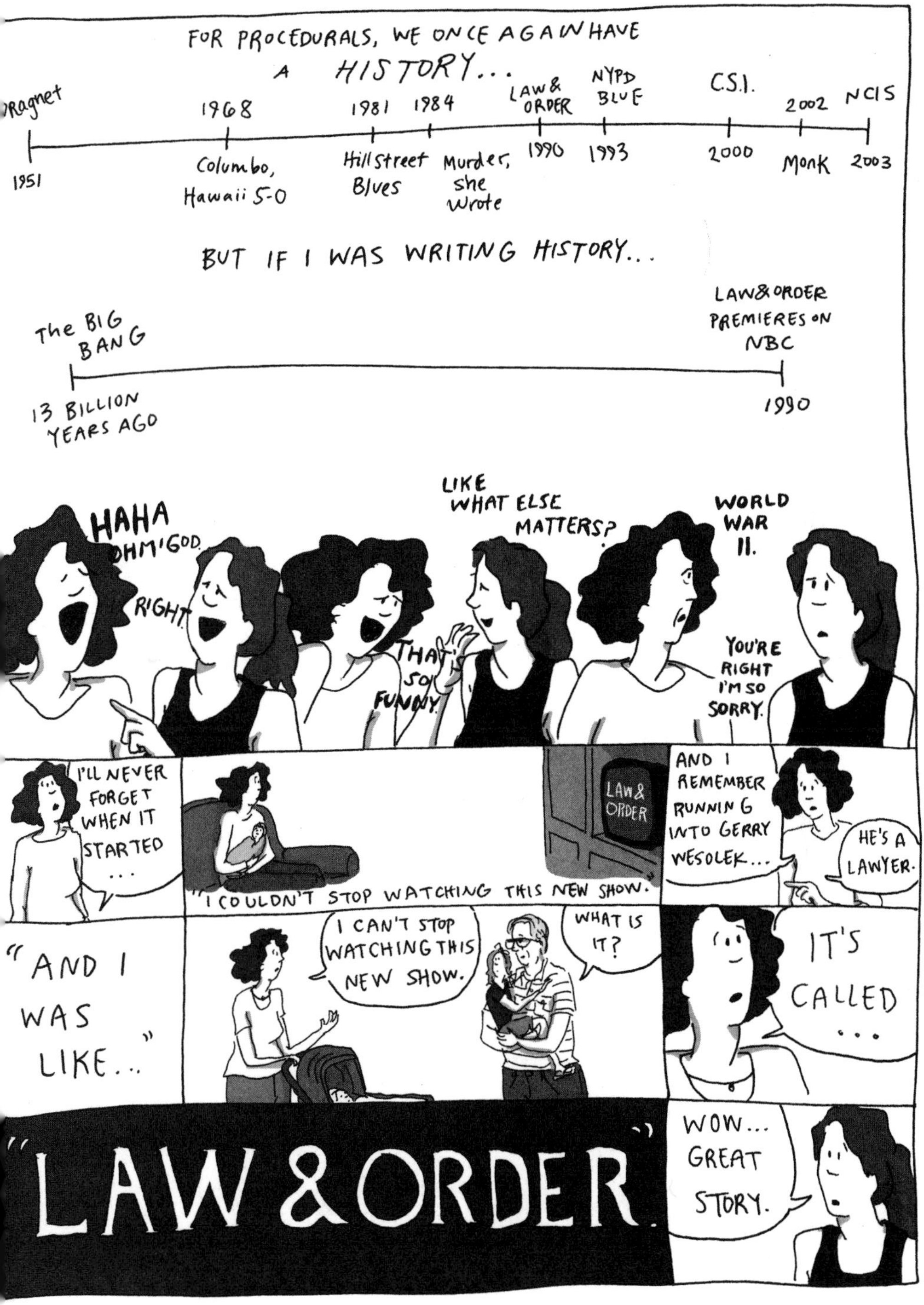
FOR PROCEDURALS, WE ONCE AGAIN HAVE A HISTORY...
Dragnet
1951
1968
Columbo, Hawaii 5-0
1981
Hill Street Blues
1984
Murder, she Wrote
LAW & ORDER
1990
NYPD BLUE
1993
C.S.I.
2000
2002
Monk
NCIS
2003
BUT IF I WAS WRITING HISTORY...
The BIG BANG
13 BILLION YEARS AGO
LAW & ORDER PREMIERES ON NBC
1990
HAHA OHM'GOD.
RIGHT.
THAT'S SO FUNNY.
LIKE WHAT ELSE MATTERS?
WORLD WAR II.
YOU'RE RIGHT I'M SO SORRY.
I'LL NEVER FORGET WHEN IT STARTED...
LAW & ORDER
"I COULDN'T STOP WATCHING THIS NEW SHOW."
AND I REMEMBER RUNNING INTO GERRY WESOLEK...
HE'S A LAWYER.
"AND I WAS LIKE..."
I CAN'T STOP WATCHING THIS NEW SHOW.
WHAT IS IT?
IT'S CALLED...
"LAW & ORDER."
WOW... GREAT STORY.

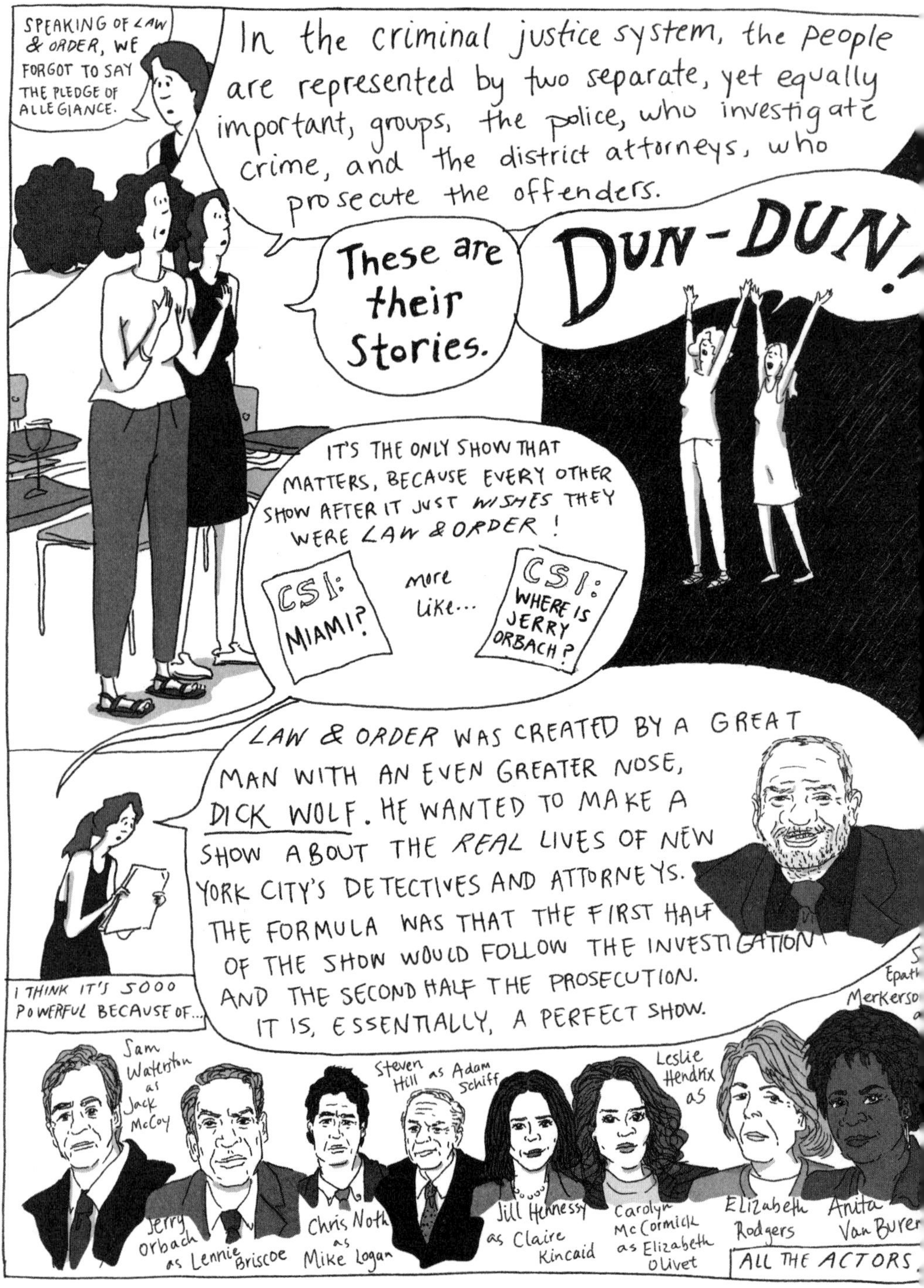
SPEAKING OF LAW & ORDER, WE FORGOT TO SAY THE PLEDGE OF ALLEGIANCE.
In the criminal justice system, the people are represented by two separate, yet equally important, groups, the police, who investigate crime, and the district attorneys, who prosecute the offenders.
These are their Stories.
DUN-DUN!
IT'S THE ONLY SHOW THAT MATTERS, BECAUSE EVERY OTHER SHOW AFTER IT JUST WISHES THEY WERE LAW & ORDER!
CSI: MIAMI?
more like...
CSI: WHERE IS JERRY ORBACH?
LAW & ORDER WAS CREATED BY A GREAT MAN WITH AN EVEN GREATER NOSE, DICK WOLF. HE WANTED TO MAKE A SHOW ABOUT THE REAL LIVES OF NEW YORK CITY'S DETECTIVES AND ATTORNEYS. THE FORMULA WAS THAT THE FIRST HALF OF THE SHOW WOULD FOLLOW THE INVESTIGATION AND THE SECOND HALF THE PROSECUTION. IT IS, ESSENTIALLY, A PERFECT SHOW.
I THINK IT'S SOOO POWERFUL BECAUSE OF...
Sam Waterston as Jack McCoy
Jerry Orbach as Lennie Briscoe
Chris Noth as Mike Logan
Steven Hill as Adam Schiff
Jill Hennessy as Claire Kincaid
Carolyn McCormick as Elizabeth Olivet
Leslie Hendrix as
Elizabeth Rodgers
Anita Van Buren
ALL THE ACTORS

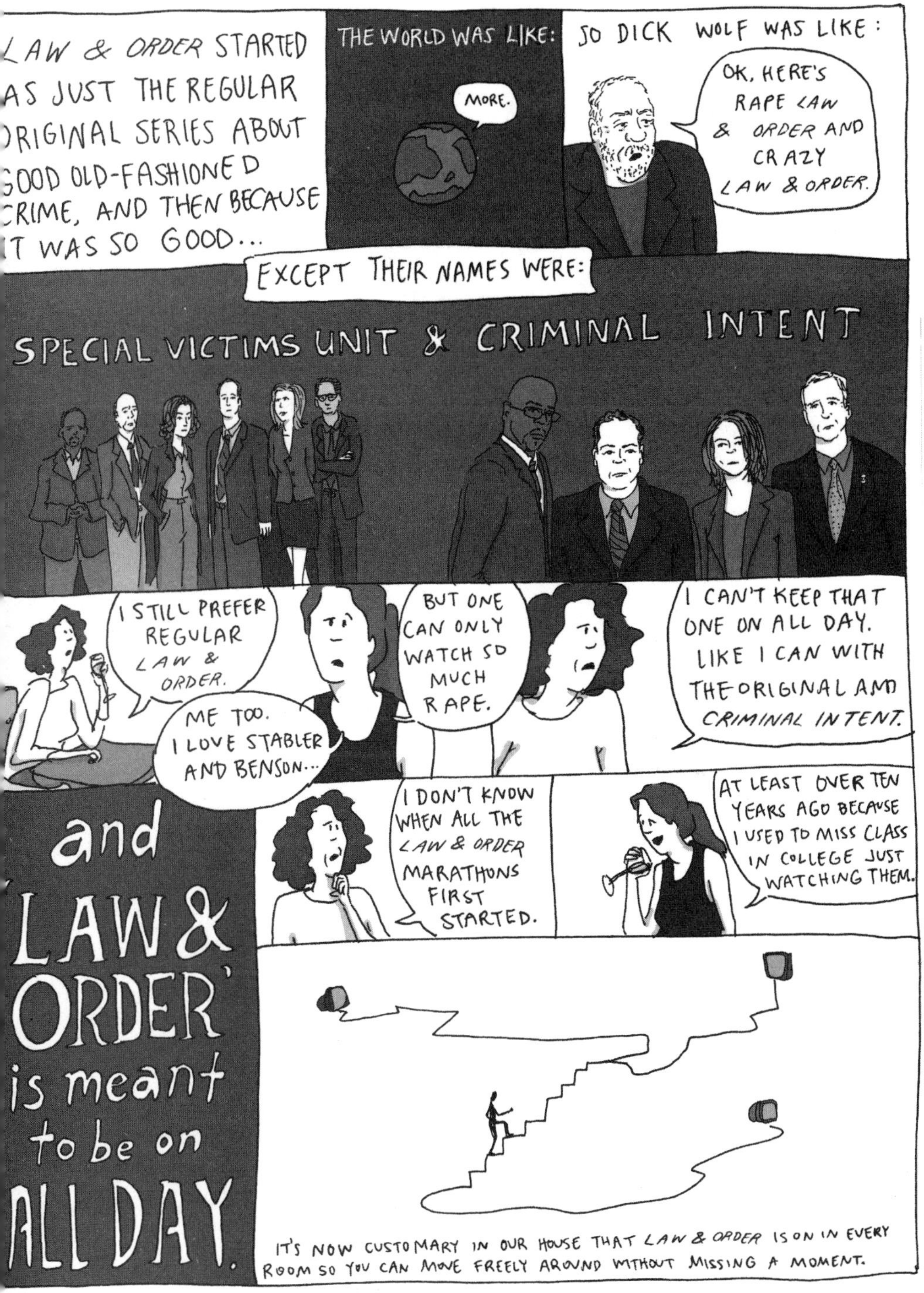
LAW & ORDER STARTED AS JUST THE REGULAR ORIGINAL SERIES ABOUT GOOD OLD-FASHIONED CRIME, AND THEN BECAUSE IT WAS SO GOOD...
THE WORLD WAS LIKE:
MORE.
SO DICK WOLF WAS LIKE:
OK, HERE'S RAPE LAW & ORDER AND CRAZY LAW & ORDER.
EXCEPT THEIR NAMES WERE:
SPECIAL VICTIMS UNIT & CRIMINAL INTENT
I STILL PREFER REGULAR LAW & ORDER.
ME TOO. I LOVE STABLER AND BENSON...
BUT ONE CAN ONLY WATCH SO MUCH RAPE.
I CAN'T KEEP THAT ONE ON ALL DAY. LIKE I CAN WITH THE ORIGINAL AND CRIMINAL INTENT.
and LAW & ORDER is meant to be on ALL DAY.
I DON'T KNOW WHEN ALL THE LAW & ORDER MARATHONS FIRST STARTED.
AT LEAST OVER TEN YEARS AGO BECAUSE I USED TO MISS CLASS IN COLLEGE JUST WATCHING THEM.
IT'S NOW CUSTOMARY IN OUR HOUSE THAT LAW & ORDER IS ON IN EVERY ROOM SO YOU CAN MOVE FREELY AROUND WITHOUT MISSING A MOMENT.

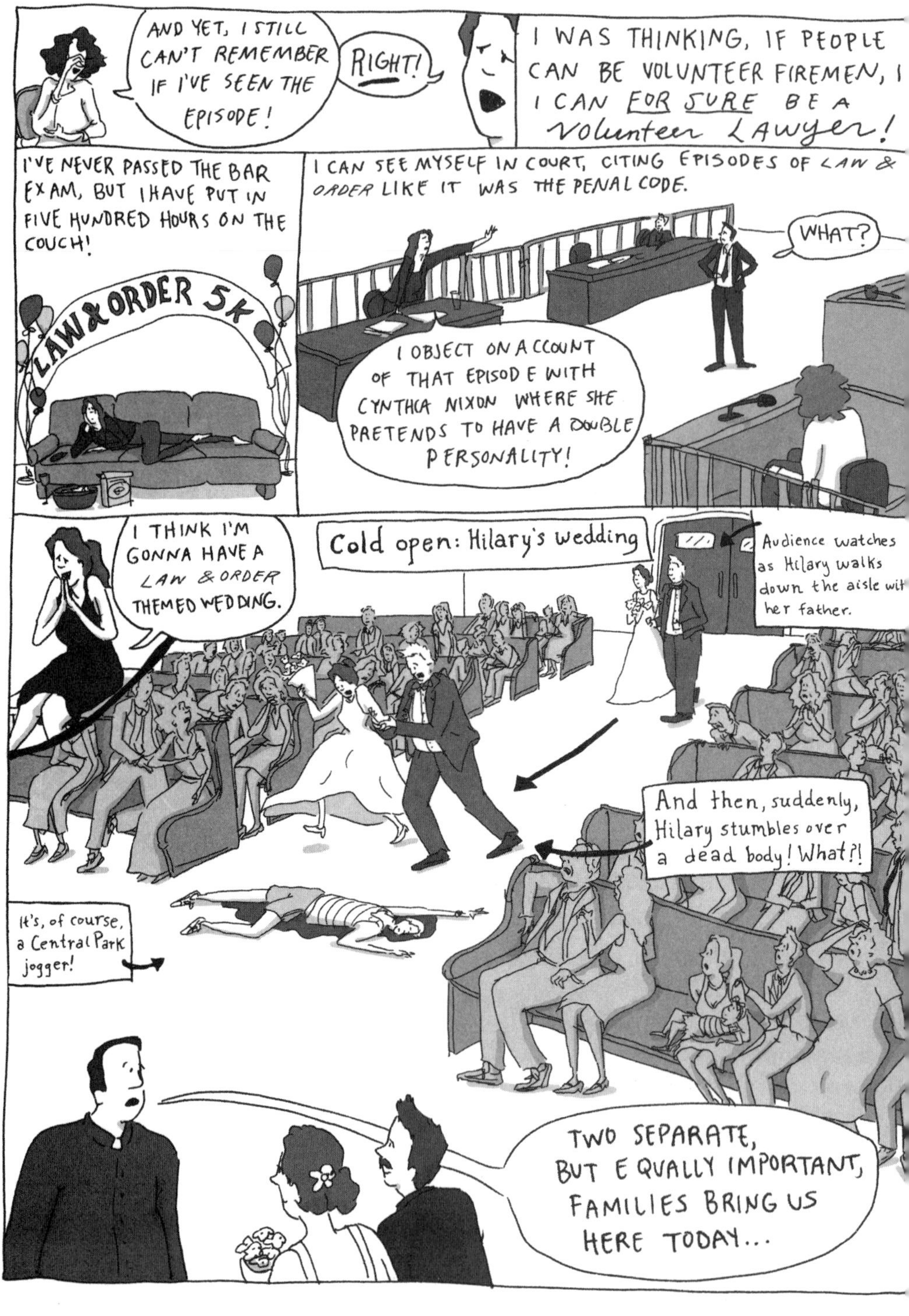
AND YET, I STILL CAN'T REMEMBER IF I'VE SEEN THE EPISODE!
RIGHT!
I WAS THINKING, IF PEOPLE CAN BE VOLUNTEER FIREMEN, I CAN FOR SURE BE A Volunteer Lawyer!
I'VE NEVER PASSED THE BAR EXAM, BUT I HAVE PUT IN FIVE HUNDRED HOURS ON THE COUCH!
LAW & ORDER 5K
I CAN SEE MYSELF IN COURT, CITING EPISODES OF LAW & ORDER LIKE IT WAS THE PENAL CODE.
WHAT?
I OBJECT ON ACCOUNT OF THAT EPISODE WITH CYNTHIA NIXON WHERE SHE PRETENDS TO HAVE A DOUBLE PERSONALITY!
I THINK I'M GONNA HAVE A LAW & ORDER THEMED WEDDING.
Cold open: Hilary's wedding
Audience watches as Hilary walks down the aisle with her father.
And then, suddenly, Hilary stumbles over a dead body! What?!
It's, of course, a Central Park jogger!
TWO SEPARATE, BUT EQUALLY IMPORTANT, FAMILIES BRING US HERE TODAY...

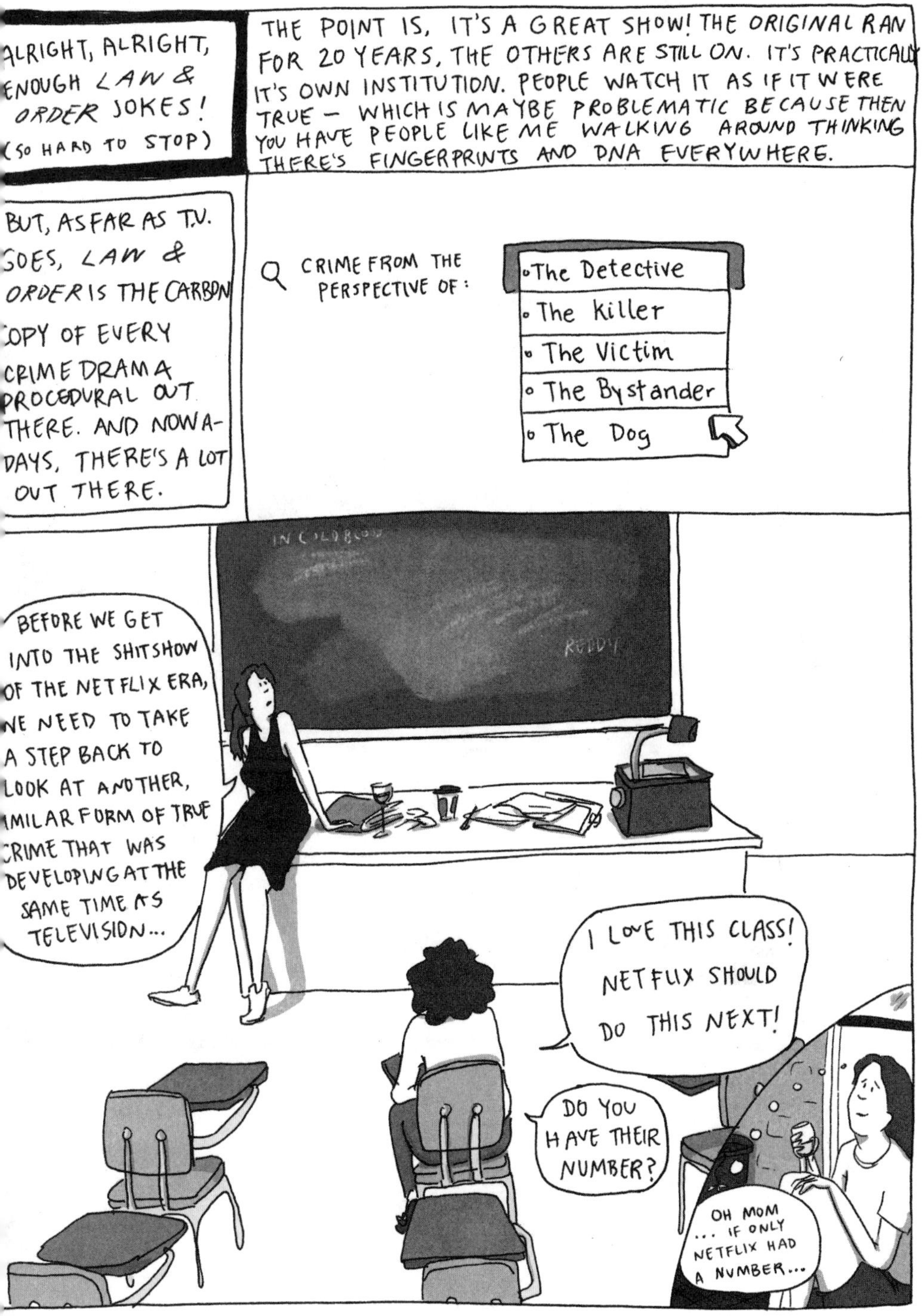
ALRIGHT, ALRIGHT, ENOUGH *LAW & ORDER* JOKES! (SO HARD TO STOP)
THE POINT IS, IT'S A GREAT SHOW! THE ORIGINAL RAN FOR 20 YEARS, THE OTHERS ARE STILL ON. IT'S PRACTICALLY IT'S OWN INSTITUTION. PEOPLE WATCH IT AS IF IT WERE TRUE — WHICH IS MAYBE PROBLEMATIC BECAUSE THEN YOU HAVE PEOPLE LIKE ME WALKING AROUND THINKING THERE'S FINGERPRINTS AND DNA EVERYWHERE.
BUT, AS FAR AS T.V. GOES, *LAW & ORDER* IS THE CARBON COPY OF EVERY CRIME DRAMA PROCEDURAL OUT THERE. AND NOWADAYS, THERE'S A LOT OUT THERE.
CRIME FROM THE PERSPECTIVE OF:
The Detective
The Killer
The Victim
The Bystander
The Dog
BEFORE WE GET INTO THE SHITSHOW OF THE NETFLIX ERA, WE NEED TO TAKE A STEP BACK TO LOOK AT ANOTHER, SIMILAR FORM OF TRUE CRIME THAT WAS DEVELOPING AT THE SAME TIME AS TELEVISION...
I LOVE THIS CLASS! NETFLIX SHOULD DO THIS NEXT!
DO YOU HAVE THEIR NUMBER?
OH MOM ... IF ONLY NETFLIX HAD A NUMBER...

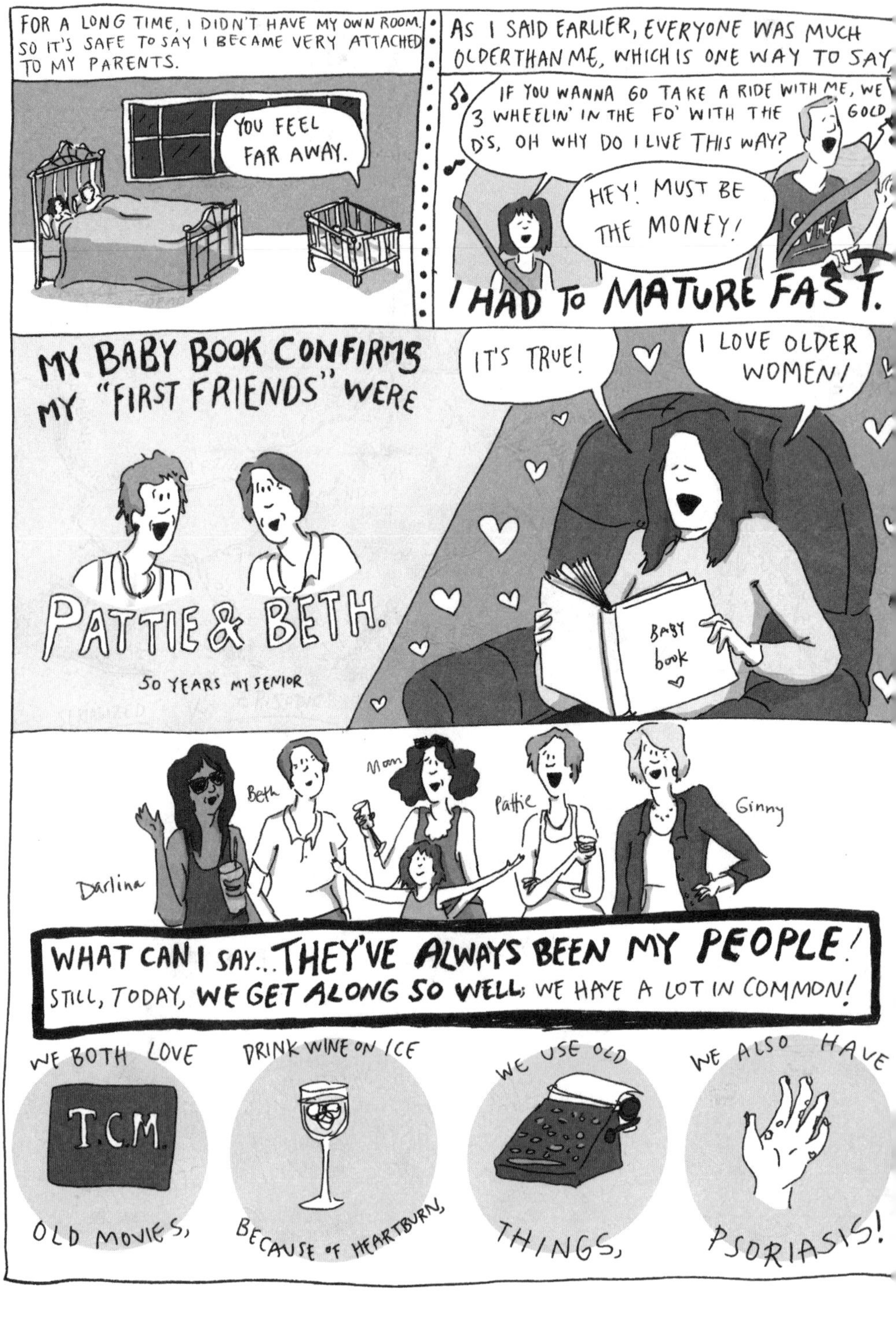

FOR A LONG TIME, I DIDN'T HAVE MY OWN ROOM. SO IT'S SAFE TO SAY I BECAME VERY ATTACHED TO MY PARENTS.
YOU FEEL FAR AWAY.
AS I SAID EARLIER, EVERYONE WAS MUCH OLDER THAN ME, WHICH IS ONE WAY TO SAY
IF YOU WANNA GO TAKE A RIDE WITH ME, WE 3 WHEELIN' IN THE FO' WITH THE GOLD D'S, OH WHY DO I LIVE THIS WAY?
HEY! MUST BE THE MONEY!
I HAD TO MATURE FAST.
MY BABY BOOK CONFIRMS MY "FIRST FRIENDS" WERE
PATTIE & BETH.
50 YEARS MY SENIOR
IT'S TRUE!
I LOVE OLDER WOMEN!
BABY book
Darlina
Beth
Mom
Pattie
Ginny
WHAT CAN I SAY... THEY'VE ALWAYS BEEN MY PEOPLE!
STILL, TODAY, WE GET ALONG SO WELL; WE HAVE A LOT IN COMMON!
WE BOTH LOVE
T.C.M.
OLD MOVIES,
DRINK WINE ON ICE
BECAUSE OF HEARTBURN,
WE USE OLD
THINGS,
WE ALSO HAVE
PSORIASIS!

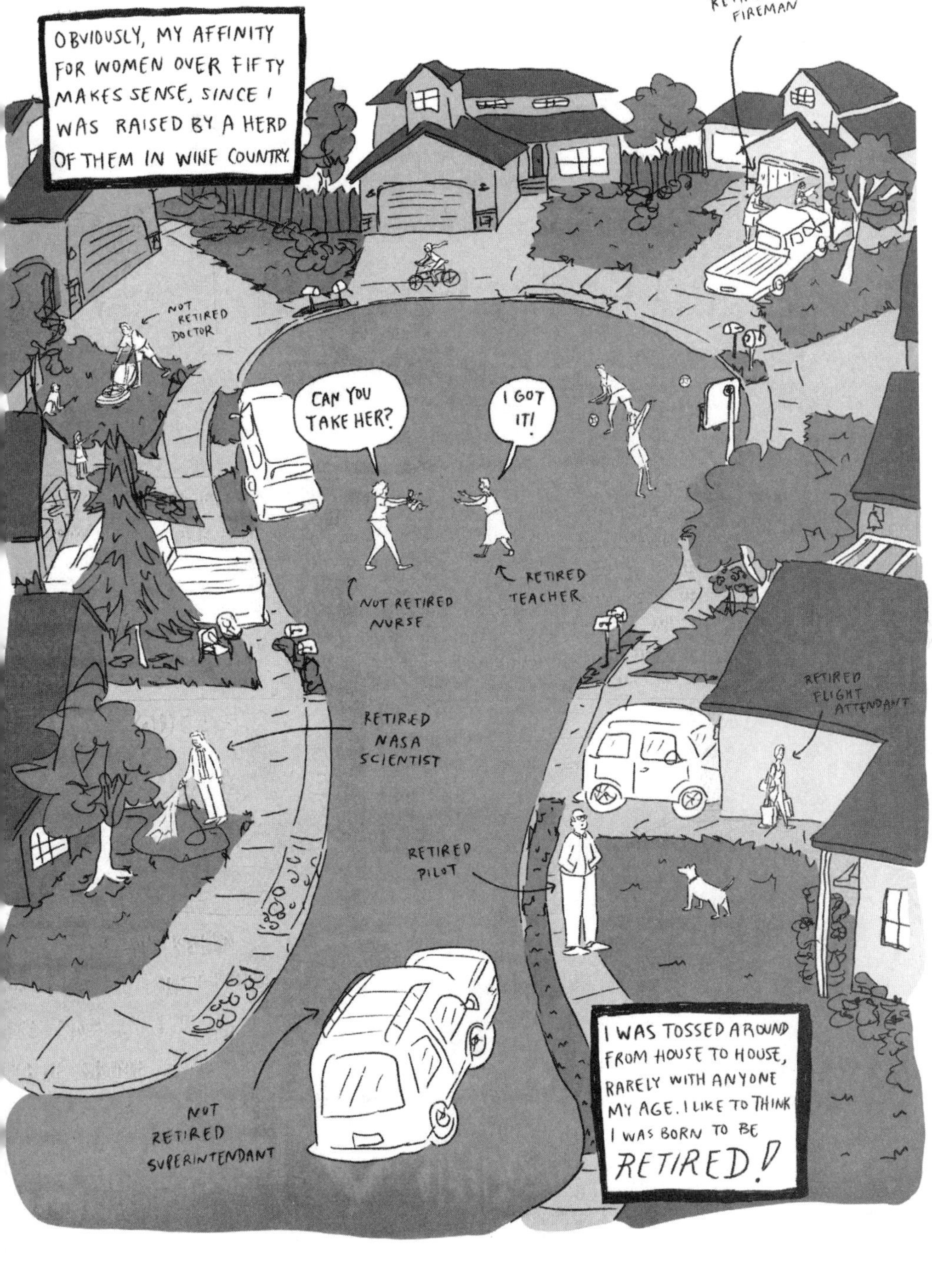
OBVIOUSLY, MY AFFINITY FOR WOMEN OVER FIFTY MAKES SENSE, SINCE I WAS RAISED BY A HERD OF THEM IN WINE COUNTRY.
RETIRED FIREMAN
NOT RETIRED DOCTOR
CAN YOU TAKE HER?
I GOT IT!
NOT RETIRED NURSE
RETIRED TEACHER
RETIRED NASA SCIENTIST
RETIRED FLIGHT ATTENDANT
RETIRED PILOT
NOT RETIRED SUPERINTENDANT
I WAS TOSSED AROUND FROM HOUSE TO HOUSE, RARELY WITH ANYONE MY AGE. I LIKE TO THINK I WAS BORN TO BE RETIRED!

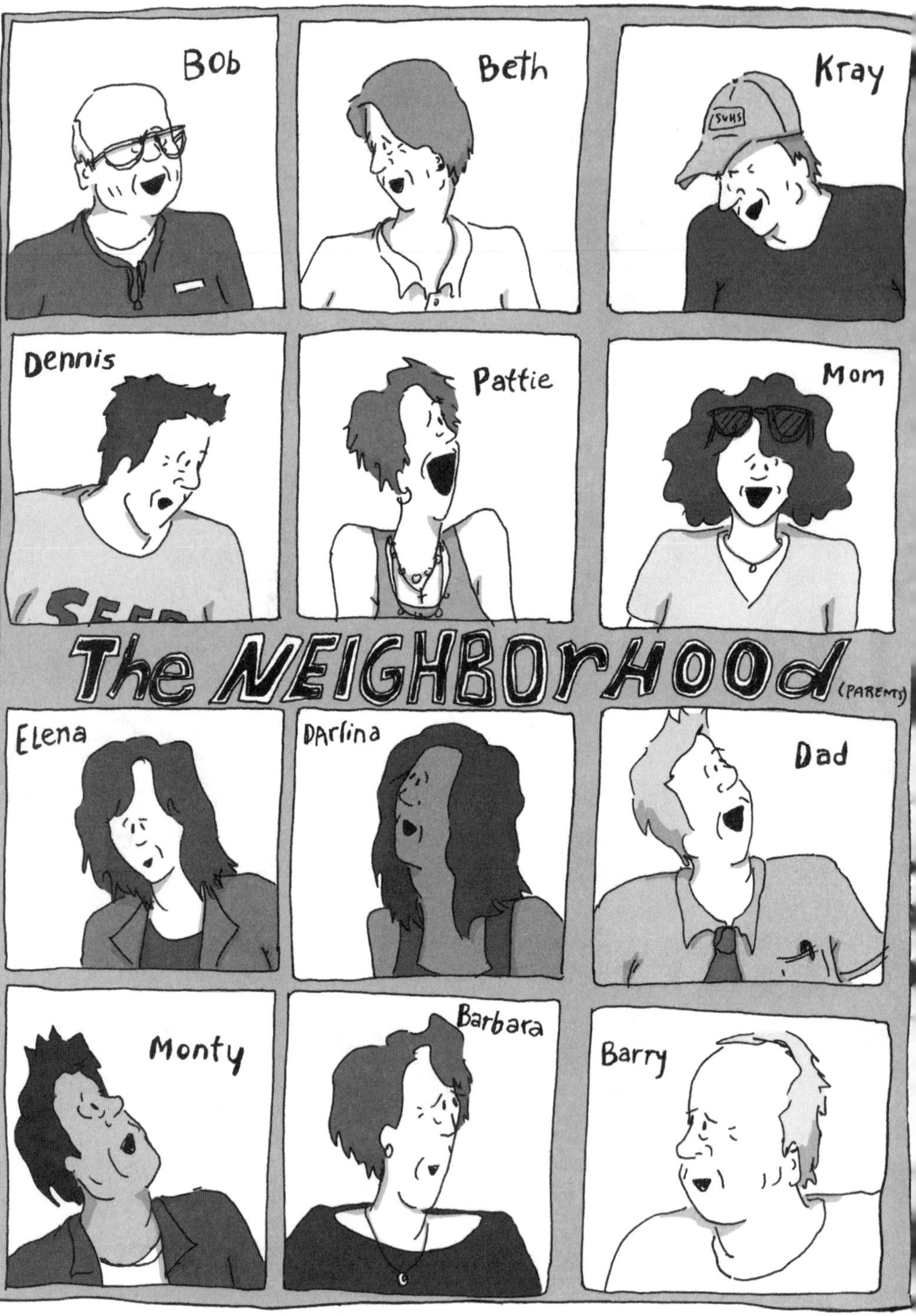

Bob
Beth
Kray
SVHS
Dennis
Pattie
Mom
The NEIGHBORHOOD (PARENTS)
Elena
DArlina
Dad
Monty
Barbara
Barry

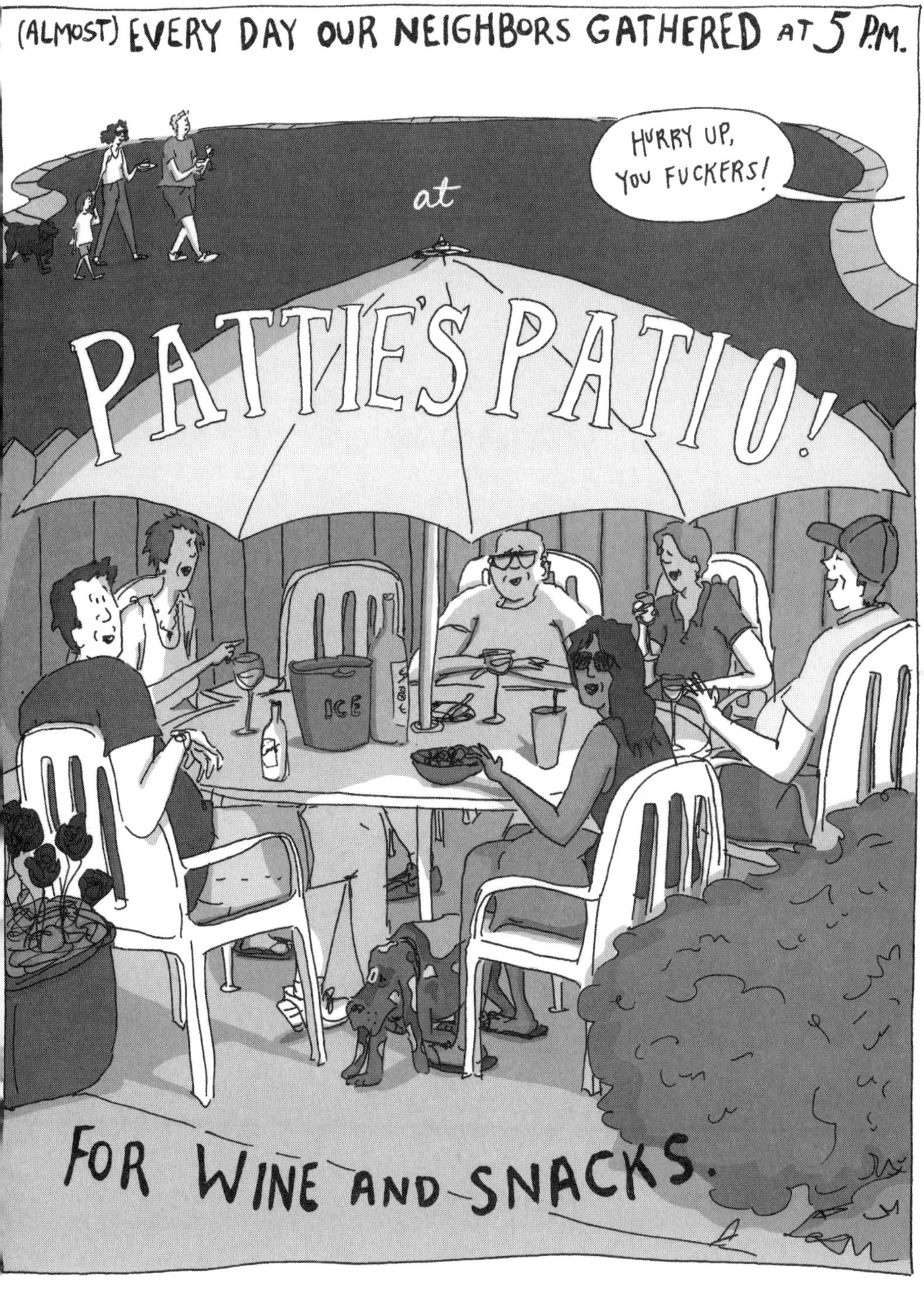

(ALMOST) EVERY DAY OUR NEIGHBORS GATHERED AT 5 P.M.
HURRY UP, YOU FUCKERS!
at
PATTIE'S PATIO!
ICE
FOR WINE AND SNACKS.

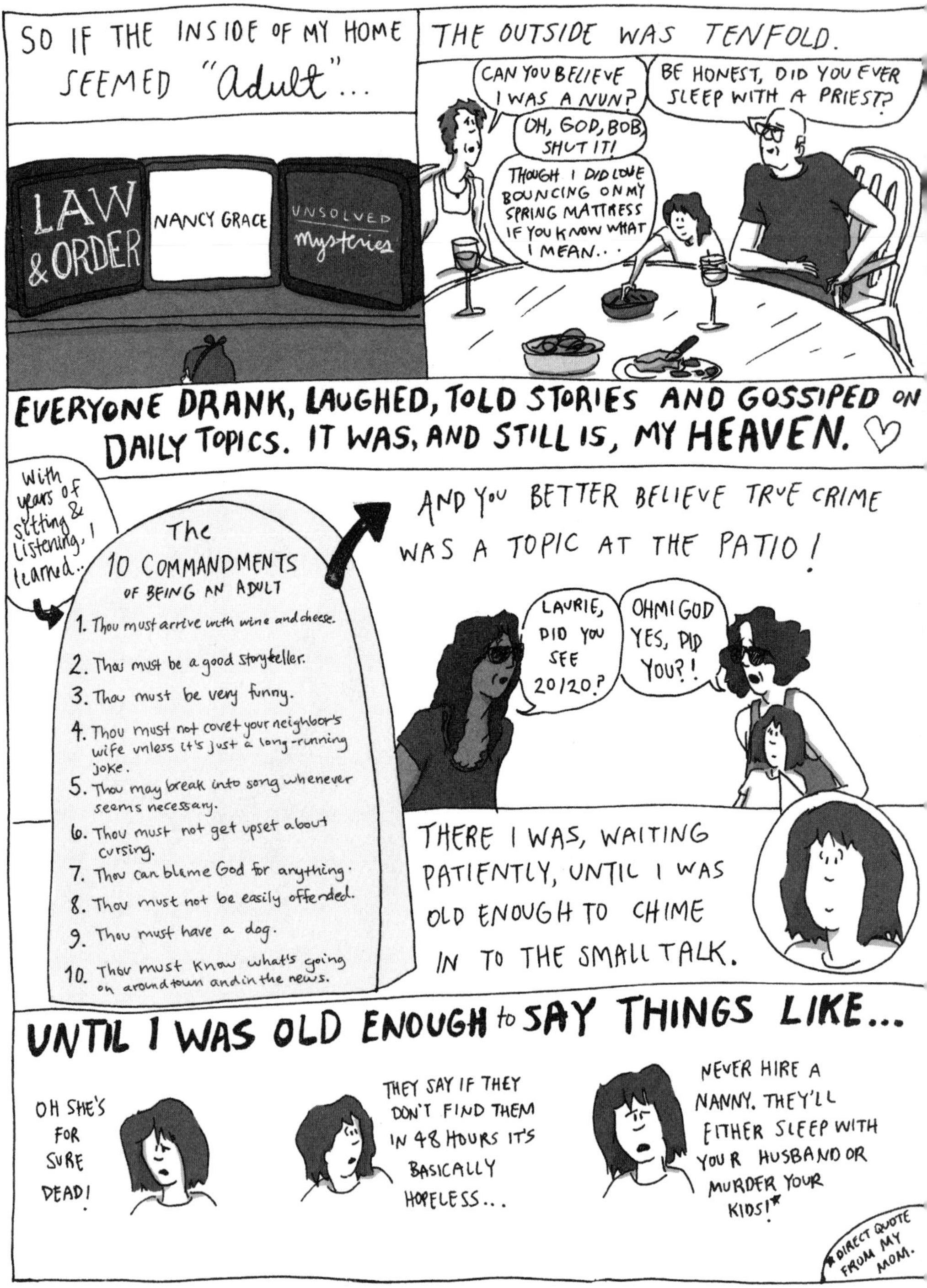
SO IF THE INSIDE OF MY HOME SEEMED "adult"...
LAW & ORDER
NANCY GRACE
UNSOLVED mysteries
THE OUTSIDE WAS TENFOLD.
CAN YOU BELIEVE I WAS A NUN?
OH, GOD, BOB, SHUT IT!
THOUGH I DID LOVE BOUNCING ON MY SPRING MATTRESS IF YOU KNOW WHAT I MEAN...
BE HONEST, DID YOU EVER SLEEP WITH A PRIEST?
EVERYONE DRANK, LAUGHED, TOLD STORIES AND GOSSIPED ON DAILY TOPICS. IT WAS, AND STILL IS, MY HEAVEN. ♡
With years of sitting & listening, I learned...
The 10 COMMANDMENTS OF BEING AN ADULT
1. Thou must arrive with wine and cheese.
2. Thou must be a good storyteller.
3. Thou must be very funny.
4. Thou must not covet your neighbor's wife unless it's just a long-running joke.
5. Thou may break into song whenever seems necessary.
6. Thou must not get upset about cursing.
7. Thou can blame God for anything.
8. Thou must not be easily offended.
9. Thou must have a dog.
10. Thou must know what's going on around town and in the news.
AND YOU BETTER BELIEVE TRUE CRIME WAS A TOPIC AT THE PATIO!
LAURIE, DID YOU SEE 20/20?
OHMIGOD YES, DID YOU?!
THERE I WAS, WAITING PATIENTLY, UNTIL I WAS OLD ENOUGH TO CHIME IN TO THE SMALL TALK.
UNTIL I WAS OLD ENOUGH to SAY THINGS LIKE...
OH SHE'S FOR SURE DEAD!
THEY SAY IF THEY DON'T FIND THEM IN 48 HOURS IT'S BASICALLY HOPELESS...
NEVER HIRE A NANNY. THEY'LL EITHER SLEEP WITH YOUR HUSBAND OR MURDER YOUR KIDS!*
*DIRECT QUOTE FROM MY MOM.

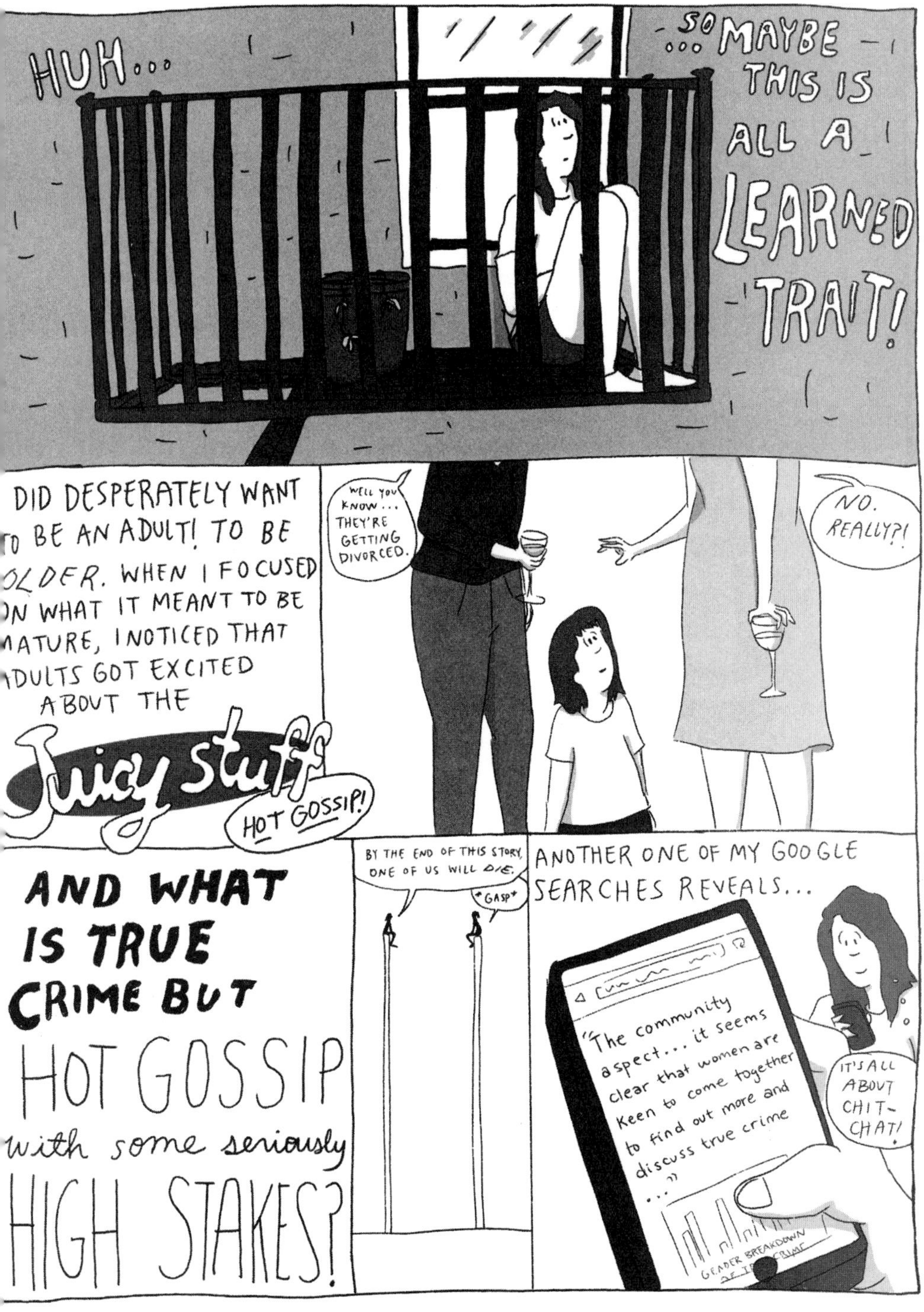

HUH...
...SO MAYBE THIS IS ALL A LEARNED TRAIT!
DID DESPERATELY WANT TO BE AN ADULT! TO BE OLDER. WHEN I FOCUSED ON WHAT IT MEANT TO BE MATURE, I NOTICED THAT ADULTS GOT EXCITED ABOUT THE
Juicy stuff
HOT GOSSIP!
WELL YOU KNOW... THEY'RE GETTING DIVORCED.
NO. REALLY?!
AND WHAT IS TRUE CRIME BUT
HOT GOSSIP
with some seriously
HIGH STAKES?
BY THE END OF THIS STORY, ONE OF US WILL DIE.
GASP
ANOTHER ONE OF MY GOOGLE SEARCHES REVEALS...
"The community aspect... it seems clear that women are keen to come together to find out more and discuss true crime ..."
GENDER BREAKDOWN
IT'S ALL ABOUT CHIT-CHAT!

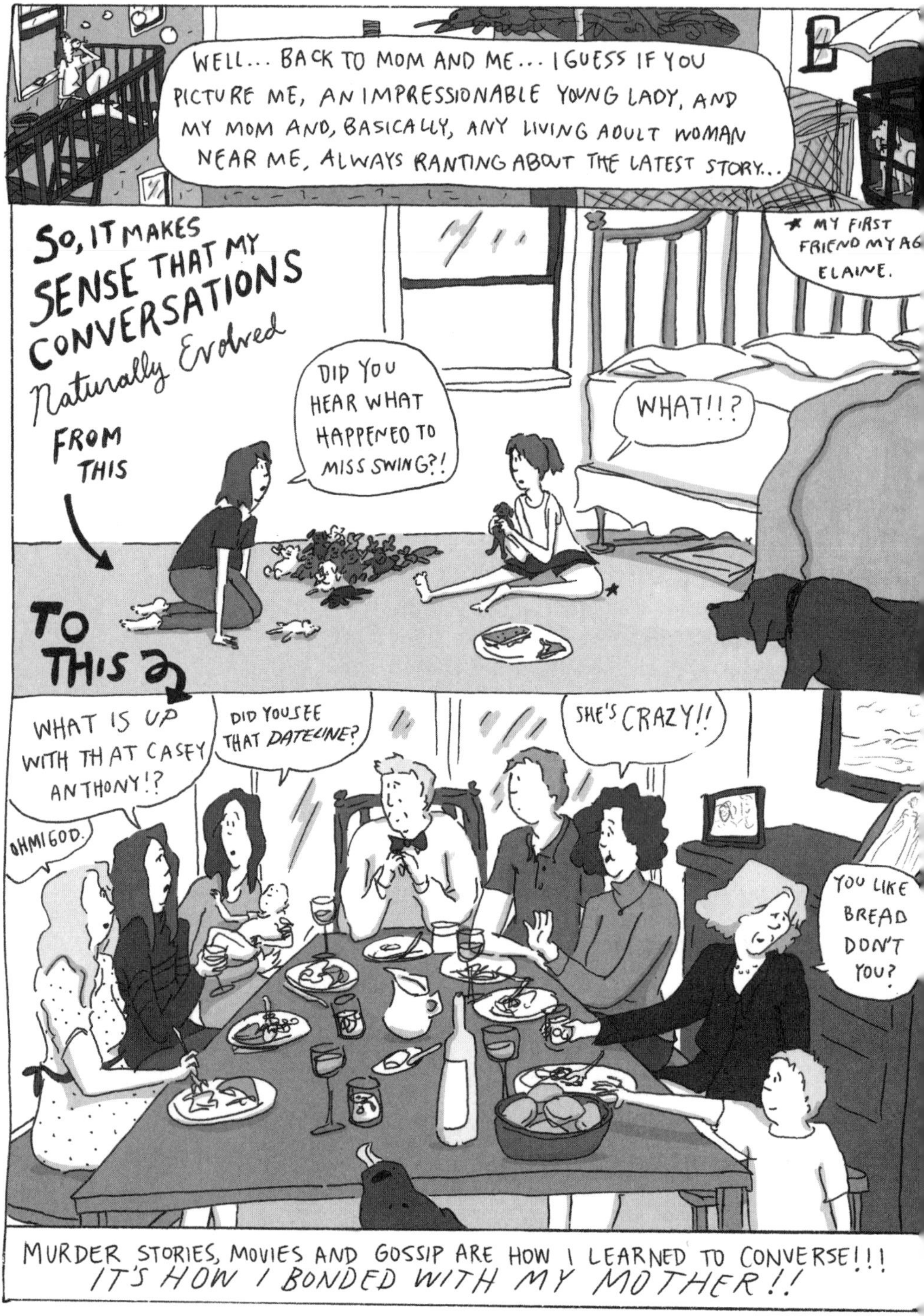

WELL... BACK TO MOM AND ME... I GUESS IF YOU PICTURE ME, AN IMPRESSIONABLE YOUNG LADY, AND MY MOM AND, BASICALLY, ANY LIVING ADULT WOMAN NEAR ME, ALWAYS RANTING ABOUT THE LATEST STORY...
SO, IT MAKES SENSE THAT MY CONVERSATIONS Naturally Evolved
FROM THIS
DID YOU HEAR WHAT HAPPENED TO MISS SWING?!
WHAT!!?
* MY FIRST FRIEND MY AG ELAINE.
TO THIS
WHAT IS UP WITH THAT CASEY ANTHONY!?
DID YOU SEE THAT *DATELINE*?
SHE'S CRAZY!!
OHMIGOD.
YOU LIKE BREAD DON'T YOU?
MURDER STORIES, MOVIES AND GOSSIP ARE HOW I LEARNED TO CONVERSE!!!
IT'S HOW I BONDED WITH MY MOTHER!!

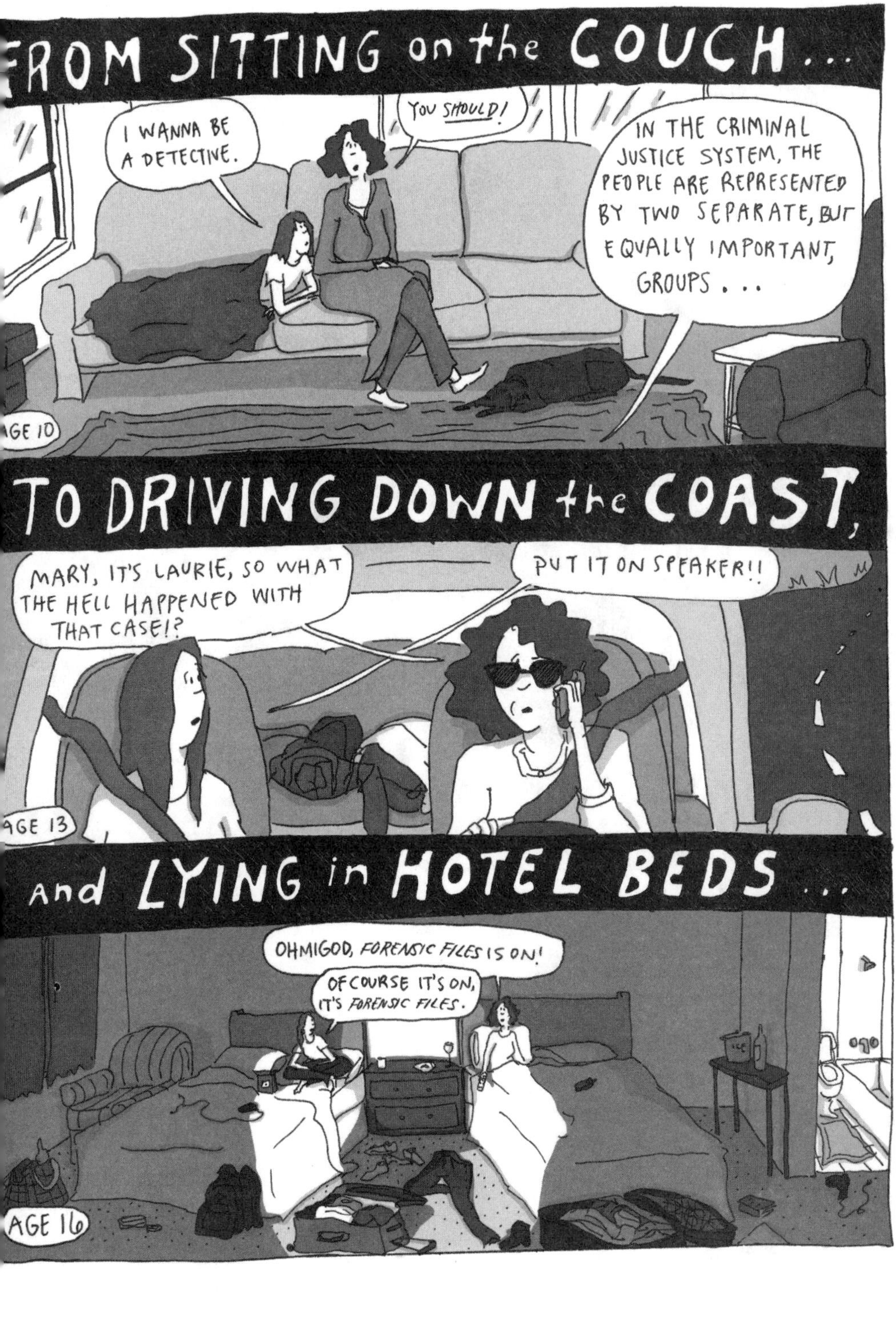
FROM SITTING on the COUCH...
I WANNA BE A DETECTIVE.
YOU SHOULD!
IN THE CRIMINAL JUSTICE SYSTEM, THE PEOPLE ARE REPRESENTED BY TWO SEPARATE, BUT EQUALLY IMPORTANT, GROUPS . . .
AGE 10
TO DRIVING DOWN the COAST,
MARY, IT'S LAURIE, SO WHAT THE HELL HAPPENED WITH THAT CASE!?
PUT IT ON SPEAKER!!
AGE 13
and LYING in HOTEL BEDS . . .
OHMIGOD, FORENSIC FILES IS ON!
OF COURSE IT'S ON, IT'S FORENSIC FILES.
AGE 16

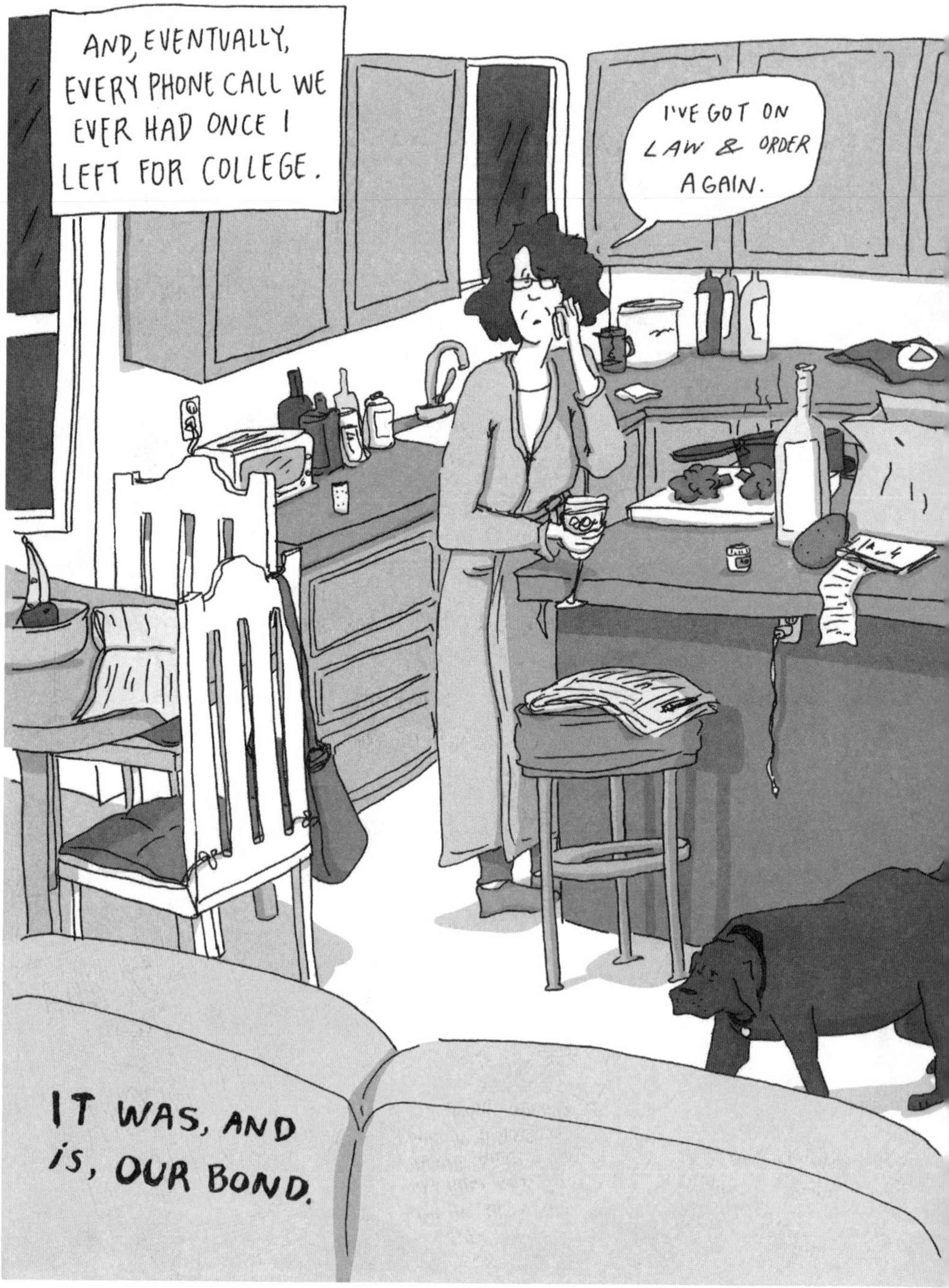
AND, EVENTUALLY, EVERY PHONE CALL WE EVER HAD ONCE I LEFT FOR COLLEGE.
I'VE GOT ON LAW & ORDER AGAIN.
IT WAS, AND IS, OUR BOND.

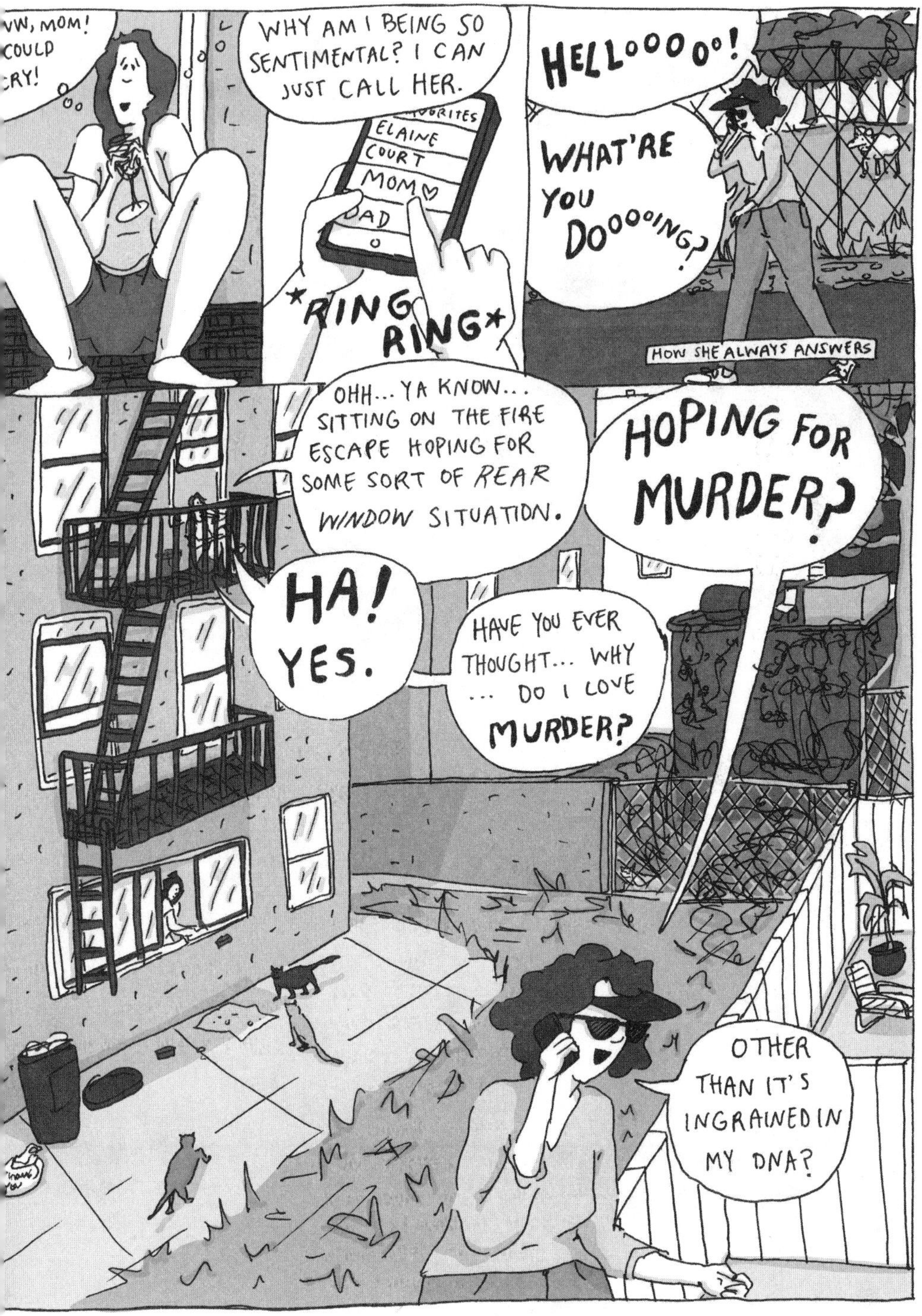

AW, MOM! COULD CRY!
WHY AM I BEING SO SENTIMENTAL? I CAN JUST CALL HER.
ELAINE
COURT
MOM
DAD
RING RING
HELLOOOOO!
WHAT'RE YOU DOOOOING?
HOW SHE ALWAYS ANSWERS
OHH... YA KNOW... SITTING ON THE FIRE ESCAPE HOPING FOR SOME SORT OF *REAR WINDOW* SITUATION.
HOPING FOR MURDER?
HA! YES.
HAVE YOU EVER THOUGHT... WHY ... DO I LOVE MURDER?
OTHER THAN IT'S INGRAINED IN MY DNA?

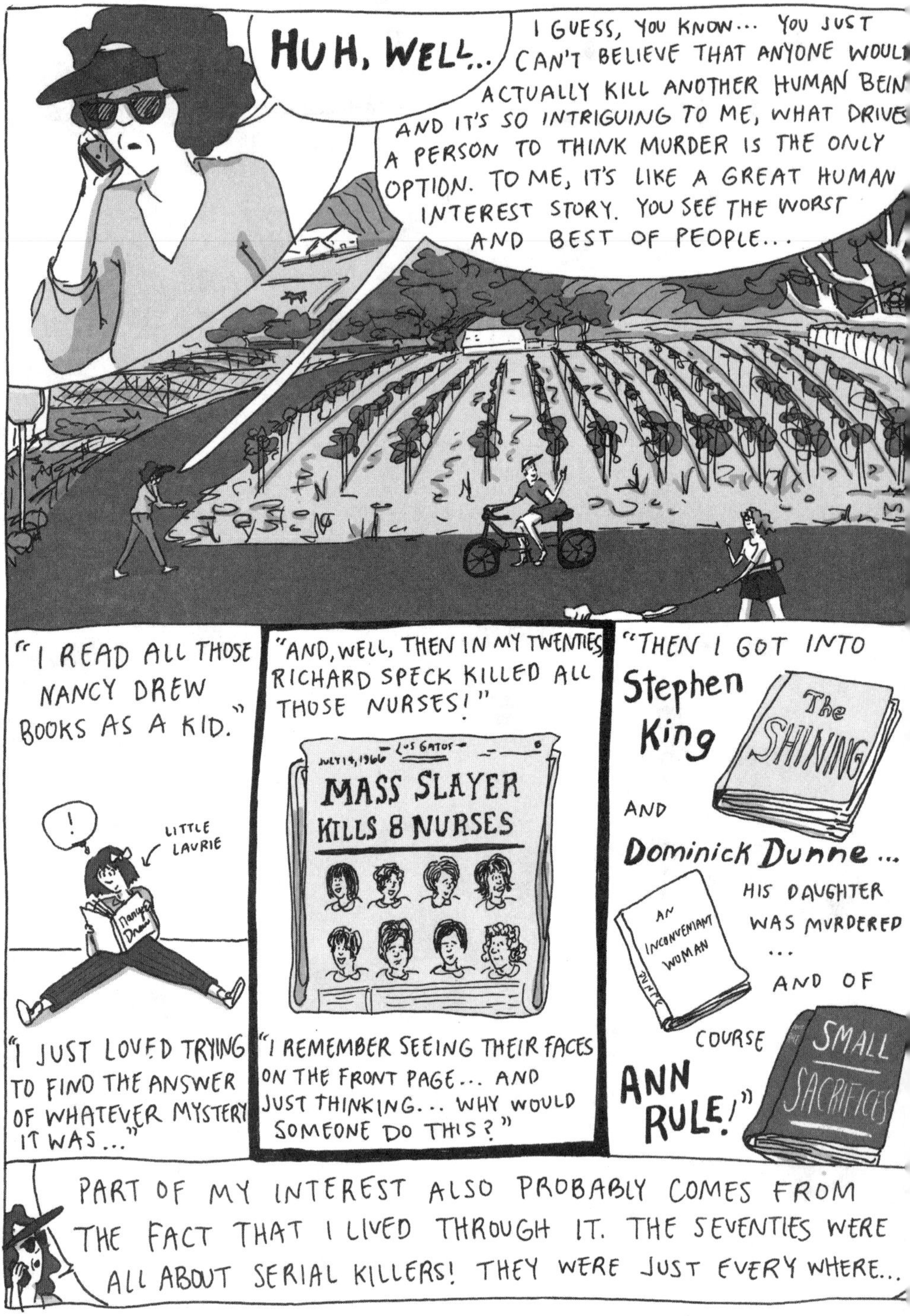

HUH, WELL...
I GUESS, YOU KNOW... YOU JUST CAN'T BELIEVE THAT ANYONE WOULD ACTUALLY KILL ANOTHER HUMAN BEING AND IT'S SO INTRIGUING TO ME, WHAT DRIVES A PERSON TO THINK MURDER IS THE ONLY OPTION. TO ME, IT'S LIKE A GREAT HUMAN INTEREST STORY. YOU SEE THE WORST AND BEST OF PEOPLE...
"I READ ALL THOSE NANCY DREW BOOKS AS A KID."
!
LITTLE LAURIE
Nancy Drew
"I JUST LOVED TRYING TO FIND THE ANSWER OF WHATEVER MYSTERY IT WAS..."
"AND, WELL, THEN IN MY TWENTIES, RICHARD SPECK KILLED ALL THOSE NURSES!"
LOS GATOS
JULY 14, 1966
MASS SLAYER KILLS 8 NURSES
"I REMEMBER SEEING THEIR FACES ON THE FRONT PAGE... AND JUST THINKING... WHY WOULD SOMEONE DO THIS?"
"THEN I GOT INTO Stephen King
The SHINING
AND
Dominick Dunne...
HIS DAUGHTER WAS MURDERED...
AN INCONVENIENT WOMAN
DUNNE
AND OF COURSE
ANN RULE!"
SMALL SACRIFICES
PART OF MY INTEREST ALSO PROBABLY COMES FROM THE FACT THAT I LIVED THROUGH IT. THE SEVENTIES WERE ALL ABOUT SERIAL KILLERS! THEY WERE JUST EVERYWHERE...

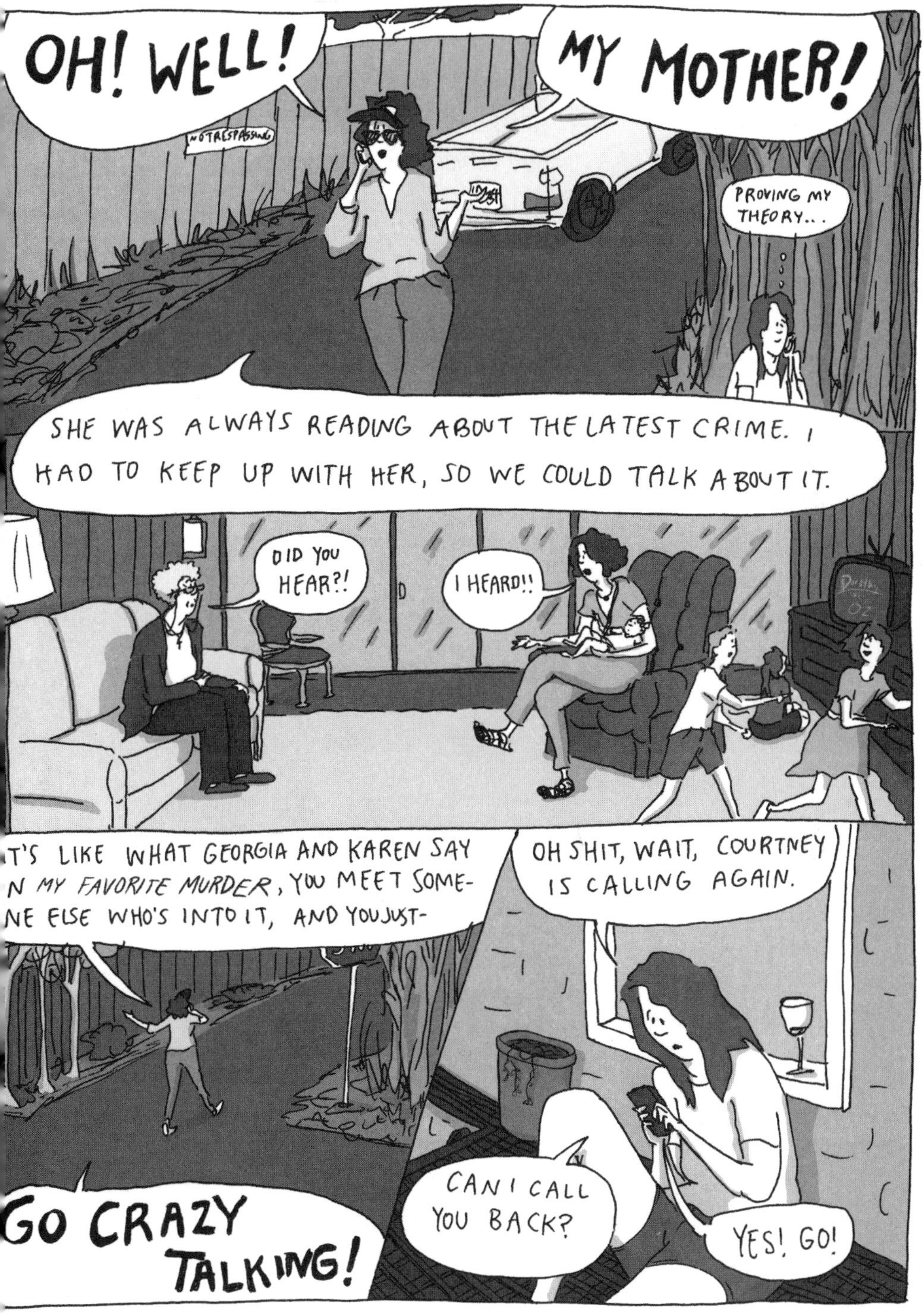
OH! WELL!
MY MOTHER!
NO TRESPASSING
PROVING MY THEORY...
SHE WAS ALWAYS READING ABOUT THE LATEST CRIME. I HAD TO KEEP UP WITH HER, SO WE COULD TALK ABOUT IT.
DID YOU HEAR?!
I HEARD!!
T'S LIKE WHAT GEORGIA AND KAREN SAY
N *MY FAVORITE MURDER*, YOU MEET SOME-
NE ELSE WHO'S INTO IT, AND YOU JUST-
GO CRAZY TALKING!
OH SHIT, WAIT, COURTNEY IS CALLING AGAIN.
CAN I CALL YOU BACK?
YES! GO!

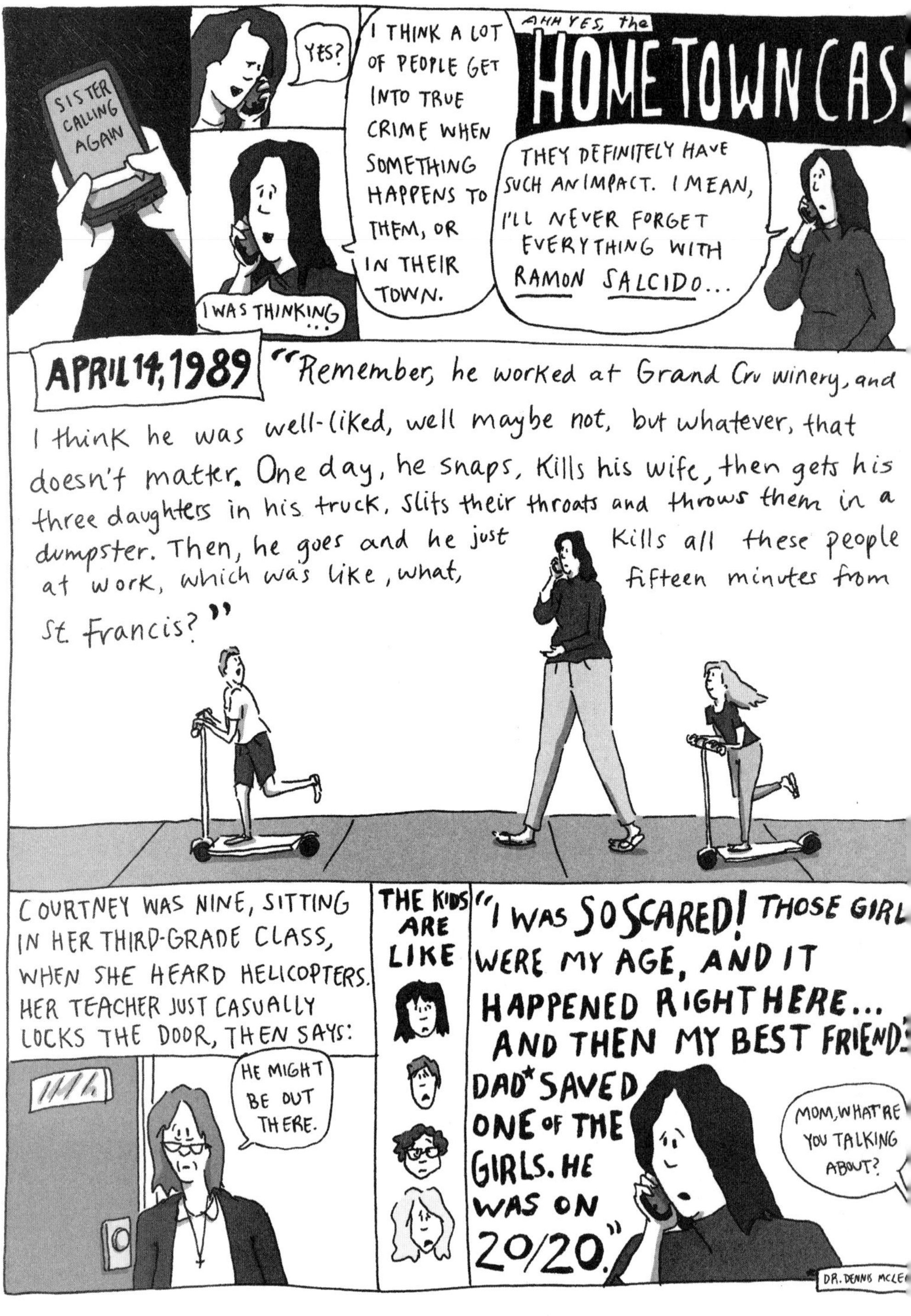
SISTER CALLING AGAIN
YES?
I WAS THINKING...
I THINK A LOT OF PEOPLE GET INTO TRUE CRIME WHEN SOMETHING HAPPENS TO THEM, OR IN THEIR TOWN.
AHH YES, the
HOMETOWN CAS
THEY DEFINITELY HAVE SUCH AN IMPACT. I MEAN, I'LL NEVER FORGET EVERYTHING WITH RAMON SALCIDO...
APRIL 14, 1989
"Remember, he worked at Grand Cru winery, and I think he was well-liked, well maybe not, but whatever, that doesn't matter. One day, he snaps, kills his wife, then gets his three daughters in his truck, slits their throats and throws them in a dumpster. Then, he goes and he just kills all these people at work, which was like, what, fifteen minutes from St. Francis?"
COURTNEY WAS NINE, SITTING IN HER THIRD-GRADE CLASS, WHEN SHE HEARD HELICOPTERS. HER TEACHER JUST CASUALLY LOCKS THE DOOR, THEN SAYS:
HE MIGHT BE OUT THERE.
THE KIDS ARE LIKE
"I WAS SO SCARED! THOSE GIRL WERE MY AGE, AND IT HAPPENED RIGHT HERE... AND THEN MY BEST FRIEND'S DAD* SAVED ONE OF THE GIRLS. HE WAS ON 20/20."
MOM, WHAT'RE YOU TALKING ABOUT?
DR. DENNIS MCLE

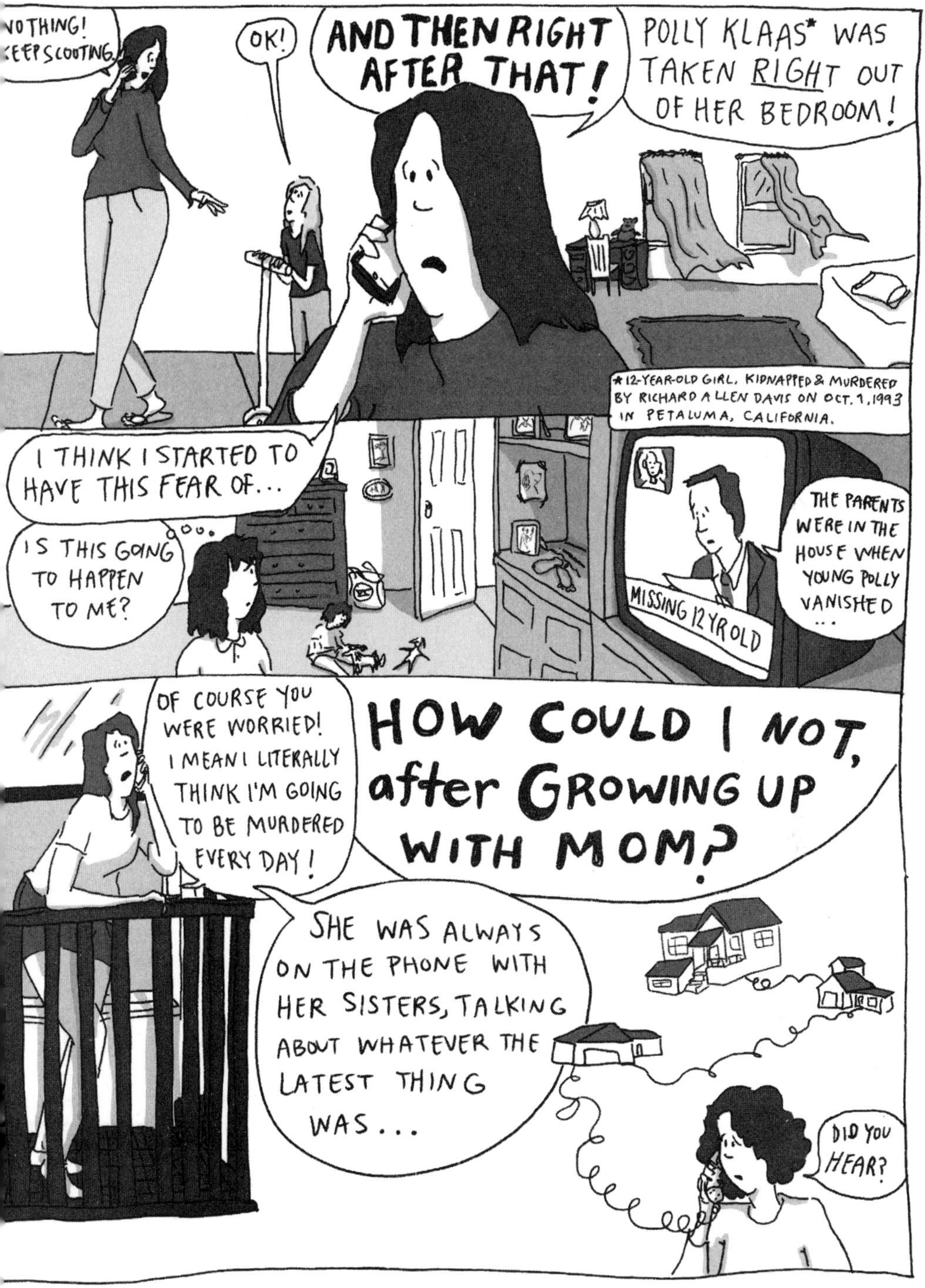
NOTHING! KEEP SCOOTING.
OK!
AND THEN RIGHT AFTER THAT!
POLLY KLAAS* WAS TAKEN RIGHT OUT OF HER BEDROOM!
*12-YEAR-OLD GIRL, KIDNAPPED & MURDERED BY RICHARD ALLEN DAVIS ON OCT. 1, 1993 IN PETALUMA, CALIFORNIA.
I THINK I STARTED TO HAVE THIS FEAR OF...
IS THIS GOING TO HAPPEN TO ME?
MISSING 12 YR OLD
THE PARENTS WERE IN THE HOUSE WHEN YOUNG POLLY VANISHED ...
OF COURSE YOU WERE WORRIED! I MEAN I LITERALLY THINK I'M GOING TO BE MURDERED EVERY DAY!
HOW COULD I NOT, after GROWING UP WITH MOM?
SHE WAS ALWAYS ON THE PHONE WITH HER SISTERS, TALKING ABOUT WHATEVER THE LATEST THING WAS...
DID YOU HEAR?

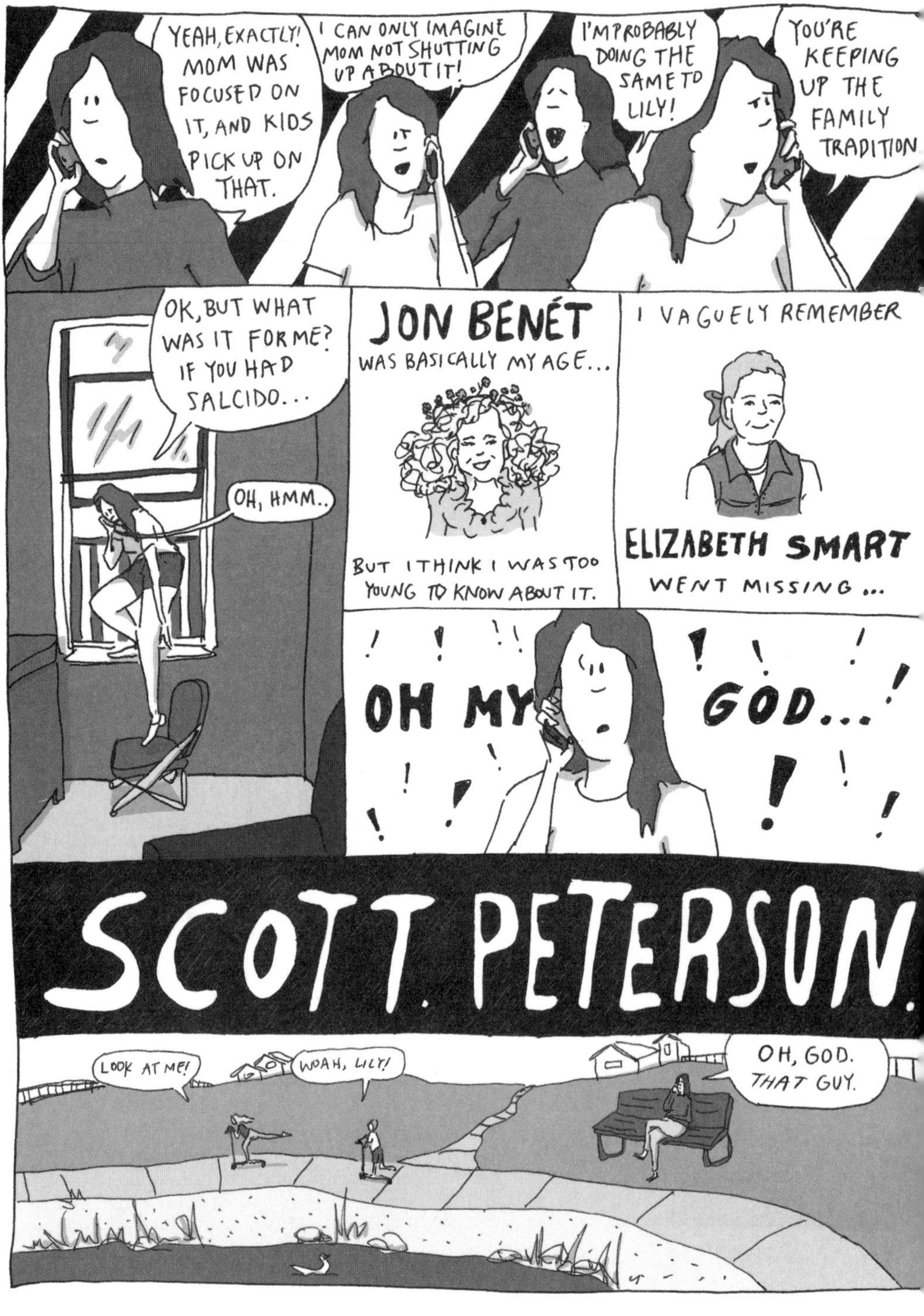
YEAH, EXACTLY! MOM WAS FOCUSED ON IT, AND KIDS PICK UP ON THAT.
I CAN ONLY IMAGINE MOM NOT SHUTTING UP ABOUT IT!
I'M PROBABLY DOING THE SAME TO LILY!
YOU'RE KEEPING UP THE FAMILY TRADITION
OK, BUT WHAT WAS IT FOR ME? IF YOU HAD SALCIDO...
OH, HMM..
JON BENÉT
WAS BASICALLY MY AGE...
BUT I THINK I WAS TOO YOUNG TO KNOW ABOUT IT.
I VAGUELY REMEMBER
ELIZABETH SMART
WENT MISSING...
OH MY GOD...
SCOTT. PETERSON.
LOOK AT ME!
WOAH, LILY!
OH, GOD. THAT GUY.

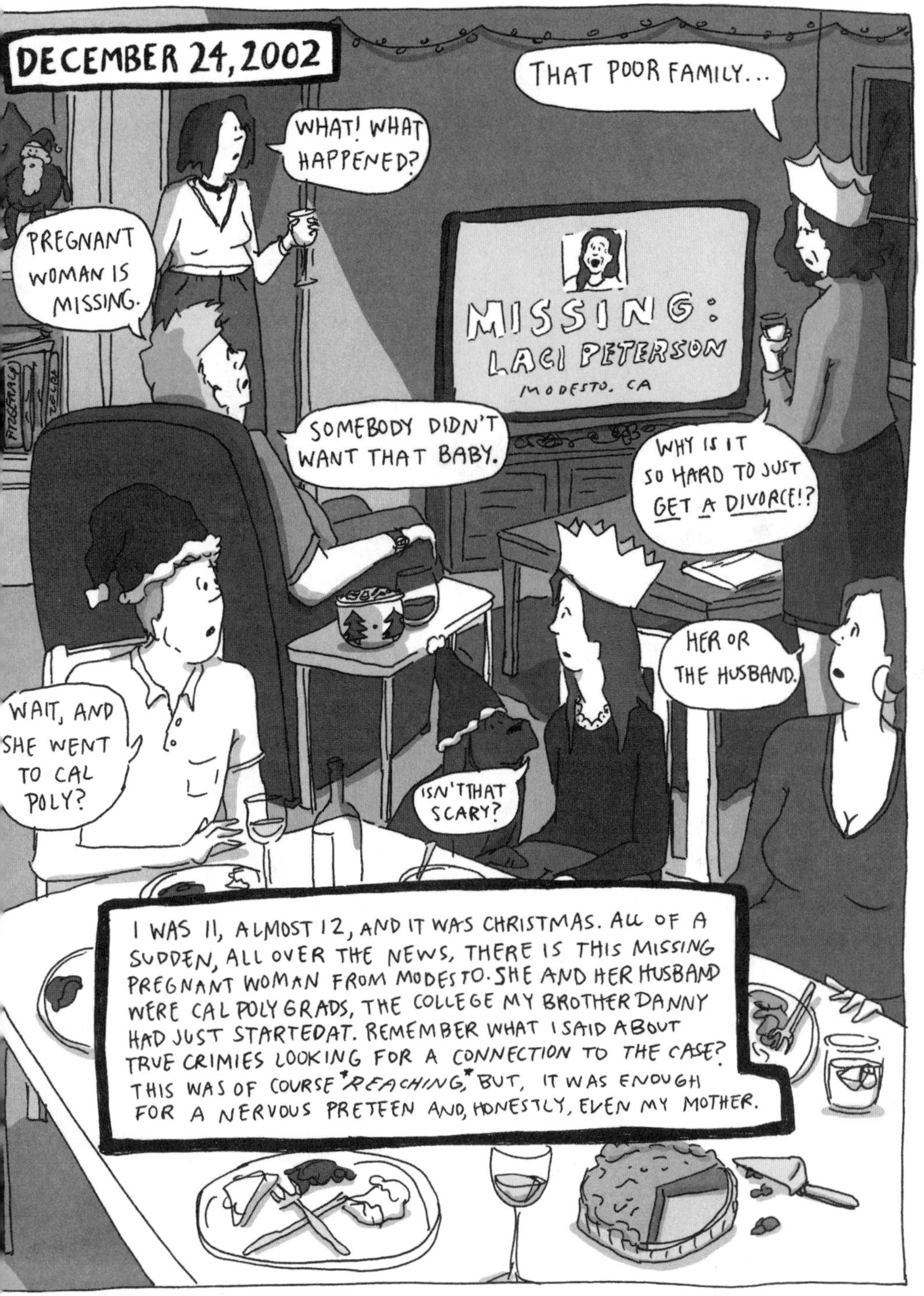
DECEMBER 24, 2002
WHAT! WHAT HAPPENED?
PREGNANT WOMAN IS MISSING.
THAT POOR FAMILY...
MISSING: LACI PETERSON MODESTO, CA
SOMEBODY DIDN'T WANT THAT BABY.
WHY IS IT SO HARD TO JUST GET A DIVORCE!?
HER OR THE HUSBAND.
WAIT, AND SHE WENT TO CAL POLY?
ISN'T THAT SCARY?
I WAS 11, ALMOST 12, AND IT WAS CHRISTMAS. ALL OF A SUDDEN, ALL OVER THE NEWS, THERE IS THIS MISSING PREGNANT WOMAN FROM MODESTO. SHE AND HER HUSBAND WERE CAL POLY GRADS, THE COLLEGE MY BROTHER DANNY HAD JUST STARTED AT. REMEMBER WHAT I SAID ABOUT TRUE CRIMIES LOOKING FOR A CONNECTION TO THE CASE? THIS WAS OF COURSE *REACHING,* BUT, IT WAS ENOUGH FOR A NERVOUS PRETEEN AND, HONESTLY, EVEN MY MOTHER.

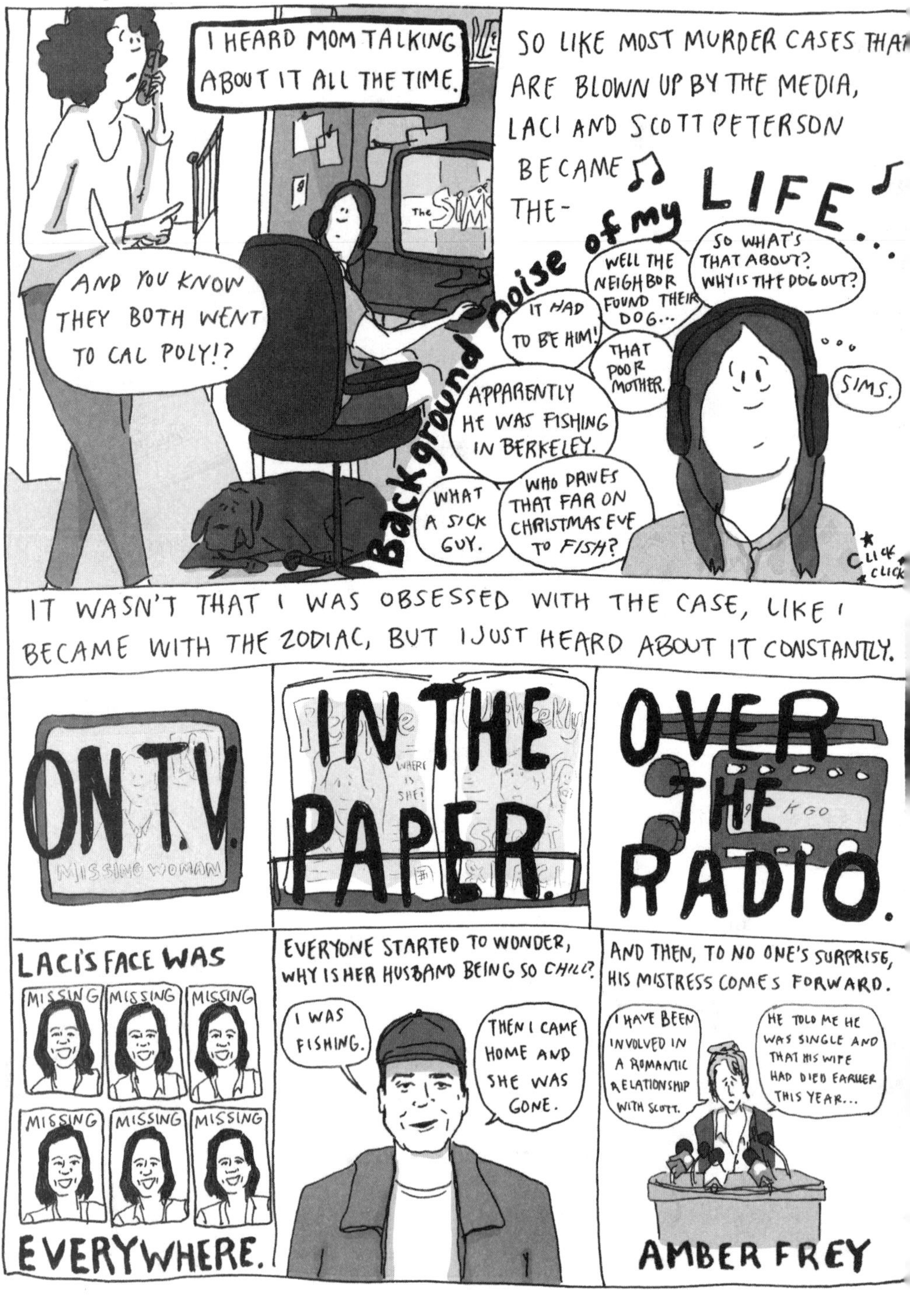

I HEARD MOM TALKING ABOUT IT ALL THE TIME.
AND YOU KNOW THEY BOTH WENT TO CAL POLY!?
SO LIKE MOST MURDER CASES THAT ARE BLOWN UP BY THE MEDIA, LACI AND SCOTT PETERSON BECAME THE-
Background noise of my LIFE...
SO WHAT'S THAT ABOUT? WHY IS THE DOG OUT?
WELL THE NEIGHBOR FOUND THEIR DOG...
IT HAD TO BE HIM!
THAT POOR MOTHER.
APPARENTLY HE WAS FISHING IN BERKELEY.
WHAT A SICK GUY.
WHO DRIVES THAT FAR ON CHRISTMAS EVE TO FISH?
SIMS.
CLICK CLICK
IT WASN'T THAT I WAS OBSESSED WITH THE CASE, LIKE I BECAME WITH THE ZODIAC, BUT I JUST HEARD ABOUT IT CONSTANTLY.
ON T.V.
MISSING WOMAN
IN THE PAPER.
WHERE IS SHE?
OVER THE RADIO.
KGO
LACI'S FACE WAS
MISSING
MISSING
MISSING
MISSING
MISSING
MISSING
EVERYWHERE.
EVERYONE STARTED TO WONDER, WHY IS HER HUSBAND BEING SO CHILL?
I WAS FISHING.
THEN I CAME HOME AND SHE WAS GONE.
AND THEN, TO NO ONE'S SURPRISE, HIS MISTRESS COMES FORWARD.
I HAVE BEEN INVOLVED IN A ROMANTIC RELATIONSHIP WITH SCOTT.
HE TOLD ME HE WAS SINGLE AND THAT HIS WIFE HAD DIED EARLIER THIS YEAR...
AMBER FREY

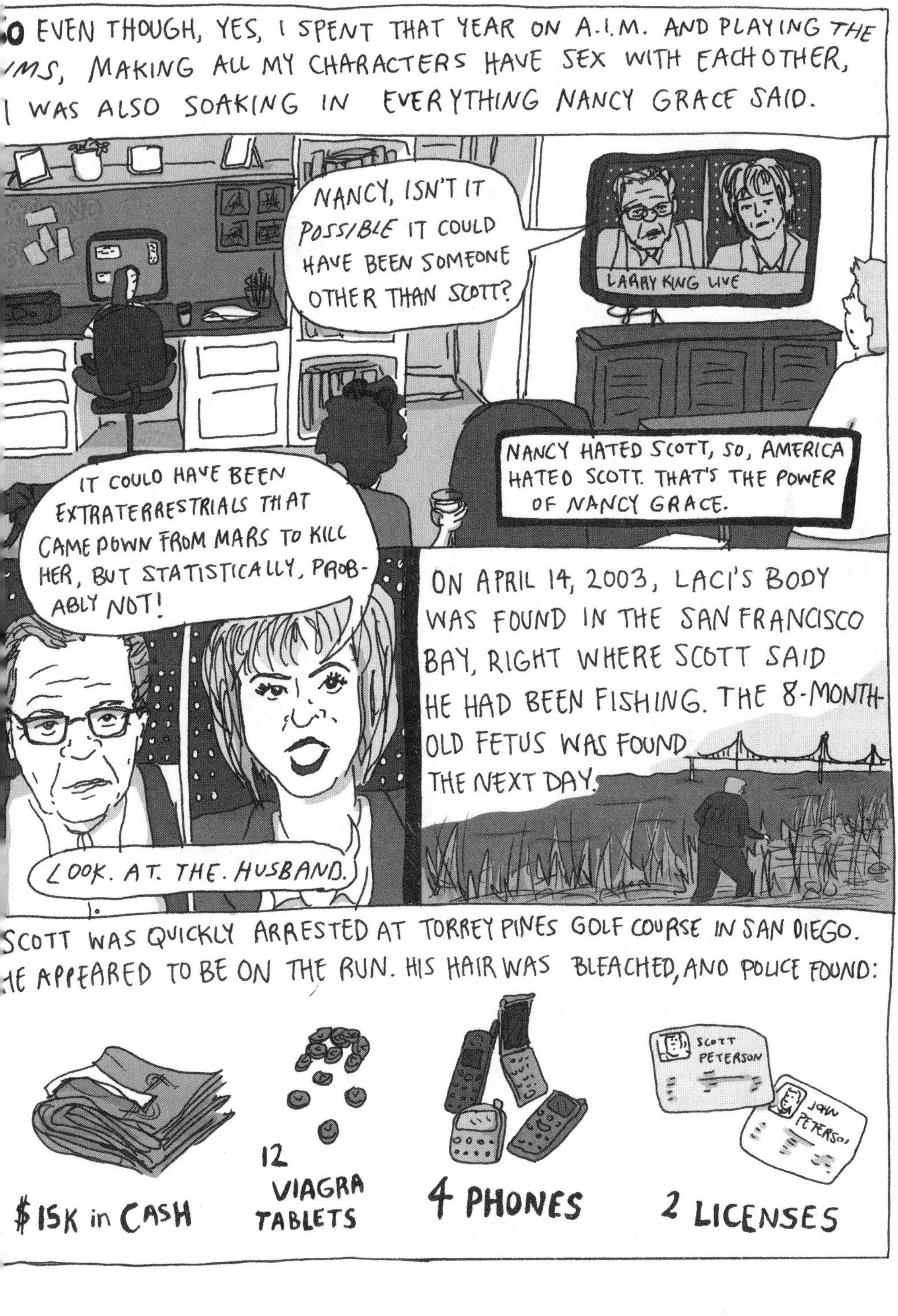
O EVEN THOUGH, YES, I SPENT THAT YEAR ON A.I.M. AND PLAYING THE IMS, MAKING ALL MY CHARACTERS HAVE SEX WITH EACHOTHER, I WAS ALSO SOAKING IN EVERYTHING NANCY GRACE SAID.
NANCY, ISN'T IT POSSIBLE IT COULD HAVE BEEN SOMEONE OTHER THAN SCOTT?
LARRY KING LIVE
IT COULD HAVE BEEN EXTRATERRESTRIALS THAT CAME DOWN FROM MARS TO KILL HER, BUT STATISTICALLY, PROBABLY NOT!
NANCY HATED SCOTT, SO, AMERICA HATED SCOTT. THAT'S THE POWER OF NANCY GRACE.
LOOK. AT. THE. HUSBAND.
ON APRIL 14, 2003, LACI'S BODY WAS FOUND IN THE SAN FRANCISCO BAY, RIGHT WHERE SCOTT SAID HE HAD BEEN FISHING. THE 8-MONTH-OLD FETUS WAS FOUND THE NEXT DAY.
SCOTT WAS QUICKLY ARRESTED AT TORREY PINES GOLF COURSE IN SAN DIEGO. E APPEARED TO BE ON THE RUN. HIS HAIR WAS BLEACHED, AND POLICE FOUND:
SCOTT PETERSON
JOHN PETERSON
$15K in CASH
12 VIAGRA TABLETS
4 PHONES
2 LICENSES

BY THAT POINT SCOTT HAD BECOME A **RUNNING** 🏃 **JOKE** 🏃 IN OUR NEIGHBORHOOD.

GOING FISHING! SO YOU CAN EXPECT A DEAD BODY SOON.

MAYBE WE CAN INVITE AMBER FREY OVER FOR A DRINK?

FREE SCOTT PETERSON

★ READ THIS IRONICALLY

SCOTT WAS EVENTUALLY CONVICTED AND IS CURRENTLY SITTING ON DEATH ROW. HE MAINTAINS HIS INNOCENCE, SAYS HE WAS FRAMED.

DID YOU EVER READ THAT BOOK?

"THAT BOOK"

Amber Frey
WITNESS

OHH, NO I DIDN'T!

OK, BUT I DID JUST WATCH THIS A&E DOC ABOUT IT ALL?

WAIT, REALLY? I HAVEN'T SEEN IT!

YOU NEED TO WATCH IT! BECAUSE IT WA[S] LIKE TOTALLY SUGGESTING HE DIDN'T IT, AND I WAS LIKE . . .

I'M SORR[Y]

WHAT!

I KNOW THERE WASN'T, LIKE, A TON OF HARD EVIDENCE, BUT DIDN'T HE MAGICALLY PREDICT HER DEATH?

YES! HE TOLD AMBER SHE WAS DEAD LIKE WEEKS BEFORE SHE DIED. AND THEN ALL THOSE TAPED PHONE CALLS WHERE HE IS HAPPY AS A CLAM!

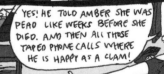
I ALWAYS THOUGHT GONE GIRL WAS BASE[D] ON HIM . . . EXCEPT HE DID IT

GOD!

MOM!! LILY FELL!

MOM, WELL, ALL THE ADULTS, REALLY CULTIVATED THIS OBSESSION. BUT HOW COULD THEY NOT?! IT WAS THE '90s!

CAN YOU IMAGINE IF HE... DIDN'T DO IT?

THAT WOULD MEAN AN INNOCENT MAN IS SITTING IN JAIL . . .

THERE'S PROBABLY WAY MORE INNOCENT PEOPLE ON DEATH ROW THAN ANYONE WOULD CARE TO ADMIT

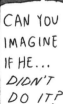
MOMMY!!! I FELL!!!!

OH SHOOT I GOTTA GO—

WATCH THE SCOTT PETERSON DOC SERIES ON A&E TO MAKE YOUR OWN OPINION!!!

220

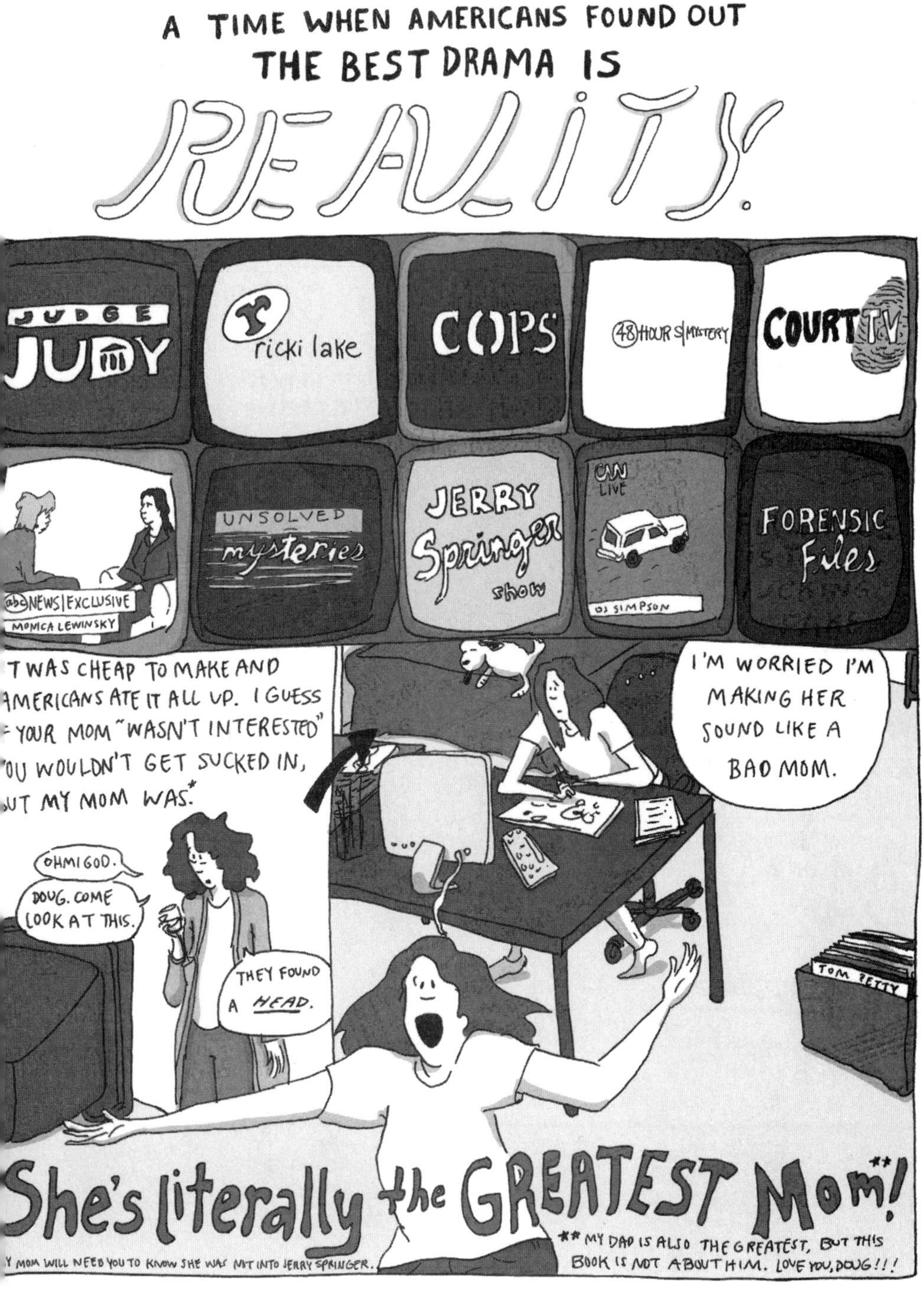
A TIME WHEN AMERICANS FOUND OUT
THE BEST DRAMA IS
REALITY.
JUDGE JUDY
ricki lake
COPS
48 HOURS MYSTERY
COURT TV
abc NEWS | EXCLUSIVE
MONICA LEWINSKY
UNSOLVED mysteries
JERRY Springer show
CNN LIVE
OJ SIMPSON
FORENSIC Files
T WAS CHEAP TO MAKE AND AMERICANS ATE IT ALL UP. I GUESS F YOUR MOM "WASN'T INTERESTED" OU WOULDN'T GET SUCKED IN, UT MY MOM WAS.*
I'M WORRIED I'M MAKING HER SOUND LIKE A BAD MOM.
OHMIGOD.
DOUG. COME LOOK AT THIS.
THEY FOUND A HEAD.
TOM PETTY
She's literally the GREATEST Mom!**
Y MOM WILL NEED YOU TO KNOW SHE WAS NOT INTO JERRY SPRINGER.
** MY DAD IS ALSO THE GREATEST, BUT THIS BOOK IS NOT ABOUT HIM. LOVE YOU, DOUG!!!

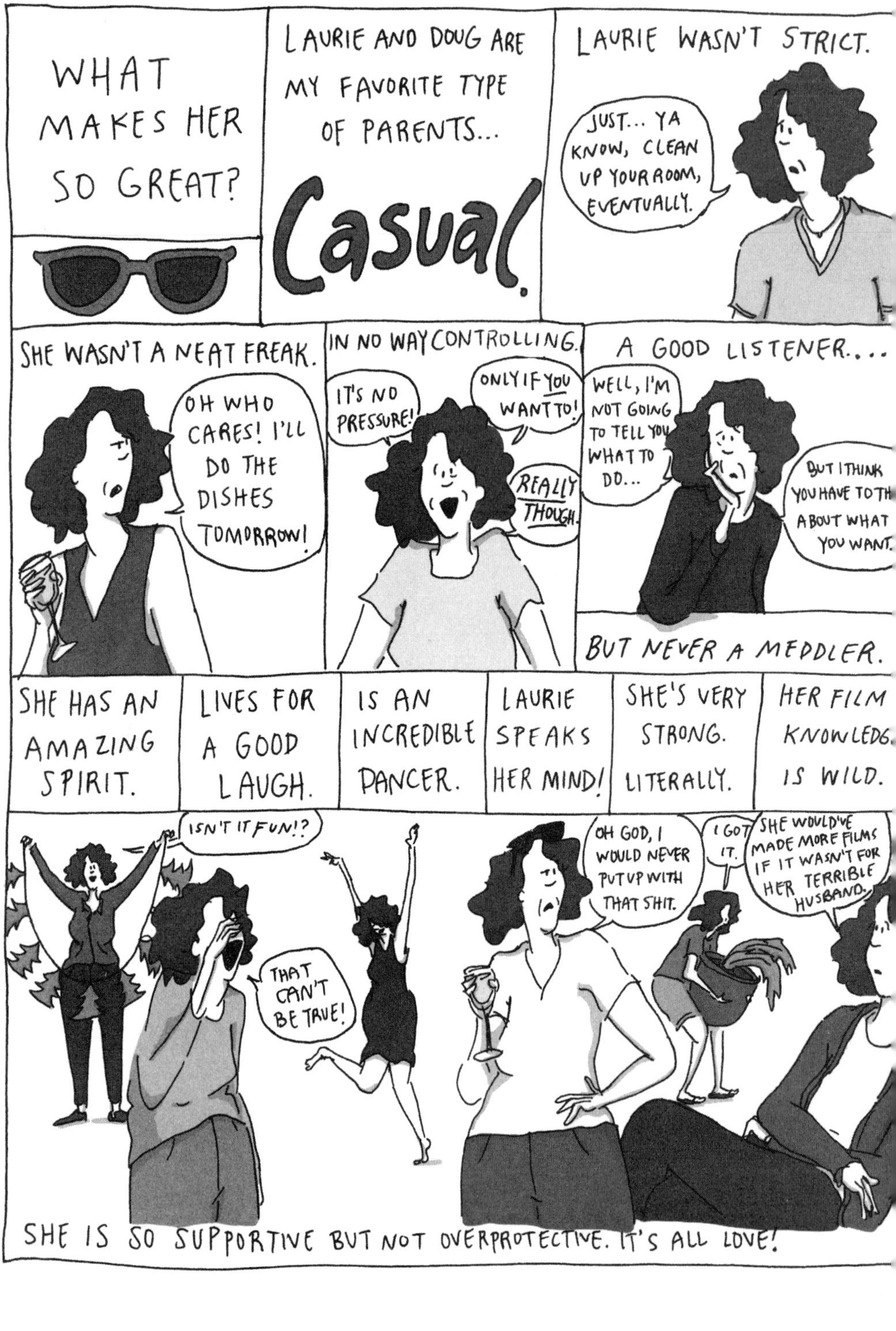
WHAT MAKES HER SO GREAT?
LAURIE AND DOUG ARE MY FAVORITE TYPE OF PARENTS...
Casual.
LAURIE WASN'T STRICT.
JUST... YA KNOW, CLEAN UP YOUR ROOM, EVENTUALLY.
SHE WASN'T A NEAT FREAK.
OH WHO CARES! I'LL DO THE DISHES TOMORROW!
IN NO WAY CONTROLLING.
IT'S NO PRESSURE!
ONLY IF YOU WANT TO!
REALLY THOUGH.
A GOOD LISTENER....
WELL, I'M NOT GOING TO TELL YOU WHAT TO DO...
BUT I THINK YOU HAVE TO TH
ABOUT WHAT YOU WANT.
BUT NEVER A MEDDLER.
SHE HAS AN AMAZING SPIRIT.
LIVES FOR A GOOD LAUGH.
IS AN INCREDIBLE DANCER.
LAURIE SPEAKS HER MIND!
SHE'S VERY STRONG. LITERALLY.
HER FILM KNOWLEDG IS WILD.
ISN'T IT FUN!?
THAT CAN'T BE TRUE!
OH GOD, I WOULD NEVER PUT UP WITH THAT SHIT.
I GOT IT.
SHE WOULD'VE MADE MORE FILMS IF IT WASN'T FOR HER TERRIBLE HUSBAND.
SHE IS SO SUPPORTIVE BUT NOT OVERPROTECTIVE. IT'S ALL LOVE!

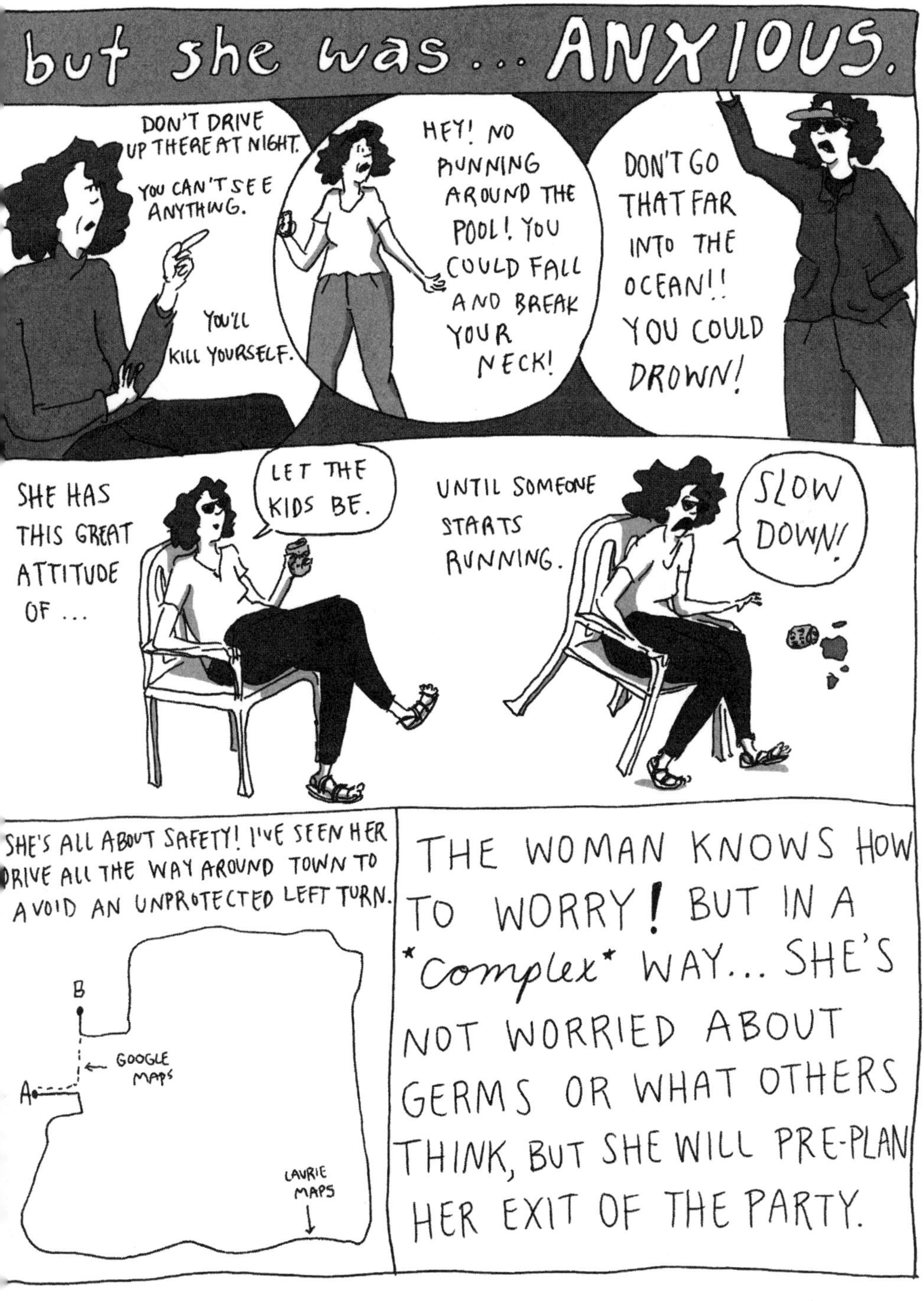

but she was... ANXIOUS.
DON'T DRIVE UP THERE AT NIGHT.
YOU CAN'T SEE ANYTHING.
YOU'LL KILL YOURSELF.
HEY! NO RUNNING AROUND THE POOL! YOU COULD FALL AND BREAK YOUR NECK!
DON'T GO THAT FAR INTO THE OCEAN!! YOU COULD DROWN!
SHE HAS THIS GREAT ATTITUDE OF ...
LET THE KIDS BE.
UNTIL SOMEONE STARTS RUNNING.
SLOW DOWN!
SHE'S ALL ABOUT SAFETY! I'VE SEEN HER DRIVE ALL THE WAY AROUND TOWN TO AVOID AN UNPROTECTED LEFT TURN.
B
A
GOOGLE MAPS
LAURIE MAPS
THE WOMAN KNOWS HOW TO WORRY! BUT IN A *complex* WAY... SHE'S NOT WORRIED ABOUT GERMS OR WHAT OTHERS THINK, BUT SHE WILL PRE-PLAN HER EXIT OF THE PARTY.

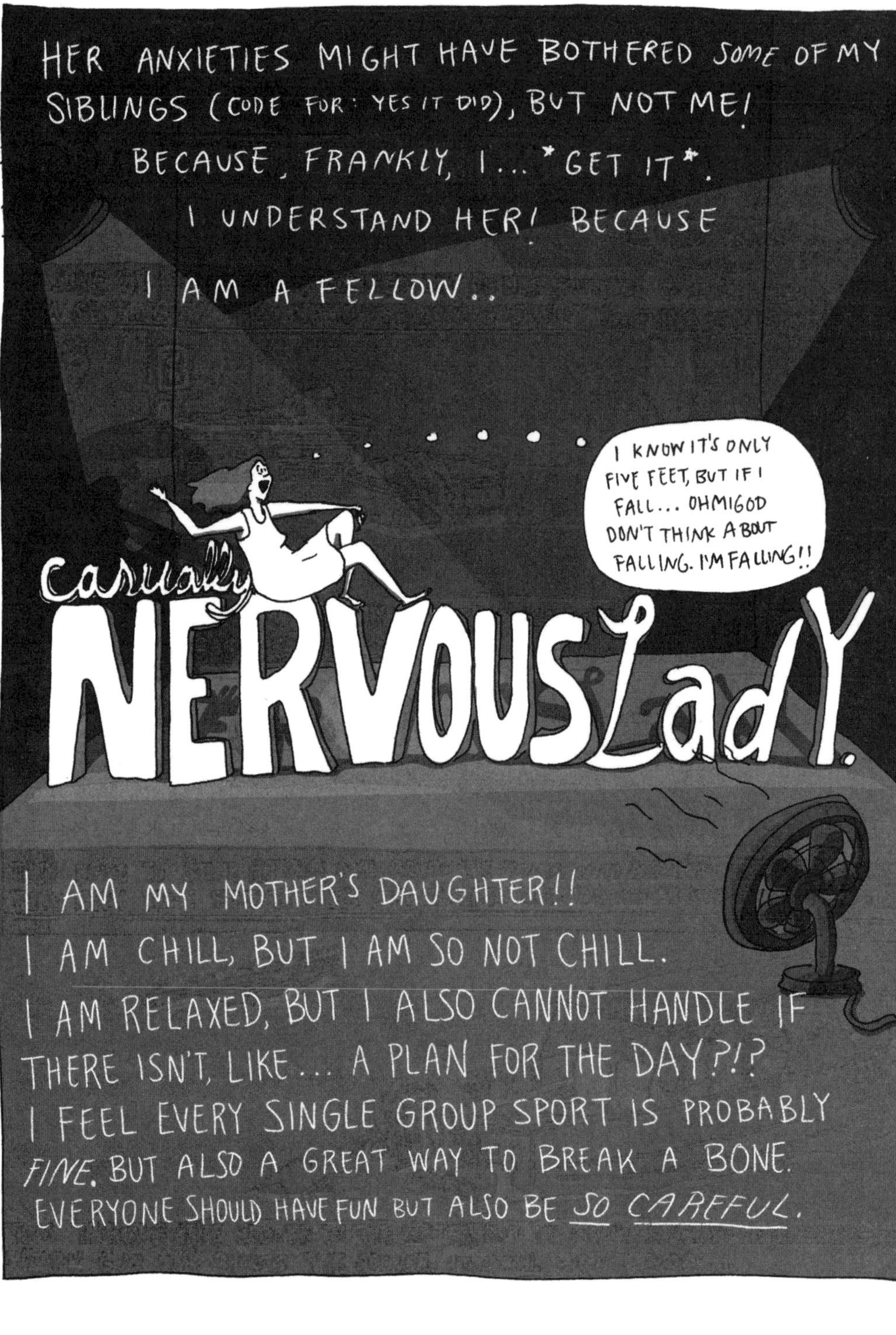
HER ANXIETIES MIGHT HAVE BOTHERED SOME OF MY SIBLINGS (CODE FOR: YES IT DID), BUT NOT ME!
BECAUSE, FRANKLY, I... *GET IT*.
I UNDERSTAND HER! BECAUSE
I AM A FELLOW..
I KNOW IT'S ONLY FIVE FEET, BUT IF I FALL... OHMIGOD DON'T THINK ABOUT FALLING. I'M FALLING!!
casually
NERVOUS LadY.
I AM MY MOTHER'S DAUGHTER!!
I AM CHILL, BUT I AM SO NOT CHILL.
I AM RELAXED, BUT I ALSO CANNOT HANDLE IF THERE ISN'T, LIKE... A PLAN FOR THE DAY?!?
I FEEL EVERY SINGLE GROUP SPORT IS PROBABLY FINE. BUT ALSO A GREAT WAY TO BREAK A BONE.
EVERYONE SHOULD HAVE FUN BUT ALSO BE SO CAREFUL.

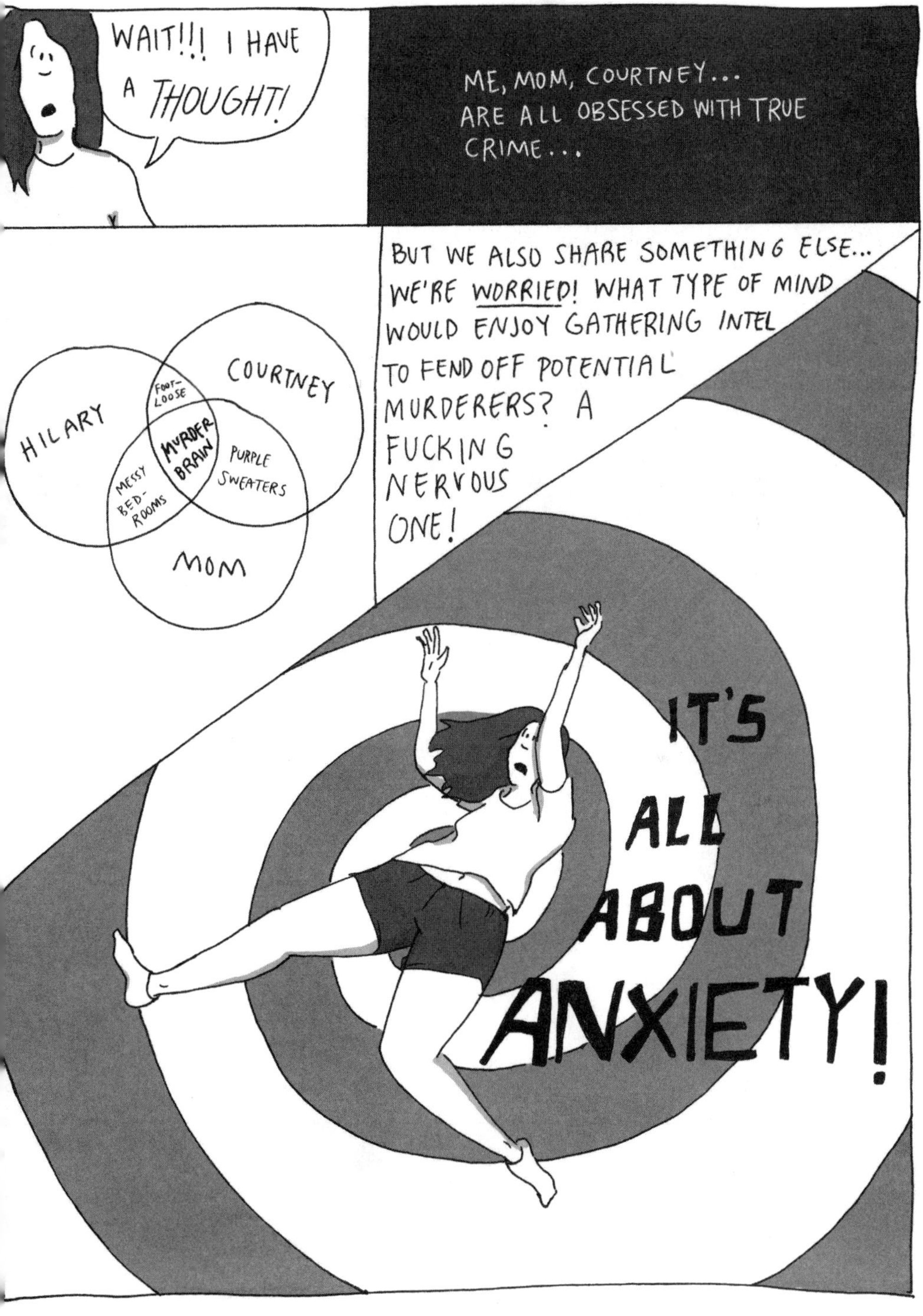
WAIT!!! I HAVE A THOUGHT!
ME, MOM, COURTNEY... ARE ALL OBSESSED WITH TRUE CRIME...
HILARY
COURTNEY
MOM
FOOT-LOOSE
MURDER BRAIN
MESSY BED-ROOMS
PURPLE SWEATERS
BUT WE ALSO SHARE SOMETHING ELSE... WE'RE WORRIED! WHAT TYPE OF MIND WOULD ENJOY GATHERING INTEL TO FEND OFF POTENTIAL MURDERERS? A FUCKING NERVOUS ONE!
IT'S ALL ABOUT ANXIETY!

ME &
ANNE MARIE
FAHEY

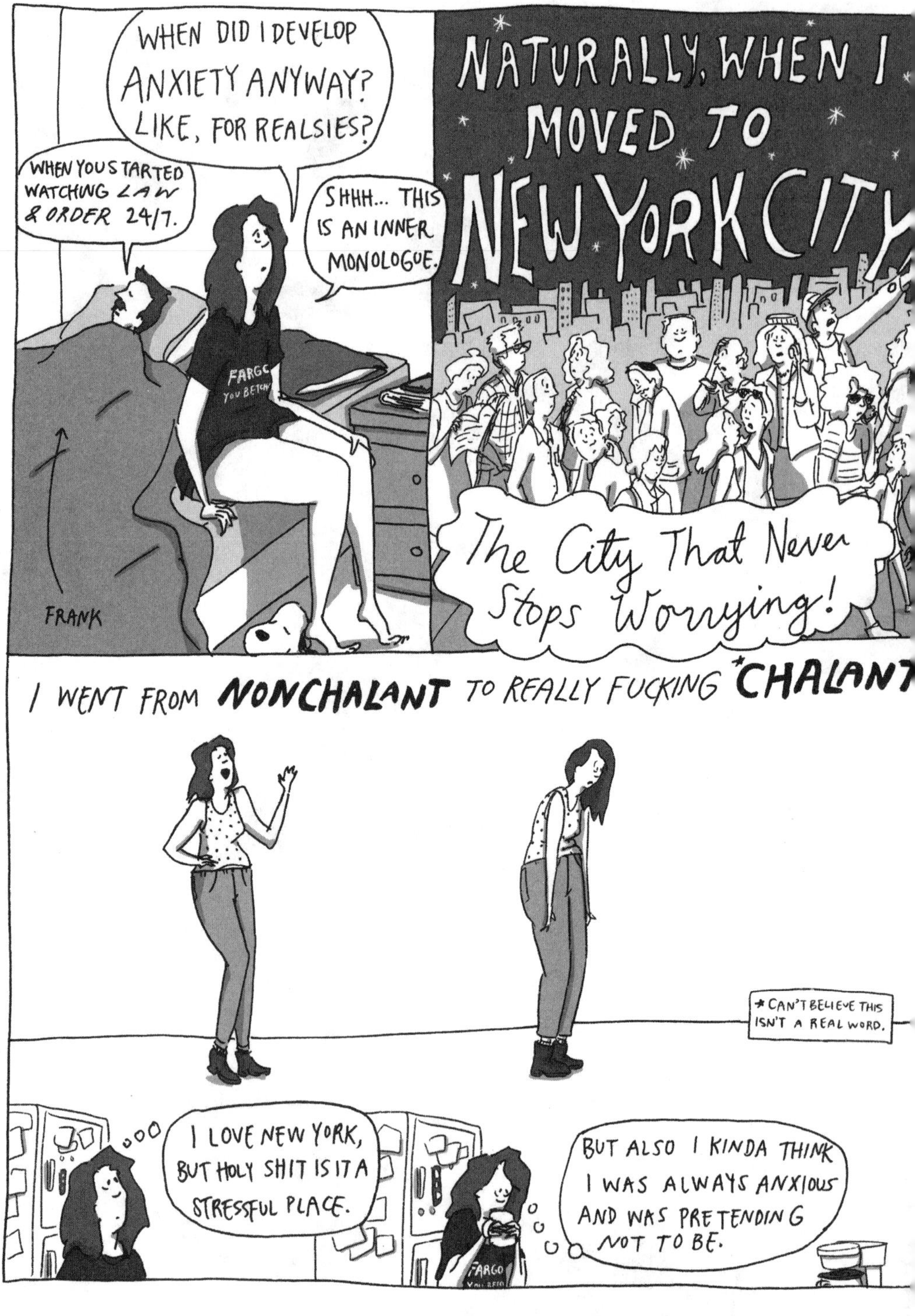
WHEN DID I DEVELOP ANXIETY ANYWAY? LIKE, FOR REALSIES?
WHEN YOU STARTED WATCHING LAW & ORDER 24/7.
SHHH... THIS IS AN INNER MONOLOGUE.
FRANK
FARGO YOU BETCHA
NATURALLY, WHEN I MOVED TO NEW YORK CITY,
The City That Never Stops Worrying!
I WENT FROM NONCHALANT TO REALLY FUCKING *CHALANT
* CAN'T BELIEVE THIS ISN'T A REAL WORD.
I LOVE NEW YORK, BUT HOLY SHIT IS IT A STRESSFUL PLACE.
BUT ALSO I KINDA THINK I WAS ALWAYS ANXIOUS AND WAS PRETENDING NOT TO BE.

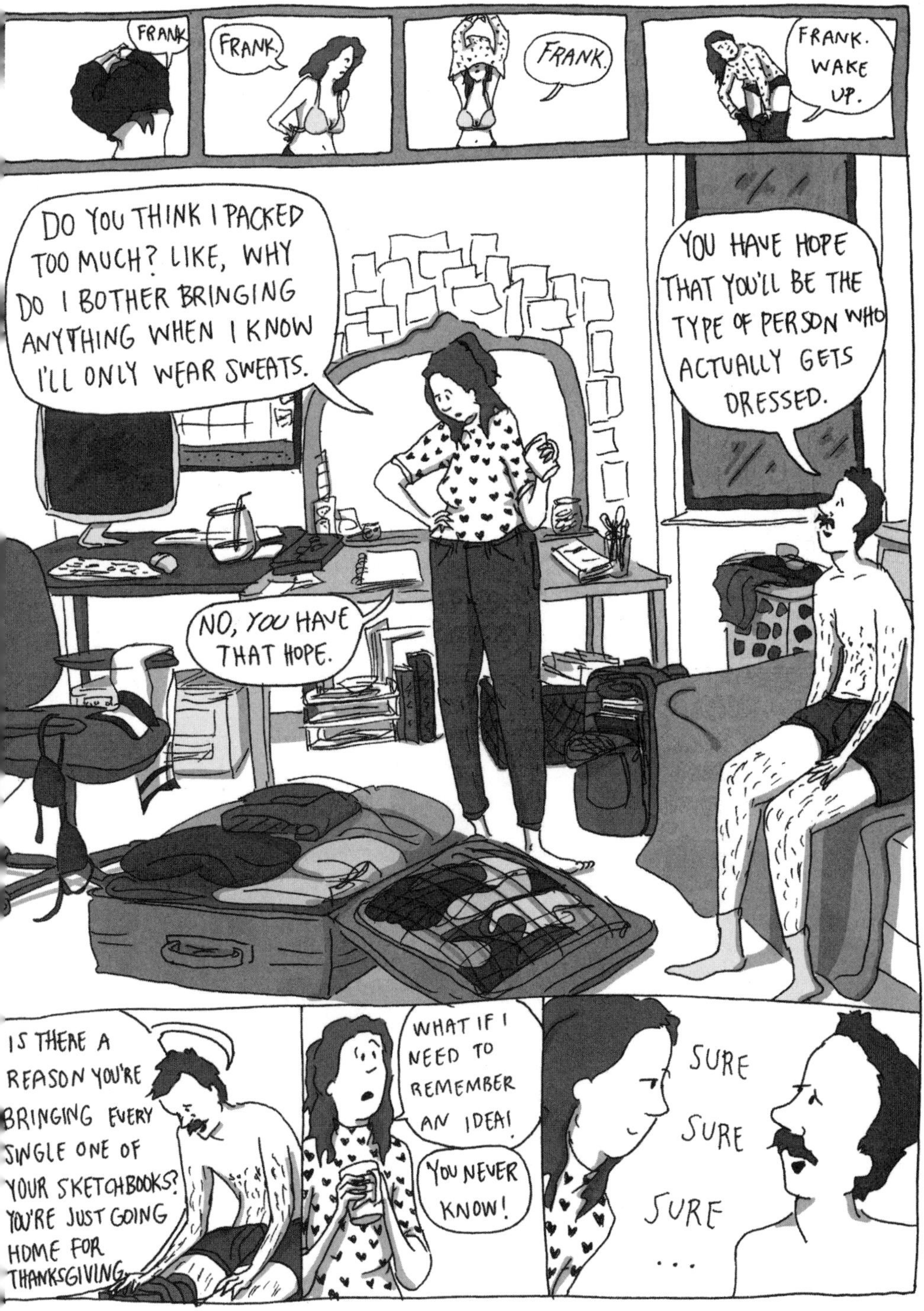
FRANK
FRANK.
FRANK.
FRANK. WAKE UP.
DO YOU THINK I PACKED TOO MUCH? LIKE, WHY DO I BOTHER BRINGING ANYTHING WHEN I KNOW I'LL ONLY WEAR SWEATS.
YOU HAVE HOPE THAT YOU'LL BE THE TYPE OF PERSON WHO ACTUALLY GETS DRESSED.
NO, YOU HAVE THAT HOPE.
IS THERE A REASON YOU'RE BRINGING EVERY SINGLE ONE OF YOUR SKETCHBOOKS? YOU'RE JUST GOING HOME FOR THANKSGIVING.
WHAT IF I NEED TO REMEMBER AN IDEA!
YOU NEVER KNOW!
SURE
SURE
SURE
...

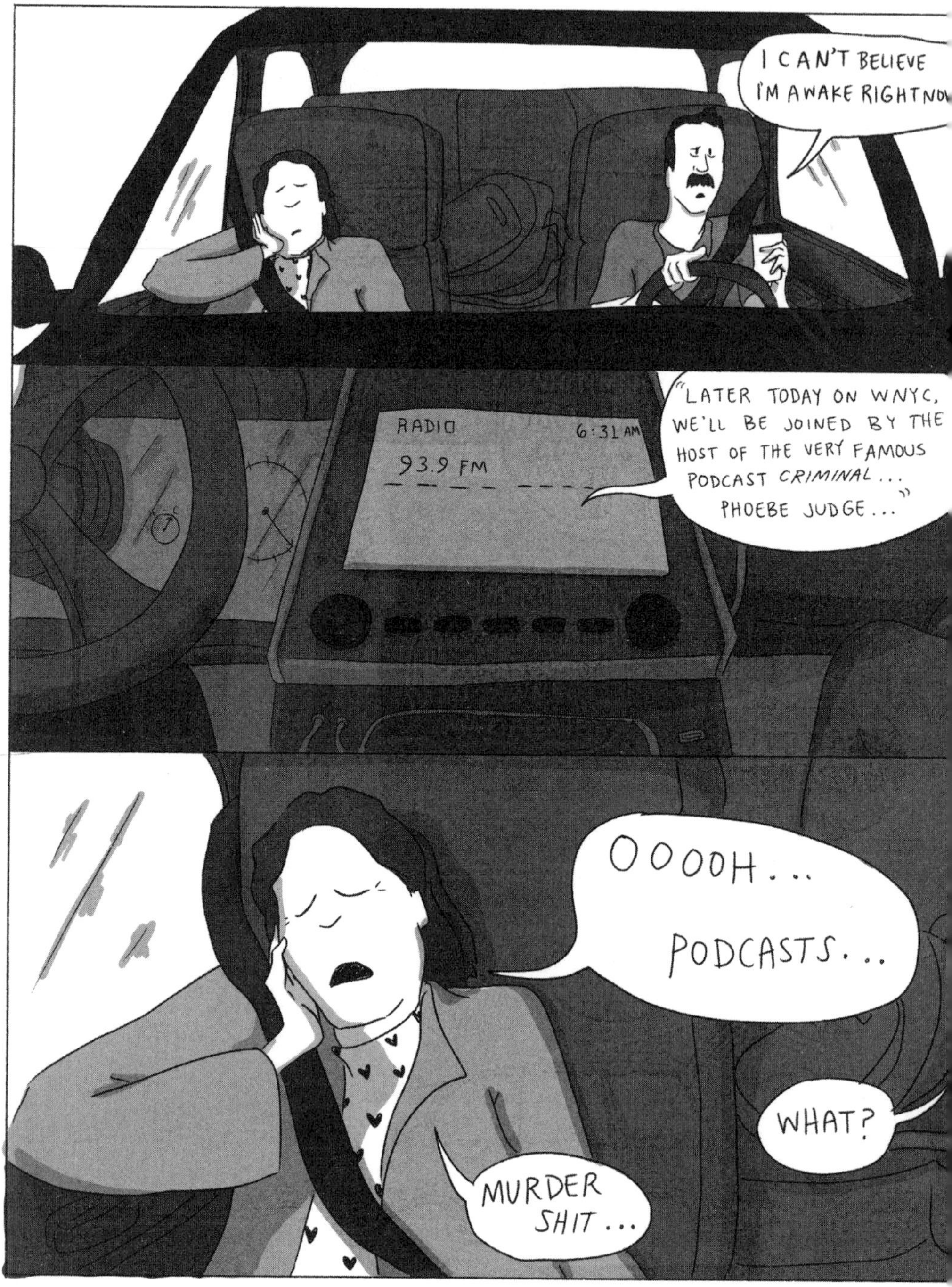
I CAN'T BELIEVE I'M AWAKE RIGHT NOW
RADIO
6:31 AM
93.9 FM
"LATER TODAY ON WNYC, WE'LL BE JOINED BY THE HOST OF THE VERY FAMOUS PODCAST *CRIMINAL*... PHOEBE JUDGE..."
OOOOH... PODCASTS...
WHAT?
MURDER SHIT...

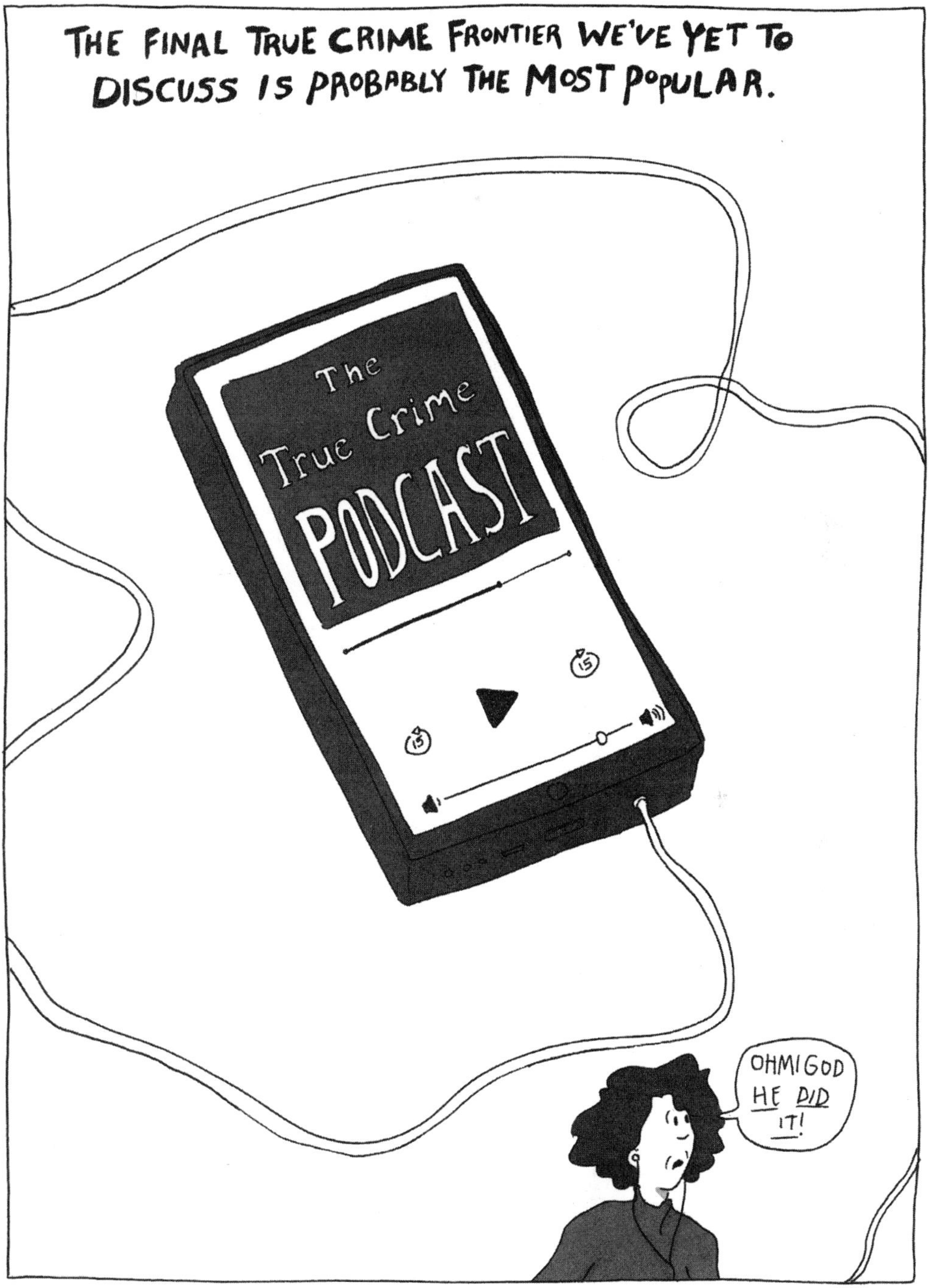
THE FINAL TRUE CRIME FRONTIER WE'VE YET TO DISCUSS IS PROBABLY THE MOST POPULAR.
The True Crime PODCAST
OHMIGOD HE DID IT!

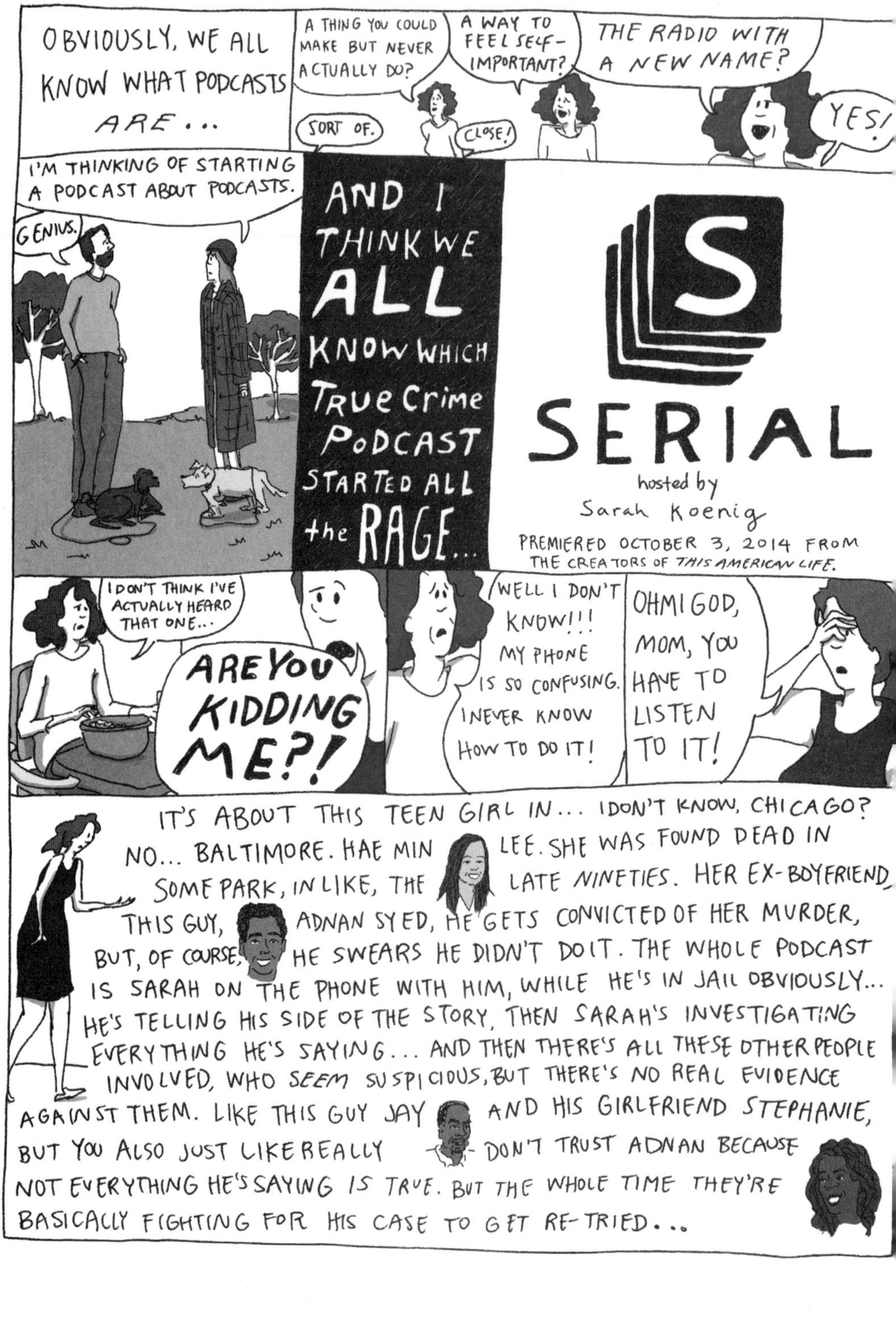

OBVIOUSLY, WE ALL KNOW WHAT PODCASTS ARE...
A THING YOU COULD MAKE BUT NEVER ACTUALLY DO?
SORT OF.
A WAY TO FEEL SELF-IMPORTANT?
CLOSE!
THE RADIO WITH A NEW NAME?
YES!
I'M THINKING OF STARTING A PODCAST ABOUT PODCASTS.
GENIUS.
AND I THINK WE ALL KNOW WHICH TRUE CRIME PODCAST STARTED ALL the RAGE...
SERIAL
hosted by
Sarah Koenig
PREMIERED OCTOBER 3, 2014 FROM THE CREATORS OF THIS AMERICAN LIFE.
I DON'T THINK I'VE ACTUALLY HEARD THAT ONE...
ARE YOU KIDDING ME?!
WELL I DON'T KNOW!!! MY PHONE IS SO CONFUSING. I NEVER KNOW HOW TO DO IT!
OHMIGOD, MOM, YOU HAVE TO LISTEN TO IT!
IT'S ABOUT THIS TEEN GIRL IN... I DON'T KNOW, CHICAGO? NO... BALTIMORE. HAE MIN LEE. SHE WAS FOUND DEAD IN SOME PARK, IN LIKE, THE LATE NINETIES. HER EX-BOYFRIEND, THIS GUY, ADNAN SYED, HE GETS CONVICTED OF HER MURDER, BUT, OF COURSE, HE SWEARS HE DIDN'T DO IT. THE WHOLE PODCAST IS SARAH ON THE PHONE WITH HIM, WHILE HE'S IN JAIL OBVIOUSLY... HE'S TELLING HIS SIDE OF THE STORY, THEN SARAH'S INVESTIGATING EVERYTHING HE'S SAYING... AND THEN THERE'S ALL THESE OTHER PEOPLE INVOLVED, WHO SEEM SUSPICIOUS, BUT THERE'S NO REAL EVIDENCE AGAINST THEM. LIKE THIS GUY JAY AND HIS GIRLFRIEND STEPHANIE, BUT YOU ALSO JUST LIKE REALLY DON'T TRUST ADNAN BECAUSE NOT EVERYTHING HE'S SAYING IS TRUE. BUT THE WHOLE TIME THEY'RE BASICALLY FIGHTING FOR HIS CASE TO GET RE-TRIED...

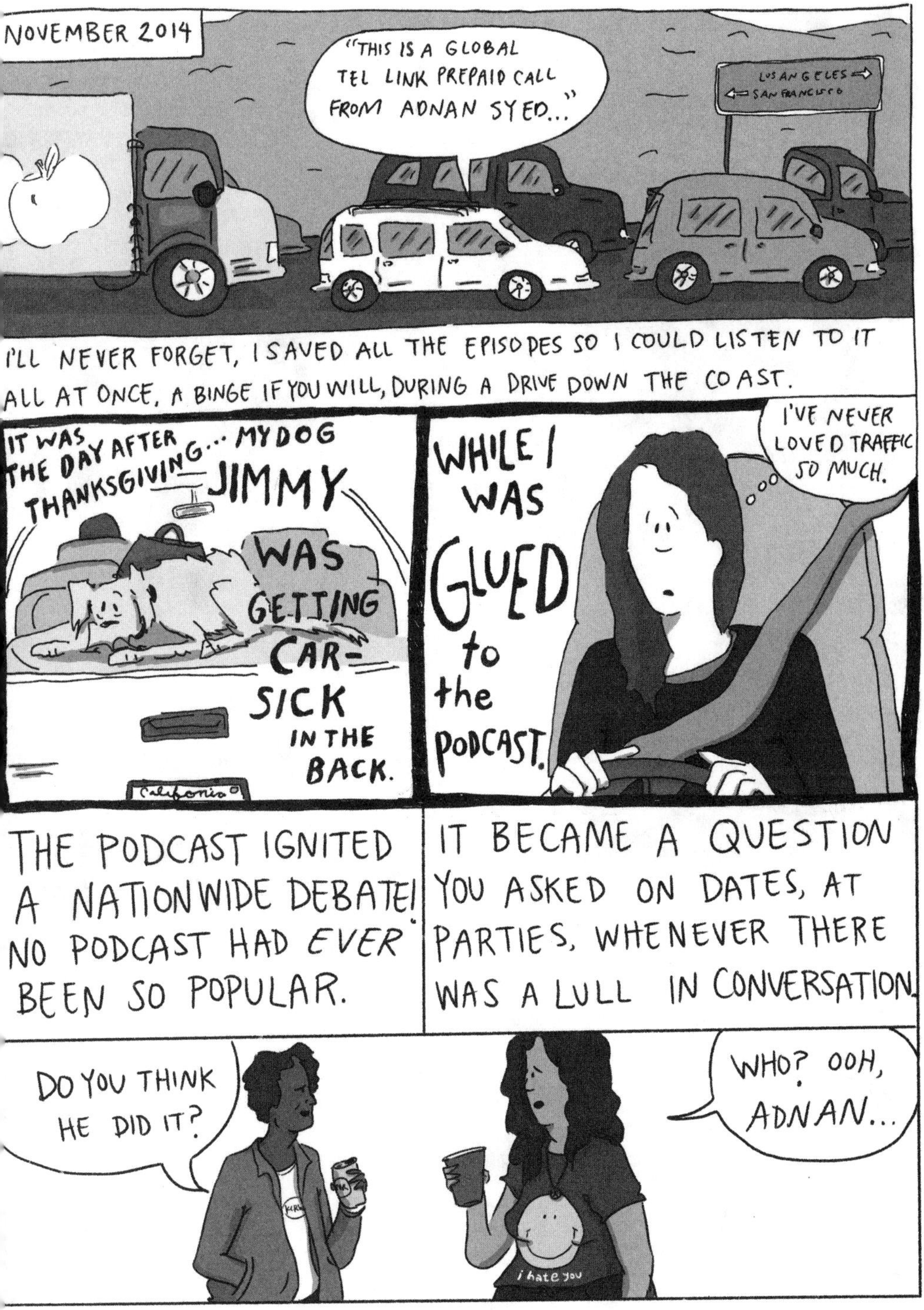
NOVEMBER 2014
"THIS IS A GLOBAL TEL LINK PREPAID CALL FROM ADNAN SYED..."
LOS ANGELES
SAN FRANCISCO
I'LL NEVER FORGET, I SAVED ALL THE EPISODES SO I COULD LISTEN TO IT ALL AT ONCE, A BINGE IF YOU WILL, DURING A DRIVE DOWN THE COAST.
IT WAS THE DAY AFTER THANKSGIVING... MY DOG JIMMY WAS GETTING CAR-SICK IN THE BACK.
California
WHILE I WAS GLUED to the PODCAST.
I'VE NEVER LOVED TRAFFIC SO MUCH.
THE PODCAST IGNITED A NATIONWIDE DEBATE! NO PODCAST HAD *EVER* BEEN SO POPULAR.
IT BECAME A QUESTION YOU ASKED ON DATES, AT PARTIES, WHENEVER THERE WAS A LULL IN CONVERSATION.
DO YOU THINK HE DID IT?
WHO? OOH, ADNAN...
i hate you

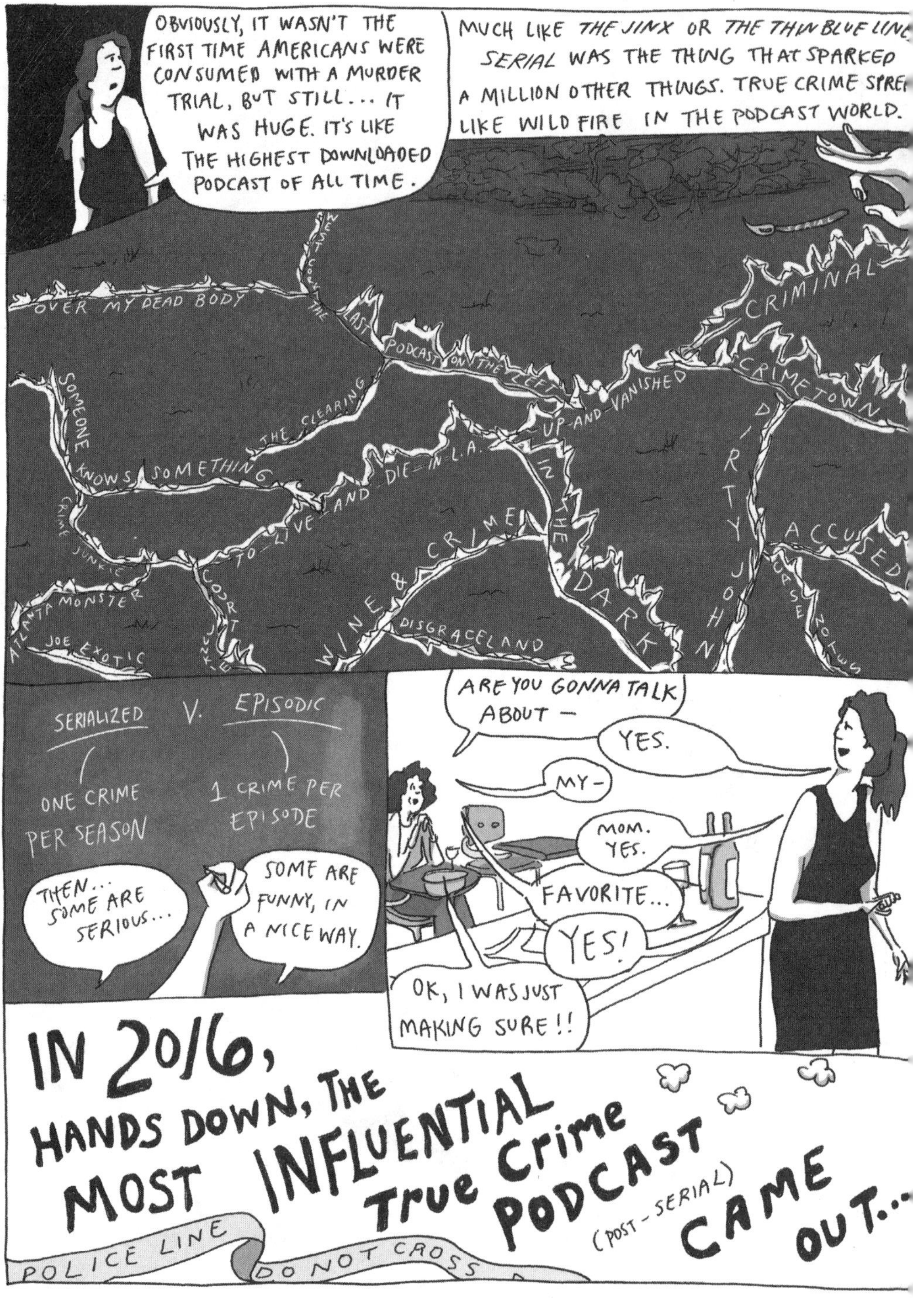
OBVIOUSLY, IT WASN'T THE FIRST TIME AMERICANS WERE CONSUMED WITH A MURDER TRIAL, BUT STILL... IT WAS HUGE. IT'S LIKE THE HIGHEST DOWNLOADED PODCAST OF ALL TIME.
MUCH LIKE THE JINX OR THE THIN BLUE LINE SERIAL WAS THE THING THAT SPARKED A MILLION OTHER THINGS. TRUE CRIME SPREAD LIKE WILD FIRE IN THE PODCAST WORLD.
OVER MY DEAD BODY
WEST COAST
THE LAST PODCAST ON THE LEFT
CRIMINAL
CRIMETOWN
UP AND VANISHED
SOMEONE KNOWS SOMETHING
THE CLEARING
CRIME JUNKIE
TO LIVE AND DIE IN L.A.
IN THE DARK
DIRTY JOHN
ACCUSED
CASE NOTES
WINE & CRIME
ATLANTA MONSTER
JOE EXOTIC
COURT JUNKIE
DISGRACELAND
SERIALIZED V. EPISODIC
ONE CRIME PER SEASON
1 CRIME PER EPISODE
THEN... SOME ARE SERIOUS...
SOME ARE FUNNY, IN A NICE WAY.
ARE YOU GONNA TALK ABOUT —
YES.
MY—
MOM. YES.
FAVORITE...
YES!
OK, I WAS JUST MAKING SURE!!
IN 2016, HANDS DOWN, THE MOST INFLUENTIAL True Crime PODCAST (POST-SERIAL) CAME OUT...
POLICE LINE DO NOT CROSS

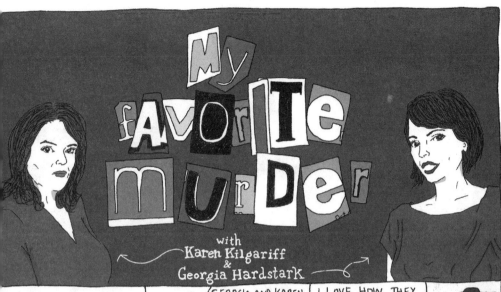

My fAVORIte murDer

with
Karen Kilgariff
&
Georgia Hardstark

IT'S A PODCAST WHERE TWO COMEDIANS TALK ABOUT THEIR LIVES AND ANXIETIES AND ALSO THEIR FAVORITE MURDER THEY LEARNED ABOUT THAT WEEK.

GEORGIA AND KAREN TAPPED INTO THIS, JUST, MASSIVE AUDIENCE OF, WELL, MOSTLY WOMEN WHO LOVE TO TALK ABOUT MURDER WITH THEIR FRIENDS.

I LOVE HOW THEY ALSO TALK ABOUT THEIR OWN MENTAL HEALTH STUFF AND HOW THEY'VE DEALT WITH IT AND HOW IT ALL KINDA RELATES.

THIS PODCAST IS SO POPULAR, IT'S *practically* A CULT!

EXCEPT IT'S FOR SURE...

NOT A CULT!

THEY JUST HAVE A VERY DEDICATED FAN BASE.

GEORGIA AND KAREN WERE THE FIRST PEOPLE TO FINALLY GIVE US TRUE CRIME FANATICS A *NAME* TO IDENTIFY OURSELVES WITH...

WE'RE MURDERINOS!

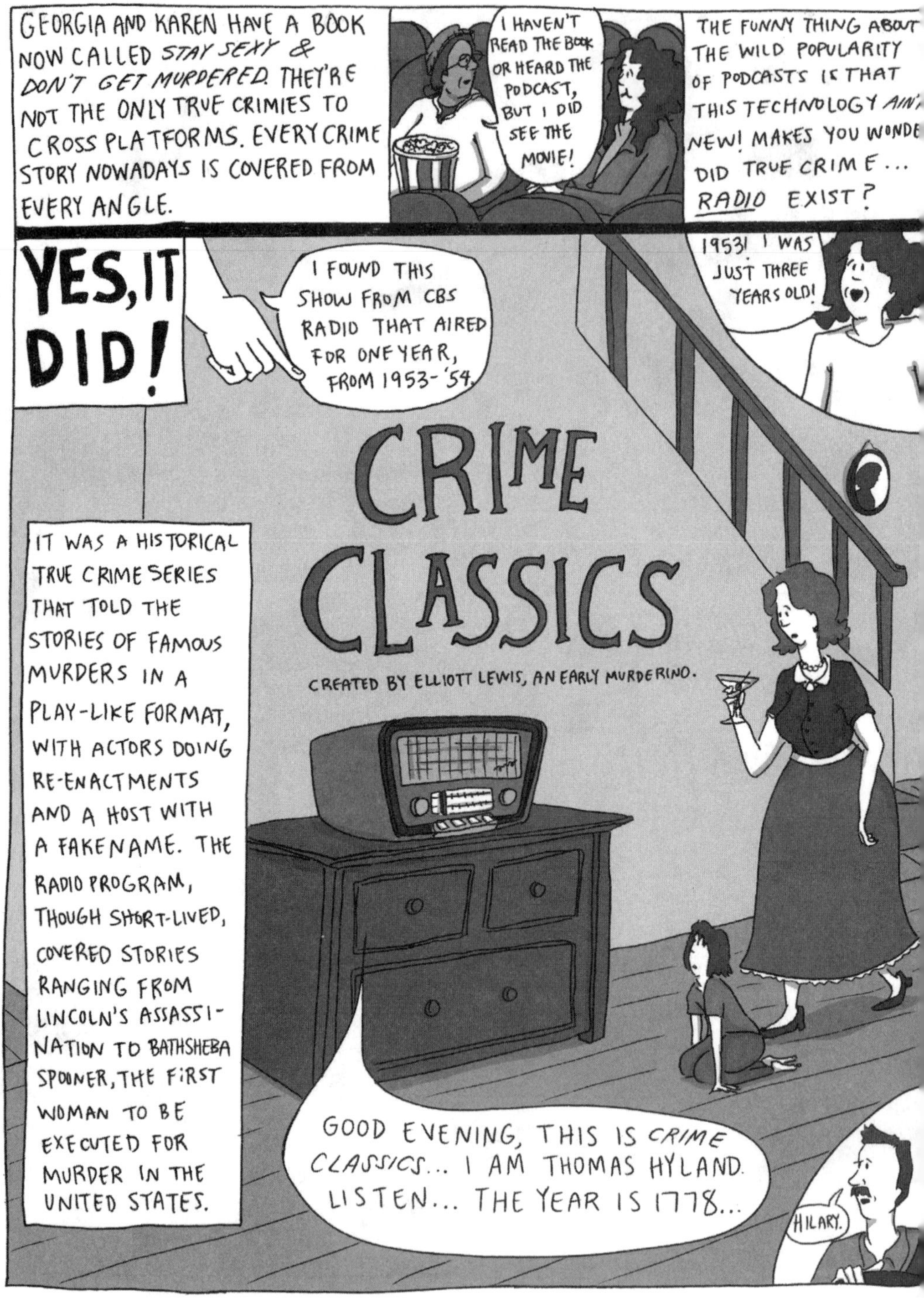
GEORGIA AND KAREN HAVE A BOOK NOW CALLED *STAY SEXY & DON'T GET MURDERED.* THEY'RE NOT THE ONLY TRUE CRIMIES TO CROSS PLATFORMS. EVERY CRIME STORY NOWADAYS IS COVERED FROM EVERY ANGLE.
I HAVEN'T READ THE BOOK OR HEARD THE PODCAST, BUT I DID SEE THE MOVIE!
THE FUNNY THING ABOUT THE WILD POPULARITY OF PODCASTS IS THAT THIS TECHNOLOGY AIN'T NEW! MAKES YOU WONDER... DID TRUE CRIME... RADIO EXIST?
YES, IT DID!
I FOUND THIS SHOW FROM CBS RADIO THAT AIRED FOR ONE YEAR, FROM 1953-'54.
1953! I WAS JUST THREE YEARS OLD!
CRIME CLASSICS
CREATED BY ELLIOTT LEWIS, AN EARLY MURDERINO.
IT WAS A HISTORICAL TRUE CRIME SERIES THAT TOLD THE STORIES OF FAMOUS MURDERS IN A PLAY-LIKE FORMAT, WITH ACTORS DOING RE-ENACTMENTS AND A HOST WITH A FAKE NAME. THE RADIO PROGRAM, THOUGH SHORT-LIVED, COVERED STORIES RANGING FROM LINCOLN'S ASSASSINATION TO BATHSHEBA SPOONER, THE FIRST WOMAN TO BE EXECUTED FOR MURDER IN THE UNITED STATES.
GOOD EVENING, THIS IS *CRIME CLASSICS*... I AM THOMAS HYLAND. LISTEN... THE YEAR IS 1778...
HILARY.

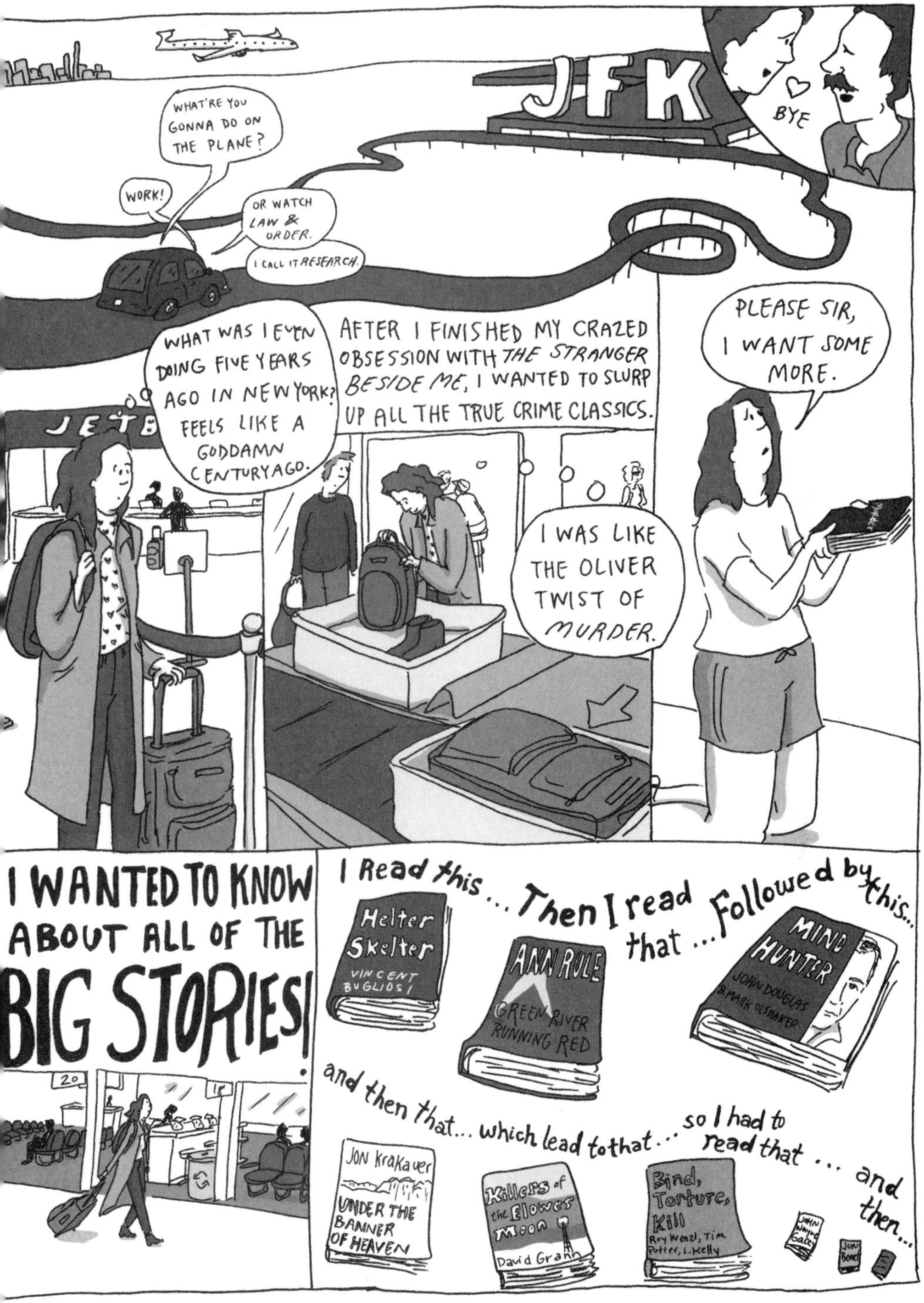

JFK
BYE
WHAT'RE YOU GONNA DO ON THE PLANE?
WORK!
OR WATCH LAW & ORDER.
I CALL IT RESEARCH.
WHAT WAS I EVEN DOING FIVE YEARS AGO IN NEW YORK? FEELS LIKE A GODDAMN CENTURY AGO.
AFTER I FINISHED MY CRAZED OBSESSION WITH THE STRANGER BESIDE ME, I WANTED TO SLURP UP ALL THE TRUE CRIME CLASSICS.
I WAS LIKE THE OLIVER TWIST OF MURDER.
PLEASE SIR, I WANT SOME MORE.
I WANTED TO KNOW ABOUT ALL OF THE BIG STORIES!
I Read this... Then I read that... Followed by this...
Helter Skelter
VINCENT BUGLIOSI
ANN RULE
GREEN RIVER RUNNING RED
MIND HUNTER
JOHN DOUGLAS & MARK OLSHAKER
and then that... which lead to that... so I had to read that... and then...
JON Krakauer
UNDER THE BANNER OF HEAVEN
Killers of the Flower Moon
David Grann
Bind, Torture, Kill
Roy Wenzl, Tim Potter, L. Kelly

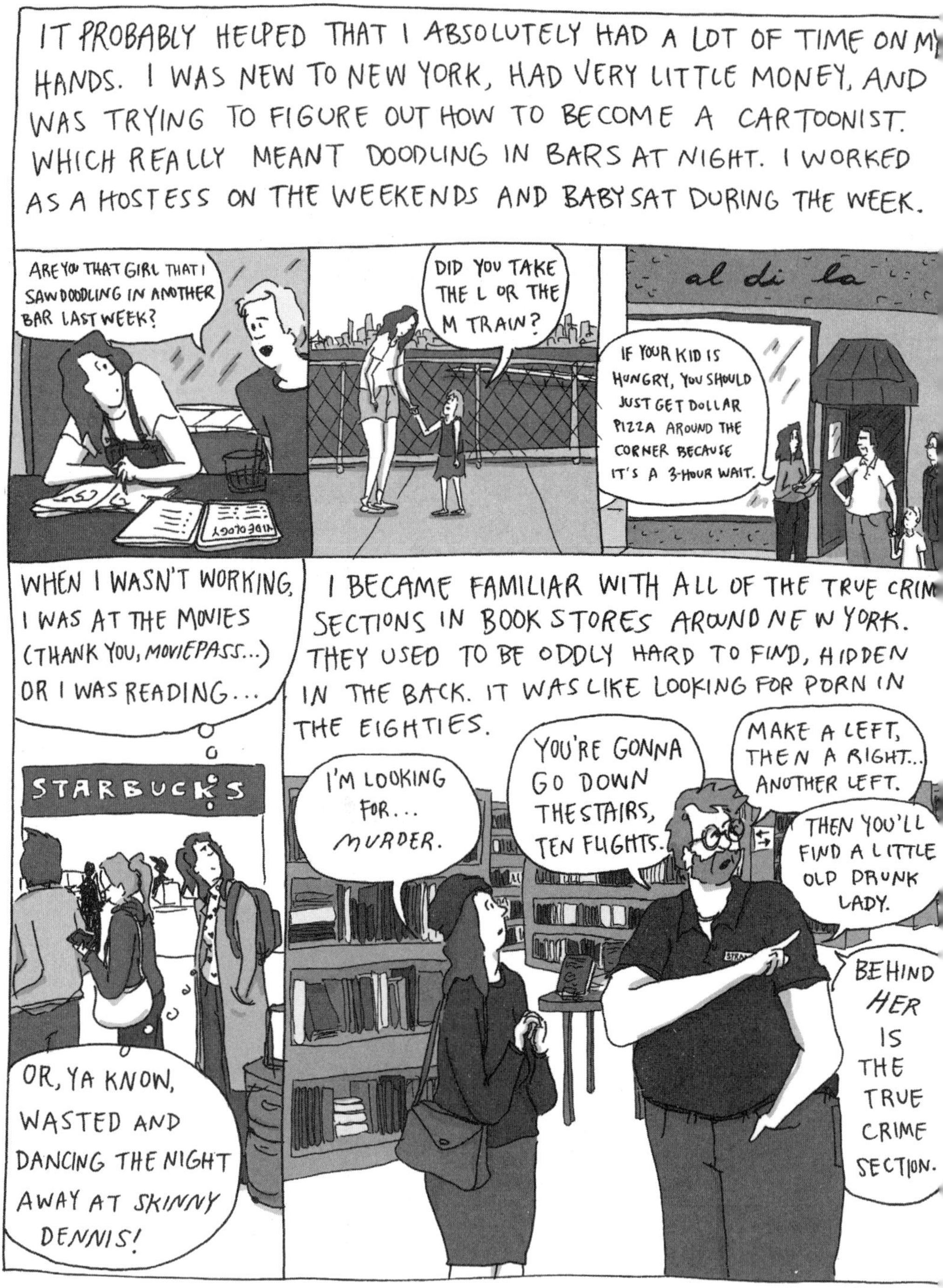
IT PROBABLY HELPED THAT I ABSOLUTELY HAD A LOT OF TIME ON MY HANDS. I WAS NEW TO NEW YORK, HAD VERY LITTLE MONEY, AND WAS TRYING TO FIGURE OUT HOW TO BECOME A CARTOONIST. WHICH REALLY MEANT DOODLING IN BARS AT NIGHT. I WORKED AS A HOSTESS ON THE WEEKENDS AND BABYSAT DURING THE WEEK.
ARE YOU THAT GIRL THAT I SAW DOODLING IN ANOTHER BAR LAST WEEK?
DID YOU TAKE THE L OR THE M TRAIN?
al di la
IF YOUR KID IS HUNGRY, YOU SHOULD JUST GET DOLLAR PIZZA AROUND THE CORNER BECAUSE IT'S A 3-HOUR WAIT.
WHEN I WASN'T WORKING, I WAS AT THE MOVIES (THANK YOU, MOVIEPASS...) OR I WAS READING...
STARBUCKS
OR, YA KNOW, WASTED AND DANCING THE NIGHT AWAY AT SKINNY DENNIS!
I BECAME FAMILIAR WITH ALL OF THE TRUE CRIME SECTIONS IN BOOK STORES AROUND NEW YORK. THEY USED TO BE ODDLY HARD TO FIND, HIDDEN IN THE BACK. IT WAS LIKE LOOKING FOR PORN IN THE EIGHTIES.
I'M LOOKING FOR... MURDER.
YOU'RE GONNA GO DOWN THE STAIRS, TEN FLIGHTS.
MAKE A LEFT, THEN A RIGHT... ANOTHER LEFT.
THEN YOU'LL FIND A LITTLE OLD DRUNK LADY.
BEHIND HER IS THE TRUE CRIME SECTION.

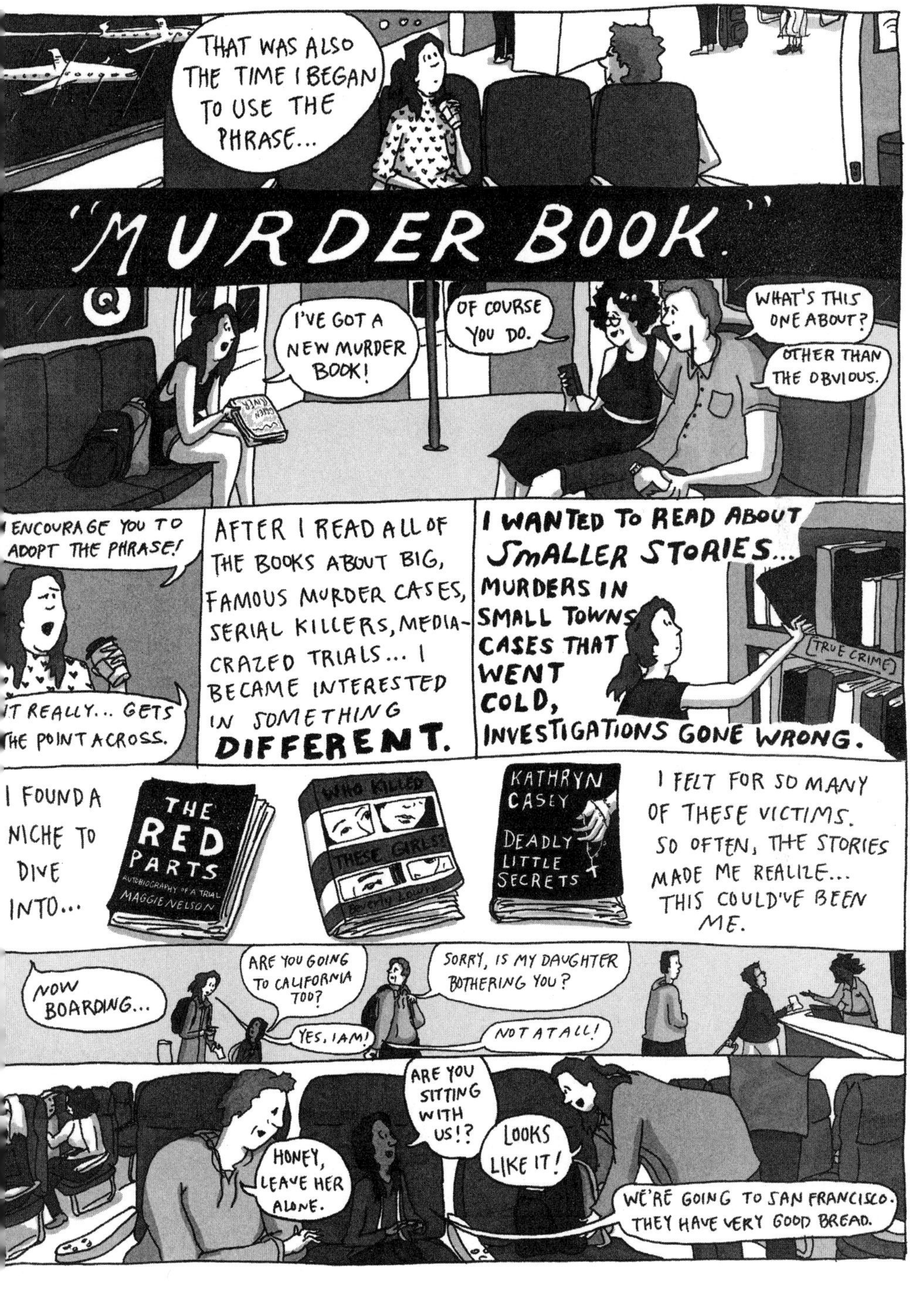
THAT WAS ALSO THE TIME I BEGAN TO USE THE PHRASE...
"MURDER BOOK."
I'VE GOT A NEW MURDER BOOK!
OF COURSE YOU DO.
WHAT'S THIS ONE ABOUT?
OTHER THAN THE OBVIOUS.
I ENCOURAGE YOU TO ADOPT THE PHRASE!
IT REALLY... GETS THE POINT ACROSS.
AFTER I READ ALL OF THE BOOKS ABOUT BIG, FAMOUS MURDER CASES, SERIAL KILLERS, MEDIA-CRAZED TRIALS... I BECAME INTERESTED IN SOMETHING DIFFERENT.
I WANTED TO READ ABOUT SMALLER STORIES... MURDERS IN SMALL TOWNS, CASES THAT WENT COLD, INVESTIGATIONS GONE WRONG.
TRUE CRIME
I FOUND A NICHE TO DIVE INTO...
THE RED PARTS
AUTOBIOGRAPHY OF A TRIAL
MAGGIE NELSON
WHO KILLED THESE GIRLS?
Beverly Lowry
KATHRYN CASEY
DEADLY LITTLE SECRETS
I FELT FOR SO MANY OF THESE VICTIMS. SO OFTEN, THE STORIES MADE ME REALIZE... THIS COULD'VE BEEN ME.
NOW BOARDING...
ARE YOU GOING TO CALIFORNIA TOO?
YES, I AM!
SORRY, IS MY DAUGHTER BOTHERING YOU?
NOT AT ALL!
ARE YOU SITTING WITH US!?
HONEY, LEAVE HER ALONE.
LOOKS LIKE IT!
WE'RE GOING TO SAN FRANCISCO. THEY HAVE VERY GOOD BREAD.

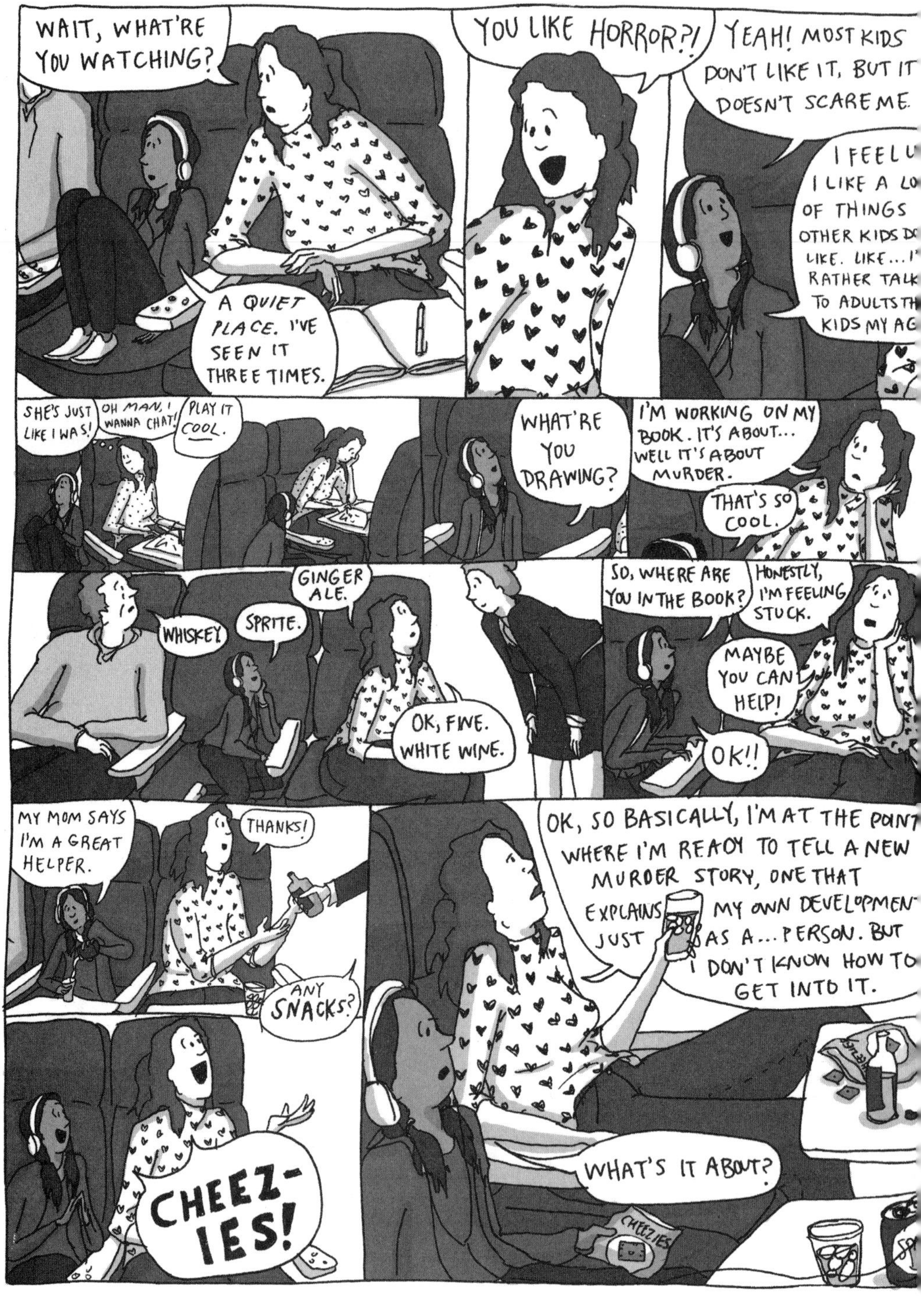
WAIT, WHAT'RE YOU WATCHING?
A QUIET PLACE. I'VE SEEN IT THREE TIMES.
YOU LIKE HORROR?!
YEAH! MOST KIDS DON'T LIKE IT, BUT IT DOESN'T SCARE ME.
I FEEL L
I LIKE A LO
OF THINGS
OTHER KIDS D
LIKE. LIKE... I'
RATHER TALK
TO ADULTS TH
KIDS MY AG
SHE'S JUST LIKE I WAS!
OH MAN, I WANNA CHAT!
PLAY IT COOL.
WHAT'RE YOU DRAWING?
I'M WORKING ON MY BOOK. IT'S ABOUT... WELL IT'S ABOUT MURDER.
THAT'S SO COOL.
WHISKEY.
SPRITE.
GINGER ALE.
OK, FINE. WHITE WINE.
SO, WHERE ARE YOU IN THE BOOK?
HONESTLY, I'M FEELING STUCK.
MAYBE YOU CAN HELP!
OK!!
MY MOM SAYS I'M A GREAT HELPER.
THANKS!
ANY SNACKS?
CHEEZ-IES!
CHEEZIES
OK, SO BASICALLY, I'M AT THE POINT WHERE I'M READY TO TELL A NEW MURDER STORY, ONE THAT EXPLAINS MY OWN DEVELOPMEN JUST AS A... PERSON. BUT I DON'T KNOW HOW TO GET INTO IT.
WHAT'S IT ABOUT?

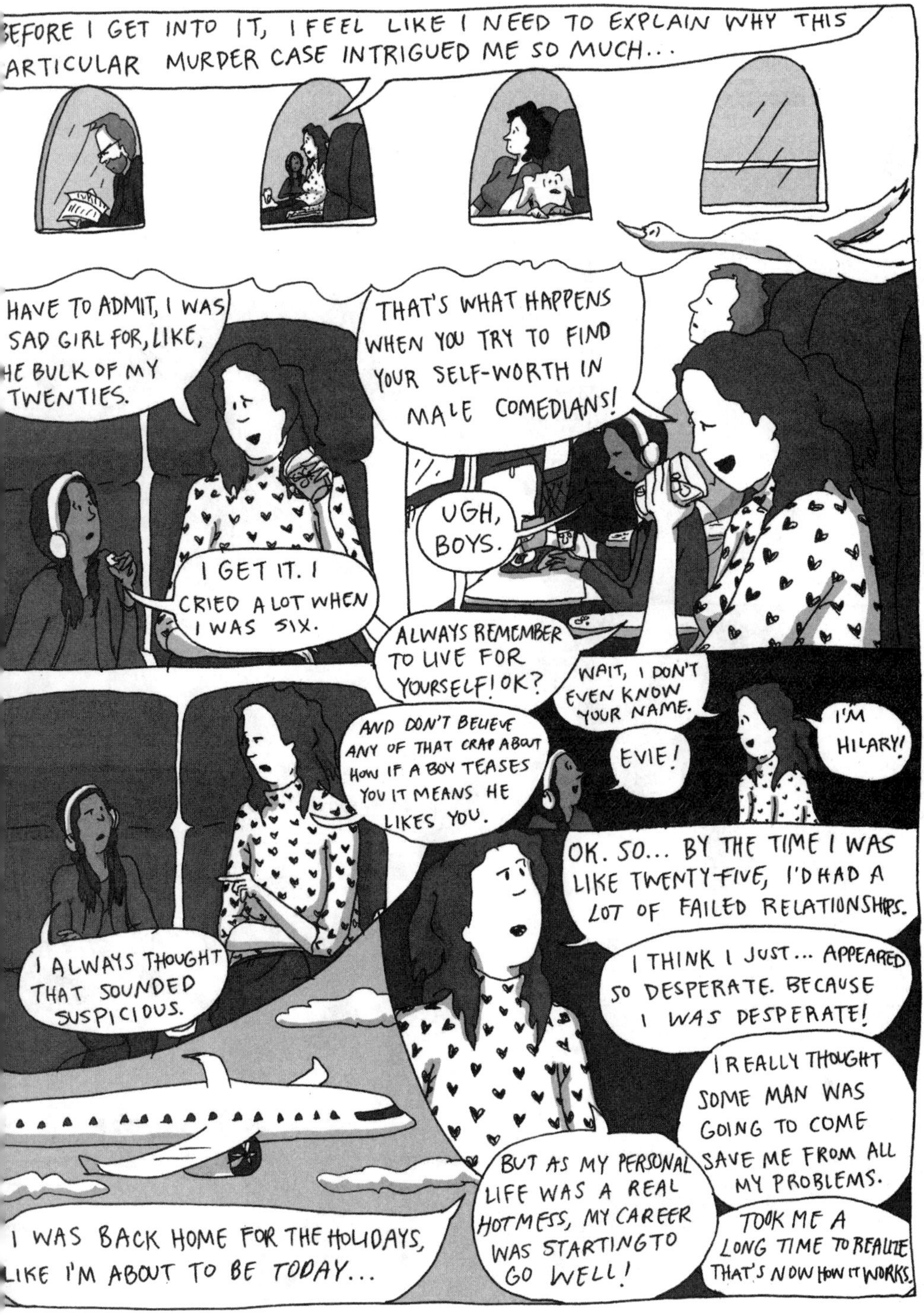

EFORE I GET INTO IT, I FEEL LIKE I NEED TO EXPLAIN WHY THIS ARTICULAR MURDER CASE INTRIGUED ME SO MUCH...
HAVE TO ADMIT, I WAS SAD GIRL FOR, LIKE, HE BULK OF MY TWENTIES.
I GET IT. I CRIED A LOT WHEN I WAS SIX.
THAT'S WHAT HAPPENS WHEN YOU TRY TO FIND YOUR SELF-WORTH IN MALE COMEDIANS!
UGH, BOYS.
ALWAYS REMEMBER TO LIVE FOR YOURSELF! OK?
AND DON'T BELIEVE ANY OF THAT CRAP ABOUT HOW IF A BOY TEASES YOU IT MEANS HE LIKES YOU.
I ALWAYS THOUGHT THAT SOUNDED SUSPICIOUS.
WAIT, I DON'T EVEN KNOW YOUR NAME.
EVIE!
I'M HILARY!
OK. SO... BY THE TIME I WAS LIKE TWENTY-FIVE, I'D HAD A LOT OF FAILED RELATIONSHIPS.
I THINK I JUST... APPEARED SO DESPERATE. BECAUSE I WAS DESPERATE!
I REALLY THOUGHT SOME MAN WAS GOING TO COME SAVE ME FROM ALL MY PROBLEMS.
TOOK ME A LONG TIME TO REALIZE THAT'S NOW HOW IT WORKS.
BUT AS MY PERSONAL LIFE WAS A REAL HOT MESS, MY CAREER WAS STARTING TO GO WELL!
I WAS BACK HOME FOR THE HOLIDAYS, LIKE I'M ABOUT TO BE TODAY...

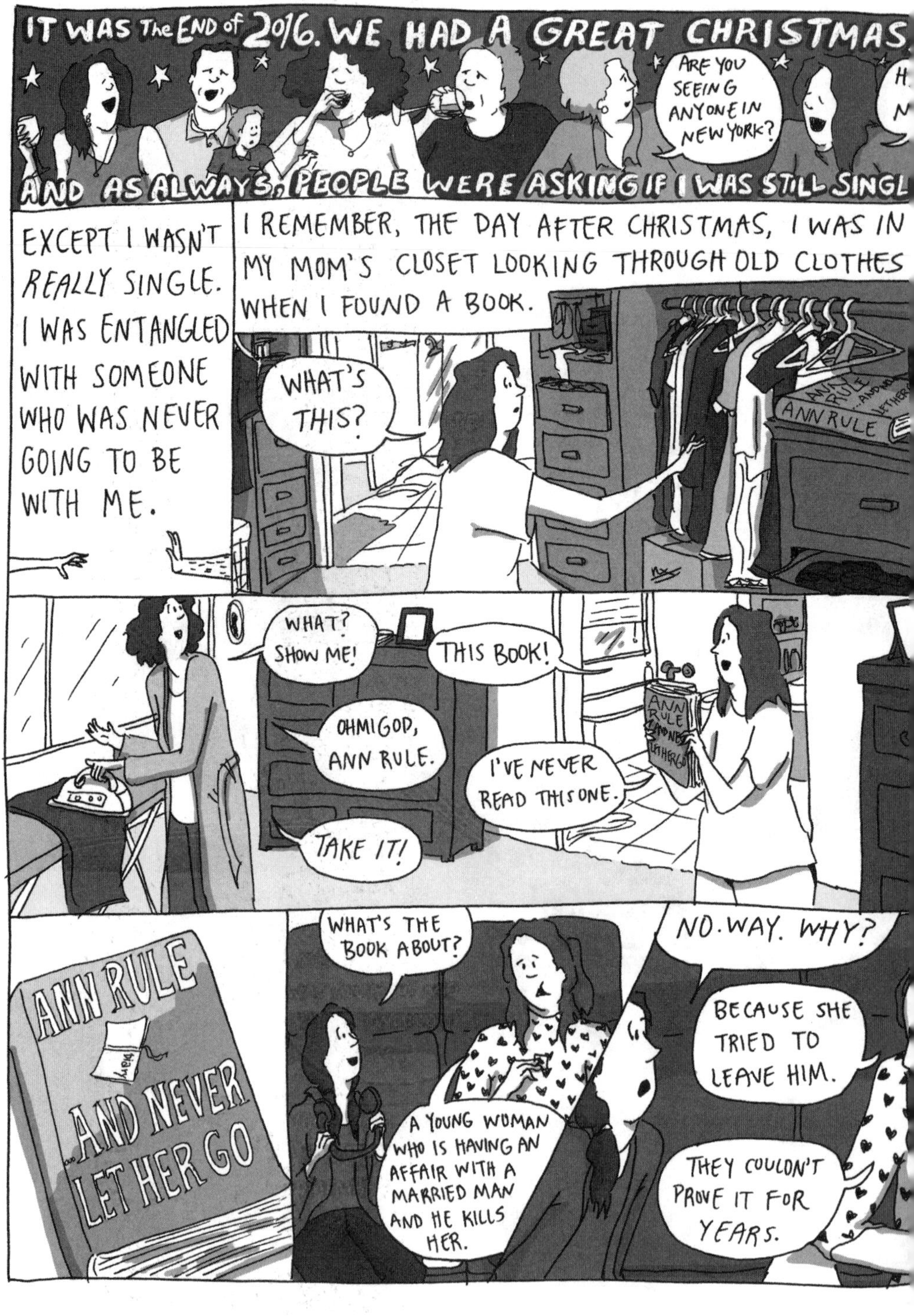
IT WAS THE END OF 2016. WE HAD A GREAT CHRISTMAS.
ARE YOU SEEING ANYONE IN NEW YORK?
AND AS ALWAYS, PEOPLE WERE ASKING IF I WAS STILL SINGL
EXCEPT I WASN'T REALLY SINGLE. I WAS ENTANGLED WITH SOMEONE WHO WAS NEVER GOING TO BE WITH ME.
I REMEMBER, THE DAY AFTER CHRISTMAS, I WAS IN MY MOM'S CLOSET LOOKING THROUGH OLD CLOTHES WHEN I FOUND A BOOK.
WHAT'S THIS?
ANN RULE
WHAT? SHOW ME!
THIS BOOK!
OHMIGOD, ANN RULE.
I'VE NEVER READ THIS ONE.
TAKE IT!
ANN RULE ...AND NEVER LET HER GO
WHAT'S THE BOOK ABOUT?
A YOUNG WOMAN WHO IS HAVING AN AFFAIR WITH A MARRIED MAN AND HE KILLS HER.
NO. WAY. WHY?
BECAUSE SHE TRIED TO LEAVE HIM.
THEY COULDN'T PROVE IT FOR YEARS.

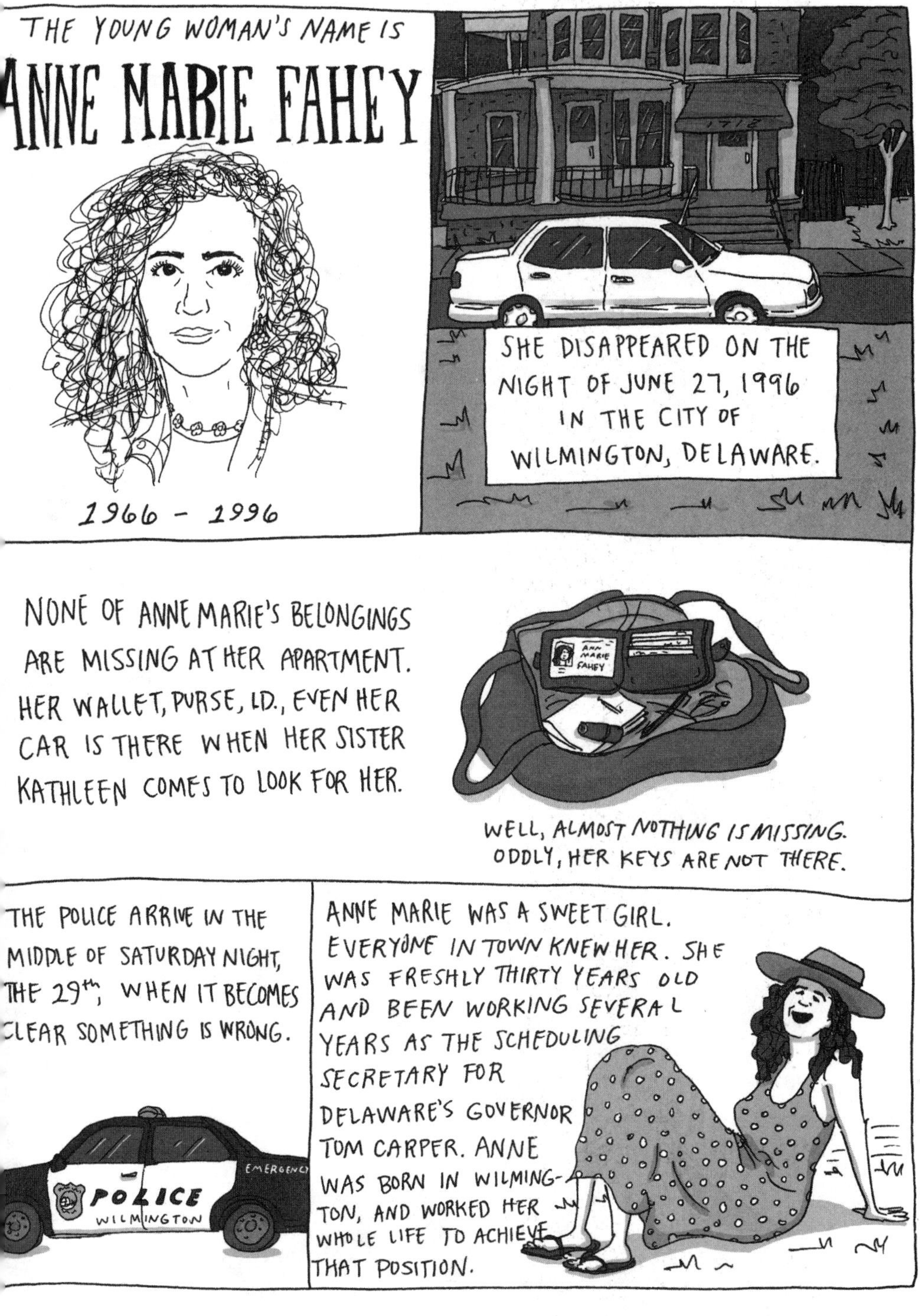
THE YOUNG WOMAN'S NAME IS
ANNE MARIE FAHEY
1966 - 1996
SHE DISAPPEARED ON THE NIGHT OF JUNE 27, 1996 IN THE CITY OF WILMINGTON, DELAWARE.
NONE OF ANNE MARIE'S BELONGINGS ARE MISSING AT HER APARTMENT. HER WALLET, PURSE, I.D., EVEN HER CAR IS THERE WHEN HER SISTER KATHLEEN COMES TO LOOK FOR HER.
ANN MARIE FAHEY
WELL, ALMOST NOTHING IS MISSING. ODDLY, HER KEYS ARE NOT THERE.
THE POLICE ARRIVE IN THE MIDDLE OF SATURDAY NIGHT, THE 29th, WHEN IT BECOMES CLEAR SOMETHING IS WRONG.
EMERGENCY
POLICE
WILMINGTON
ANNE MARIE WAS A SWEET GIRL. EVERYONE IN TOWN KNEW HER. SHE WAS FRESHLY THIRTY YEARS OLD AND BEEN WORKING SEVERAL YEARS AS THE SCHEDULING SECRETARY FOR DELAWARE'S GOVERNOR TOM CARPER. ANNE WAS BORN IN WILMINGTON, AND WORKED HER WHOLE LIFE TO ACHIEVE THAT POSITION.

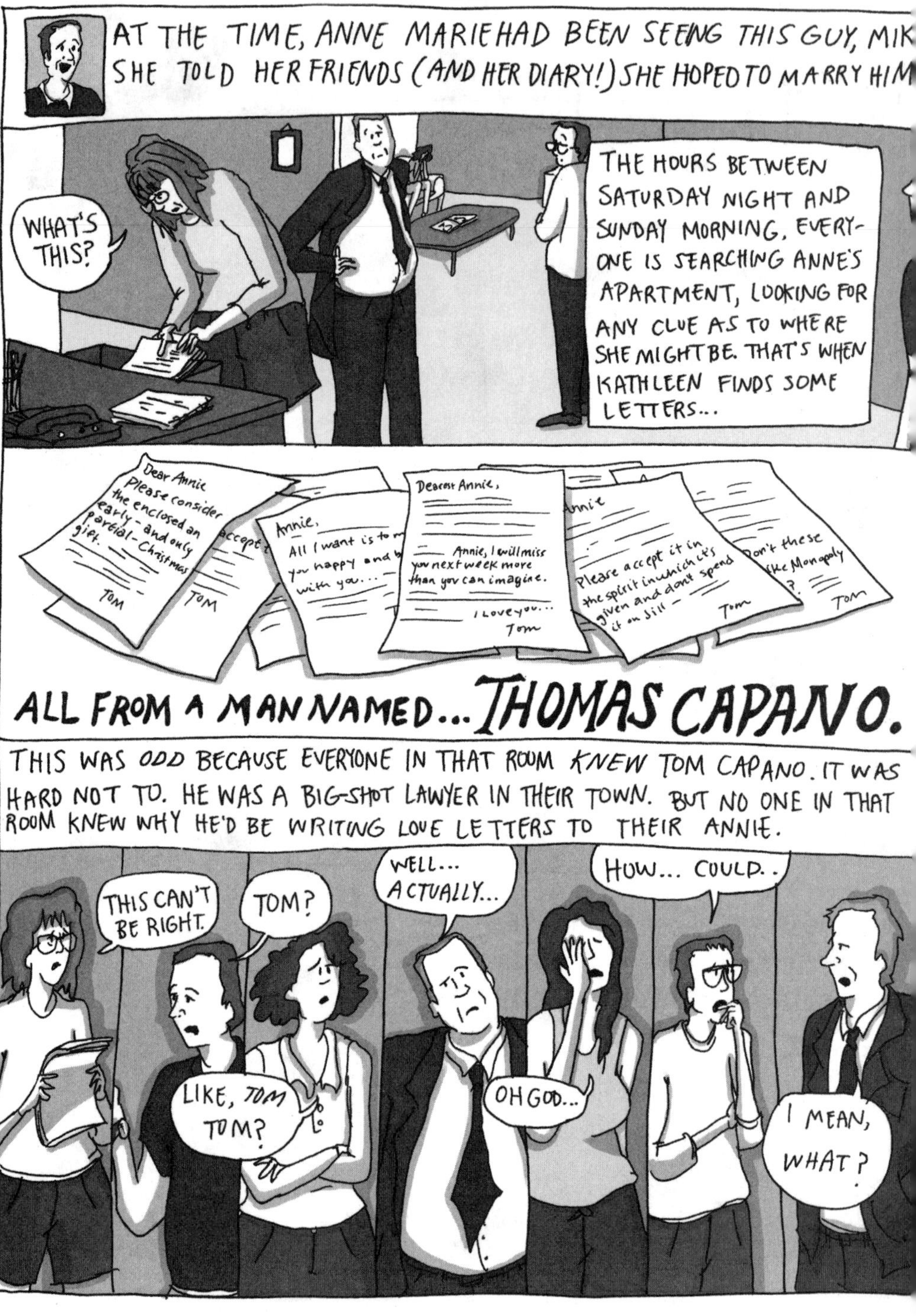

AT THE TIME, ANNE MARIEHAD BEEN SEEING THIS GUY, MIK
SHE TOLD HER FRIENDS (AND HER DIARY!) SHE HOPED TO MARRY HIM
WHAT'S THIS?
THE HOURS BETWEEN SATURDAY NIGHT AND SUNDAY MORNING, EVERYONE IS SEARCHING ANNE'S APARTMENT, LOOKING FOR ANY CLUE AS TO WHERE SHE MIGHT BE. THAT'S WHEN KATHLEEN FINDS SOME LETTERS...
Dear Annie
Please consider the enclosed an early - and only partial - Christmas gift.
TOM
TOM
Annie,
All I want is to
you happy and
with you...
Dearest Annie,
Annie, I will miss you next week more than you can imagine.
I Love you...
Tom
Please accept it in the spirit in which it's given and don't spend it on Jill -
Tom
Don't these
like Monopoly
TOM
ALL FROM A MAN NAMED... THOMAS CAPANO.
THIS WAS ODD BECAUSE EVERYONE IN THAT ROOM KNEW TOM CAPANO. IT WAS HARD NOT TO. HE WAS A BIG-SHOT LAWYER IN THEIR TOWN. BUT NO ONE IN THAT ROOM KNEW WHY HE'D BE WRITING LOVE LETTERS TO THEIR ANNIE.
THIS CAN'T BE RIGHT.
TOM?
LIKE, TOM TOM?
WELL... ACTUALLY...
OH GOD...
HOW... COULD..
I MEAN, WHAT?

TOM CAPANO WAS *MORE* THAN JUST A LAWYER IN TOWN. THE CAPANO FAMILY WAS A BIG DEAL IN WILMINGTON. THEY WERE WORTH MILLIONS WITH THEIR CONSTRUCTION AND REAL ESTATE BUSINESS FOUNDED BY THEIR FATHER. LOUIS SR. HAD BUILT THE WHOLE GODDAMN TOWN, FROM LUXURY HOMES TO APARTMENTS TO CITY BUILDINGS AND SHOPPING MALLS. THEY OWNED EVERYTHING.

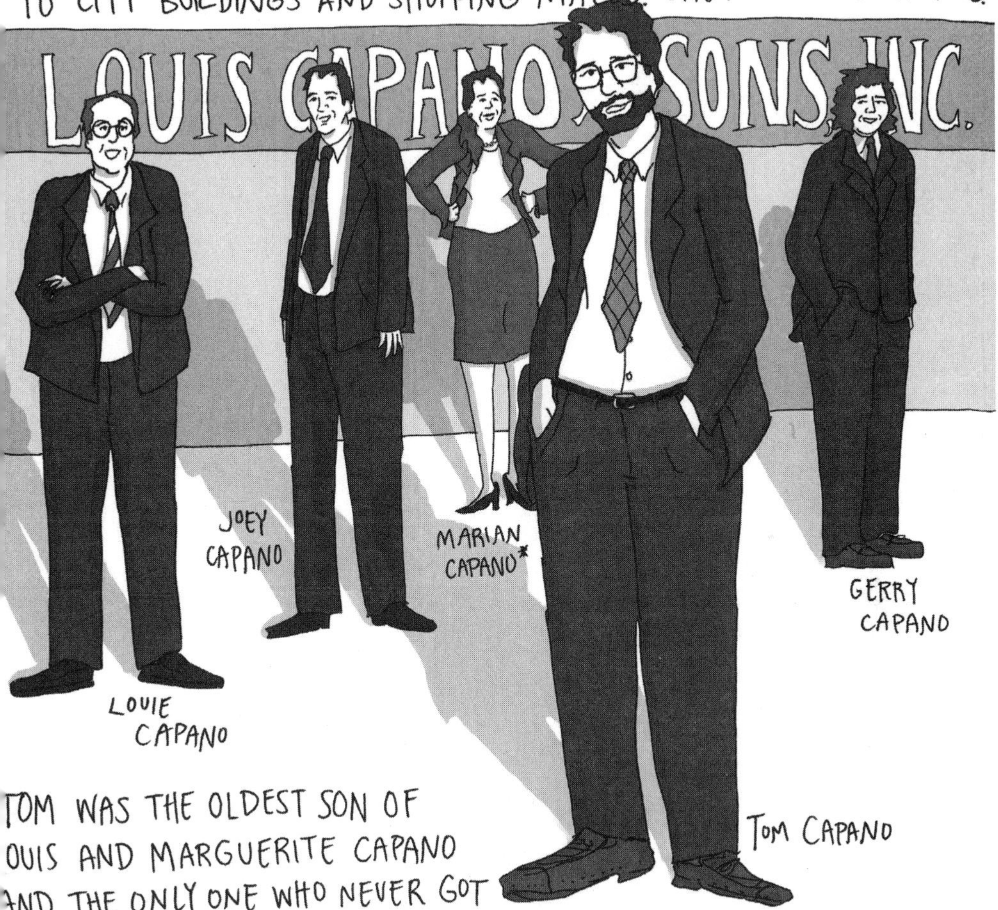

LOUIS CAPANO SONS, INC.
JOEY CAPANO
MARIAN CAPANO*
GERRY CAPANO
LOUIE CAPANO
TOM CAPANO

TOM WAS THE OLDEST SON OF OUIS AND MARGUERITE CAPANO AND THE ONLY ONE WHO NEVER GOT N TROUBLE WITH THE COPS. OVER THE YEARS, HE HELD POSITIONS LIKE HIEF OF STAFF FOR THE MAYOR, DELAWARE'S DEPUTY ATTORNEY ENERAL AND PARTNER AT A LOCAL PRIVATE FIRM. HE WAS ENTRENCHED IN LOCAL AND STATE POLITICS.

* THE DAUGHTER WAS COMPLETELY CUT OUT OF THE FAMILY FORTUNE FOR NOT BEING A MAN!!

THOUGH ANNE MARIE WAS ALSO BORN AND RAISED IN WILMINGTON, SHE HAD A VERY DIFFERENT UPBRINGING THAN TOM. ANNE WAS THE YOUNGE OF SIX CHILDREN. WHEN THEIR MOTHER DIED OF LUNG CANCER IN 1975 SHE WAS ONLY NINE YEARS OLD. THEIR FATHER WAS A MESS AFTER AND FELL TO ALCOHOLISM. HE STOPPED WORKING AND COMPLETELY GAVE UP ON RAISING THE KIDS. MOST OF THE SIBLINGS WERE ALREADY OLD ENOUGH TO FEND FOR THEMSELVES, BUT LITTLE ANNIE WAS SO YOUNG AND WAS SUBJECTED TO THE TERRORS OF HER DAD'S DISEASE.

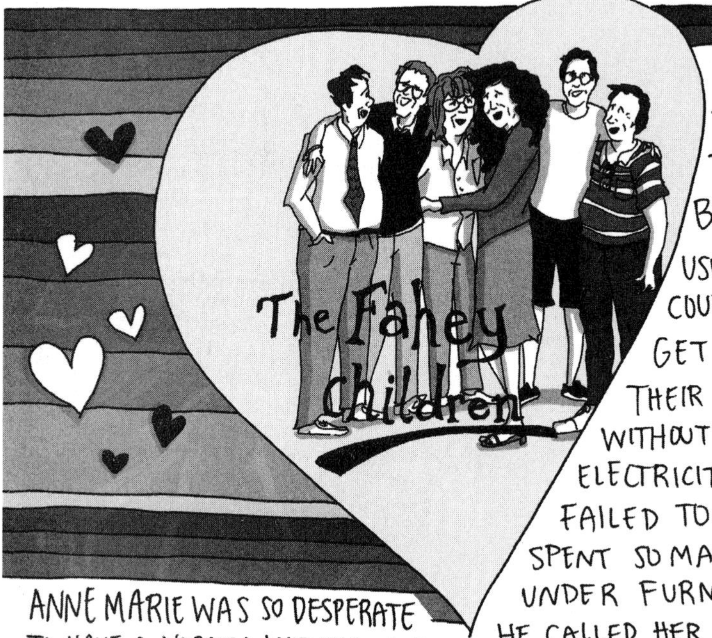
The Fahey Children

HER SIBLINGS TRIED TO PROTECT HER, BUT THEY COULDN'T ALWAYS BE THERE. ANNE MARIE USUALLY HAD NOT EVEN A COUPLE OF DOLLARS TO GET HERSELF SOME FOOD. THEIR HOUSE OFTEN WENT WITHOUT RUNNING WATER OR ELECTRICITY BECAUSE HER DAD FAILED TO PAY THE BILLS. SHE SPENT SO MANY NIGHTS HIDING UNDER FURNITURE TO ESCAPE HIM. HE CALLED HER NAMES LIKE UGLY AND FAT... ANYTHING HE COULD DO TO RIDICULE HER.

ANNE MARIE WAS SO DESPERATE TO HAVE A NORMAL LIFE THAT SHE NEVER LET ON AT SCHOOL WHAT WAS HAPPENING AT HOME. SHE GOT REALLY GOOD AT PUTTING A SMILE ON HER FACE. SOMEHOW, SHE MADE IT THROUGH AND WENT OFF TO COLLEGE, WHERE SHE THOUGHT SHE MIGHT FINALLY BE HAPPY AND FREE.

THE FAHEY CHILDREN HAD A STRONG BOND BECAUSE THEY SURVIVED HELL TOGETHER. IN SO MANY WAYS, THEY WERE ALL EACH OTHER HAD!

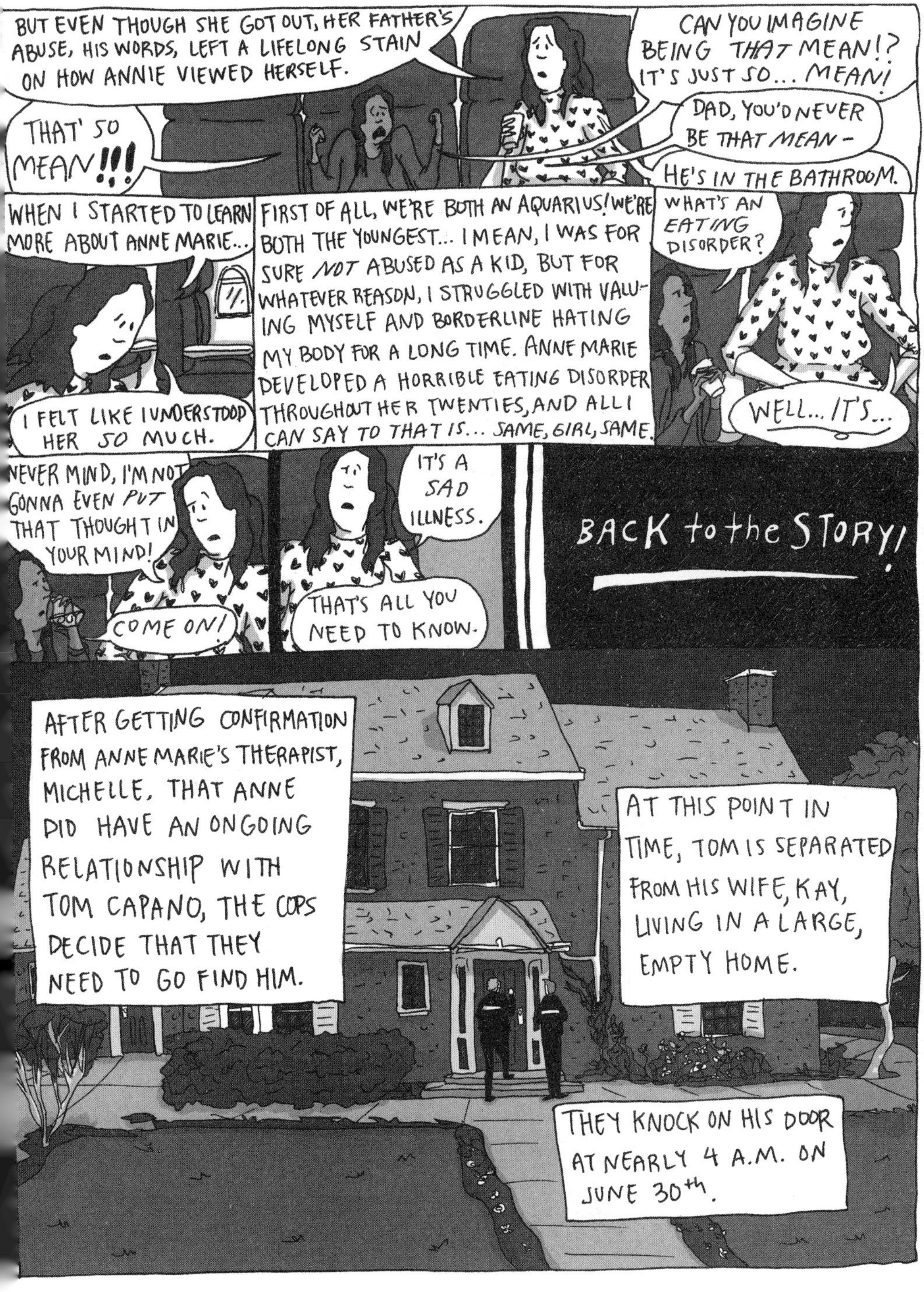
BUT EVEN THOUGH SHE GOT OUT, HER FATHER'S ABUSE, HIS WORDS, LEFT A LIFELONG STAIN ON HOW ANNIE VIEWED HERSELF.
CAN YOU IMAGINE BEING THAT MEAN!? IT'S JUST SO... MEAN!
THAT' SO MEAN!!!
DAD, YOU'D NEVER BE THAT MEAN -
HE'S IN THE BATHROOM.
WHEN I STARTED TO LEARN MORE ABOUT ANNE MARIE...
I FELT LIKE I UNDERSTOOD HER SO MUCH.
FIRST OF ALL, WE'RE BOTH AN AQUARIUS! WE'RE BOTH THE YOUNGEST... I MEAN, I WAS FOR SURE NOT ABUSED AS A KID, BUT FOR WHATEVER REASON, I STRUGGLED WITH VALUING MYSELF AND BORDERLINE HATING MY BODY FOR A LONG TIME. ANNE MARIE DEVELOPED A HORRIBLE EATING DISORDER THROUGHOUT HER TWENTIES, AND ALL I CAN SAY TO THAT IS... SAME, GIRL, SAME.
WHAT'S AN EATING DISORDER?
WELL... IT'S...
NEVER MIND, I'M NOT GONNA EVEN PUT THAT THOUGHT IN YOUR MIND!
COME ON!
IT'S A SAD ILLNESS.
THAT'S ALL YOU NEED TO KNOW.
BACK to the STORY!
AFTER GETTING CONFIRMATION FROM ANNE MARIE'S THERAPIST, MICHELLE, THAT ANNE DID HAVE AN ONGOING RELATIONSHIP WITH TOM CAPANO, THE COPS DECIDE THAT THEY NEED TO GO FIND HIM.
AT THIS POINT IN TIME, TOM IS SEPARATED FROM HIS WIFE, KAY, LIVING IN A LARGE, EMPTY HOME.
THEY KNOCK ON HIS DOOR AT NEARLY 4 A.M. ON JUNE 30th.

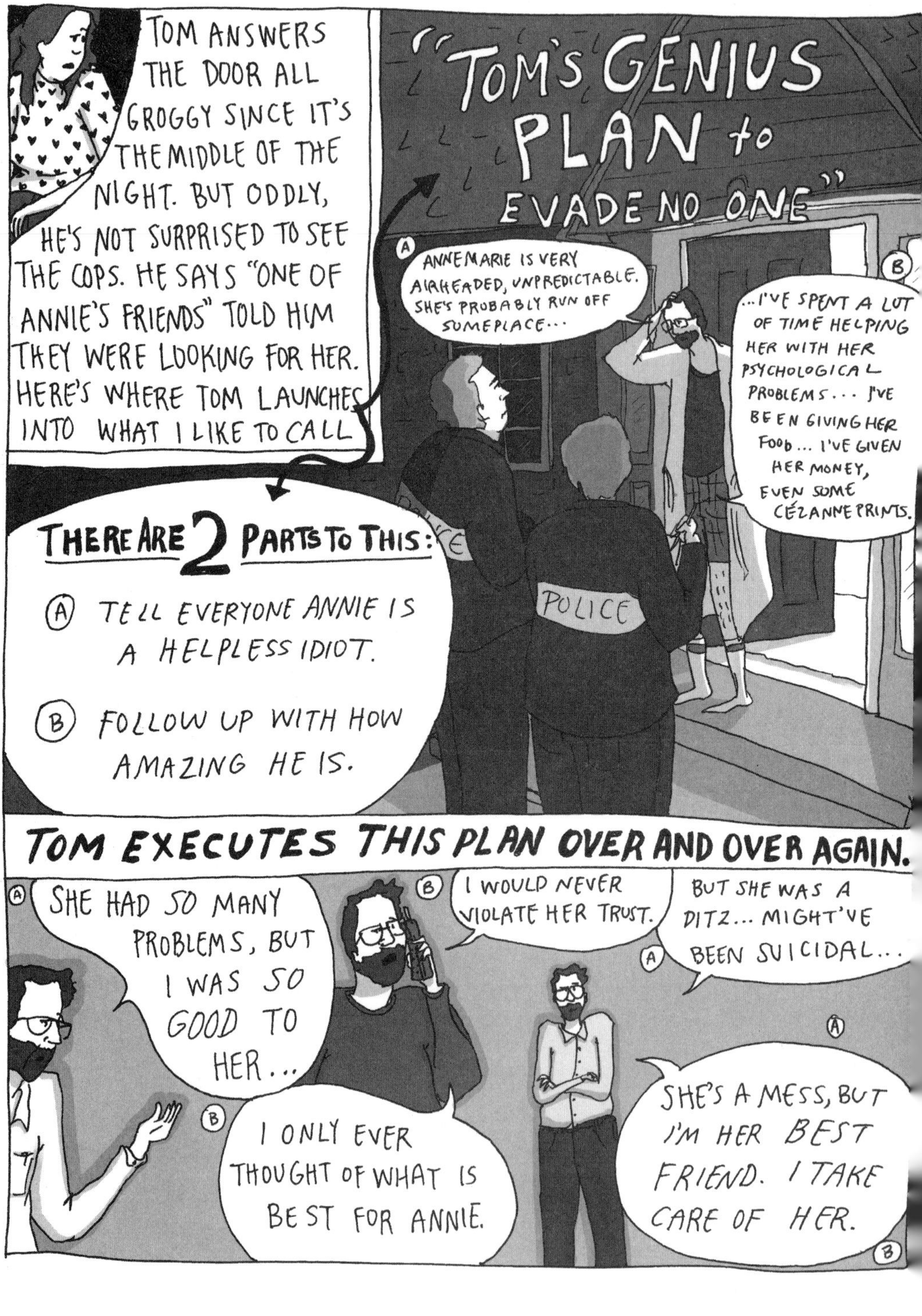
TOM ANSWERS THE DOOR ALL GROGGY SINCE IT'S THE MIDDLE OF THE NIGHT. BUT ODDLY, HE'S NOT SURPRISED TO SEE THE COPS. HE SAYS "ONE OF ANNIE'S FRIENDS" TOLD HIM THEY WERE LOOKING FOR HER. HERE'S WHERE TOM LAUNCHES INTO WHAT I LIKE TO CALL
"TOM'S GENIUS PLAN to EVADE NO ONE"
A
ANNEMARIE IS VERY AIRHEADED, UNPREDICTABLE. SHE'S PROBABLY RUN OFF SOMEPLACE...
B
...I'VE SPENT A LOT OF TIME HELPING HER WITH HER PSYCHOLOGICAL PROBLEMS... I'VE BEEN GIVING HER FOOD... I'VE GIVEN HER MONEY, EVEN SOME CÉZANNE PRINTS.
THERE ARE 2 PARTS TO THIS:
(A) TELL EVERYONE ANNIE IS A HELPLESS IDIOT.
(B) FOLLOW UP WITH HOW AMAZING HE IS.
POLICE
POLICE
TOM EXECUTES THIS PLAN OVER AND OVER AGAIN.
A
SHE HAD SO MANY PROBLEMS, BUT I WAS SO GOOD TO HER...
B
I ONLY EVER THOUGHT OF WHAT IS BEST FOR ANNIE.
B
I WOULD NEVER VIOLATE HER TRUST.
A
BUT SHE WAS A DITZ... MIGHT'VE BEEN SUICIDAL...
A
SHE'S A MESS, BUT I'M HER BEST FRIEND. I TAKE CARE OF HER.
B

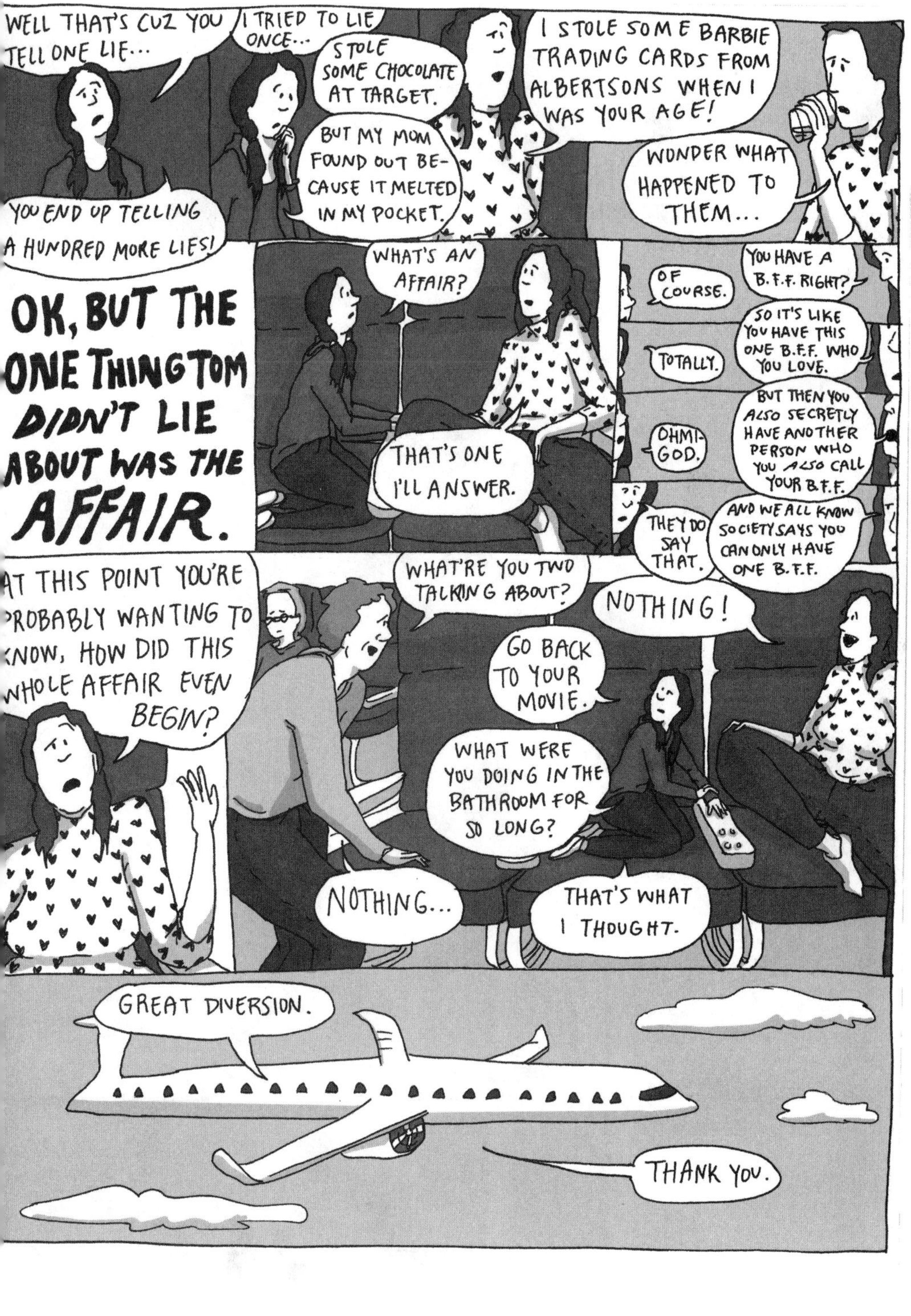
WELL THAT'S CUZ YOU TELL ONE LIE...
YOU END UP TELLING A HUNDRED MORE LIES!
I TRIED TO LIE ONCE...
STOLE SOME CHOCOLATE AT TARGET.
BUT MY MOM FOUND OUT BE-CAUSE IT MELTED IN MY POCKET.
I STOLE SOME BARBIE TRADING CARDS FROM ALBERTSONS WHEN I WAS YOUR AGE!
WONDER WHAT HAPPENED TO THEM...
OK, BUT THE ONE THING TOM DIDN'T LIE ABOUT WAS THE AFFAIR.
WHAT'S AN AFFAIR?
THAT'S ONE I'LL ANSWER.
YOU HAVE A B.F.F. RIGHT?
OF COURSE.
SO IT'S LIKE YOU HAVE THIS ONE B.F.F. WHO YOU LOVE.
TOTALLY.
BUT THEN YOU ALSO SECRETLY HAVE ANOTHER PERSON WHO YOU ALSO CALL YOUR B.F.F.
OHMI-GOD.
AND WE ALL KNOW SOCIETY SAYS YOU CAN ONLY HAVE ONE B.F.F.
THEY DO SAY THAT.
AT THIS POINT YOU'RE PROBABLY WANTING TO KNOW, HOW DID THIS WHOLE AFFAIR EVEN BEGIN?
WHAT'RE YOU TWO TALKING ABOUT?
NOTHING!
GO BACK TO YOUR MOVIE.
WHAT WERE YOU DOING IN THE BATHROOM FOR SO LONG?
NOTHING...
THAT'S WHAT I THOUGHT.
GREAT DIVERSION.
THANK YOU.

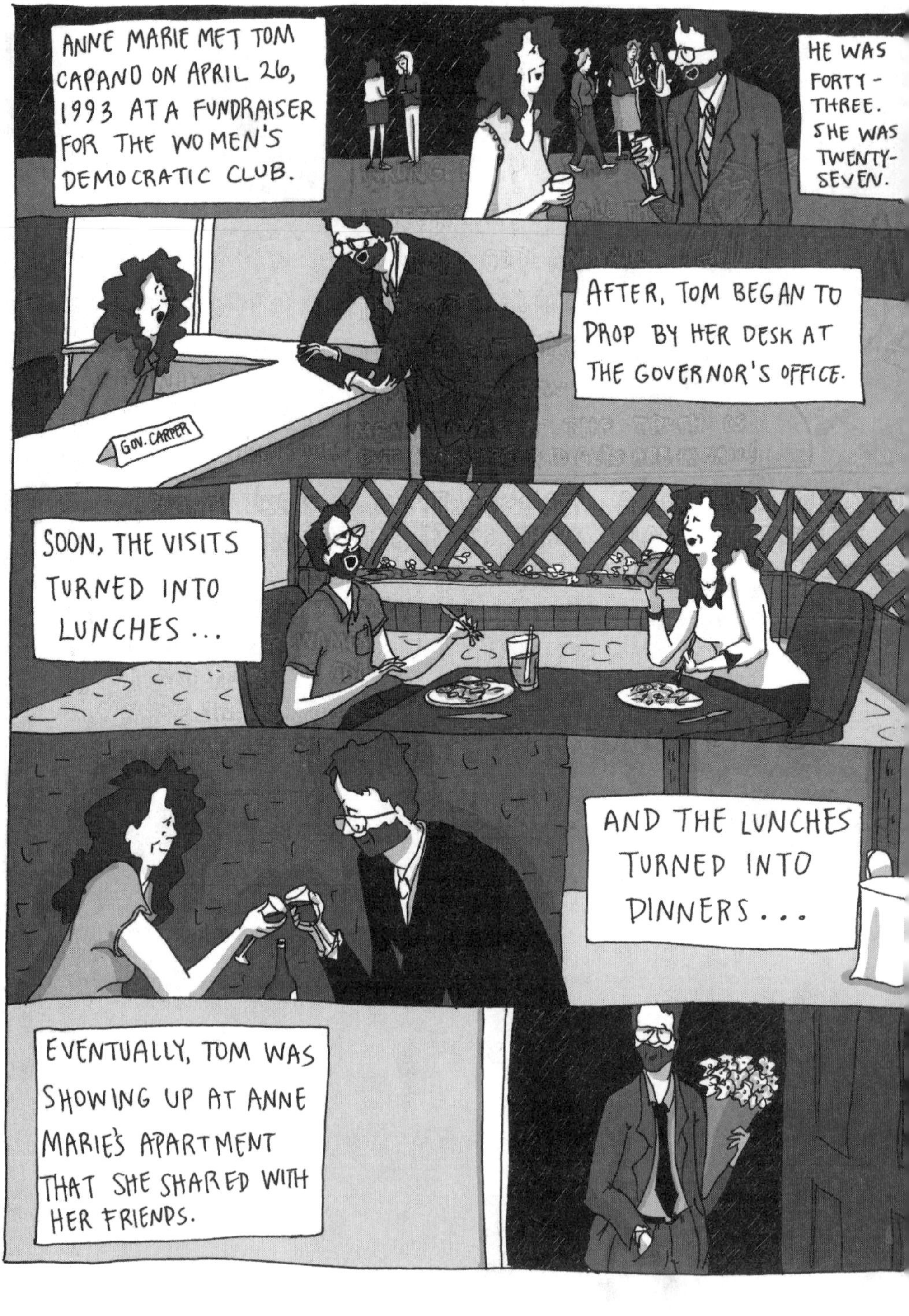
ANNE MARIE MET TOM CAPANO ON APRIL 26, 1993 AT A FUNDRAISER FOR THE WOMEN'S DEMOCRATIC CLUB.
HE WAS FORTY-THREE. SHE WAS TWENTY-SEVEN.
GOV. CARPER
AFTER, TOM BEGAN TO DROP BY HER DESK AT THE GOVERNOR'S OFFICE.
SOON, THE VISITS TURNED INTO LUNCHES...
AND THE LUNCHES TURNED INTO DINNERS...
EVENTUALLY, TOM WAS SHOWING UP AT ANNE MARIE'S APARTMENT THAT SHE SHARED WITH HER FRIENDS.

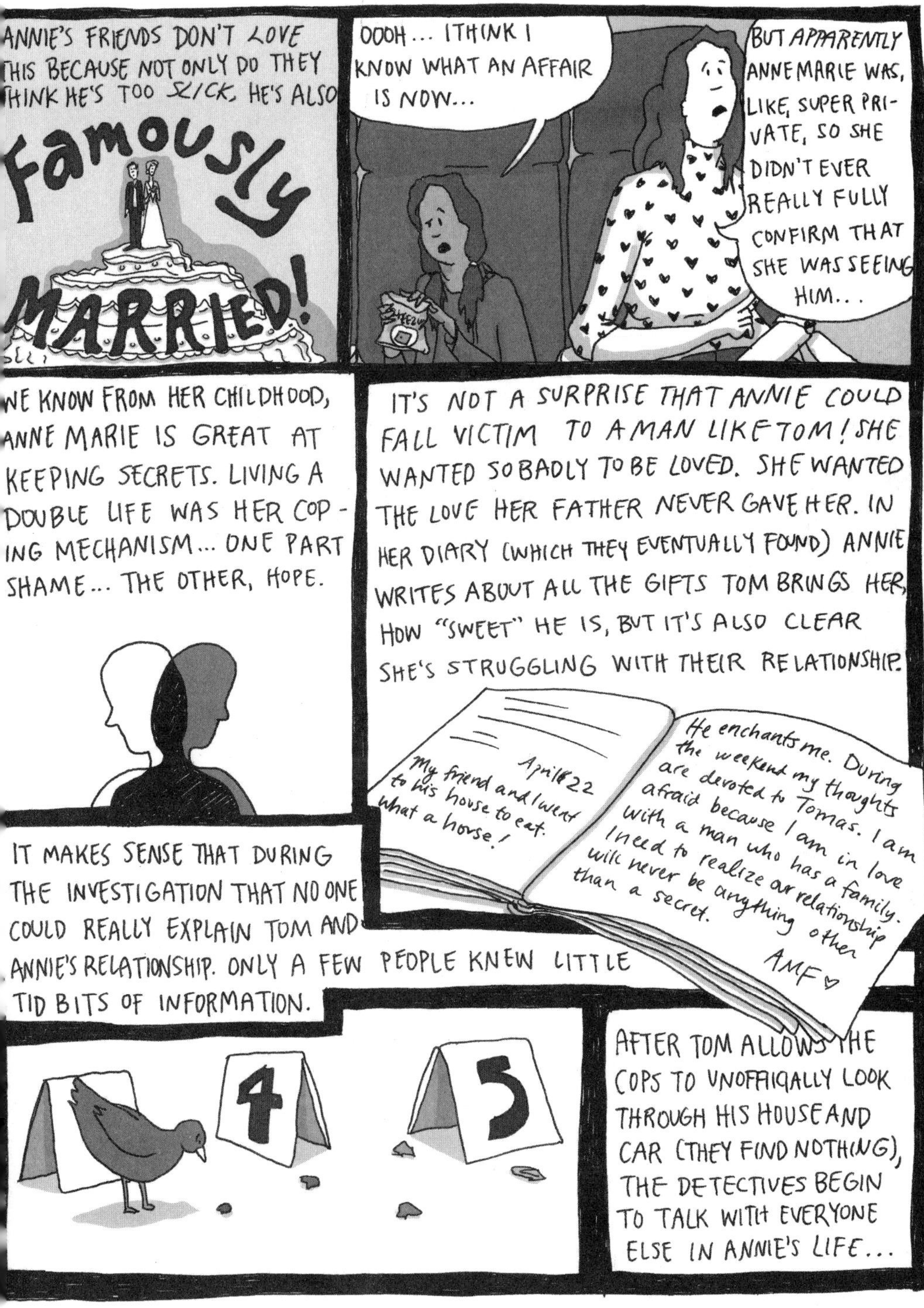
ANNIE'S FRIENDS DON'T LOVE THIS BECAUSE NOT ONLY DO THEY THINK HE'S TOO SLICK, HE'S ALSO
FAMOUSLY MARRIED!
OOOH... I THINK I KNOW WHAT AN AFFAIR IS NOW...
BUT APPARENTLY ANNEMARIE WAS, LIKE, SUPER PRIVATE, SO SHE DIDN'T EVER REALLY FULLY CONFIRM THAT SHE WAS SEEING HIM...
WE KNOW FROM HER CHILDHOOD, ANNE MARIE IS GREAT AT KEEPING SECRETS. LIVING A DOUBLE LIFE WAS HER COPING MECHANISM... ONE PART SHAME... THE OTHER, HOPE.
IT'S NOT A SURPRISE THAT ANNIE COULD FALL VICTIM TO A MAN LIKE TOM! SHE WANTED SO BADLY TO BE LOVED. SHE WANTED THE LOVE HER FATHER NEVER GAVE HER. IN HER DIARY (WHICH THEY EVENTUALLY FOUND) ANNIE WRITES ABOUT ALL THE GIFTS TOM BRINGS HER, HOW "SWEET" HE IS, BUT IT'S ALSO CLEAR SHE'S STRUGGLING WITH THEIR RELATIONSHIP.
April 22
My friend and I went to his house to eat. What a horse!
He enchants me. During the weekend my thoughts are devoted to Tomas. I am afraid because I am in love with a man who has a family. I need to realize our relationship will never be anything other than a secret.
AMF ♡
IT MAKES SENSE THAT DURING THE INVESTIGATION THAT NO ONE COULD REALLY EXPLAIN TOM AND ANNIE'S RELATIONSHIP. ONLY A FEW PEOPLE KNEW LITTLE TID BITS OF INFORMATION.
4
5
AFTER TOM ALLOWS THE COPS TO UNOFFICIALLY LOOK THROUGH HIS HOUSE AND CAR (THEY FIND NOTHING), THE DETECTIVES BEGIN TO TALK WITH EVERYONE ELSE IN ANNIE'S LIFE...

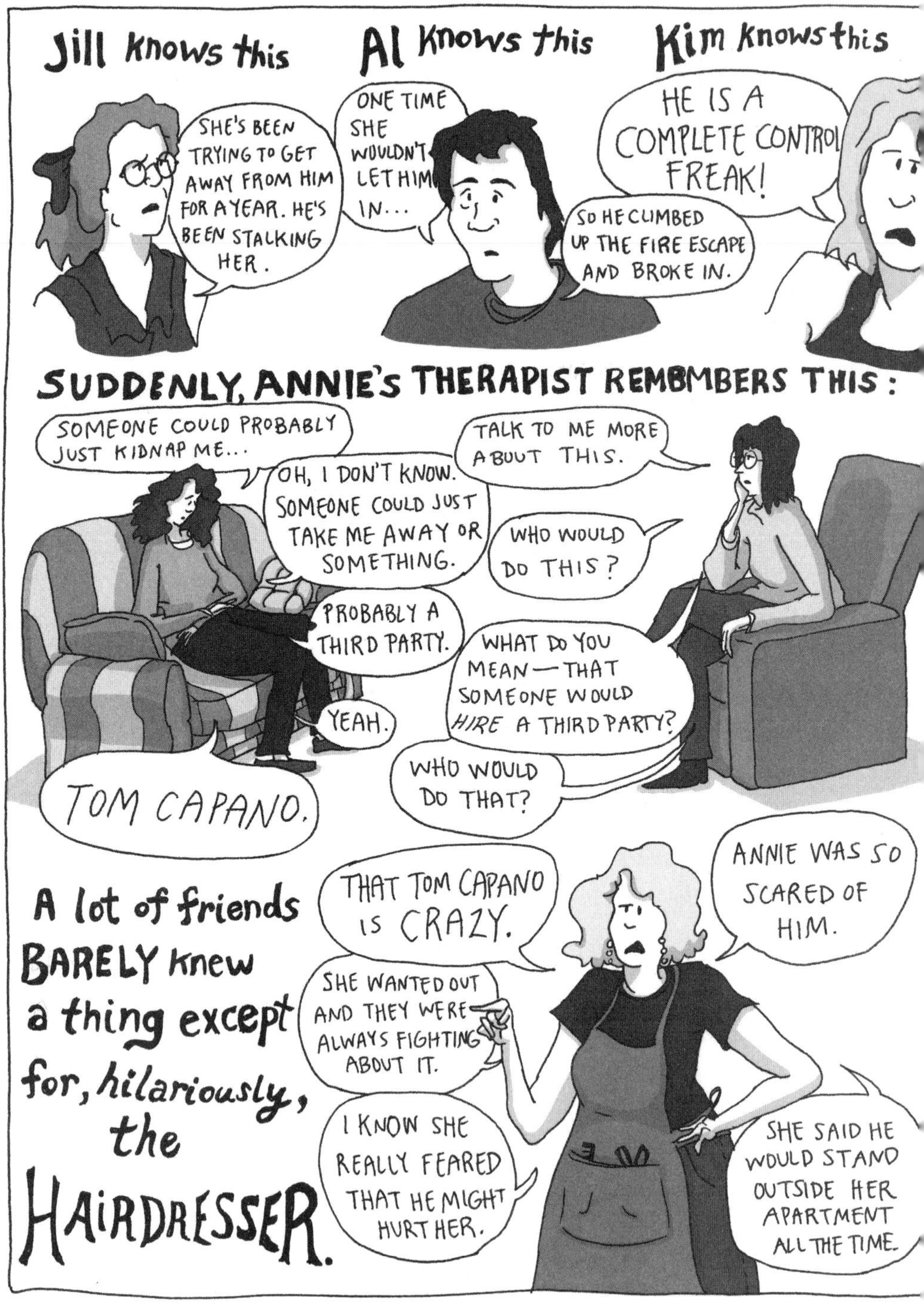
Jill knows this
SHE'S BEEN TRYING TO GET AWAY FROM HIM FOR A YEAR. HE'S BEEN STALKING HER.
Al knows this
ONE TIME SHE WOULDN'T LET HIM IN...
SO HE CLIMBED UP THE FIRE ESCAPE AND BROKE IN.
Kim knows this
HE IS A COMPLETE CONTROL FREAK!
SUDDENLY, ANNIE'S THERAPIST REMBMBERS THIS:
SOMEONE COULD PROBABLY JUST KIDNAP ME...
TALK TO ME MORE ABOUT THIS.
OH, I DON'T KNOW. SOMEONE COULD JUST TAKE ME AWAY OR SOMETHING.
WHO WOULD DO THIS?
PROBABLY A THIRD PARTY.
WHAT DO YOU MEAN—THAT SOMEONE WOULD HIRE A THIRD PARTY?
YEAH.
WHO WOULD DO THAT?
TOM CAPANO.
A lot of friends BARELY knew a thing except for, hilariously, the HAIRDRESSER.
THAT TOM CAPANO IS CRAZY.
ANNIE WAS SO SCARED OF HIM.
SHE WANTED OUT AND THEY WERE ALWAYS FIGHTING ABOUT IT.
I KNOW SHE REALLY FEARED THAT HE MIGHT HURT HER.
SHE SAID HE WOULD STAND OUTSIDE HER APARTMENT ALL THE TIME.

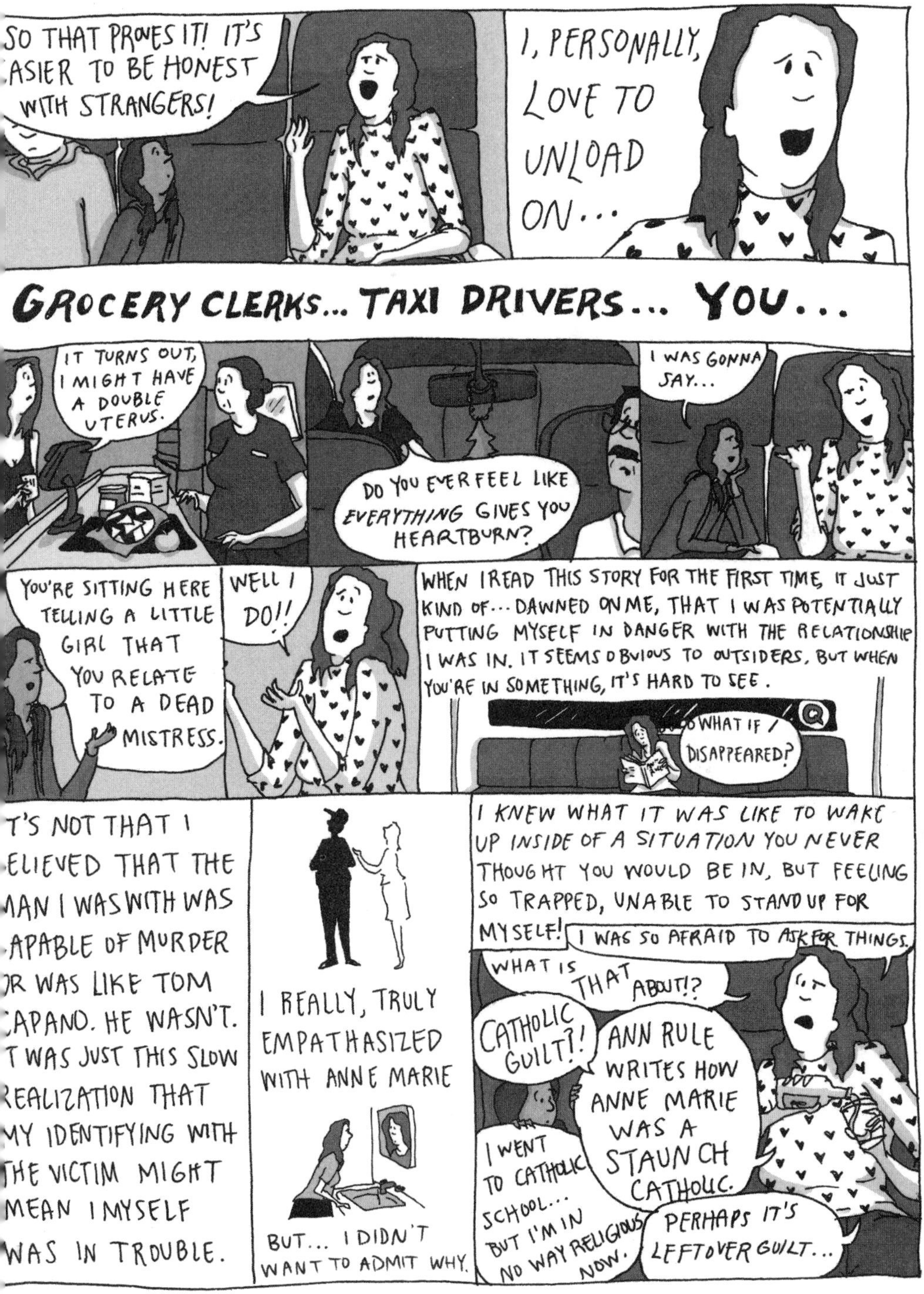
SO THAT PROVES IT! IT'S EASIER TO BE HONEST WITH STRANGERS!
I, PERSONALLY, LOVE TO UNLOAD ON...
GROCERY CLERKS... TAXI DRIVERS... YOU...
IT TURNS OUT, I MIGHT HAVE A DOUBLE UTERUS.
DO YOU EVER FEEL LIKE EVERYTHING GIVES YOU HEARTBURN?
I WAS GONNA SAY...
YOU'RE SITTING HERE TELLING A LITTLE GIRL THAT YOU RELATE TO A DEAD MISTRESS.
WELL I DO!!
WHEN I READ THIS STORY FOR THE FIRST TIME, IT JUST KIND OF... DAWNED ON ME, THAT I WAS POTENTIALLY PUTTING MYSELF IN DANGER WITH THE RELATIONSHIP I WAS IN. IT SEEMS OBVIOUS TO OUTSIDERS, BUT WHEN YOU'RE IN SOMETHING, IT'S HARD TO SEE.
WHAT IF I DISAPPEARED?
IT'S NOT THAT I BELIEVED THAT THE MAN I WAS WITH WAS CAPABLE OF MURDER OR WAS LIKE TOM CAPANO. HE WASN'T. IT WAS JUST THIS SLOW REALIZATION THAT MY IDENTIFYING WITH THE VICTIM MIGHT MEAN I MYSELF WAS IN TROUBLE.
I REALLY, TRULY EMPATHASIZED WITH ANNE MARIE
BUT... I DIDN'T WANT TO ADMIT WHY.
I KNEW WHAT IT WAS LIKE TO WAKE UP INSIDE OF A SITUATION YOU NEVER THOUGHT YOU WOULD BE IN, BUT FEELING SO TRAPPED, UNABLE TO STAND UP FOR MYSELF!
I WAS SO AFRAID TO ASK FOR THINGS.
WHAT IS THAT ABOUT!?
CATHOLIC GUILT?!
ANN RULE WRITES HOW ANNE MARIE WAS A STAUNCH CATHOLIC.
I WENT TO CATHOLIC SCHOOL... BUT I'M IN NO WAY RELIGIOUS NOW.
PERHAPS IT'S LEFTOVER GUILT...

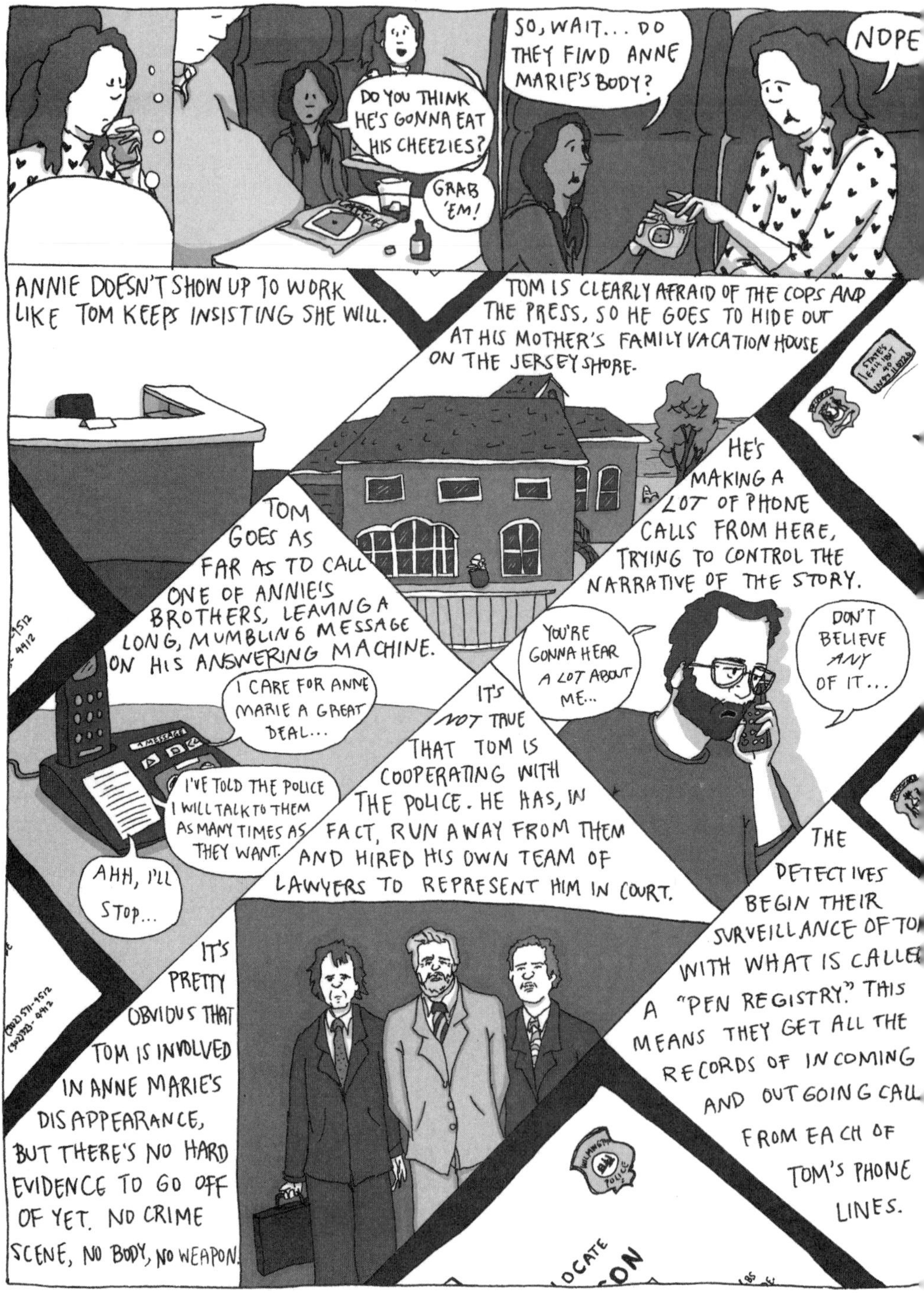
DO YOU THINK HE'S GONNA EAT HIS CHEEZIES?
GRAB 'EM!
SO, WAIT... DO THEY FIND ANNE MARIE'S BODY?
NOPE
ANNIE DOESN'T SHOW UP TO WORK LIKE TOM KEEPS INSISTING SHE WILL.
TOM IS CLEARLY AFRAID OF THE COPS AND THE PRESS, SO HE GOES TO HIDE OUT AT HIS MOTHER'S FAMILY VACATION HOUSE ON THE JERSEY SHORE.
TOM GOES AS FAR AS TO CALL ONE OF ANNIE'S BROTHERS, LEAVING A LONG, MUMBLING MESSAGE ON HIS ANSWERING MACHINE.
I CARE FOR ANNE MARIE A GREAT DEAL...
I'VE TOLD THE POLICE I WILL TALK TO THEM AS MANY TIMES AS THEY WANT.
AHH, I'LL STOP...
HE'S MAKING A LOT OF PHONE CALLS FROM HERE, TRYING TO CONTROL THE NARRATIVE OF THE STORY.
YOU'RE GONNA HEAR A LOT ABOUT ME...
DON'T BELIEVE ANY OF IT...
IT'S NOT TRUE THAT TOM IS COOPERATING WITH THE POLICE. HE HAS, IN FACT, RUN AWAY FROM THEM AND HIRED HIS OWN TEAM OF LAWYERS TO REPRESENT HIM IN COURT.
IT'S PRETTY OBVIOUS THAT TOM IS INVOLVED IN ANNE MARIE'S DISAPPEARANCE, BUT THERE'S NO HARD EVIDENCE TO GO OFF OF YET. NO CRIME SCENE, NO BODY, NO WEAPON.
THE DETECTIVES BEGIN THEIR SURVEILLANCE OF TOM WITH WHAT IS CALLED A "PEN REGISTRY." THIS MEANS THEY GET ALL THE RECORDS OF INCOMING AND OUTGOING CALLS FROM EACH OF TOM'S PHONE LINES.

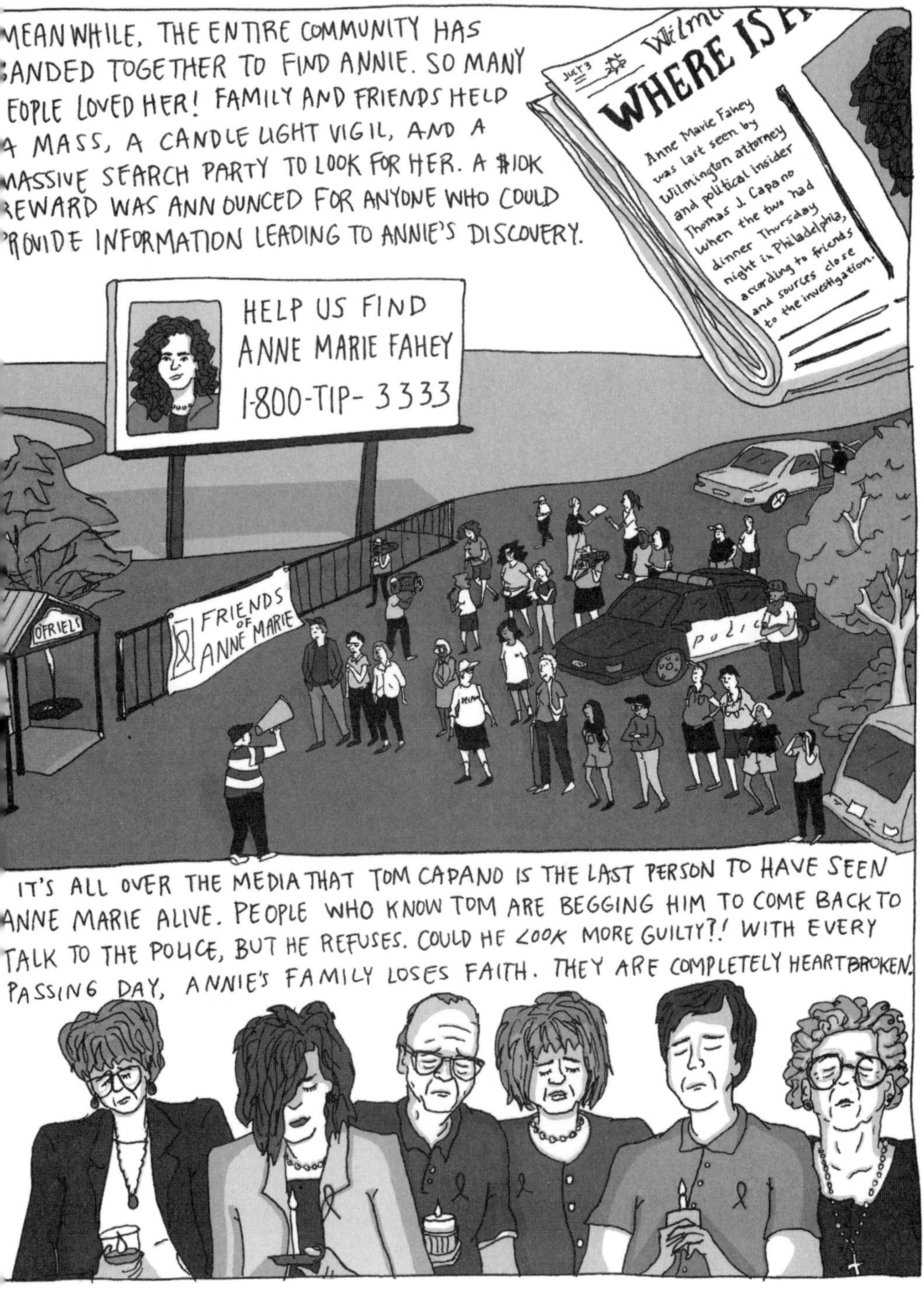
MEANWHILE, THE ENTIRE COMMUNITY HAS
ANDED TOGETHER TO FIND ANNIE. SO MANY
EOPLE LOVED HER! FAMILY AND FRIENDS HELD
A MASS, A CANDLE LIGHT VIGIL, AND A
ASSIVE SEARCH PARTY TO LOOK FOR HER. A $10K
EWARD WAS ANNOUNCED FOR ANYONE WHO COULD
ROVIDE INFORMATION LEADING TO ANNIE'S DISCOVERY.
JULY 3
Wilm
WHERE IS
Anne Marie Fahey was last seen by Wilmington attorney and political insider Thomas J. Capano when the two had dinner Thursday night in Philadelphia, according to friends and sources close to the investigation.
HELP US FIND ANNE MARIE FAHEY
1-800-TIP-3333
O'FRIEL'S
FRIENDS OF ANNE MARIE
POLIC
IT'S ALL OVER THE MEDIA THAT TOM CAPANO IS THE LAST PERSON TO HAVE SEEN
ANNE MARIE ALIVE. PEOPLE WHO KNOW TOM ARE BEGGING HIM TO COME BACK TO
TALK TO THE POLICE, BUT HE REFUSES. COULD HE LOOK MORE GUILTY?! WITH EVERY
PASSING DAY, ANNIE'S FAMILY LOSES FAITH. THEY ARE COMPLETELY HEARTBROKEN.

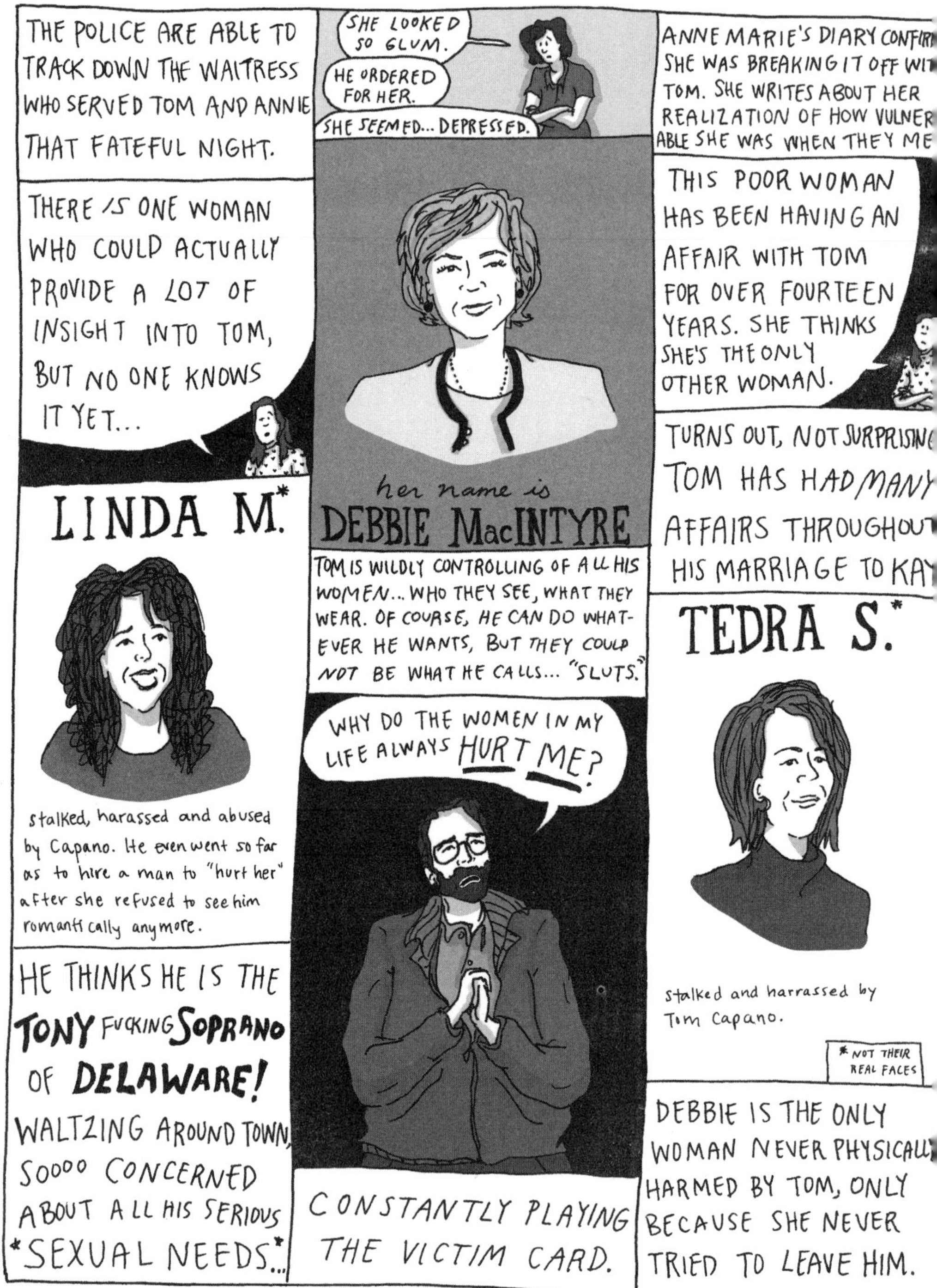
THE POLICE ARE ABLE TO TRACK DOWN THE WAITRESS WHO SERVED TOM AND ANNIE THAT FATEFUL NIGHT.
SHE LOOKED SO GLUM.
HE ORDERED FOR HER.
SHE SEEMED... DEPRESSED.
ANNE MARIE'S DIARY CONFIR
SHE WAS BREAKING IT OFF WI
TOM. SHE WRITES ABOUT HER
REALIZATION OF HOW VULNER
ABLE SHE WAS WHEN THEY ME
THERE IS ONE WOMAN WHO COULD ACTUALLY PROVIDE A LOT OF INSIGHT INTO TOM, BUT NO ONE KNOWS IT YET...
her name is
DEBBIE MacINTYRE
THIS POOR WOMAN HAS BEEN HAVING AN AFFAIR WITH TOM FOR OVER FOURTEEN YEARS. SHE THINKS SHE'S THE ONLY OTHER WOMAN.
TOM IS WILDLY CONTROLLING OF ALL HIS WOMEN... WHO THEY SEE, WHAT THEY WEAR. OF COURSE, HE CAN DO WHATEVER HE WANTS, BUT THEY COULD NOT BE WHAT HE CALLS... "SLUTS."
TURNS OUT, NOT SURPRISIN
TOM HAS HAD MANY
AFFAIRS THROUGHOU
HIS MARRIAGE TO KA
LINDA M.*
stalked, harassed and abused by Capano. He even went so far as to hire a man to "hurt her" after she refused to see him romantically anymore.
WHY DO THE WOMEN IN MY LIFE ALWAYS HURT ME?
TEDRA S.*
stalked and harrassed by Tom Capano.
* NOT THEIR REAL FACES
HE THINKS HE IS THE TONY FUCKING SOPRANO OF DELAWARE! WALTZING AROUND TOWN, SOOOO CONCERNED ABOUT ALL HIS SERIOUS *SEXUAL NEEDS*...
CONSTANTLY PLAYING THE VICTIM CARD.
DEBBIE IS THE ONLY WOMAN NEVER PHYSICALLY HARMED BY TOM, ONLY BECAUSE SHE NEVER TRIED TO LEAVE HIM.

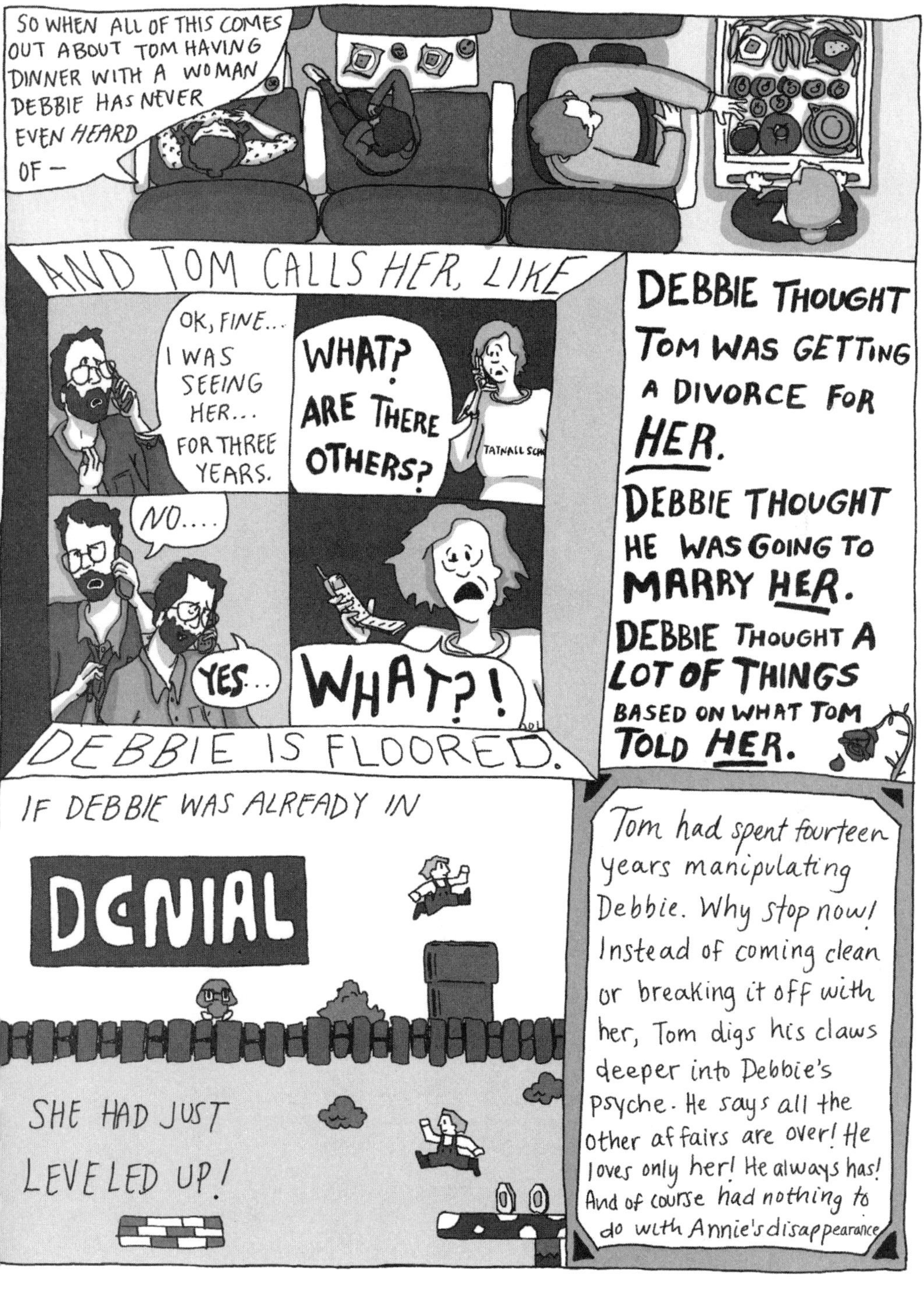
SO WHEN ALL OF THIS COMES OUT ABOUT TOM HAVING DINNER WITH A WOMAN DEBBIE HAS NEVER EVEN HEARD OF —
AND TOM CALLS HER, LIKE
OK, FINE... I WAS SEEING HER... FOR THREE YEARS.
WHAT? ARE THERE OTHERS?
TATNALL SCH
NO....
YES...
WHAT?!
DEBBIE IS FLOORED.
DEBBIE THOUGHT TOM WAS GETTING A DIVORCE FOR HER.
DEBBIE THOUGHT HE WAS GOING TO MARRY HER.
DEBBIE THOUGHT A LOT OF THINGS BASED ON WHAT TOM TOLD HER.
IF DEBBIE WAS ALREADY IN
DENIAL
SHE HAD JUST LEVELED UP!
Tom had spent fourteen years manipulating Debbie. Why stop now! Instead of coming clean or breaking it off with her, Tom digs his claws deeper into Debbie's psyche. He says all the other affairs are over! He loves only her! He always has! And of course had nothing to do with Annie's disappearance

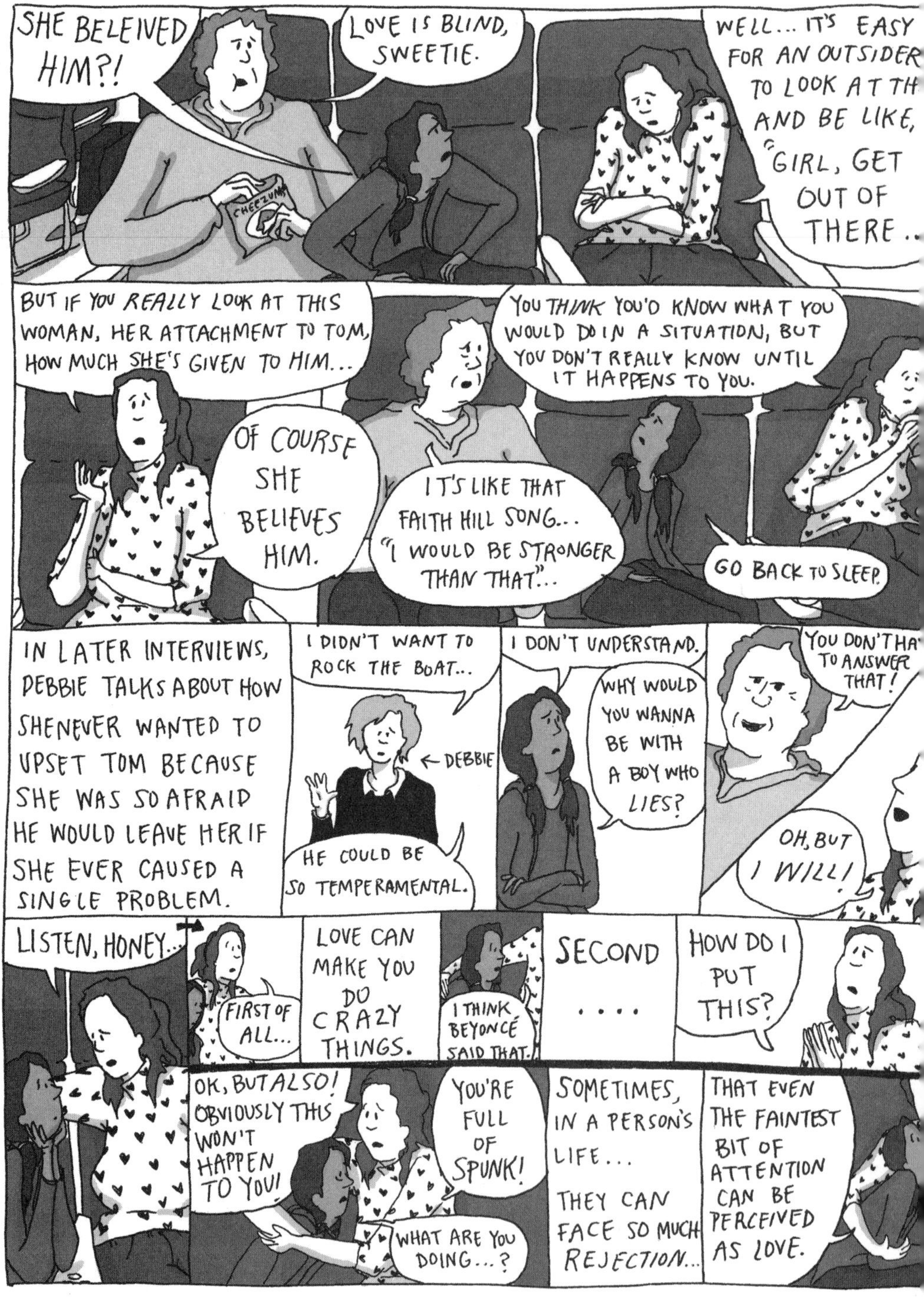
SHE BELEIVED HIM?!
LOVE IS BLIND, SWEETIE.
WELL... IT'S EASY FOR AN OUTSIDER TO LOOK AT TH AND BE LIKE, "GIRL, GET OUT OF THERE...
CHEEZUMS
BUT IF YOU REALLY LOOK AT THIS WOMAN, HER ATTACHMENT TO TOM, HOW MUCH SHE'S GIVEN TO HIM...
OF COURSE SHE BELIEVES HIM.
YOU THINK YOU'D KNOW WHAT YOU WOULD DO IN A SITUATION, BUT YOU DON'T REALLY KNOW UNTIL IT HAPPENS TO YOU.
IT'S LIKE THAT FAITH HILL SONG... "I WOULD BE STRONGER THAN THAT"...
GO BACK TO SLEEP.
IN LATER INTERVIEWS, DEBBIE TALKS ABOUT HOW SHE NEVER WANTED TO UPSET TOM BECAUSE SHE WAS SO AFRAID HE WOULD LEAVE HER IF SHE EVER CAUSED A SINGLE PROBLEM.
I DIDN'T WANT TO ROCK THE BOAT...
← DEBBIE
HE COULD BE SO TEMPERAMENTAL.
I DON'T UNDERSTAND.
WHY WOULD YOU WANNA BE WITH A BOY WHO LIES?
YOU DON'T HA TO ANSWER THAT!
OH, BUT I WILL!
LISTEN, HONEY...
FIRST OF ALL...
LOVE CAN MAKE YOU DO CRAZY THINGS.
I THINK BEYONCÉ SAID THAT.
SECOND ....
HOW DO I PUT THIS?
OK, BUT ALSO! OBVIOUSLY THIS WON'T HAPPEN TO YOU!
YOU'RE FULL OF SPUNK!
WHAT ARE YOU DOING...?
SOMETIMES, IN A PERSON'S LIFE...
THEY CAN FACE SO MUCH REJECTION...
THAT EVEN THE FAINTEST BIT OF ATTENTION CAN BE PERCEIVED AS LOVE.

AND SOMETIMES WHEN YOU FEEL LIKE YOU'RE IN LOVE... YOU DON'T WANT TO SEE A PERSON'S FLAWS. YOU LITERALLY CANNOT SEE THEM!

AND THERE ARE PEOPLE OUT THERE WHO CAN DETECT THAT VULNERABILITY ... THAT... WHAT SOME MIGHT CALL, WEAKNESS...

(AND THEY USE IT AGAINST YOU.)

SO, LIKE A BULLY?

AN EMOTIONAL BULLY.

YOU TOO?

BUT WHY WOULD YOU LIKE A BULLY?!

MY COLLEGE GIRLFRIEND. MESSED ME UP FOR YEARS.

MOM?

NO!

YOU LOVED SOME- ONE WHO ISN'T MOM??

I GET IT. I'M IN A GOOD RELATIONSHIP NOW, BUT IT TOOK A LOT OF THERAPY.

BUT WHY WOULD YOU LIKE A BULLY?

WHAT IS THE LESSON TO LEARN HERE?!?

BOYS... LIE?

LOVE... HURTS?

NEVER GROW UP.

UNAVAILABLE MEN AREN'T AS INTERESTING AS THEY SEEM!

OOOH! GOOD ONE!

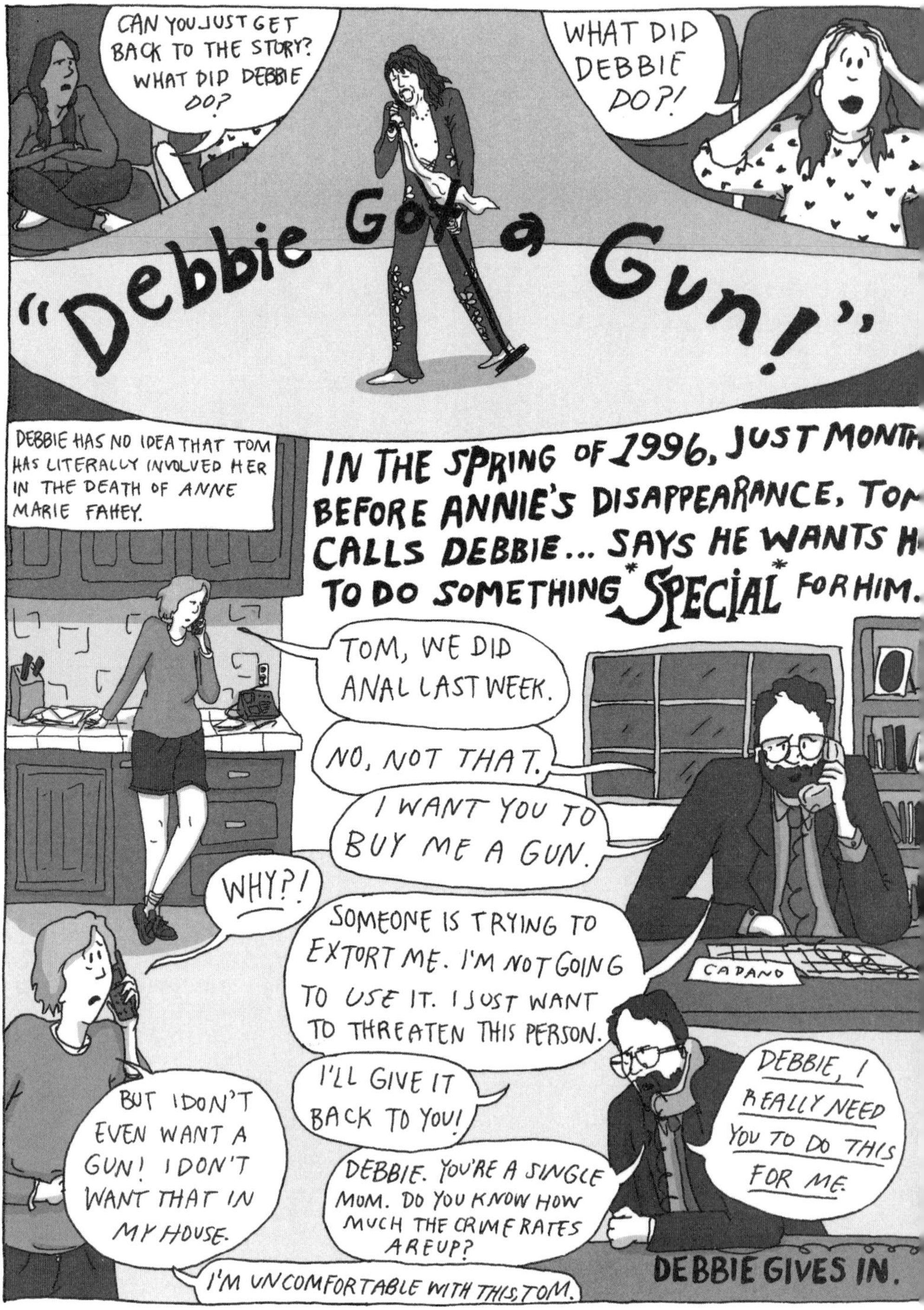
CAN YOU JUST GET BACK TO THE STORY? WHAT DID DEBBIE DO?
WHAT DID DEBBIE DO?!
"Debbie Got a Gun!"
DEBBIE HAS NO IDEA THAT TOM HAS LITERALLY INVOLVED HER IN THE DEATH OF ANNE MARIE FAHEY.
IN THE SPRING OF 1996, JUST MONTH
BEFORE ANNIE'S DISAPPEARANCE, TOM
CALLS DEBBIE... SAYS HE WANTS H
TO DO SOMETHING *SPECIAL* FOR HIM.
TOM, WE DID ANAL LAST WEEK.
NO, NOT THAT.
I WANT YOU TO BUY ME A GUN.
WHY?!
SOMEONE IS TRYING TO EXTORT ME. I'M NOT GOING TO USE IT. I JUST WANT TO THREATEN THIS PERSON.
CAPANO
I'LL GIVE IT BACK TO YOU!
BUT I DON'T EVEN WANT A GUN! I DON'T WANT THAT IN MY HOUSE.
DEBBIE. YOU'RE A SINGLE MOM. DO YOU KNOW HOW MUCH THE CRIME RATES ARE UP?
DEBBIE, I REALLY NEED YOU TO DO THIS FOR ME.
I'M UNCOMFORTABLE WITH THIS, TOM.
DEBBIE GIVES IN.

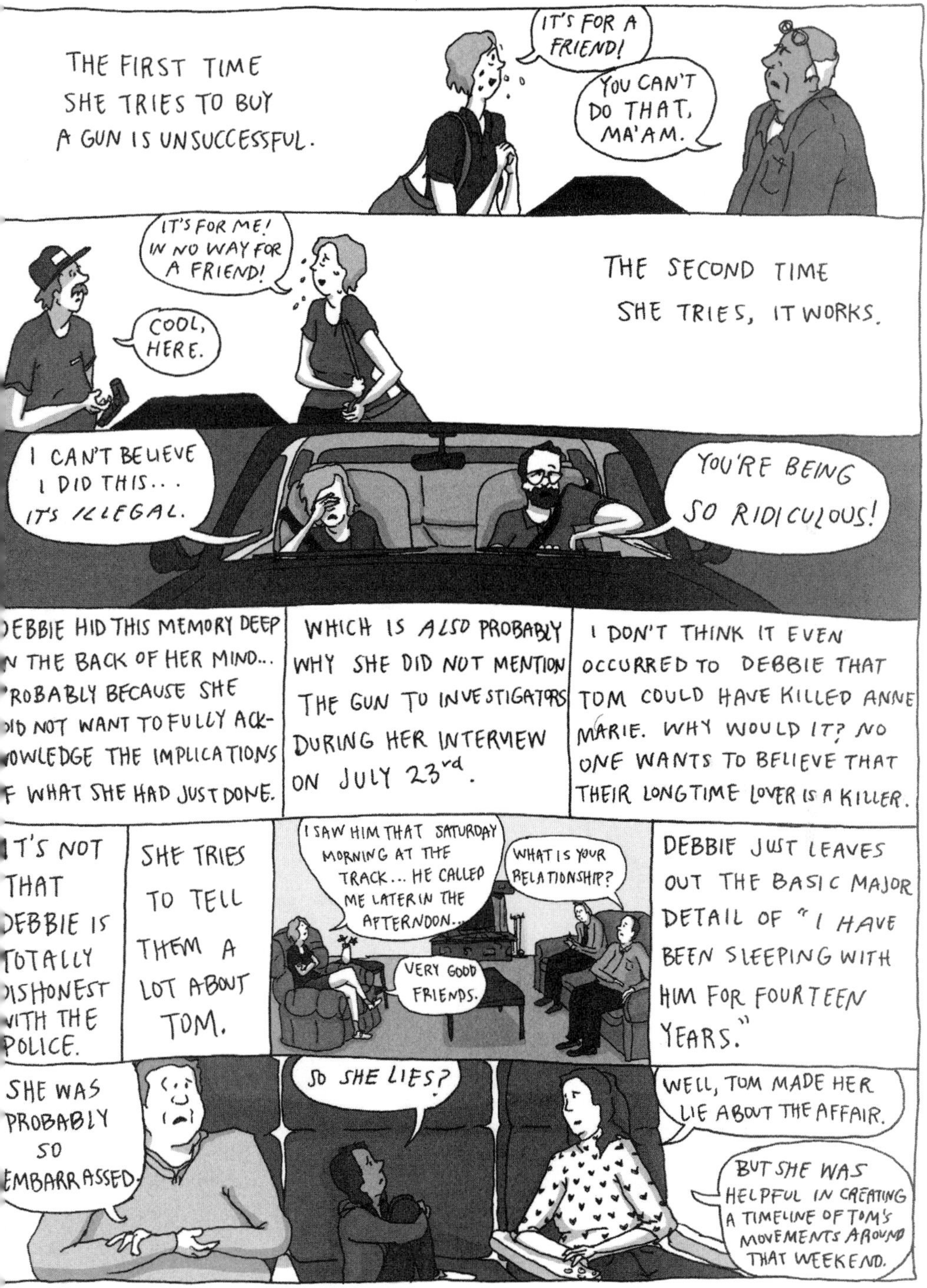
THE FIRST TIME SHE TRIES TO BUY A GUN IS UNSUCCESSFUL.
IT'S FOR A FRIEND!
YOU CAN'T DO THAT, MA'AM.
IT'S FOR ME! IN NO WAY FOR A FRIEND!
COOL, HERE.
THE SECOND TIME SHE TRIES, IT WORKS.
I CAN'T BELIEVE I DID THIS... IT'S ILLEGAL.
YOU'RE BEING SO RIDICULOUS!
EBBIE HID THIS MEMORY DEEP N THE BACK OF HER MIND... ROBABLY BECAUSE SHE ID NOT WANT TO FULLY ACK- OWLEDGE THE IMPLICATIONS F WHAT SHE HAD JUST DONE.
WHICH IS ALSO PROBABLY WHY SHE DID NOT MENTION THE GUN TO INVESTIGATORS DURING HER INTERVIEW ON JULY 23rd.
I DON'T THINK IT EVEN OCCURRED TO DEBBIE THAT TOM COULD HAVE KILLED ANNE MARIE. WHY WOULD IT? NO ONE WANTS TO BELIEVE THAT THEIR LONGTIME LOVER IS A KILLER.
T'S NOT THAT EBBIE IS TOTALLY ISHONEST ITH THE OLICE.
SHE TRIES TO TELL THEM A LOT ABOUT TOM.
I SAW HIM THAT SATURDAY MORNING AT THE TRACK... HE CALLED ME LATER IN THE AFTERNOON...
WHAT IS YOUR RELATIONSHIP?
VERY GOOD FRIENDS.
DEBBIE JUST LEAVES OUT THE BASIC MAJOR DETAIL OF "I HAVE BEEN SLEEPING WITH HIM FOR FOURTEEN YEARS."
SHE WAS PROBABLY SO EMBARRASSED.
SO SHE LIES?
WELL, TOM MADE HER LIE ABOUT THE AFFAIR.
BUT SHE WAS HELPFUL IN CREATING A TIMELINE OF TOM'S MOVEMENTS AROUND THAT WEEKEND.

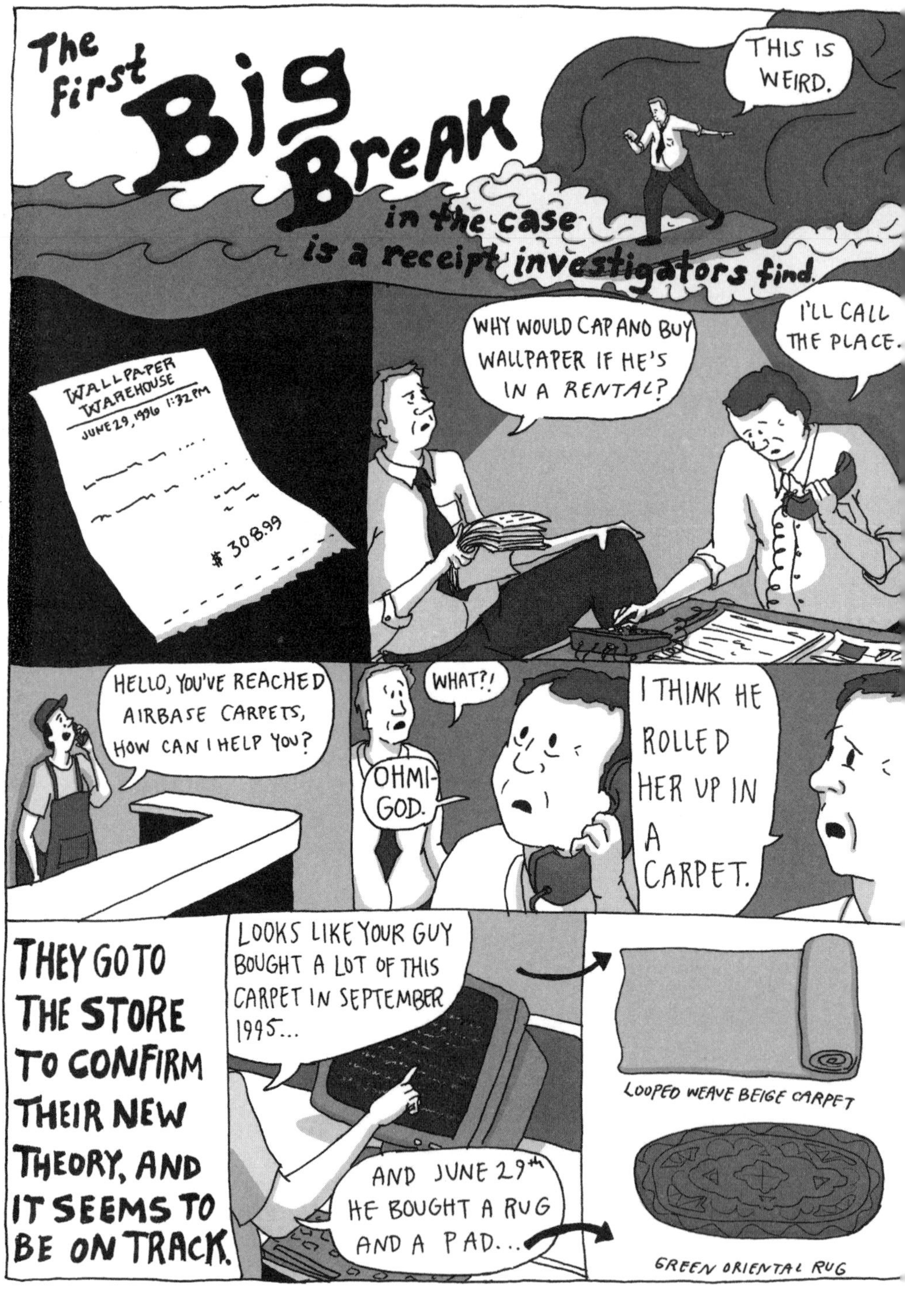
The first Big Break in the case is a receipt investigators find.
THIS IS WEIRD.
WALLPAPER WAREHOUSE
JUNE 29, 1996 1:32 PM
$ 308.99
WHY WOULD CAP AND BUY WALLPAPER IF HE'S IN A RENTAL?
I'LL CALL THE PLACE.
HELLO, YOU'VE REACHED AIRBASE CARPETS, HOW CAN I HELP YOU?
WHAT?!
OHMI-GOD.
I THINK HE ROLLED HER UP IN A CARPET.
THEY GO TO THE STORE TO CONFIRM THEIR NEW THEORY, AND IT SEEMS TO BE ON TRACK.
LOOKS LIKE YOUR GUY BOUGHT A LOT OF THIS CARPET IN SEPTEMBER 1995...
AND JUNE 29th HE BOUGHT A RUG AND A PAD...
LOOPED WEAVE BEIGE CARPET
GREEN ORIENTAL RUG

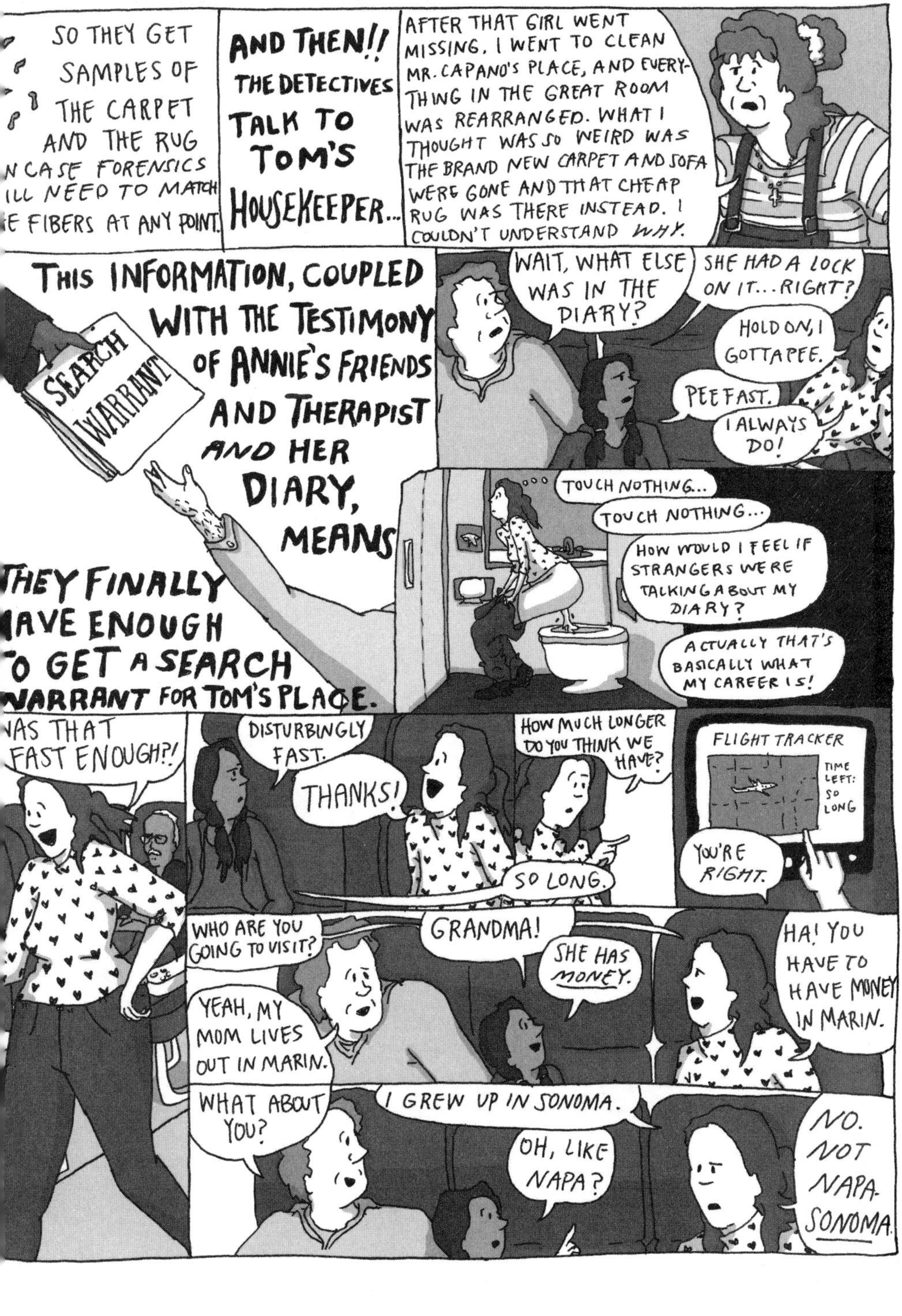
SO THEY GET SAMPLES OF THE CARPET AND THE RUG N CASE FORENSICS ILL NEED TO MATCH E FIBERS AT ANY POINT.
AND THEN!! THE DETECTIVES TALK TO TOM'S HOUSEKEEPER...
AFTER THAT GIRL WENT MISSING, I WENT TO CLEAN MR. CAPANO'S PLACE, AND EVERYTHING IN THE GREAT ROOM WAS REARRANGED. WHAT I THOUGHT WAS SO WEIRD WAS THE BRAND NEW CARPET AND SOFA WERE GONE AND THAT CHEAP RUG WAS THERE INSTEAD. I COULDN'T UNDERSTAND WHY.
THIS INFORMATION, COUPLED WITH THE TESTIMONY OF ANNIE'S FRIENDS AND THERAPIST AND HER DIARY, MEANS
SEARCH WARRANT
HEY FINALLY AVE ENOUGH O GET A SEARCH WARRANT FOR TOM'S PLACE.
WAIT, WHAT ELSE WAS IN THE DIARY?
SHE HAD A LOCK ON IT... RIGHT?
HOLD ON, I GOTTA PEE.
PEE FAST.
I ALWAYS DO!
TOUCH NOTHING...
TOUCH NOTHING...
HOW WOULD I FEEL IF STRANGERS WERE TALKING ABOUT MY DIARY?
ACTUALLY THAT'S BASICALLY WHAT MY CAREER IS!
AS THAT FAST ENOUGH?!
DISTURBINGLY FAST.
THANKS!
HOW MUCH LONGER DO YOU THINK WE HAVE?
FLIGHT TRACKER
TIME LEFT: SO LONG
YOU'RE RIGHT.
SO LONG.
WHO ARE YOU GOING TO VISIT?
GRANDMA!
SHE HAS MONEY.
YEAH, MY MOM LIVES OUT IN MARIN.
HA! YOU HAVE TO HAVE MONEY IN MARIN.
WHAT ABOUT YOU?
I GREW UP IN SONOMA.
OH, LIKE NAPA?
NO. NOT NAPA. SONOMA.

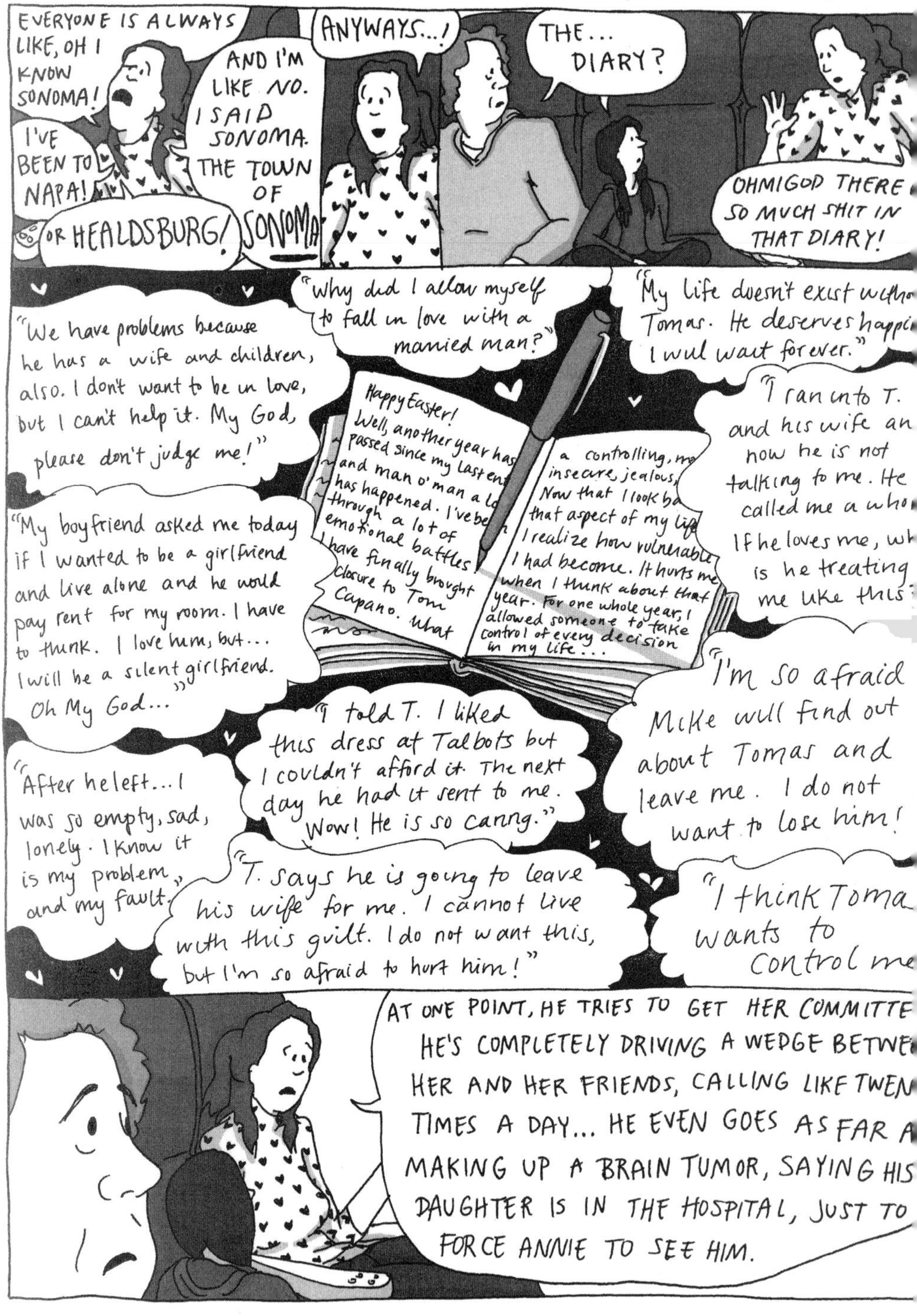
EVERYONE IS ALWAYS LIKE, OH I KNOW SONOMA!
I'VE BEEN TO NAPA!
OR HEALDSBURG!
AND I'M LIKE NO. I SAID SONOMA. THE TOWN OF SONOMA
ANYWAYS...!
THE... DIARY?
OHMIGOD THERE SO MUCH SHIT IN THAT DIARY!
"We have problems because he has a wife and children, also. I don't want to be in love, but I can't help it. My God, please don't judge me!"
"Why did I allow myself to fall in love with a married man?"
"My life doesn't exist with Tomas. He deserves happi I will wait forever."
Happy Easter! Well, another year has passed since my last en and man o' man a lo has happened. I've be through a lot of emotional battles! I have finally brought closure to Tom Capano. What
a controlling, m insecure, jealous, Now that I look b that aspect of my lif I realize how vulnerable I had become. It hurts me when I think about that year. For one whole year, I allowed someone to take control of every decision in my life...
"I ran into T. and his wife an now he is not talking to me. He called me a who If he loves me, wh is he treating me like this?
"My boyfriend asked me today if I wanted to be a girlfriend and live alone and he would pay rent for my room. I have to think. I love him, but... I will be a silent girlfriend. Oh My God..."
"I told T. I liked this dress at Talbots but I couldn't afford it. The next day he had it sent to me. Wow! He is so caring."
"I'm so afraid Mike will find out about Tomas and leave me. I do not want to lose him!
"After he left... I was so empty, sad, lonely. I know it is my problem and my fault."
"T. says he is going to leave his wife for me. I cannot live with this guilt. I do not want this, but I'm so afraid to hurt him!"
"I think Toma wants to control me
AT ONE POINT, HE TRIES TO GET HER COMMITTE HE'S COMPLETELY DRIVING A WEDGE BETWE HER AND HER FRIENDS, CALLING LIKE TWEN TIMES A DAY... HE EVEN GOES AS FAR A MAKING UP A BRAIN TUMOR, SAYING HIS DAUGHTER IS IN THE HOSPITAL, JUST TO FORCE ANNIE TO SEE HIM.

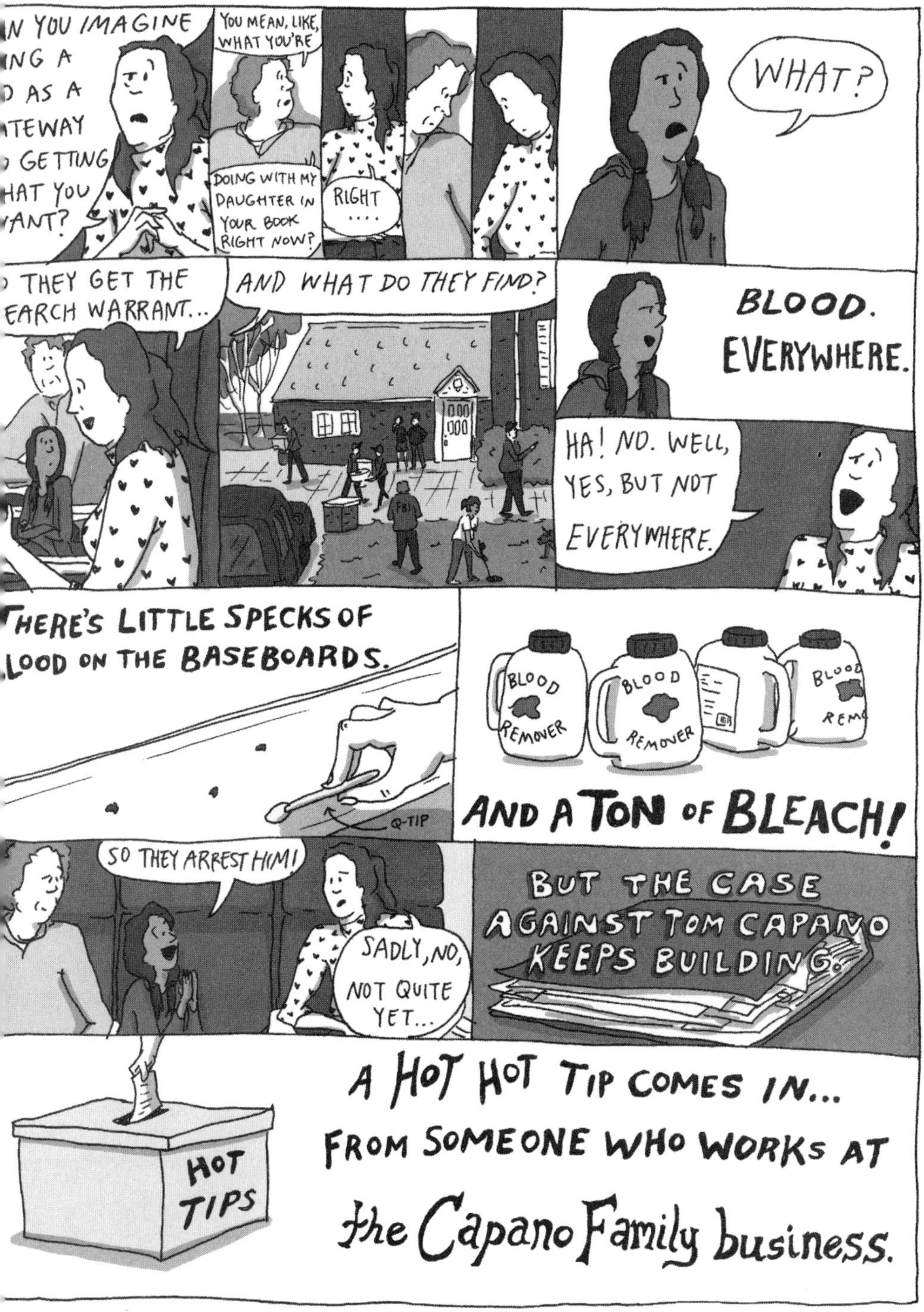
N YOU IMAGINE ING A D AS A ITEWAY GETTING HAT YOU ANT?
YOU MEAN, LIKE, WHAT YOU'RE
DOING WITH MY DAUGHTER IN YOUR BOOK RIGHT NOW?
RIGHT ....
WHAT?
THEY GET THE EARCH WARRANT...
AND WHAT DO THEY FIND?
BLOOD. EVERYWHERE.
HA! NO. WELL, YES, BUT NOT EVERYWHERE.
THERE'S LITTLE SPECKS OF LOOD ON THE BASEBOARDS.
Q-TIP
BLOOD REMOVER
BLOOD REMOVER
AND A TON OF BLEACH!
SO THEY ARREST HIM!
SADLY, NO, NOT QUITE YET...
BUT THE CASE AGAINST TOM CAPANO KEEPS BUILDING.
HOT TIPS
A HOT HOT TIP COMES IN... FROM SOMEONE WHO WORKS AT the Capano Family business.

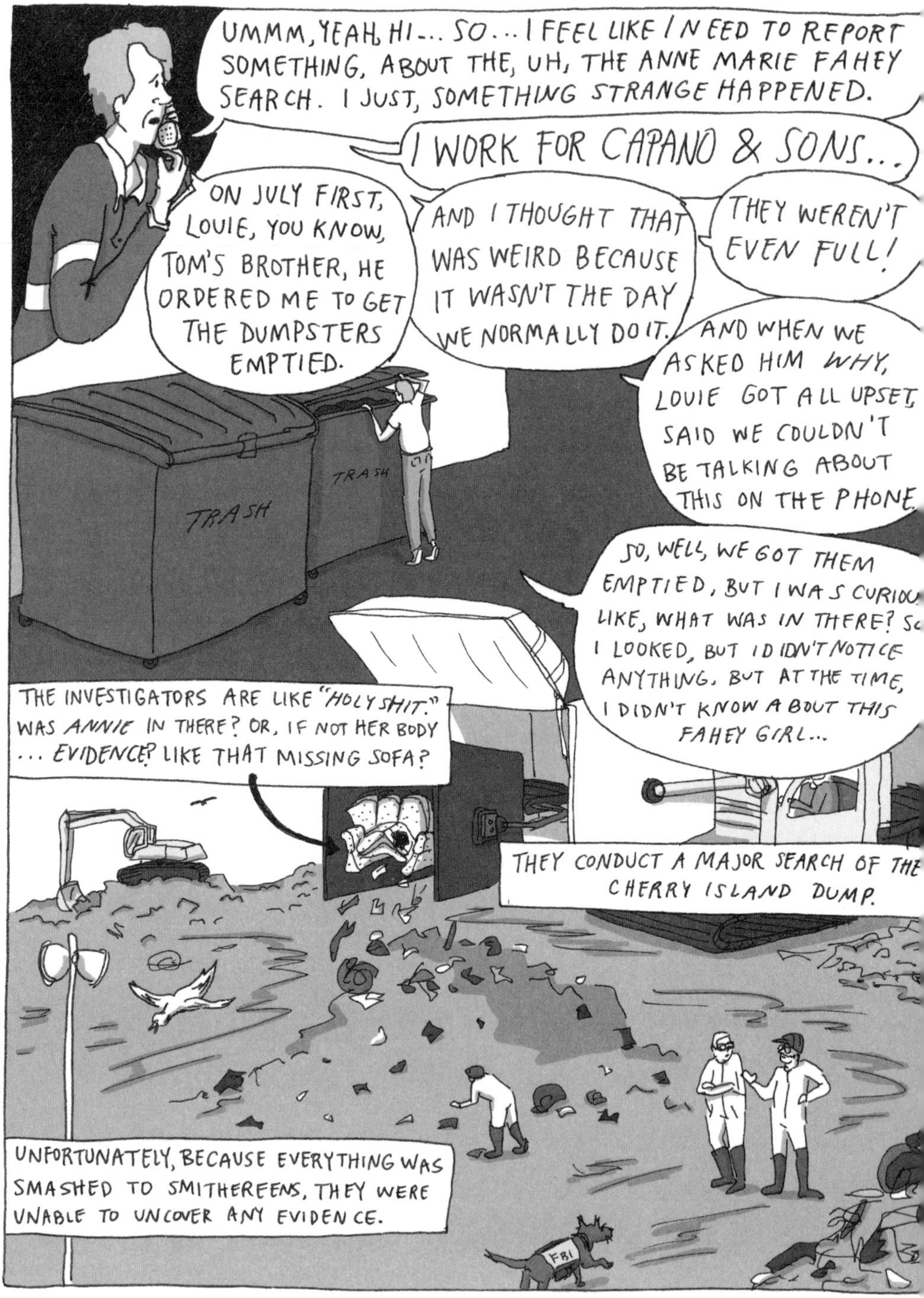
UMMM, YEAH, HI... SO... I FEEL LIKE I NEED TO REPORT SOMETHING, ABOUT THE, UH, THE ANNE MARIE FAHEY SEARCH. I JUST, SOMETHING STRANGE HAPPENED.
I WORK FOR CAPANO & SONS...
ON JULY FIRST, LOUIE, YOU KNOW, TOM'S BROTHER, HE ORDERED ME TO GET THE DUMPSTERS EMPTIED.
AND I THOUGHT THAT WAS WEIRD BECAUSE IT WASN'T THE DAY WE NORMALLY DO IT.
THEY WEREN'T EVEN FULL!
AND WHEN WE ASKED HIM WHY, LOUIE GOT ALL UPSET, SAID WE COULDN'T BE TALKING ABOUT THIS ON THE PHONE.
TRASH
TRASH
SO, WELL, WE GOT THEM EMPTIED, BUT I WAS CURIOU LIKE, WHAT WAS IN THERE? SO I LOOKED, BUT I DIDN'T NOTICE ANYTHING. BUT AT THE TIME, I DIDN'T KNOW ABOUT THIS FAHEY GIRL...
THE INVESTIGATORS ARE LIKE "HOLY SHIT." WAS ANNIE IN THERE? OR, IF NOT HER BODY ... EVIDENCE? LIKE THAT MISSING SOFA?
THEY CONDUCT A MAJOR SEARCH OF THE CHERRY ISLAND DUMP.
UNFORTUNATELY, BECAUSE EVERYTHING WAS SMASHED TO SMITHEREENS, THEY WERE UNABLE TO UNCOVER ANY EVIDENCE.
FBI

SO, AT THIS POINT, IT'S LIKE THE END OF AUGUST, AND TO THE FAHEYS IT FEELS LIKE NOTHING IS GETTING DONE. EVEN THOUGH THE INVESTIGATORS ARE GATHERING REALLY STRONG EVIDENCE AGAINST CAPANO, THEY CAN'T TELL ANYONE ABOUT IT! WHICH LEAVES CAPANO WALKING AROUND TOWN, SUPER CONFIDENT...

IT WASN'T ME. THE BLOOD IN MY HOUSE IS FROM ONE OF MY DAUGHTERS. I LOVED ANNE MARIE FAHEY!

Anne-Marie

ANNIE'S FAMILY IS LOST... FEELING LIKE THERE WILL NEVER BE JUSTICE FOR THEIR SWEET SISTER.

BUT THEY WOULD HAVE HOPE IF THEY KNEW...

EVIDENCE

THE FIBERS FOUND IN THE TRUNK OF KAY CAPANO'S SUBURBAN MATCH THE BEIGE CARPET TOM PURCHASED IN SEPTEMBER '95.

SWORN AFFADAVIT

Ginny Columbus

ALL OF ANNIE'S FRIENDS CONFIRM THAT TOM WAS STALKING AND HARASSING HER.

Diary

EVERYTHING IN ANNIE'S DIARY AND ALL OF THE EMAILS BETWEEN HER AND TOM.

MOST IMPORTANTLY! THE BLOOD IN CAPANO'S HOUSE

... WAS A MATCH TO ANNE MARIE FAHEY!

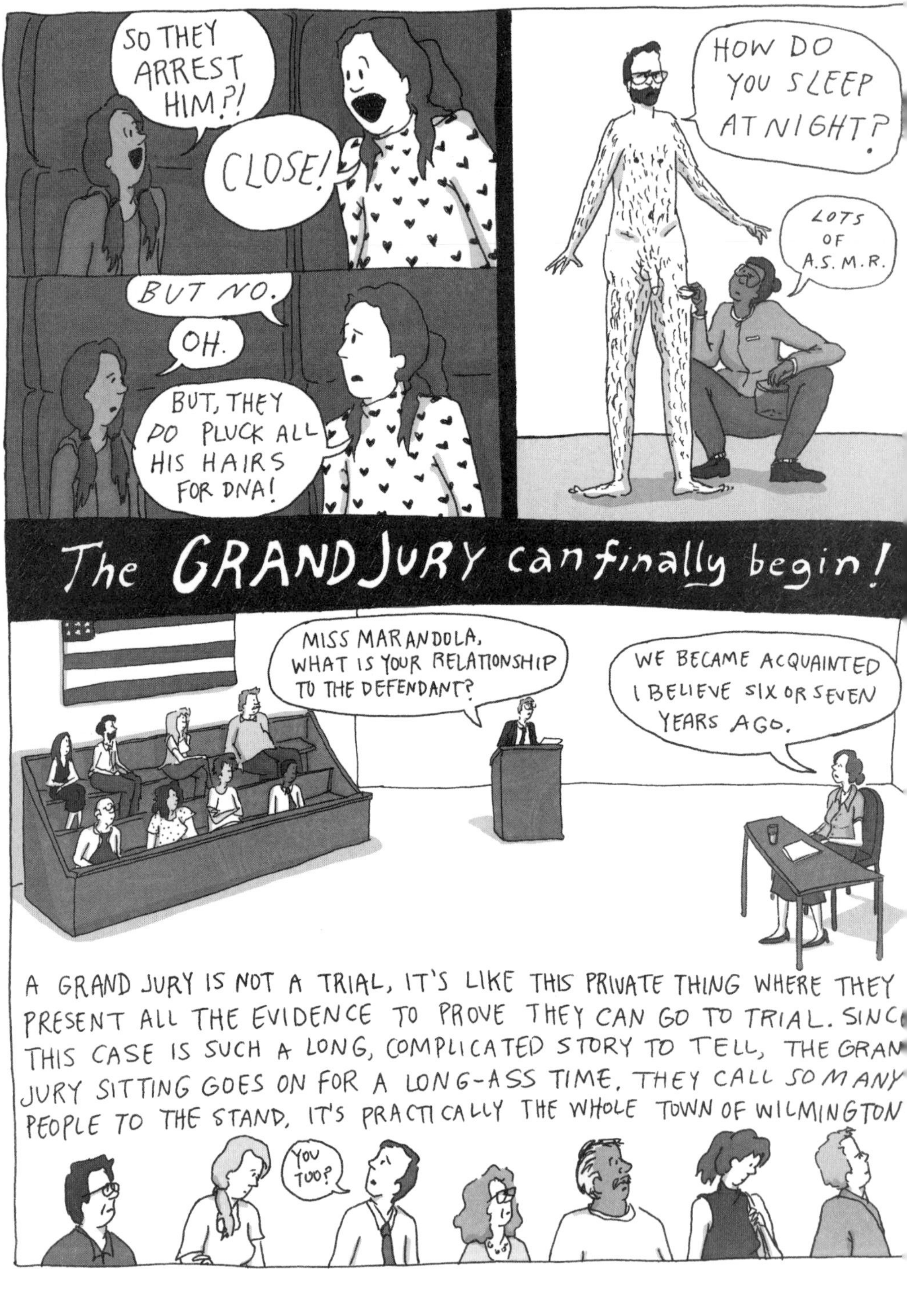
SO THEY ARREST HIM?!
CLOSE!
BUT NO.
OH.
BUT, THEY DO PLUCK ALL HIS HAIRS FOR DNA!
HOW DO YOU SLEEP AT NIGHT?
LOTS OF A.S.M.R.
The GRAND JURY can finally begin!
MISS MARANDOLA, WHAT IS YOUR RELATIONSHIP TO THE DEFENDANT?
WE BECAME ACQUAINTED I BELIEVE SIX OR SEVEN YEARS AGO.
A GRAND JURY IS NOT A TRIAL, IT'S LIKE THIS PRIVATE THING WHERE THEY PRESENT ALL THE EVIDENCE TO PROVE THEY CAN GO TO TRIAL. SINC THIS CASE IS SUCH A LONG, COMPLICATED STORY TO TELL, THE GRAN JURY SITTING GOES ON FOR A LONG-ASS TIME. THEY CALL SO MANY PEOPLE TO THE STAND, IT'S PRACTICALLY THE WHOLE TOWN OF WILMINGTON
YOU TOO?

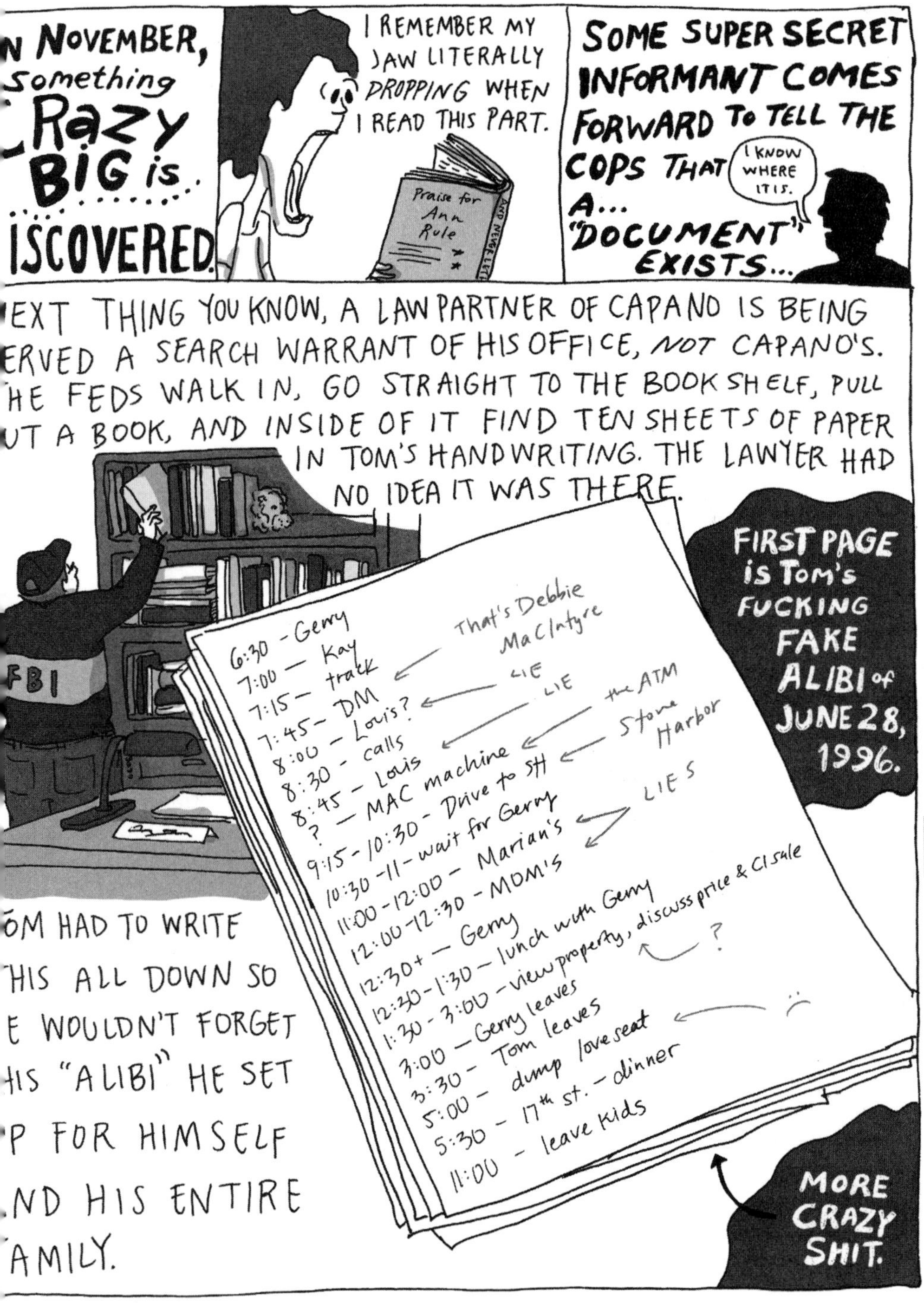

N NOVEMBER, something
RaZY
BIG is
ISCOVERED.
I REMEMBER MY JAW LITERALLY DROPPING WHEN I READ THIS PART.
Praise for Ann Rule
SOME SUPER SECRET INFORMANT COMES FORWARD TO TELL THE COPS THAT
I KNOW WHERE IT IS.
A... "DOCUMENT" EXISTS...
EXT THING YOU KNOW, A LAW PARTNER OF CAPANO IS BEING ERVED A SEARCH WARRANT OF HIS OFFICE, NOT CAPANO'S. HE FEDS WALK IN, GO STRAIGHT TO THE BOOK SHELF, PULL UT A BOOK, AND INSIDE OF IT FIND TEN SHEETS OF PAPER IN TOM'S HANDWRITING. THE LAWYER HAD NO IDEA IT WAS THERE.
FBI
6:30 - Gerry
7:00 — Kay
7:15 — track
7:45 — DM
8:00 — Louis?
8:30 - calls
8:45 - Louis
? — MAC machine
9:15 - 10:30 - Drive to SH
10:30 - 11 - wait for Gerry
11:00 - 12:00 - Marian's
12:00 - 12:30 - MOM'S
12:30+ — Gerry
12:30 - 1:30 — lunch with Gerry
1:30 - 3:00 - view property, discuss price & CI sale
3:00 — Gerry leaves
3:30 - Tom leaves
5:00 - dump love seat
5:30 - 17th st. - dinner
11:00 - leave kids
That's Debbie MacIntyre
LIE
LIE
the ATM
Stone Harbor
LIES
?
FIRST PAGE IS TOM'S FUCKING FAKE ALIBI OF JUNE 28, 1996.
OM HAD TO WRITE HIS ALL DOWN SO E WOULDN'T FORGET HIS "ALIBI" HE SET P FOR HIMSELF ND HIS ENTIRE AMILY.
MORE CRAZY SHIT.

WHO TIPPED OFF THE COPS?

NO CLUE. THEY NEVER SAID.

WHAT WAS IN THE REST OF THOSE PAGES? A MAP?! TO THE BODY!

PASSENGERS, WE ARE NEARING OUR DESTINATION.

MOST OF THE OTHER PAGES THEY FOUND WERE TOM'S THOUGHTS ABOUT ANNE MARIE FAHEY, PAINTING HER AS A "HEADCASE," BUT THE INVESTIGATORS WERE MORE INTRIGUED BY THAT TIMELINE AND HOW MANY TIMES TOM'S BROTHER GERRY APPEARED ON IT. WAS HE... INVOLVED IN THE MURDER? GERRY WAS THE YOUNGEST BROTHER AND DEFINITELY THE WEAKEST LINK. HE WAS A DRUGGIE, OWNED GUNS, HUNG WITH EX—CONVICTS.

Gerry Capano

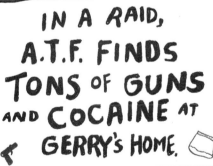

OH THIS.

AND THIS.

OH I HAVE TRASH.

THE PROSECUTION GETS THE A.T.F. TO START LOOKING AT GERRY... TO PUT PRESSURE ON HIM SO HE WOULD TURN ON HIS BROTHER

IN A RAID, A.T.F. FINDS TONS OF GUNS AND COCAINE AT GERRY'S HOME.

APPARENTLY, THERE'S A LAW AGAINST DRUG USERS OWNING WEAPONS. SO THAT'S COOL.

INSTEAD OF BRINGING GERRY IN FOR QUESTIONING, THEY LET HIM SIT IN PANIC FOR MONTHS.

THEY'RE COMING FOR ME.

THEY'RE HERE.

WHAT HAVE I DONE.

AND IT WORKS.

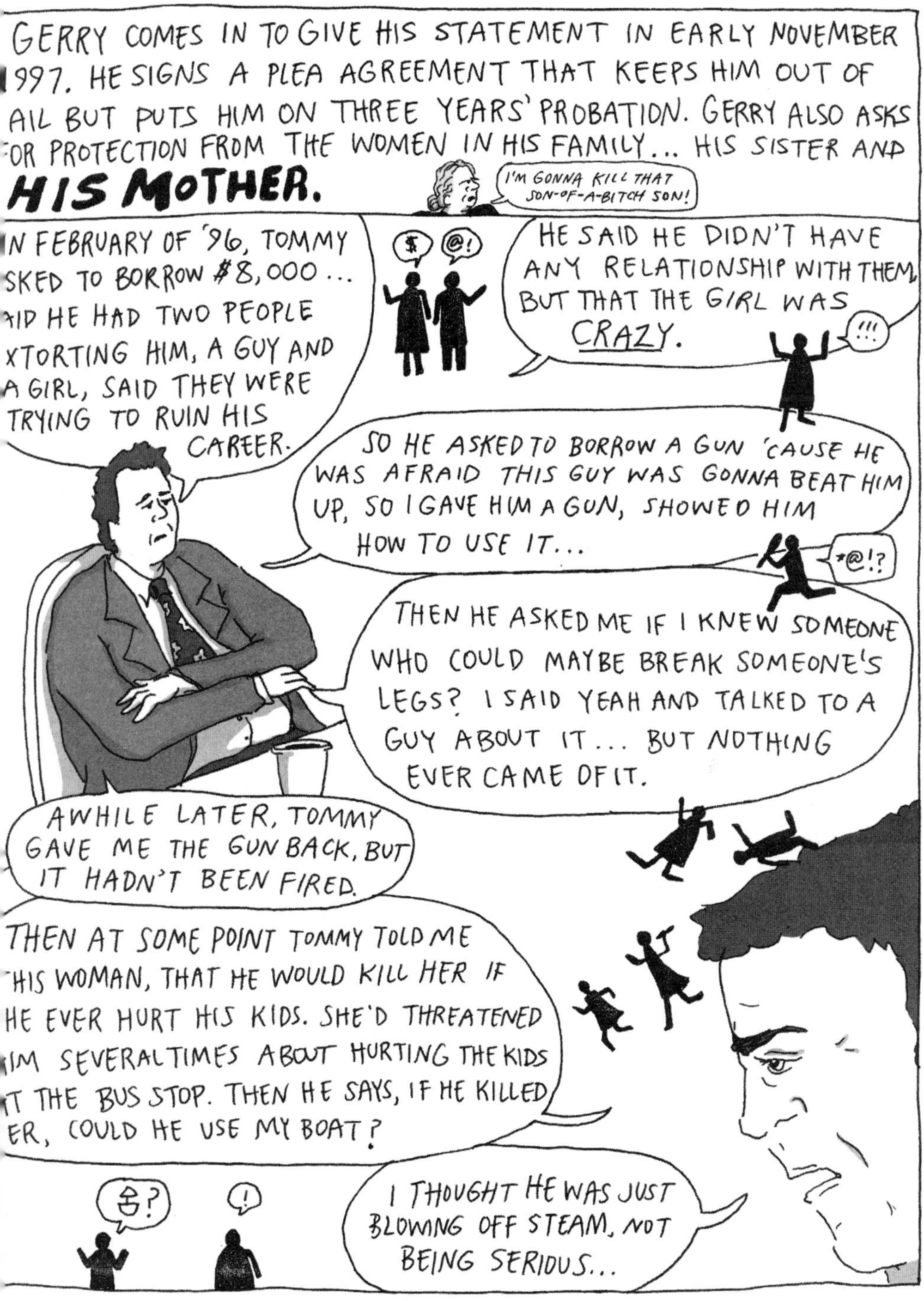
GERRY COMES IN TO GIVE HIS STATEMENT IN EARLY NOVEMBER 1997. HE SIGNS A PLEA AGREEMENT THAT KEEPS HIM OUT OF JAIL BUT PUTS HIM ON THREE YEARS' PROBATION. GERRY ALSO ASKS FOR PROTECTION FROM THE WOMEN IN HIS FAMILY... HIS SISTER AND HIS MOTHER.
I'M GONNA KILL THAT SON-OF-A-BITCH SON!
IN FEBRUARY OF '96, TOMMY ASKED TO BORROW $8,000... SAID HE HAD TWO PEOPLE EXTORTING HIM, A GUY AND A GIRL, SAID THEY WERE TRYING TO RUIN HIS CAREER.
HE SAID HE DIDN'T HAVE ANY RELATIONSHIP WITH THEM, BUT THAT THE GIRL WAS CRAZY.
!!!
SO HE ASKED TO BORROW A GUN 'CAUSE HE WAS AFRAID THIS GUY WAS GONNA BEAT HIM UP, SO I GAVE HIM A GUN, SHOWED HIM HOW TO USE IT...
*@!?
THEN HE ASKED ME IF I KNEW SOMEONE WHO COULD MAYBE BREAK SOMEONE'S LEGS? I SAID YEAH AND TALKED TO A GUY ABOUT IT... BUT NOTHING EVER CAME OF IT.
AWHILE LATER, TOMMY GAVE ME THE GUN BACK, BUT IT HADN'T BEEN FIRED.
THEN AT SOME POINT TOMMY TOLD ME THIS WOMAN, THAT HE WOULD KILL HER IF SHE EVER HURT HIS KIDS. SHE'D THREATENED HIM SEVERAL TIMES ABOUT HURTING THE KIDS AT THE BUS STOP. THEN HE SAYS, IF HE KILLED HER, COULD HE USE MY BOAT?
I THOUGHT HE WAS JUST BLOWING OFF STEAM, NOT BEING SERIOUS...

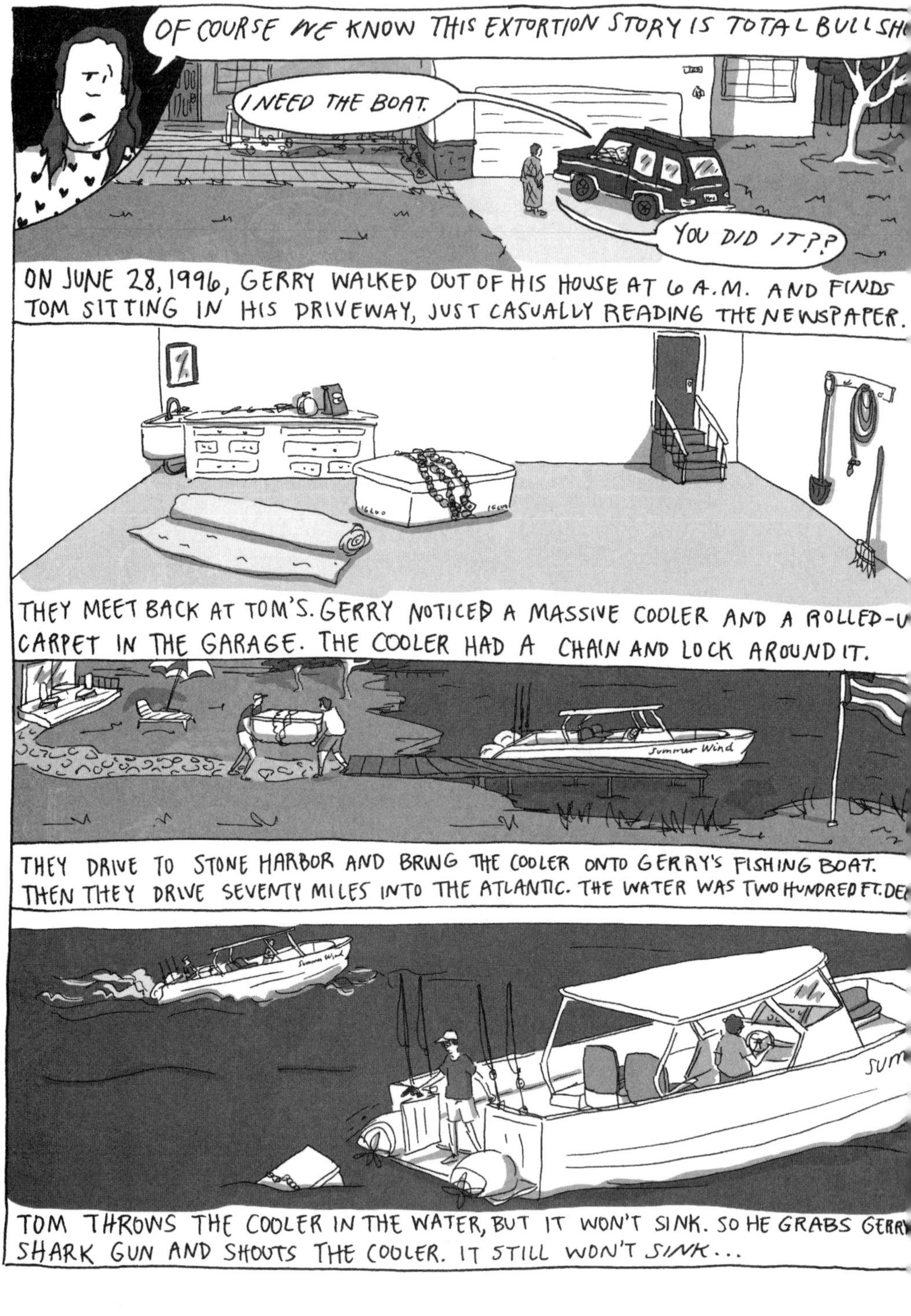
OF COURSE WE KNOW THIS EXTORTION STORY IS TOTAL BULLSH
I NEED THE BOAT.
YOU DID IT??
ON JUNE 28, 1996, GERRY WALKED OUT OF HIS HOUSE AT 6 A.M. AND FINDS TOM SITTING IN HIS DRIVEWAY, JUST CASUALLY READING THE NEWSPAPER.
THEY MEET BACK AT TOM'S. GERRY NOTICED A MASSIVE COOLER AND A ROLLED-U CARPET IN THE GARAGE. THE COOLER HAD A CHAIN AND LOCK AROUND IT.
Summer Wind
THEY DRIVE TO STONE HARBOR AND BRING THE COOLER ONTO GERRY'S FISHING BOAT. THEN THEY DRIVE SEVENTY MILES INTO THE ATLANTIC. THE WATER WAS TWO HUNDRED FT. DE
TOM THROWS THE COOLER IN THE WATER, BUT IT WON'T SINK. SO HE GRABS GERR SHARK GUN AND SHOUTS THE COOLER. IT STILL WON'T SINK...

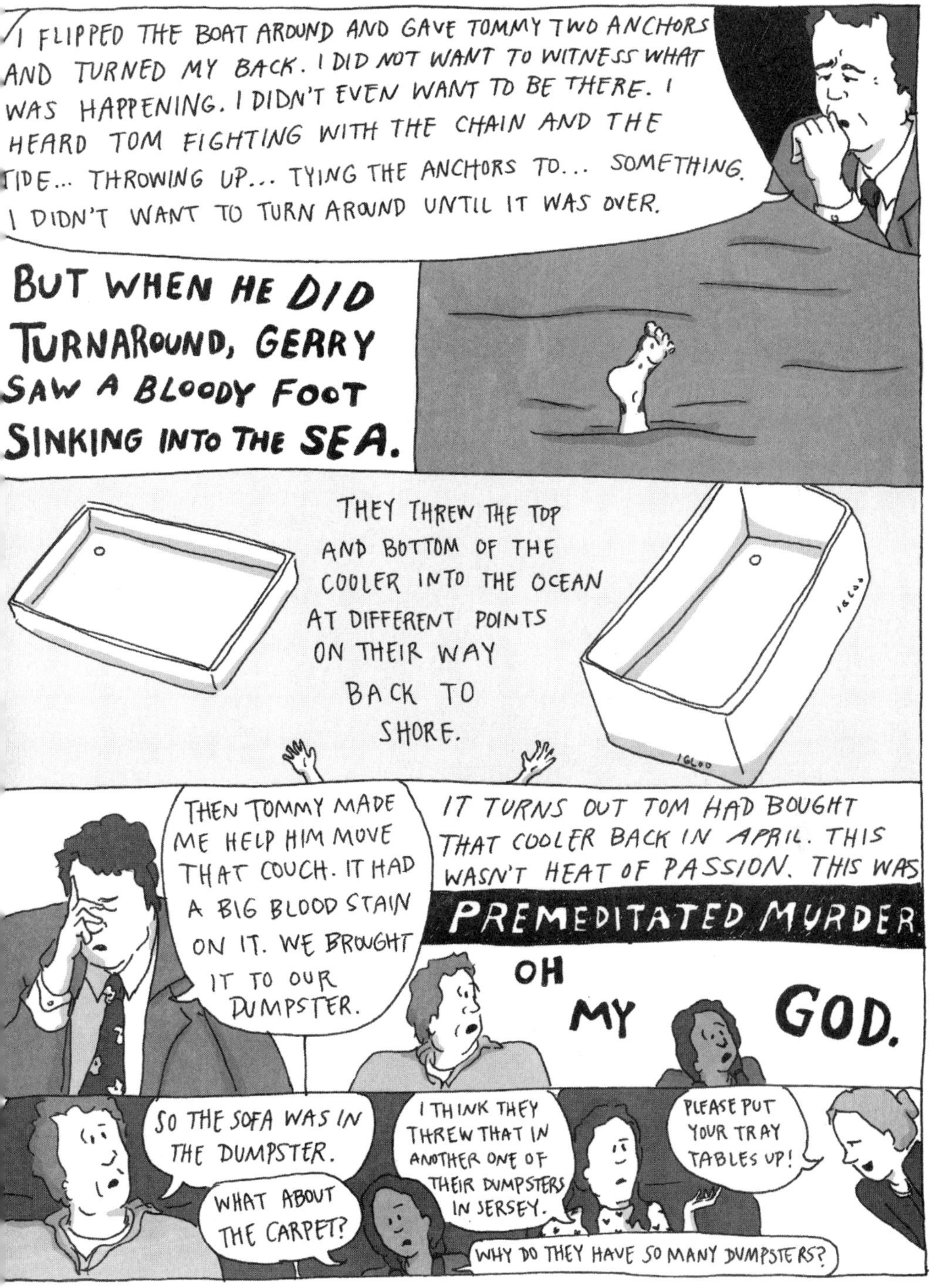
I FLIPPED THE BOAT AROUND AND GAVE TOMMY TWO ANCHORS AND TURNED MY BACK. I DID NOT WANT TO WITNESS WHAT WAS HAPPENING. I DIDN'T EVEN WANT TO BE THERE. I HEARD TOM FIGHTING WITH THE CHAIN AND THE TIDE... THROWING UP... TYING THE ANCHORS TO... SOMETHING. I DIDN'T WANT TO TURN AROUND UNTIL IT WAS OVER.
BUT WHEN HE DID TURNAROUND, GERRY SAW A BLOODY FOOT SINKING INTO THE SEA.
THEY THREW THE TOP AND BOTTOM OF THE COOLER INTO THE OCEAN AT DIFFERENT POINTS ON THEIR WAY BACK TO SHORE.
IGLOO
THEN TOMMY MADE ME HELP HIM MOVE THAT COUCH. IT HAD A BIG BLOOD STAIN ON IT. WE BROUGHT IT TO OUR DUMPSTER.
IT TURNS OUT TOM HAD BOUGHT THAT COOLER BACK IN APRIL. THIS WASN'T HEAT OF PASSION. THIS WAS
PREMEDITATED MURDER.
OH MY GOD.
SO THE SOFA WAS IN THE DUMPSTER.
WHAT ABOUT THE CARPET?
I THINK THEY THREW THAT IN ANOTHER ONE OF THEIR DUMPSTERS IN JERSEY.
PLEASE PUT YOUR TRAY TABLES UP!
WHY DO THEY HAVE SO MANY DUMPSTERS?

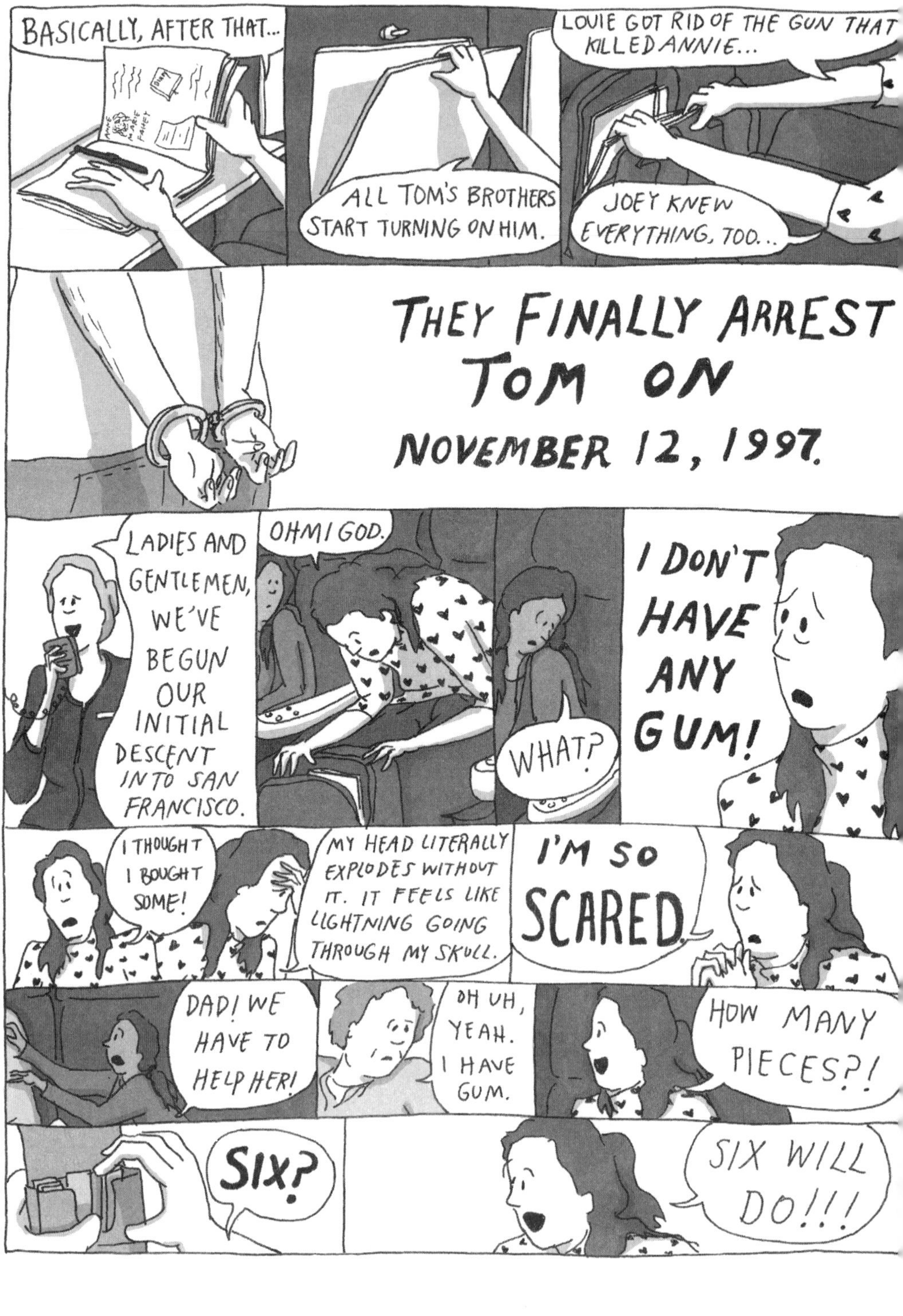
BASICALLY, AFTER THAT...
ALL TOM'S BROTHERS START TURNING ON HIM.
LOUIE GOT RID OF THE GUN THAT KILLED ANNIE...
JOEY KNEW EVERYTHING, TOO...
THEY FINALLY ARREST TOM ON NOVEMBER 12, 1997.
LADIES AND GENTLEMEN, WE'VE BEGUN OUR INITIAL DESCENT INTO SAN FRANCISCO.
OHMIGOD.
WHAT?
I DON'T HAVE ANY GUM!
I THOUGHT I BOUGHT SOME!
MY HEAD LITERALLY EXPLODES WITHOUT IT. IT FEELS LIKE LIGHTNING GOING THROUGH MY SKULL.
I'M SO SCARED.
DAD! WE HAVE TO HELP HER!
OH UH, YEAH. I HAVE GUM.
HOW MANY PIECES?!
SIX?
SIX WILL DO!!!

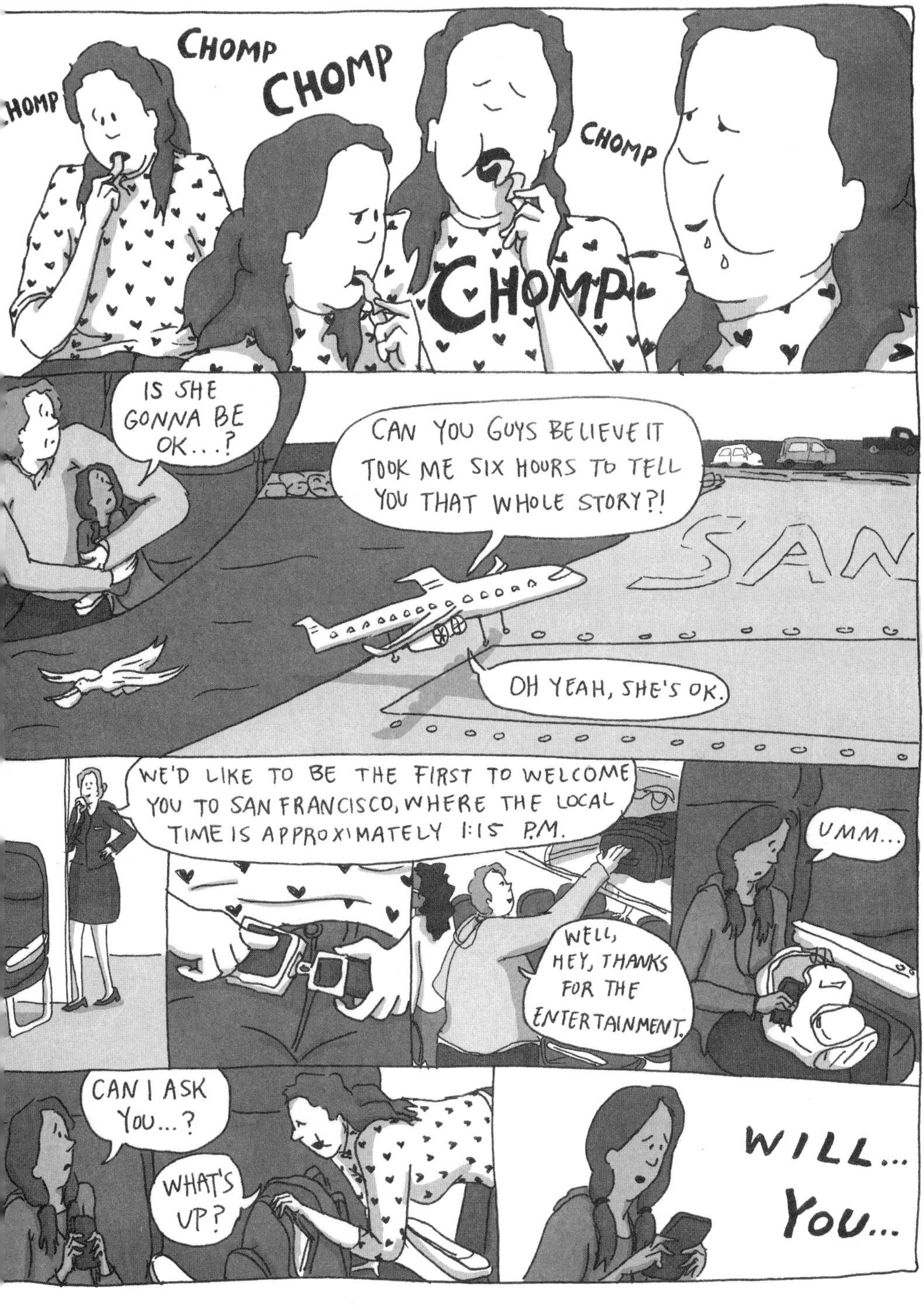
CHOMP
CHOMP
CHOMP
CHOMP
CHOMP
IS SHE GONNA BE OK...?
CAN YOU GUYS BELIEVE IT TOOK ME SIX HOURS TO TELL YOU THAT WHOLE STORY?!
SAN
OH YEAH, SHE'S OK.
WE'D LIKE TO BE THE FIRST TO WELCOME YOU TO SAN FRANCISCO, WHERE THE LOCAL TIME IS APPROXIMATELY 1:15 P.M.
UMM...
WELL, HEY, THANKS FOR THE ENTERTAINMENT.
CAN I ASK YOU...?
WHAT'S UP?
WILL...
YOU...

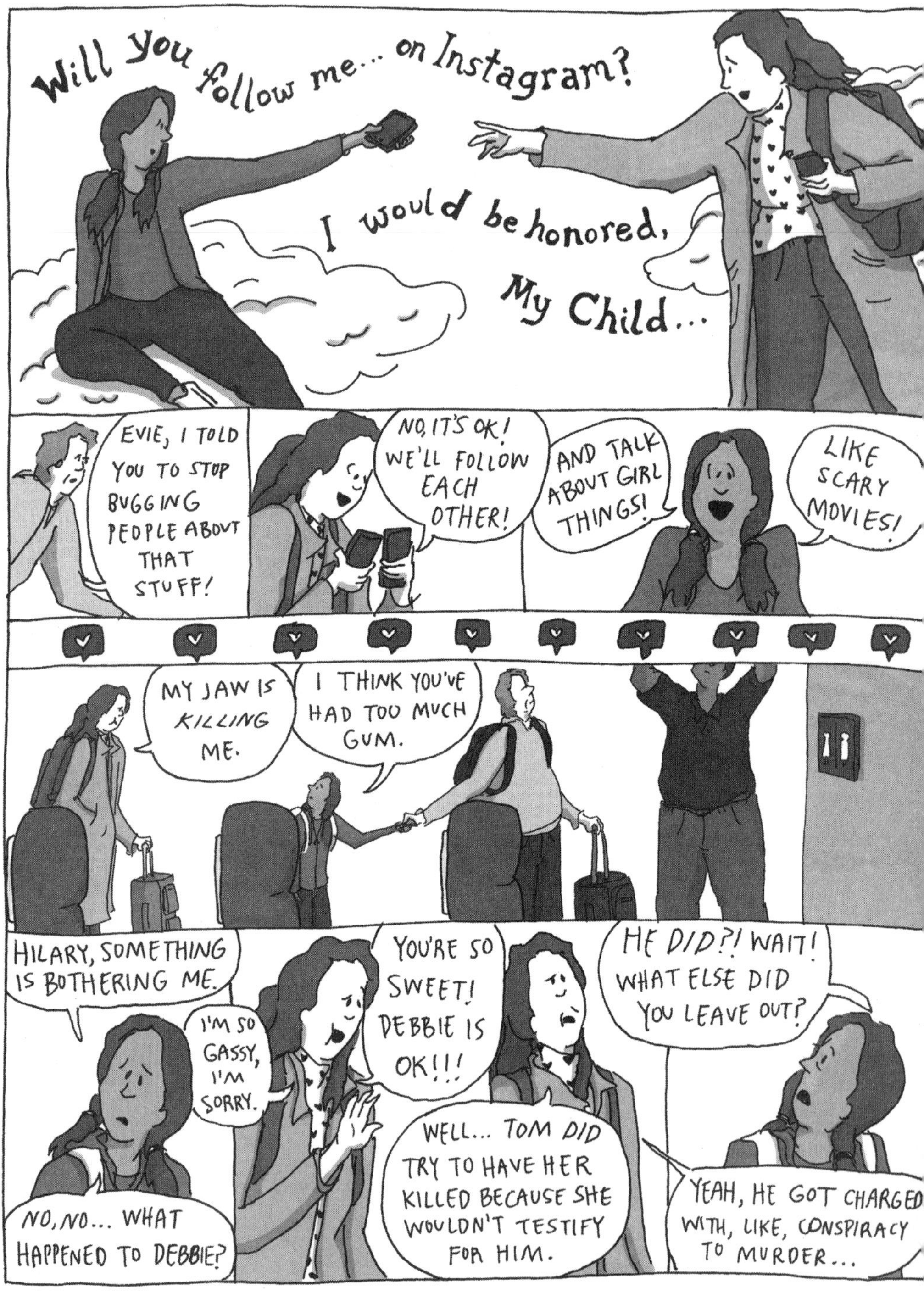
Will you follow me... on Instagram?
I would be honored, My Child...
EVIE, I TOLD YOU TO STOP BUGGING PEOPLE ABOUT THAT STUFF!
NO, IT'S OK! WE'LL FOLLOW EACH OTHER!
AND TALK ABOUT GIRL THINGS!
LIKE SCARY MOVIES!
MY JAW IS KILLING ME.
I THINK YOU'VE HAD TOO MUCH GUM.
HILARY, SOMETHING IS BOTHERING ME.
I'M SO GASSY, I'M SORRY.
NO, NO... WHAT HAPPENED TO DEBBIE?
YOU'RE SO SWEET! DEBBIE IS OK!!!
WELL... TOM DID TRY TO HAVE HER KILLED BECAUSE SHE WOULDN'T TESTIFY FOR HIM.
HE DID?! WAIT! WHAT ELSE DID YOU LEAVE OUT?
YEAH, HE GOT CHARGED WITH, LIKE, CONSPIRACY TO MURDER...

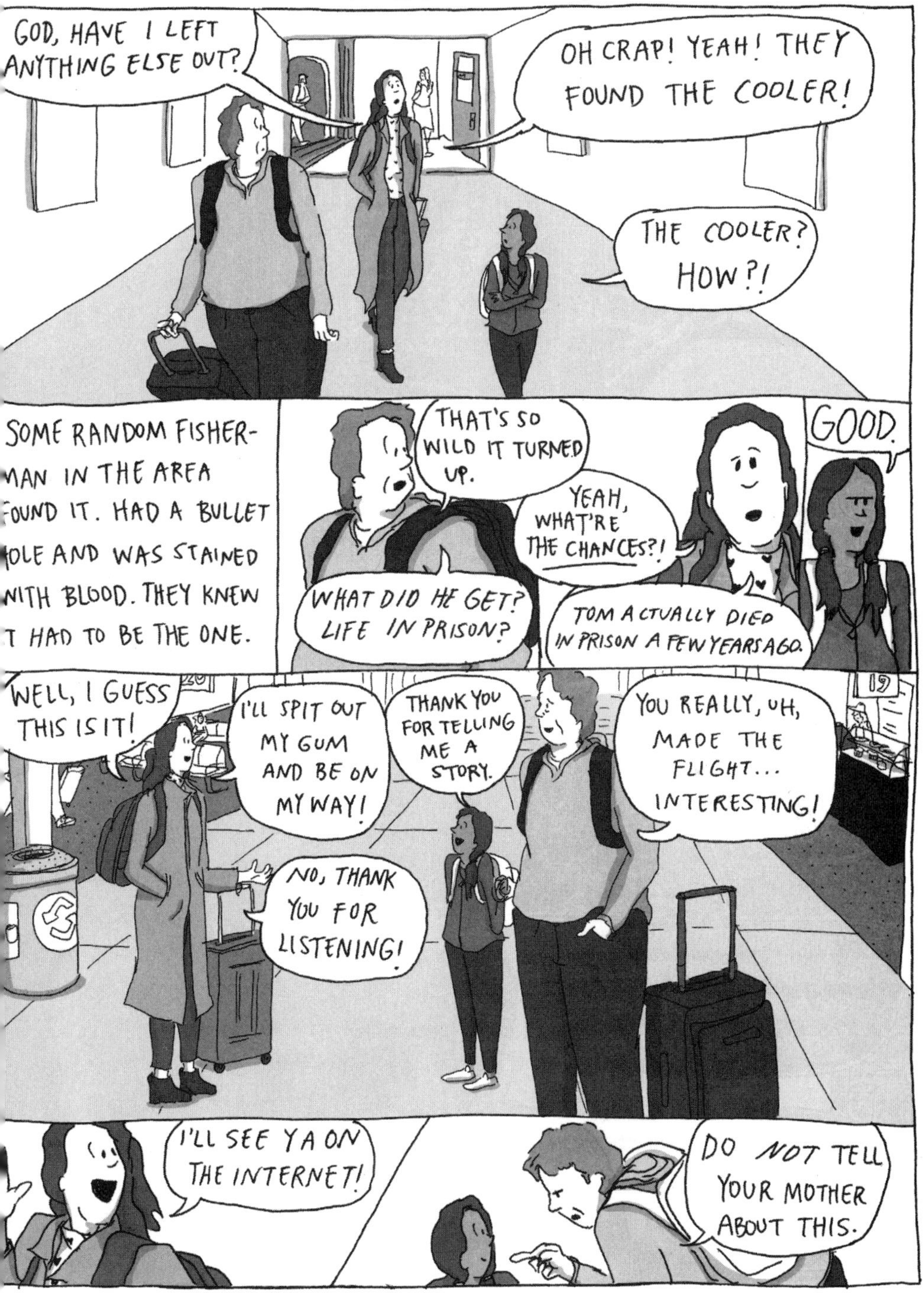
GOD, HAVE I LEFT ANYTHING ELSE OUT?
OH CRAP! YEAH! THEY FOUND THE COOLER!
THE COOLER? HOW?!
SOME RANDOM FISHERMAN IN THE AREA FOUND IT. HAD A BULLET HOLE AND WAS STAINED WITH BLOOD. THEY KNEW IT HAD TO BE THE ONE.
THAT'S SO WILD IT TURNED UP.
YEAH, WHAT'RE THE CHANCES?!
WHAT DID HE GET? LIFE IN PRISON?
TOM ACTUALLY DIED IN PRISON A FEW YEARS AGO.
GOOD.
WELL, I GUESS THIS IS IT!
I'LL SPIT OUT MY GUM AND BE ON MY WAY!
THANK YOU FOR TELLING ME A STORY.
YOU REALLY, UH, MADE THE FLIGHT... INTERESTING!
NO, THANK YOU FOR LISTENING!
I'LL SEE YA ON THE INTERNET!
DO NOT TELL YOUR MOTHER ABOUT THIS.

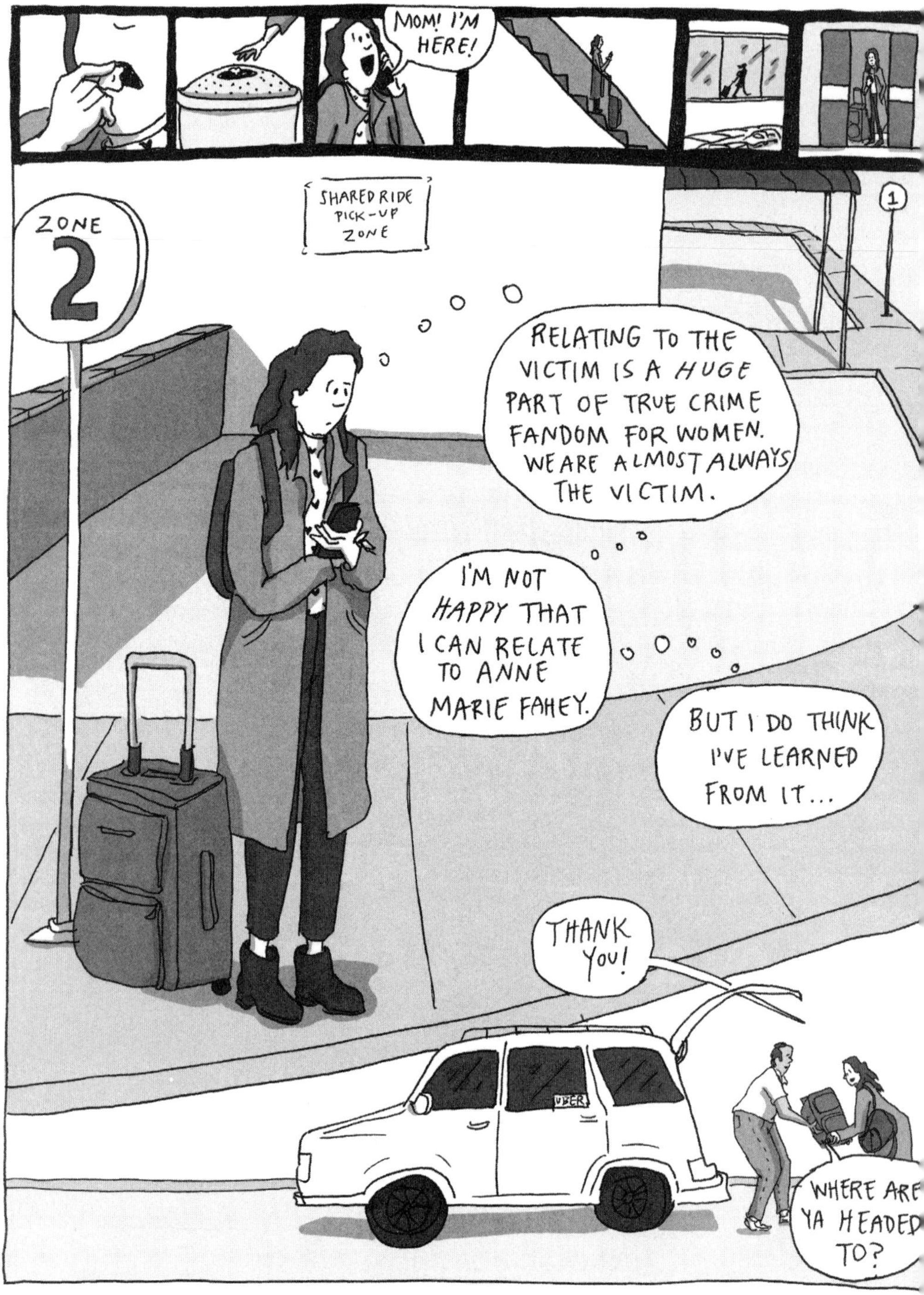
MOM! I'M HERE!
SHARED RIDE PICK-UP ZONE
ZONE 2
1
RELATING TO THE VICTIM IS A *HUGE* PART OF TRUE CRIME FANDOM FOR WOMEN. WE ARE ALMOST ALWAYS THE VICTIM.
I'M NOT *HAPPY* THAT I CAN RELATE TO ANNE MARIE FAHEY.
BUT I DO THINK I'VE LEARNED FROM IT...
THANK YOU!
UBER
WHERE ARE YA HEADED TO?

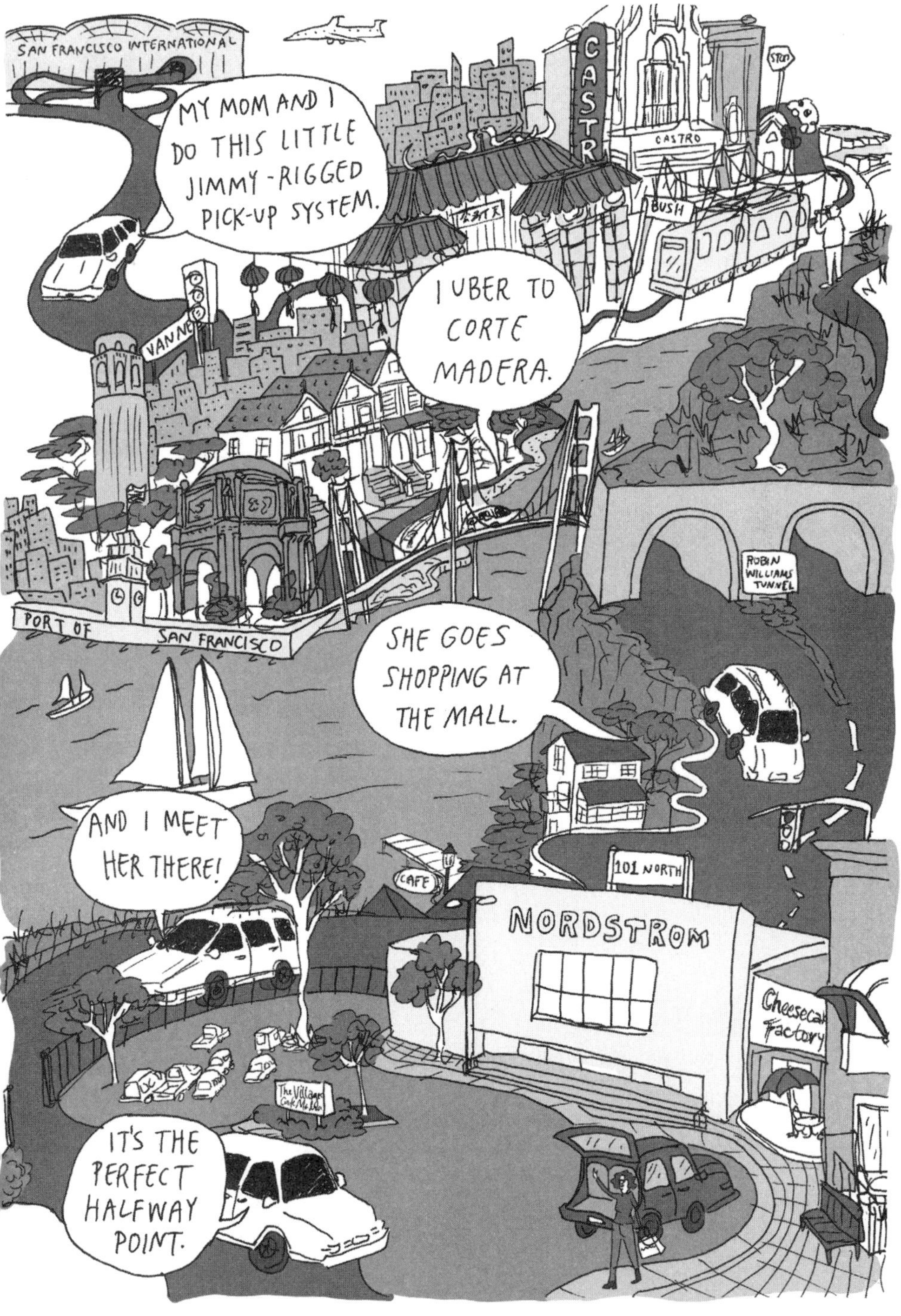
SAN FRANCISCO INTERNATIONAL
MY MOM AND I DO THIS LITTLE JIMMY-RIGGED PICK-UP SYSTEM.
CASTR
CASTRO
BUSH
VANN
I UBER TO CORTE MADERA.
ROBIN WILLIAMS TUNNEL
PORT OF SAN FRANCISCO
SHE GOES SHOPPING AT THE MALL.
AND I MEET HER THERE!
CAFE
101 NORTH
NORDSTROM
Cheesecak Factory
IT'S THE PERFECT HALFWAY POINT.

CASUALLY TERRIFIED

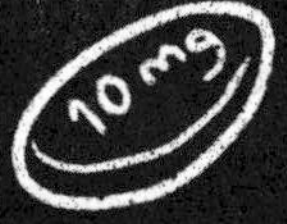
10 mg

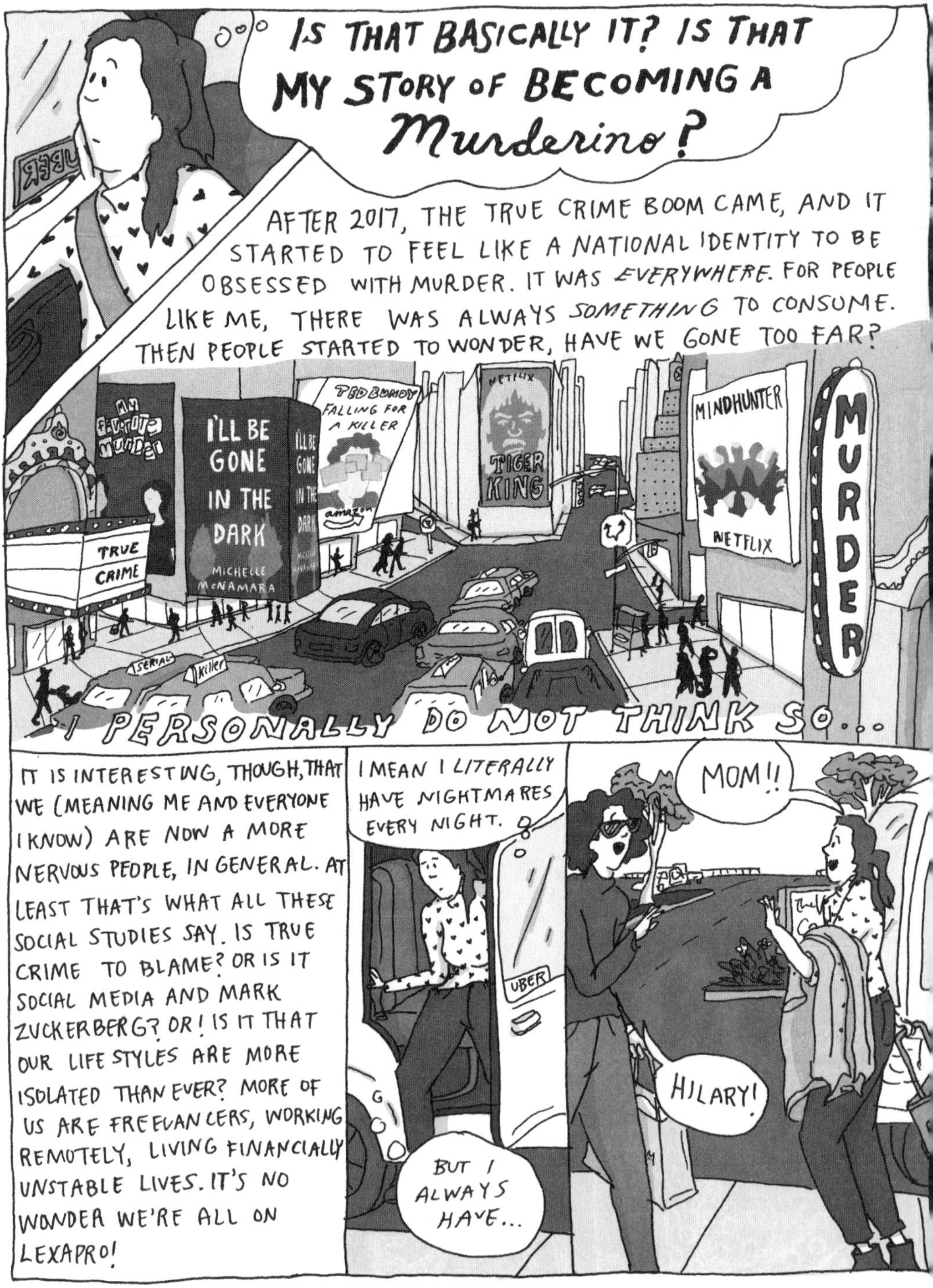
IS THAT BASICALLY IT? IS THAT MY STORY OF BECOMING A Murderino?
AFTER 2017, THE TRUE CRIME BOOM CAME, AND IT STARTED TO FEEL LIKE A NATIONAL IDENTITY TO BE OBSESSED WITH MURDER. IT WAS EVERYWHERE. FOR PEOPLE LIKE ME, THERE WAS ALWAYS SOMETHING TO CONSUME. THEN PEOPLE STARTED TO WONDER, HAVE WE GONE TOO FAR?
UBER
MY FAVORITE MURDER
I'LL BE GONE IN THE DARK
MICHELLE McNAMARA
TED BUNDY FALLING FOR A KILLER
amazon
NETFLIX
TIGER KING
MINDHUNTER
NETFLIX
MURDER
TRUE CRIME
SERIAL
Killer
I PERSONALLY DO NOT THINK SO...
IT IS INTERESTING, THOUGH, THAT WE (MEANING ME AND EVERYONE I KNOW) ARE NOW A MORE NERVOUS PEOPLE, IN GENERAL. AT LEAST THAT'S WHAT ALL THESE SOCIAL STUDIES SAY. IS TRUE CRIME TO BLAME? OR IS IT SOCIAL MEDIA AND MARK ZUCKERBERG? OR! IS IT THAT OUR LIFESTYLES ARE MORE ISOLATED THAN EVER? MORE OF US ARE FREELANCERS, WORKING REMOTELY, LIVING FINANCIALLY UNSTABLE LIVES. IT'S NO WONDER WE'RE ALL ON LEXAPRO!
I MEAN I LITERALLY HAVE NIGHTMARES EVERY NIGHT.
UBER
BUT I ALWAYS HAVE...
MOM!!
HILARY!

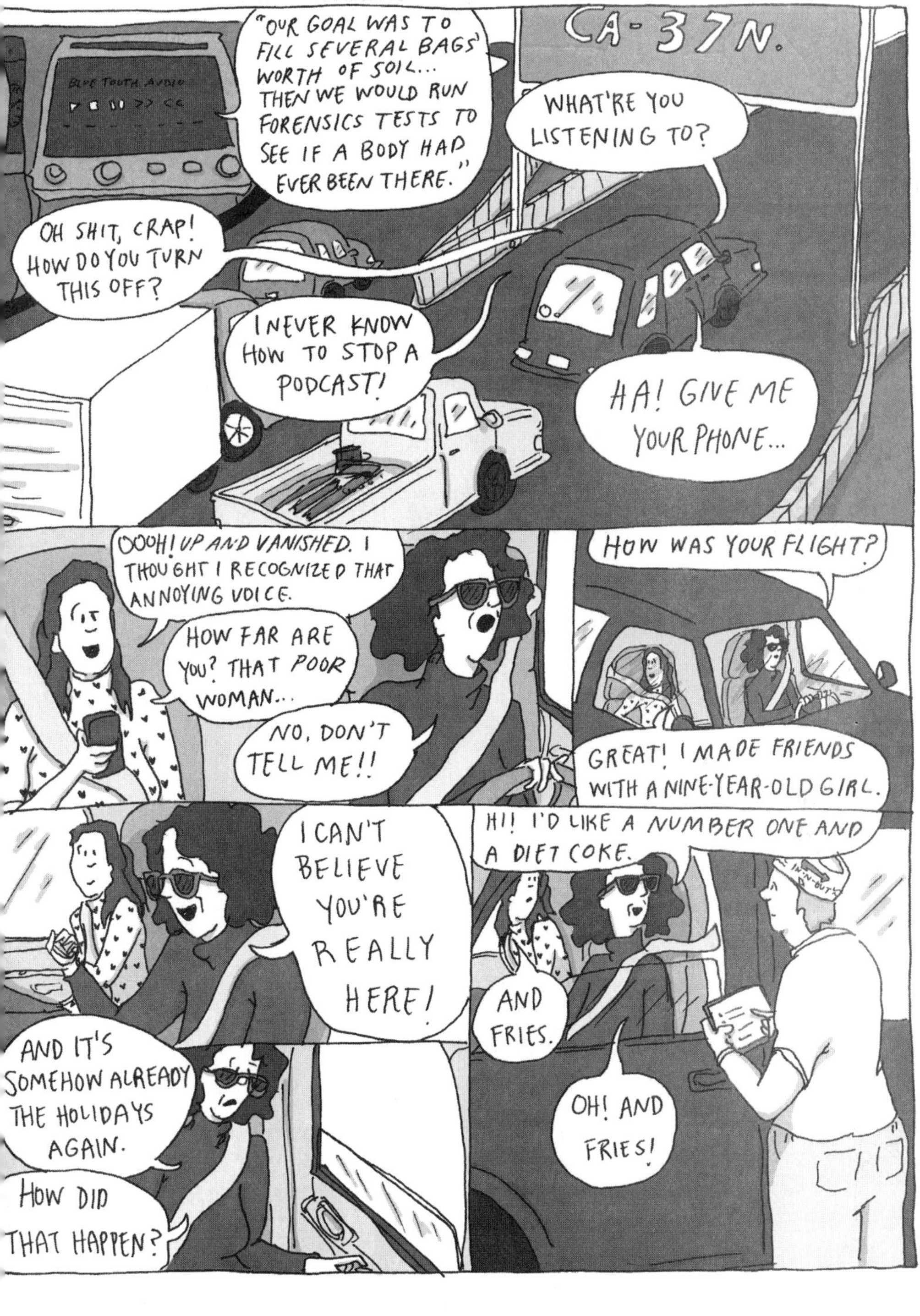
"OUR GOAL WAS TO FILL SEVERAL BAGS' WORTH OF SOIL... THEN WE WOULD RUN FORENSICS TESTS TO SEE IF A BODY HAD EVER BEEN THERE."
CA-37N.
WHAT'RE YOU LISTENING TO?
OH SHIT, CRAP! HOW DO YOU TURN THIS OFF?
I NEVER KNOW HOW TO STOP A PODCAST!
HA! GIVE ME YOUR PHONE...
OOOH! *UP AND VANISHED.* I THOUGHT I RECOGNIZED THAT ANNOYING VOICE.
HOW FAR ARE YOU? THAT *POOR* WOMAN...
NO, DON'T TELL ME!!
HOW WAS YOUR FLIGHT?
GREAT! I MADE FRIENDS WITH A NINE-YEAR-OLD GIRL.
I CAN'T BELIEVE YOU'RE REALLY HERE!
AND IT'S SOMEHOW ALREADY THE HOLIDAYS AGAIN.
HOW DID THAT HAPPEN?
HI! I'D LIKE A *NUMBER ONE* AND A DIET COKE.
AND FRIES.
OH! AND FRIES!

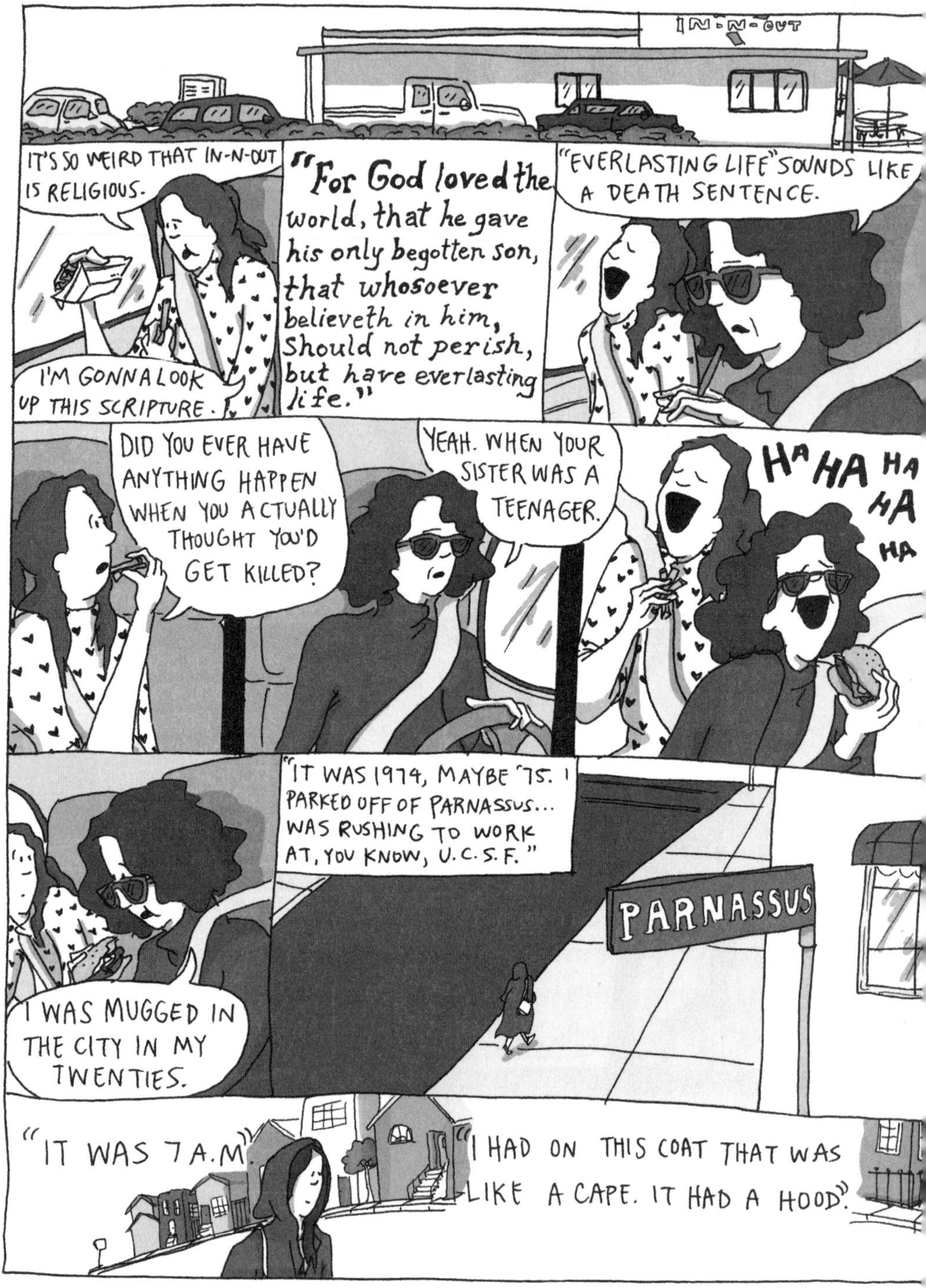
IN-N-OUT
IT'S SO WEIRD THAT IN-N-OUT IS RELIGIOUS.
I'M GONNA LOOK UP THIS SCRIPTURE.
"For God loved the world, that he gave his only begotten son, that whosoever believeth in him, Should not perish, but have everlasting life."
"EVERLASTING LIFE" SOUNDS LIKE A DEATH SENTENCE.
DID YOU EVER HAVE ANYTHING HAPPEN WHEN YOU ACTUALLY THOUGHT YOU'D GET KILLED?
YEAH. WHEN YOUR SISTER WAS A TEENAGER.
HA HA HA HA HA HA
I WAS MUGGED IN THE CITY IN MY TWENTIES.
"IT WAS 1974, MAYBE '75. I PARKED OFF OF PARNASSUS... WAS RUSHING TO WORK AT, YOU KNOW, U.C.S.F."
PARNASSUS
"IT WAS 7 A.M."
"I HAD ON THIS COAT THAT WAS LIKE A CAPE. IT HAD A HOOD."

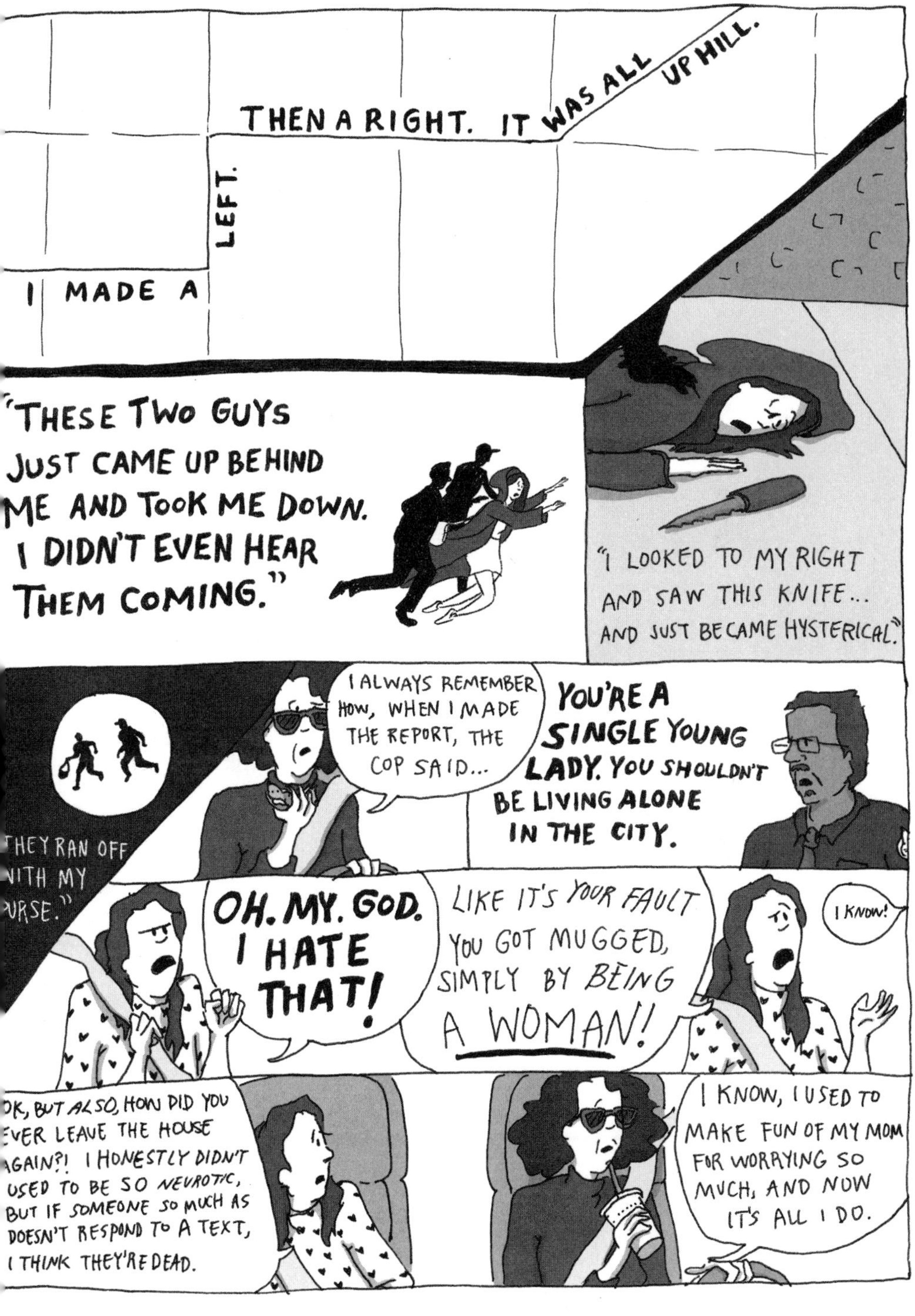

I MADE A
LEFT.
THEN A RIGHT. IT WAS ALL UP HILL.
"THESE TWO GUYS JUST CAME UP BEHIND ME AND TOOK ME DOWN. I DIDN'T EVEN HEAR THEM COMING."
"I LOOKED TO MY RIGHT AND SAW THIS KNIFE... AND JUST BECAME HYSTERICAL."
THEY RAN OFF WITH MY PURSE."
I ALWAYS REMEMBER HOW, WHEN I MADE THE REPORT, THE COP SAID...
YOU'RE A SINGLE YOUNG LADY. YOU SHOULDN'T BE LIVING ALONE IN THE CITY.
OH. MY. GOD. I HATE THAT!
LIKE IT'S YOUR FAULT YOU GOT MUGGED, SIMPLY BY BEING A WOMAN!
I KNOW!
OK, BUT ALSO, HOW DID YOU EVER LEAVE THE HOUSE AGAIN?! I HONESTLY DIDN'T USED TO BE SO NEUROTIC, BUT IF SOMEONE SO MUCH AS DOESN'T RESPOND TO A TEXT, I THINK THEY'RE DEAD.
I KNOW, I USED TO MAKE FUN OF MY MOM FOR WORRYING SO MUCH, AND NOW IT'S ALL I DO.

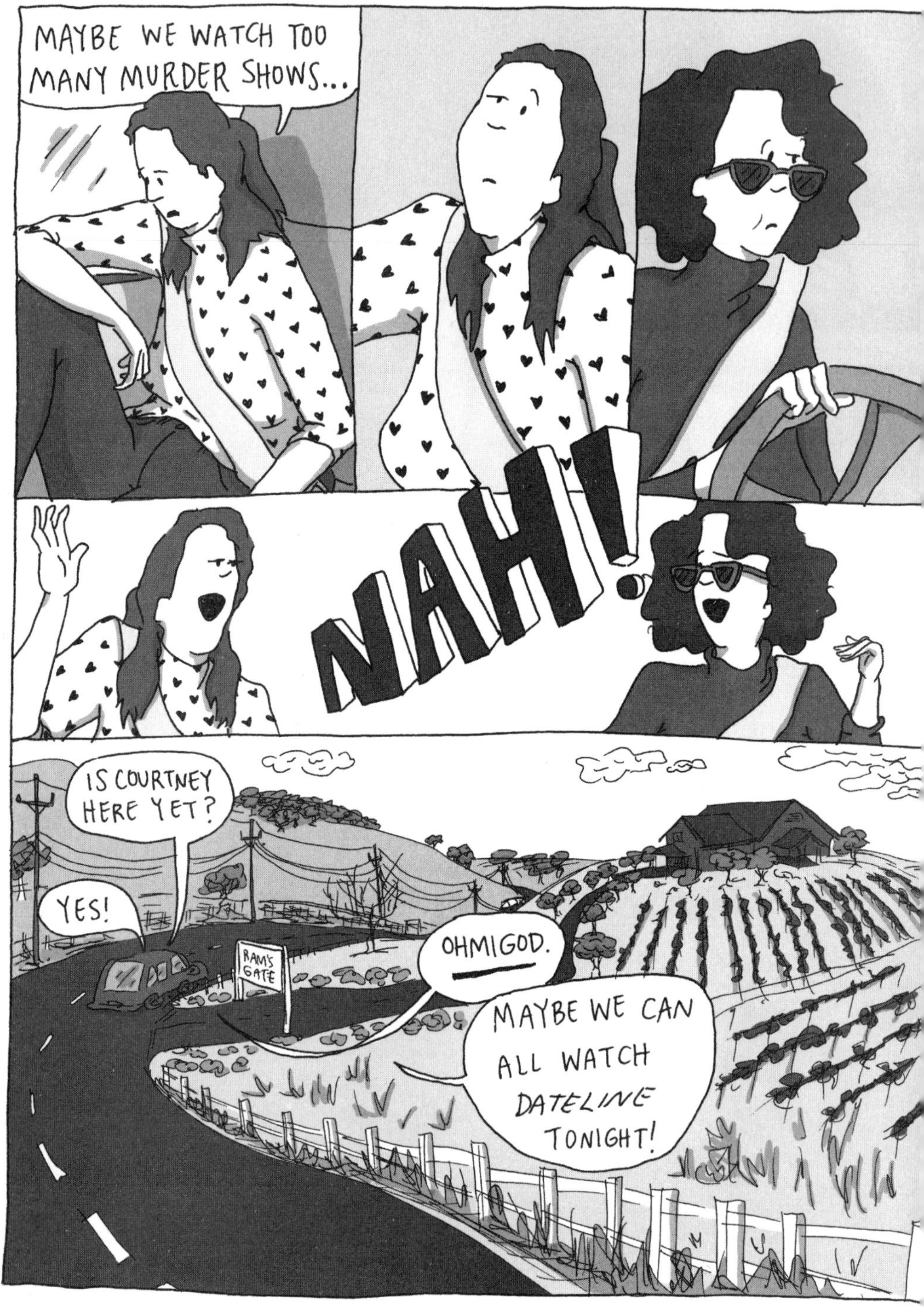
MAYBE WE WATCH TOO MANY MURDER SHOWS...
NAH!
IS COURTNEY HERE YET?
YES!
RAM'S GATE
OHMIGOD.
MAYBE WE CAN ALL WATCH *DATELINE* TONIGHT!

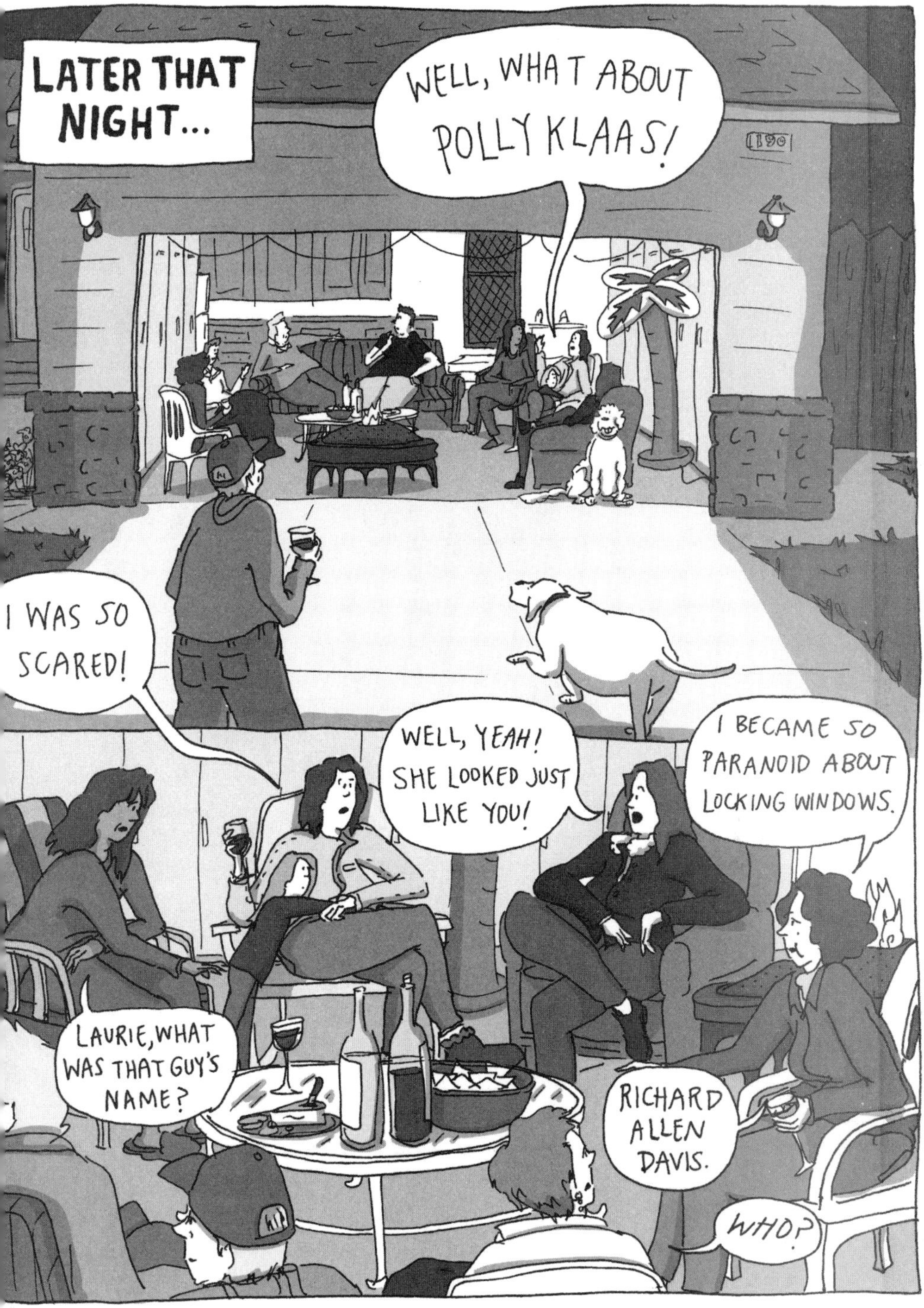
LATER THAT NIGHT...
WELL, WHAT ABOUT POLLY KLAAS!
1890
I WAS SO SCARED!
WELL, YEAH! SHE LOOKED JUST LIKE YOU!
I BECAME SO PARANOID ABOUT LOCKING WINDOWS.
LAURIE, WHAT WAS THAT GUY'S NAME?
RICHARD ALLEN DAVIS.
WHO?

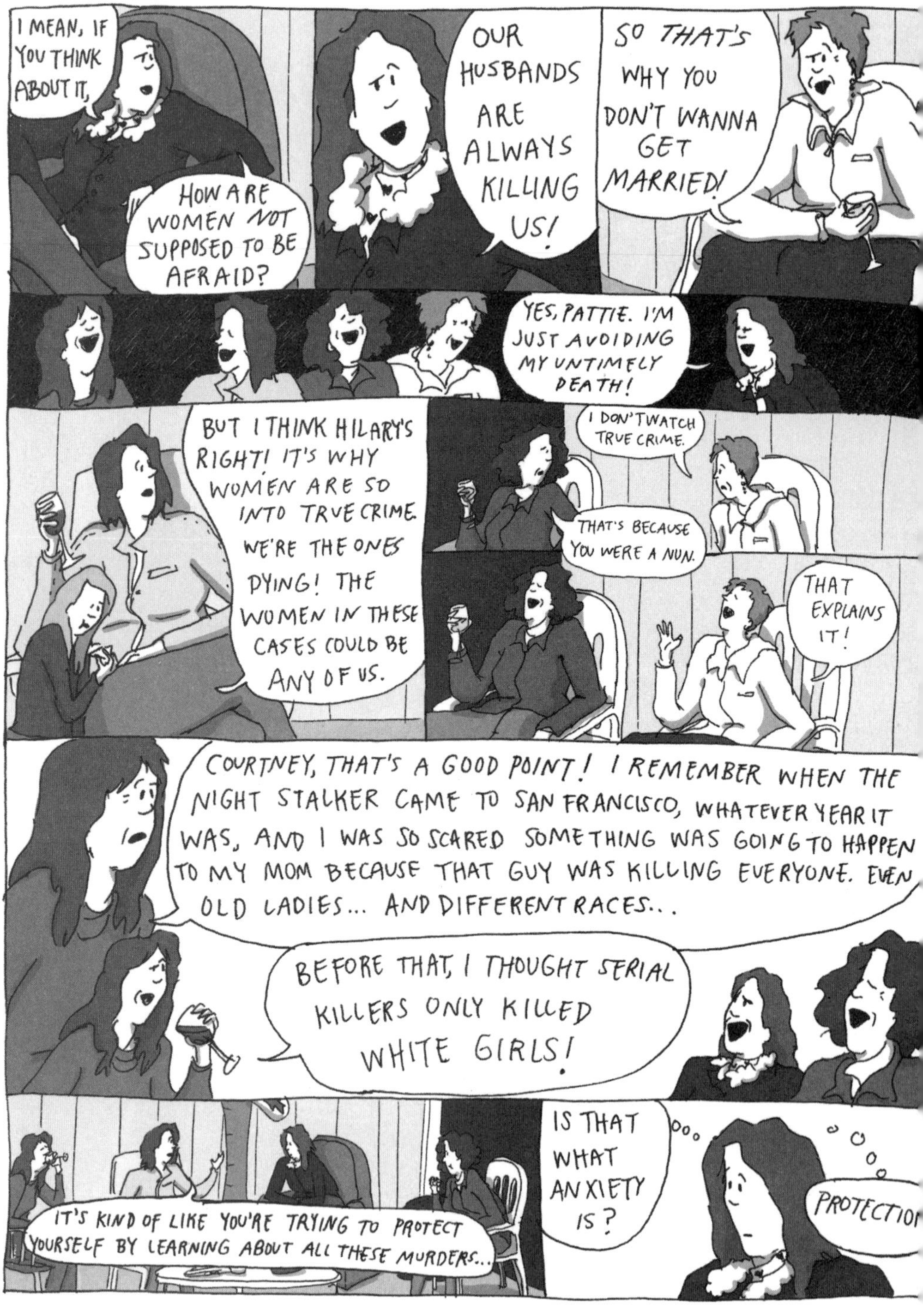
I MEAN, IF YOU THINK ABOUT IT,
HOW ARE WOMEN NOT SUPPOSED TO BE AFRAID?
OUR HUSBANDS ARE ALWAYS KILLING US!
SO THAT'S WHY YOU DON'T WANNA GET MARRIED!
YES, PATTIE. I'M JUST AVOIDING MY UNTIMELY DEATH!
BUT I THINK HILARY'S RIGHT! IT'S WHY WOMEN ARE SO INTO TRUE CRIME. WE'RE THE ONES DYING! THE WOMEN IN THESE CASES COULD BE ANY OF US.
I DON'T WATCH TRUE CRIME.
THAT'S BECAUSE YOU WERE A NUN.
THAT EXPLAINS IT!
COURTNEY, THAT'S A GOOD POINT! I REMEMBER WHEN THE NIGHT STALKER CAME TO SAN FRANCISCO, WHATEVER YEAR IT WAS, AND I WAS SO SCARED SOMETHING WAS GOING TO HAPPEN TO MY MOM BECAUSE THAT GUY WAS KILLING EVERYONE. EVEN OLD LADIES... AND DIFFERENT RACES...
BEFORE THAT, I THOUGHT SERIAL KILLERS ONLY KILLED WHITE GIRLS!
IT'S KIND OF LIKE YOU'RE TRYING TO PROTECT YOURSELF BY LEARNING ABOUT ALL THESE MURDERS...
IS THAT WHAT ANXIETY IS?
PROTECTIO

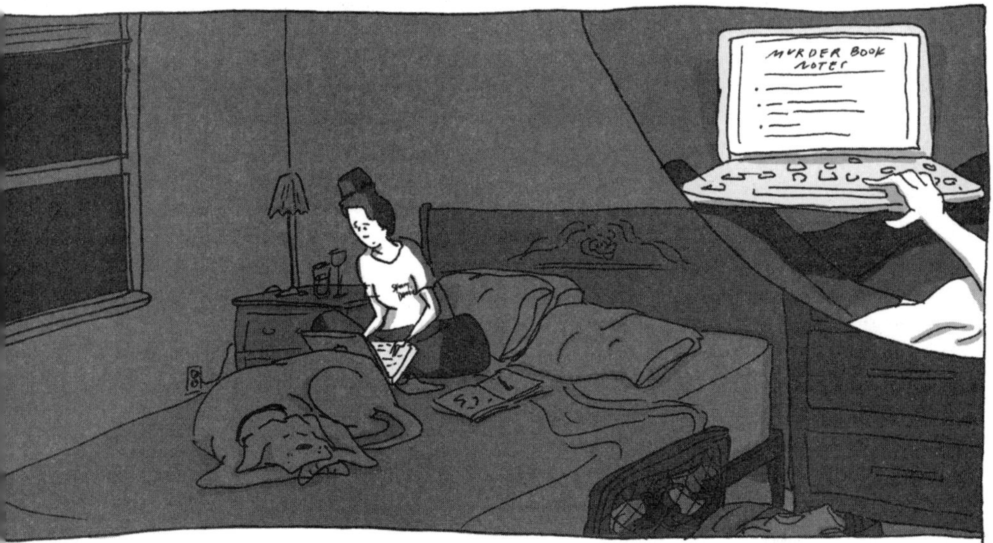
MURDER BOOK NOTES
Skinny Dennis

hough, statistically, men are more likely to be murdered, the cases that get attention, that fill the public eye, the ones that all these movies, books, and podcasts are about, are almost always *THE WRONGFUL DEATH* of a *WOMAN*. More specifically, a white woman - because f systemic *racism!!!* Obviously people of color get murdered, but their stories are often kept from being highlighted at a national level like these:

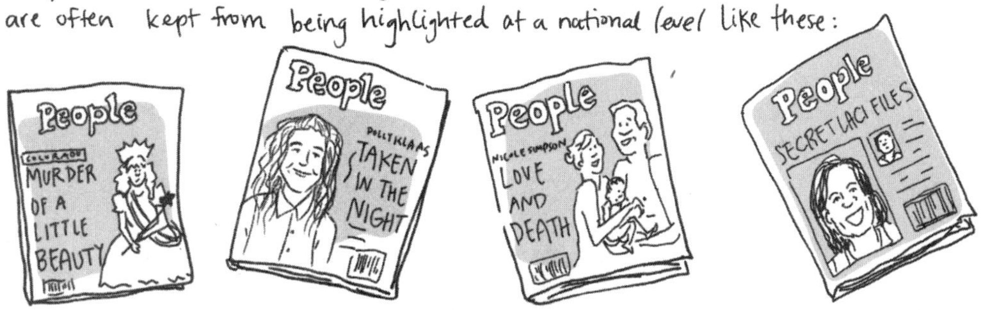
People
COLORADO
MURDER OF A LITTLE BEAUTY
People
POLLY KLAAS
TAKEN IN THE NIGHT
People
NICOLE SIMPSON
LOVE AND DEATH
People
SECRET LACI FILES

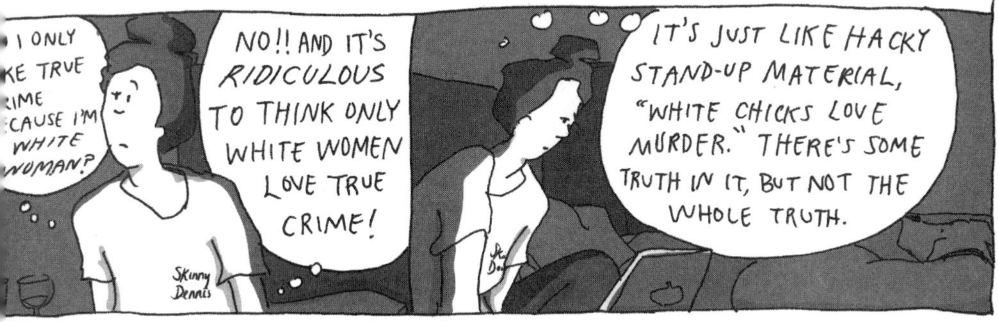
I ONLY KE TRUE IME CAUSE I'M WHITE WOMAN?
NO!! AND IT'S *RIDICULOUS* TO THINK ONLY WHITE WOMEN LOVE TRUE CRIME!
Skinny Dennis
IT'S JUST LIKE HACKY STAND-UP MATERIAL, "WHITE CHICKS LOVE MURDER." THERE'S SOME TRUTH IN IT, BUT NOT THE WHOLE TRUTH.

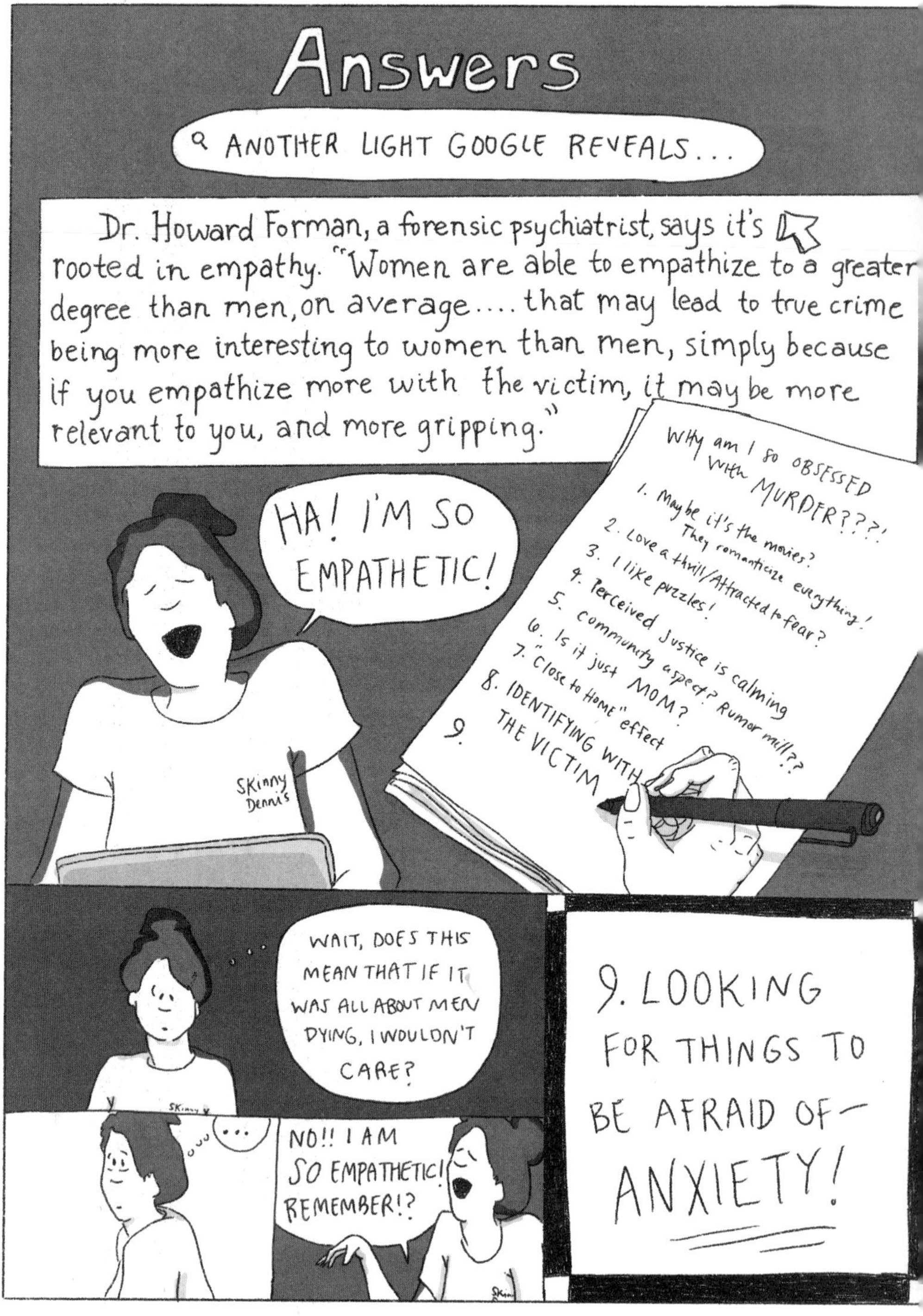
Answers
ANOTHER LIGHT GOOGLE REVEALS...
Dr. Howard Forman, a forensic psychiatrist, says it's rooted in empathy. "Women are able to empathize to a greater degree than men, on average.... that may lead to true crime being more interesting to women than men, simply because if you empathize more with the victim, it may be more relevant to you, and more gripping."
HA! I'M SO EMPATHETIC!
WHY am I so OBSESSED WITH MURDER???!
1. Maybe it's the movies? They romanticize everything!
2. Love a thrill/Attracted to fear?
3. I like puzzles!
4. Perceived Justice is calming
5. community aspect? Rumor mill??
6. Is it just MOM?
7. "Close to Home" effect
8. IDENTIFYING WITH THE VICTIM
9.
SKinny Dennis
WAIT, DOES THIS MEAN THAT IF IT WAS ALL ABOUT MEN DYING, I WOULDN'T CARE?
...
NO!! I AM SO EMPATHETIC! REMEMBER!?
9. LOOKING FOR THINGS TO BE AFRAID OF— ANXIETY!

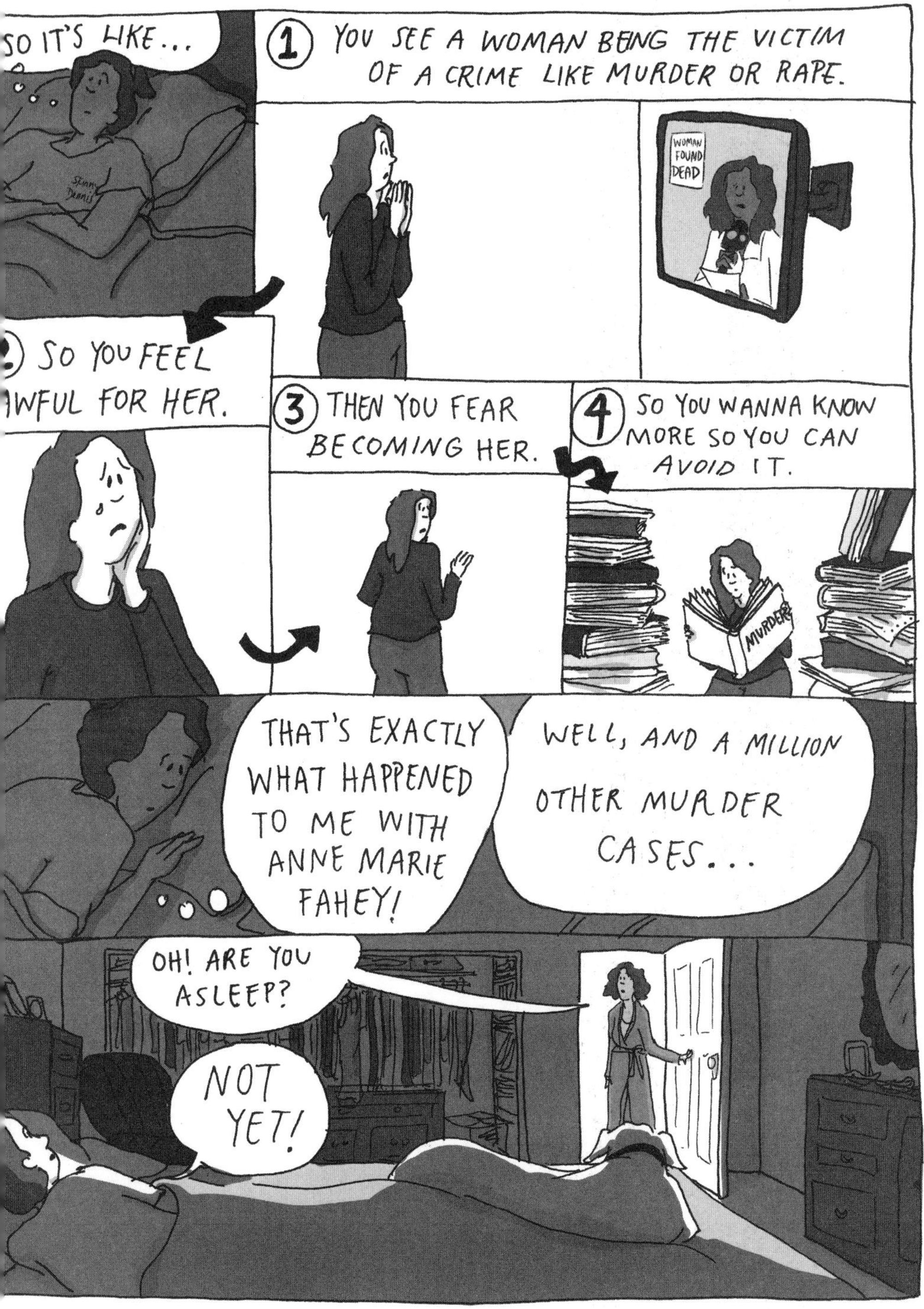
SO IT'S LIKE...
1 YOU SEE A WOMAN BEING THE VICTIM OF A CRIME LIKE MURDER OR RAPE.
WOMAN FOUND DEAD
2 SO YOU FEEL AWFUL FOR HER.
3 THEN YOU FEAR BECOMING HER.
4 SO YOU WANNA KNOW MORE SO YOU CAN AVOID IT.
MURDER
THAT'S EXACTLY WHAT HAPPENED TO ME WITH ANNE MARIE FAHEY!
WELL, AND A MILLION OTHER MURDER CASES...
OH! ARE YOU ASLEEP?
NOT YET!

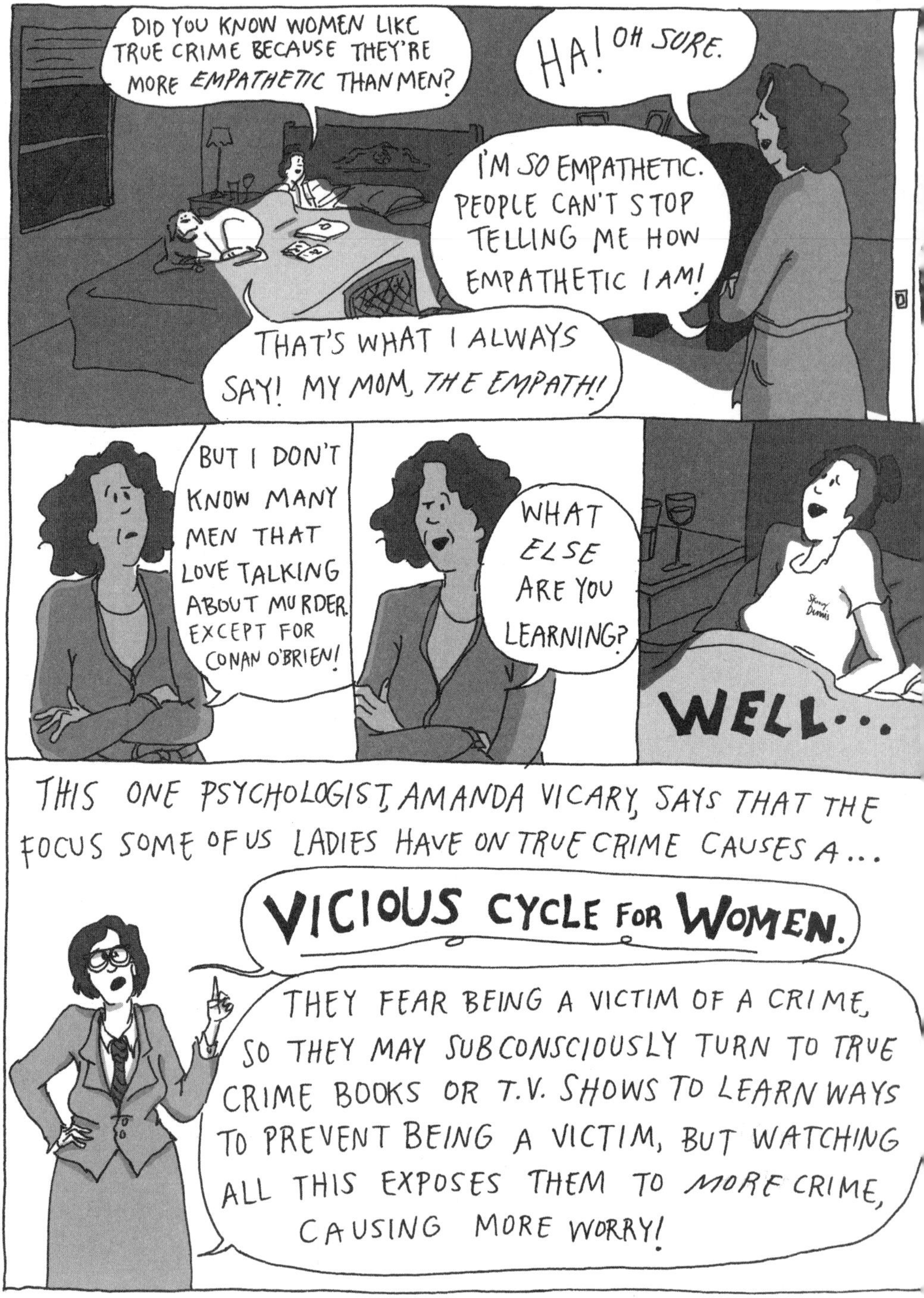
DID YOU KNOW WOMEN LIKE TRUE CRIME BECAUSE THEY'RE MORE EMPATHETIC THAN MEN?
HA! OH SURE.
I'M SO EMPATHETIC. PEOPLE CAN'T STOP TELLING ME HOW EMPATHETIC I AM!
THAT'S WHAT I ALWAYS SAY! MY MOM, THE EMPATH!
BUT I DON'T KNOW MANY MEN THAT LOVE TALKING ABOUT MURDER. EXCEPT FOR CONAN O'BRIEN!
WHAT ELSE ARE YOU LEARNING?
WELL...
THIS ONE PSYCHOLOGIST, AMANDA VICARY, SAYS THAT THE FOCUS SOME OF US LADIES HAVE ON TRUE CRIME CAUSES A...
VICIOUS CYCLE FOR WOMEN.
THEY FEAR BEING A VICTIM OF A CRIME, SO THEY MAY SUBCONSCIOUSLY TURN TO TRUE CRIME BOOKS OR T.V. SHOWS TO LEARN WAYS TO PREVENT BEING A VICTIM, BUT WATCHING ALL THIS EXPOSES THEM TO MORE CRIME, CAUSING MORE WORRY!

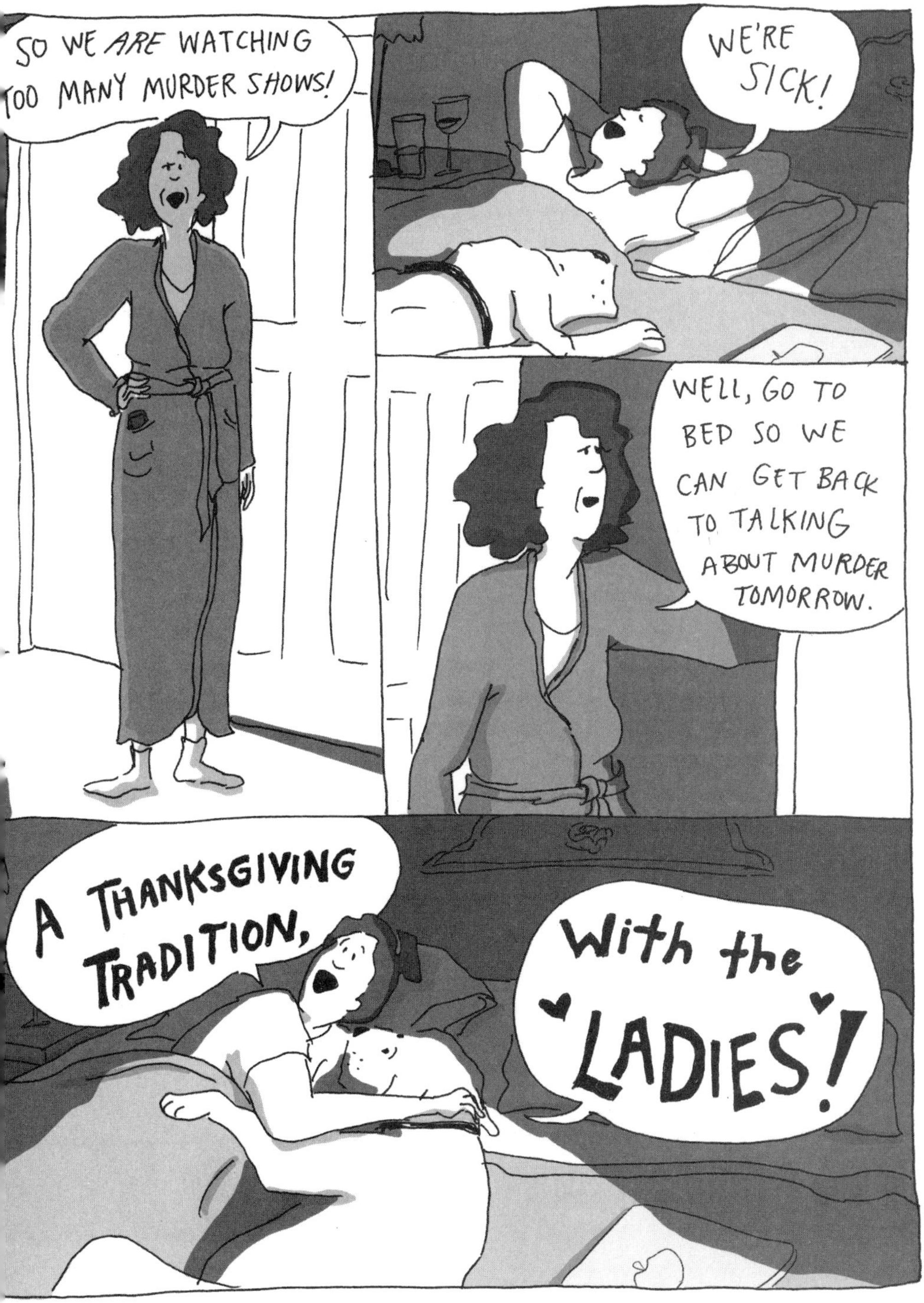
SO WE ARE WATCHING TOO MANY MURDER SHOWS!
WE'RE SICK!
WELL, GO TO BED SO WE CAN GET BACK TO TALKING ABOUT MURDER TOMORROW.
A THANKSGIVING TRADITION,
With the "LADIES"!

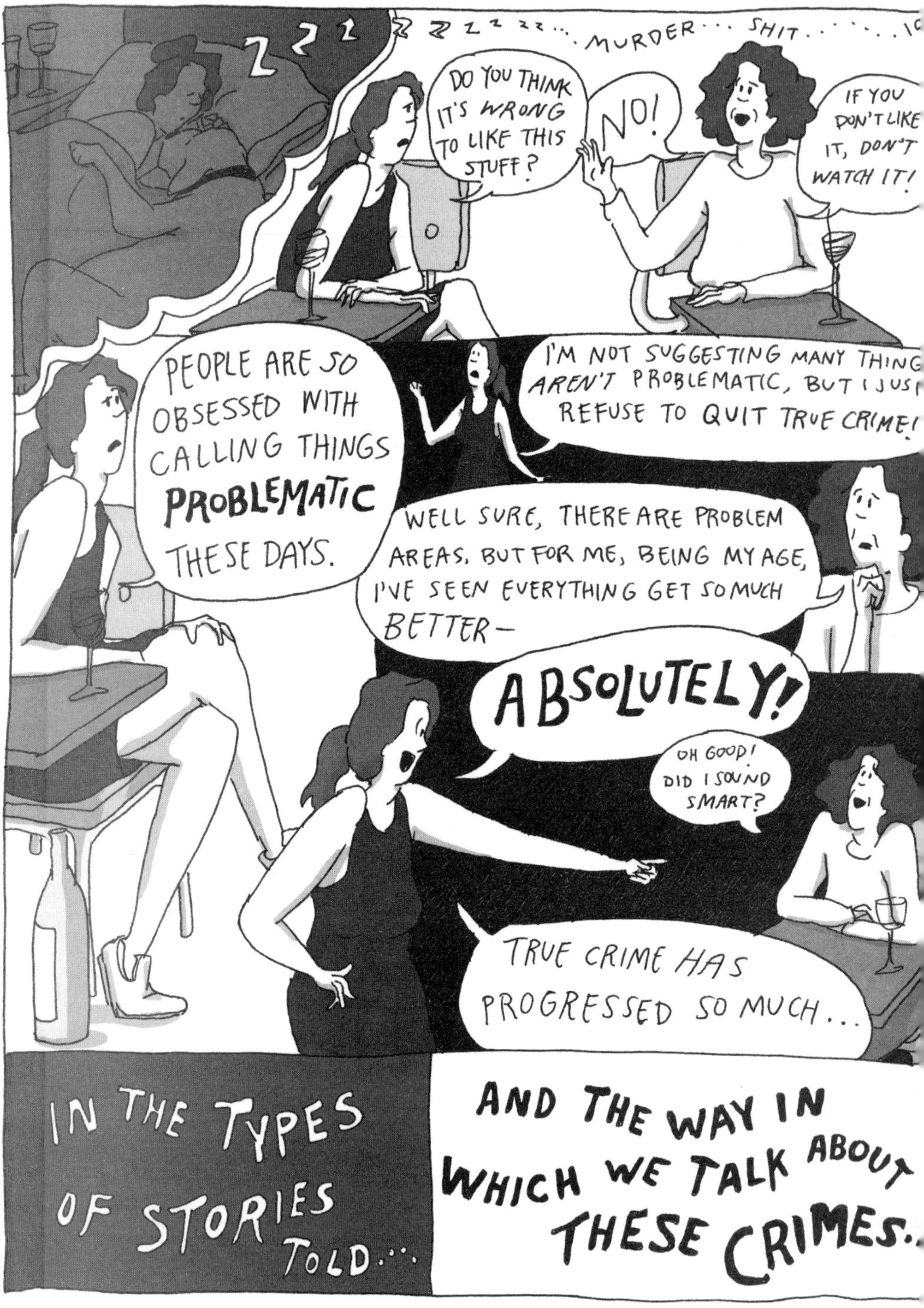
Z Z Z
Z Z Z Z Z Z Z... MURDER... SHIT...
DO YOU THINK IT'S *WRONG* TO LIKE THIS STUFF?
NO!
IF YOU DON'T LIKE IT, DON'T WATCH IT!
PEOPLE ARE SO OBSESSED WITH CALLING THINGS **PROBLEMATIC** THESE DAYS.
I'M NOT SUGGESTING MANY THING AREN'T PROBLEMATIC, BUT I JUS REFUSE TO QUIT TRUE CRIME!
WELL SURE, THERE ARE PROBLEM AREAS, BUT FOR ME, BEING MY AGE, I'VE SEEN EVERYTHING GET SO MUCH BETTER—
ABSOLUTELY!
OH GOOD! DID I SOUND SMART?
TRUE CRIME *HAS* PROGRESSED SO MUCH...
IN THE TYPES OF STORIES TOLD...
AND THE WAY IN WHICH WE TALK ABOUT THESE CRIMES..

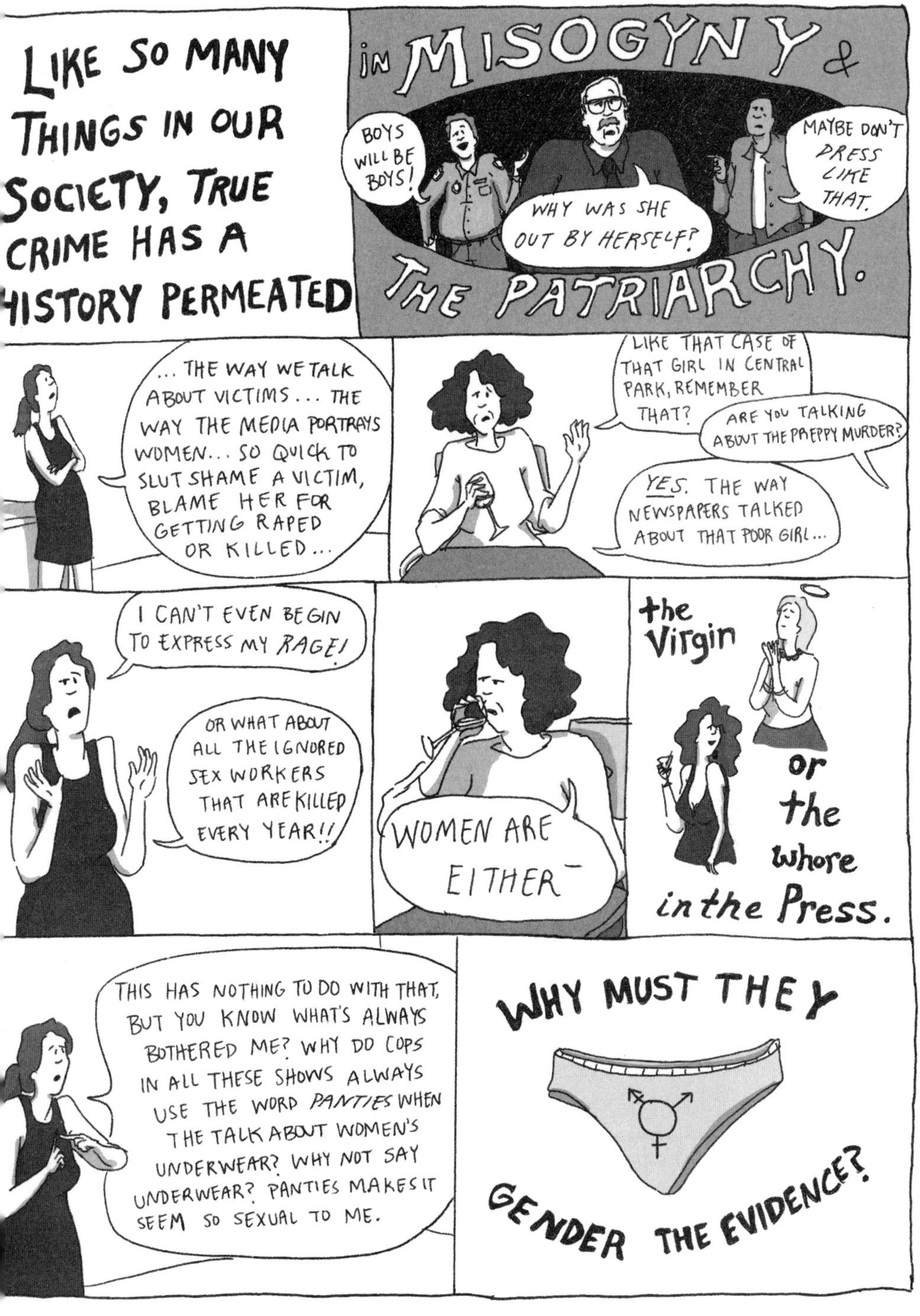
LIKE SO MANY THINGS IN OUR SOCIETY, TRUE CRIME HAS A HISTORY PERMEATED
IN MISOGYNY &
BOYS WILL BE BOYS!
WHY WAS SHE OUT BY HERSELF?
MAYBE DON'T DRESS LIKE THAT.
THE PATRIARCHY.
... THE WAY WE TALK ABOUT VICTIMS ... THE WAY THE MEDIA PORTRAYS WOMEN... SO QUICK TO SLUT SHAME A VICTIM, BLAME HER FOR GETTING RAPED OR KILLED...
LIKE THAT CASE OF THAT GIRL IN CENTRAL PARK, REMEMBER THAT?
ARE YOU TALKING ABOUT THE PREPPY MURDER?
YES. THE WAY NEWSPAPERS TALKED ABOUT THAT POOR GIRL...
I CAN'T EVEN BEGIN TO EXPRESS MY RAGE!
OR WHAT ABOUT ALL THE IGNORED SEX WORKERS THAT ARE KILLED EVERY YEAR!!
WOMEN ARE EITHER
the Virgin or the whore in the Press.
THIS HAS NOTHING TO DO WITH THAT, BUT YOU KNOW WHAT'S ALWAYS BOTHERED ME? WHY DO COPS IN ALL THESE SHOWS ALWAYS USE THE WORD PANTIES WHEN THE TALK ABOUT WOMEN'S UNDERWEAR? WHY NOT SAY UNDERWEAR? PANTIES MAKES IT SEEM SO SEXUAL TO ME.
WHY MUST THEY GENDER THE EVIDENCE?

ON TOP OF THE SEXISM...

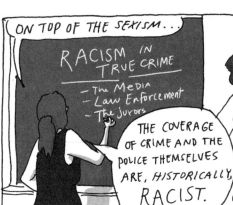

RACISM IN TRUE CRIME
- The Media
- Law Enforcement
- The Jurors

THE COVERAGE OF CRIME AND THE POLICE THEMSELVES ARE, HISTORICALLY, RACIST.

RIGHT... IF JONBENÉT RAMSEY WAS A LITTLE BLACK GIRL, WOULD I EVEN KNOW HER NAME?

PROBABLY NOT. WHY DO WE KNOW ALL THESE NAMES? LIKE JONBENÉT, LACI PETERSON, ELIZABETH SMART, EVEN AMANDA KNOX! BECAUSE THEY'RE WHITE WOMEN.

THINK OF HOW LONG IT TOOK FOR THE POLICE TO EVEN ACKNOWLEDGE ALL THE BLACK KIDS DISAPPEARING IN ATLANTA IN THE '80s.

IT COULD BE ME

AND ON THE OTHER SIDE OF THINGS, NOT THE VICTIMS BUT THE PERPETRATORS... EVEN THE IDEA THAT BLACK SERIAL KILLERS DON'T EXIST IS NOT TRUE! THEY DO!

BLACK SERIAL KILLERS IN AMERICA

SAMUEL LITTLE
KILLED 60

HENRY WALLACE
KILLED 10

CHESTER TURNER
KILLED 10

PAUL DUROUSSEAU
KILLED 7

LORENZO GILYARD
KILLED 13

MARK GOUDEAU
KILLED 9

(AND MORE...)

RICHARD RAMIREZ IS ONE OF THE SCARIEST KILLERS OF ALL TIME! AND HE ISN'T WHITE! WHY DON'T PEOPLE TALK ABOUT THAT?

RICHARD RAMIREZ
THE NIGHT STALKER

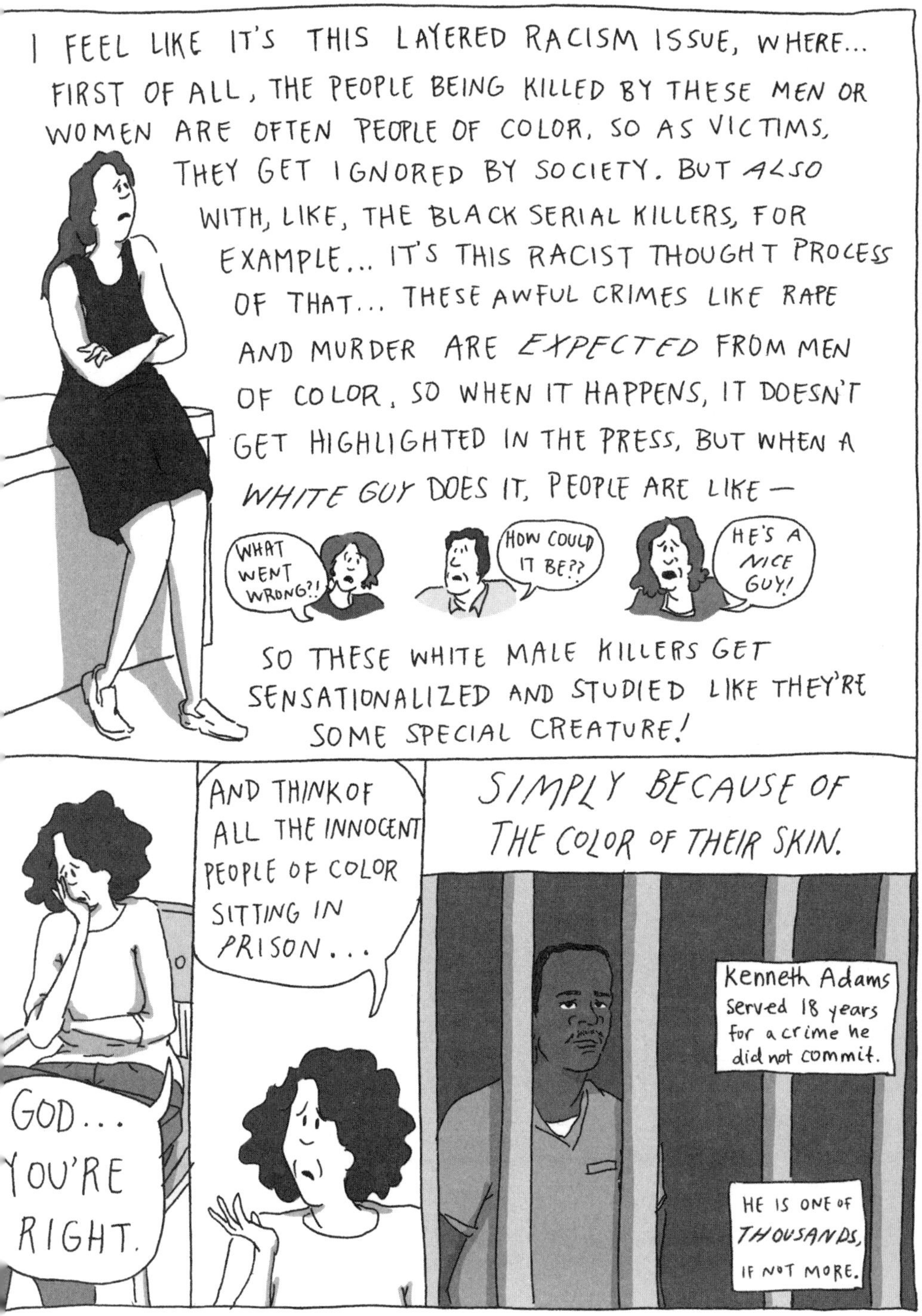
I FEEL LIKE IT'S THIS LAYERED RACISM ISSUE, WHERE... FIRST OF ALL, THE PEOPLE BEING KILLED BY THESE MEN OR WOMEN ARE OFTEN PEOPLE OF COLOR, SO AS VICTIMS, THEY GET IGNORED BY SOCIETY. BUT ALSO WITH, LIKE, THE BLACK SERIAL KILLERS, FOR EXAMPLE... IT'S THIS RACIST THOUGHT PROCESS OF THAT... THESE AWFUL CRIMES LIKE RAPE AND MURDER ARE EXPECTED FROM MEN OF COLOR, SO WHEN IT HAPPENS, IT DOESN'T GET HIGHLIGHTED IN THE PRESS, BUT WHEN A WHITE GUY DOES IT, PEOPLE ARE LIKE—
WHAT WENT WRONG?!
HOW COULD IT BE??
HE'S A NICE GUY!
SO THESE WHITE MALE KILLERS GET SENSATIONALIZED AND STUDIED LIKE THEY'RE SOME SPECIAL CREATURE!
GOD... YOU'RE RIGHT.
AND THINK OF ALL THE INNOCENT PEOPLE OF COLOR SITTING IN PRISON...
SIMPLY BECAUSE OF THE COLOR OF THEIR SKIN.
Kenneth Adams served 18 years for a crime he did not commit.
HE IS ONE OF THOUSANDS, IF NOT MORE.

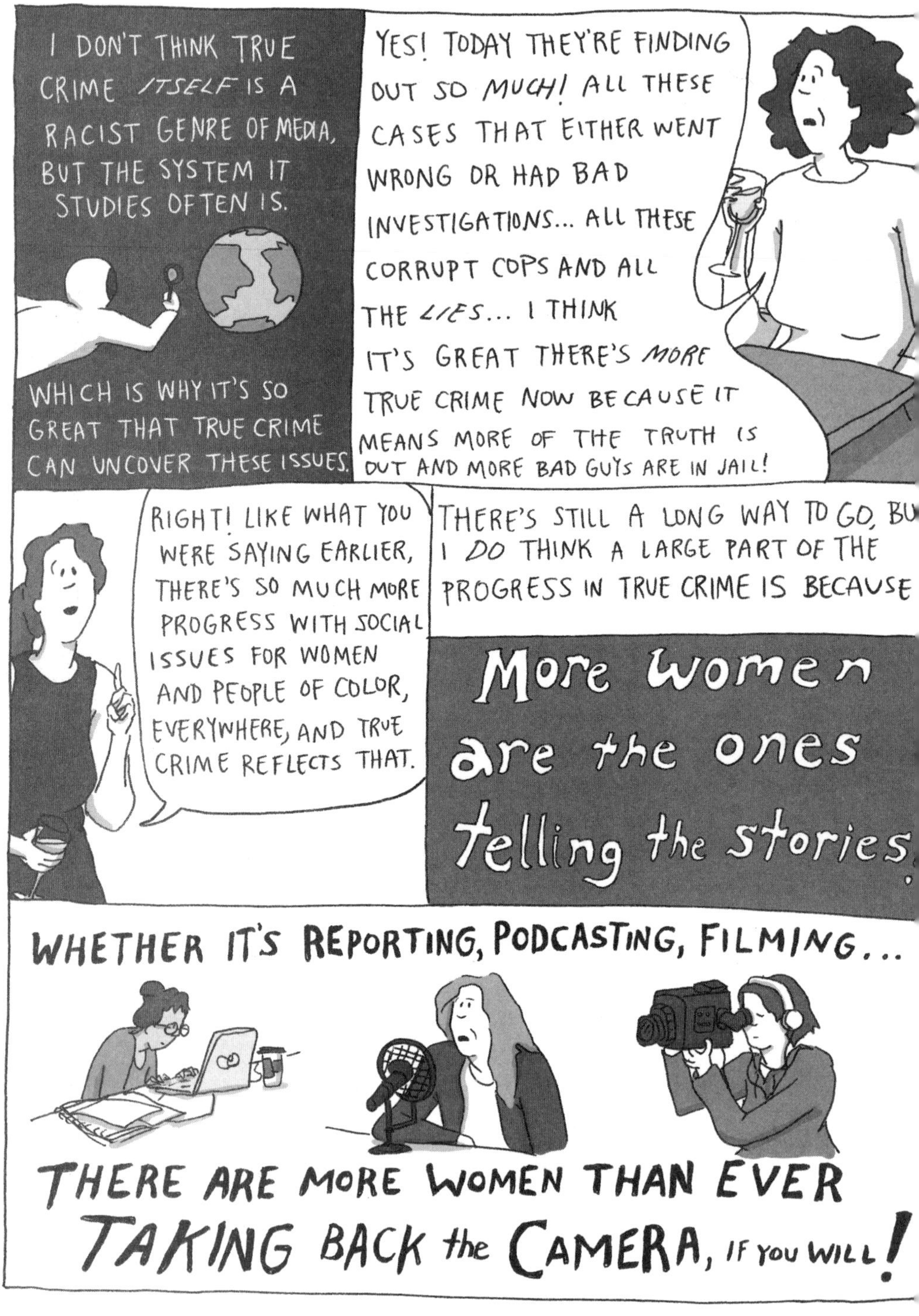
I DON'T THINK TRUE CRIME ITSELF IS A RACIST GENRE OF MEDIA, BUT THE SYSTEM IT STUDIES OFTEN IS.
WHICH IS WHY IT'S SO GREAT THAT TRUE CRIME CAN UNCOVER THESE ISSUES.
YES! TODAY THEY'RE FINDING OUT SO MUCH! ALL THESE CASES THAT EITHER WENT WRONG OR HAD BAD INVESTIGATIONS... ALL THESE CORRUPT COPS AND ALL THE LIES... I THINK IT'S GREAT THERE'S MORE TRUE CRIME NOW BECAUSE IT MEANS MORE OF THE TRUTH IS OUT AND MORE BAD GUYS ARE IN JAIL!
RIGHT! LIKE WHAT YOU WERE SAYING EARLIER, THERE'S SO MUCH MORE PROGRESS WITH SOCIAL ISSUES FOR WOMEN AND PEOPLE OF COLOR, EVERYWHERE, AND TRUE CRIME REFLECTS THAT.
THERE'S STILL A LONG WAY TO GO, BU I DO THINK A LARGE PART OF THE PROGRESS IN TRUE CRIME IS BECAUSE
More women are the ones telling the stories.
WHETHER IT'S REPORTING, PODCASTING, FILMING...
THERE ARE MORE WOMEN THAN EVER TAKING BACK the CAMERA, IF YOU WILL!

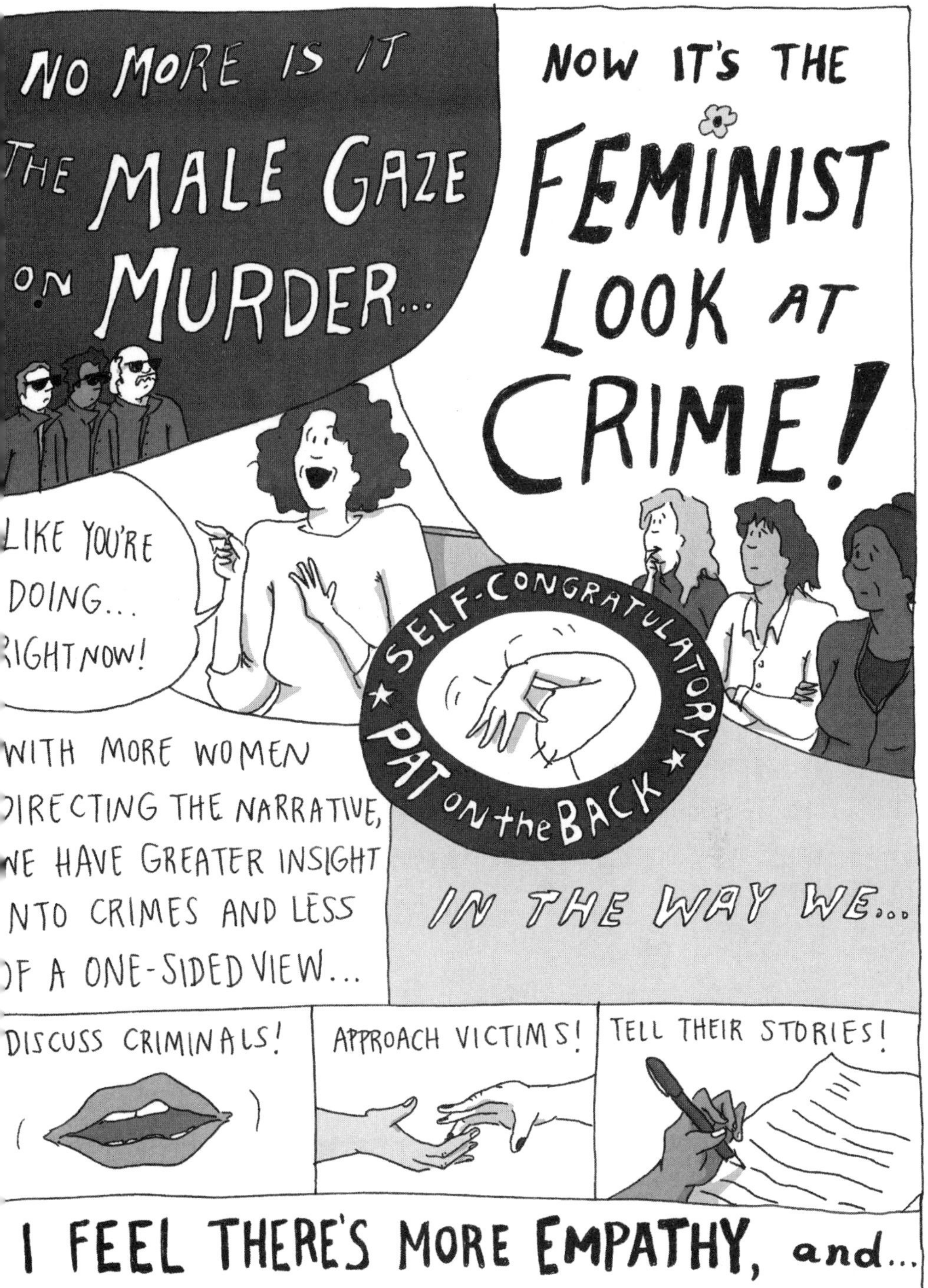
NO MORE IS IT THE MALE GAZE ON MURDER...
NOW IT'S THE FEMINIST LOOK AT CRIME!
LIKE YOU'RE DOING... RIGHT NOW!
SELF-CONGRATULATORY PAT ON THE BACK
WITH MORE WOMEN DIRECTING THE NARRATIVE, WE HAVE GREATER INSIGHT INTO CRIMES AND LESS OF A ONE-SIDED VIEW...
IN THE WAY WE...
DISCUSS CRIMINALS!
APPROACH VICTIMS!
TELL THEIR STORIES!
I FEEL THERE'S MORE EMPATHY, and...

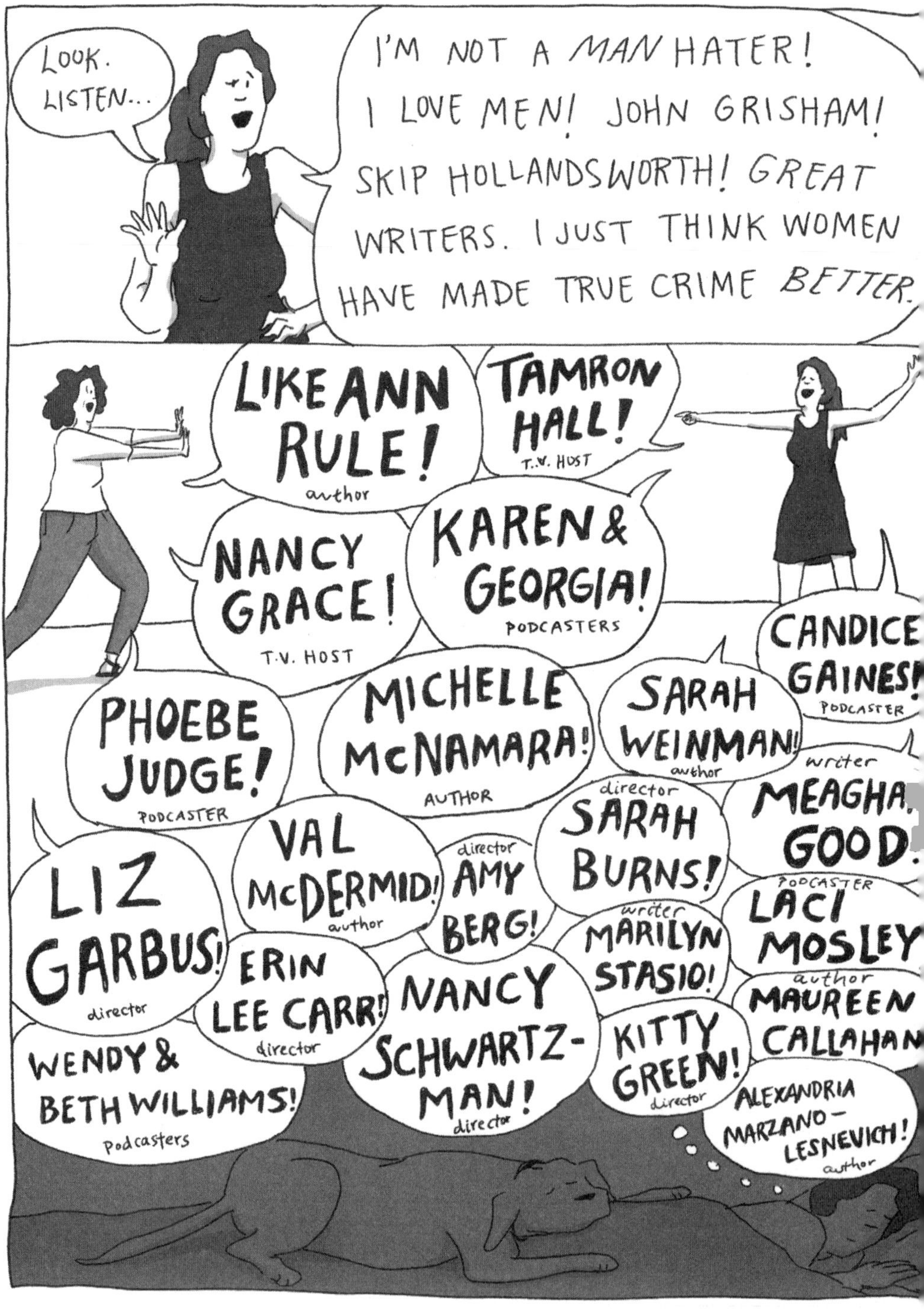

LOOK. LISTEN...
I'M NOT A MAN HATER! I LOVE MEN! JOHN GRISHAM! SKIP HOLLANDSWORTH! GREAT WRITERS. I JUST THINK WOMEN HAVE MADE TRUE CRIME BETTER.
LIKE ANN RULE! author
TAMRON HALL! T.V. HOST
NANCY GRACE! T.V. HOST
KAREN & GEORGIA! PODCASTERS
CANDICE GAINES! PODCASTER
PHOEBE JUDGE! PODCASTER
MICHELLE McNAMARA! AUTHOR
SARAH WEINMAN! author
writer MEAGHA[N] GOOD!
LIZ GARBUS! director
VAL McDERMID! author
director AMY BERG!
director SARAH BURNS!
PODCASTER LACI MOSLEY
writer MARILYN STASIO!
author MAUREEN CALLAHAN
ERIN LEE CARR! director
NANCY SCHWARTZ-MAN! director
KITTY GREEN! director
WENDY & BETH WILLIAMS! podcasters
ALEXANDRIA MARZANO-LESNEVICH! author

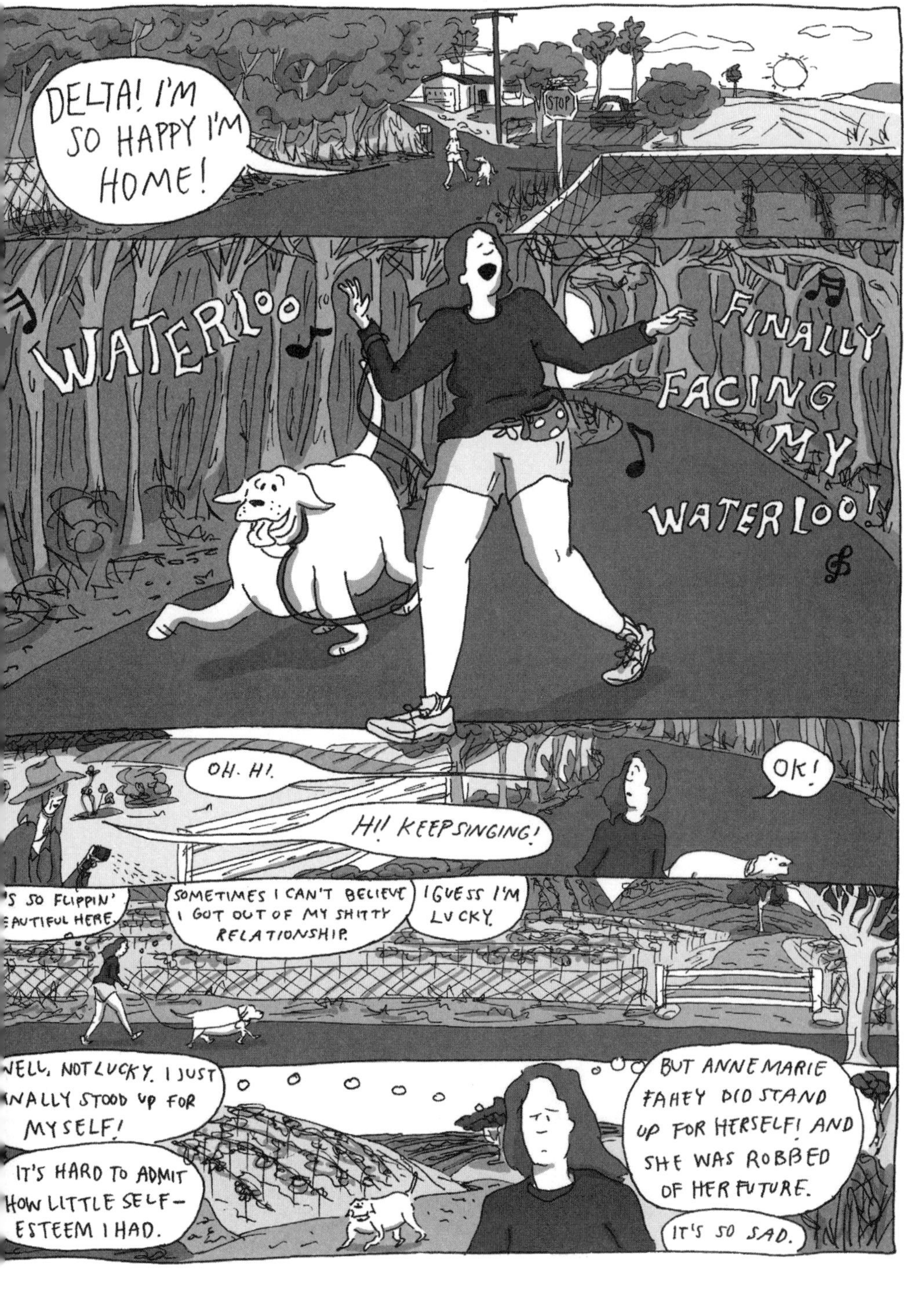
DELTA! I'M SO HAPPY I'M HOME!
WATERLOO
FINALLY FACING MY WATERLOO!
STOP
OH. HI.
HI! KEEP SINGING!
OK!
'S SO FLIPPIN' EAUTIFUL HERE.
SOMETIMES I CAN'T BELIEVE I GOT OUT OF MY SHITTY RELATIONSHIP.
I GUESS I'M LUCKY.
VELL, NOT LUCKY. I JUST NALLY STOOD UP FOR MYSELF!
IT'S HARD TO ADMIT HOW LITTLE SELF-ESTEEM I HAD.
BUT ANNE MARIE FAHEY DID STAND UP FOR HERSELF! AND SHE WAS ROBBED OF HER FUTURE.
IT'S SO SAD.

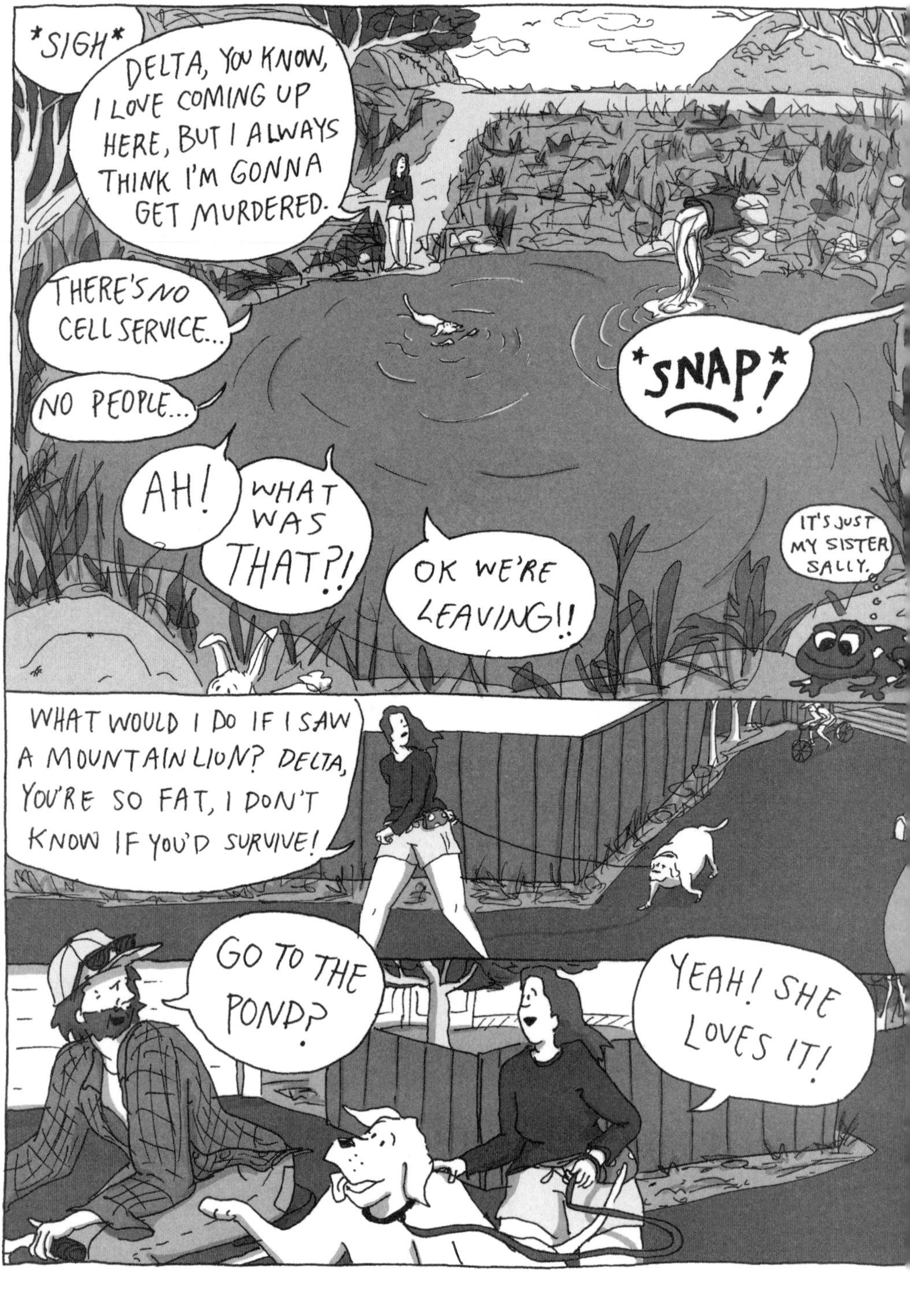
SIGH
DELTA, YOU KNOW, I LOVE COMING UP HERE, BUT I ALWAYS THINK I'M GONNA GET MURDERED.
THERE'S NO CELL SERVICE...
NO PEOPLE...
SNAP!
AH!
WHAT WAS THAT?!
OK WE'RE LEAVING!!
IT'S JUST MY SISTER SALLY.
WHAT WOULD I DO IF I SAW A MOUNTAIN LION? DELTA, YOU'RE SO FAT, I DON'T KNOW IF YOU'D SURVIVE!
GO TO THE POND?
YEAH! SHE LOVES IT!

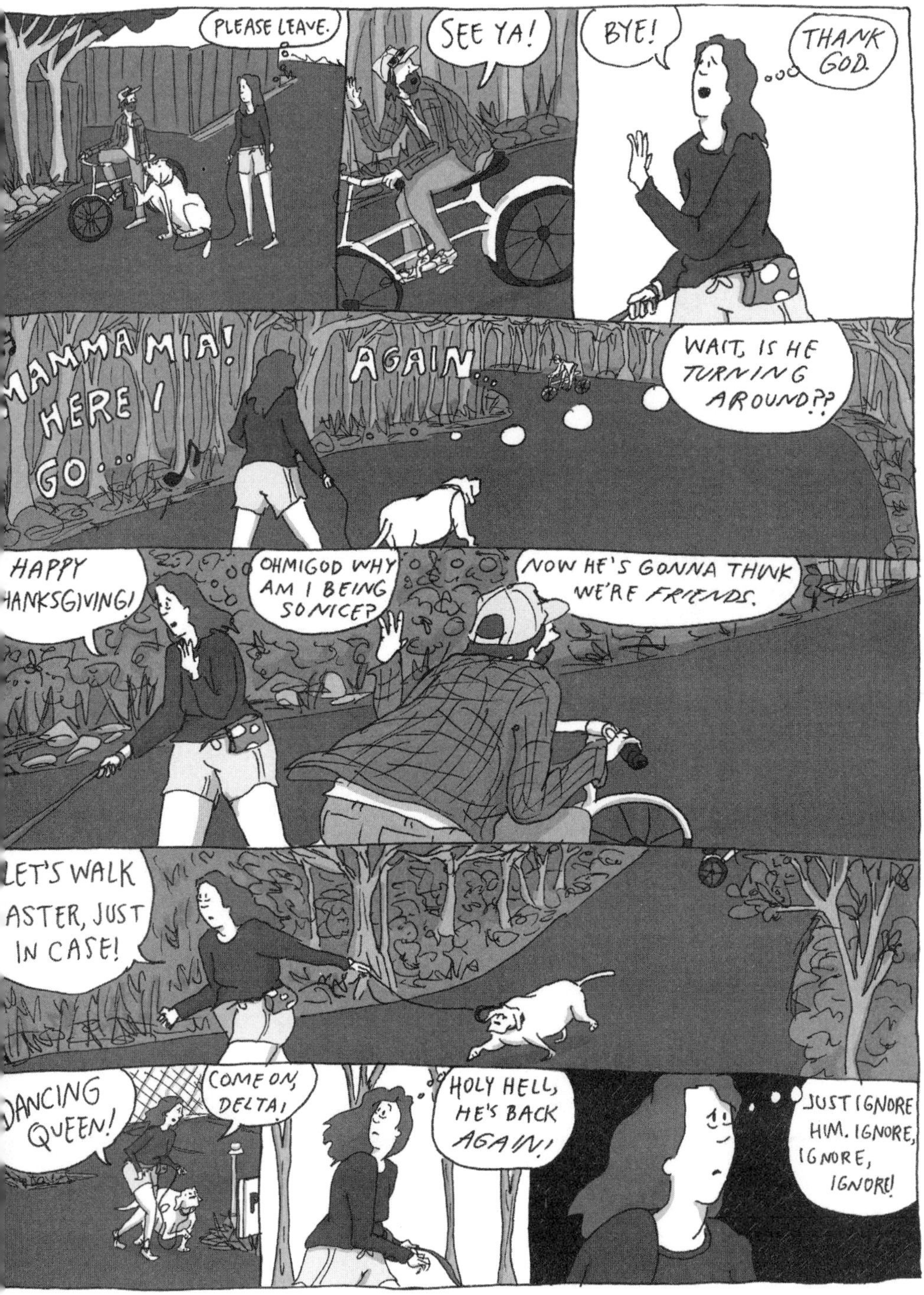
PLEASE LEAVE.
SEE YA!
BYE!
THANK GOD.
MAMMA MIA! HERE I GO... AGAIN...
WAIT, IS HE TURNING AROUND??
HAPPY
HANKSGIVING!
OHMIGOD WHY AM I BEING SO NICE?
NOW HE'S GONNA THINK WE'RE FRIENDS.
LET'S WALK
ASTER, JUST IN CASE!
ANCING QUEEN!
COME ON, DELTA!
HOLY HELL, HE'S BACK AGAIN!
JUST IGNORE HIM. IGNORE, IGNORE, IGNORE!

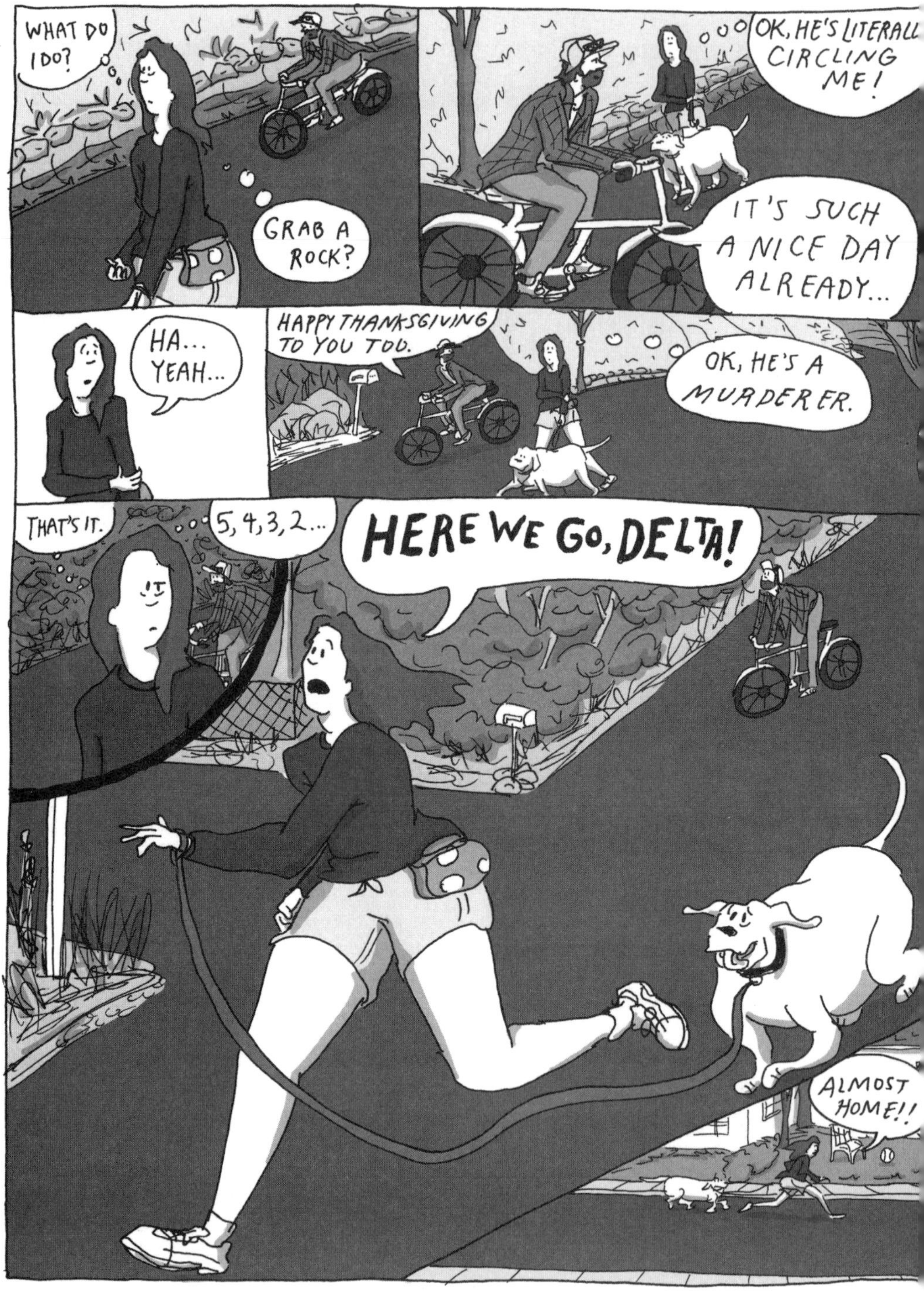
WHAT DO I DO?
GRAB A ROCK?
OK, HE'S LITERALL CIRCLING ME!
IT'S SUCH A NICE DAY ALREADY...
HA... YEAH...
HAPPY THANKSGIVING TO YOU TOO.
OK, HE'S A MURDERER.
THAT'S IT.
5, 4, 3, 2...
HERE WE GO, DELTA!
ALMOST HOME!!

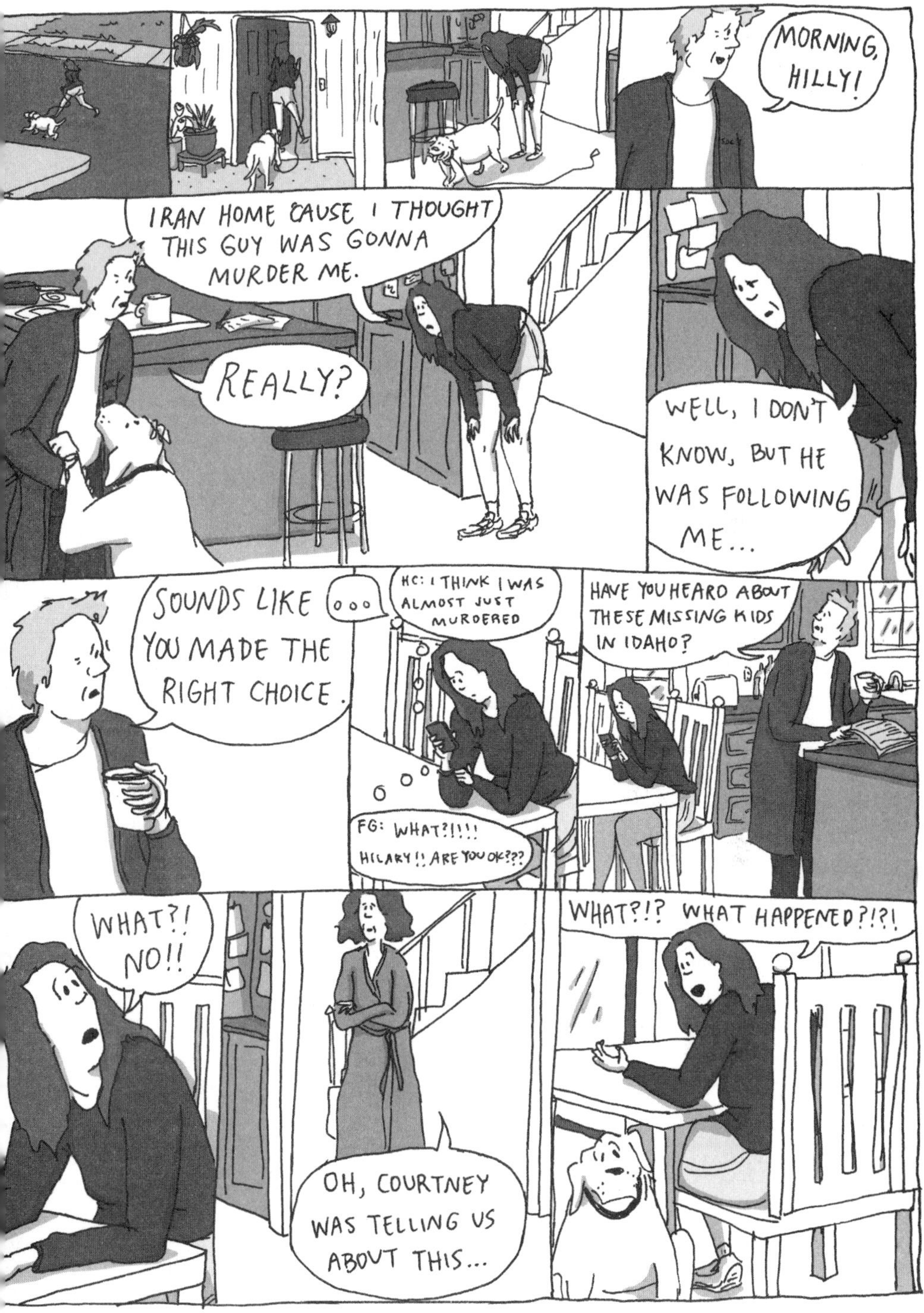
MORNING, HILLY!
I RAN HOME CAUSE I THOUGHT THIS GUY WAS GONNA MURDER ME.
REALLY?
WELL, I DON'T KNOW, BUT HE WAS FOLLOWING ME...
SOUNDS LIKE YOU MADE THE RIGHT CHOICE.
...
HC: I THINK I WAS ALMOST JUST MURDERED
FG: WHAT?!!!!
HILARY!! ARE YOU OK???
HAVE YOU HEARD ABOUT THESE MISSING KIDS IN IDAHO?
WHAT?! NO!!
OH, COURTNEY WAS TELLING US ABOUT THIS...
WHAT?!? WHAT HAPPENED?!?!

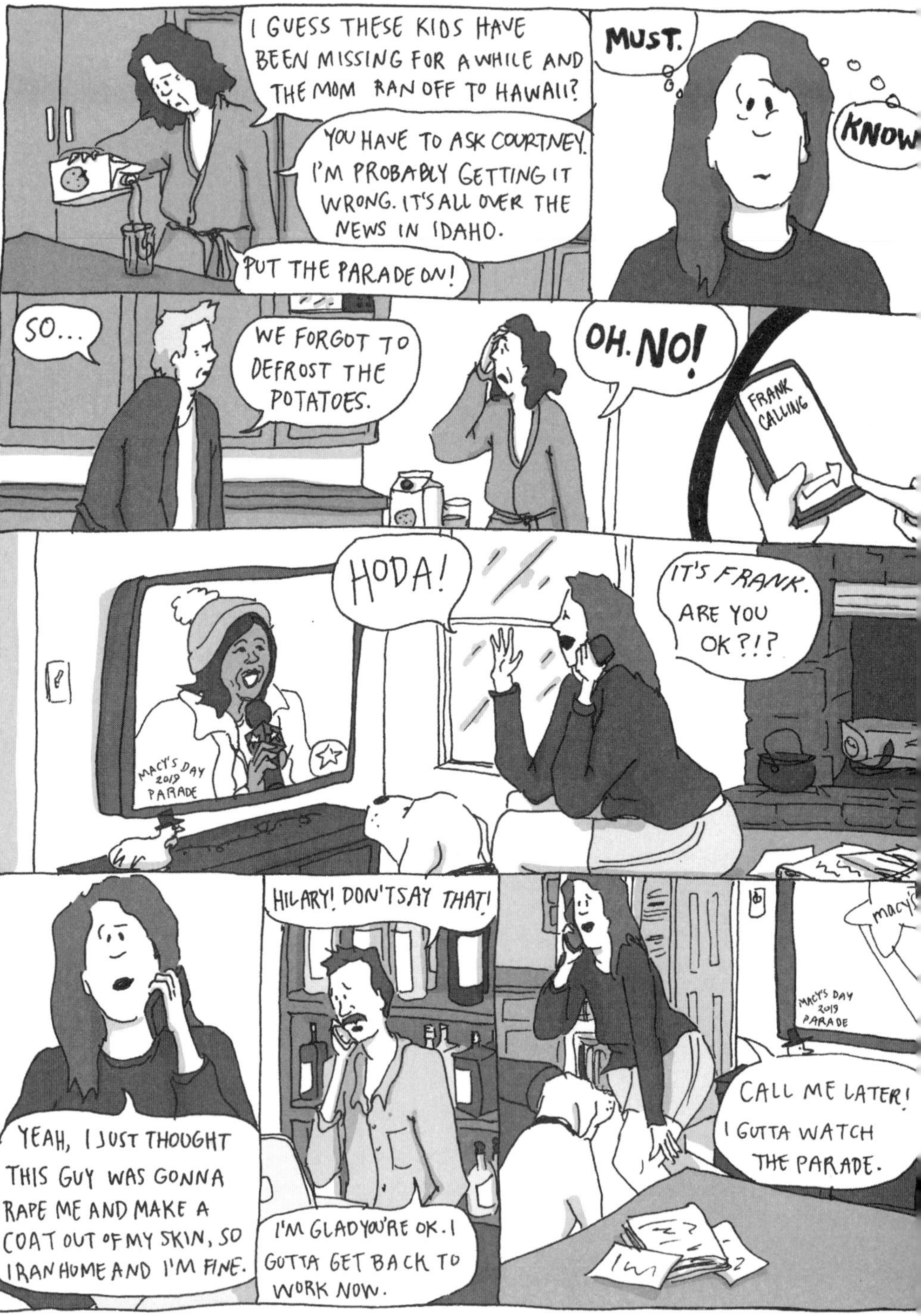

I GUESS THESE KIDS HAVE BEEN MISSING FOR A WHILE AND THE MOM RAN OFF TO HAWAII?
YOU HAVE TO ASK COURTNEY. I'M PROBABLY GETTING IT WRONG. IT'S ALL OVER THE NEWS IN IDAHO.
PUT THE PARADE ON!
MUST.
KNOW
SO...
WE FORGOT TO DEFROST THE POTATOES.
OH. NO!
FRANK CALLING
HODA!
MACY'S DAY 2019 PARADE
IT'S FRANK. ARE YOU OK?!?
YEAH, I JUST THOUGHT THIS GUY WAS GONNA RAPE ME AND MAKE A COAT OUT OF MY SKIN, SO I RAN HOME AND I'M FINE.
HILARY! DON'T SAY THAT!
I'M GLAD YOU'RE OK. I GOTTA GET BACK TO WORK NOW.
macy's
MACY'S DAY 2019 PARADE
CALL ME LATER! I GOTTA WATCH THE PARADE.

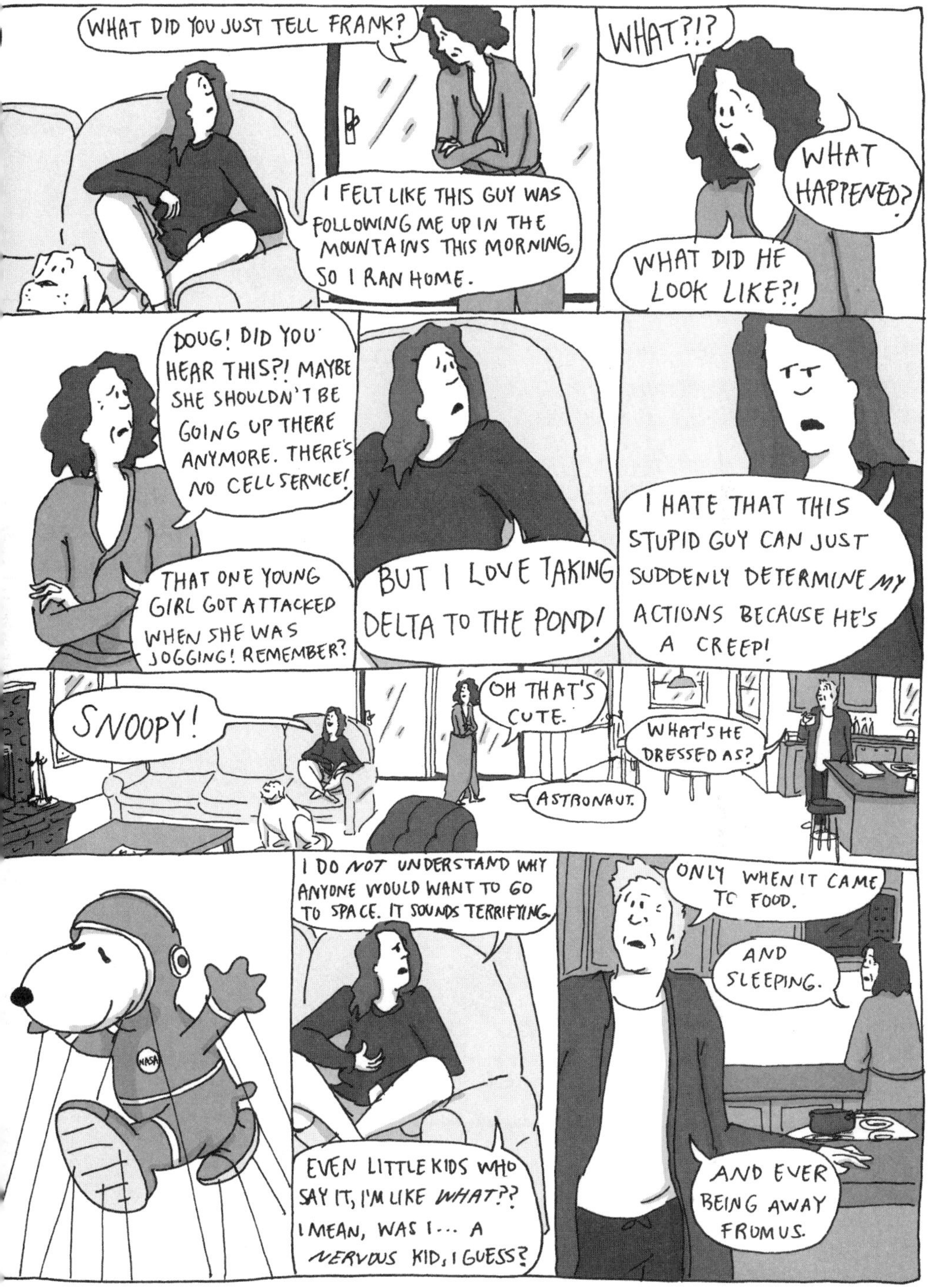
WHAT DID YOU JUST TELL FRANK?
I FELT LIKE THIS GUY WAS FOLLOWING ME UP IN THE MOUNTAINS THIS MORNING, SO I RAN HOME.
WHAT?!?
WHAT HAPPENED?
WHAT DID HE LOOK LIKE?!
DOUG! DID YOU HEAR THIS?! MAYBE SHE SHOULDN'T BE GOING UP THERE ANYMORE. THERE'S NO CELL SERVICE!
THAT ONE YOUNG GIRL GOT ATTACKED WHEN SHE WAS JOGGING! REMEMBER?
BUT I LOVE TAKING DELTA TO THE POND!
I HATE THAT THIS STUPID GUY CAN JUST SUDDENLY DETERMINE MY ACTIONS BECAUSE HE'S A CREEP!
SNOOPY!
OH THAT'S CUTE.
WHAT'S HE DRESSED AS?
ASTRONAUT.
NASA
I DO NOT UNDERSTAND WHY ANYONE WOULD WANT TO GO TO SPACE. IT SOUNDS TERRIFYING.
EVEN LITTLE KIDS WHO SAY IT, I'M LIKE WHAT?? I MEAN, WAS I... A NERVOUS KID, I GUESS?
ONLY WHEN IT CAME TO FOOD.
AND SLEEPING.
AND EVER BEING AWAY FROM US.

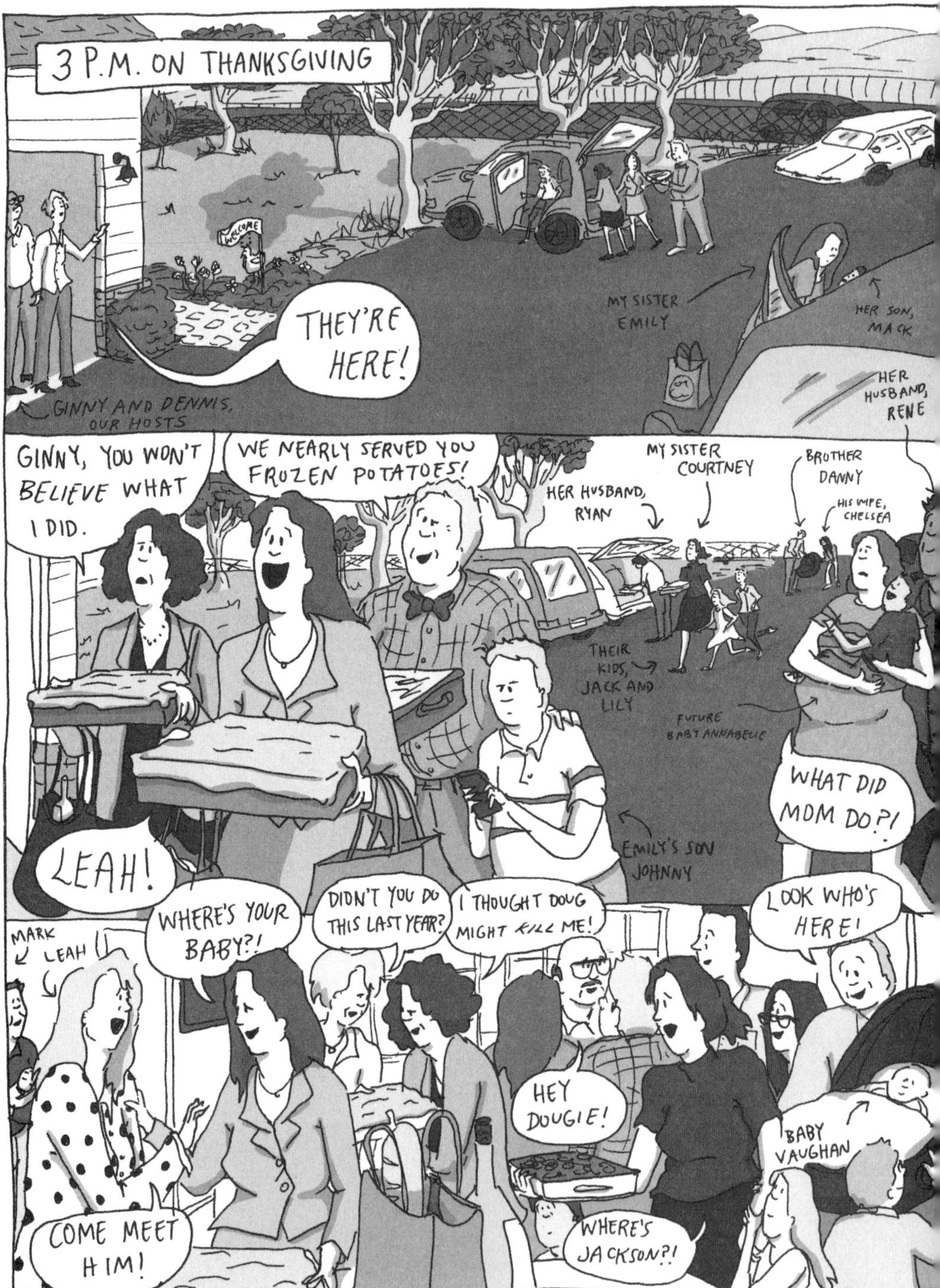
3 P.M. ON THANKSGIVING
THEY'RE HERE!
GINNY AND DENNIS, OUR HOSTS
MY SISTER EMILY
HER SON, MACK
HER HUSBAND, RENE
GINNY, YOU WON'T BELIEVE WHAT I DID.
WE NEARLY SERVED YOU FROZEN POTATOES!
HER HUSBAND, RYAN
MY SISTER COURTNEY
BROTHER DANNY
HIS WIFE, CHELSEA
THEIR KIDS, JACK AND LILY
FUTURE BABY ANNABELLE
WHAT DID MOM DO?!
LEAH!
EMILY'S SON JOHNNY
MARK
LEAH
WHERE'S YOUR BABY?!
DIDN'T YOU DO THIS LAST YEAR?
I THOUGHT DOUG MIGHT KILL ME!
LOOK WHO'S HERE!
HEY DOUGIE!
BABY VAUGHAN
COME MEET HIM!
WHERE'S JACKSON?!

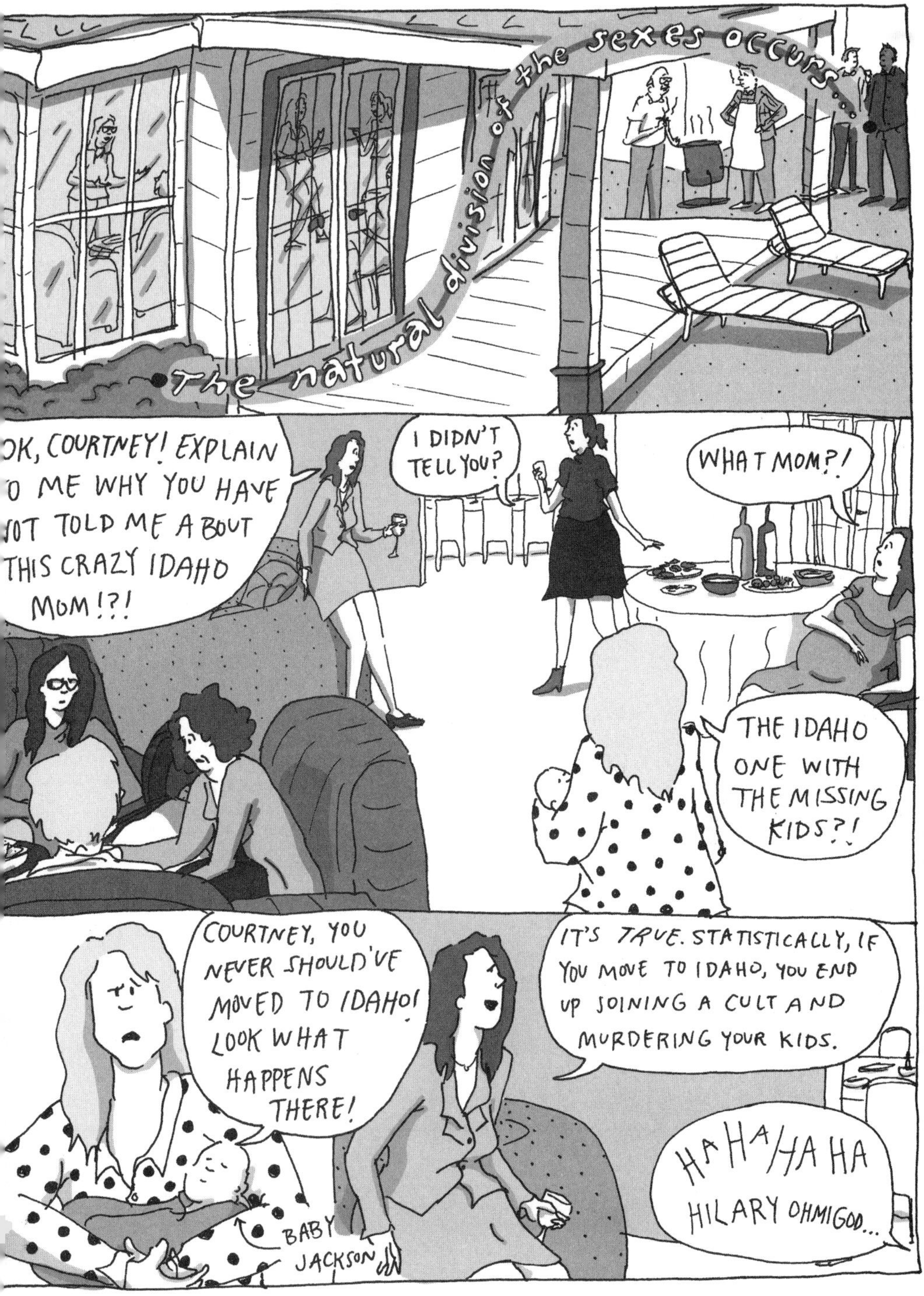

The natural division of the sexes occurs...
OK, COURTNEY! EXPLAIN TO ME WHY YOU HAVE NOT TOLD ME ABOUT THIS CRAZY IDAHO MOM!?!
I DIDN'T TELL YOU?
WHAT MOM?!
THE IDAHO ONE WITH THE MISSING KIDS?!
COURTNEY, YOU NEVER SHOULD'VE MOVED TO IDAHO! LOOK WHAT HAPPENS THERE!
IT'S TRUE. STATISTICALLY, IF YOU MOVE TO IDAHO, YOU END UP JOINING A CULT AND MURDERING YOUR KIDS.
BABY JACKSON
HA HA HA HA HA HA
HILARY OHMIGOD...

 OK, BUT, SERIOUSLY. TELL ME.

 IT'S LIKE THE CRAZIEST STORY I'VE EVER HEARD.

"WHERE DO I EVEN BEGIN?"

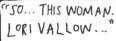 "SO... THIS WOMAN. LORI VALLOW..."

 "SHE HAS TWO KIDS, ONE IS ADOPTED. NO ONE HAS SEEN THEM IN MONTHS." TYLEE JOSH

 "SO FINALLY THE GRANDPARENTS CALL THE COPS BECAUSE THEY'RE LIKE —"

 WE WANT TO KNOW WHERE OUR GRANDCHILDREN ARE!

 "AND IT'S LIKE... ANY NORMAL MOM WOULDN'T HIDE HER KIDS, SO OBVIOUSLY SOMETHING IS WRONG."

 "THE POLICE GO OVER..." OH, THEY'RE NOT HERE RIGHT NOW. "AND SHE JUST HAS SOME RANDOM EXCUSE."

 "AND NOW APPARENTLY SHE'S RUN OFF TO HAWAII?"

 "WITH SOME GUY WHO'S A PASTOR?!"

 OOOH... MORMONS.

 YEP.

"IT'S STARTING TO BE ALL OVER THE NEWS NOW AND PEOPLE WANT TO FIND THESE POOR KIDS! BUT NOW IT JUST COME OUT THAT ALL OF HER EX-HUSBANDS *MYSTERIOUSLY* 1 2 3 *DIED.*"

 STOP IT.

 YEAH.

 SHE'S LIKE THE BLACK WIDOW.

 PEOPLE SHOULD NEED A LICENSE TO HAVE A BABY. IT'S INSANE.

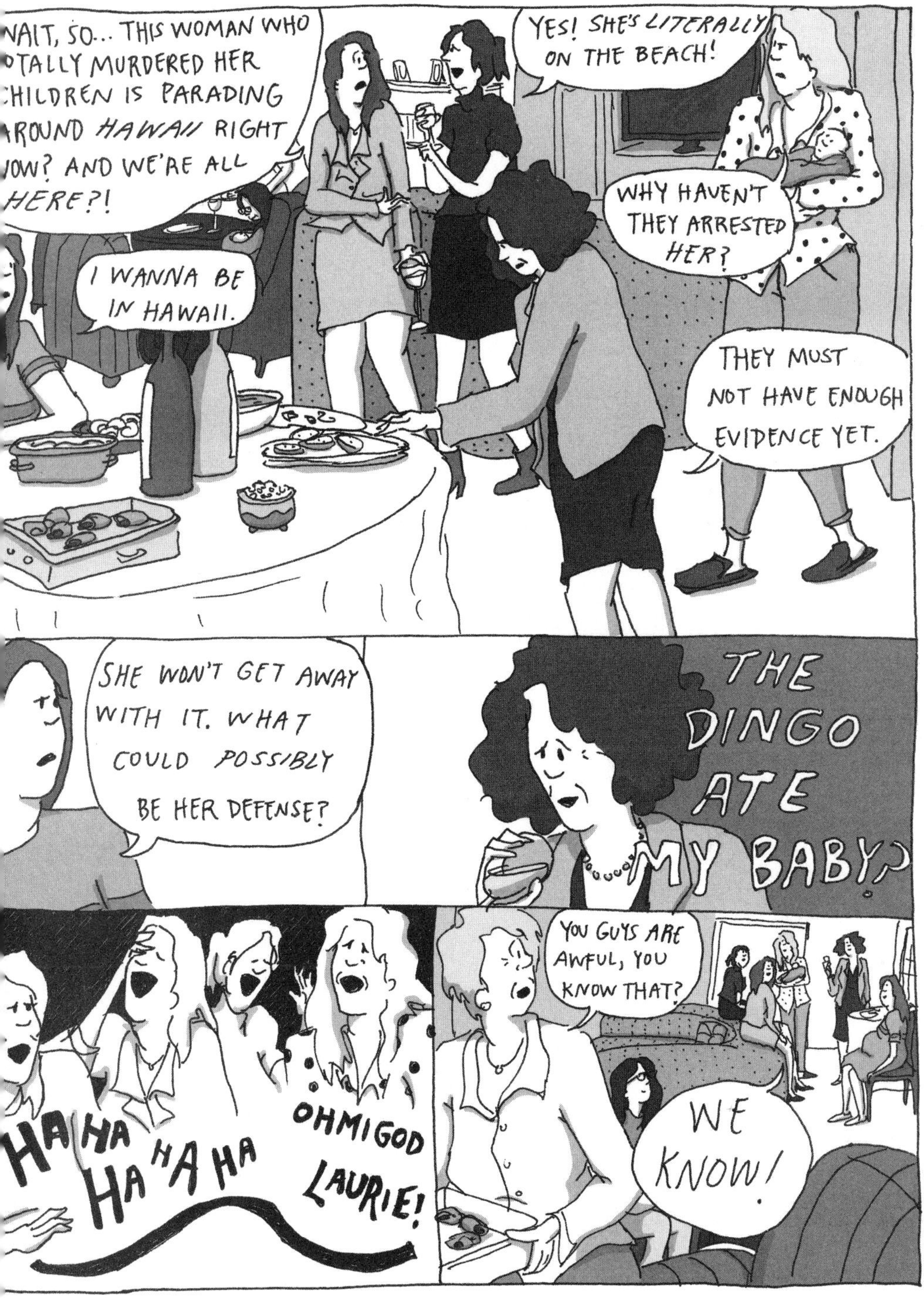
AIT, SO... THIS WOMAN WHO TALLY MURDERED HER HILDREN IS PARADING ROUND HAWAII RIGHT OW? AND WE'RE ALL HERE?!
YES! SHE'S LITERALLY ON THE BEACH!
I WANNA BE IN HAWAII.
WHY HAVEN'T THEY ARRESTED HER?
THEY MUST NOT HAVE ENOUGH EVIDENCE YET.
SHE WON'T GET AWAY WITH IT. WHAT COULD POSSIBLY BE HER DEFENSE?
THE DINGO ATE MY BABY?
HA HA HA HA HA HA
OHMIGOD LAURIE!
YOU GUYS ARE AWFUL, YOU KNOW THAT?
WE KNOW!

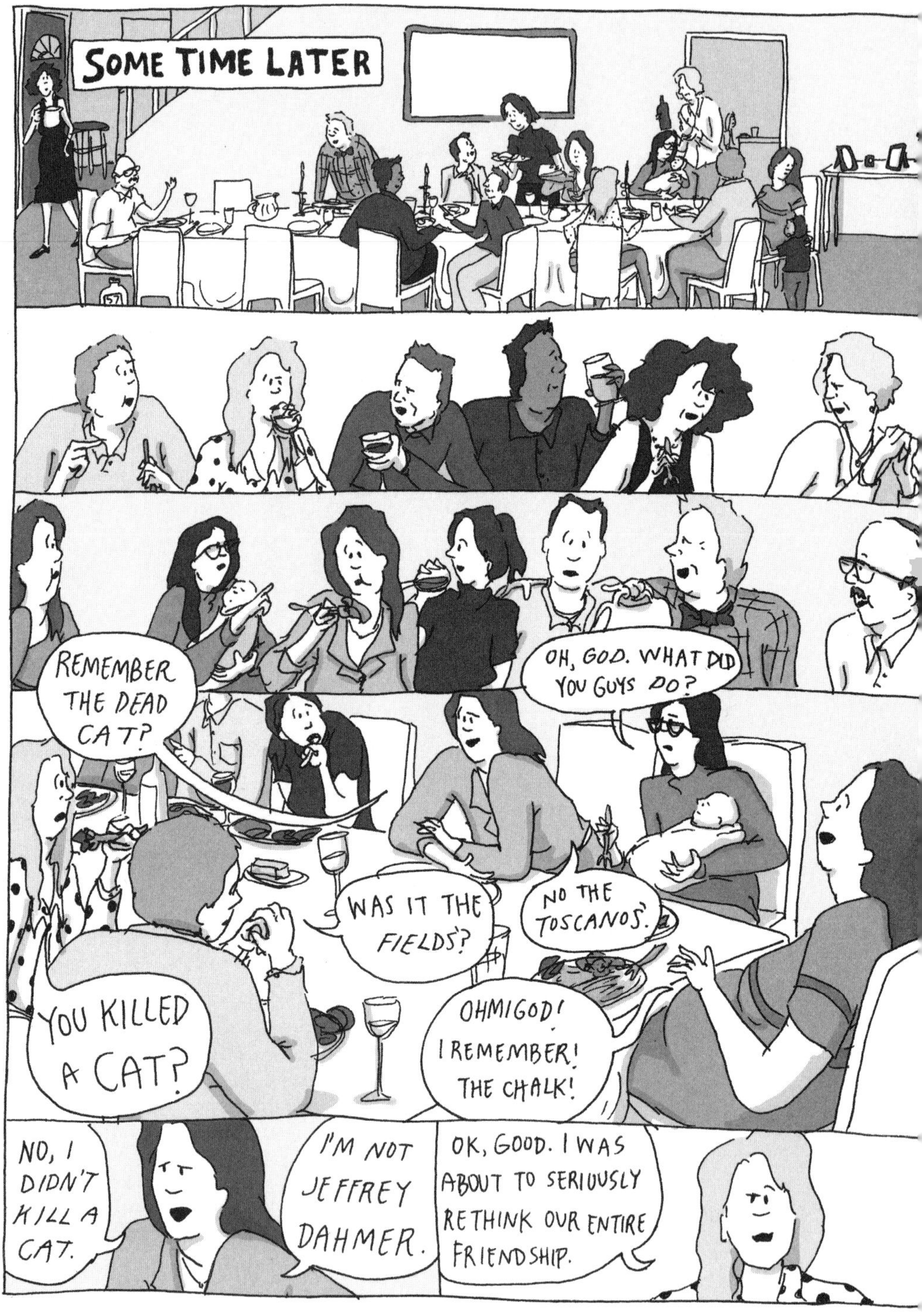
SOME TIME LATER
REMEMBER THE DEAD CAT?
OH, GOD. WHAT DID YOU GUYS DO?
WAS IT THE FIELDS'?
NO THE TOSCANOS'.
YOU KILLED A CAT?
OHMIGOD! I REMEMBER! THE CHALK!
NO, I DIDN'T KILL A CAT.
I'M NOT JEFFREY DAHMER.
OK, GOOD. I WAS ABOUT TO SERIOUSLY RETHINK OUR ENTIRE FRIENDSHIP.

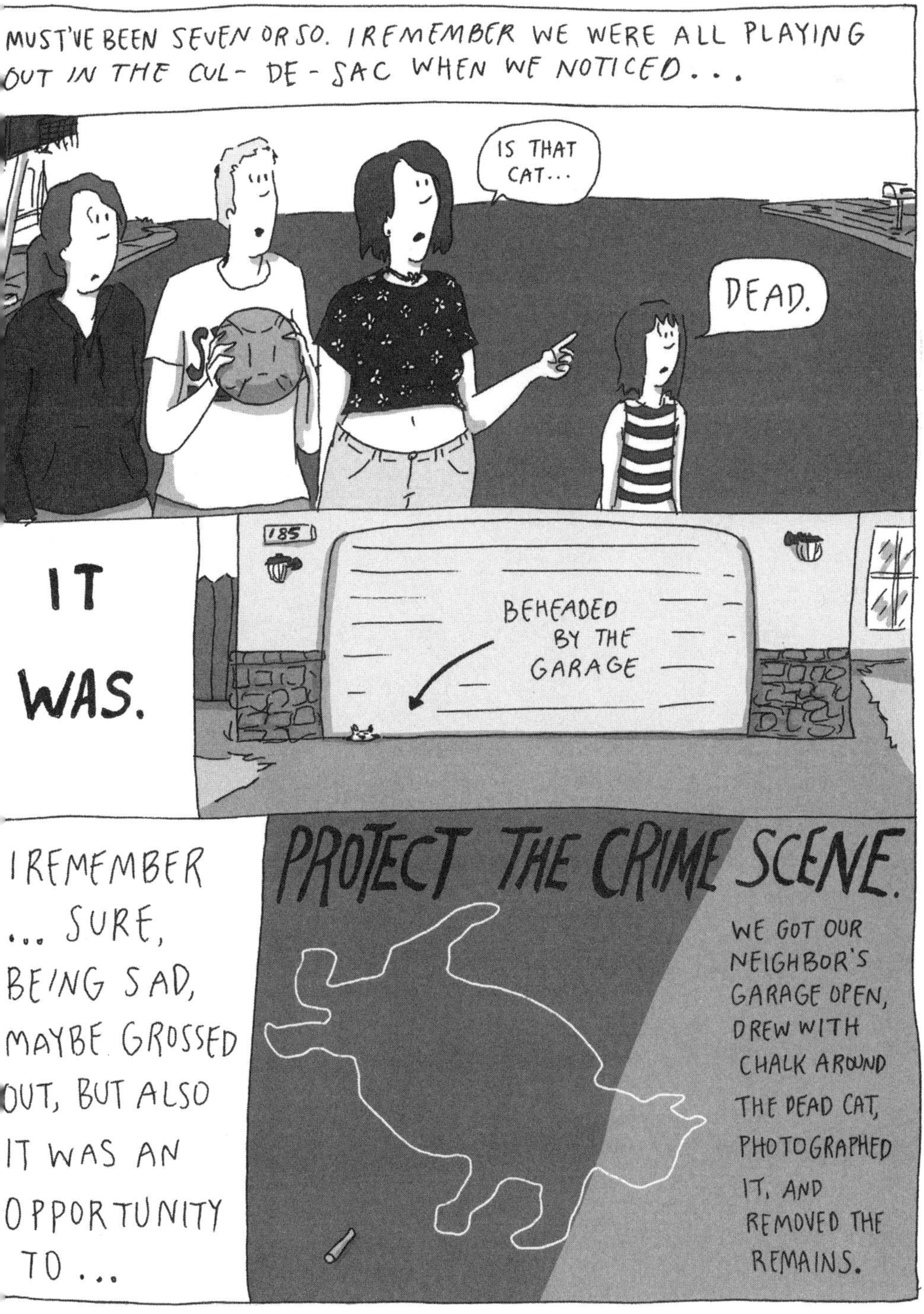
MUST'VE BEEN SEVEN OR SO. I REMEMBER WE WERE ALL PLAYING OUT IN THE CUL-DE-SAC WHEN WE NOTICED...
IS THAT CAT...
DEAD.
IT WAS.
185
BEHEADED BY THE GARAGE
I REMEMBER ... SURE, BEING SAD, MAYBE GROSSED OUT, BUT ALSO IT WAS AN OPPORTUNITY TO...
PROTECT THE CRIME SCENE.
WE GOT OUR NEIGHBOR'S GARAGE OPEN, DREW WITH CHALK AROUND THE DEAD CAT, PHOTOGRAPHED IT, AND REMOVED THE REMAINS.

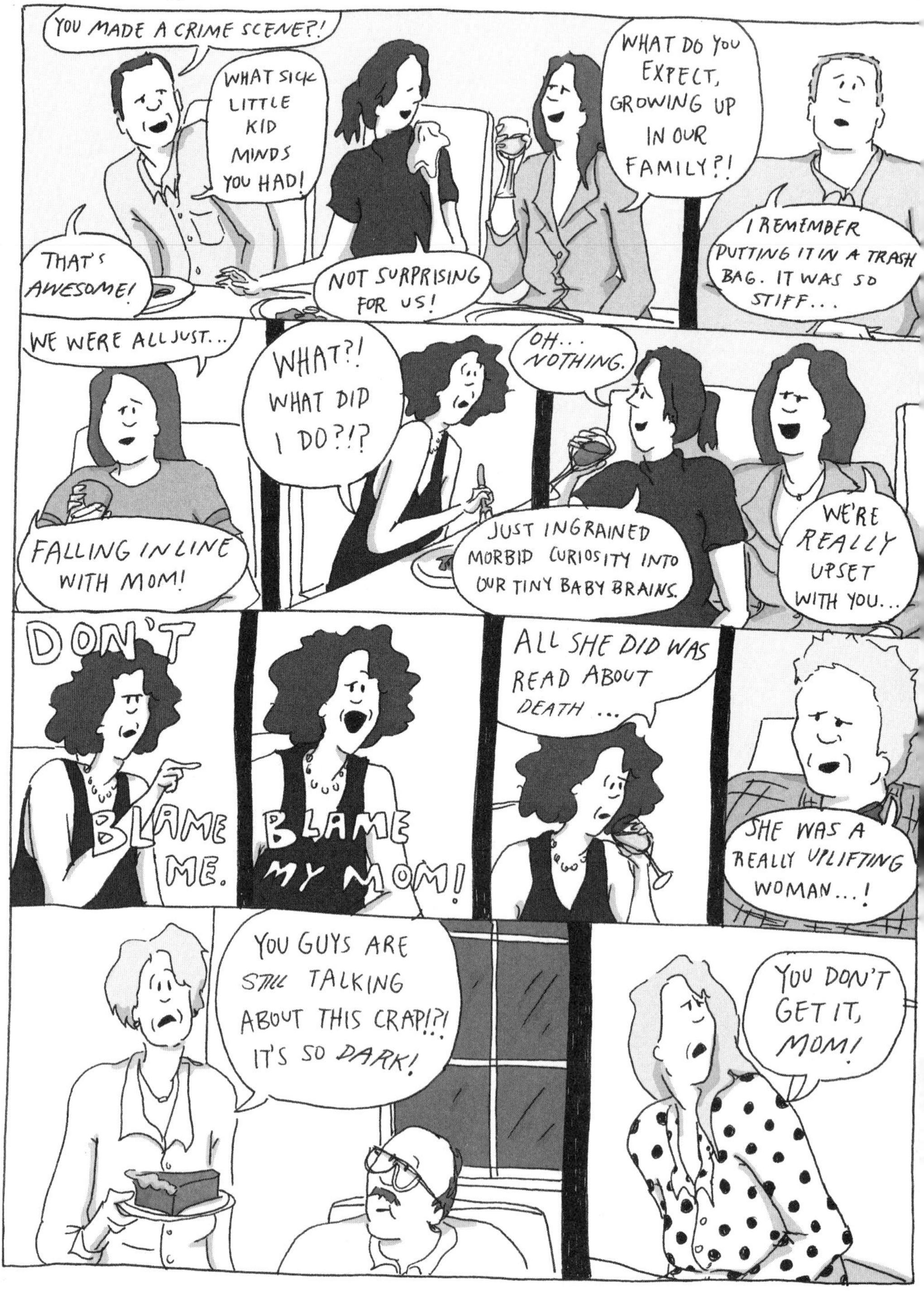
YOU MADE A CRIME SCENE?!
WHAT SICK LITTLE KID MINDS YOU HAD!
THAT'S AWESOME!
NOT SURPRISING FOR US!
WHAT DO YOU EXPECT, GROWING UP IN OUR FAMILY?!
I REMEMBER PUTTING IT IN A TRASH BAG. IT WAS SO STIFF...
WE WERE ALL JUST...
FALLING IN LINE WITH MOM!
WHAT?! WHAT DID I DO?!?
OH... NOTHING.
JUST INGRAINED MORBID CURIOSITY INTO OUR TINY BABY BRAINS.
WE'RE REALLY UPSET WITH YOU...
DON'T BLAME ME.
BLAME MY MOM!
ALL SHE DID WAS READ ABOUT DEATH ...
SHE WAS A REALLY UPLIFTING WOMAN...!
YOU GUYS ARE STILL TALKING ABOUT THIS CRAP!?!... IT'S SO DARK!
YOU DON'T GET IT, MOM!

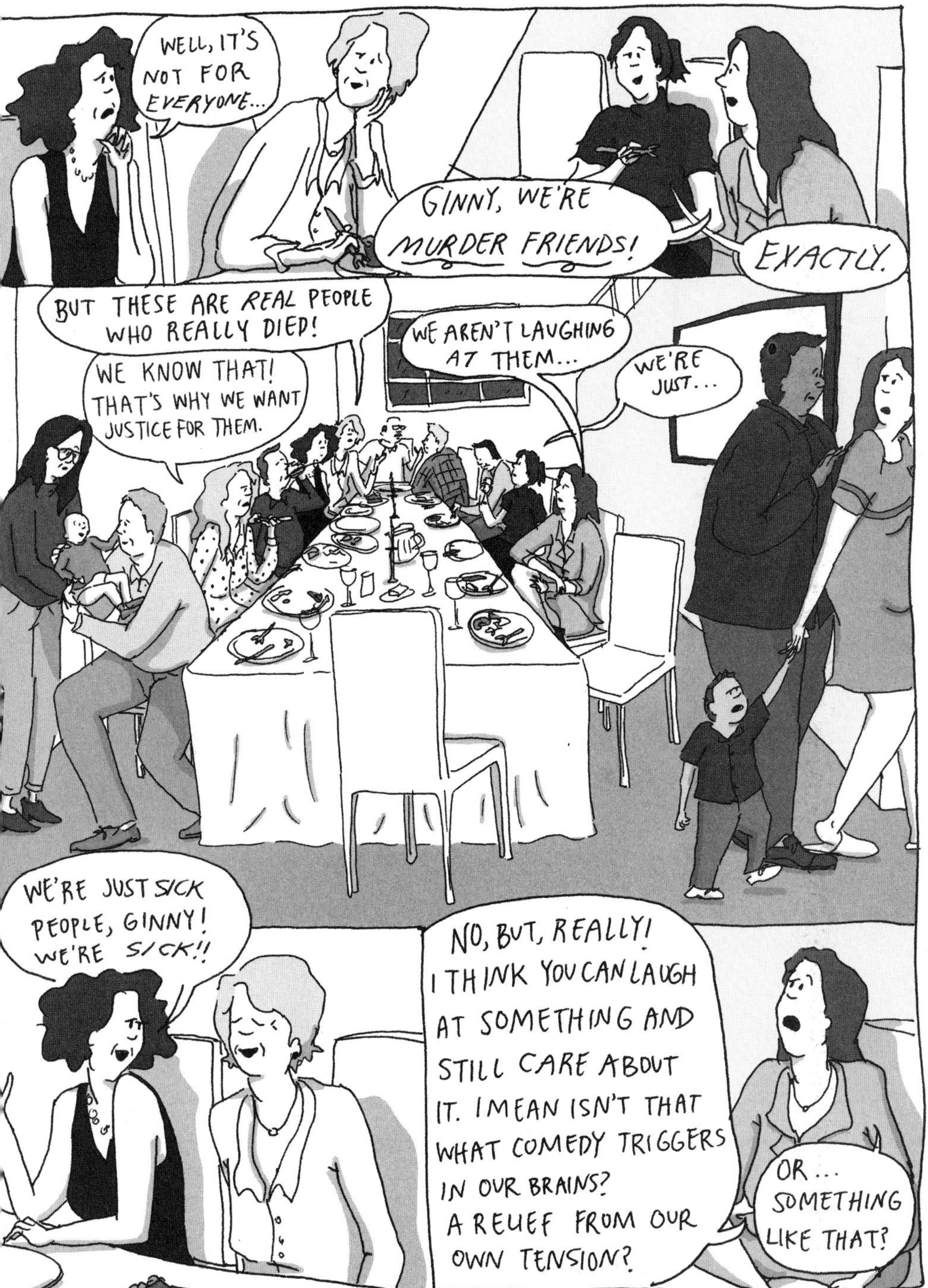
WELL, IT'S NOT FOR EVERYONE...
GINNY, WE'RE MURDER FRIENDS!
EXACTLY.
BUT THESE ARE REAL PEOPLE WHO REALLY DIED!
WE KNOW THAT! THAT'S WHY WE WANT JUSTICE FOR THEM.
WE AREN'T LAUGHING AT THEM...
WE'RE JUST...
WE'RE JUST SICK PEOPLE, GINNY! WE'RE SICK!!
NO, BUT, REALLY! I THINK YOU CAN LAUGH AT SOMETHING AND STILL CARE ABOUT IT. I MEAN ISN'T THAT WHAT COMEDY TRIGGERS IN OUR BRAINS? A RELIEF FROM OUR OWN TENSION?
OR... SOMETHING LIKE THAT?

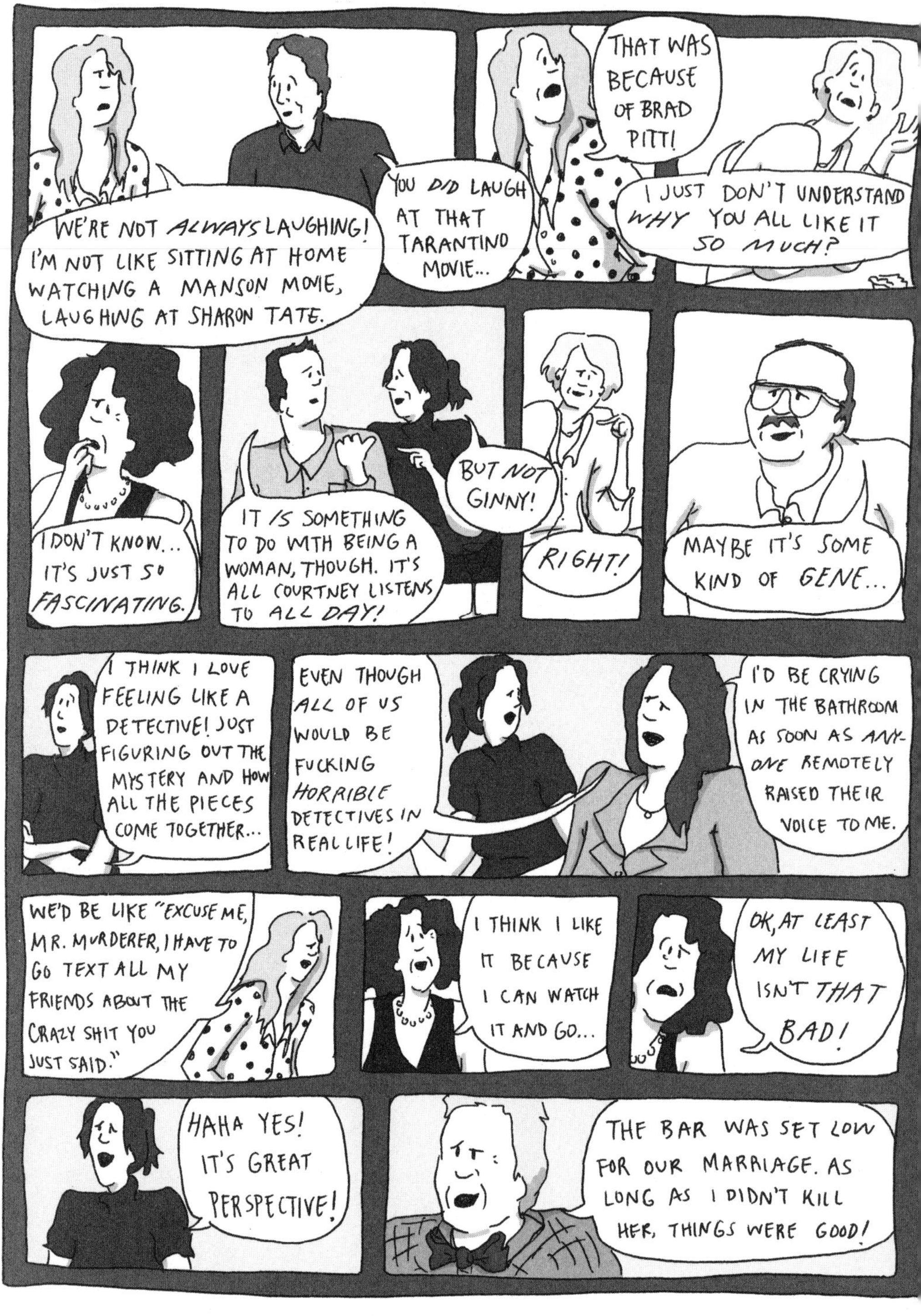
WE'RE NOT ALWAYS LAUGHING! I'M NOT LIKE SITTING AT HOME WATCHING A MANSON MOVIE, LAUGHING AT SHARON TATE.
YOU DID LAUGH AT THAT TARANTINO MOVIE...
THAT WAS BECAUSE OF BRAD PITT!
I JUST DON'T UNDERSTAND WHY YOU ALL LIKE IT SO MUCH?
I DON'T KNOW... IT'S JUST SO FASCINATING.
IT IS SOMETHING TO DO WITH BEING A WOMAN, THOUGH. IT'S ALL COURTNEY LISTENS TO ALL DAY!
BUT NOT GINNY!
RIGHT!
MAYBE IT'S SOME KIND OF GENE...
I THINK I LOVE FEELING LIKE A DETECTIVE! JUST FIGURING OUT THE MYSTERY AND HOW ALL THE PIECES COME TOGETHER...
EVEN THOUGH ALL OF US WOULD BE FUCKING HORRIBLE DETECTIVES IN REAL LIFE!
I'D BE CRYING IN THE BATHROOM AS SOON AS ANY-ONE REMOTELY RAISED THEIR VOICE TO ME.
WE'D BE LIKE "EXCUSE ME, MR. MURDERER, I HAVE TO GO TEXT ALL MY FRIENDS ABOUT THE CRAZY SHIT YOU JUST SAID."
I THINK I LIKE IT BECAUSE I CAN WATCH IT AND GO...
OK, AT LEAST MY LIFE ISN'T THAT BAD!
HAHA YES! IT'S GREAT PERSPECTIVE!
THE BAR WAS SET LOW FOR OUR MARRIAGE. AS LONG AS I DIDN'T KILL HER, THINGS WERE GOOD!

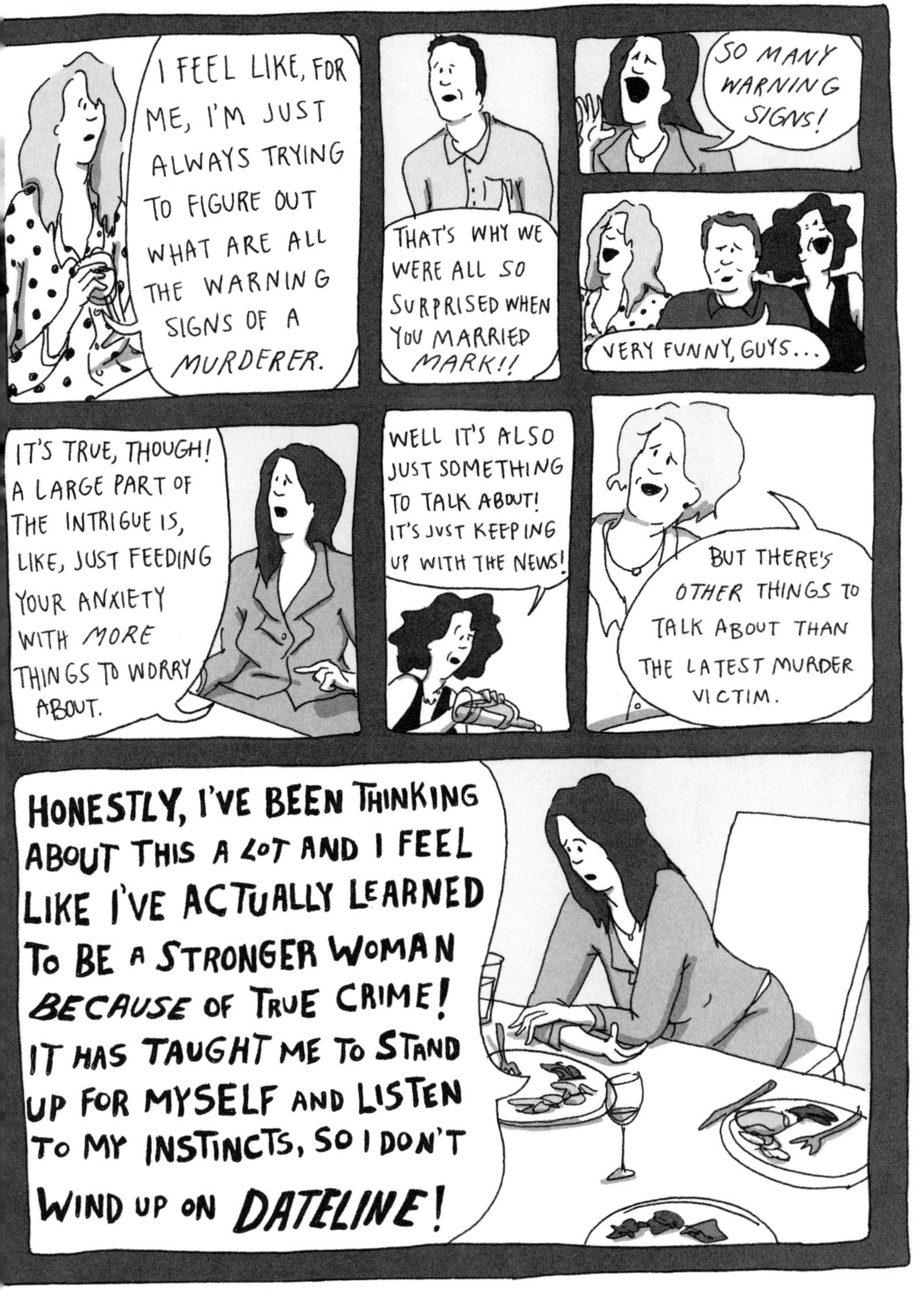
I FEEL LIKE, FOR ME, I'M JUST ALWAYS TRYING TO FIGURE OUT WHAT ARE ALL THE WARNING SIGNS OF A *MURDERER*.
THAT'S WHY WE WERE ALL *SO* SURPRISED WHEN YOU MARRIED *MARK!!*
SO MANY WARNING SIGNS!
VERY FUNNY, GUYS...
IT'S TRUE, THOUGH! A LARGE PART OF THE INTRIGUE IS, LIKE, JUST FEEDING YOUR ANXIETY WITH *MORE* THINGS TO WORRY ABOUT.
WELL IT'S ALSO JUST SOMETHING TO TALK ABOUT! IT'S JUST KEEPING UP WITH THE NEWS!
BUT THERE'S *OTHER* THINGS TO TALK ABOUT THAN THE LATEST MURDER VICTIM.
HONESTLY, I'VE BEEN THINKING ABOUT THIS A *LOT* AND I FEEL LIKE I'VE ACTUALLY LEARNED TO BE A STRONGER WOMAN *BECAUSE* OF TRUE CRIME! IT HAS TAUGHT ME TO STAND UP FOR MYSELF AND LISTEN TO MY INSTINCTS, SO I DON'T WIND UP ON *DATELINE*!

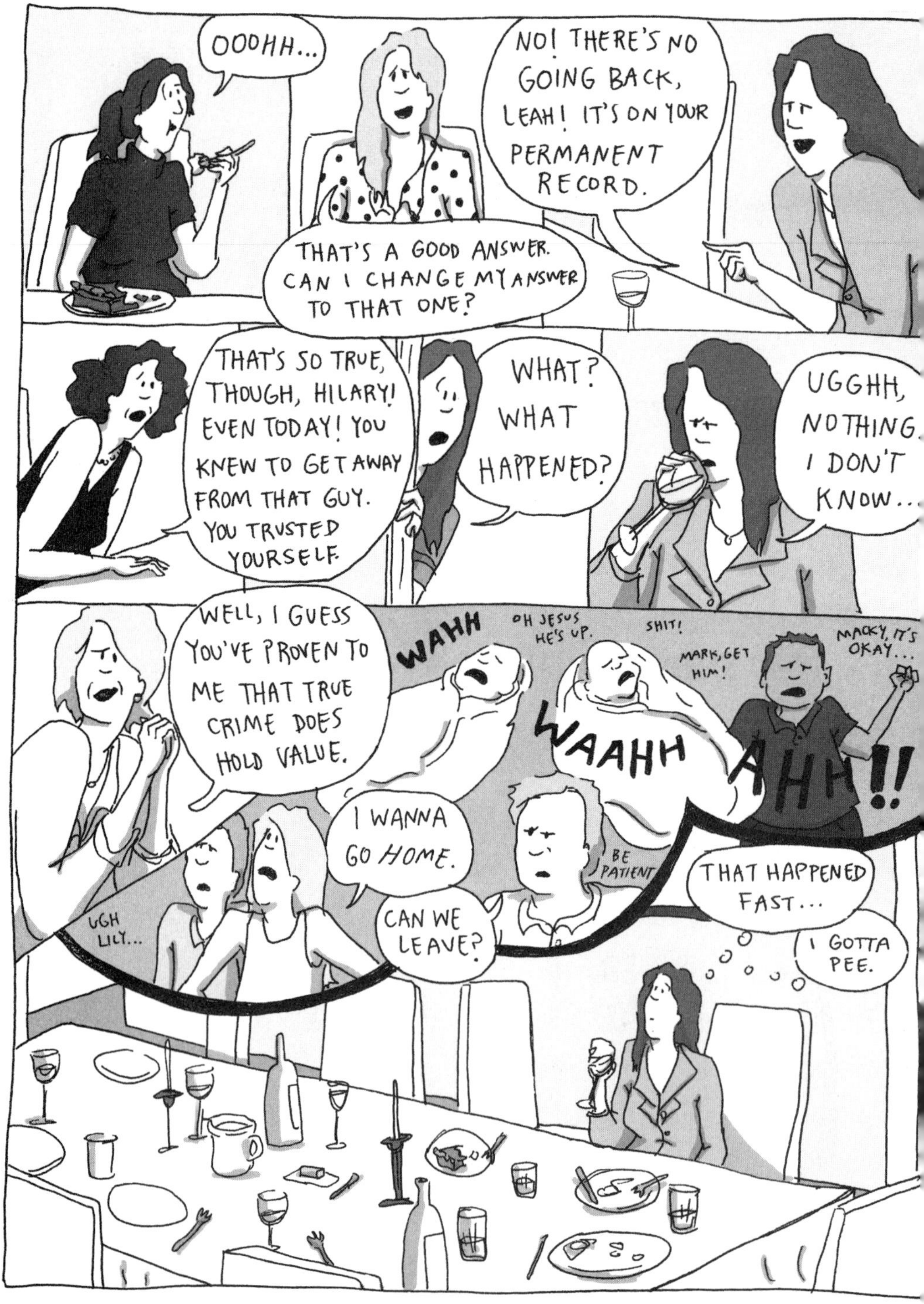
OOOHH...
NO! THERE'S NO GOING BACK, LEAH! IT'S ON YOUR PERMANENT RECORD.
THAT'S A GOOD ANSWER. CAN I CHANGE MY ANSWER TO THAT ONE?
THAT'S SO TRUE, THOUGH, HILARY! EVEN TODAY! YOU KNEW TO GET AWAY FROM THAT GUY. YOU TRUSTED YOURSELF.
WHAT? WHAT HAPPENED?
UGGHH, NOTHING. I DON'T KNOW...
WELL, I GUESS YOU'VE PROVEN TO ME THAT TRUE CRIME DOES HOLD VALUE.
WAHH
OH JESUS HE'S UP.
SHIT!
MARK, GET HIM!
MACKY, IT'S OKAY...
WAAHH
AHH!!
I WANNA GO HOME.
BE PATIENT
THAT HAPPENED FAST...
UGH LILY...
CAN WE LEAVE?
I GOTTA PEE.

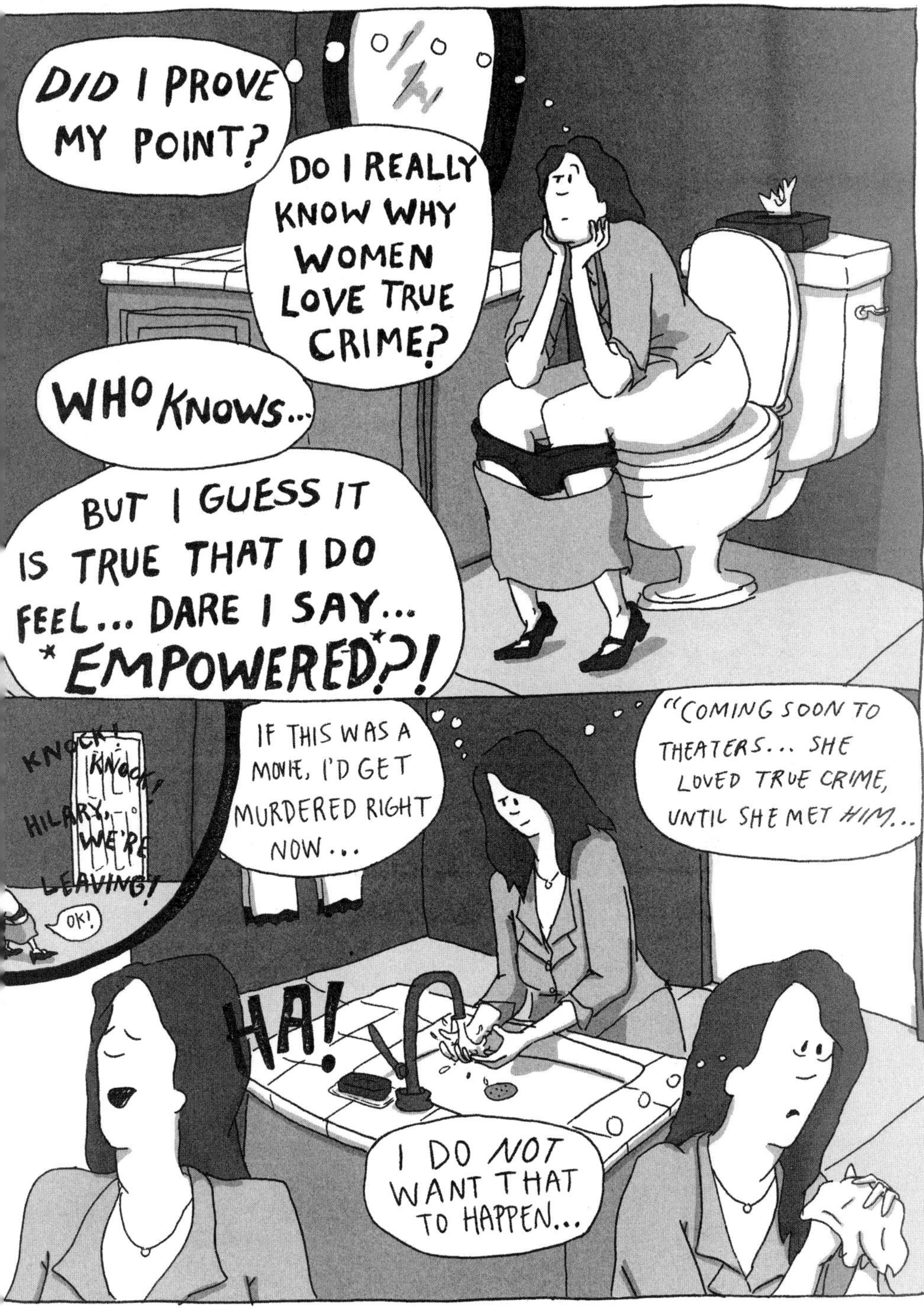
DID I PROVE MY POINT?
DO I REALLY KNOW WHY WOMEN LOVE TRUE CRIME?
WHO KNOWS...
BUT I GUESS IT IS TRUE THAT I DO FEEL... DARE I SAY... *EMPOWERED*?!
KNOCK! KNOCK! HILARY, WE'RE LEAVING!
OK!
IF THIS WAS A MOVIE, I'D GET MURDERED RIGHT NOW...
"COMING SOON TO THEATERS... SHE LOVED TRUE CRIME, UNTIL SHE MET HIM...
HA!
I DO NOT WANT THAT TO HAPPEN...

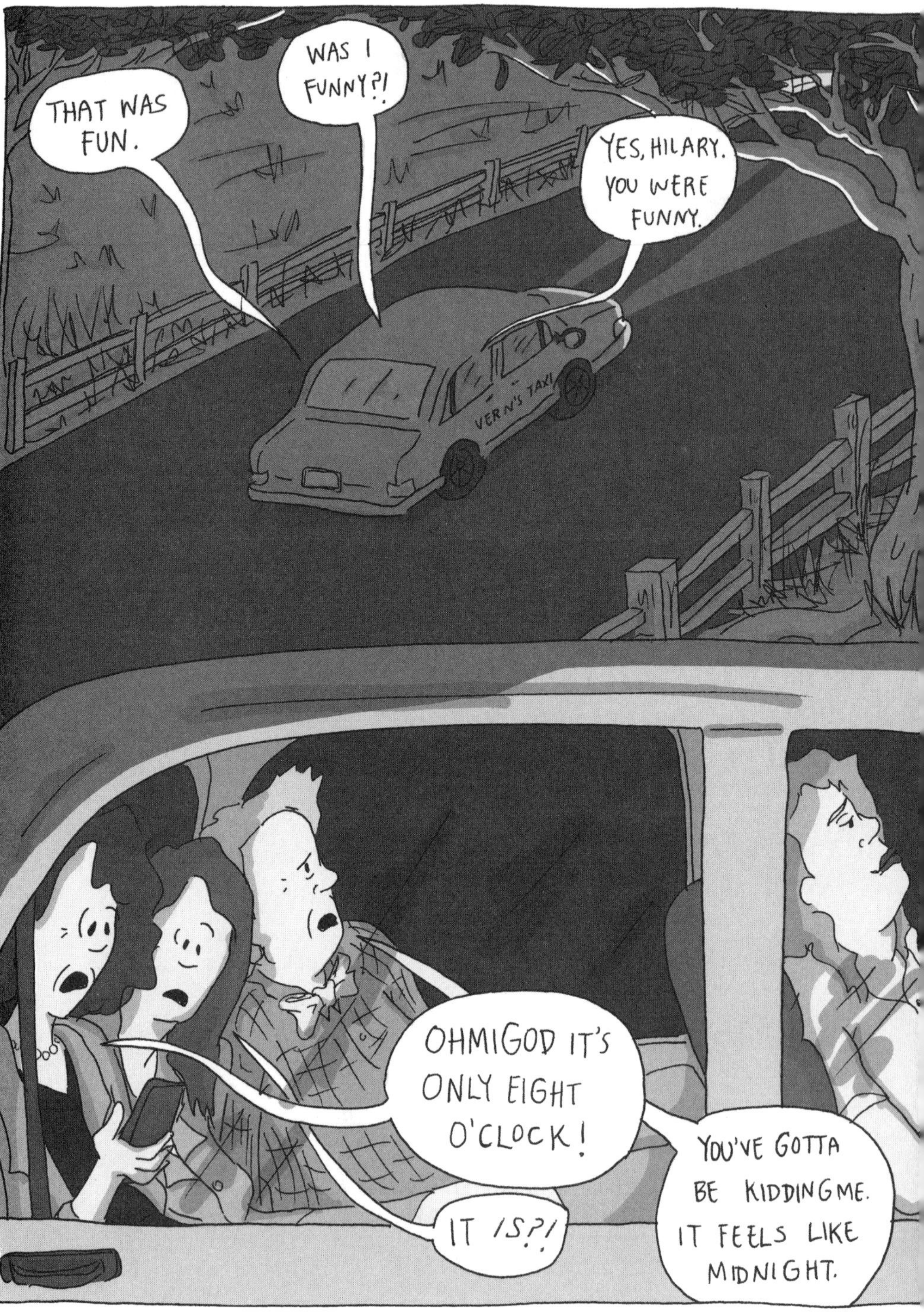
THAT WAS FUN.
WAS I FUNNY?!
YES, HILARY. YOU WERE FUNNY.
VERN'S TAXI
OHMIGOD IT'S ONLY EIGHT O'CLOCK!
IT IS?!
YOU'VE GOTTA BE KIDDING ME. IT FEELS LIKE MIDNIGHT.

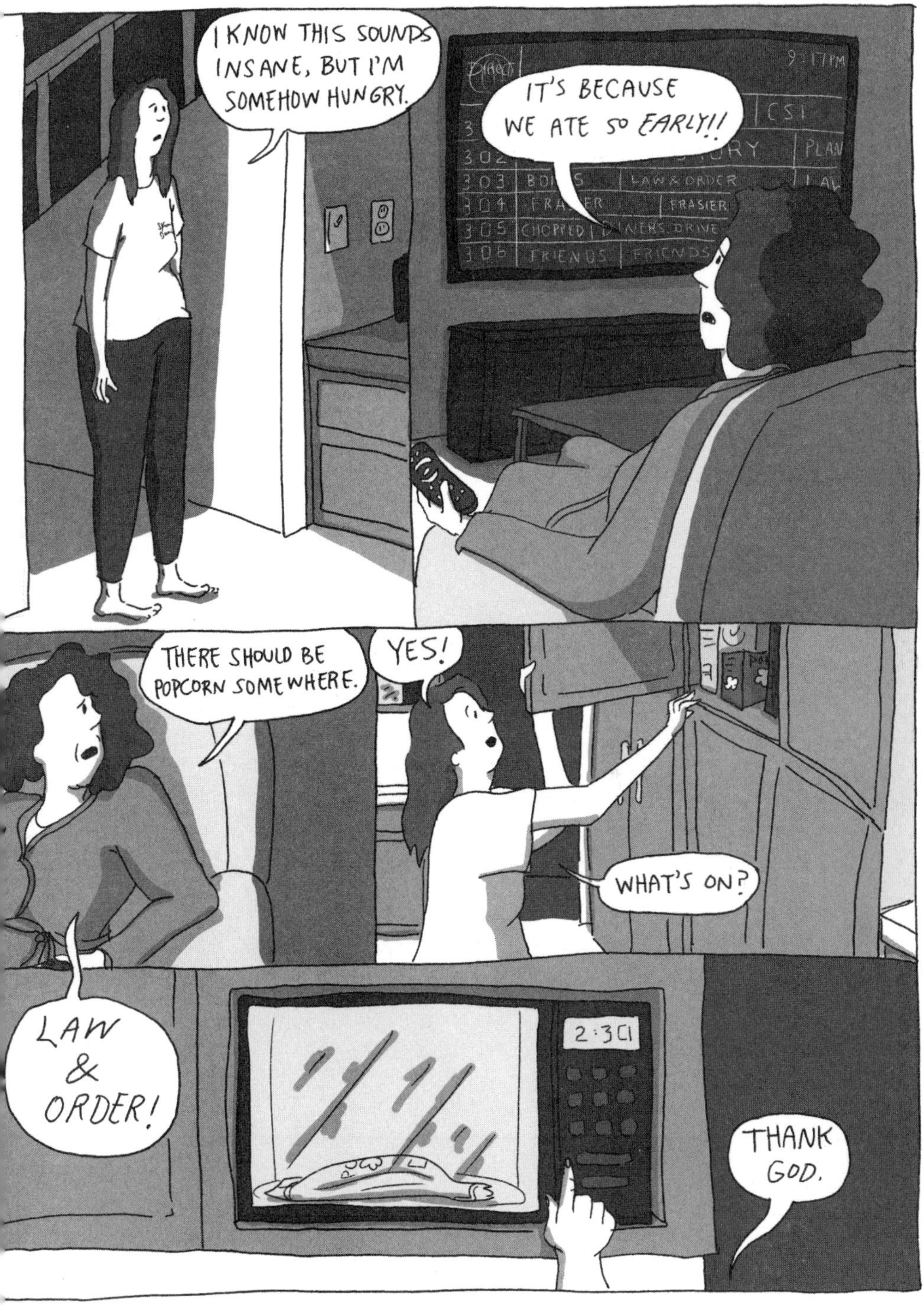
I KNOW THIS SOUNDS INSANE, BUT I'M SOMEHOW HUNGRY.
IT'S BECAUSE WE ATE SO *EARLY*!!
THERE SHOULD BE POPCORN SOMEWHERE.
YES!
WHAT'S ON?
LAW & ORDER!
THANK GOD.

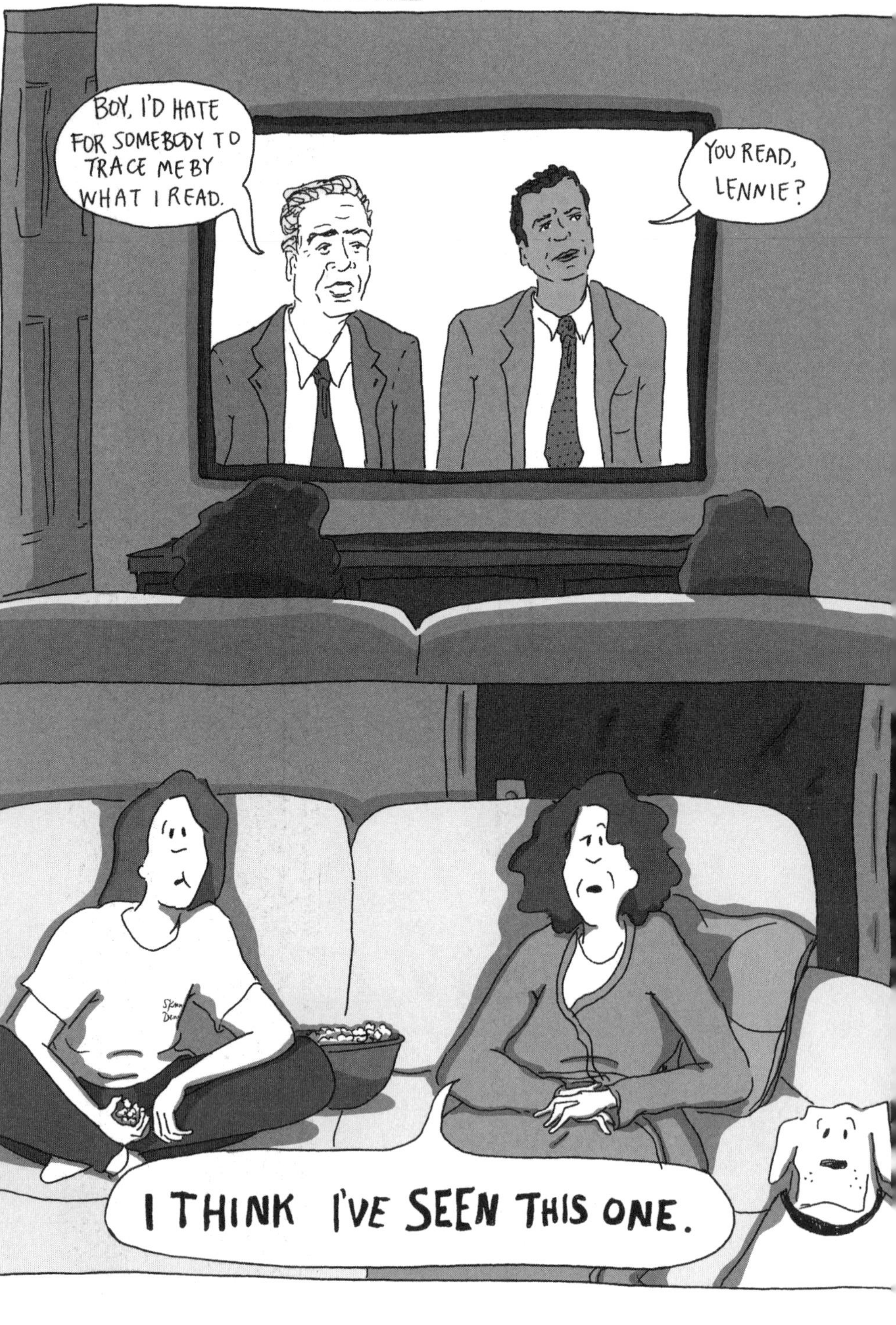
BOY, I'D HATE FOR SOMEBODY TO TRACE ME BY WHAT I READ.
YOU READ, LENNIE?
I THINK I'VE SEEN THIS ONE.

Dun-

Dun!

♡ Thank you to ♡

My mom, my dad, my sisters, my brother, my aunts and uncles and everyone in between. My lover, Frank. All of my murder friends— Kristin, Leah, Jasmine, Kelsey, Kitty, Lynn, Erin, Summre, Beth, MaryBeth and surely more. Andrews McMeel and my editor, Allison Adler. My Agent, Michelle Brower. Additional coloring and emotional support from Rita Sapunor. My assistant, Angaelica LaPasta. My supports, Elaine, Willa and Derek. My dog, Margie. My cartoon friends Sofia Warren, Ellis Rosen, Amy Kurzweil, Jason Katzenstein, Kendra Allenby, Jason Chatfield, Hallie Bateman, Johnny DiNapoli, Neil Dvorak, Karen Sneider, Liana Finck, Emma Allen and Colin Stokes.

The pack of wolves who raised me—Pattie, Kray, Bob, Beth, Dennis, Darlina, Elena, Barbara and anyone who has ever had a drink at Pattie's Patio.

My inspiration, Charles Schulz, Ann Rule, Robert Graysmith, Roz Chast, Sidney Harris, Melissa Broder, Nora Ephron, Liza Donnelly, Maria Bamford, Ellen Forney, Ruby Elliot, Diane Keaton and all the writers of Law & Order.

The bartenders at Erv's, the waiters at Little Purity and the flight attendants who served me as I wrote.

Hilary Fitzgerald Campbell is a writer, comedian, and *New Yorker* cartoonist who has illustrated books such as *Feminist Fight Club* and *Are You My Uber?* She lives in Brooklyn with her dog and her vast collection of *Law & Order* DVDs and can be found on Instagram @cartoonsbyhilary.

Explore more of *Murder Book* at www.hilarysmurderbook.com.

Andrews McMeel Publishing
a division of Andrews McMeel Universal
1130 Walnut Street, Kansas City, Missouri 64106

www.andrewsmcmeel.com

21 22 23 24 25 RR4 10 9 8 7 6 5 4 3 2 1

ISBN: 978-1-5248-6116-2

Library of Congress Control Number: 2021938794

Author photo credit: Kristen Bartley

Editor: Allison Adler
Art Director: Sierra S. Stanton
Production Editor: Elizabeth A. Garcia
Production Manager: Carol Coe

ATTENTION: SCHOOLS AND BUSINESSES
Andrews McMeel books are available at quantity discounts with bulk purchase for educational, business, or sales promotional use. For information, please e-mail the Andrews McMeel Publishing Special Sales Department: specialsales@amuniversal.com.